Electromagnetics

Electromagnetics

Fifth Edition

Mahmood Nahvi, PhD
Professor Emeritus of Electrical Engineering
California Polytechnic State University

Joseph A. Edminister
Professor Emeritus of Electrical Engineering
The University of Akron

Schaum's Outline Series

New York   Chicago   San Francisco   Athens   London   Madrid
Mexico City   Milan   New Delhi   Singapore   Sydney   Toronto

MAHMOOD NAHVI is professor emeritus of electrical engineering at California Polytechnic State University (Cal Poly) in San Luis Obispo, California. He earned B.Sc., M.Sc., and PhD degrees in electrical engineering, and has more than 55 years of educational, academic, research, and industrial experience in this field. He has taught undergraduate and graduate courses on various subjects including electric circuits, electronics, signals and systems, electromagnetics, random signals and noise, digital signal and image processing, and communications and control. Dr. Nahvi's areas of special interest and expertise include network theory, control theory, adaptation and learning in synthetic and living systems, communication and control in living systems, neural networks for pattern recognition and motor control, satellite communication, digital signal and image processing, and engineering education. In the area of engineering education, he has developed computer modules for electric circuits, signals, and systems which improve the teaching and learning of the fundamentals of electrical engineering. Dr Nahvi is the author of *Signals and Systems*, McGraw-Hill, 2014. He is also the co-author, with Joseph A. Edminister, of *Schaum's Outline of Electric Circuits*.

JOSEPH A. EDMINISTER is professor emeritus of Electrical Engineering at the University of Akron in Akron, Ohio, where he also served as assistant dean and acting dean of Engineering. He was a member or the faculty from 1957 until his retirement in 1983. In 1984 he served on the staff of Congressman Dennis Eckart (D-11-OH) on an IEEE Congressional Fellowship. He then joined Cornell University as a patent attorney and later as Director of Corporate Relations for the College of Engineering until his retirement in 1995. He received his B.S.E.E. in 1957 and his M.S.E. in 1960 from the University of Akron. In 1974 he received his J.D., also from Akron. Professor Edminister is a registered Professional Engineer in Ohio, a member of the bar in Ohio, and a registered patent attorney.

1 2 3 4 5 6 7 8 9   LOV   23 22 21 20 19 18

ISBN   978-1-260-12097-4
MHID   1-260-12097-X

e-ISBN   978-1-260-12098-1
e-MHID   1-260-12098-8

Library of Congress Control Number: 2013946487

Preface

The fifth edition of *Schaum's Outline of Electromagnetics* offers several new features which make it a more powerful tool for students and practitioners of electromagnetic field theory. It expands upon the presentation of transmission lines in Chapter 15. It adds new materials on the admittance plane, *y*- and *z*-mapping, and their navigation in the Smith Chart. A new Chapter 18 on *Propagation of Electromagnetic Waves in the Atmosphere* is added, along with examples, problems, and references. The book is designed for use as a textbook for a first course in electromagnetics or as a supplement to other standard textbooks, as well as a reference and aid to professionals.

Chapter 1 presents an overview of the subject including fundamental theories, new examples and problems (from static fields through Maxwell's equations), wave propagation, and transmission lines. Chapters 2–4 introduce vector analysis and the electric field. Mathematical tools such as the gradient, divergence, curl, and Laplacian are presented in Chapter 5. Chapters 6, 7, and 8 present electrostatics, electric currents, and dielectric materials. Laplace's equation is treated in Chapter 9. The magnetic field, boundary conditions, and magnetic circuits are covered in Chapters 10–12. Time-varying fields, Maxwell's equations, and electromagnetic waves are presented in Chapters 13 and 14. Transmission lines are discussed in Chapter 15 in a now expanded form with new material. (This chapter can be used independently from other chapters should the program of study recommend it.)

The basic approach of the previous editions has been retained. As in other Schaum's Outlines, the emphasis is on how to solve problems and learn through examples. Each chapter includes statements of pertinent definitions and simplified outlines of the principles and theoretical foundations needed to understand the subject, all interleaved with illustrative examples. Each chapter then contains an ample set of problems with detailed solutions and another set of problems with answers.

The study of electromagnetics requires the use of rather advanced mathematics, specifically vector analysis in Cartesian, cylindrical, and spherical coordinates. Throughout the book the mathematical treatment has been kept as simple as possible and an abstract approach has been avoided. Concrete examples are liberally used and numerous graphs and sketches are given. We have in many years of teaching found that the solution of most problems begins with a carefully drawn and labeled sketch.

This book is dedicated to our students from whom we have learned to teach well. Contributions of Messrs M.L. Kult and K.F. Lee to the material on transmission lines, waveguides, and antennas are acknowledged. We would like to thank our colleagues at Cal Poly State University in San Luis Obispo for their comments. Specifically, the review and input by Professor Dean Arakaki is greatly appreciated. Special thanks are due to Reza Nahvi for reviewing the material, accuracy checking, and editorial work. Finally, we wish to thank our wives Zahra Nahvi and Nina Edminister for their continuing support.

MAHMOOD NAHVI
JOSEPH A. EDMINISTER

Contents

CHAPTER 1   The Subject of Electromagnetics   **1**

    1.1 Historical Background   1
    1.2 Objectives of the Chapter   1
    1.3 Electric Charge   2
    1.4 Units   2
    1.5 Vectors   4
    1.6 Electrical Force, Field, Flux, and Potential   4
    1.7 Magnetic Force, Field, Flux, and Potential   7
    1.8 Electromagnetic Induction   9
    1.9 Mathematical Operators and Identities   10
    1.10 Maxwell's Equations   10
    1.11 Electromagnetic Waves   11
    1.12 Trajectory of a Sinusoidal Motion in Two Dimensions   14
    1.13 Wave Polarization   15
    1.14 Electromagnetic Spectrum   16
    1.15 Transmission Lines   17

CHAPTER 2   Vector Analysis   **31**

    2.1 Introduction   31
    2.2 Vector Notation   31
    2.3 Vector Functions   32
    2.4 Vector Algebra   32
    2.5 Coordinate Systems   34
    2.6 Differential Volume, Surface, and Line Elements   35

CHAPTER 3   Electric Field   **44**

    3.1 Introduction   44
    3.2 Coulomb's Law in Vector Form   44
    3.3 Superposition   45
    3.4 Electric Field Intensity   45
    3.5 Charge Distributions   46
    3.6 Standard Charge Configurations   48

CHAPTER 4   Electric Flux   **63**

    4.1 Net Charge in a Region   63
    4.2 Electric Flux and Flux Density   63
    4.3 Gauss's Law   65
    4.4 Relation between Flux Density and Electric Field Intensity   65
    4.5 Special Gaussian Surfaces   66

CHAPTER 5   Gradient, Divergence, Curl, and Laplacian   78

    5.1 Introduction   78
    5.2 Gradient   78
    5.3 The Del Operator   79
    5.4 The Del Operator and Gradient   80
    5.5 Divergence   80
    5.6 Expressions for Divergence in Coordinate Systems   80
    5.7 The Del Operator and Divergence   82
    5.8 Divergence of D   83
    5.9 The Divergence Theorem   83
  5.10 Curl   84
  5.11 Laplacian   86
  5.12 Summary of Vector Operations   86

CHAPTER 6   Electrostatics: Work, Energy, and Potential   97

    6.1 Work Done in Moving a Point Charge   97
    6.2 Conservative Property of the Electrostatic Field   98
    6.3 Electric Potential between Two Points   99
    6.4 Potential of a Point Charge   99
    6.5 Potential of a Charge Distribution   99
    6.6 Relationship between E and V   100
    6.7 Energy in Static Electric Fields   101

CHAPTER 7   Electric Current   113

    7.1 Introduction   113
    7.2 Charges in Motion   113
    7.3 Convection Current Density J   114
    7.4 Conduction Current Density J   114
    7.5 Conductivity σ 115
    7.6 Current I 116
    7.7 Resistance R 117
    7.8 Current Sheet Density K   118
    7.9 Continuity of Current   119
  7.10 Conductor-Dielectric Boundary Conditions   120

CHAPTER 8   Capacitance and Dielectric Materials   131

    8.1 Polarization P and Relative Permittivity ϵ_r 131
    8.2 Capacitance   132
    8.3 Multiple-Dielectric Capacitors   133
    8.4 Energy Stored in a Capacitor   134
    8.5 Fixed-Voltage D and E   135
    8.6 Fixed-Charge D and E   135
    8.7 Boundary Conditions at the Interface of Two Dielectrics   136
    8.8 Method of Images   137

CHAPTER 9   Laplace's Equation   151

    9.1 Introduction   151
    9.2 Poisson's Equation and Laplace's Equation   151

9.3 Explicit Forms of Laplace's Equation   151
9.4 Uniqueness Theorem   152
9.5 Mean Value and Maximum Value Theorems   153
9.6 Cartesian Solution in One Variable   153
9.7 Cartesian Product Solution   154
9.8 Cylindrical Product Solution   155
9.9 Spherical Product Solution   156

CHAPTER 10 Magnetic Field and Boundary Conditions   172

10.1 Introduction   172
10.2 Biot-Savart Law   172
10.3 Ampère's Law   174
10.4 Relationship of J and H   174
10.5 Magnetic Flux Density B   175
10.6 Boundary Relations for Magnetic Fields   176
10.7 Current Sheet at the Boundary   177
10.8 Summary of Boundary Conditions   178
10.9 Vector Magnetic Potential A   178
10.10 Stokes' Theorem   179

CHAPTER 11 Forces and Torques in Magnetic Fields   193

11.1 Magnetic Force on Particles   193
11.2 Electric and Magnetic Fields Combined   194
11.3 Magnetic Force on a Current Element   195
11.4 Work and Power   195
11.5 Torque   196
11.6 Magnetic Moment of a Planar Coil   197

CHAPTER 12 Inductance and Magnetic Circuits   209

12.1 Inductance   209
12.2 Standard Conductor Configurations   211
12.3 Faraday's Law and Self-Inductance   212
12.4 Internal Inductance   212
12.5 Mutual Inductance   213
12.6 Magnetic Circuits   214
12.7 The B-H Curve   215
12.8 Ampère's Law for Magnetic Circuits   216
12.9 Cores with Air Gaps   217
12.10 Multiple Coils   217
12.11 Parallel Magnetic Circuits   218

CHAPTER 13 Time-Varying Fields and Maxwell's Equations   233

13.1 Introduction   233
13.2 Maxwell's Equations for Static Fields   233
13.3 Faraday's Law and Lenz's Law   233
13.4 Conductors' Motion in Time-Independent Fields   234
13.5 Conductors' Motion in Time-Dependent Fields   235
13.6 Displacement Current   236
13.7 Ratio of J_c to J_D 238
13.8 Maxwell's Equations for Time-Varying Fields   238

CHAPTER 14 Electromagnetic Waves   251

    14.1 Introduction   251
    14.2 Wave Equations   251
    14.3 Solutions in Cartesian Coordinates   252
    14.4 Plane Waves   253
    14.5 Solutions for Partially Conducting Media   254
    14.6 Solutions for Perfect Dielectrics   255
    14.7 Solutions for Good Conductors; Skin Depth   255
    14.8 Interface Conditions at Normal Incidence   256
    14.9 Oblique Incidence and Snell's Laws   258
    14.10 Perpendicular Polarization   259
    14.11 Parallel Polarization   259
    14.12 Standing Waves   260
    14.13 Power and the Poynting Vector   261

CHAPTER 15 Transmission Lines   273

    15.1 Introduction   273
    15.2 Distributed Parameters   273
    15.3 Incremental Models   274
    15.4 Transmission Line Equation   275
    15.5 Impedance, Admittance, and Other Features of Interest   275
    15.6 Sinusoidal Steady-State Excitation   276
    15.7 Lossless Lines   278
    15.8 The Smith Chart   279
    15.9 Admittance Plane   282
    15.10 Quarter-Wave Transformer   282
    15.11 Impedance Matching   283
    15.12 Single-Stub Matching   284
    15.13 Double-Stub Matching   285
    15.14 Impedance Measurement   287
    15.15 Transients in Lossless Lines   288

CHAPTER 16 Waveguides   316

    16.1 Introduction   316
    16.2 Transverse and Axial Fields   316
    16.3 TE and TM Modes; Wave Impedances   318
    16.4 Determination of the Axial Fields   318
    16.5 Mode Cutoff Frequencies   319
    16.6 Dominant Mode   320
    16.7 Power Transmitted in a Lossless Waveguide   322
    16.8 Power Dissipation in a Lossy Waveguide   322

CHAPTER 17 Antennas   335

    17.1 Introduction   335
    17.2 Current Source and the E and H Fields   335
    17.3 Electric (Hertzian) Dipole Antenna   335
    17.4 Antenna Parameters   336
    17.5 Small Circular-Loop Antenna   338
    17.6 Finite-Length Dipole   338
    17.7 Monopole Antenna   339

17.8   Self- and Mutual Impedances   340
17.9   The Receiving Antenna   341
17.10 Linear Arrays   342
17.11 Reflectors   343

CHAPTER 18 Propagation of Electromagnetic Waves in the Atmosphere   354

18.1   Introduction and Summary   354
18.2   Plane Waves in Homogeneous Media   354
18.3   Propagation Parameters   355
18.4   Complex Dielectric Constant   357
18.5   Power Equation   358
18.6   Refraction   359
18.7   Reflection, Diffraction, and Scattering   360
18.8   The Atmosphere   361
18.9   Atmospheric Effects on Propagation of Radio Waves   362
18.10 Attenuation by Gaseous Absorption   362
18.11 Attenuation by Hydrometeors   363
18.12 Ground and Sky Waves   364
18.13 Models of the Troposphere   366
18.14 Tropospheric Refractivity   366
18.15 Tropospheric Excess Delay   367
18.16 Bending Effect of Tropospheric Refraction   368
18.17 Conductivity, Permittivity, and Refraction Index
           of the Ionosphere   369
18.18 Satellite Microwave Ranging   370
18.19 Ionospheric Range Error   371
18.20 Tropospheric Range Error   372

APPENDIX   **384**

INDEX   **385**

The Subject of Electromagnetics

1.1 Historical Background

Electric and magnetic phenomena have been known to mankind since early times. The amber effect is an example of an electrical phenomenon: a piece of amber rubbed against the sleeve becomes electrified, acquiring a force field which attracts light objects such as chaff and paper. Rubbing one's woolen jacket on the hair of one's head elicits sparks which can be seen in the dark. Lightning between clouds (or between clouds and the earth) is another example of familiar electrical phenomena. The woolen jacket and the clouds are electrified, acquiring a force field which leads to sparks. Examples of familiar magnetic phenomena are natural or magnetized mineral stones that attract metals such as iron. The magical magnetic force, it is said, had even kept some objects in temples floating in the air.

The scientific and quantitative exploration of electric and magnetic phenomena started in the seventeenth and eighteenth centuries (Gilbert, 1600; Guericke, 1660; Dufay, 1733; Franklin, 1752; Galvani, 1771; Cavendish, 1775; Coulomb, 1785; Volta, 1800). Forces between stationary electric charges were explained by Coulomb's law. Electrostatics and magnetostatics (fields which do not change with time) were formulated and modeled mathematically. The study of the interrelationship between electric and magnetic fields and their time-varying behavior progressed in the nineteenth century (Oersted, 1820 and 1826; Ampère, 1820; Faraday, 1831; Henry, 1831; Maxwell, 1856 and 1873; Hertz, 1893).[1] Oersted observed that an electric current produces a magnetic field. Faraday verified that a time-varying magnetic field produces an electric field (emf). Henry constructed electromagnets and discovered self-inductance. Maxwell, by introducing the concept of the displacement current, developed a mathematical foundation for electromagnetic fields and waves currently known as Maxwell's equations. Hertz verified, experimentally, propagation of electromagnetic waves predicted by Maxwell's equations. Despite their simplicity, Maxwell's equations are comprehensive in that they account for all classical electromagnetic phenomena, from static fields to electromagnetic induction and wave propagation. Since publication of Maxwell's historical manuscript in 1873 more advances have been made in the field, culminating in what is presently known as classical electromagnetics (EM). Currently, the important applications of EM are in radiation and propagation of electromagnetic waves in free space by transmission lines, waveguides, fiber optics, and other methods. The power of these applications far surpasses any alleged historical magical powers of healing patients or suspending objects in the air.

In order to study the subject of electromagnetics, one may start with electrostatic and magnetostatic fields, continue with time-varying fields and Maxwell's equations, and move on to electromagnetic wave propagation and radiation. Alternatively, one may start with Maxwell's equations. This book uses the first approach, starting with the Coulomb force law between two charges. Vector algebra and vector calculus are introduced early and as needed throughout the book.

1.2 Objectives of the Chapter

This chapter is intended to provide a brief glance (and be easily understood by an undergraduate student in the sciences and engineering) of some basic concepts and methods of the subject of electromagnetics. The objective

---

[1] For some historical timelines see the references at the end of this chapter.

is to familiarize the reader with the subject and let him or her know what to expect from it. The chapter can also serve as a short summary of the main tools and techniques used throughout the book. Detailed treatments of the concepts are provided throughout the rest of the book.

1.3   Electric Charge

The source of the force field associated with an electrified object (such as the amber rubbed against the sleeve) is a quantity called electric charge which we will denote by Q or q. The unit of electric charge is the coulomb, shown by the letter C (see the next section for a definition). Electric charges are of two types, labeled positive and negative. Charges of the same type repel while those of the opposite type attract each other. At the atomic level we recognize two types of charged particles of equal numbers in the natural state: electrons and protons. An electron has a negative charge of 1.60219×10^{-9} C (sometimes shown by the letter e) and a proton has a positive charge of precisely the same amount as that of an electron. The choice of negative and positive labels for electric charges on electrons and protons is accidental and rooted in history. The electric charge on an electron is the smallest amount one may find. This quantization of charge, however, is not of interest in classical electromagnetics and will not be discussed. Instead we will have charges as a continuous quantity concentrated at a point or distributed on a line, a surface, or in a volume, with the charge density normally denoted by the letter ρ.

It is much easier to remove electrons from their host atoms than protons. If some electrons leave a piece of matter which is electrically neutral, then that matter becomes positively charged. To take our first example again, electrons are transferred from cloth to amber when they are rubbed together. The amber then accumulates a negative charge which becomes the source of an electric field. Some numerical properties of electrons are given in Table 1-1.

TABLE **1-1 Some Numerical Properties of Electrons**

Electric charge	-1.60219×10^{-19} C
Resting mass	9.10939×10^{-31} kg
Charge to mass ratio	1.75×10^{11} C/kg
Order of radius	3.8×10^{-15} m
Number of electrons per 1 C	6.24×10^{18}

1.4   Units

In electromagnetics we use the International System of Units, abbreviated SI from the French *le Système international d'unités* (also called the rationalized MKS system). The SI system has seven basic units for seven basic quantities. Three units come from the MKS mechanical system (the *meter*, the *kilogram*, and the *second*). The fourth unit is the *ampere* for electric current. One *ampere* is the amount of constant current in each of two infinitely long parallel conductors with negligible diameters separated by one meter with a resulting force between them of 2×10^{-7} newtons per meter. These basic units are summarized in Table 1-2.

TABLE **1-2 Four Basic Units in the SI System**

QUANTITY	SYMBOL	SI UNIT	ABBREVIATION
Length	L, ℓ	Meter	m
Mass	M, m	Kilogram	kg
Time	T, t	Second	s
Current	I, i	Ampere	A

The other three basic quantities and their corresponding SI units are the temperature in degrees kelvin (K), the luminous intensity in candelas (cd), and the amount of a substance in moles (mol). These are not of interest to us. Units for all other quantities of interest are derived from the four basic units of *length, mass, time,* and *current* using electromechanical formulae. For example, the unit of electric charge is found from its relationship with current and time to be $q = \int i \, dt$. Thus, one coulomb is the amount of charge passed by one ampere in one second, $1 \, C = 1 \, A \times 1 \, s$. The derived units are shown in Table 1-3.

TABLE 1-3 Additional Units in the SI System Derived from the Basic Units

QUANTITY	SYMBOL	SI UNIT	ABBREVIATION
Force	F, f	Newton	N
Energy, work	W, w	Joule	J
Power	P, p	Watt	W
Electric charge	Q, q	Coulomb	C
Electric field	E, e	Volt/meter	V/m
Electric potential	V, v	Volt	V
Displacement	D	Coulomb/meter^2	C/m^2
Resistance	R	Ohm	Ω
Conductance	G	Siemens	S
Capacitance	C	Farad	F
Inductance	L	Henry	H
Magnetic field intensity	H	Ampere/meter	A/m
Magnetic flux	ϕ	Weber	Wb
Magnetic flux density	B	Tesla	T
Frequency	f	Hertz	Hz

Magnetic flux density B is sometimes measured in gauss, where 10^4 gauss = 1 tesla. The decimal multiples and submultiples of SI units will be used whenever possible. The symbols given in Table 1-4 are prefixed to the unit symbols of Tables 1-2 and 1-3.

TABLE 1-4 Decimal Multiples and Submultiples of Units in the SI System

PREFIX	FACTOR	SYMBOL
Atto	10^{-18}	a
Femto	10^{-15}	f
Pico	10^{-12}	p
Nano	10^{-9}	n
Micro	10^{-6}	μ
Milli	10^{-3}	m
Centi	10^{-2}	c
Deci	10^{-1}	d
Kilo	10^{3}	k
Mega	10^{6}	M
Giga	10^{9}	G
Tera	10^{12}	T
Peta	10^{15}	P
Exa	10^{18}	E

1.5   Vectors

In electromagnetics we use vectors to facilitate our calculations and explanations. A vector is a quantity speci-fied by its magnitude and direction. Forces and force fields are examples of quantities expressed by vectors. To distinguish vectors from scalar quantities, bold-face letters are used for the former. A vector whose magnitude is 1 is called a *unit vector*. To represent vectors in the Cartesian coordinate space, we employ three basic unit vectors: $\mathbf{a}_x$, $\mathbf{a}_y$, and $\mathbf{a}_z$ in the x, y, and z directions, respectively. For example, a vector connecting the origin to point A at $(x = 2, y = -1, z = 3)$ is shown by $\mathbf{A} = 2\mathbf{a}_x - \mathbf{a}_y + 3\mathbf{a}_z$. Its magnitude is $|\mathbf{A}| = A = \sqrt{2^2 + (-1)^2 + 3^2} = \sqrt{14}$. Its direction is given by the unit vector

$$\frac{\mathbf{A}}{\sqrt{14}} = 0.5345\mathbf{a}_x - 0.2673\mathbf{a}_y + 0.8018\mathbf{a}_z$$

Three basic vector operations are

addition and subtraction, $\mathbf{A} \pm \mathbf{B} = (A_x \pm B_x)\mathbf{a}_x + (A_y \pm B_y)\mathbf{a}_y + (A_z \pm B_z)\mathbf{a}_z$,

dot product, $\mathbf{A} \cdot \mathbf{B} = AB \cos \theta$, where θ is the smaller angle between $\mathbf{A}$ and $\mathbf{B}$,

cross product, $\mathbf{A} \times \mathbf{B} = AB \sin \theta\, \mathbf{a}_n$, where $\mathbf{a}_n$ is the unit vector normal to the plane parallel to $\mathbf{A}$ and $\mathbf{B}$.

The dot product results in a scalar quantity; hence it is also called the scalar product. It can easily be shown that $\mathbf{A} \cdot \mathbf{B} = A_x B_x + A_y B_y + A_z B_z$. The cross product results in a vector quantity; hence, it is also called the vector product. $\mathbf{A} \times \mathbf{B}$ is normal to both $\mathbf{A}$ and $\mathbf{B}$ and follows the *right-hand rule*: With the fingers of the right hand rotating from $\mathbf{A}$ to $\mathbf{B}$ through angle θ, the thumb points in the direction of $\mathbf{A} \times \mathbf{B}$. It can easily be shown that

$$\left. \begin{array}{l} \mathbf{a}_x \times \mathbf{a}_y = \mathbf{a}_z \\ \mathbf{a}_y \times \mathbf{a}_z = \mathbf{a}_x \\ \mathbf{a}_z \times \mathbf{a}_x = \mathbf{a}_y \end{array} \right\} \Rightarrow \mathbf{A} \times \mathbf{B} = (A_y B_z - A_z B_y)\mathbf{a}_x + (A_z B_x - A_x B_z)\mathbf{a}_y + (A_x B_x - A_y B_x)\mathbf{a}_z$$

1.6   Electrical Force, Field, Flux, and Potential

Electrical Force.   There is a force between two point charges. The force is directly proportional to the charge magnitudes and inversely proportional to the square of their separation distance. The direction of the force is along the line joining the two charges. For point charges of like sign the force is one of repulsion, while for unlike charges the force is attractive. The magnitude of the force is given by

$$F = \frac{Q_1 Q_2}{4\pi\epsilon d^2}$$

This is *Coulomb's law*, which was developed from work with small charged bodies (spheres) and a delicate torsion balance (Coulomb 1785). Rationalized SI units are used. The force is in newtons (N), the distance is in meters (m), and the charge is in units called the coulomb (C). The SI system is rationalized by the factor 4π, introduced in Coulomb's law in order that it not appear later in Maxwell's equation. ϵ is the *permittivity* of the medium with the unit $C^2/(N \cdot m^2)$ or, equivalently, farads per meter (F/m). For free space or vacuum,

$$\epsilon = \epsilon_0 = 8.854 \times 10^{-12} \text{ F/m} \approx \frac{10^{-9}}{36\pi} \text{ F/m}$$

For media other than free space, $\epsilon = \epsilon_0 \epsilon_r$, where ϵ_r is the *relative permittivity* or *dielectric constant*. Free space is to be assumed in all problems and examples as well as the approximate value for ϵ_0, unless there is a state-ment to the contrary.

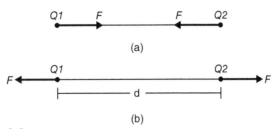

Fig. 1-1 Coulomb's law $F = \frac{Q_1 Q_2}{4\pi \epsilon d^2}$. In (a) Q_1 and Q_2 are unlike charges, and in (b) they are of the same type.

EXAMPLE 1.   Two electrons in free space are separated by 1 $A°$ (1 Angstrom = 10^{-10} m). We want to find and compare Coulomb's electrostatic force and Newton's gravitational force between them. Since the distance between the two electrons, 10^{-10} m, is much more than their radii, $\approx 3.8 \times 10^{-15}$ m, they can be considered point charges and masses. Coulomb's electrostatic force between them is

$$F_e = \frac{Q_1 Q_2}{4\pi\epsilon_0 d^2} = \frac{\left[1.60219 \times 10^{-19}\right]^2}{4\pi \times \frac{10^{-9}}{4\pi} \times 10^{-20}} \approx 23.1 \times 10^{-9} \text{ N}$$

Newton's gravitational force between two masses M_1 and M_2 separated by a distance d is $F_g = GM_1 M_2/d^2$, where F_g is in newtons, M_1 and M_2 are in kg, d is in meters, and G, the gravitational constant, is $G = 6.674 \times 10^{-11}$. With the resting mass of an electron being 9.10939×10^{-31} kg, the gravitational force between them is

$$F_g = G \frac{M_1 M_2}{d^2} = 6.674 \times 10^{-11} \frac{\left[9.10939 \times 10^{-31}\right]^2}{10^{-20}} \approx 55.4 \times 10^{-52} \text{ N}$$

Therefore, the electrical force between two electrons is approximately 42 orders of magnitude stronger than their gravitational force.

Superposition Property.   The presence of a third charge doesn't change the mutual force between the other two charges, but rather adds (vectorially) its own force contribution. This is called the linear superposition property. It helps us define a vector quantity called the field intensity and use it in order to find the force on a charge at any point in the field.

Electric Field.   The force field associated with a charge configuration is called an electric field. It is a vector field specified by a quantity called the electric field intensity, shown by vector **E**. The electric field intensity at a given point is the force on a positive unit charge, called the test charge, placed at that point. The intensity of the electric field due to a point charge Q at a distance d is a vector directed away from the point charge (if Q is positive) or toward it (if Q is negative). Its magnitude is

$$E = \frac{Q}{4\pi\epsilon d^2}$$

In vector notation

$$\mathbf{E} = \frac{Q}{4\pi\epsilon d^2} \mathbf{a}$$

where **a** is the unit vector directed from the point charge to the test point. The unit of the electric field intensity is V/m. The superposition property of electric field is used to find the field due to any spatial charge configuration.

EXAMPLE 2.   The electric field intensity at 10 cm away from a point charge of 0.1 μC in vacuum is

$$\mathbf{E} = \frac{10^{-7}}{4\pi\left(\dfrac{10^{-9}}{36\pi}\right)10^{-2}}\,\mathbf{a}_r = 90\,\mathbf{a}_r\ \text{kV/m}$$

where $\mathbf{a}_r$ is the radial unit vector with the charge at the center. At the distance of 1 m its magnitude is reduced to 900 V/m. If the medium is a dielectric with relative permittivity $\epsilon_r = 100$ (such as titanium dioxide), the above field intensities are reduced to 900 and 9 V/m, respectively.

Electric Flux.   An electric field is completely specified by its intensity vector. However, to help better explain some phenomena, we also define a scalar field called the electric flux. Electric flux is considered a quantity, albeit an imaginary one, which originates on the positive charge, moves along a stream of directional lines (called flux lines), and terminates on the negative charge, or at infinity if there are no other charges in the field. Electrical forces are thus experienced when an electric charge encounters lines of electric flux. This is analogous to the example of fluid flow where the flux originates from a source and terminates at a sink or dissipates into the environment. In this case, a vector field such as velocity defines the flux density, from which one can determine the amount of fluid flow passing through a surface. Faraday envisioned the concept of electric flux, shown by Ψ, to explain how a positive charge induces an equal but negative charge on a shell which encloses it. His experimental setup consisted of an inner shell enclosed by an outer sphere. Unlike flux, which is a scalar field, its density is a vector field.

Electric Flux Density.   Flux density $\mathbf{D}$ in an electric field is defined by $\mathbf{D} = \epsilon\mathbf{E}$. In the SI system, the unit of electric flux is the coulomb (C) and that of flux density is C/m². The flux passing through a differential surface element $d\mathbf{s}$ is the *dot* product $\mathbf{D}\cdot d\mathbf{s}$, which numerically is equal to the product of the differential surface element's area, with the magnitude of the component of the flux density perpendicular to it.

Gauss's Law.   The total flux out of a closed surface is equal to the net charge enclosed within the surface.

EXAMPLE 3.   Flux density through a spherical surface with radius d enclosing a point charge Q is

$$\mathbf{D} = \epsilon\mathbf{E} = \frac{Q}{4\pi d^2}\,\mathbf{a}$$

where $\mathbf{a}$ is the radial unit vector from the point charge to the test point on the sphere. The total flux coming out of the sphere is

$$\Psi = 4\pi d^2 \times D = 4\pi d^2 \times \frac{Q}{4\pi d^2} = Q$$

Electric Potential.   The work done to move a unit charge from point B to point A in an electric field is called the potential of point A with reference to point B and shown by V_{AB}. It is equal to the line integral

$$V_{AB} = -\int_B^A \mathbf{E}\cdot d\mathbf{l}$$

The value of the integral depends only on the electric field and the two end-points. It is independent of the path traversed by the charge as long as all attempted paths share the same initial and destination points. The value of the integral over a closed path is, therefore, zero. This is a property of a conservative field such as $\mathbf{E}$. If the reference point B is moved to infinity, the integral defines a scalar field called the potential field. The unit of the potential is the volt (V), the work needed to move one C of charge a distance of 1 m along a field of $E = 1$ V/m.

The electric potential is introduced as a line integral of the electric field. It can also be found from charge distributions. Conversely, field intensity and flux can be obtained from the potential (see Chapter 6).

EXAMPLE 4.   There exists a static electric field in the atmosphere directed downward which depends on weather conditions and decreases with height. Assuming that its intensity near the ground is about 150 V/m and remains the same within the tropospheric height, find the electric potential at a height of 333 m with respect to the ground.

$$V = 150 \text{ V/m} \times 333 \text{ m} \approx 50 \text{ kV}$$

1.7   Magnetic Force, Field, Flux, and Potential

Magnetic Force.   Permanent magnets, be they natural, such as a lodestone (Gilbert, 1600 AD), or manufactured, such as one bought from a store, establish a force field in their vicinity which exerts a force on some metallic objects. The force here is called the magnetic force, and the field is called a magnetic field. The source of the magnetic field is the motion of electric charges within the atomic structure of such permanent magnets. Moving electric charges (such as an electric current) also produce a magnetic field which may be detected in the same way as that of a permanent magnet. Hold a compass needle close to a wire carrying a DC current and the needle will align itself, at a right angle with the current. Change the current direction in the wire and the needle will change its direction. This experiment, performed by Oersted in 1820, indicates that the electric current produces a magnetic field in its surroundings which exerts a force on the compass needle. Replace the compass with a solenoid carrying a DC current and the solenoid will align itself, just like the compass, in a direction perpendicular to the current. With a DC current, such generated magnetic fields are static in nature. In a similar experiment, a wire suspended along the direction of a magnetic field and carrying a sinusoidal current will vibrate at the frequency of the current. (This effect was used in the early days of EKG monitoring. Passage of electrical heart pulses through a wire suspended in the field of a permanent magnet causes it to deflect and vibrate, with a pen recording the vibrations and hence the electrical activity of the heart.) These observations indicate that the magnetic field exerts a force on the compass, another magnet, or a current-carrying wire or solenoid. They specifically show that a current-carrying wire generates a magnetic field in its neighborhood which exerts a force on another current-carrying wire placed there.

Force Between Two Wires.   Two infinitely long parallel wires carrying currents I_1 and I_2 and separated by distance d experience a mutual force. They are pushed apart (when currents are in the same direction) or pulled together (when currents are in opposite directions). The magnitude of the magnetic force between the two wires in free space is given by the following:

$$F = \frac{\mu_0}{2\pi} \frac{I_1 I_2}{d}$$

where $\mu_0 = 4\pi \times 10^{-7}$ (H/m) is the permeability of free space. The force is in newtons (N), the distance is in meters (m), and the currents are in amperes (A).

Magnetic Field Strength.   The magnetic field strength is a vector quantity, specified by a magnitude and a direction. In this book we work with magnetic fields whose sources are electric currents and moving charges. The magnitude of the differential field strength of a small element of conducting wire dl carrying a current I is

$$dH = \frac{I \, dl \sin \theta}{4\pi R^2}$$

where R is the distance from the current element to the test point at which dH is being measured and θ is the angle between the current element and the line connecting it to the test point. The direction of the field is normal to the plane made of the current element and the connecting line, following the right-hand rule: With the right thumb pointing along the direction of current, the fingers point in the direction of the field. This is called the Biot-Savart law. In vector notation it is given by

$$d\mathbf{H} = \frac{I \, d\mathbf{l} \times \mathbf{a}_R}{4\pi R^2}$$

where $d\mathbf{l}$ is the differential current element vector and $\mathbf{a}_R$ is the unit vector directed from it to the test point.

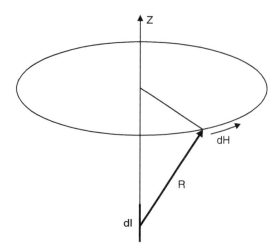

Fig. 1-2 Differential magnetic field $d\mathbf{H}$ at the distance $\mathbf{R}$ due to a differential current element $d\mathbf{l}$.

The unit of magnetic field strength is A/m. The superposition property is used to find the magnetic field due to any current configuration.

Magnetic Field Strength of a Long Wire.   By using the superposition property, we can integrate the above differential field to find the magnetic field strength due to a given current configuration. For example, the magnetic field strength at a radial distance r from a straight, long wire carrying current I is

$$\mathbf{H} = \frac{I}{2\pi r}\,\mathbf{a}_\phi$$

The direction of $\mathbf{H}$, shown by the unit vector $\mathbf{a}_\phi$, again follows the right-hand rule: Grasp the conductor with the right hand such that the thumb points in the direction of the current, and the fingers will point in the direction of the field. As an example, the strength of the magnetic field at 1 meter away from a long cable carrying a current of 10 A is $H = 10/(2\pi) = 1.6$ A/m.

Ampère's Law.   The line integral of the tangential component of the magnetic field strength around a closed path is equal to the current enclosed by the path.

EXAMPLE 5.   Consider a circular path of radius r surrounding an infinitely long, straight, thin wire carrying current I. The magnetic field strength surrounding the circle is a vector $\mathbf{H}$ tangent to the circle. Its magnitude is $H = I/(2\pi r)$ and the line integral around the path is $2\pi r \times H = 2\pi r \times I/(2\pi r) = I$, thus confirming Ampère's law.

Magnetic Flux and Its Density.   Associated with a magnetic field $\mathbf{H}$ is a force field $\mathbf{B} = \mu\mathbf{H}$, called the magnetic flux density (also known as magnetic induction). Like $\mathbf{H}$, $\mathbf{B}$ is a vector field—that is, a quantity with a magnitude and a direction—but unlike $\mathbf{H}$, which is independent of the medium, $\mathbf{B}$ depends on the medium through a factor μ called the permeability. For free space, the permeability is $\mu_0 = 4\pi \times 10^{-7}$ H/m.
   Having defined its density, we can find the magnetic flux Φ through a given surface by integrating the flux passing through a differential surface element's area $d\mathbf{s}$: $\Phi = \int \mathbf{B} \cdot d\mathbf{s}$, where the dot (·) shows the product of the differential surface element's area and the magnitude of the component of flux density normal to it. In the SI system, the unit of magnetic flux is the *weber*, shown by *Wb*, and that of flux density is the *tesla*, shown by T (where $Wb/m^2 = T$).

EXAMPLE 6.   The magnetic flux density at a distance 10 meters away from a long cable carrying a DC current of 100 A in free space is

$$B = \mu_0 H = \frac{\mu_0 I}{2\pi d} = \frac{4\pi \times 10^{-7} \times 100}{2\pi \times 10} = 2 \times 10^{-6}\ T = 2\ \mu T$$

The magnetic flux through a rectangular area (1 m × 10 cm) coplanar with the cable and placed length-wise along it at a distance of 10 m is $\Phi = \int \mathbf{B} \cdot \mathbf{ds} \approx B \times S = 2\,\mu T \times 10^{-1}\,m^2 = 2 \times 10^{-7}\,Wb$. The flux is constant.

Force on a Moving Charge.   Motion of a charged particle in a magnetic field generates a force on the particle. The magnitude of the force is proportional to the charge Q, magnetic flux density B, velocity of motion v, and the sine of the angle θ between the velocity and magnetic vectors, $F = QvB \sin \theta$. Its direction is perpendicular to the flux density vector $\mathbf{B}$ and the velocity vector $\mathbf{v}$. In vector notation, the force is expressed by the vector product

$$\mathbf{F}_{magnetic} = Q\mathbf{v} \times \mathbf{B}$$

If the field combines an electric field with the magnetic field, the total force on the moving particle is

$$\mathbf{F}_{total} = Q\,(\mathbf{E} + \mathbf{v} \times \mathbf{B})$$

Vector Magnetic Potential.   In Section 1.6 we introduced the scalar quantity called electric potential which can serve as an intermediate quantity for field computations. Similarly, for magnetic fields we define *a vector magnetic potential* $\mathbf{A}$ such that

$$\nabla \times \mathbf{A} = \mathbf{B}$$

where $\nabla \times \mathbf{A}$ is a vector called the *curl* of $\mathbf{A}$ (see Section 1.9 for the definition of curl). The vector magnetic potential can be obtained from the current distribution in the media and thus can serve as an intermediate quantity for calculation of $\mathbf{B}$ and $\mathbf{H}$ (see Chapter 10). The unit of the vector magnetic potential is the *weber per meter* (Wb/m).

1.8   Electromagnetic Induction

Static electric and magnetic fields are decoupled from each other. Each field works and exists by itself and can be treated separately. Time variation couples them together. An early discovery of electromagnetic coupling was made by Faraday, who observed that a time-varying magnetic field generates a time-varying electric field, which produces a voltage and current in a conducting loop placed in the field. This is known as Faraday's law of induction. The effect was verified experimentally for the first time by Faraday in 1831. (Faraday also hypothesized that in a similar way a time-varying electric field should produce a magnetic field, but he did not predict it theoretically or demonstrated it experimentally. That was left to Maxwell's equations in 1873 and Hertz in 1893.) It is said that the time-varying magnetic flux induces an electric potential. The voltage is called the electromotive force (*emf*). An *emf* can also be produced by a moving magnetic field or by a conductor moving in a magnetic field, even when that field is constant. Using the concept of magnetic flux linkage ϕ (the total magnetic flux linking the circuit), Faraday's law, stated in mathematical form, is

$$emf = -\frac{d\phi}{dt}$$

where ϕ is the total magnetic flux linking the circuit. ϕ is called the magnetic flux linkage.

EXAMPLE 7.   A very long straight wire carries a 60-Hz current with an *RMS* value I_0 in free space. To determine I_0, a single-strand rectangular test loop (1 m × 10 cm) is placed coplanar with the wire and length-wise in parallel with it at a distance of 10 m. The *rms* of the induced *emf* in the loop is 95 μV. Find I_0.

$$i(t) = \sqrt{2}I_0 \sin(377t)$$

$$H = \frac{i}{2\pi r}, \quad B = \mu_0 H = 4\pi \times 10^{-7} \times \frac{i}{2\pi \times 10} = 2 \times 10^{-8} i$$

$$\phi = B \times S = (2 \times 10^{-8} i) \times (1 \times 10^{-1}) = 2 \times 10^{-9} i = 2\sqrt{2} \times 10^{-9} I_0 \sin(377t)$$

$$emf = -\frac{d\phi}{dt} = -377 \times 2\sqrt{2} \times 10^{-9} I_0 \cos(377t), \quad \text{with an } rms \text{ of } 0.754 I_0 \ \mu V$$

From the measured $emf = 95\ \mu V$ we find $I_0 = 95/0.754 = 126$ A.

Increasing Flux Linkage.   Flux linkage is increased by a factor *n* if the test loop has *n* turns. Let the test loop of Example 7 have 100 turns and the induced *emf* will become 9.5 mV.

1.9   Mathematical Operators and Identities

Electromagnetic fields and forces are vector quantities specified by their magnitude and direction and shown by boldface letters, as seen in the previous sections. So far we have been content with simple cases and examples which are handled without resorting to vector algebra and calculus. To analyze and study the subject of electromagnetics rigorously, however, we need vector algebra and mathematical operators such as the *gradient, divergence, curl*, and *Laplacian*. These will be discussed in Chapter 5 and throughout the book as the need arises. Some important vector operators used in electromagnetics are briefly summarized in Table 1-5. They are given in the Cartesian coordinate system. The unit vectors in the *x*, *y*, and *z* directions are shown by $\mathbf{a}_x$, $\mathbf{a}_y$, and $\mathbf{a}_z$, respectively.

TABLE 1-5 Some Useful Vector Operators and Identities

(1) Cartesian vector: $\mathbf{A} = A_x\mathbf{a}_x + A_y\mathbf{a}_y + A_z\mathbf{a}_z$

(2) Time-derivative of a vector: $\dfrac{\partial \mathbf{A}}{\partial t} = \dfrac{\partial A_x}{\partial t}\mathbf{a}_x + \dfrac{\partial A_y}{\partial t}\mathbf{a}_y + \dfrac{\partial A_z}{\partial t}\mathbf{a}_z$

(3) Dot product of two vectors: $\mathbf{A}\cdot\mathbf{B} = A_xB_x + A_yB_y + A_zB_z$

(4) Cross product of two vectors: $\mathbf{A}\times\mathbf{B} = (A_yB_z - A_zB_y)\mathbf{a}_x + (A_zB_x - A_xB_z)\mathbf{a}_y + (A_xB_y - A_yB_x)\mathbf{a}_z$

(5) Del operator: $\nabla \equiv \dfrac{\partial(\ )}{\partial x}\mathbf{a}_x + \dfrac{\partial(\ )}{\partial y}\mathbf{a}_y + \dfrac{\partial(\ )}{\partial z}\mathbf{a}_z$

(6) Gradient of a scalar field: $\nabla F = \dfrac{\partial F}{\partial x}\mathbf{a}_x + \dfrac{\partial F}{\partial y}\mathbf{a}_y + \dfrac{\partial F}{\partial z}\mathbf{a}_z$

(7) Divergence of a vector field: $\nabla\cdot\mathbf{A} = \dfrac{\partial A_x}{\partial x} + \dfrac{\partial A_y}{\partial y} + \dfrac{\partial A_z}{\partial z}$

(8) Curl of a vector field: $\nabla\times\mathbf{A} = \left(\dfrac{\partial A_z}{\partial y} - \dfrac{\partial A_y}{\partial z}\right)\mathbf{a}_x + \left(\dfrac{\partial A_x}{\partial z} - \dfrac{\partial A_z}{\partial x}\right)\mathbf{a}_y + \left(\dfrac{\partial A_y}{\partial x} - \dfrac{\partial A_x}{\partial y}\right)\mathbf{a}_z$

(9) Laplacian (divergence of gradient) of a scalar field: $\nabla^2 F \equiv \nabla\cdot\nabla F = \dfrac{\partial^2 F}{\partial x^2} + \dfrac{\partial^2 F}{\partial y^2} + \dfrac{\partial^2 F}{\partial z^2}$

(10) Curl curl of a vector field: $\nabla\times(\nabla\times\mathbf{A}) = \nabla(\nabla\cdot\mathbf{A}) - \nabla^2\mathbf{A}$

(11) Vector identities:
 (a) Divergence of the curl is zero $\nabla\cdot(\nabla\times\mathbf{A}) = 0$
 (b) Curl of the gradient is zero $\nabla\times(\nabla F) = \mathbf{0}$

1.10   Maxwell's Equations

James Clerk Maxwell (1831–1879) was inspired by Faraday's discovery in 1831 that a time-varying magnetic field generates an electric field and his hypothesis that a time-varying electric field would similarly generate a magnetic field (an idea that Faraday had neither demonstrated experimentally nor predicted theoretically).

In his theoretical attempt to formulate the coupling between time-varying electric and magnetic fields, Maxwell recognized the inadequancy of Ampère's law when applied to time-varying fields, as it contradicted the conservation of electric charge principle (see Problem 1.17). Maxwell introduced the concept of a *displacement current density* $\frac{\partial \mathbf{D}}{\partial t}$ in Ampère's law to supplement the current density due to moving charges. The introduction of the *displacement current* removed that contradiction and predicted that a time-varying electric field would also produce a (time-varying) magnetic field. The collective set of the following four equations (written in vector form) are called Maxwell's equations.

$$\nabla \times \mathbf{E} = -\frac{\partial \mathbf{B}}{\partial t} \qquad \text{(Faraday's law)}$$

$$\nabla \times \mathbf{H} = \mathbf{J} + \frac{\partial \mathbf{D}}{\partial t} \qquad \text{(Ampère's law supplemented by Maxwell's displacement current)}$$

$$\nabla \cdot \mathbf{D} = \rho \qquad \text{(Gauss's law for the electric field)}$$

$$\nabla \cdot \mathbf{B} = 0 \qquad \text{(Gauss's law for the magnetic field)}$$

Here ρ is the charge density and $\mathbf{J}$ is the current density. Maxwell's equations form the main tenet of classical electromagnetics. They provide a general and complete framework for time-varying electromagnetic fields from which the special case of static fields can also be deduced. But more importantly, the equations predict electromagnetic waves which propagate through space at the speed of light.

In the case of sinusoidal time-variation (time dependence through $e^{j\omega t}$, also called time harmonics), we obtain the phasor representation (also called the time harmonic form) of Maxwell's equations.

$$\nabla \times \mathbf{E} = -j\omega \mathbf{B} \qquad\qquad \nabla \cdot \mathbf{D} = \rho$$
$$\nabla \times \mathbf{H} = \mathbf{J} + j\omega \mathbf{D} \qquad\qquad \nabla \cdot \mathbf{B} = 0$$

In the phasor domain, $\mathbf{E}$ and $\mathbf{B}$ are complex-valued vectors and functions of space (x, y, z) only. They share the same time dependency through $e^{j\omega t}$. The phasor representation of Maxwell's equations does not impose any limitations and can be used without loss of generality.

Maxwell's Equations in Source-Free Media.   Maxwell's equations in a linear medium with permeability μ, permittivity ϵ, and containing no charges or currents ($\rho = 0$ and $J = 0$) become

$$\nabla \times \mathbf{E} = -\mu \frac{\partial \mathbf{H}}{\partial t} \qquad\qquad \nabla \cdot \mathbf{E} = 0$$

$$\nabla \times \mathbf{H} = \epsilon \frac{\partial \mathbf{E}}{\partial t} \qquad\qquad \nabla \cdot \mathbf{H} = 0$$

These provide two first-order partial differential equations in $\mathbf{E}$ and $\mathbf{H}$ which couple derivatives with respect to space and time. To find wave equations for $\mathbf{E}$ and $\mathbf{H}$, we take the derivatives of the above equations and obtain two second-order partial differential equations in $\mathbf{E}$ and $\mathbf{H}$, resulting in a decoupling of these two fields. Some wave equations for special and important situations are derived in the next section.

1.11   Electromagnetic Waves

Electromagnetic waves are time-varying field patterns which travel through space. An example is the sinusoidal plane wave in free space with constitutive fields given by

$$\mathbf{E} = E_0 \sin \omega (t - \sqrt{\epsilon_0 \mu_0}\ z)\ \mathbf{a}_x$$
$$\mathbf{H} = H_0 \sin \omega (t - \sqrt{\epsilon_0 \mu_0}\ z)\ \mathbf{a}_y$$

where $\mathbf{a}_x$ and $\mathbf{a}_y$ are unit vectors in the x and y directions, respectively. The electric field has a component in the x direction only, and the magnetic field is at a right angle to it. They are functions of $(t - \sqrt{\epsilon_0 \mu_0}\, z)$, with a time delay of $\sqrt{\epsilon_0 \mu_0}\, z$ seconds from $z = 0$. This indicates that the field pattern propagates in the positive z direction at a speed of $u = 1/\sqrt{\epsilon_0 \mu_0}$, which is the speed of light. Note that $\mathbf{E}$, $\mathbf{H}$, and the propagation direction z form a right-handed coordinate system. In conformity with Maxwell's equations, $H_0 = E_0 \sqrt{\epsilon_0 / \mu_0}$ (see Problem 1.18).

In this book we will also study electromagnetic waves in media other than free space; e.g., dielectrics, lossy matter, dispersive media, transmission lines, waveguides, and antennas. Equations governing waves and their propagations are called wave equations. They are derived from Maxwell's equations and are in the form of partial differential equations. The solution to a wave equation determines $\mathbf{E}$ and $\mathbf{H}$ as functions of space and time (x, y, z, and t). In this section we illustrate wave equations for several simple cases, starting with plane waves in source-free media. Full derivations and solutions are left until Chapter 14.

Plane Waves in Source-Free Media. In a plane wave, the electric and magnetic field intensities depend on time and only one spatial coordinate: z. This also happens to be the direction of propagation and transmission of energy. The fields are also normal to each other. The electric field has only an x component $E_x(z, t)$ and the magnetic field only a y component $H_y(z, t)$. Faraday's and Ampère's laws provide two first-order partial differential equations coupling the derivatives of E_x and H_y with respect to z and t. With regard to the steps shown in Table 1-6, the equations are decoupled and the wave equations shown below are derived.

$$\frac{\partial^2 E_x}{\partial z^2} = \mu\epsilon \frac{\partial^2 E_x}{\partial t^2} \quad \text{and} \quad \frac{\partial^2 H_y}{\partial z^2} = \mu\epsilon \frac{\partial^2 H_y}{\partial t^2}$$

The wave equation in the phasor domain can be derived from its time-domain counterpart. See Problem 1.19.

TABLE 1-6 Derivation of the Plane Wave Equation

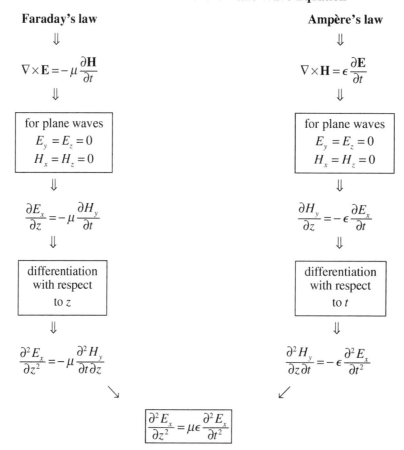

Faraday's law	Ampère's law
$\Downarrow$	$\Downarrow$
$\nabla \times \mathbf{E} = -\mu \dfrac{\partial \mathbf{H}}{\partial t}$	$\nabla \times \mathbf{H} = \epsilon \dfrac{\partial \mathbf{E}}{\partial t}$
$\Downarrow$	$\Downarrow$
for plane waves $E_y = E_z = 0$ $H_x = H_z = 0$	for plane waves $E_y = E_z = 0$ $H_x = H_z = 0$
$\Downarrow$	$\Downarrow$
$\dfrac{\partial E_x}{\partial z} = -\mu \dfrac{\partial H_y}{\partial t}$	$\dfrac{\partial H_y}{\partial z} = -\epsilon \dfrac{\partial E_x}{\partial t}$
$\Downarrow$	$\Downarrow$
differentiation with respect to z	differentiation with respect to t
$\Downarrow$	$\Downarrow$
$\dfrac{\partial^2 E_x}{\partial z^2} = -\mu \dfrac{\partial^2 H_y}{\partial t\, \partial z}$	$\dfrac{\partial^2 H_y}{\partial z\, \partial t} = -\epsilon \dfrac{\partial^2 E_x}{\partial t^2}$

$$\boxed{\frac{\partial^2 E_x}{\partial z^2} = \mu\epsilon \frac{\partial^2 E_x}{\partial t^2}}$$

The wave equations have the form of the following general one-dimensional scalar equation:

$$\frac{\partial^2 F}{\partial z^2} = \frac{1}{u^2}\frac{\partial^2 F}{\partial t^2}$$

where F is the magnitude of a field intensity at location z and time t and u is the wave velocity. Solutions to the above equation are the wave patterns $F = f(z - ut)$ and $F = g(z + ut)$. The electric and magnetic field intensity vectors are perpendicular to the z direction and the waves are plane waves traveling in the $+z$ and $-z$ directions, respectively. For harmonic waves (having a time dependency of $e^{j\omega t}$), the above equation becomes

$$\frac{d^2 F(z)}{dz^2} + \frac{\omega^2}{u^2}F(z) = 0$$

Solutions to this equation are $F = Ce^{j(\omega t - \beta z)}$ and $F = De^{j(\omega t + \beta z)}$ or any real and imaginary parts of them such as $F = C\sin(\omega t - \beta z)$, which was introduced as the sinusoidal plane wave at the beginning of this section. ω is the angular frequency of time variation and $\beta = \omega/u$. The waveform repeats itself when z changes by $\lambda = 2\pi/\beta$, called the wavelength. The frequency of the wave is $f = \omega/(2\pi)$. The wavelength and frequency are related by $f \times \lambda = u$.

Wave Equation in Source-Free Media.   From Maxwell's equations one obtains the second-order partial differential equations for **E** and **H** in source-free media. They are called the classical (*Helmholtz*) wave equations. See Table 1-7.

TABLE 1-7 Classical Wave Equations in Time and Phasor Domains

Time domain:	$\nabla^2\mathbf{E} = \mu\epsilon\frac{\partial^2\mathbf{E}}{\partial t^2}$	$\nabla^2\mathbf{H} = \mu\epsilon\frac{\partial^2\mathbf{H}}{\partial t^2}$
Phasor domain:	$\nabla^2\mathbf{E} + \omega^2\mu\epsilon\mathbf{E} = 0$	$\nabla^2\mathbf{H} + \omega^2\mu\epsilon\mathbf{H} = 0$
where ∇^2 is the Laplacian operator	$\nabla^2\mathbf{E} = \left(\frac{\partial^2}{\partial x^2} + \frac{\partial^2}{\partial y^2} + \frac{\partial^2}{\partial z^2}\right)\mathbf{E}$	

These are waves which travel at a speed of $u = 1/\sqrt{\mu\epsilon}$, which is the speed of light in the given medium. To derive the wave equations, start with Maxwell's equations in a medium with permeability μ and permittivity ϵ, containing no charges or currents ($\rho = 0$ and $J = 0$). Then proceed as shown in Table 1-8 for the case of the **E** field.

TABLE 1-8 Derivation of the Wave Equation for the Electric Field in Source-Free Media

Step 1. Take the curl of both sides in Faraday's law	$\nabla \times (\nabla \times \mathbf{E}) = -\mu\frac{\partial}{\partial t}(\nabla \times \mathbf{H})$
Step 2. Substitute for $\nabla \times \mathbf{H}$ from Ampère's law	$\nabla \times (\nabla \times \mathbf{E}) = -\mu\epsilon\frac{\partial^2\mathbf{E}}{\partial t^2}$
Step 3. Note that the curl of **E** is	$\nabla \times (\nabla \times \mathbf{E}) = \nabla(\nabla \cdot \mathbf{E}) - \nabla^2\mathbf{E}$
Step 4. Also note that the divergence of **E** is zero.	$\nabla \cdot \mathbf{E} = 0$
Step 5. Therefore,	$\nabla \times (\nabla \times \mathbf{E}) = -\nabla^2\mathbf{E}$
Step 6. Substitute the result of Step 5 into Step 2 to find	$\boxed{\nabla^2\mathbf{E} = \mu\epsilon\frac{\partial^2\mathbf{E}}{\partial t^2}}$

The wave equation for the **H** field is found in a similar way. Start Step 1 by taking the curl of both sides in Ampère's law and proceed as in Table 1-8. See Problem 1.20.

Power Flow and Poynting Vector.　Electromagnetic waves, propagated from a source such as a radio station or radiated from the sun, carry energy. The instantaneous density of power flow at a location and time is given by the *Poynting vector* $\mathbf{S} = \mathbf{E} \times \mathbf{H}$, where **E** and **H** are real functions of space and time. For plane waves, power flow is in the direction of propagation. In the SI system, the unit of **S** is $(\mathrm{V/m}) \times (\mathrm{A/m}) = (\mathrm{W/m^2})$.

EXAMPLE 8.　Consider the plane wave propagating in the positive z direction and given by $\mathbf{E} = E_0 \sin(\omega t - \beta z)\, \mathbf{a}_x$ and $\mathbf{H} = H_0 \sin(\omega t - \beta z)\, \mathbf{a}_y$, where $H_0 = E_0 \sqrt{\epsilon_0 \mu_0}$ and $\beta = \omega\sqrt{\epsilon_0\mu_0}$. The Poynting vector is $\mathbf{S} = \mathbf{E} \times \mathbf{H} = E_0 H_0$ $\sin^2(\omega t - \beta z)\, \mathbf{a}_z = \dfrac{E_0^2}{2}\sqrt{\epsilon_0/\mu_0}\,[1 - \sin 2(\omega t - \beta z)]\, \mathbf{a}_z$, Average power flow is found by integrating the instantaneous power over one period and dividing the result by the period. In this example, $P_{Avg} = \dfrac{E_0^2}{2}\sqrt{\epsilon_0/\mu_0}$ $(\mathrm{W/m^2})$.

For harmonic waves the fields are given by $\mathcal{RE}\{\mathbf{E}e^{j\omega t}\}$ and $\mathcal{RE}\{\mathbf{H}e^{j\omega t}\}$, where the complex-valued vectors **E** and **H** are the electric and magnetic field phasors, respectively. We define the complex Poynting vector to be $\mathbf{S} = \mathbf{E} \times \mathbf{H}^*/2$. The average power is then

$$P_{avg} = \frac{1}{2}\mathcal{RE}\{\mathbf{E} \times \mathbf{H}^*\}$$

EXAMPLE 9.　The electric field in an FM radio signal in free space is measured to be 5 μV/m (rms). Find the average power of the signal impinging on an area of 1 $\mathrm{m^2}$.

In conformity with Faraday's law, $H_0 = E_0 \sqrt{\epsilon/\mu} = 2.6526 \times 10^{-3}\, E_0 = 13.263 \times 10^{-9}$ T (rms). The average power flow is $P_{avg} = E_0 \times H_0 = (5 \times 10^{-15}) \times (13.263 \times 10^{-9}) = 66.214 \times 10^{-15}\ \mathrm{W/m^2} = 66.214\ \mathrm{fW/m^2}$.

1.12　Trajectory of a Sinusoidal Motion in Two Dimensions

Consider the time-varying vector $\mathbf{E} = E_x \cos \omega t\, \mathbf{a}_x + E_y \cos(\omega t + \theta)\, \mathbf{a}_y$, drawn from the origin to the tip at

$$\begin{cases} x = E_x \cos \omega t \\ y = E_y \cos(\omega t + \theta) \end{cases}$$

Assume E_x, E_y, and θ are positive constants. As time goes on, the tip moves in the xy plane. The trajectory of the tip is found by eliminating the variable t from the above equations as shown in the following.

　(a)　**Linear Trajectory.**　For $\theta = 0$ (in phase) or π (out of phase):

$$\begin{cases} x = E_x \cos \omega t \\ y = \pm E_y \cos \omega t \end{cases}$$

and the tip has a linear trajectory $y = \pm \dfrac{E_y}{E_x} x$. See Fig. 1-3(a). Rotate the x and y axes by an angle ϕ with $\tan \phi = E_y/E_x$, $0 \le \phi \le \pi/2$, (in the clockwise direction for $\theta = 0$ and the counterclockwise direction for $\theta = \pi$), and the vector is then given by $\mathbf{E} = E \cos \omega t\, \mathbf{a}_{x'}$, where $E = \sqrt{E_x^2 + E_y^2}$ and $\mathbf{a}_{x'}$ is the unit vector in the new x direction.

　(b)　**Circular Trajectory.**　For $E_y = E_x = E$ and $\theta = \pi/2$ or $-\pi/2$

$$\begin{cases} x = E \cos \omega t \\ y = \mp E \sin \omega t \end{cases}$$

The tip has a circular trajectory $x^2 + y^2 = E^2$. For $\theta = \pi/2$ it moves in the clockwise direction, and for $\theta = -\pi/2$ it moves in the counterclockwise direction. See Fig. 1-3(b).

(c) Elliptical Trajectory. For the general case (but with still constant values for E_x, E_y, and θ),

$$\begin{cases} x = E_x \cos \omega t \\ y = E_y (\cos \omega t \cos \theta - \sin \omega t \sin \theta) \end{cases} \Rightarrow \begin{cases} \cos \omega t = \dfrac{x}{E_x} \\ \sin \omega t = \dfrac{(x/E_x) \cos \theta - (y/E_y)}{\sin \theta} \end{cases}$$

But $\cos^2 \omega t + \sin^2 \omega t = 1$. Therefore,

$$\left(\frac{x}{E_x}\right)^2 + \left(\frac{y}{E_y}\right)^2 - \frac{2xy}{E_x E_y} \cos \theta = \sin^2 \theta$$

The tip of the vector moves along an elliptical trajectory. See Fig. 1-3(c).

The cross-product term xy in the above equation may be eliminated by aligning the major and minor axes of the ellipse in Fig. 1-3(c) with the horizontal and vertical directions. This is done by rotating the x and y axes by an angle γ in the counterclockwise direction, where $\cot(2\gamma) = (k^2 - 1)/2k \cos \theta$, $k = E_x/E_y$, and $0 \le \gamma \le pi/2$.

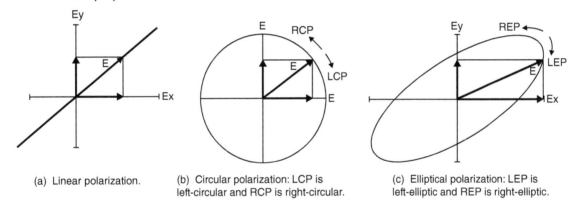

(a) Linear polarization.   (b) Circular polarization: LCP is   (c) Elliptical polarization: LEP is
                                              left-circular and RCP is right-circular.   left-elliptic and REP is right-elliptic.

Fig. 1-3 Three types of polarization and trajectories of the tip of the **E** vector in a plane wave propagating in the +z direction (out of the page).

1.13 Wave Polarization

All plane waves share the property that the **E** (and **H**) fields are perpendicular to the direction of propagation (e.g., the z axis). In general, the electric field (as well as the magnetic field) has two components: namely, those in the x and y directions. In the case of sinusoidal time variation (also called time harmonics) and dielectric media (e.g., free space), the fields are functions of $e^{j(\omega t - \beta z)}$. For any given value of z, the electric field is given by the time-varying vector

$$\mathbf{E} = \mathcal{RE}\{(E_x \mathbf{a}_x + E_y e^{j\theta} \mathbf{a}_y)e^{j\omega t}\}$$

where $\mathbf{a}_x$ and $\mathbf{a}_y$ are unit vectors in the x and y directions, respectively, and θ is the phase difference between the x and y components of the field. Simply expressed, the electric field is an **E** vector with x and y components (each of which vary sinusoidally with time)

$$\begin{cases} x = E_x \cos \omega t \\ y = E_y \cos(\omega t + \theta) \end{cases}$$

This is the same vector we discussed in Section 1.12 with three possible tip trajectories. Each trajectory is associated with one type of wave polarization as summarized below.

(a) **Linear Polarization.** In a linearly polarized wave, the tip of the field vector moves back and forth along a line in the *xy* plane as time goes by. See Fig. 1-3(a). The *x* and *y* components of the field can be combined, representing **E** by a one-dimensional vector which oscillates in time, as we have generally considered plane waves with one component only. It is seen that the sum of several linearly polarized waves is linearly polarized as well. Linearly polarized waves are also called uniform plane waves.

(b) **Circular Polarization.** In a circularly polarized wave, the tip of the field vector moves along a circle as time goes by. With propagation in the +*z* direction, if the motion of the tip is in the counterclockwise direction (direction of the right-hand fingers with the thumb pointing in the direction of propagation), the wave has right circular (also called right-hand circular) polarization. If the motion of the tip is in the clockwise direction (direction of the left-hand fingers with the thumb pointing in the direction of propagation), the wave has left circular (also called left-hand circular) polarization. See Fig. 1-3(b).

(c) **Elliptical Polarization.** In an elliptically polarized wave, the tip of the field vector moves on an ellipse as time goes by. See Fig. 1-3(c). Here, as in the case of circular polarization, the rotation of the tip can be left-handed or right-handed, resulting in left elliptical or right elliptical polarizations.

(d) **Some Practical Effects of Polarization.** There are several practical correlates of, and benefits to, recognizing the polarization of a plane wave. Some examples are the following. The polarization of an antenna and the radiated energy from it are related. Similarly, the energy collected by an antenna from an incident wave is related to its polarization. On the other hand, orientation in some cases such as a dipole antenna is not a critical factor in signal reception if it is carried by circularly polarized waves. In electromagnetics, the term "polarization" is also used in relation to a medium such as a dielectric. Although this second usage is unrelated to wave polarization, polarization of a medium can change its relative permittivity (see Section 8.1) and also influence polarization of the wave passing through it.

1.14   Electromagnetic Spectrum

A plane wave in free space propagating in the positive *z* direction is given by $\sin(\omega t - \beta z)$, where $f = \omega/(2\pi)$ is the frequency of the wave and $\lambda = 2\pi/\beta$ is its wavelength. At any time the waveform repeats itself when *z* changes by λ. The wavelength and frequency are related by $f \times \lambda = u$, where *u* is the speed of light. The electromagnetic spectrum ranges from extremely low frequencies (ELF, 3-30 Hz) in the radio range to gamma rays (up to 10^{23} Hz). It is summarized in Table 1-9a. The radio frequency bands are summarized in Table 1-9b.

TABLE 1-9a Electromagnetic Spectrum

100 Mm	1 mm	750 nm	380 nm	600 pm	3 fm
Radio and microwave	Infrared	Visible light	Ultraviolet	X rays	γ rays
3 Hz	300 GHz	400 THz	760 THz	500 PHz	10^{23} Hz

TABLE 1-9b Radio Frequency Bands

NAME	FREQUENCY	WAVELENGTH	APPLICATIONS
ELF	3–30 Hz	100 Mm to 10 Mm	
SLF	30–300 Hz	10 Mm to 1 Mm	Power grids
ULF	300–3000 Hz	1 Mm to 100 km	
VLF	3–30 kHz	100 km to 10 km	
LF	30–300 kHz	10 km to 1 km	
MF	300–3000 kHz	1 km to 100 m	AM broadcast
HF	3–30 MHz	100 m to 10 m	Shortwave
VHF	30–300 MHz	10 m to 1 m	FM, TV
UHF	300–3000 MHz	1 m to 10 cm	TV, cellular
SHF	3–30 GHz	10 cm to 1 cm	Radar, data
EHF	30–300 GHz	1 cm to 1 mm	Radar, data

E = Extremely, S = Super, U = Ultra, V = Very, L = Low, M = Medium, H = High, F = Frequency.

1.15   Transmission Lines

Transmission lines are structures consisting of two conductors which guide electromagnetic waves between two devices over a distance. Examples are power lines, telephone wires, coaxial cables, and microstrips. A transmission line has resistance, capacitance, and inductance, all distributed throughout the structure. The wave equations for and behavior of a transmission line can be derived from a model with distributed parameters.

Transmission Line Equation.   Consider an incremental line segment of length Δx and model it by the lumped-element two-terminal circuit shown in Fig. 1-4.

Fig. 1-4 Incremental lumped-element model of a segment of a transmission line.

By applying Kirchhoff's current and voltage laws at the terminals of the incremental segment and dividing all sides by Δx, we obtain the following equations:

$$\frac{\Delta v(x,t)}{\Delta x} = Ri(x,t) + L\frac{\partial i(x,t)}{\partial t}$$

$$\frac{\Delta i(x,t)}{\Delta x} = Gv(x,t) + C\frac{\partial v(x,t)}{\partial t}$$

where R and L are the resistance and inductance per unit length of the conductor. Similarly, G and C are the conductance and capacitance per unit length of the line dielectric. In the limit $\Delta x \to 0$, the equations become first-order partial differential equations:

$$\frac{\partial v(x,t)}{\partial x} = Ri(x,t) + L\frac{\partial i(x,t)}{\partial t}$$

$$\frac{\partial i(x,t)}{\partial x} = Gv(x,t) + C\frac{\partial v(x,t)}{\partial t}$$

Sinusoidal (AC) Steady State Excitation.   In the sinusoidal (AC) steady state, the voltage and current can be expressed as phasors, resulting in the equations derived in Table 1-10.

TABLE **1-10 Derivation of Transmission Line Equations in Phasor Form**

$v(x,t) = \mathcal{RE}\{\hat{V}(x)e^{j\omega t}\}$	$i(x,t) = \mathcal{RE}\{\hat{I}(x)e^{j\omega t}\}$
$\dfrac{d\hat{V}(x)}{dx} = Z\hat{I}(x)$	$\dfrac{d\hat{I}(x)}{dx} = Y\hat{V}(x)$

$$\frac{d^2\hat{V}(x)}{dx^2} = \gamma^2\hat{V}(x)$$

$$\frac{d^2\hat{I}(x)}{dx^2} = \gamma^2\hat{I}(x)$$

where $Z = R + jL\omega$, $Y = G + jC\omega$, and $\gamma = \sqrt{ZY} = \sqrt{(R + jL\omega)(G + jC\omega)} = a + j\beta$ is called the propagation constant. The resulting equations have the same form as that of wave propagation. The solutions are

$$\hat{V}(x) = V_0^+ e^{-\gamma x} + V_0^- e^{\gamma x}$$

$$\hat{I}(x) = I_0^+ e^{-\gamma x} + I_0^- e^{\gamma x}$$

where the complex numbers V_0^+, V_0^-, I_0^+, and I_0^- are constants of integration (and are constrained by the line's boundary conditions as illustrated in Example 10). These constants are also related by the line equation $\dfrac{d\hat{V}(x)}{dx} = Z\hat{I}(x)$ (Table 1-10). Therefore,

$$I_0^+ = \frac{V_0^+}{Z_0} \quad \text{and} \quad I_0^- = -\frac{V_0^-}{Z_0}$$

where $Z_0 = \sqrt{Z/Y}$ (called the line's characteristic impedance). These phasors can readily be transformed into their time-domain counterparts. For example, the time-domain representation of the voltage along the line is

$$v(x, t) = \mathcal{RE}\{\hat{V}(x)\, e^{j\omega t}\} = |V_0^+|e^{-\alpha x}\cos(\omega t - \beta x + \phi^+) + |V_0^-|e^{\alpha x}\cos(\omega t + \beta x + \phi^-)$$

where

$$V_0^+ = |V_0^+|e^{-\phi+} \quad \text{and} \quad V_0^- = |V_0^-|e^{-\phi-}$$

At any point on the line, the current and voltage are made of two sinusoidal waves with decaying amplitudes and angular frequency ω; one wave, called the incident wave $\hat{V}_{\text{inc}}$, travels to the right (in the $+x$ direction) with decaying amplitude $V_0^+e^{-\alpha x}$. The other, called the reflected wave $\hat{V}_{\text{refl}}$, travels to the left (in the $-x$ direction) with decaying amplitude $V_0^-e^{\alpha x}$. The following pointwise parameters are defined for a transmission line and are used in its analysis.

Reflection coefficent: $\qquad\qquad\qquad\qquad\qquad \Gamma(x) = \dfrac{\hat{V}_{\text{refl}}(x)}{\hat{V}_{\text{inc}}(x)}$

Impedance (looking back toward the receiving end): $\quad Z(x) = \dfrac{\hat{V}(x)}{\hat{I}(x)} = Z_0\dfrac{1 + \Gamma(x)}{1 - \Gamma(x)}$

AC Steady State in a Lossless Line.   If $R = G = 0$ (or, at high frequencies, when their contribution to γ can be ignored), the propagation constant becomes purely imaginary, $\gamma = j\beta$. The solutions to the transmission line equations then become

$$\hat{V}(x) = V_0^+e^{-j\beta x} + V_0^-e^{j\beta x}$$

$$\hat{I}(x) = \frac{V_0^+}{Z_0}e^{-j\beta x} - \frac{V_0^-}{Z_0}e^{j\beta x}$$

where $\beta = \omega\sqrt{LC}$, $Z_0 = \sqrt{L/C}$. V_0^+ and V_0^- are determined from the boundary conditions (see Example 10).

EXAMPLE 10.   A lossless transmission line connects an AC generator ($V_g = 10\ V_{rms}$ at 750 MHz with an output impedance of $Z_g = 10\ \Omega$) to the load $Z_R = 150\ \Omega$. See Fig. 1-5. The line is 20 cm long and has distributed parameters $L = 0.2\ \mu H/m$ and $C = 80\ pF/m$. Find the voltage and current in the line.

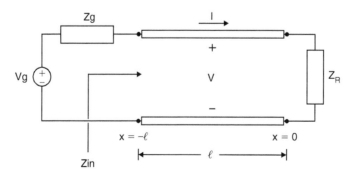

Fig. 1-5 A transmission line connecting a generator to a load.

Expressions developed for $\hat{V}(x)$ and $\hat{I}(x)$ in the AC steady state will be used. From the given values for the line, $Z_0 = \sqrt{L/C} = 50\ \Omega$, $\beta = \omega\sqrt{LC} = 6\pi$, and $\beta\ell = 1.2\pi$. Let $x = 0$ at the load and $x = -\ell$ at the generator. Apply the boundary conditions at those two ends of the line to find V_0^+ and V_0^-.

(a) At $x = 0$ (the load)

$$\hat{V}(0) = V_0^+ + V_0^-$$

$$\hat{I}(0) = \frac{V_0^+}{Z_0} - \frac{V_0^-}{Z_0}$$

However, the $i - v$ characteristic of the load requires that $\hat{V}(0) = Z_R\hat{I}(0)$. Therefore,

$$V_0^+ + V_0^- = \frac{Z_R}{Z_0}[V_0^+ - V_0^-]$$

from which

$$V_0^- = \Gamma V_0^+, \text{ where } \Gamma = \frac{Z_R - Z_0}{Z_R + Z_0} = 0.5.$$

(b) At $x = -\ell$ (the generator end of the line)

$$\hat{V}(-\ell) = V_0^+e^{j\beta\ell} + V_0^-e^{-j\beta\ell}$$

$$\hat{I}(-\ell) = \frac{V_0^+}{Z_0}e^{j\beta\ell} - \frac{V_0^-}{Z_0}e^{-j\beta\ell}$$

However, application of Kirchhoff's voltage law at $x = -\ell$ results in $\hat{V}(-\ell) = V_g - Z_g\hat{I}(-\ell)$. Therefore,

$$V_0^+e^{j\beta\ell} + V_0^-e^{-j\beta\ell} = V_g - \frac{Z_g}{Z_0}[V_0^+e^{j\beta\ell} - V_0^-e^{-j\beta\ell}]$$

from which

$$V_0^+ = \frac{V_gZ_0}{Z_0(e^{j\beta\ell} + \Gamma e^{-j\beta\ell}) + Z_g(e^{j\beta\ell} - \Gamma e^{-j\beta\ell})}$$

By substituting for $V_g = 10\sqrt{2}$, $Z_0 = 50$, $\beta\ell = 1.2\pi$, $\Gamma = 0.5$, and $Z_g = 10$ in the above equation, we find $V_0^+ = 10.27\angle160°$ and $V_0^- = 5.13\angle160°$. The voltage and current throughout the line $(-0.2 \le x \le 0)$ are

$$v(t) = 10.27\cos(\omega t - \beta x + 2.7925) + 5.13\cos(\omega t + \beta x + 2.7925)$$
$$i(t) = 0.2054\cos(\omega t - \beta x + 2.7925) - 0.1027\cos(\omega t + \beta x + 2.7925)$$

where the 160° phase angle is converted to $160\pi/180 = 2.7925$ radians. A right-shift (delay) of $2.7925/\omega = 593$ ps in the time origin produces $V_g = 10\sqrt{2}\angle-160°$ and

$$v(t) = 10.27\cos(\omega t - \beta x) + 5.13\cos(\omega t + \beta x)$$
$$i(t) = 0.2054\cos(\omega t - \beta x) - 0.1027\cos(\omega t + \beta x)$$

Input Impedance of a Lossless Line.   The input impedance of a lossless line is the ratio of the voltage to current phasors at $x = -\ell$. It may be expressed in terms of the reflection coefficient:

$$Z_{in} = Z(-\ell) = \frac{\hat{V}(-\ell)}{\hat{I}(-\ell)} = Z_0\frac{V_0^+e^{\beta\ell} + V_0^-e^{-\beta\ell}}{V_0^+e^{\beta\ell} - V_0^-e^{-\beta\ell}} = Z_0\frac{1 + \Gamma e^{-2\beta\ell}}{1 - \Gamma e^{-2\beta\ell}}$$

where $\Gamma = \dfrac{V_0^-}{V_0^+}$ is the reflection coefficent at the load. The input impedance may also be expressed in terms of the load impedance by substituting in the above expression for $\Gamma = \dfrac{Z_R - Z_0}{Z_R + Z_0}$. The result is

$$Z_{in} = \frac{\hat{V}(-\ell)}{\hat{I}(-\ell)} = Z_0 \frac{Z_R + jZ_0 \tan \beta \ell}{Z_0 + jZ_R \tan \beta \ell}$$

EXAMPLE 11.　Replace the circuit of Fig. 1-5 by the equivalent circuit of Fig. 1-6 and use it to obtain V_0^+.

Fig. 1-6　Equivalent circuit of the transmission line of Fig. 1-5.

From Fig. 1-5,　　　　　　　　$\hat{V}(-\ell) = V_0^+ e^{\beta \ell} + V_0^- e^{-\beta \ell} = V_0^+ (e^{\beta \ell} + \Gamma e^{-\beta \ell})$,　where $\Gamma = \dfrac{Z_R - Z_0}{Z_R + Z_0}$

From Fig. 1-6,　　　　　　　　$\hat{V}(-\ell) = V_g \dfrac{Z_{in}}{Z_g + Z_{in}}$

From equating the above expressions,　$V_0^+ = V_g \left(\dfrac{Z_{in}}{Z_g + Z_{in}} \right) \left(\dfrac{1}{e^{\beta \ell} + \Gamma e^{-\beta \ell}} \right)$

EXAMPLE 12.　In the circuit of Example 10, (a) find the input impedance of the line (at the generator end looking toward the load), and (b) use the equivalent circuit of Fig. 1-6 to calculate V_0^+.

(a)　Having $Z_0 = 50$, $Z_R = 150$, $\beta \ell = 1.2\pi$, and $\tan \beta \ell = 0.7265$, we calculate Z_{in}:

$$Z_{in} = Z_0 \frac{Z_R + jZ_0 \tan \beta \ell}{Z_0 + jZ_R \tan \beta \ell} = 50 \frac{150 + j50 \times 0.7265}{50 + j150 \times 0.7265} = 64.36 \angle -51.74° \, \Omega$$

(b)　Having $V_g = 10\sqrt{2}$, $Z_q = 10$, $Z_{in} = 64.36 \angle -51.74°$, $\beta \ell = 1.2\pi$, and $\Gamma = 0.5$, we calculate V_0^+:

$$V_0^+ = V_g \left(\frac{Z_{in}}{Z_g + Z_{in}} \right) \left(\frac{1}{e^{\beta \ell} + \Gamma e^{-\beta \ell}} \right) = \frac{10\sqrt{2} \times 64.36 \angle -51.74°}{10 + 64.36 \angle -51.74° \times (1.5 \cos \beta \ell + j0.5 \sin \beta \ell)} = 10.27 \angle 160° \, V$$

Some Parameters of Lossless Transmission.　The angular frequency is ω (frequency $f = \omega/(2\pi)$ Hz and period $T = 1/f$ seconds). The incident and reflected waves are sinusoids with constant amplitudes V_0^+ and V_0^-, respectively. Each wave repeats itself after traveling a distance of $\lambda = 2\pi/\beta$, which is called the wavelength. The phase velocity of the traveling wave in a lossless line is $\mu_p = \lambda/T = \omega/\beta = 1/\sqrt{LC}$. For two-wire or coaxial transmission lines (made of perfect conductors and dielectrics), $LC = \mu \epsilon$, which results in a phase velocity $\mu_p = 1\sqrt{\mu \epsilon}$, where μ and ϵ are the permeability and permittivity, respectively, of the insulation between the conductors. Because permeability and permittivity are specified in terms of their relative values to those of free space, $\mu = \mu_r \mu_0$ and $\epsilon = \epsilon_r \epsilon_0$, the phase velocity becomes $\mu_p = c/\sqrt{\mu_r \epsilon_r}$, where $c = 1/\sqrt{\mu_0 \epsilon_0}$ is the speed of light in free space.

The amplitude of the voltage wave has a maximum and a minimum value, whose ratio is called the *voltage standing wave ratio*, VSWR, and is defined by

$$S = \frac{\left|\hat{V}\right|_{max}}{\left|\hat{V}\right|_{min}} = \frac{1+\Gamma}{1-\Gamma}, \quad \text{where } \Gamma = \frac{V_0^-}{V_0^+} \text{ is the reflection coefficient.}$$

Short-Circuited Line.   If the line terminates in a short circuit ($Z_R = 0$ in Fig. 1-5), then

$$\hat{V}(0) = V_0^+ + V_0^- = 0, V_0^+ = -V_0^-, \hat{I}(0) = 2\frac{V_0^+}{Z_0}, \quad \Gamma = -1$$

$$\hat{V}(x) = V_0^+(e^{-j\beta x} - e^{j\beta x}) = -j2V_0^+ \sin \beta x, \quad \text{and} \quad \hat{I}(x) = \frac{V_0^+}{Z_0}(e^{-j\beta x} + e^{j\beta x}) = 2\frac{V_0^+}{Z_0}\cos \beta x$$

$$Z_{in} = Z(-\ell) = \frac{\hat{V}(-\ell)}{\hat{I}(-\ell)} = jZ_0 \tan \beta\ell$$

The input impedance of the line is reactive (inductive when $\tan \beta\ell > 0$ and capacitive when $\tan \beta\ell < 0$). Note that $\beta\ell = 2\pi\ell/\lambda$. For $\ell = k\lambda/2$, k an integer (line length being a multiple of the half-wavelength), $\beta\ell = k\pi\ell$, $\tan \beta\ell = 0$, and the line appears as a short circuit.

Open-Circuited Line.   If the line terminates in an open circuit ($Z_R = \infty$ in Fig. 1-5), then

$$\hat{I}(0) = \frac{V_0^+ - V_0^-}{Z_0} = 0, V_0^+ = V_0^-, \hat{V}(0) = 2V_0^+, \quad \Gamma = 1$$

$$\hat{V}(x) = V_0^+(e^{-j\beta x} + e^{j\beta x}) = 2V_0^+ \cos \beta x, \quad \text{and} \quad \hat{I}(x) = \frac{V_0^+}{Z_0}(e^{-j\beta x} - e^{j\beta x}) = j2\frac{V_0^+}{Z_0}\sin \beta x$$

$$Z_{in} = Z(-\ell) = \frac{\hat{V}(-\ell)}{\hat{I}(-\ell)} = -jZ_0 \cot \beta\ell$$

The input impedance of the line is reactive. Again, note that for $\ell = (2k+1)\lambda/4$, k an integer, $\beta\ell = (2k+1)\pi/2$, $\cot \beta\ell = 0$, and the line appears as a short circuit.

Matched Line.   If the line terminates in an impedance equal to its characteristic value ($Z_R = Z_0$ in Fig. 1-5), then

$$\Gamma = \frac{Z_R - Z_0}{Z_R - Z_0} = 0, \quad \hat{V}(0) = V_0^+, \quad \hat{I}(0) = \frac{V_0^+}{Z_0}$$

$$\hat{V}(x) = V_0^+ e^{-j\beta x}, \quad \text{and} \quad \hat{I}(x) = \frac{V_0^+}{Z_0}e^{-j\beta x}$$

$$Z(x) = \frac{\hat{V}(x)}{\hat{I}(x)} = V_0^+ e^{-j\beta x} \times \frac{Z_0}{V_0^+ e^{-j\beta x}} = Z_0$$

At any point on the line, the voltage and current are in phase with a constant ratio. The impedance is Z_0.

Power in a Lossless Line.   The instantaneous power delivered to a load is $p(t) = v(t)i(t)$, where $v(t)$ and $i(t)$ are the voltage and current, respectively. Average power during the period from t to $t + T$ is

$$P = \frac{1}{T}\int_t^{t+T} p(t)\,dt$$

In the sinusoidal steady state,

$$v(t) = V \cos(\omega t), \quad i(t) = I \cos(\omega t + \theta), \quad p(t) = VI\frac{\cos\theta + \cos(2\omega t + \theta)}{2}, \quad \text{and } P = \frac{VI}{2}$$

In the phasor domain,

$$v(t) = \mathcal{RE}\{\hat{V}e^{j\omega t}\}, \quad i(t) = \mathcal{RE}\{\hat{I}e^{j\omega t}\}, \quad \text{and} \quad P = \frac{1}{2}\mathcal{RE}\{\hat{V}\cdot\hat{I}^*\} = \frac{1}{2}\left|\hat{V}\right|\left|\hat{I}\right|\cos\theta$$

where $\hat{V}$ is the voltage phasor across the load, $\hat{I}^*$ is the complex conjugate of its current phasor, and θ is the phase angle of the current with reference to the voltage. Accordingly, in a lossless transmission line, the average powers delivered to the load by the incident wave or reflected from it by the reflected wave are, respectively,

$$P_{inc} = \frac{\left|V_0^+\right|^2}{2\left|Z_0\right|}, \quad \text{and} \quad P_{refl} = \frac{-\Gamma^2\left|V_0^+\right|^2}{2\left|Z_0\right|}$$

The net average power delivered to the load is

$$P = P_{inc} + P_{refl} = \frac{\left|V_0^+\right|^2}{2\left|Z_0\right|}(1-\Gamma^2)$$

(Superposition of power applies because the incident and reflected waves have the same frequency.)

SOLVED PROBLEMS

Note: A Cartesian coordinate system (x, y, z) with unit vectors $\mathbf{a}_x$, $\mathbf{a}_y$, and $\mathbf{a}_z$ is assumed in the problems below. Thus, by (a, b, c) is meant a point in three dimensional space with $x = a$, $y = b$, and $z = c$. Similarly, a point in the xy plane is shown by (a, b).

1.1.   Two identical point charges Q are separated by distance d in a homogeneous medium. Find the electric field intensity at a point r m away from each charge. See Fig. 1-7. Find the near and far field intensities.

By the superposition principle, $\mathbf{E} = \mathbf{E}_1 + \mathbf{E}_2$, where $\mathbf{E}_1$ and $\mathbf{E}_2$, each with magnitude $Q/(4\pi\epsilon r^2)$, are the field intensities due to each charge. Designate the line connecting the two charges as the x axis with the origin at its middle. The test charge will be at $y = \sqrt{r^2 - d^2/4}$. The x components of $\mathbf{E}_1$ and $\mathbf{E}_2$ cancel each other, while their y components add. From Coulomb's law and the geometry of the problem we find the field intensity at a point on the y axis to be

$$\mathbf{E} = 2E_1 \frac{y}{r}\mathbf{a}_y = \frac{Q}{2\pi\epsilon}\frac{\sqrt{r^2 - d^2/4}}{r^3}\mathbf{a}_y$$

where $\mathbf{a}_y$ is the unit vector in the y direction. At the origin, $r = d/2$, and the field is zero. At $r >> d$, the field is $\mathbf{E} \approx \frac{Q}{2\pi\epsilon r^2}\mathbf{a}_y$, which is nearly the field intensity due to a point charge of $2Q$.

1.2.   Repeat Problem 1.1 for two equal charges of opposite signs.

Here the y components of $\mathbf{E}_1$ and $\mathbf{E}_2$ cancel each other and the x components add. See Fig. 1-8. From the geometry of the problem,

$$\mathbf{E} = E_1\frac{d}{r}\mathbf{a}_x = \frac{Qd}{4\pi\epsilon r^3}\mathbf{a}_x$$

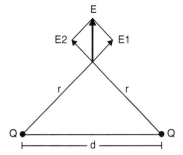

Fig. 1-7 Electric field intensity along the orthogonal bisector of the line connecting two like charges $+Q$.

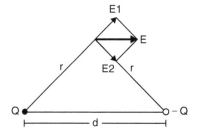

Fig. 1-8 Electric field intensity along the orthogonal bisector of the line connecting two unlike charges $\pm Q$.

The field is inversely proportional to r^3. At $r = d/2$, it becomes $\mathbf{E} = \dfrac{Q}{2\pi\epsilon r^2}\mathbf{a}_x$, which is the field intensity due to a point charge of $2Q$.

1.3. Two point charges of magnitude $0.1\ \mu C$ and opposite signs are placed in vacuum on the x axis at positions ∓ 1 m, respectively. (*a*) Calculate the field intensity at the point $(0, 1)$. (*b*) Approximate the value of intensity at a point 10 cm away from one charge by ignoring the effect of the other charge and determine the percentage of error due to such an approximation.

(*a*) As in Fig. 1-8, the y components of the fields produced by each point charge cancel each other and their x components add, resulting in $\mathbf{E} = \dfrac{Qd}{4\pi\epsilon r^3}\mathbf{a}_x$. With $Q = 0.1\ \mu C$, $d = 2$ m, and $r = \sqrt{2}$, we find $\mathbf{E} = 636.4\ \mathbf{a}_x$ V/m.

(*b*) Each point charge dominates the field in its 10-cm vicinity, resulting in $\mathbf{E} \approx \pm 180\ \mathbf{a}_r$ kV/m, where $\mathbf{a}_r$ is the radial unit vector with that charge as the center. The field is directed outward at $x = -1$ and inward at $x = 1$. The most error occurs when the test point is at $(\pm.9, 0)$, with a relative percentage error of $100 \times 1/(1 + 19^2) = 0.275\%$.

1.4. Three point charges Q, Q_1, and Q_2 are separated by a distance d from each other in a homogeneous medium. Find the electric force on Q.

Let the line connecting Q_1 and Q_2 be the y axis with the origin at its center. The forces exerted by Q_1 and Q_2 on Q are given by the vectors $\mathbf{F}_1$ and $\mathbf{F}_2$.

$$\mathbf{F}_1 = kQ_1\mathbf{a}_1 \quad \text{and} \quad \mathbf{F}_2 = kQ_2\mathbf{a}_2$$

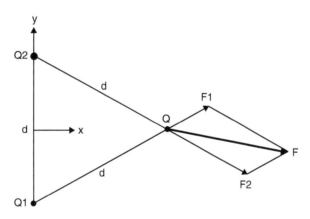

Fig. 1-9 Forces on charge Q due to charges Q_1 and Q_2.

where $\mathbf{a}_1$ and $\mathbf{a}_2$ are unit vectors from Q_1 and Q_2, respectively, toward Q, and $k = Q/(4\pi\epsilon d^2)$. See Fig. 1-9. The total force on Q is the vectorial addition $\mathbf{F} = \mathbf{F}_1 + \mathbf{F}_2$ found by adding the x and y components of the two forces. Hence,

$$F_{1x} = \sqrt{3}kQ_1/2 \qquad\qquad F_{1y} = kQ_1/2$$
$$F_{2x} = \sqrt{3}kQ_2/2 \qquad\qquad F_{2y} = -kQ_2/2$$
$$F_x = F_{1x} + F_{2x} = \sqrt{3}k(Q_1+Q_2)/2 \qquad F_y = F_{1y} + F_{2y} = k(Q_1-Q_2)/2$$
$$\mathbf{F} = \frac{Q}{2\pi\epsilon d^2}\left[\sqrt{3}(Q_1+Q_2)\mathbf{a}_x + (Q_1-Q_2)\mathbf{a}_y\right]$$

1.5. A charge Q_1 is placed at the point $(0, -d)$ and another charge Q_2 at $(0, d)$. Develop an equation for the electric field intensity at a test point (x, y) as a function of d, Q_1, Q_2, x, and y.

Let $\mathbf{R}_1$ and $\mathbf{R}_2$ represent vectors connecting Q_1 and Q_2, respectively, to (x, y).

$$\mathbf{R}_1 = x\mathbf{a}_x + (y+d)\mathbf{a}_y, \quad R_1 = [x^2 + (y+d)^2]^{\frac{1}{2}}, \quad \mathbf{a}_{R1} = \frac{\mathbf{R}_1}{R_1} = \frac{x\mathbf{a}_x + (y+d)\mathbf{a}_y}{R_1}$$

$$\mathbf{R}_2 = x\mathbf{a}_x + (y-d)\mathbf{a}_y, \quad R_1 = [x^2 + (y-d)^2]^{\frac{1}{2}}, \quad \mathbf{a}_{R2} = \frac{\mathbf{R}_2}{R_2} = \frac{x\mathbf{a}_x + (y+d)\mathbf{a}_y}{R_2}$$

$$\mathbf{E}_1 = \frac{Q_1}{4\pi\epsilon R_1^2}\mathbf{a}_{R1} = \frac{Q_1}{4\pi\epsilon R_1^3}[x\mathbf{a}_x + (y+d)\mathbf{a}_y]$$

$$\mathbf{E}_2 = \frac{Q_2}{4\pi\epsilon R_2^2}\mathbf{a}_{R2} = \frac{Q_2}{4\pi\epsilon R_2^3}[x\mathbf{a}_x + (y-d)\mathbf{a}_y]$$

$$\mathbf{E} = \mathbf{E}_1 + \mathbf{E}_2 = \frac{x}{4\pi\epsilon}\left[\frac{Q_1}{R_1^3} + \frac{Q_2}{R_2^3}\right]\mathbf{a}_x + \frac{1}{4\pi\epsilon}\left[\frac{Q_1(y+d)}{R_1^3} + \frac{Q_2(y-d)}{R_2^3}\right]\mathbf{a}_y$$

1.6. Flux lines at any point in an electric field in a homogeneous medium are tangent to the field intensity at that point. Consider the electric field in such a medium produced by two point charges $\pm Q$ placed at $\pm d$ m on the x axis, respectively. Find the direction of the flux lines at locations $(\pm d, 0)$ and $(0, y)$.

Each point charge dominates the field in its vicinity, resulting in a radial direction for the field intensity and flux lines (originating from $x = d$ and sinking at $x = -d$). The flux lines become horizontal (going from right to left) when they cross the y axis because the y components of the individual fields cancel each other and their x components add.

1.7. Two small spherical bodies each with mass $m = 1$ gram are suspended near each other by two strings of length $\ell = 10$ cm as in Fig. 1-10(a). Assume that the spheres are placed in a vacuum and experience a gravitational pull ($g = 9.81$ m/s^2). When each is loaded with a charge Q, the spheres separate by a distance of $d = 1$ cm as in Fig. 1-10(b). Find Q.

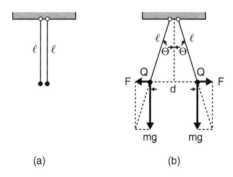

(a)   (b)

Fig. 1-10 Two charged bodies repel each other with a force $F = \dfrac{Q^2}{4\pi\epsilon d^2}$.

The charge may be calculated from the separation distance d. The gravitational force on each sphere is mg in the downward vertical direction. The Coulomb force is $F = Q^2/(4\pi\epsilon d^2)$ in the horizontal direction, pushing the spheres away from each other. At equilibrium, each string aligns itself with the direction of the total force on its bob. From the similarity of the force- and string-triangles we find

$$\frac{F}{\sqrt{m^2g^2 + F^2}} = \frac{d/2}{\ell} \quad \Rightarrow \quad F = \frac{mgd/2}{\sqrt{\ell^2 - (d/2)^2}}$$

Substituting $Q^2/(4\pi\epsilon d^2)$ for F and solving for Q we find

$$Q^2 = \frac{2\pi\epsilon_0 d^3}{\sqrt{\ell^2 - (d/2)^2}}mg$$

With $\epsilon_0 = 8.854 \times 10^{-12}$ F/m, $d = 0.01$ m, $\ell = 0.1$ m, and $m = 10^{-3}$ kg, we obtain $Q = 2.3376$ nC.

1.8. An infinitely long, straight line has a uniform charge distribution of ρ C/m. Use Gauss's law to find the electric field at a point r m away from it.

Consider a cylindrical volume of height ℓ with circular cross sectional area of radius r, which has the line as its axis. The volume contains a total charge of $Q = \rho\ell$. By symmetry, the **E** field is radial in direction and has the same magnitude on the surface of the cylinder. The total flux through the surface is $\Psi = \epsilon E \times \ell \times \pi r^2$. By Gauss' law, $\Psi = Q$ from which $E = \rho/\pi\epsilon r^2$.

1.9. An infinite plane is uniformly charged with a distribution of ρ C/m². Use Gauss's law to find the electric field at a point r m away from it.

Consider a cylindrical volume with the cross-section area S normal to the plane and bisected by it in two equal lengths. The volume contains a total charge of $Q = \rho S$. By symmetry, the **E** field is directed away from the plane and normal to it with the same magnitude on the cylinder's cross sections. The total flux through the surface of the cylinder is $\Psi = \epsilon E \times 2 \times S$. By Gauss's law, $\Psi = Q$ from which $E = \rho/(2\epsilon)$, which is independent of the distance from the plane.

1.10. A uniform charge distribution with density ρ C/m² is established on the infinite xy plane ($z = 0$). Find the electric potential at points above or below the plane.

For $z > 0$, the electric field intensity is $\mathbf{E} = \rho/(2\epsilon)\,\mathbf{a}_z$ and $V = E \times z = \rho z/(2\epsilon)$. For $z < 0$, $\mathbf{E} = -\rho/(2\epsilon)\mathbf{a}_z$ and $V = -\rho z/(2\epsilon)$.

1.11. An infinite plane at $z = d$ is uniformly charged with a density ρ C/m² and a second plane at $z = 0$ with density $-\rho$ C/m². Find the electric field intensity **E** and potential V at $-\infty < z < -\infty$ with reference to $z = 0$.

Let $\mathbf{E}_1$ and $\mathbf{E}_2$ represent the electric fields due to the first and second planes, respectively. From the result of Problem 1.10 and using the superposition principle we obtain

$$\mathbf{E}_1 = \begin{cases} \dfrac{\rho}{2\epsilon}\mathbf{a}_z, & z > d \\[2mm] -\dfrac{\rho}{2\epsilon}\mathbf{a}_z, & z < d \end{cases} \qquad \mathbf{E}_2 = \begin{cases} -\dfrac{\rho}{2\epsilon}\mathbf{a}_z, & z > 0 \\[2mm] \dfrac{\rho}{2\epsilon}\mathbf{a}_z, & z < 0 \end{cases} \quad \text{and} \quad \mathbf{E} = \mathbf{E}_1 + \mathbf{E}_2 = \begin{cases} -\dfrac{\rho}{\epsilon}\mathbf{a}_z, & 0 < z < d \\[2mm] 0, & \text{elsewhere} \end{cases}$$

By integrating **E** along the z axis with reference to the potential at $z = 0$ we obtain $V = \begin{cases} \rho d/\epsilon, & z > d \\ \rho z/\epsilon, & 0 \geq z \geq d \\ 0, & z < 0 \end{cases}$

1.12. Two infinite parallel planes carry uniform charge distributions of $\pm\rho_0\cos(\omega t)$, respectively. Find the electric field intensity, the electric potential, and the displacement current in the space between them if the gap separating them is filled with (*a*) air, (*b*) a dielectric material with $\epsilon_r = 100$.

(*a*) $\epsilon \approx \epsilon_0$ $\qquad E = \dfrac{\rho_0}{\epsilon_0}\cos(\omega t),$ $\qquad V = \dfrac{\rho_0 d}{\epsilon_0}\cos(\omega t),$ $\qquad \dfrac{\partial D}{\partial t} = -\omega\rho_0\sin(\omega t)$

(*b*) $\epsilon = 100\epsilon_0$ $\qquad E = \dfrac{1}{100}\dfrac{\rho_0}{\epsilon_0}\cos(\omega t),$ $\qquad V = \dfrac{1}{100}\dfrac{\rho_0 d}{\epsilon_0}\cos(\omega t),$ $\qquad \dfrac{\partial D}{\partial t} = -\omega\rho_0\sin(\omega t)$

Note that the displacement current remains the same in (*a*) and (*b*). The electric field intensity and the electric potential are reduced by a factor of 100 in (*b*).

1.13. Find the average and *rms* values of the force per unit length between two infinitely long wires that are separated by 1 m and carry 60-Hz AC currents of 100 amperes (*rms*) in opposing directions in air.

$$i(t) = 100\sqrt{2}\sin(377t), \quad i^2(t) = 10^4[1 - \cos(754t)]$$

$$F = \frac{\mu_0}{2\pi}\frac{i^2(t)}{d} = \frac{4\pi \times 10^{-7}}{2\pi} \times 10^4[1 - \cos(754t)] = 2 \times 10^{-3}[1 - \cos(754t)] \ (N)$$

Average of F is 2×10^{-3} N. Its *rms* value is $2 \times 10^{-3}\sqrt{1 + \dfrac{1}{2}} = 2.45 \times 10^{-3}$ N.

1.14. Two infinitely long parallel wires separated by 1 m are at 6 m above ground. Each carries a 60-Hz AC current of 100 amperes (*rms*), but in opposing directions. See Fig. 1-11. Find the magnetic flux density **B** at a test location on the ground which is at an equal distance from the wires.

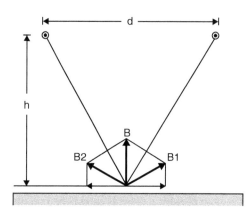

Fig. 1-11 Magnetic flux density $\mathbf{B} = \mathbf{B}_1 + \mathbf{B}_2$ due to a pair of overhead lines carrying currents in opposite directions.

The instantaneous current in the wires is $i(t) = 100\sqrt{2}\ \sin(377t)$. The magnetic flux density due to each wire is

$$B = \frac{\mu_0 i}{2\pi R} = \frac{4\pi \times 10^{-7}}{2\pi \times \sqrt{36 + 0.25}} 100\sqrt{2}\ \sin(377t) = 4.7\ \sin(377t)\ (\mu T)$$

directed at a right angle to the line connecting the test point to that wire. The horizontal components of $\mathbf{B}_1$ and $\mathbf{B}_2$ cancel each other, but the vertical components add. From the similarity between the vector- and distance triangles, we find $\mathbf{B} = 0.78\ \mathbf{a}_y\ \mu T$.

1.15. An AC current in an overhead wire generates an AC magnetic field with $B_{AC} = 50\ \sin(377t)\ \mu T$ at a test location below. The earth's static magnetic field at that location is $B_{DC} = 50\ \mu T$, directed toward the magnetic north. Find the total field (instantaneous, average, and *rms* values) at that location if the current runs in a (*a*) west-east, or (*b*) south-north direction.

Let the west-east direction be the x axis and the south-north direction be the y axis, with unit vectors $\mathbf{a}_x$ and $\mathbf{a}_y$, respectively. Then, $\mathbf{B} = \mathbf{B}_{DC} + \mathbf{B}_{AC}$, where $\mathbf{B}_{DC} = 50\mathbf{a}_y\ \mu T$.

(*a*) $\mathbf{I} = \mathbf{I}_0 \sin(377t)\mathbf{a}_x,$ $\mathbf{B}_{AC} = 50 \sin(377t)\mathbf{a}_y,$ $\mathbf{B} = 50\ [\sin(377t) + 1]\ \mathbf{a}_y,$ $B_{avg} = 50,$ $B_{rms} = 61.23$

(*b*) $\mathbf{I} = \mathbf{I}_0 \sin(377t)\mathbf{a}_y,$ $\mathbf{B}_{AC} = -50 \sin(377t)\mathbf{a}_x,$ $\mathbf{B} = 50\ [-\sin(377t)\mathbf{a}_x + \mathbf{a}_y],$ $B_{avg} = 60.8,$ $B_{rms} = 43.3$

All magnetic field values are in μT.

1.16. A single-strand rectangular test loop (1 m × 10 cm) is placed length-wise in parallel with, and at a distance of 10 m from, a very long straight wire such that they form a plane. The wire carries a 50-A (rms) sinusoidal current at the frequency f Hz, and the medium is free space. Obtain the *emf* induced in the loop as a function of f, and find its *rms* values at 60 Hz and 60 kHz.

$$i = 50\sqrt{2}\ \sin(2\pi f t)$$

$$B = \mu_0 H = \frac{\mu_0 i}{2\pi r} = \frac{4\pi \times 10^{-7}}{2\pi \times 10} \times 50\sqrt{2}\ \sin(2\pi f t) = 10^{-6}\sqrt{2}\ \sin(2\pi f t)$$

$$\phi = B \times S = 10^{-7}\sqrt{2}\ \sin(2\pi f t)$$

$$emf = -\frac{d\phi}{dt} = 2\sqrt{2}\pi f \times 10^{-7}\ \cos(2\pi f t)$$

The *rms* value of the induced *emf* is $0.2\pi f\ (\mu V)$. At 60 Hz it is 37.7 μV, and at 60 kHz it becomes 37.7 mV.

1.17. Prove the necessity for the displacement current introduced by Maxwell in Ampère's law.

First consider Ampère's law in its original form, $\nabla \times \mathbf{H} = \mathbf{J}$, and then take the divergence of both sides of it: $\nabla \cdot (\nabla \times \mathbf{H}) = \nabla \cdot \mathbf{J}$. But $\nabla \cdot (\nabla \times \mathbf{H}) = 0$ (divergence of the curl is always zero according to line 11(a) in Table 1-5). This would require $\nabla \cdot \mathbf{J} = 0$, contradicting, in time-varying fields, conservation of charge which states that $\nabla \cdot \mathbf{J} + \frac{\partial \rho}{\partial t} = 0$. Now consider Ampère's law in the modified form with Maxwell's displacement current included, $\nabla \times \mathbf{H} = \mathbf{J} + \frac{\partial \mathbf{D}}{\partial t}$, and take the divergence of both sides: $\nabla \cdot (\nabla \times \mathbf{H}) = \nabla \cdot \mathbf{J} + \frac{\partial (\nabla \cdot \mathbf{D})}{\partial t}$.

By Gauss's law, $\frac{\partial (\nabla \cdot \mathbf{D})}{\partial t} = \frac{\partial \rho}{\partial t}$. Therefore, $\nabla \cdot (\nabla \times \mathbf{H}) = \nabla \cdot \mathbf{J} + \frac{\partial \rho}{\partial t} = 0$, which is the statement of conservation of charge for a time-varying field. Adding the displacement current to Ampère's law resolves the contradiction.

1.18. Consider the pair of vectors $\mathbf{E} = E_0 \sin \omega(t - \sqrt{\epsilon\mu}\, z)\, \mathbf{a}_x$ and $\mathbf{H} = H_0 \sin \omega(t - \sqrt{\epsilon\mu}\, z)\, \mathbf{a}_y$, where $\mathbf{a}_x$ and $\mathbf{a}_y$ are unit vectors in the x and y directions, respectively. Show that in order to conform with Maxwell's equations (i.e., represent electromagnetic waves in a homogeneous medium), $H_0 = E_0 \sqrt{\epsilon/\mu}$.

Faraday's law requires $\nabla \times \mathbf{E} = -\mu \frac{\partial \mathbf{H}}{\partial t}$. In this problem we have $\nabla \times \mathbf{E} = \frac{\partial E_x}{\partial z} \mathbf{a}_y = -E_0 \omega \sqrt{\epsilon\mu} \cos \omega(t - \sqrt{\epsilon\mu}z)\, \mathbf{a}_y$ and $\frac{\partial \mathbf{H}}{\partial t} = \omega H_0 \cos \omega(t - \sqrt{\epsilon\mu}z)\, \mathbf{a}_y$. To conform with Faraday's law, we need $E_0 \omega \sqrt{\epsilon\mu} = \mu \omega H_0$, or $H_0 = E_0 \sqrt{\epsilon/\mu}$. In free space, $H_0 = 2.65258 \times 10^{-3} E_0$.

1.19. Derive the source-free wave equation for $\mathbf{E}$ in the phasor domain from its time-domain form.

The time-domain wave equation for the $\mathbf{E}$ field is $\nabla^2 \mathbf{E} = \mu\epsilon \frac{\partial^2 \mathbf{E}}{\partial t^2}$. For harmonic waves

$$\mathbf{E} = \mathbf{E}(x, y, z)e^{j\omega t}, \quad \frac{\partial^2 \mathbf{E}}{\partial t^2} = -\omega^2 \mathbf{E}(x, y, z)e^{j\omega t}, \quad \text{and} \quad \nabla^2 \mathbf{E} = \nabla^2 \mathbf{E}(\mathbf{x}, \mathbf{y}, \mathbf{z})e^{j\omega t}.$$

Substitute the above in the time-domain equation and drop the common term $e^{j\omega t}$ from both sides to obtain $\nabla^2 \mathbf{E} + \omega^2 \mu\epsilon \mathbf{E} = 0$. This is the phasor-domain wave equation.

1.20. Derive the phasor-domain wave equation for a magnetic field in source-free media from Maxwell's equations.

Start with Maxwell's equations given below and proceed through Steps 1, 2, and 3.

Faraday's law: $\nabla \times \mathbf{E} = -j\omega\mu\mathbf{H}$ Gauss's law for the electric field: $\nabla \cdot \mathbf{E} = 0$

Ampère's law: $\nabla \times \mathbf{H} = j\omega\epsilon\mathbf{E}$ Gauss's law for the magnetic field: $\nabla \cdot \mathbf{H} = 0$

Step 1.   Take the curl of both sides in Ampère's law $\Rightarrow$ $\nabla \times (\nabla \times \mathbf{H}) = j\omega\mu(\nabla \times \mathbf{E})$

          From Faraday's law, $\Rightarrow$ $\nabla \times \mathbf{E} = -j\omega\mu(j\omega\epsilon\mathbf{H}) = \omega^2 \mu\epsilon\mathbf{H}$

          As a result, $\Rightarrow$ $\nabla \times (\nabla \times \mathbf{H}) = \omega^2 \mu\epsilon\mathbf{H}$

Step 2.   From mathematical identities, $\Rightarrow$ $\nabla \times (\nabla \times \mathbf{H}) = \nabla(\nabla \cdot \mathbf{H}) - \nabla^2 \mathbf{H}$

          But, divergence of $\mathbf{H}$ is zero. $\Rightarrow$ $\nabla \cdot \mathbf{H} = 0$

          Therefore, $\Rightarrow$ $\nabla \times (\nabla \times \mathbf{H}) = -\nabla^2 \mathbf{H}$

Step 3.   Equate results of Steps 1 and 2 to find that $\Rightarrow$ $\boxed{\nabla^2 \mathbf{H} = -\omega^2 \mu\epsilon\mathbf{H}}$

SUPPLEMENTARY PROBLEMS

1.21. Two identical point charges each of the same sign and magnitude Q are placed in the xy plane at $(-d/2, 0)$ and $(d/2, 0)$. (*a*) Find the electric field on the z axis at a distance z from the origin. (*b*) Obtain its value for $Q = 0.5\ nC$, $d = 2$ m, and $z = 1$ m.

1.22. Four equal electric charges of magnitude 0.25 nC are placed in the xy plane at the four corners of a square of side $\sqrt{2}$ m centered at the origin. Find the electric field intensity at $z = 1$ m.

1.23. A total charge of 1 nC is equally distributed among $2n$ points which are placed equidistantly on a circle with a 1 m radius centered at the origin in the xy plane. Find the electric field intensity on the axis of the circle at $z = \pm 1$ m.

1.24. A sum of 0.5 nC is distributed equally at n points and placed at random locations on a unit circle in the xy plane. Another identical set is then placed on the circle at locations which are the mirror images of the first set with respect to the origin. Find the electric field intensity on the axis of the circle at $z = \pm 1$ m.

1.25. A charge Q is distributed uniformly on a circular ring with radius r centered at the origin in the xy plane. (*a*) Find the electric field on the z axis at a distance z from the center. (*b*) Obtain its value for $Q = 1\ nC$ and $r = z = 1$ m.

1.26. Nine cocentric rings carry charge densities of $e^{-\frac{(k-5)^2}{8}}$ nC/m, where $k = 1, 2, ..., 9$ m is the radius of a ring. (*a*) Find the total charge Q on the ensemble. (*b*) Find the electric field intensity on the axis of the rings at a distance 5 m from the center. (*c*) Determine the radius m of an equivalent ring with a uniform density $Q/(2\pi n)$ which would generate the same electric field intensity $\mathbf{E}$ on its axis 5 m away from the center.

1.27. Two point charges of 0.5 nC each are placed in the xy plane at $(1, 1)$ and $(-1, 1)$. Two other charges of $-0.5\ nC$ each are placed at $(-1, -1)$ and $(1, -1)$. Find the electric field on the z-axis at $z = 1$.

1.28. Two point charges of 0.5 nC each are placed in the xy plane at $(1, 0)$ and $(0, 1)$. Two other charges of $-0.5\ nC$ each are placed at $(-1, 0)$ and $(0, -1)$. Find the electric field on the z-axis at $z = 1$.

1.29. Twenty point charges are placed equidistantly on a unit circle starting at $(1, 0)$ and progressing counter-clockwise. The first 10 points (on the upper half-circle) are 50 pC each and the next 10 points (on the lower half-circle) are -50 pC each. Find the electric field at a vertical distance of 1 m from the center of the circle.

1.30. The infinite sheet at $z = 0$ is uniformly charged with a density of 2 nC/m^2. On the $z > 0$ side, the sheet is covered by a 1-cm thick layer of dielectric material with $\epsilon_r = 100$. Find the flux density $\mathbf{D}$ and electric field strength $\mathbf{E}$ for $z > 0$.

1.31. The electric potential between two infinite parallel plates which are 10 cm apart is set to 100 V. Find the electric field in the space between them.

1.32. An electric potential $v(t) = 100 \cos(36000\pi t)$ is established between two infinite parallel plates which are separated from each other by 1 cm. Find the displacement current in the space between the plates if it is filled with (*a*) air, (*b*) a dielectric material with $\epsilon_r = 100$.

1.33. An electric charge with a density of 0.25 nC/cm^3 is uniformly distributed throughout the spherical volume $r < 1$ cm. The sphere is enclosed by a dielectric shell with $\epsilon_r = 10$ and $1 < r < 2$ cm. Find $\mathbf{D}$ and $\mathbf{E}$ for $1 < r < \infty$.

1.34. Find the magnitude of magnetic flux density 8 m away from an infinitely long, straight wire carrying a 60-Hz AC current of 60 A (*rms*) in air.

1.35. Derive the wave equation for the magnetic field of a plane wave using the method of Table 1-6.

1.36. A 75-Ω lossless transmission line is terminated on a 33.33-Ω load. To match the load to the line, we place a segment of 50-Ω transmission line between the load and the 75-Ω line. Find the length of the 50-Ω line.

1.37. Find the characteristic impedance of a lossless line from two measurements Z_{in}^{sc} and Z_{in}^{oc}, the short-circuited and open-circuited input impedances, respectively.

1.38. A sinusoidal signal generator feeds a distant load Z_L through a transmission line. Determine the length of the line if it is desired that the input impedance of the line as seen by the generator remain at Z_L regardless of the line's characteristic impedance.

1.39. A sinusoidal signal generator ($V_g = 10$ V$_{rms}$, $Z_g = 25$ Ω) feeds a 100 Ω resistor as in Fig. 1-12(a). (*a*) Find the average power delivered to the resistor. (*b*) To maximize the power delivered to the resistor, a lossless transmission line is placed between the generator and the load as in Fig. 1-12(b). Determine the length and characteristic impedance of the line. Then find the power delivered to the 100 Ω resistor.

(a)   (b)

Fig. 1-12 By employing a quarter-wave section of a lossless transmission line with an appropriate characteristic impedance, a load is matched to the source resulting in maximum power transfer. In (a), power delivered to the 100-Ω load is 640 mW. By placing a quarter-section ($\ell = \lambda/4$) of a lossless line, as in (b), with characteristic impedance $Z_0 = \sqrt{25 \times 100} = 50$ Ω, the impedance seen by the generator becomes 25 Ω and power delivered is maximized to the value 4 W.

1.40. Using the time-domain expressions given in Example 10 for a line's voltage and current, find the instantaneous and average powers delivered to the load.

ANSWERS TO SUPPLEMENTARY PROBLEMS

1.21. (*a*) $\mathbf{E} = Qz\,\mathbf{a}_z/\,[2\pi\epsilon(z^2 + d^2/4)^{3/2}]$,   (*b*) $3.18\,\mathbf{a}_z$ V/m

1.22. *Hint:*   Use superposition and the answer to problem 1.21.
    $\mathbf{E} = 3.18\,\mathbf{a}_z$ V/m

1.23. $\mathbf{E} = \pm 3.18\,\mathbf{a}_z$ V/m

1.24. $\mathbf{E} = \pm 3.18\,\mathbf{a}_z$ V/m

1.25. (*a*) $\mathbf{E} = Qz\,\mathbf{a}_z/[4\pi\epsilon(z^2 + r^2)^{3/2}]$,   (*b*) $3.18\,\mathbf{a}_z$ V/m

1.26. (*a*) $Q = 153.9$ *n*C,   (*b*) $\mathbf{E} = 8.078\,\mathbf{a}_z$ V/m,   (*c*) $m = 8.753$ m

1.27. *Hint:*   Use superposition and the answer to problem 1.2.
    $\mathbf{E} = -3.46\,\mathbf{a}_y$ V/m

1.28. $\mathbf{E} = -3.18(\mathbf{a}_x + \mathbf{a}_y)$ V/m

1.29. $\mathbf{E} = -0.318\,\mathbf{a}_r - 2.009\,\mathbf{a}_\phi$ V/m

1.30. $\mathbf{D} = 10^{-9}\mathbf{a}_z$ c/m^2, $\mathbf{E} = \begin{cases} 1.131\mathbf{a}_z \text{ V/m}, & 0 < z < 1\,\text{cm} \\ 113.1\mathbf{a}_z \text{ V/m}, & z > 1\,\text{cm} \end{cases}$

1.31. $\mathbf{E} = 1$ kV from the positive to the negative plate.

1.32. (*a*) $\frac{\partial D}{\partial t} = -10 \sin(36000\pi t)$ mA/m^2,   (*b*) $\frac{\partial D}{\partial t} = -\sin(36000\pi t)$ A/m^2

1.33. $\mathbf{D} = \dfrac{10^{-9}}{12r^2}\mathbf{a}_r$ C/m^2, $\mathbf{E} = \begin{cases} \dfrac{3\pi}{r^2}\mathbf{a}_r \text{ V/m,} & 1 < r < 2 \text{ cm} \\ \dfrac{3\pi}{10r^2}\mathbf{a}_r \text{ V/m,} & r > 2 \text{ cm} \end{cases}$,

where $\mathbf{a}_r$ is the radial unit vector away from the center of the sphere.

1.34. $B = 2.12 \sin(377t)$ (μT)

1.35. *Hint:* In both columns of Table 1-6 switch differentiations with respect to z and t.

1.36. $\ell = \lambda/4$

1.37. $Z^{oc}_{in} = -jZ_0 \cot(\beta\ell)$, $Z^{sc}_{in} = jZ_0 \tan(\beta\ell)$, $Z_o = \sqrt{Z^{oc}_{in}Z^{sc}_{in}}$

1.38. $\ell = n\lambda/2$

1.39. (*a*) 640 mW, (*b*) $Z_0 = 50\ \Omega$, $\ell = \lambda/4$, $P = 4$ W

1.40. $p(t) = v(t)i(t) = (15.4 \cos \omega t) \times (0.1025 \cos \omega t) = 1.5785 \cos^2 \omega t = 0.78925(1 + \cos 2\omega t)$. $P_{avg} = 789.25$ mW

SOME REFERENCES FOR HISTORICAL BACKGROUND

Following are some of the original works of the period before the twentieth century:

Gilbert, William (1540–1603), *De magnete*, 1600, 1893 translation by P. Fleury Mottelay, Dover Publications, New York, 1958.

Cavendish, Henry (1731–1810), *The electrical researches of the Honourable Henry Cavendish written between 1771 and 1781*, ed. by J. Clerk Maxwell, Cambridge, 1879. A new impression of the first edition is published by Frank Cass & Co., London, 1967.

Henry, Joseph (1797–1878), *On a reciprocating motion produced by magnetic attraction and repulsion*, first published in *Silliman's Journal, 1831*. The paper is reprinted in *Turning Points in American Electrical History*, pp. 31–34, IEEE Press, New York, 1977.

Maxwell, James Clerk (1831–1879), *A dynamical theory of electromagnetic field*, Royal Society Transactions, Vol. CLV, 1864. Reproduced in *The scientific papers of James Clerk Maxwell*, pp. 527–597, edited by W.D. Niven (1890), Dover Publications, New York, 1965.

Maxwell, James Clerk (1831–1879), *A treatise on electricity and magnetism*, Oxford, Clarendon, 1892. 3d ed., Oxford University Press (Vol I and II, 1873), 1955.

Hertz, Heinrich (1857–1894), *Electric Waves, being researches on the propagation of electric action with finite velocity through space*, 1893 translation by D.E. Jones, with a preface by Lord Kelvin, Dover Publications, 1962.

For some historical accounts see the following:

Appleyard, Rollo, *Pioneers of electrical communication*, Books for Libraries Press, Freeport, New York, 1930, reprinted in 1968.

Dibner, Bern, *Oersted and the discovery of electromagnetism*, Blaisdell Publishing Company, New York, London, 1962.

Dunsheath, Percy, *A history of electrical engineering*, Faber and Faber Publishing, London, 1962.

Heilbron, J.L., *Electricity in the 17th and 18th centuries: a study of early modern physics*, University of California Press, Berkeley, 1979.

Meyer, Herbert W., *A history of electricity and magnetism*, MIT Press, Cambridge, Massachusetts, 1971.

National Electrical Manufacturers Association, *A chronological history of electrical development from 600 B.C.*, New York, 1946.

Vector Analysis

2.1 Introduction

In electromagnetics, vectors are used extensively as the main tool of analysis. They were introduced briefly in Section 1.5, along with some vector operations in the Cartesian coordinate system. This chapter expands the scope of vector algebra to a level needed throughout the rest of the book. It also introduces the cylindrical and spherical coordinate systems, as all three coordinate systems are used in electromagnetics. As the notation, both for the vectors and the coordinate systems, differs from one text to another, a thorough understanding of the notation employed herein is essential for setting up the problems and obtaining solutions. In addition to this chapter, more vector operations (gradient, divergence, and curl) are introduced in Chapter 5.

2.2 Vector Notation

In order to distinguish *vectors* (quantities having magnitude and direction) from *scalars* (quantities having magnitude only), the vectors are denoted by boldface symbols. A *unit vector*, one of absolute value (or magnitude or length) 1, will in this book always be indicated by a boldface, lowercase $\mathbf{a}$. The unit vector in the direction of a vector $\mathbf{A}$ is determined by dividing $\mathbf{A}$ by its absolute value:

$$\mathbf{a}_A = \frac{\mathbf{A}}{|\mathbf{A}|} \quad \text{or} \quad \frac{\mathbf{A}}{A}$$

By use of the unit vectors $\mathbf{a}_x, \mathbf{a}_y, \mathbf{a}_z$ along the x, y, and z axes, respectively, of a Cartesian coordinate system, an arbitrary vector can be written in *component form*:

$$\mathbf{A} = A_x \mathbf{a}_x + A_y \mathbf{a}_y + A_z \mathbf{a}_z$$

In terms of components, the absolute value of a vector is defined by

$$|\mathbf{A}| = A = \sqrt{A_x^2 + A_y^2 + A_z^2}$$

EXAMPLE 1. A vector drawn from point M (2, 2, 0) to point N (4, 5, 6) is shown by $\mathbf{A} = 2\mathbf{a}_x + 3\mathbf{a}_y + 6\mathbf{a}_z$. Its magnitude is $|\mathbf{A}| = \sqrt{2^2 + 3^2 + 6^2} = 7$. Its direction is given by the unit vector

$$\mathbf{a}_A = \frac{\mathbf{A}}{|\mathbf{A}|} = \frac{2}{7}\mathbf{a}_x + \frac{3}{7}\mathbf{a}_y + \frac{6}{7}\mathbf{a}_z$$

2.3   Vector Functions

A vector function in a three-dimensional space assigns a vector to each point in that space. It specifies the magnitude and direction of the vector at that point. The spatial components of the vector are, in general, functions of the coordinates of the location. Electric and magnetic fields are examples of vector functions.

EXAMPLE 2.   The electric field intensity due to a point charge Q placed at the origin is

$$\mathbf{E} = \frac{Q}{4\pi\epsilon R^2}\,\mathbf{a}_R$$

where $\mathbf{a}_R$ is the radial unit vector. Express $\mathbf{E}$ in the Cartesian coordinate system and find its value at the points $K(3, 4, 12)$, $L(2, 6, 9)$, $M(1, 4, 8)$, and $N(4, 5, 6)$.

$$\mathbf{E}\,(x,y,z) = \frac{Q(x\mathbf{a}_x + y\mathbf{a}_y + z\mathbf{a}_z)}{4\pi\epsilon[x^2 + y^2 + z^2]^{\frac{3}{2}}}$$

$$\mathbf{E}\,(3,4,12) = \frac{Q(3\mathbf{a}_x + 4\mathbf{a}_y + 12\mathbf{a}_z)}{4\pi\epsilon \times 13^3}$$

$$\mathbf{E}\,(2,6,9) = \frac{Q(2\mathbf{a}_x + 6\mathbf{a}_y + 9\mathbf{a}_z)}{4\pi\epsilon \times 11^3}$$

$$\mathbf{E}\,(1,4,8) = \frac{Q(\mathbf{a}_x + 4\mathbf{a}_y + 8\mathbf{a}_z)}{4\pi\epsilon \times 9^3}$$

$$\mathbf{E}\,(4,5,6) = \frac{Q(2\mathbf{a}_x + 3\mathbf{a}_y + 6\mathbf{a}_z)}{4\pi\epsilon \times 7^3}$$

These points are located on concentric spheres with radii 13, 11, 9, and 7, respectively.

2.4   Vector Algebra

1.   Vectors may be added and subtracted.

$$\mathbf{A} \pm \mathbf{B} = (A_x\mathbf{a}_x + A_y\mathbf{a}_y + A_z\mathbf{a}_z) \pm (B_x\mathbf{a}_x + B_y\mathbf{a}_y + B_z\mathbf{a}_z)$$
$$= (A_x \pm B_x)\mathbf{a}_x + (A_y \pm B_y)\mathbf{a}_y + (A_z \pm B_z)\mathbf{a}_z$$

2.   The associative, distributive, and commutative laws apply.

$$\mathbf{A} + (\mathbf{B} + \mathbf{C}) = (\mathbf{A} + \mathbf{B}) + \mathbf{C}$$
$$k(\mathbf{A} + \mathbf{B}) = k\mathbf{A} + k\mathbf{B} \qquad (k_1 + k_2)\mathbf{A} = k_1\mathbf{A} + k_2\mathbf{A}$$
$$\mathbf{A} + \mathbf{B} = \mathbf{B} + \mathbf{A}$$

3.   The *dot product* of two vectors is, by definition,

$$\mathbf{A} \cdot \mathbf{B} = AB\cos\theta \qquad \text{(read ``A dot B'')}$$

where θ is the smaller angle between $\mathbf{A}$ and $\mathbf{B}$. In Example 3 it is shown that

$$\mathbf{A} \cdot \mathbf{B} = A_x B_x + A_y B_y + A_z B_z$$

which gives, in particular, $|\mathbf{A}| = \sqrt{\mathbf{A} \cdot \mathbf{A}}$.

EXAMPLE 3.   The dot product obeys the distributive and scalar multiplication laws

$$\mathbf{A} \cdot (\mathbf{B} + \mathbf{C}) = \mathbf{A} \cdot \mathbf{B} + \mathbf{A} \cdot \mathbf{C} \qquad \mathbf{A} \cdot k\mathbf{B} = k(\mathbf{A} \cdot \mathbf{B})$$

This being the case,

$$\mathbf{A} \cdot \mathbf{B} = (A_x\mathbf{a}_x + A_y\mathbf{a}_y + A_z\mathbf{a}_z) \cdot (B_x\mathbf{a}_x + B_y\mathbf{a}_y + B_z\mathbf{a}_z)$$
$$= A_xB_x(\mathbf{a}_x \cdot \mathbf{a}_x) + A_yB_y(\mathbf{a}_y \cdot \mathbf{a}_y) + A_zB_z(\mathbf{a}_z \cdot \mathbf{a}_z)$$
$$+ A_xB_y(\mathbf{a}_x \cdot \mathbf{a}_y) + \cdots + A_zB_y(\mathbf{a}_z \cdot \mathbf{a}_y)$$

However, $\mathbf{a}_x \cdot \mathbf{a}_x = \mathbf{a}_y \cdot \mathbf{a}_y = \mathbf{a}_z \cdot \mathbf{a}_z = 1$ because the $\cos\theta$ in the dot product is unity when the angle is zero. And when $\theta = 90°$, $\cos\theta$ is zero; hence, all other dot products of the unit vectors are zero. Thus,

$$\mathbf{A} \cdot \mathbf{B} = A_xB_x + A_yB_y + A_zB_z$$

4. The *cross product* of two vectors is, by definition,

$$\mathbf{A} \times \mathbf{B} = (AB \sin \theta)\mathbf{a}_n \qquad \text{(read ``A cross B'')}$$

where θ is the smaller angle between $\mathbf{A}$ and $\mathbf{B}$, and $\mathbf{a}_n$ is a unit vector normal to the plane determined by $\mathbf{A}$ and $\mathbf{B}$ when they are drawn from a common point. There are two normals to the plane, so further specification is needed. The normal selected is the one in the direction of advance of a right-hand screw when $\mathbf{A}$ is turned toward $\mathbf{B}$ (Fig. 2-1). Because of this direction requirement, the commutative law does not apply to the cross product; instead,

$$\mathbf{A} \times \mathbf{B} = -\mathbf{B} \times \mathbf{A}$$

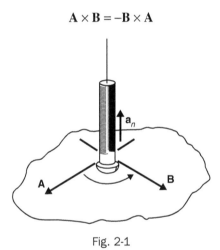

Fig. 2-1

Expanding the cross product in component form,

$$\mathbf{A} \times \mathbf{B} = (A_x\mathbf{a}_x + A_y\mathbf{a}_y + A_z\mathbf{a}_z) \times (B_x\mathbf{a}_x + B_y\mathbf{a}_y + B_z\mathbf{a}_z)$$
$$= (A_yB_z - A_zB_y)\mathbf{a}_x + (A_zB_x - A_xB_z)\mathbf{a}_y + (A_xB_y - A_yB_x)\mathbf{a}_z$$

which is conveniently expressed as a determinant:

$$\mathbf{A} \times \mathbf{B} = \begin{vmatrix} \mathbf{a}_x & \mathbf{a}_y & \mathbf{a}_z \\ A_x & A_y & A_z \\ B_x & B_y & B_z \end{vmatrix}$$

EXAMPLE 4. Given $\mathbf{A} = 2\mathbf{a}_x + 4\mathbf{a}_y - 3\mathbf{a}_z$ and $\mathbf{B} = \mathbf{a}_x - \mathbf{a}_y$, find $\mathbf{A} \cdot \mathbf{B}$ and $\mathbf{A} \times \mathbf{B}$.

$$\mathbf{A} \cdot \mathbf{B} = (2)(1) + (4)(-1) + (-3)(0) = -2$$

$$\mathbf{A} \times \mathbf{B} = \begin{vmatrix} \mathbf{a}_x & \mathbf{a}_y & \mathbf{a}_z \\ 2 & 4 & -3 \\ 1 & -1 & 0 \end{vmatrix} = -3\mathbf{a}_x - 3\mathbf{a}_y - 6\mathbf{a}_z$$

2.5   Coordinate Systems

A problem which has cylindrical or spherical symmetry could be expressed and solved in the familiar Cartesian coordinate system. However, the solution would fail to show the symmetry and in most cases would be needlessly complex. Therefore, throughout this book, in addition to the Cartesian coordinate system, the circular cylindrical and the spherical coordinate systems will be used. All three will be examined together in order to illustrate the similarities and the differences.

A point P is described by three coordinates: in Cartesian (x, y, z), in circular cylindrical (r, ϕ, z), and in spherical (r, θ, ϕ), as shown in Fig. 2-2. The order of specifying the coordinates is important and should be carefully followed. The angle ϕ is the same angle in both the cylindrical and spherical systems. But, in the order of the coordinates, ϕ appears in the second position in cylindrical, (r, ϕ, z), and the third position in spherical, (r, θ, ϕ). The same symbol, r, is used in both cylindrical and spherical coordinate systems for two quite different things. In cylindrical coordinates r measures the distance from the z axis in a plane normal to the z axis, while in the spherical system r measures the distance from the origin to the point. It should be clear from the context of the problem which r is intended.

(a) Cartesian   (b) Cylindrical   (c) Spherical

Fig. 2-2

A point is also defined by the intersection of three orthogonal surfaces, as shown in Fig. 2-3. In Cartesian coordinates the surfaces are the infinite planes $x = $ const., $y = $ const., and $z = $ const. In cylindrical coordinates, $z = $ const. is the same infinite plane as in the Cartesian case; $\phi = $ const., is a half plane with its edge along the z axis; $r = $ const. is a right circular cylinder. These three surfaces are orthogonal and their intersection locates point P. In spherical coordinates, $\phi = $ const. is the same half plane as the one in cylindrical coordinates; $r = $ const. is a sphere with its center at the origin; $\theta = $ const. is a right circular cone whose axis is the z axis and whose vertex is at the origin. Note that θ is limited to the range $0 \le \theta \le \pi$.

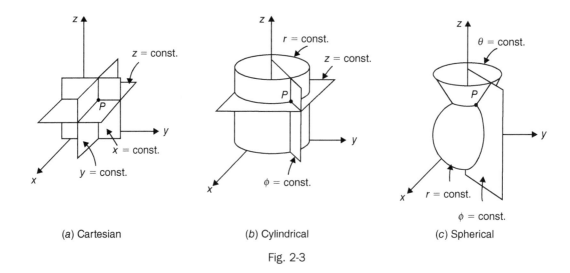

(a) Cartesian   (b) Cylindrical   (c) Spherical

Fig. 2-3

Fig. 2-4 shows the three unit vectors at point P. In the Cartesian system the unit vectors have fixed directions, independent of the location of P. This is not true for the other two systems (except in the case of $\mathbf{a}_z$). Each unit vector is normal to its coordinate surface and is in the direction in which the coordinate increases. Notice that all these systems are right-handed:

$$\mathbf{a}_x \times \mathbf{a}_y = \mathbf{a}_z \qquad \mathbf{a}_r \times \mathbf{a}_\phi = \mathbf{a}_z \qquad \mathbf{a}_r \times \mathbf{a}_\theta = \mathbf{a}_\phi$$

The component forms of a vector in the three systems are

$$\mathbf{A} = A_x \mathbf{a}_x + A_y \mathbf{a}_y + A_z \mathbf{a}_z \quad \text{(Cartesian)}$$
$$\mathbf{A} = A_r \mathbf{a}_r + A_\phi \mathbf{a}_\phi + A_z \mathbf{a}_z \quad \text{(cylindrical)}$$
$$\mathbf{A} = A_r \mathbf{a}_r + A_\theta \mathbf{a}_\theta + A_\phi \mathbf{a}_\phi \quad \text{(spherical)}$$

It should be noted that the components A_x, A_r, A_ϕ, etc., are not generally constants but more often are functions of the coordinates in that particular system.

(a) Cartesian   (b) Cylindrical   (c) Spherical

Fig. 2-4

2.6   Differential Volume, Surface, and Line Elements

There are relatively few problems in electromagnetics that can be solved without some sort of integration—along a curve, over a surface, or throughout a volume. Hence, the corresponding differential elements must be clearly understood.

When the coordinates of point P are expanded to $(x + dx, y + dy, z + dz)$ or $(r + dr, \phi + d\phi, z + dz)$, or $(r + dr, \theta + d\theta, \phi + d\phi)$, a differential volume dv is formed. To the first order in infinitesimal quantities, the differential volume is, in all three coordinate systems, a rectangular box. The value of dv in each system is given in Fig. 2-5.

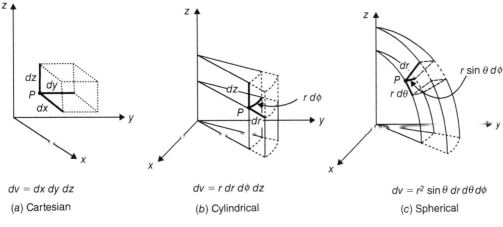

$dv = dx\, dy\, dz$ $dv = r\, dr\, d\phi\, dz$ $dv = r^2 \sin\theta\, dr\, d\theta\, d\phi$

(a) Cartesian   (b) Cylindrical   (c) Spherical

Fig. 2-5

From Fig. 2-5 may also be read the areas of the surface elements that bound the differential volume. For instance, in spherical coordinates, the differential surface element perpendicular to $\mathbf{a}_r$ is

$$dS = (r\,d\theta)(r\sin\theta\,d\phi) = r^2\sin\theta\,d\theta\,d\phi$$

The differential line element, $d\ell$ is the diagonal through P. Thus,

$$d\ell^2 = dx^2 + dy^2 + dz^2 \qquad \text{(Cartesian)}$$
$$d\ell^2 = dr^2 + r^2\,d\phi^2 + dz^2 \qquad \text{(cylindrical)}$$
$$d\ell^2 = dr^2 + r^2\,d\theta^2 + r^2\sin^2\theta\,d\phi^2 \qquad \text{(spherical)}$$

SOLVED PROBLEMS

2.1. Show that the vector directed from $M(x_1, y_1, z_1)$ to $N(x_2, y_2, z_2)$ in Fig. 2-6 is given by

$$(x_2 - x_1)\mathbf{a}_x + (y_2 - y_1)\mathbf{a}_y + (z_2 - z_1)\mathbf{a}_z$$

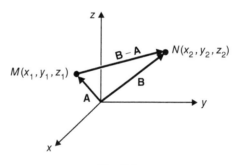

Fig. 2-6

The coordinates of M and N are used to write the two position vectors $\mathbf{A}$ and $\mathbf{B}$ in Fig. 2-6.

$$\mathbf{A} = x_1\mathbf{a}_x + y_1\mathbf{a}_y + z_1\mathbf{a}_z$$
$$\mathbf{B} = x_2\mathbf{a}_x + y_2\mathbf{a}_y + z_2\mathbf{a}_z$$

Then
$$\mathbf{B} - \mathbf{A} = (x_2 - x_1)\mathbf{a}_x + (y_2 - y_1)\mathbf{a}_y + (z_2 - z_1)\mathbf{a}_z$$

2.2. Find the vector $\mathbf{A}$ directed from $(2, -4, 1)$ to $(0, -2, 0)$ in Cartesian coordinates and find the unit vector along $\mathbf{A}$.

$$\mathbf{A} = (0-2)\mathbf{a}_x + [-2-(-4)]\mathbf{a}_y + (0-1)\mathbf{a}_z = -2\mathbf{a}_x + 2\mathbf{a}_y - \mathbf{a}_z$$
$$|\mathbf{A}|^2 = (-2)^2 + (2)^2 + (-1)^2 = 9$$
$$\mathbf{a}_A = \frac{\mathbf{A}}{|\mathbf{A}|} = -\frac{2}{3}\mathbf{a}_x + \frac{2}{3}\mathbf{a}_y - \frac{1}{3}\mathbf{a}_z$$

2.3. Find the distance between $(5, 3\pi/2, 0)$ and $(5, \pi/2, 10)$ in cylindrical coordinates.

First, obtain the *Cartesian* position vectors $\mathbf{A}$ and $\mathbf{B}$ (see Fig. 2-7).

$$\mathbf{A} = -5\mathbf{a}_y \qquad \mathbf{B} = 5\mathbf{a}_y + 10\mathbf{a}_z$$

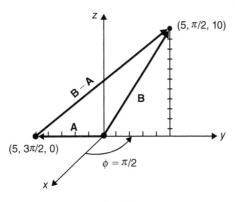

Fig. 2-7

Then $\mathbf{B} - \mathbf{A} = 10\mathbf{a}_y + 10\mathbf{a}_z$ and the required distance between the points is

$$|\mathbf{B} - \mathbf{A}| = 10\sqrt{2}$$

The cylindrical coordinates of the points cannot be used to obtain a vector between the points in the same manner as was employed in Problem 2.1 in Cartesian coordinates.

2.4. Show that $\mathbf{A} = 4\mathbf{a}_x - 2\mathbf{a}_y - \mathbf{a}_z$ and $\mathbf{B} = \mathbf{a}_x + 4\mathbf{a}_y - 4\mathbf{a}_z$ are mutually perpendicular.

Since the dot product contains $\cos\theta$, a dot product of zero from any two nonzero vectors implies that $\theta = 90°$.

$$\mathbf{A} \cdot \mathbf{B} = (4)(1) + (-2)(4) + (-1)(-4) = 0$$

2.5. Given $\mathbf{A} = 2\mathbf{a}_x + 4\mathbf{a}_y$ and $\mathbf{B} = 6\mathbf{a}_y - 4\mathbf{a}_z$, find the smaller angle between them using (*a*) the cross product, (*b*) the dot product.

(*a*)
$$\mathbf{A} \times \mathbf{B} = \begin{vmatrix} \mathbf{a}_x & \mathbf{a}_y & \mathbf{a}_z \\ 2 & 4 & 0 \\ 0 & 6 & -4 \end{vmatrix} = -16\mathbf{a}_x + 8\mathbf{a}_y + 12\mathbf{a}_z$$

$$|\mathbf{A}| = \sqrt{(2)^2 + (4)^2 + (0)^2} = 4.47$$

$$|\mathbf{B}| = \sqrt{(0)^2 + (6)^2 + (-4)^2} = 7.21$$

$$|\mathbf{A} \times \mathbf{B}| = \sqrt{(-16)^2 + (8)^2 + (12)^2} = 21.54$$

Then, since $|\mathbf{A} \times \mathbf{B}| = |\mathbf{A}|\,|\mathbf{B}|\sin\theta$,

$$\sin\theta = \frac{21.54}{(4.47)(7.21)} = 0.668 \quad \text{or} \quad \theta = 41.9°$$

(*b*)
$$\mathbf{A} \cdot \mathbf{B} = (2)(0) + (4)(6) + (0)(-4) = 24$$

$$\cos\theta = \frac{\mathbf{A} \cdot \mathbf{B}}{|\mathbf{A}||\mathbf{B}|} = \frac{24}{(4.47)(7.21)} = 0.745 \quad \text{or} \quad \theta = 41.9°$$

2.6. Given $\mathbf{F} = (y - 1)\mathbf{a}_x + 2x\mathbf{a}_y$, find the vector at $(2, 2, 1)$ and its projection on $\mathbf{B}$, where $\mathbf{B} = 5\mathbf{a}_x - \mathbf{a}_y + 2\mathbf{a}_z$.

$$\mathbf{F}(2, 2, 1) = (2 - 1)\mathbf{a}_x + (2)(2)\mathbf{a}_y$$
$$= \mathbf{a}_x + 4\mathbf{a}_y$$

As indicated in Fig. 2-8, the projection of one vector on a second vector is obtained by expressing the unit vector in the direction of the second vector and taking the dot product.

$$\text{Proj. } \mathbf{A} \text{ on } \mathbf{B} = \mathbf{A} \cdot \mathbf{a}_B = \frac{\mathbf{A} \cdot \mathbf{B}}{|\mathbf{B}|}$$

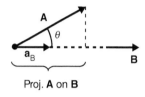

Proj. **A** on **B**

Fig. 2-8

Thus, at (2, 2, 1),

$$\text{Proj. } \mathbf{F} \text{ on } \mathbf{B} = \frac{\mathbf{F} \cdot \mathbf{B}}{|\mathbf{B}|} = \frac{(1)(5) + (4)(-1) + (0)(2)}{\sqrt{30}} = \frac{1}{\sqrt{30}}$$

2.7. Given $\mathbf{A} = \mathbf{a}_x + \mathbf{a}_y$, $\mathbf{B} = \mathbf{a}_x + 2\mathbf{a}_z$ and $\mathbf{C} = 2\mathbf{a}_y + \mathbf{a}_z$, find $(\mathbf{A} \times \mathbf{B}) \times \mathbf{C}$ and compare it with $\mathbf{A} \times (\mathbf{B} \times \mathbf{C})$.

$$\mathbf{A} \times \mathbf{B} = \begin{vmatrix} \mathbf{a}_x & \mathbf{a}_y & \mathbf{a}_z \\ 1 & 1 & 0 \\ 1 & 0 & 2 \end{vmatrix} = 2\mathbf{a}_x - 2\mathbf{a}_y - \mathbf{a}_z$$

Then

$$(\mathbf{A} \times \mathbf{B}) \times \mathbf{C} = \begin{vmatrix} \mathbf{a}_x & \mathbf{a}_y & \mathbf{a}_z \\ 2 & -2 & -1 \\ 0 & 2 & 1 \end{vmatrix} = -2\mathbf{a}_y + 4\mathbf{a}_z$$

A similar calculation gives $\mathbf{A} \times (\mathbf{B} \times \mathbf{C}) = 2\mathbf{a}_x - 2\mathbf{a}_y + 3\mathbf{a}_z$. Thus, the cross product does not obey the vector triple associative law.

2.8. Using the vectors **A**, **B**, and **C** of Problem 2.7, find $\mathbf{A} \cdot \mathbf{B} \times \mathbf{C}$ and compare it with $\mathbf{A} \times \mathbf{B} \cdot \mathbf{C}$.

From Problem 2.7, $\mathbf{B} \times \mathbf{C} = -4\mathbf{a}_x - \mathbf{a}_y + 2\mathbf{a}_z$. Then

$$\mathbf{A} \cdot \mathbf{B} \times \mathbf{C} = (1)(-4) + (1)(-1) + (0)(2) = -5$$

Also from Problem 2.7, $\mathbf{A} \times \mathbf{B} = 2\mathbf{a}_x - 2\mathbf{a}_y - \mathbf{a}_z$. Then

$$\mathbf{A} \times \mathbf{B} \cdot \mathbf{C} = (2)(0) + (-2)(2) + (-1)(1) = -5$$

Parentheses are not needed in the scalar triple product, since it has meaning only when the cross product is taken first. In general, it can be shown that

$$\mathbf{A} \cdot \mathbf{B} \times \mathbf{C} = \begin{vmatrix} A_x & A_y & A_z \\ B_x & B_y & B_z \\ C_x & C_y & C_z \end{vmatrix}$$

As long as the vectors appear in the same cyclic order, the result is the same. The scalar triple products not in this cyclic order have a change in sign.

2.9. Express the unit vector which points from $z = h$ on the z axis toward $(r, \phi, 0)$ in cylindrical coordinates. See Fig. 2-9.

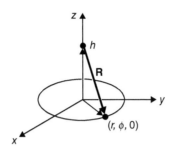

Fig. 2-9

The vector **R** is the difference of two vectors:

$$\mathbf{R} = r\mathbf{a}_r - h\mathbf{a}_z$$

$$\mathbf{a}_R = \frac{\mathbf{R}}{|\mathbf{R}|} = \frac{r\mathbf{a}_r - h\mathbf{a}_z}{\sqrt{r^2 + h^2}}$$

The angle ϕ does not appear explicitly in these expressions. Nevertheless, both **R** and $\mathbf{a}_R$ vary with ϕ through $\mathbf{a}_r$.

2.10. Express the unit vector which is directed toward the origin from an arbitrary point on the plane $z = -5$, as shown in Fig. 2-10.

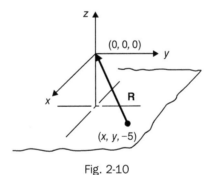

Fig. 2-10

Since the problem is in Cartesian coordinates, the two-point formula of Problem 2.1 applies.

$$\mathbf{R} = -x\mathbf{a}_x - y\mathbf{a}_y + 5\mathbf{a}_z$$

$$\mathbf{a}_R = \frac{-x\mathbf{a}_x - y\mathbf{a}_y + 5\mathbf{a}_z}{\sqrt{x^2 + y^2 + 25}}$$

2.11. Use the spherical coordinate system to find the area of the strip $\alpha \le \theta \le \beta$ on the spherical shell of radius a (Fig. 2-11). What results when $\alpha = 0$ and $\beta = \pi$?

The differential surface element is [see Fig. 2-5(*c*)]

$$dS = r^2 \sin \theta \, d\theta \, d\phi$$

Fig. 2-11

Then
$$A = \int_0^{2\pi} \int_\alpha^\beta a^2 \sin\theta \, d\theta \, d\phi$$
$$= 2\pi a^2 (\cos\alpha - \cos\beta)$$

When $\alpha = 0$ and $\beta = \pi$, $A = 4\pi a^2$, the surface area of the entire sphere.

2.12. Obtain the expression for the volume of a sphere of radius a from the differential volume.

From Fig. 2-5(c), $dv = r^2 \sin\theta \, dr \, d\theta \, d\phi$. Then

$$v = \int_0^{2\pi} \int_0^\pi \int_0^a r^2 \sin\theta \, dr \, d\theta \, d\phi = \frac{4}{3}\pi a^3$$

2.13. Use the cylindrical coordinate system to find the area of the curved surface of a right circular cylinder where $r = 2$ m, $h = 5$ m, and $30° \le \phi \le 120°$ (see Fig. 2-12).

Fig. 2-12

The differential surface element is $dS = r \, d\phi \, dz$. Then

$$A = \int_0^5 \int_{\pi/6}^{2\pi/3} 2 \, d\phi \, dz$$
$$= 5\pi \text{ m}^2$$

2.14. Transform

$$\mathbf{A} = y\mathbf{a}_x + x\mathbf{a}_y + \frac{x^2}{\sqrt{x^2 + y^2}} \mathbf{a}_z$$

from Cartesian to cylindrical coordinates.

Referring to Fig. 2-2(b),

$$x = r \cos \phi \qquad y = r \sin \phi \qquad r = \sqrt{x^2 + y^2}$$

Hence, $$\mathbf{A} = r \sin \phi \mathbf{a}_x + r \cos \phi \mathbf{a}_y + r \cos^2 \phi \mathbf{a}_z$$

Now the projections of the Cartesian unit vectors on $\mathbf{a}_r$, $\mathbf{a}_\phi$, and $\mathbf{a}_z$ are obtained:

$$\begin{array}{lll}
\mathbf{a}_x \cdot \mathbf{a}_r = \cos \phi & \mathbf{a}_x \cdot \mathbf{a}_\phi = -\sin \phi & \mathbf{a}_x \cdot \mathbf{a}_z = 0 \\
\mathbf{a}_y \cdot \mathbf{a}_r = \sin \phi & \mathbf{a}_y \cdot \mathbf{a}_\phi = \cos \phi & \mathbf{a}_y \cdot \mathbf{a}_z = 0 \\
\mathbf{a}_z \cdot \mathbf{a}_r = 0 & \mathbf{a}_z \cdot \mathbf{a}_\phi = 0 & \mathbf{a}_z \cdot \mathbf{a}_z = 1
\end{array}$$

Therefore, $$\begin{aligned}
\mathbf{a}_x &= \cos \phi \mathbf{a}_r - \sin \phi \mathbf{a}_\phi \\
\mathbf{a}_y &= \sin \phi \mathbf{a}_r + \cos \phi \mathbf{a}_\phi \\
\mathbf{a}_z &= \mathbf{a}_z
\end{aligned}$$

and $$\mathbf{A} = 2r \sin \phi \cos \phi \mathbf{a}_r + (r \cos^2 \phi - r \sin^2 \phi)\mathbf{a}_\phi + r \cos^2 \phi \mathbf{a}_z$$

2.15. A vector of magnitude 10 points from $(5, 5\pi/4, 0)$ in cylindrical coordinates toward the origin (Fig. 2-13). Express the vector in Cartesian coordinates.

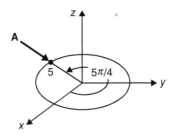

Fig. 2-13

In cylindrical coordinates, the vector may be expressed as $10\mathbf{a}_r$, where $\phi = \pi/4$. Hence,

$$A_x = 10 \cos \frac{\pi}{4} = \frac{10}{\sqrt{2}} \qquad A_y = 10 \sin \frac{\pi}{4} = \frac{10}{\sqrt{2}} \qquad A_z = 0$$

so that

$$\mathbf{A} = \frac{10}{\sqrt{2}} \mathbf{a}_x + \frac{10}{\sqrt{2}} \mathbf{a}_y$$

Notice that the value of the radial coordinate, 5, is immaterial.

SUPPLEMENTARY PROBLEMS

2.16. Given $\mathbf{A} = 4\mathbf{a}_y + 10\mathbf{a}_z$ and $\mathbf{B} = 2\mathbf{a}_x + 3\mathbf{a}_y$, find the projection of $\mathbf{A}$ on $\mathbf{B}$.

2.17. Given $\mathbf{A} = (10/\sqrt{2})(\mathbf{a}_x + \mathbf{a}_z)$ and $\mathbf{B} = 3(\mathbf{a}_y + \mathbf{a}_z)$, express the projection of $\mathbf{B}$ on $\mathbf{A}$ as a vector in the direction of $\mathbf{A}$.

2.18. Find the angle between $\mathbf{A} = 10\mathbf{a}_y + 2\mathbf{a}_z$ and $\mathbf{B} = -4\mathbf{a}_y + 0.5\mathbf{a}_z$ using both the dot product and the cross product.

2.19. Find the angle between $\mathbf{A} = 5.8\mathbf{a}_y + 1.55\mathbf{a}_z$ and $\mathbf{B} = -6.93\mathbf{a}_y + 4.0\mathbf{a}_z$ using both the dot product and the cross product.

2.20. Given the plane $4x + 3y + 2z = 12$, find the unit vector normal to the surface in the direction away from the origin.

2.21. Find the relationship which the Cartesian components of **A** and **B** must satisfy if the vector fields are to be everywhere parallel.

2.22. Express the unit vector directed toward the origin from an arbitrary point on the line described by $x = 0$, $y = 3$.

2.23. Express the unit vector directed toward the point (x_1, y_1, z_1) from an arbitrary point in the plane $y = -5$.

2.24. Express the unit vector directed toward the point $(0, 0, h)$ from an arbitrary point in the plane $z = -2$.

2.25. Given $\mathbf{A} = 5\mathbf{a}_x$ and $\mathbf{B} = 4\mathbf{a}_x + B_y\mathbf{a}_y$, find B_y such that the angle between **A** and **B** is $45°$. If **B** also has a term $B_z\mathbf{a}_z$, what relationship must exist between B_y and B_z?

2.26. Show that the absolute value of $\mathbf{A} \cdot \mathbf{B} \times \mathbf{C}$ is the volume of the parallelepiped with edges **A**, **B**, and **C**.

2.27. Given $\mathbf{A} = 2\mathbf{a}_x - \mathbf{a}_z$, $\mathbf{B} = 3\mathbf{a}_x + \mathbf{a}_y$, and $\mathbf{C} = -2\mathbf{a}_x + 6\mathbf{a}_y - 4\mathbf{a}_z$, show that **C** is $\perp$ to both **A** and **B**.

2.28. Given $\mathbf{A} = \mathbf{a}_x - \mathbf{a}_y$, $\mathbf{B} = 2\mathbf{a}_z$, and $\mathbf{C} = -\mathbf{a}_x + 3\mathbf{a}_y$, find $\mathbf{A} \cdot \mathbf{B} \times \mathbf{C}$. Examine other variations of this scalar triple product.

2.29. Using the vectors of Problem 2.28 find $(\mathbf{A} \times \mathbf{B}) \times \mathbf{C}$.

2.30. Find the unit vector directed from $(2, -5, -2)$ toward $(14, -5, 3)$.

2.31. Find the vector directed from $(10, 3\pi/4, \pi/6)$ to $(5, \pi/4, \pi)$, where the endpoints are given in spherical coordinates.

2.32. Find the distance between $(2, \pi/6, 0)$ and $(1, \pi, 2)$, where the points are given in cylindrical coordinates.

2.33. Find the distance between $(1, \pi/4, 0)$ and $(1, 3\pi/4, \pi)$, where the points are given in spherical coordinates.

2.34. Use spherical coordinates and integrate to find the area of the region $0 \le \phi \le \alpha$ on the spherical shell of radius a. What is the result when $\alpha = 2\pi$?

2.35. Use cylindrical coordinates to find the area of the curved surface of a right circular cylinder of radius a and height h.

2.36. Use cylindrical coordinates and integrate to obtain the volume of the right circular cylinder of Problem 2.35.

2.37. Use spherical coordinates to write the differential surface areas dS_1 and dS_2 and then integrate to obtain the areas of the surfaces marked 1 and 2 in Fig. 2-14.

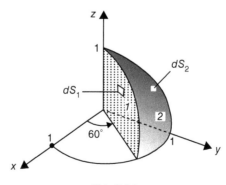

Fig. 2-14

2.38. Use spherical coordinates to find the volume of a hemispherical shell of inner radius 2.00 m and outer radius 2.02 m.

2.39. Using spherical coordinates to express the differential volume, integrate to obtain the volume defined by $1 \le r \le 2$ m, $0 \le \theta \le \pi/2$, and $0 \le \phi \le \pi/2$.

ANSWERS TO SUPPLEMENTARY PROBLEMS

2.16. $12/\sqrt{13}$

2.17. $1.50(\mathbf{a}_x + \mathbf{a}_z)$

2.18. $161.5°$

2.19. $135°$

2.20. $(4\mathbf{a}_x + 3\mathbf{a}_y + 2\mathbf{a}_z)/\sqrt{29}$

2.21. $\dfrac{A_x}{B_x} = \dfrac{A_y}{B_y} = \dfrac{A_z}{B_z}$

2.22. $\mathbf{a} = \dfrac{-3\mathbf{a}_y - z\mathbf{a}_z}{\sqrt{9+z^2}}$

2.23. $\mathbf{a} = \dfrac{(x_1-x)\mathbf{a}_x + (y_1+5)\mathbf{a}_y + (z_1-z)\mathbf{a}_z}{\sqrt{(x_1-x)^2 + (y_1-5)^2 + (z_1-z)^2}}$

2.24. $\mathbf{a} = \dfrac{-x\mathbf{a}_x - y\mathbf{a}_y + (h+2)\mathbf{a}_z}{\sqrt{x^2 + y^2 + (h+2)^2}}$

2.25. $B_y = \pm 4$, $\sqrt{B_y^2 + B_z^2} = 4$

2.26. *Hint*: First show that the base has area $|\mathbf{B} \times \mathbf{C}|$.

2.28. $-4, \pm 4$

2.29. $-8\mathbf{a}_z$

2.30. $\mathbf{a} = \dfrac{12}{13}\mathbf{a}_x + \dfrac{5}{13}\mathbf{a}_z$

2.31. $-9.66\mathbf{a}_x - 3.54\mathbf{a}_y + 10.61\mathbf{a}_z$

2.32. 3.53

2.33. 2.0

2.34. $2\alpha a^2$, $A = 4\pi a^2$

2.35. $2\pi a h$

2.36. $\pi a^2 h$

2.37. $\pi/4, \pi/6$

2.38. $0.162\,\pi$ m³

2.39. $\dfrac{7\pi}{6}$ m³

CHAPTER 3

Electric Field

3.1 Introduction

The concepts of electric force and field intensity were introduced in Chapter 1. This chapter elaborates further on those concepts and formulates them using vector notations, a necessary framework in electromagnetics. In doing so, it expands upon, and refers to, some examples and problems from Chapter 1.

3.2 Coulomb's Law in Vector Form

The force between two charges Q_1 and Q_2 is given by Coulomb's law. This was introduced in Section 1.6 in scalar form. In vector form Coulomb's law incorporates both the magnitude and direction of the force as follows:

$$\mathbf{F}_1 = \frac{Q_1 Q_2}{4\pi\epsilon R_{21}^2}\mathbf{a}_{21} = \frac{Q_1 Q_2}{4\pi\epsilon R_{21}^3}\mathbf{R}_{21}$$

where $\mathbf{F}_1$ is the force on charge Q_1 due to a second charge Q_2, $\mathbf{a}_{21}$ is the unit vector *directed from Q_2 to Q_1*, $\mathbf{R}_{21} = R_{21}\mathbf{a}_{21}$, and ϵ is the *permittivity* of the medium.

EXAMPLE 1. Find the force on charge Q_1, 20 μC, due to charge Q_2, -300 μC, where Q_1 is at (0, 1, 2) m and Q_2 at (2, 0, 0) m.

Because 1 C is a rather large unit, charges are often given in microcoulombs (μC), nanocoulombs (nC), or picocoulombs (pC). (See Appendix for the SI prefix system.) Referring to Fig. 3-1,

$$\mathbf{R}_{21} = -2\mathbf{a}_x + \mathbf{a}_y + 2\mathbf{a} \qquad R_{21} = \sqrt{(-2)^2 + 1^2 + 2^2} = 3$$

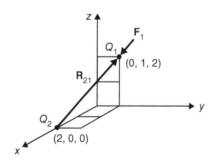

Fig. 3-1

and

$$\mathbf{a}_{21} = \frac{1}{3}(-2\mathbf{a}_x + \mathbf{a}_y + 2\mathbf{a}_z)$$

Then

$$\mathbf{F}_1 = \frac{(20 \times 10^{-6})(-300 \times 10^{-6})}{4\pi(10^{-9}/36\pi)(3)^2} \left(\frac{-2\mathbf{a}_x + \mathbf{a}_y + 2\mathbf{a}_z}{3} \right)$$

$$= 6 \left(\frac{2\mathbf{a}_x - \mathbf{a}_y - \mathbf{a}_z}{3} \right) \text{N}$$

The force magnitude is 6 N and the direction is such that Q_1 is attracted to Q_2 (unlike charges attract).

The force field in the region of an isolated charge Q is spherically symmetric. This is made evident by locating Q at the origin of a spherical coordinate system, so that the position vector $\mathbf{R}$, from Q to a small test charge $Q_t \ll Q$, is simply $r\mathbf{a}_r$. Then

$$\mathbf{F}_t = \frac{Q_t Q}{4\pi\epsilon_0 r^2} \mathbf{a}_r$$

showing that on the spherical surface $r = $ constant, $|\mathbf{F}_t|$ is constant, and $\mathbf{F}_t$ is radial.

3.3   Superposition

The force on a charge Q_1 due to $n-1$ other charges $Q_2, \ldots, Q_n$ is the *vector sum* of the individual charge forces:

$$\mathbf{F}_1 = \frac{Q_1 Q_2}{4\pi\epsilon_0 R_{21}^2} \mathbf{a}_{21} + \frac{Q_1 Q_3}{4\pi\epsilon_0 R_{31}^2} \mathbf{a}_{31} + \cdots = \frac{Q_1}{4\pi\epsilon_0} \sum_{k=2}^{n} \frac{Q_k}{R_{k1}^2} \mathbf{a}_{k1}$$

This superposition extends in a natural way to the case where charge is continuously distributed through some spatial region: One simply replaces the above vector sum by a *vector integral* (see Section 3.5).

3.4   Electric Field Intensity

Suppose that the above-considered test charge Q_t is sufficiently small so as not to disturb significantly the field of the fixed point charge Q. Then the *electric field intensity*, $\mathbf{E}$, due to Q is defined to be the force per unit charge on Q_t: $\mathbf{E} = \mathbf{F}_t / Q_t$.

For Q at the origin of a spherical coordinate system [see Fig. 3-2(a)], the electric field intensity at an arbitrary point P is, from Section 3.2,

$$\mathbf{E} = \frac{Q}{4\pi\epsilon_0 r^2} \mathbf{a}_r$$

(a) Spherical   (b) Cartesian

Fig. 3-2

In an arbitrary Cartesian coordinate system [see Fig. 3-2(b)],

$$\mathbf{E} = \frac{Q}{4\pi\epsilon_0 R^2}\,\mathbf{a}_R$$

The units of $\mathbf{E}$ are newtons per coulomb (N/C) or the equivalent, volts per meter (V/m).

EXAMPLE 2.   Find $\mathbf{E}$ at $(0, 3, 4)$ m in Cartesian coordinates due to a point charge $Q = 0.5\ \mu$C at the origin. In this case,

$$\mathbf{R} = 3\mathbf{a}_y + 4\mathbf{a}_z \qquad R = 5 \qquad \mathbf{a}_R = 0.6\mathbf{a}_y + 0.8\mathbf{a}_z$$

$$\mathbf{E} = \frac{0.5\times 10^{-6}}{4\pi(10^{-9}/36\pi)(5)^2}\,(0.6\mathbf{a}_y + 0.8\mathbf{a}_z)$$

Thus, $|\mathbf{E}| = 180$ V/m in the direction $\mathbf{a}_R = 0.6\mathbf{a}_y + 0.8\mathbf{a}_z$.

3.5   Charge Distributions

Volume Charge

When charge is distributed throughout a specified volume, each charge element contributes to the electric field at an external point. A summation or integration is then required to obtain the total electric field. Even though electric charge in its smallest division is found to be an electron or proton, it is useful to consider continuous (in fact, differentiable) charge distributions and to define a *charge density* by

$$\rho = \frac{dQ}{dv}\ (\text{C/m}^3)$$

Note the units in parentheses, which is meant to signify that ρ will be in C/m³ provided that the variables are expressed in proper SI units (C for Q and m³ for v). This convention will be used throughout this book.

    With reference to volume v in Fig. 3-3, each differential charge dQ produces a differential electric field

$$d\mathbf{E} = \frac{dQ}{4\pi\epsilon_0 R^2}\,\mathbf{a}_R$$

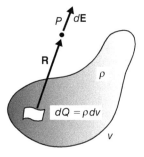

Fig. 3-3

at the observation point P. Assuming that the only charge in the region is contained within the volume, the total electric field at P is obtained by integration over the volume:

$$\mathbf{E} = \int_v \frac{\rho\,\mathbf{a}_R}{4\pi\epsilon_0 R^2}\,dv$$

Sheet Charge

Charge may also be distributed over a surface or a sheet. Then each differential charge dQ on the sheet results in a differential electric field

$$d\mathbf{E} = \frac{dQ}{4\pi\epsilon_0 R^2}\,\mathbf{a}_R$$

at point P (see Fig. 3-4). If the *surface charge density* is ρ_s (C/m²) and if no other charge is present in the region, then the total electric field at P is

$$\mathbf{E} = \int_S \frac{\rho_s \mathbf{a}_R}{4\pi\epsilon_0 R^2}\,dS$$

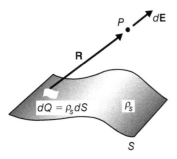

Fig. 3-4

Line Charge

If charge is distributed over a (curved) line, each differential charge dQ along the line produces a differential electric field

$$d\mathbf{E} = \frac{dQ}{4\pi\epsilon_0 R^2}\,\mathbf{a}_R$$

at P (see Fig. 3-5). And if the *line charge density* is ρ_ℓ (C/m), and no other charge is in the region, then the total electric field at P is

$$\mathbf{E} = \int_L \frac{\rho_\ell \mathbf{a}_R}{4\pi\epsilon_0 R^2}\,d\ell$$

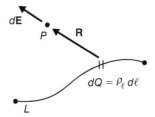

Fig. 3-5

It should be emphasized that in all three of the above charge distributions and corresponding integrals for $\mathbf{E}$, the unit vector $\mathbf{a}_R$ is variable, depending on the coordinates of the charge element dQ. Thus, $\mathbf{a}_R$ cannot be removed from the integrand. It should also be noticed that whenever the appropriate integral converges, it defines $\mathbf{E}$ at an *internal* point of the charge distribution.

3.6 Standard Charge Configurations

In three special cases the integration discussed in Section 3.5 is either unnecessary or easily carried out. In regard to these standard configurations (and to others which will be covered in this chapter), it should be noted that the charge is not "on a conductor." When a problem states that charge is distributed in the form of a disk, for example, it does not mean that we have a disk-shaped conductor with charge on the surface. (In Chapter 7, conductors with surface charge will be examined.) Although it may now require a stretch of the imagination, these charges should be thought of as somehow suspended in space, fixed in the specified configuration.

Point Charge

As previously determined, the field of a single point charge Q is given by

$$E = \frac{Q}{4\pi\epsilon_0 r^2}\, \mathbf{a}_r \quad \text{(spherical coordinates)}$$

See Fig. 3-2(*a*). This is a spherically symmetric field that follows an *inverse-square law* (like gravitation).

Infinite Line Charge

If charge is distributed with *uniform* density ρ_ℓ (C/m) along an *infinite, straight* line—which will be chosen as the z axis—then the field is given by

$$E = \frac{\rho_\ell}{2\pi\epsilon_0 r}\, \mathbf{a}_r \quad \text{(cylindrical coordinates)}$$

See Fig. 3-6. This field has cylindrical symmetry and is inversely proportional to the *first power* of the distance from the line charge. For a derivation of **E**, see Problem 3.9.

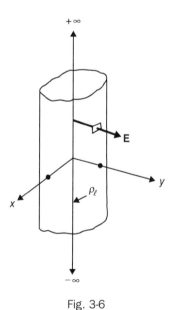

Fig. 3-6

EXAMPLE 3.   A uniform line charge, infinite in extent, with $\rho_1 = 20$ nC/m, lies along the z axis. Find **E** at (6, 8, 3) m.

In cylindrical coordinates $r = \sqrt{6^2 + 8^2} = 10$ m. The field is constant with z. Thus,

$$E = \frac{20\times 10^{-9}}{2\pi(10^{-9}/36\pi)(10)}\, \mathbf{a}_r = 36\mathbf{a}_r\, \text{V/m}$$

Infinite Plane Charge

If charge is distributed with *uniform* density ρ_s (C/m^2) over an *infinite plane*, then the field is given by

$$\mathbf{E} = \frac{\rho_s}{2\epsilon_0}\,\mathbf{a}_n$$

See Fig. 3-7. This field is of constant magnitude and has mirror symmetry about the plane charge. For a derivation of this expression, see Problem 3.12.

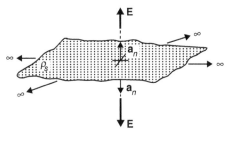

Fig. 3-7

EXAMPLE 4.   Charge is distributed uniformly over the plane $z = 10$ cm with a density $\rho_s = (1/3\pi)$ nC/m^2. Find **E**.

$$|\mathbf{E}| = \frac{\rho_s}{2\epsilon_0} = \frac{(1/3\pi)10^{-9}}{2(10^{-9}/36\pi)} = 6\,\text{V/m}$$

Above the sheet ($z > 10$ cm), $\mathbf{E} = 6\mathbf{a}_z$ V/m; and for $z < 10$ cm, $\mathbf{E} = -6\mathbf{a}_z$ V/m.

SOLVED PROBLEMS

3.1. Two point charges, $Q_1 = 50$ μC and $Q_2 = 10$ μC, are located at $(-1, 1, -3)$ m and $(3, 1, 0)$ m, respectively (Fig. 3-8). Find the force on Q_1.

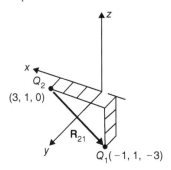

Fig. 3-8

$$\mathbf{R}_{21} = -4\mathbf{a}_x - 3\mathbf{a}_z$$
$$\mathbf{a}_{21} = \frac{-4\mathbf{a}_x - 3\mathbf{a}_z}{5}$$
$$\mathbf{F}_1 = \frac{Q_1 Q_2}{4\pi\epsilon_0 R_{21}^2}\mathbf{a}_{21}$$
$$= \frac{(50\times10^{-6})(10^{-5})}{4\pi(10^{-9}/36\pi)(5)^2}\left(\frac{-4\mathbf{a}_x - 3\mathbf{a}_z}{5}\right)$$
$$= (0.18)(-0.8\mathbf{a}_x - 0.6\mathbf{a}_z)\,\text{N}$$

The force has a magnitude of 0.18 N and a direction given by the unit vector $-0.8\mathbf{a}_x -0.6\mathbf{a}_z$. In component form,

$$\mathbf{F}_1 = 0.144\mathbf{a}_x - 0.108\mathbf{a}_z\,\text{N}$$

3.2. Refer to Fig. 3-9. Find the force on a 100 μC charge at (0, 0, 3) m if four like charges of 20 μC are located on the x and y axes at ± 4 m.

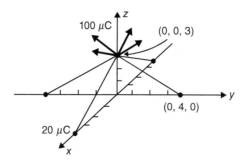

Fig. 3-9

Consider the force due to the charge at $y = 4$,

$$\frac{(10^{-4})(20\times10^{-6})}{4\pi(10^{-9}/36\pi)(5)^2}\left(\frac{-4\mathbf{a}_y+3\mathbf{a}_z}{5}\right)$$

The y component will be canceled by the charge at $y = -4$. Similarly, the x components due to the other two charges will cancel. Hence,

$$\mathbf{F} = 4\left(\frac{18}{25}\right)\left(\frac{3}{5}\mathbf{a}_z\right) = 1.73\mathbf{a}_z \text{ N}$$

3.3. Refer to Fig. 3-10. Point charge $Q_1 = 300$ μC, located at $(1, -1, -3)$ m, experiences a force

$$\mathbf{F}_1 = 8\mathbf{a}_x - 8\mathbf{a}_y + 4\mathbf{a}_z \text{ N}$$

Fig. 3-10

due to point charge Q_2 at $(3, -3, -2)$ m. Determine Q_2.

$$\mathbf{R}_{21} = -2\mathbf{a}_x + 2\mathbf{a}_y - \mathbf{a}_z$$

Note that, because

$$\frac{8}{-2} = \frac{-8}{2} = \frac{4}{-1}$$

the given force is along $\mathbf{R}_{21}$ (see Problem 2.21), as it must be.

$$\mathbf{F}_1 = \frac{Q_1 Q_2}{4\pi\epsilon_0 R^2}\mathbf{a}_R$$

$$8\mathbf{a}_x - 8\mathbf{a}_y + 4\mathbf{a}_z = \frac{(300\times10^{-6})Q_2}{4\pi(10^{-9}/36\pi)(3)^2}\left(\frac{-2\mathbf{a}_x+2\mathbf{a}_y-\mathbf{a}_z}{3}\right)$$

Hence, $Q_2 = -40$ μC.

3.4. Find the force on a point charge of 50 μC at (0, 0, 5) m due to a charge of 500π μC that is uniformly distributed over the circular disk $r \leq 5$ m, $z = 0$ m (see Fig. 3-11).

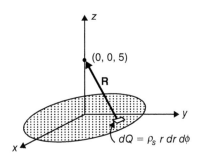

Fig. 3-11

The charge density is

$$\rho_s = \frac{Q}{A} = \frac{500\pi \times 10^{-6}}{\pi(5)^2} = 0.2 \times 10^{-4} \, C/m^2$$

In cylindrical coordinates,

$$\mathbf{R} = -r\mathbf{a}_r + 5\mathbf{a}_z$$

Then each differential charge results in a differential force

$$d\mathbf{F} = \frac{(50 \times 10^{-6})(\rho_s r \, dr \, d\phi)}{4\pi(10^{-9}/36\pi)(r^2 + 25)} \left(\frac{-r\mathbf{a}_r + 5\mathbf{a}_z}{\sqrt{r^2 + 25}} \right)$$

Before integrating, note that the radial components will cancel and that $\mathbf{a}_z$ is constant. Hence,

$$\mathbf{F} = \int_0^{2\pi} \int_0^5 \frac{(50 \times 10^{-6})(0.2 \times 10^{-4}) 5r \, dr \, d\phi}{4\pi(10^{-9}/36\pi)(r^2 + 25)^{3/2}} \mathbf{a}_z$$

$$= 90\pi \int_0^5 \frac{r \, dr}{(r^2 + 25)^{3/2}} \mathbf{a}_z = 90\pi \left[\frac{-1}{\sqrt{r^2 + 25}} \right]_0^5 \mathbf{a}_z = 16.56\mathbf{a}_z \, N$$

3.5. Repeat Problem 3.4 for a disk of radius 2 m.

Reducing the radius has two effects: the charge density is increased by a factor

$$\frac{\rho_2}{\rho_1} = \frac{(5)^2}{(2)^2} = 6.25$$

while the integral over r becomes

$$\int_0^2 \frac{r \, dr}{(r^2 + 25)^{3/2}} = 0.0143 \quad \text{instead of} \quad \int_0^5 \frac{r \, dr}{(r^2 + 25)^{3/2}} = 0.0586$$

The resulting force is

$$\mathbf{F} = (6.25) \left(\frac{0.0143}{0.0586} \right) (16.56\mathbf{a}_z \, N) = 25.27\mathbf{a}_z \, N$$

3.6. Find the expression for the electric field at P due to a point charge Q at (x_1, y_1, z_1). Repeat with the charge placed at the origin.

As shown in Fig. 3-12,

$$\mathbf{R} = (x - x_1)\mathbf{a}_x + (y - y_1)\mathbf{a}_y + (z - z_1)\mathbf{a}_z$$

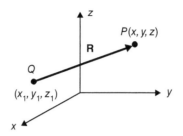

Fig. 3-12

Then
$$\mathbf{E} = \frac{Q}{4\pi\epsilon_0 R^2}\,\mathbf{a}_R$$

$$= \frac{Q}{4\pi\epsilon_0}\frac{(x-x_1)\mathbf{a}_x + (y-y_1)\mathbf{a}_y + (z-z_1)\mathbf{a}_z}{[(x-x_1)^2 + (y-y_1)^2 + (z-z_1)^2]^{3/2}}$$

When the charge is at the origin,

$$\mathbf{E} = \frac{Q}{4\pi\epsilon_0}\frac{x\mathbf{a}_x + y\mathbf{a}_y + z\mathbf{a}_z}{(x^2 + y^2 + z^2)^{3/2}}$$

but this expression fails to show the symmetry of the field. In spherical coordinates with Q at the origin,

$$\mathbf{E} = \frac{Q}{4\pi\epsilon_0 r^2}\,\mathbf{a}_r$$

and now the symmetry is apparent.

3.7. Find **E** at the origin due to a point charge of 64.4 nC located at $(-4, 3, 2)$ m in Cartesian coordinates.

The electric field intensity due to a point charge Q at the origin in spherical coordinates is

$$\mathbf{E} = \frac{Q}{4\pi\epsilon_0 r^2}\,\mathbf{a}_r$$

In this problem the distance is $\sqrt{29}$ m and the vector from the charge to the origin, where **E** is to be evaluated, is $\mathbf{R} = 4\mathbf{a}_x - 3\mathbf{a}_y - 2\mathbf{a}_z$.

$$\mathbf{E} = \frac{64.4\times 10^{-9}}{4\pi(10^{-9}/36\pi)\,(29)}\left(\frac{4\mathbf{a}_x - 3\mathbf{a}_y - 2\mathbf{a}_z}{\sqrt{29}}\right) = (20.0)\left(\frac{4\mathbf{a}_x - 3\mathbf{a}_y - 2\mathbf{a}_z}{\sqrt{29}}\right) \text{V/m}$$

3.8. Find **E** at $(0, 0, 5)$ m due to $Q_1 = 0.35\ \mu$C at $(0, 4, 0)$ m and $Q_2 = -0.55\ \mu$C at $(3, 0, 0)$ m (see Fig. 3-13).

$$\mathbf{R}_1 = -4\mathbf{a}_y + 5\mathbf{a}_z$$
$$\mathbf{R}_2 = -3\mathbf{a}_x + 5\mathbf{a}_z$$

$$\mathbf{E}_1 = \frac{0.35\times 10^{-6}}{4\pi(10^{-9}/36\pi)\,(41)}\left(\frac{-4\mathbf{a}_y + 5\mathbf{a}_z}{\sqrt{41}}\right)$$
$$= -48.0\mathbf{a}_y + 60.0\mathbf{a}_z \text{ V/m}$$

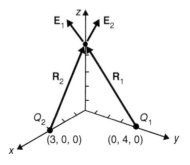

Fig. 3-13

$$E_2 = \frac{-0.55 \times 10^{-6}}{4\pi(10^{-9}/36\pi)(34)}\left(\frac{-3\mathbf{a}_x + 5\mathbf{a}_z}{\sqrt{34}}\right)$$

$$= 74.9\mathbf{a}_x - 124.9\mathbf{a}_z \ \text{V/m}$$

and
$$\mathbf{E} = \mathbf{E}_1 + \mathbf{E}_2 = 74.9\mathbf{a}_x - 48.0\mathbf{a}_y - 64.9\mathbf{a}_z \ \text{V/m}$$

3.9. Charge is distributed uniformly along an infinite straight line with constant density ρ_ℓ. Develop the expression for $\mathbf{E}$ at the general point P.

Cylindrical coordinates will be used, with the line charge as the z axis (see Fig. 3-14). At P,

$$d\mathbf{E} = \frac{dQ}{4\pi\epsilon_0 R^2}\left(\frac{r\mathbf{a}_r - z\mathbf{a}_z}{\sqrt{r^2 + z^2}}\right)$$

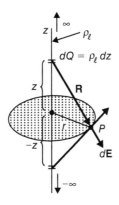

Fig. 3-14

Since for every dQ at z there is another charge dQ at $-z$, the z components cancel. Then

$$\mathbf{E} = \int_{-\infty}^{\infty} \frac{\rho_\ell r \, dz}{4\pi\epsilon_0 (r^2 + z^2)^{3/2}} \mathbf{a}_r$$

$$= \frac{\rho_\ell r}{4\pi\epsilon_0}\left[\frac{z}{r^2\sqrt{r^2 + z^2}}\right]_{-\infty}^{\infty} \mathbf{a}_r = \frac{\rho_\ell}{2\pi\epsilon_0 r} \mathbf{a}_r$$

3.10. On the line described by $x = 2$ m, $y = -4$ m there is a uniform charge distribution of density $\rho_\ell = 20$ nC/m. Determine the electric field $\mathbf{E}$ at $(-2, -1, 4)$ m.

With some modification for Cartesian coordinates the expression obtained in Problem 3.9 can be used with this uniform line charge. Since the line is parallel to $\mathbf{a}_z$, the field has no z component. Referring to Fig. 3-15,

$$\mathbf{R} = -4\mathbf{a}_x + 3\mathbf{a}_y$$

and
$$\mathbf{E} = \frac{20 \times 10^{-9}}{2\pi\epsilon_0(5)}\left(\frac{-4\mathbf{a}_x + 3\mathbf{a}_y}{5}\right) = -57.6\mathbf{a}_x + 43.2\mathbf{a}_y \ \text{V/m}$$

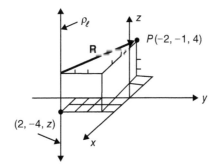

Fig. 3-15

3.11. As shown in Fig. 3-16, two uniform line charges of density $\rho_\ell = 4$ nC/m lie in the $x = 0$ plane at $y = \pm 4$ m. Find **E** at $(4, 0, 10)$ m.

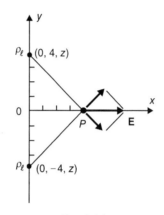

Fig. 3-16

The line charges are both parallel to $\mathbf{a}_z$; their fields are radial and parallel to the xy plane. For either line charge, the magnitude of the field at P would be

$$\mathbf{E} = \frac{\rho_\ell}{2\pi\epsilon_0 r} = \frac{18}{\sqrt{2}} \text{ V/m}$$

The field due to both line charges is, by superposition,

$$\mathbf{E} = 2\left(\frac{18}{\sqrt{2}} \cos 45°\right)\mathbf{a}_x = 18\mathbf{a}_x \text{ V/m}$$

3.12. Develop an expression for **E** due to charge uniformly distributed over an infinite plane with density ρ_s.

The cylindrical coordinate system will be used, with the charge in the $z = 0$ plane as shown in Fig. 3-17.

$$d\mathbf{E} = \frac{\rho_s r \, dr \, d\phi}{4\pi\epsilon_0 (r^2 + z^2)}\left(\frac{-r\mathbf{a}_r + z\mathbf{a}_z}{\sqrt{r^2 + x^2}}\right)$$

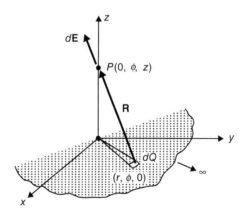

Fig. 3-17

Symmetry about the z axis results in cancellation of the radial components.

$$\mathbf{E} = \int_0^{2\pi} \int_0^{\infty} \frac{\rho_s rz\, dr\, d\phi}{4\pi\epsilon_0 (r^2 + z^2)^{3/2}}\, \mathbf{a}_z$$

$$= \frac{\rho_s z}{2\epsilon_0}\left[\frac{-1}{\sqrt{r^2 + z^2}}\right]_0^{\infty} \mathbf{a}_z = \frac{\rho_s}{2\epsilon_0}\, \mathbf{a}_z$$

This result is for points above the xy plane. Below the xy plane the unit vector changes to $2\mathbf{a}_z$. The generalized form may be written using $\mathbf{a}_n$, the unit normal vector:

$$\mathbf{E} = \frac{\rho_s}{2\epsilon_0}\, \mathbf{a}_n$$

The electric field is everywhere normal to the plane of the charge, and its magnitude is independent of the distance from the plane.

3.13. As shown in Fig. 3-18, the plane $y = 3$ m contains a uniform charge distribution of density $\rho_s = (10^{-8}/6\pi)$ C/m^2. Determine $\mathbf{E}$ at all points.

Fig. 3-18

For $y > 3$ m,

$$\mathbf{E} = \frac{\rho_s}{2\epsilon_0}\, \mathbf{a}_n$$
$$= 30\mathbf{a}_y \text{ V/m}$$

and for $y < 3$ m,

$$\mathbf{E} = -30\mathbf{a}_y \text{ V/m}$$

3.14. Two infinite uniform sheets of charge, each with density ρ_s, are located at $x = \pm 1$ (Fig. 3-19). Determine $\mathbf{E}$ in all regions.

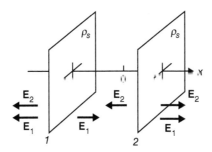

Fig. 3-19

Only parts of the two sheets of charge are shown in Fig. 3-19. Both sheets result in **E** fields that are directed along x, independent of the distance. Then

$$\mathbf{E}_1 + \mathbf{E}_2 = \begin{cases} -(\rho_s/\epsilon_0)\,\mathbf{a}_x & x < -1 \\ 0 & -1 < x < 1 \\ (\rho_s/\epsilon_0)\,\mathbf{a}_x & x > 1 \end{cases}$$

3.15. Repeat Problem 3.14 with ρ_s on $x = -1$ and $-\rho_s$ on $x = 1$.

$$\mathbf{E}_1 + \mathbf{E}_2 = \begin{cases} 0 & x < -1 \\ (\rho_s/\epsilon_0)\,\mathbf{a}_x & -1 < x < 1 \\ 0 & x > 1 \end{cases}$$

3.16. A uniform sheet charge with $\rho_s = (1/3\pi)$ nC/m^2 is located at $z = 5$ m and a uniform line charge with $\rho_\ell = (-25/9)$ nC/m at $z = -3$ m, $y = 3$ m. Find **E** at $(x, -1, 0)$ m.

The two charge configurations are parallel to the x axis. Hence the view in Fig. 3-20 is taken looking at the yz plane from positive x. Due to the sheet charge,

$$\mathbf{E}_s = \frac{\rho_2}{2\epsilon_0}\,\mathbf{a}_n$$

Fig. 3-20

At P, $\mathbf{a}_n = -\mathbf{a}_z$ and

$$\mathbf{E}_s = -6\mathbf{a}_z \text{ V/m}$$

Due to the line charge,

$$\mathbf{E}_\ell = \frac{\rho_\ell}{2\pi\epsilon_0 r}\,\mathbf{a}_r$$

and at P

$$\mathbf{E}_\ell = 8\mathbf{a}_y - 6\mathbf{a}_z \text{ V/m}$$

The total electric field is the sum, $\mathbf{E} = \mathbf{E}_\ell + \mathbf{E}_s = 8\mathbf{a}_y - 12\mathbf{a}_z$ V/m.

3.17. Determine **E** at $(2, 0, 2)$ m due to three standard charge distributions as follows: a uniform sheet at $x = 0$ m with $\rho_{s1} = (1/3\pi)$ nC/m^2, a uniform sheet at $x = 4$ m with $\rho_{s2} = (-1/3\pi)$ nC/m^2, and a uniform line at $x = 6$ m, $y = 0$ m with $\rho_\ell = -2$ nC/m.

Since the three charge configurations are parallel with $\mathbf{a}_z$, there will be no z component of the field. Point $(2, 0, 2)$ will have the same field as any point $(2, 0, z)$. In Fig. 3-21, P is located between the two sheet charges, where the fields add due to the difference in sign.

$$\mathbf{E} = \frac{\rho_{s1}}{2\epsilon_0}\mathbf{a}_n + \frac{\rho_{s2}}{2\epsilon_0}\mathbf{a}_n + \frac{\rho_\ell}{2\pi\epsilon_0 r}\mathbf{a}_r$$
$$= 6\mathbf{a}_x + 6\mathbf{a}_x + 9\mathbf{a}_x$$
$$= 21\mathbf{a}_x \text{ V/m}$$

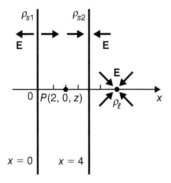

Fig. 3-21

3.18. As shown in Fig. 3-22, charge is distributed along the z axis between $z = \pm 5$ m with a uniform density $\rho_\ell = 20$ nC/m. Determine $\mathbf{E}$ at $(2, 0, 0)$ m in Cartesian coordinates. Also express the answer in cylindrical coordinates.

$$d\mathbf{E} = \frac{20\times 10^{-9}\,dz}{4\pi(10^{-9}/36\pi)\,(4+z^2)}\left(\frac{2\mathbf{a}_x - z\mathbf{a}_z}{\sqrt{4+z^2}}\right) \text{ (V/m)}$$

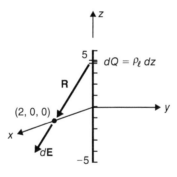

Fig. 3-22

Symmetry with respect to the $z = 0$ plane eliminates any z component in the result.

$$\mathbf{E} = 180 \int_{-5}^{5} \frac{2\,dz}{(4+z^2)^{3/2}}\,\mathbf{a}_x = 167\mathbf{a}_x \text{ V/m}$$

In cylindrical coordinates, $\mathbf{E} = 167\mathbf{a}_r$ V/m.

3.19. Charge is distributed along the z axis from $z = 5$ m to ∞ and from $z = -5$ m to $-\infty$ (see Fig. 3-23) with the same density as in Problem 3.18, 20 nC/m. Find $\mathbf{E}$ at $(2, 0, 0)$ m.

$$d\mathbf{E} = \frac{20\times 10^{-9}\,dz}{4\pi(10^{-9}/36\pi)\,(4+z^2)}\left(\frac{2\mathbf{a}_x - z\mathbf{a}_z}{\sqrt{4+z^2}}\right) \text{ (V/m)}$$

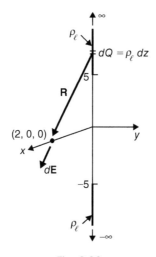

Fig. 3-23

Again the z component vanishes.

$$\mathbf{E} = 180 \left[\int_{5}^{\infty} \frac{2\,dz}{(4+z^2)^{3/2}} + \int_{-\infty}^{-5} \frac{2\,dz}{(4+z^2)^{3/2}} \right] \mathbf{a}_x$$

$$= 13\mathbf{a}_x \text{ V/m}$$

In cylindrical coordinates, $\mathbf{E} = 13\mathbf{a}_r$ V/m.

When the charge configurations of Problems 3.18 and 3.19 are superimposed, the result is a uniform line charge.

$$\mathbf{E} = \frac{\rho_\ell}{2\pi\epsilon_0 r}\,\mathbf{a}_r = 180\mathbf{a}_r \text{ V/m}$$

3.20. Find the electric field intensity $\mathbf{E}$ at $(0, \phi, h)$ in cylindrical coordinates due to the uniformly charged disk $r \leq a$, $z = 0$ (see Fig. 3-24).

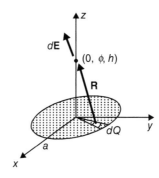

Fig. 3-24

If the constant charge density is ρ_s,

$$d\mathbf{E} = \frac{\rho_s r\,dr\,d\phi}{4\pi\epsilon_0(r^2+h^2)}\left(\frac{-r\mathbf{a}_r + h\mathbf{a}_z}{\sqrt{r^2+h^2}} \right)$$

The radial components cancel. Therefore,

$$\mathbf{E} = \frac{\rho_s h}{4\pi\epsilon_0} \int_0^{2\pi} \int_0^a \frac{r\,dr\,d\phi}{(r^2+h^2)^{3/2}}\,\mathbf{a}_z$$

$$= \frac{\rho_s h}{2\epsilon_0}\left(\frac{-1}{\sqrt{a^2+h^2}} + \frac{1}{h} \right)\mathbf{a}_z$$

Note that as $a \to \infty$, $\mathbf{E} \to (\rho_s/2\epsilon_0)\mathbf{a}_z$, the field due to a uniform plane sheet.

3.21. Charge lies on the circular disk $r \le a$, $z = 0$ with density $\rho_s = \rho_0 \sin^2 \phi$. Determine **E** at $(0, \phi, h)$.

$$d\mathbf{E} = \frac{\rho_0 (\sin^2 \phi) r\, dr\, d\phi}{4\pi\epsilon_0 (r^2 + h^2)} \left(\frac{-r\mathbf{a}_r + h\mathbf{a}_z}{\sqrt{r^2 + h^2}} \right)$$

The charge distribution, though not uniform, still is symmetrical such that all radial components cancel.

$$\mathbf{E} = \frac{\rho_0 h}{4\pi\epsilon_0} \int_0^{2\pi} \int_0^a \frac{(\sin^2 \phi) r\, dr\, d\phi}{(r^2 + h^2)^{3/2}} \mathbf{a}_z = \frac{\rho_0 h}{4\epsilon_0} \left(\frac{-1}{\sqrt{a^2 + h^2}} + \frac{1}{h} \right) \mathbf{a}_z$$

3.22. Charge lies on the circular disk $r \le 4$ m, $z = 0$ with density $\rho_s = (10^{-4}/r)$ (C/m^2). Determine **E** at $r = 0$, $z = 3$ m.

$$d\mathbf{E} = \frac{(10^{-4}/r) r\, dr\, d\phi}{4\pi\epsilon_0 (r^2 + 9)} \left(\frac{-r\mathbf{a}_r + 3\mathbf{a}_z}{\sqrt{r^2 + 9}} \right) \; (V/m)$$

As in Problems 3.20 and 3.21, the radial component vanishes by symmetry.

$$\mathbf{E} = (2.7 \times 10^6) \int_0^{2\pi} \int_0^4 \frac{dr\, d\phi}{(r^2 + 9)^{3/2}} \mathbf{a}_z = 1.51 \times 10^6 \mathbf{a}_z \; V/m \quad \text{or} \quad 1.51 \mathbf{a}_z \; MV/m$$

3.23. Charge lies in the $z = -3$ m plane in the form of a square sheet defined by $-2 \le x \le 2$ m, $-2 \le y \le 2$ m with charge density $\rho_s = 2(x^2 + y^2 + 9)^{3/2}$ nC/m^2. Find **E** at the origin.

From Fig. 3-25,

$$\mathbf{R} = -x\mathbf{a}_x - y\mathbf{a}_y + 3\mathbf{a}_z \quad (m)$$
$$dQ = \rho_s\, dx\, dy = 2(x^2 + y^2 + 9)^{3/2} \times 10^{-9}\, dx\, dy \quad (C)$$

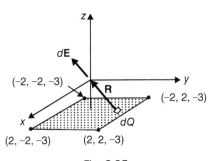

Fig. 3-25

and so

$$d\mathbf{E} = \frac{2(x^2 + y^2 + 9)^{3/2} \times 10^{-9}\, dx\, dy}{4\pi\epsilon_0 (x^2 + y^2 + 9)} \left(\frac{-x\mathbf{a}_x - y\mathbf{a}_y + 3\mathbf{a}_z}{\sqrt{x^2 + y^2 + 9}} \right) \; (V/m)$$

Due to symmetry, only the z component of **E** exists.

$$\mathbf{E} = \int_{-2}^{2} \int_{-2}^{2} \frac{6 \times 10^{-9}\, dx\, dy}{4\pi\epsilon_0} \mathbf{a}_z = 864 \mathbf{a}_z \; V/m$$

3.24. A charge of uniform density $\rho_s = 0.3$ nC/m^2 covers the plane $2x - 3y + z = 6$ m. Find **E** on the side of the plane containing the origin.

Since this charge configuration is a uniform sheet, $E = \rho_s / 2\epsilon_0$ and $\mathbf{E} = (17.0)\mathbf{a}_n$ V/m. The unit normal vectors for a plane $Ax + By + Cz = D$ are

$$\mathbf{a}_n = \pm \frac{A\mathbf{a}_x + B\mathbf{a}_y + C\mathbf{a}_z}{\sqrt{A^2 + B^2 + C^2}}$$

Therefore, the unit normal vectors for this plane are

$$\mathbf{a}_n = \pm \frac{2\mathbf{a}_x - 3\mathbf{a}_y + \mathbf{a}_z}{\sqrt{14}}$$

From Fig. 3-26 it is evident that the unit vector on the side of the plane containing the origin is produced by the negative sign. The electric field at the origin is

$$\mathbf{E} = (17.0)\left(\frac{-2\mathbf{a}_x + 3\mathbf{a}_y - \mathbf{a}_z}{\sqrt{14}}\right) \mathrm{V/m}$$

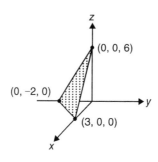

Fig. 3-26

SUPPLEMENTARY PROBLEMS

3.25. Two point charges, $Q_1 = 250 \ \mu\mathrm{C}$ and $Q_2 = -300 \ \mu\mathrm{C}$, are located at $(5, 0, 0)$ m and $(0, 0, -5)$ m, respectively. Find the force on Q_2.

3.26. Two point charges, $Q_1 = 30 \ \mu\mathrm{C}$ and $Q_2 = -100 \ \mu\mathrm{C}$, are located at $(2, 0, 5)$ m and $(-1, 0, -2)$ m, respectively. Find the force on Q_1.

3.27. In Problem 3.26 find the force on Q_2.

3.28. Four point charges, each $20 \ \mu\mathrm{C}$, are on the x and y axes at ± 4 m. Find the force on a 100-$\mu\mathrm{C}$ point charge at $(0, 0, 3)$ m.

3.29. Ten identical charges of $500 \ \mu\mathrm{C}$ each are spaced equally around a circle of radius 2 m. Find the force on a charge of $-20 \ \mu\mathrm{C}$ located on the axis, 2 m from the plane of the circle.

3.30. Determine the force on a point charge of $50 \ \mu\mathrm{C}$ at $(0, 0, 5)$ m due to a point charge of $500\pi \ \mu\mathrm{C}$ at the origin. Compare the answer with Problems 3.4 and 3.5, where this same total charge is distributed over a circular disk.

3.31. Find the force on a point charge of $30 \ \mu\mathrm{C}$ at $(0, 0, 5)$ m due to a 4 m square in the $z = 0$ plane between $x = \pm 2$ m and $y = \pm 2$ m with a total charge of $500 \ \mu\mathrm{C}$, distributed uniformly.

3.32. Two identical point charges of $Q(\mathrm{C})$ each are separated by a distance $d(\mathrm{m})$. Express the electric field $\mathbf{E}$ for points along the line joining the two charges.

3.33. Identical charges of $Q(\mathrm{C})$ are located at the eight corners of a cube with a side $\ell(\mathrm{m})$. Show that the Coulombic force on each charge has magnitude $(3.29 Q^2 / 4\pi \varepsilon_0 \ell^2)$ N.

3.34. Show that the electric field $\mathbf{E}$ outside a spherical shell of uniform charge density ρ_s is the same as $\mathbf{E}$ due to the total charge on the shell located at the center.

3.35. Develop the expression in Cartesian coordinates for $\mathbf{E}$ due to an infinitely long, straight charge configuration of uniform density ρ_ℓ.

3.36. Two uniform line charges of $\rho_\ell = 4$ nC/m each are parallel to the z axis at $x = 0$, $y = \pm 4$ m. Determine the electric field **E** at $(\pm 4, 0, z)$ m.

3.37. Two uniform line charges of $p_\ell = 5$ nC/m each are parallel to the x axis, one at $z = 0$, $y = -2$ m and the other at $z = 0$, $y = 4$ m. Find **E** at $(4, 1, 3)$ m.

3.38. Determine **E** at the origin due to a uniform line charge distribution with $\rho_1 = 3.30$ nC/m located at $x = 3$ m, $y = 4$ m.

3.39. Referring to Problem 3.38, at what other points will the value of **E** be the same?

3.40. Two meters from the z axis, $|\mathbf{E}|$ due to a uniform line charge along the z axis is known to be 1.80×10^4 V/m. Find the uniform charge density ρ_ℓ.

3.41. The plane $-x + 3y - 6z = 6$ m contains a uniform charge distribution $\rho_s = 0.53$ nC/m². Find **E** on the side containing the origin.

3.42. Two infinite sheets of uniform charge density $\rho_s = (10^{-9}/6\pi)$ C/m² are located at $z = -5$ m and $y = -5$ m. Determine the uniform line charge density ρ_ℓ necessary to produce the same value of **E** at $(4, 2, 2)$ m, if the line charge is located at $z = 0$, $y = 0$.

3.43. Two uniform charge distributions are as follows: a sheet of uniform charge density $\rho_s = -50$ nC/m² at $y = 2$ m and a uniform line of $\rho_\ell = 0.2$ μC/m at $z = 2$ m, $y = -1$ m. At what points in the region will **E** be zero?

3.44. A uniform sheet of charge with $\rho_s = (-1/3\pi)$ nC/m² is located at $z = 5$ m and a uniform line of charge with $\rho_\ell = (-25/9)$ nC/m is located at $z = -3$ m, $y = 3$ m. Find the electric field **E** at $(0, -1, 0)$ m.

3.45. A uniform line charge of $\rho_\ell = (\sqrt{2} \times 10^{-8}/6)$ C/m lies along the x axis and a uniform sheet of charge is located at $y = 5$m. Along the line $y = 3$m, $z = 3$ m the electric field **E** has only a z component. What is ρ_s for the sheet?

3.46. A uniform line charge of $\rho_\ell = 3.30$ nC/m is located at $x = 3$ m, $y = 4$ m. A point charge Q is 2 m from the origin. Find the charge Q and its location such that the electric field is zero at the origin.

3.47. A circular ring of charge with radius 2 m lies in the $z = 0$ plane, with center at the origin. If the uniform charge density is $\rho_\ell = 10$ nC/m, find the point charge Q at the origin which would produce the same electric field **E** at $(0, 0, 5)$ m.

3.48. The circular disk $r \leq 2$ m in the $z = 0$ plane has a charge density $\rho_s = 10^{-8}/r$ (C/m²). Determine the electric field **E** for the point $(0, \phi, h)$.

3.49. Examine the result in Problem 3.48 as h becomes much greater than 2 m and compare it to the field at h which results when the total charge on the disk is concentrated at the origin.

3.50. A finite sheet of charge, of density $\rho_s = 2x(x^2 + y^2 + 4)^{3/2}$ (C/m²), lies in the $z = 0$ plane for $0 \leq x \leq 2$ m and $0 \leq y \leq 2$ m. Determine **E** at $(0, 0, 2)$m.

3.51. Determine the electric field **E** at $(8, 0, 0)$ m due to a charge of 10 nC distributed uniformly along the x axis between $x = -5$ m and $x = 5$ m. Repeat for the same charge distributed between $x = -1$ m and $x = 1$ m.

3.52. The circular disk $r \leq 1$ m, $z = 0$ has a charge density $\rho_s = 2(r^2 + 25)^{3/2}e^{-10r}$ (C/m²). Find **E** at $(0, 0, 5)$ m.

3.53. Show that the electric field is zero everywhere inside a uniformly charged spherical shell.

3.54. Charge is distributed with constant density ρ throughout a spherical volume of radius a. By using the results of Problems 3.34 and 3.53, show that

$$\mathbf{E} = \begin{cases} \dfrac{r\rho}{3\epsilon_0}\mathbf{a}_r & r \leq a \\[2mm] \dfrac{a^3\rho}{3\epsilon_0 r^2}\mathbf{a}_r & r \geq a \end{cases}$$

where r is the distance from the center of the sphere.

ANSWERS TO SUPPLEMENTARY PROBLEMS

3.25. $\mathbf{F}_2 = (13.5)\left(\dfrac{\mathbf{a}_x + \mathbf{a}_z}{\sqrt{2}}\right)\mathbf{N}$

3.26. $\mathbf{F}_1 = (0.465)\left(\dfrac{-3\mathbf{a}_x - 7\mathbf{a}_z}{\sqrt{58}}\right)\mathbf{N}$

3.27. $-\mathbf{F}_1$

3.28. $1.73\mathbf{a}_z\ \mathbf{N}$

3.29. $(79.5)(-\mathbf{a}_n)\ \mathbf{N}$

3.30. $28.3\mathbf{a}_z\ \mathbf{N}$

3.31. $4.66\mathbf{a}_z\ \mathbf{N}$

3.32. If the charges are at $x = 0$ and $x = d$, then, for $0 < x < d$,

$$\mathbf{E} = \frac{Q}{4\pi\epsilon_0}\left[\frac{1}{x^2} - \frac{1}{(d-x)^2}\right]\mathbf{a}_x\ (\mathrm{V/m})$$

3.35. $\mathbf{E} = \dfrac{\rho_\ell}{2\pi\epsilon_0}\dfrac{x\mathbf{a}_x + y\mathbf{a}_y}{x^2 + y^2}$

3.36. $\pm 18\mathbf{a}_x\ \mathrm{V/m}$

3.37. $30\mathbf{a}_z\ \mathrm{V/m}$

3.38. $-7.13\mathbf{a}_x - 9.50\mathbf{a}_y\ \mathrm{V/m}$

3.39. $(0, 0, z)$

3.40. $2.0\ \mu\mathrm{C/m}$

3.41. $30\left(\dfrac{\mathbf{a}_x - 3\mathbf{a}_y + 6\mathbf{a}_z}{\sqrt{46}}\right)\mathrm{V/m}$

3.42. $0.667\ \mathrm{nC/m}$

3.43. $(x, -2.273, 2.0)\ \mathrm{m}$

3.44. $8\mathbf{a}_y\ \mathrm{V/m}$

3.45. $125\ \mathrm{pC/m^2}$

3.46. $5.28\ \mathrm{nC}$ at $(-1.2, -1.6, 0)\ \mathrm{m}$

3.47. $100.5\ \mathrm{nC}$

3.48. $\dfrac{1.13\times 10^3}{h\sqrt{4+h^2}}\,\mathbf{a}_z\ (\mathrm{V/m})$

3.50. $(18\times 10^9)\left(-\dfrac{16}{3}\mathbf{a}_x - 4\mathbf{a}_y + 8\mathbf{a}_z\right)\mathrm{V/m} = 18\left(-\dfrac{16}{3}\mathbf{a}_x - 4\mathbf{a}_y + 8\mathbf{a}_z\right)\mathrm{GV/m}$

3.51. $2.31\mathbf{a}_x\ \mathrm{V/m}$ $1.43\mathbf{a}_x\ \mathrm{V/m}$

3.52. $5.66\mathbf{a}_x\ \mathrm{GV/m}$

CHAPTER 4

Electric Flux

4.1 Net Charge in a Region

With charge density defined as in Section 3.5, it is possible to obtain the net charge contained in a specified volume by integration. From

$$dQ = \rho \, dv \qquad \text{(C)}$$

it follows that

$$Q = \int_v \rho \, dv \qquad \text{(C)}$$

In general, ρ will not be constant throughout the volume v.

EXAMPLE 1. Find the charge in the volume defined by $1 \le r \le 2$ m in spherical coordinates, if

$$\rho = \frac{5\cos^2\phi}{r^4} \quad \text{(C/m}^3)$$

By integration,

$$Q = \int_0^{2\pi} \int_0^{\pi} \int_1^{2} \left(\frac{5\cos^2\phi}{r^4} \right) r^2 \sin\theta \, dr \, d\theta \, d\phi = 5\pi \text{ C}$$

4.2 Electric Flux and Flux Density

Electric flux Ψ, a scalar field, and its density $\mathbf{D}$, a vector field, are useful quantities in solving certain problems, as will be seen in this and subsequent chapters. Unlike $\mathbf{E}$, these fields are not directly measurable; their existence was inferred from nineteenth-century experiments in electrostatics.

EXAMPLE 2. Referring to Fig. 4-1, a charge $+Q$ is first fixed in place and a spherical, concentric, conducting shell is then closed around it. Initially the shell has no net charge on its surface. Now if a conducting path to ground is *momentarily* completed by closing a switch, a charge $-Q$, equal in magnitude but of opposite sign, is discovered on the shell. This charge $-Q$ might be accounted for by a transient flow of negative charge from the ground, through the switch, and onto the shell. But what could provoke such a flow? The early experimenters suggested that a *flux* from $+Q$ to the conductor surface induced, or *displaced*, the charge $-Q$ onto the surface. Consequently, it has also been called *displacement flux*, and the use of the symbol D is a reminder of this early concept.

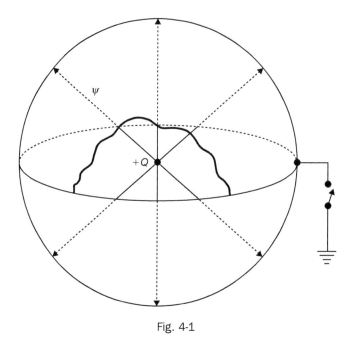

Fig. 4-1

By definition, electric flux Ψ originates on positive charge and terminates on negative charge. In the absence of negative charge, the flux Ψ terminates at infinity. Also by definition, one coulomb of electric charge gives rise to one coulomb of electric flux. Hence,

$$\Psi = Q \quad (C)$$

In Fig. 4-2(*a*) the flux lines leave $+Q$ and terminate on $-Q$. This assumes that the two charges are of equal magnitude. The case of positive charge with no negative charge in the region is illustrated in Fig. 4-2(*b*). Here the flux lines are equally spaced throughout the solid angle and reach out toward infinity.

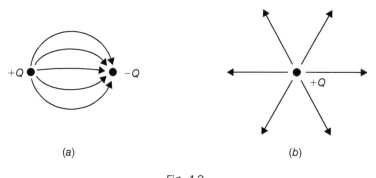

(a)   (b)

Fig. 4-2

If in the neighborhood of point P the lines of flux have the direction of the unit vector $\mathbf{a}$ (see Fig. 4-3) and if an amount of flux $d\Psi$ crosses the differential area dS, which is a normal to $\mathbf{a}$, then the *electric flux density* at P is

$$\mathbf{D} = \frac{d\Psi}{dS}\mathbf{a} \quad (C/m^2)$$

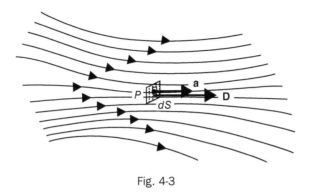

Fig. 4-3

A volume charge distribution of density ρ (C/m³) is shown enclosed by surface S in Fig. 4-4. Since each coulomb of charge Q has, by definition, one coulomb of flux Ψ, it follows that the net flux crossing the closed surface S is an exact measure of the net charge enclosed. However, the density $\mathbf{D}$ may vary in magnitude and direction from point to point of S; in general, $\mathbf{D}$ will not be along the normal to S. If, at the surface element dS, $\mathbf{D}$ makes an angle θ with the normal, then the differential flux crossing dS is given by

$$d\Psi = D\,dS\cos\theta = \mathbf{D}\cdot dS\mathbf{a}_n = \mathbf{D}\cdot d\mathbf{S}$$

where $d\mathbf{S}$ is the vector surface element, of magnitude dS and direction $\mathbf{a}_n$. The unit vector $\mathbf{a}_n$ is always taken to point out of S, so that $d\Psi$ is the amount of flux passing from the interior of S to the exterior of S through dS.

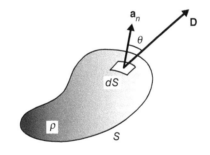

Fig. 4-4

4.3 Gauss's Law

Gauss's law states that *the total flux out of a closed surface is equal to the net charge within the surface*. This can be written in integral form as

$$\oint \mathbf{D}\cdot d\mathbf{S} = Q_{\text{enc}}$$

A great deal of valuable information can be obtained from Gauss's law through clever choice of the surface of integration; see Section 3.5.

4.4 Relation between Flux Density and Electric Field Intensity

Consider a point charge Q (assumed positive, for simplicity) at the origin (Fig. 4-5). If this is enclosed by a spherical surface of radius r, then, by symmetry, $\mathbf{D}$ due to Q is of constant magnitude over the surface and is everywhere normal to the surface. Gauss's law then gives

$$Q = \oint \mathbf{D}\cdot d\mathbf{S} = D\oint dS = D(4\pi r^2)$$

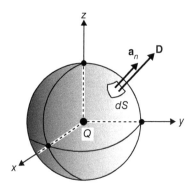

Fig. 4-5

from which $D = Q/4\pi r^2$. Therefore,

$$\mathbf{D} = \frac{Q}{4\pi r^2}\mathbf{a}_n = \frac{Q}{4\pi r^2}\mathbf{a}_r$$

But, from Section 3.4, the electric field intensity due to Q is

$$\mathbf{E} = \frac{Q}{4\pi\epsilon_0 r^2}\mathbf{a}_r$$

It follows that $\mathbf{D} = \epsilon_0\mathbf{E}$.

　　More generally, for any electric field in an isotropic medium of permittivity ϵ,

$$\mathbf{D} = \epsilon\mathbf{E}$$

Thus, $\mathbf{D}$ and $\mathbf{E}$ fields will have exactly the same form, since they differ only by a factor which is a constant of the medium. While the electric field $\mathbf{E}$ due to a charge configuration is a function of the permittivity ϵ, the electric flux density $\mathbf{D}$ is not. In problems involving multiple dielectrics, a distinct advantage will be found in first obtaining $\mathbf{D}$, then converting to $\mathbf{E}$ within each dielectric.

4.5 Special Gaussian Surfaces

The surface over which Gauss's law is applied must be closed, but it can be made up of several surface elements. If these surface elements can be selected so that $\mathbf{D}$ is either normal or tangential, and if $|\mathbf{D}|$ is constant over any element to which $\mathbf{D}$ is normal, then the integration becomes very simple. Thus, the defining conditions of a *special Gaussian surface* are

1. The surface is closed.
2. At each point of the surface $\mathbf{D}$ is either normal or tangential to the surface.
3. D is sectionally constant over that part of the surface where $\mathbf{D}$ is normal.

EXAMPLE 3.　Use a special Gaussian surface to find $\mathbf{D}$ due to a uniform line change with density ρ_ℓ (C/m). Take the line charge as the z axis of the cylindrical coordinate system (Fig. 4-6). By cylindrical symmetry, $\mathbf{D}$ can only have an r component, and this component can only depend on r. Thus, the special Gaussian surface for this problem is a closed right circular cylinder whose axis is the z axis (Fig. 4-7). Applying Gauss's law,

$$Q = \int_1 \mathbf{D}\cdot d\mathbf{S} + \int_2 \mathbf{D}\cdot d\mathbf{S} + \int_3 \mathbf{D}\cdot d\mathbf{S}$$

Fig. 4-6

Fig. 4-7

Over surfaces *1* and *3*, **D** and *d***S** are orthogonal, and so the integrals vanish. Over *2*, **D** and *d***S** are parallel (or antiparallel, if ρ_ℓ is negative), and *D* is constant because *r* is constant. Thus,

$$Q = D \int_2 dS = D(2\pi rL)$$

where *L* is the length of the cylinder. But the enclosed charge is $Q = \rho_\ell L$. Hence,

$$D = \frac{\rho_\ell}{2\pi r} \quad \text{and} \quad \mathbf{D} = \frac{\rho_\ell}{2\pi r}\mathbf{a}_r$$

Observe the simplicity of the above derivation as compared to Problem 3.9.

The one serious limitation of the method of special Gaussian surfaces is that it can be utilized only for highly symmetrical charge configurations. However, for other configurations, the method can still provide quick approximations to the field at locations very close to or very far from the charges. See Problem 4.36.

SOLVED PROBLEMS

4.1. Find the charge in the volume defined by $0 \leq x \leq 1$ m, $0 \leq y \leq 1$ m, and $0 \leq z \leq 1$ m if $\rho = 30x^2y$ (μC/m^3). What change occurs for the limits $-1 \leq y \leq 0$ m?

Since $dQ = \rho \, dv$,

$$Q = \int_0^1 \int_0^1 \int_0^1 30x^2 y \, dx \, dy \, dz = 5 \, \mu C$$

For the change in limits on y,

$$Q = \int_0^1 \int_{-1}^0 \int_0^1 30x^2 y \, dx \, dy \, dz = -5 \, \mu C$$

4.2. Three point charges, $Q_1 = 30$ nC, $Q_2 = 150$ nC, and $Q_3 = -70$ nC, are enclosed by surface S. What net flux crosses S?

Since electric flux was defined as originating on positive charge and terminating on negative charge, part of the flux from the positive charges terminates on the negative charge.

$$\Psi_{net} = Q_{net} = 30 + 150 - 70 = 110 \text{ nC}$$

4.3. What net flux crosses the closed surface S shown in Fig. 4-8, which contains a charge distribution in the form of a plane disk of radius 4 m with a density $\rho_s = (\sin^2 \phi)/2r$ (C/m^2)?

$$\Psi = Q = \int_0^{2\pi} \int_0^4 \left(\frac{\sin^2 \phi}{2r} \right) r \, dr \, d\phi = 2\pi \text{ C}$$

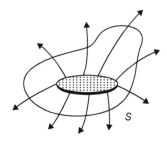

Fig. 4-8

4.4. A circular disk of radius 4 m with a charge density $\rho_s = 12 \sin \phi$ μC/m^2 is enclosed by surface S. What net flux crosses S?

$$\Psi = Q = \int_0^{2\pi} \int_0^4 (12 \sin \phi) r \, dr \, d\phi = 0 \, \mu C$$

Since the disk contains equal amounts of positive and negative charge [$\sin (\phi + \pi) = -\sin \phi$], no net flux crosses S.

4.5. Charge in the form of a plane sheet with density $\rho_s = 40$ μC/m^2 is located at $z = -0.5$ m. A uniform line charge of $\rho_\ell = -6$ μC/m lies along the y axis. What net flux crosses the surface of a cube 2 m on an edge, centered at the origin, as shown in Fig. 4-9?

$$\Psi = Q_{enc}$$

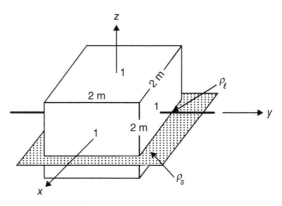

Fig. 4-9

The charge enclosed from the plane is

$$Q = (4 \text{ m}^2)(40 \ \mu\text{C/m}^2) = 160 \ \mu\text{C}$$

and from the line

$$Q = (2 \text{ m})(-6 \ \mu\text{C/m}) = -12 \ \mu\text{C}$$

Thus, $Q_{\text{enc}} = \Psi = 160 - 12 = 148 \ \mu\text{C}$.

4.6. A point charge Q is at the origin of a spherical coordinate system. Find the flux which crosses the portion of a spherical shell described by $\alpha \le \theta \le \beta$ (Fig. 4-10). What is the result if $\alpha = 0$ and $\beta = \pi/2$?

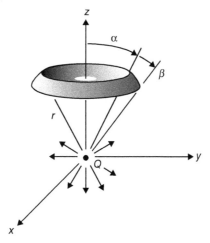

Fig. 4-10

The total flux $\Psi = Q$ crosses a complete spherical shell of area $4\pi r^2$. The area of the strip is given by

$$A = \int_0^{2\pi} \int_\alpha^\beta r^2 \sin\theta \ d\theta \ d\phi$$
$$- 2\pi r^2 (\cos\alpha - \cos\beta)$$

Then the flux through the strip is

$$\Psi_{\text{net}} = \frac{A}{4\pi r^2} Q = \frac{Q}{2}(\cos\alpha - \cos\beta)$$

For $\alpha = 0$, $\beta = \pi/2$ (a hemisphere), this becomes $\Psi_{\text{net}} = Q/2$.

4.7. A uniform line charge with $\rho_\ell = 50 \ \mu\text{C/m}$ lies along the x axis. What flux per unit length, Ψ/L, crosses the portion of the $z = -3$ m plane bounded by $y = \pm 2$ m?

The flux is uniformly distributed around the line charge. Thus the amount crossing the strip is obtained from the angle subtended compared to 2π. In Fig. 4-11,

$$\alpha = 2 \arctan\left(\frac{2}{3}\right) = 1.176 \text{ rad}$$

Then
$$\frac{\Psi}{L} = 50\left(\frac{1.176}{2\pi}\right) = 9.36 \ \mu\text{C/m}$$

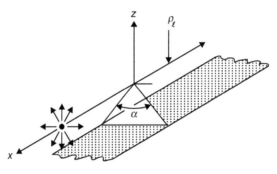

Fig. 4-11

4.8. A point charge, $Q = 30$ nC, is located at the origin in Cartesian coordinates. Find the electric flux density $\mathbf{D}$ at $(1, 3, -4)$ m.

Referring to Fig. 4-12,

$$\mathbf{D} = \frac{Q}{4\pi R^2}\mathbf{a}_R$$

$$= \frac{30 \times 10^{-9}}{4\pi(26)}\left(\frac{\mathbf{a}_x + 3\mathbf{a}_y - 4\mathbf{a}_z}{\sqrt{26}}\right)$$

$$= (9.18 \times 10^{-11})\left(\frac{\mathbf{a}_x + 3\mathbf{a}_y - 4\mathbf{a}_z}{\sqrt{26}}\right) \ \text{C/m}^2$$

or, more conveniently, $D = 91.8 \ \text{pC/m}^2$.

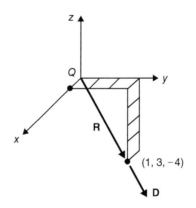

Fig. 4-12

4.9. Two identical uniform line charges lie along the x and y axes with charge densities $\rho_\ell = 20\ \mu C/m$. Obtain **D** at $(3, 3, 3)$ m.

The distance from the observation point to either line charge is $3\sqrt{2}$ m. Considering first the line charge on the x axis,

$$\mathbf{D}_1 = \frac{\rho_\ell}{2\pi r_1}\mathbf{a}_{r1} = \frac{20\ \mu C/m}{2\pi(3\sqrt{2}\,\text{m})}\left(\frac{\mathbf{a}_y + \mathbf{a}_z}{\sqrt{2}}\right)$$

and now the y axis line charge,

$$\mathbf{D}_2 = \frac{\rho_\ell}{2\pi r_2}\mathbf{a}_{r2} = \frac{20\ \mu C/m}{2\pi(3\sqrt{2}\,\text{m})}\left(\frac{\mathbf{a}_x + \mathbf{a}_z}{\sqrt{2}}\right)$$

The total flux density is the vector sum,

$$\mathbf{D} = \frac{20}{2\pi(3\sqrt{2})}\left(\frac{\mathbf{a}_x + \mathbf{a}_y + 2\mathbf{a}_z}{\sqrt{2}}\right) = (2.25)\left(\frac{\mathbf{a}_x + \mathbf{a}_y + 2\mathbf{a}_z}{\sqrt{6}}\right)\ \mu C/m^2$$

4.10. Given that $\mathbf{D} = 10x\mathbf{a}_x$ (C/m^2), determine the flux crossing a 1-m^2 area that is normal to the x axis at $x = 3$ m.

Since **D** is constant over the area and perpendicular to it,

$$\Psi = DA = (30\ \text{C/m}^2)(1\ \text{m}^2) = 30\ \text{C}$$

4.11. Determine the flux crossing a 1 mm by 1 mm area on the surface of a cylindrical shell at $r = 10$ m, $z = 2$ m, $\phi = 53.2°$ if

$$\mathbf{D} = 2x\mathbf{a}_x + 2(1-y)\mathbf{a}_y + 4z\mathbf{a}_z\ \ (\text{C/m}^2)$$

At point P (see Fig. 4-13),

$$x = 10\cos 53.2° = 6$$
$$y = 10\sin 53.2° = 8$$

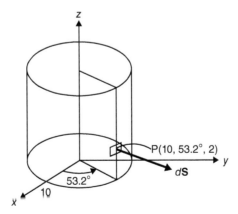

Fig. 4-13

Then, at P,

$$\mathbf{D} = 12\mathbf{a}_x - 14\mathbf{a}_y + 8\mathbf{a}_z\ \ \text{C/m}^2$$

Now, on a cylinder of radius 10 m, a 1-mm^2 patch is essentially planar, with directed area

$$d\mathbf{S} = 10^{-6}(0.6\mathbf{a}_x + 0.8\mathbf{a}_y) \quad \text{m}^2$$

Then $d\Psi = \mathbf{D} \cdot d\mathbf{S} = (12\mathbf{a}_x - 14\mathbf{a}_y + 8\mathbf{a}_z) \cdot 10^{-6}(0.6\mathbf{a}_x + 0.8\mathbf{a}_y) = -4.0 \ \mu C$

The negative sign indicates that flux crosses this differential surface in a direction toward the *z* axis rather than outward in the direction of *d*$\mathbf{S}$.

4.12. A uniform line charge of $\rho_\ell = 3 \ \mu C/m$ lies along the *z* axis, and a concentric circular cylinder of radius 2 m has $\rho_s = (-1.5/4\pi) \ \mu C/m^2$. Both distributions are infinite in extent with *z*. Use Gauss's law to find $\mathbf{D}$ in all regions.

Using the special Gaussian surface *A* in Fig. 4-14 and processing as in Example 3,

$$\mathbf{D} = \frac{\rho_\ell}{2\pi r}\mathbf{a}_r \qquad 0 < r < 2$$

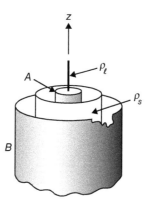

Fig. 4-14

Using the special Gaussian surface *B*,

$$Q_{enc} = \oint \mathbf{D} \cdot d\mathbf{S}$$
$$(\rho_\ell + 4\pi\rho_s)L = D(2\pi rL)$$

from which

$$\mathbf{D} = \frac{\rho_\ell + 4\pi\rho_s}{2\pi r}\mathbf{a}_r \qquad r > 2$$

For the numerical data,

$$\mathbf{D} = \begin{cases} \dfrac{0.477}{r}\mathbf{a}_r \quad (\mu C/m^2) & 0 < r < 2m \\[2mm] \dfrac{0.239}{r}\mathbf{a}_r \quad (\mu C/m^2) & r > 2m \end{cases}$$

4.13. Use Gauss's law to show that $\mathbf{D}$ and $\mathbf{E}$ are zero at all points in the plane of a uniformly charged circular ring that are inside the ring.

Consider, instead of one ring, the charge configuration shown in Fig. 4-15, where the uniformly charged cylinder is infinite in extent, made up of many rings. For Gaussian surface *1*,

$$Q_{enc} = 0 = D \oint dS$$

Fig. 4-15

Hence, $\mathbf{D} = 0$ for $r < R$. Since Ψ is completely in the radial direction, a slice dz can be taken from the cylinder of charge and the result found above will still apply to this ring. For all points within the ring, in the plane of the ring, $\mathbf{D}$ and $\mathbf{E}$ are zero.

4.14. A charge configuration in cylindrical coordinates is given by $\rho = 5re^{-2r}$ (C/m³). Use Gauss's law to find $\mathbf{D}$.

Since ρ is not a function of ϕ or z, the flux Ψ is completely radial. It is also true that, for r constant, the flux density $\mathbf{D}$ must be of constant magnitude. Then a proper special Gaussian surface is a closed right circular cylinder. The integrals over the plane ends vanish, so that Gauss's law becomes

$$Q_{\text{enc}} = \int_{\substack{\text{lateral} \\ \text{surface}}} \mathbf{D} \cdot d\mathbf{S}$$

$$\int_0^L \int_0^{2\pi} \int_0^r 5re^{-2r} r\, dr\, d\phi\, dz = D(2\pi rL)$$

$$5\pi L \left[e^{-2r} \left(-r^2 - r - \frac{1}{2} \right) + \frac{1}{2} \right] = D(2\pi rL)$$

Hence,
$$\mathbf{D} = \frac{2.5}{r} \left[\frac{1}{2} - e^{-2r} \left(r^2 + r + \frac{1}{2} \right) \right] \mathbf{a}_r \quad \text{(C/m}^2\text{)}$$

4.15. The volume in cylindrical coordinates between $r = 2$ m and $r = 4$ m contains a uniform charge density ρ (C/m³). Use Gauss's law to find $\mathbf{D}$ in all regions.

From Fig. 4-16, for $0 < r < 2$ m,

$$Q_{\text{enc}} = D(2\pi rL)$$
$$\mathbf{D} = 0$$

Fig. 4-16

For $2 \leq r \leq 4$ m,

$$\pi \rho L(r^2 - 4) = D(2\pi rL)$$

$$\mathbf{D} = \frac{\rho}{2r}(r^2 - 4)\mathbf{a}_r \quad (\text{C/m}^2)$$

For $r > 4$ m,

$$12\pi \rho L = D(2\pi rL)$$

$$\mathbf{D} = \frac{6\rho}{r}\mathbf{a}_r \quad (\text{C/m}^2)$$

4.16. The volume in spherical coordinates described by $r \leq a$ contains a uniform charge density ρ. Use Gauss's law to determine $\mathbf{D}$ and compare your results with those for the corresponding $\mathbf{E}$ field, found in Problem 3.54. What point charge at the origin will result in the same $\mathbf{D}$ field for $r > a$?

For a Gaussian surface such as Σ in Fig. 4-17,

$$Q_{\text{enc}} = \oint \mathbf{D} \cdot d\mathbf{S}$$

$$\frac{4}{3}\pi r^3 \rho = D(4\pi r^2)$$

and

$$\mathbf{D} = \frac{\rho r}{3}\mathbf{a}_r \qquad r \leq a$$

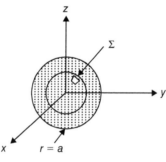

Fig. 4-17

For points outside the charge distribution,

$$\frac{4}{3}\pi a^3 \rho = D(4\pi r^2) \qquad \text{whence} \qquad \mathbf{D} = \frac{\rho a^3}{3r^2}\mathbf{a}_r \qquad r > a$$

If a point charge $Q = \frac{4}{3}\pi a^3 \rho$ is placed at the origin, the $\mathbf{D}$ field for $r > a$ will be the same. This point charge is the same as the total charge contained in the volume.

4.17. A parallel-plate capacitor has a surface charge on the lower side of the upper plate of $+\rho_s$ (C/m²). The upper surface of the lower plate contains $-\rho_s$ (C/m²). Neglect fringing and use Gauss's law to find $\mathbf{D}$ and $\mathbf{E}$ in the region between the plates.

All flux leaving the positive charge on the upper plate terminates on the equal negative charge on the lower plate. The statement *neglect fringing* insures that all flux is normal to the plates. For the special Gaussian surface shown in Fig. 4-18,

$$Q_{\text{enc}} = \int_{\text{top}} \mathbf{D} \cdot d\mathbf{S} + \int_{\text{bottom}} \mathbf{D} \cdot d\mathbf{S} + \int_{\text{side}} \mathbf{D} \cdot d\mathbf{S}$$

$$= 0 + \int_{\text{bottom}} \mathbf{D} \cdot d\mathbf{S} + 0$$

or

$$\rho_s A = D\int dS = DA$$

where A is the area. Consequently,

$$\mathbf{D} = \rho_s \mathbf{a}_n \ (\text{C/m}^2) \qquad \text{and} \qquad \mathbf{E} = \frac{\rho_s}{\epsilon_0} \mathbf{a}_n \ (\text{V/m})$$

Both are directed from the positive to the negative plate.

Fig. 4-18

SUPPLEMENTARY PROBLEMS

4.18. Find the net charge enclosed in a cube 2 m on an edge, parallel to the axes and centered at the origin, if the charge density is

$$\rho = 50x^2 \cos\left(\frac{\pi}{2} y\right) \ (\mu\text{C/m}^3)$$

4.19. Find the charge enclosed in the volume $1 \le r \le 3$ m, $0 \le \phi \le \pi/3$, $0 \le z \le 2$ m given the charge density $\rho = 2z \sin^2 \phi \ (\text{C/m}^3)$.

4.20. Given a charge density in spherical coordinates

$$\rho = \frac{\rho_0}{(r/r_0)^2} e^{-r/r_0} \cos^2 \phi$$

find the amounts of charge in the spherical volumes enclosed by $r = r_0$, $r = 5r_0$, and $r = \infty$.

4.21. A closed surface S contains a finite line charge distribution, $0 \le \ell \le \pi$ m, with charge density

$$\rho_\ell = -\rho_0 \sin \frac{\ell}{2} \ (\text{C/m})$$

What net flux crosses the surface S?

4.22. Charge is distributed in the spherical region $r \le 2$ m with density

$$\rho = \frac{-200}{r^2} \ (\mu\text{C/m}^3)$$

What net flux crosses the surfaces $r = 1$ m, $r = 4$ m, and $r = 500$ m?

4.23. A point charge Q is at the origin of a spherical coordinate system and a spherical shell charge distribution at $r = a$ has a total charge of $Q' - Q$, uniformly distributed. What flux crosses the surfaces $r = k$ for $k < a$ and $k > a$?

4.24. A uniform line charge with $\rho_\ell = 3 \ \mu\text{C/m}$ lies along the x axis. What flux crosses a spherical surface centered at the origin with $r = 3$ m?

4.25. If a point charge Q is at the origin, find an expression for the flux which crosses the portion of a sphere, centered at the origin, described by $\alpha \le \phi \le \beta$.

4.26. A point charge of Q (C) is at the center of a spherical coordinate system. Find the flux Ψ which crosses an area of 4π m^2 on a concentric spherical shell of radius 3 m.

4.27. An area of 40.2 m^2 on the surface of a spherical shell of radius 4 m is crossed by 10 μC of flux in an inward direction. What is the point charge at the origin?

4.28. A uniform line charge ρ_ℓ lies along the x axis. What percent of the flux from the line crosses the strip of the $y = 6$ plane having $-1 \leq z \leq 1$?

4.29. A point charge, $Q = 3$ nC, is located at the origin of a Cartesian coordinate system. What flux Ψ crosses the portion of the $z = 2$ m plane for which $-4 \leq x \leq 4$ m and $-4 \leq y \leq 4$ m?

4.30. A uniform line charge with $\rho_\ell = 5$ μC/m lies along the x axis. Find $\mathbf{D}$ at (3, 2, 1) m.

4.31. A point charge of $+Q$ is at the origin of a spherical coordinate system, surrounded by a concentric uniform distribution of charge on a spherical shell at $r = a$ for which the total charge is $-Q$. Find the flux Ψ crossing spherical surfaces at $r < a$ and $r > a$. Obtain D in all regions.

4.32. Given that $\mathbf{D} = 500e^{-0.1x}\mathbf{a}_x$ (μC/m^2), find the flux Ψ crossing surfaces of area 1 m^2 normal to the x axis and located at $x = 1$ m, $x = 5$ m, and $x = 10$ m.

4.33. Given that $\mathbf{D} = 5x^2\mathbf{a}_x + 10z\mathbf{a}_z$ (C/m^2), find the net outward flux crossing the surface of a cube 2 m on an edge centered at the origin. The edges of the cube are parallel to the axes.

4.34. Given that

$$\mathbf{D} = 30e^{-r/b}\mathbf{a}_r - 2\frac{z}{b}\mathbf{a}_z \quad (\text{C/m}^2)$$

in cylindrical coordinates, find the outward flux crossing the right circular cylinder described by $r = 2b$, $z = 0$, and $z = 5b$ (m).

4.35. Given that

$$\mathbf{D} = 2r\cos\phi\mathbf{a}_\phi - \frac{\sin\phi}{3r}\mathbf{a}_z$$

in cylindrical coordinates, find the flux crossing the portion of the $z = 0$ plane defined by $r \leq a$, $0 \leq \phi \leq \pi/2$. Repeat for $3\pi/2 \leq \phi \leq 2\pi$. Assume flux is positive in the $\mathbf{a}_z$ direction.

4.36. In cylindrical coordinates, the disk $r \leq a$, $z = 0$ carries charge with nonuniform density $\rho_s(r, \phi)$. Use appropriate special Gaussian surfaces to find approximate values of D on the z axis (a) very close to the disk ($0 < z \ll a$), (b) very far from the disk ($z \gg a$).

4.37. A point charge, $Q = 2000$ pC, is at the origin of spherical coordinates. A concentric spherical distribution of charge at $r = 1$ m has a charge density $\rho_s = 40\pi$ pC/m^2. What surface charge density on a concentric shell at $r = 2$ m would result in $\mathbf{D} = 0$ for $r > 2$ m?

4.38. Given a charge distribution with density $\rho = 5r$ (C/m^3) in spherical coordinates, use Gauss's law to find $\mathbf{D}$.

4.39. A uniform charge density of 2 C/m^3 exists in the volume $2 \leq x \leq 4$ m (Cartesian coordinates). Use Gauss's law to find $\mathbf{D}$ in all regions.

4.40. Use Gauss's law to find $\mathbf{D}$ and $\mathbf{E}$ in the region between the concentric conductors of a cylindrical capacitor. The inner cylinder is of radius a. Neglect fringing.

4.41. A conductor of substantial thickness has a surface charge of density ρ_s. Assuming that $\Psi = 0$ within the conductor, show that $D = \pm\rho_s$ just outside the conductor, by constructing a small special Gaussian surface.

ANSWERS TO SUPPLEMENTARY PROBLEMS

4.18. $84.9\ \mu C$

4.19. $4.91\ C$

4.20. $3.97\rho_0\,r_0^3,\ 6.24\rho_0\,r_0^3,\ 6.28\rho_0\,r_0^3$

4.21. $-2\rho_0$ (C)

4.22. $-800\pi\ \mu C,\ -1600\pi\ \mu C,\ -1600\pi\ \mu C$

4.23. $Q,\ Q'$

4.24. $18\ \mu C$

4.25. $\dfrac{\beta-\alpha}{2\pi}Q$

4.26. $Q/9$ (C)

4.27. $-50\ \mu C$

4.28. 5.26%

4.29. $0.5\ nC$

4.30. $(0.356)\left(\dfrac{2\mathbf{a}_y+\mathbf{a}_z}{\sqrt{5}}\right)\ \mu C/m^2$

4.31. $\Psi=4\pi r^2 D=\begin{cases} +Q & r<a \\ 0 & r>a \end{cases}$

4.32. $452\ \mu C,\ 303\ \mu C,\ 184\ \mu C$

4.33. $80\ C$

4.34. $129b^2$ (C)

4.35. $-\dfrac{a}{3},\dfrac{a}{3}$

4.36. (a) $\dfrac{\rho_s(0,\phi)}{2}$;   (b) $\dfrac{Q}{4\pi z^2}$ where $Q=\displaystyle\int_0^{2\pi}\int_0^a \rho_s(r,\phi)r\,dr\,d\phi$

4.37. $-71.2\ pC/m^2$

4.38. $(5r^2/4)\mathbf{a}_r$ (C/m^2)

4.39. $-2\mathbf{a}_x\ C/m^2,\ 2(x-3)\mathbf{a}_x\ (C/m^2),\ 2\mathbf{a}_x\ C/m^2$

4.40. $\rho_{sa}(a/r),\ \rho_{sa}(a/\epsilon_0 r)$

CHAPTER 5

Gradient, Divergence, Curl, and Laplacian

5.1 Introduction

In electromagnetics we need indicators for how a field, whether a scalar or a vector, changes within a segment of space or integrates over that segment. In this chapter we present three operators for such purposes: gradient, divergence, and curl. The gradient provides a measure of how a scalar field changes. For vector fields we use the divergence and the curl. For convenience, we may start with the Cartesian coordinate system. (However, note that the above operators are definable and usable in all three coordinate systems.)

5.2 Gradient

The gradient is a vector defined for each point in a scalar field (e.g., potential in an electric field or the height of points in a terrain). It is shown by the symbol ∇ applied to the scalar field (e.g., ∇V is the gradient of V). The gradient will be defined such that the change in the scalar function, dV, when traversed over a path $d\mathbf{r}$ is the dot product of ∇V and $d\mathbf{r}$.

$$dV = \nabla V \cdot d\mathbf{r}$$

In the Cartesian coordinate system, this leads to the following expression for the gradient ∇V.

$$\nabla V = \frac{\partial V}{\partial x}\,\mathbf{a}_x + \frac{\partial V}{\partial y}\,\mathbf{a}_y + \frac{\partial V}{\partial z}\,\mathbf{a}_z$$

To verify this, refer to Fig. 5-1(a). It shows two neighboring points, M and N, of the region in which a scalar function V is defined.

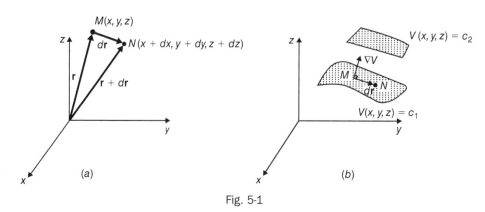

Fig. 5-1

The vector separation of the two points is

$$d\mathbf{r} = dx\mathbf{a}_x + dy\mathbf{a}_y + dz\mathbf{a}_z$$

Construction of the dot product of ∇V and $d\mathbf{r}$ results in

$$\nabla V \cdot d\mathbf{r} = \left(\frac{\partial V}{\partial x}\mathbf{a}_x + \frac{\partial V}{\partial y}\mathbf{a}_y + \frac{\partial V}{\partial z}\mathbf{a}_z\right) \cdot (dx\mathbf{a}_x + dy\mathbf{a}_y + dz\mathbf{a}_z)$$

$$\mathbf{a}_i \cdot \mathbf{a}_j = \begin{cases} 1 & i = j \\ 0 & i \neq j \end{cases}$$

$$\nabla V \cdot d\mathbf{r} = \frac{\partial V}{\partial x}dx + \frac{\partial V}{\partial y}dy + \frac{\partial V}{\partial z}dz$$

But, from the calculus, the change in V from M to N is

$$dV = \frac{\partial V}{\partial x}dx + \frac{\partial V}{\partial y}dy + \frac{\partial V}{\partial z}dz$$

and it follows that

$$dV = \nabla V \cdot d\mathbf{r}$$

The vector field ∇V (also written grad V) is called the *gradient* of the scalar function V. It is seen that, for fixed $|d\mathbf{r}|$, the change in V in a given direction $d\mathbf{r}$ is proportional to the projection of ∇V in that direction. Thus, ∇V *lies in the direction of maximum increase of the function V.*

Another view of the gradient is obtained by allowing the points M and N to lie on the same *equipotential* (if V is a potential) *surface*, $V(x, y, z) = c_1$ [see Fig. 5-1(b)]. Then $dV = 0$, which implies that ∇V is perpendicular to $d\mathbf{r}$. But $d\mathbf{r}$ is tangent to the equipotential surface; indeed, for a suitable location of N, it represents *any* tangent through M. Therefore, ∇V must be along the surface normal at M. Since ∇V is in the direction of increasing V, it points from $V(x, y, z) = c_1$ to $V(x, y, z) = c_2$, where $c_2 > c_1$. *The gradient of a potential function is a vector field that is everywhere normal to the equipotential surfaces.*

The gradient in the cylindrical and spherical coordinate systems follows directly from that in the Cartesian system. It is noted that each term contains the partial derivative of V with respect to distance in the direction of that particular unit vector.

$$\nabla V = \frac{\partial V}{\partial x}\mathbf{a}_x + \frac{\partial V}{\partial y}\mathbf{a}_y + \frac{\partial V}{\partial z}\mathbf{a}_z \qquad \text{(Cartesian)}$$

$$\nabla V = \frac{\partial V}{\partial r}\mathbf{a}_r + \frac{\partial V}{r\partial\phi}\mathbf{a}_\phi + \frac{\partial V}{\partial z}\mathbf{a}_z \qquad \text{(cylindrical)}$$

$$\nabla V = \frac{\partial V}{\partial r}\mathbf{a}_r + \frac{\partial V}{r\partial\theta}\mathbf{a}_\theta + \frac{\partial V}{r\sin\theta\,\partial\phi}\mathbf{a}_\phi \qquad \text{(spherical)}$$

While ∇V is written for grad V in any coordinate system, it must be remembered that the del operator is defined only in Cartesian coordinates.

5.3   The Del Operator

Vector analysis has its own shorthand notation which the reader must note with care. The ∇ vector operator *in Cartesian coordinates* is defined by

$$\nabla \equiv \frac{\partial(\ )}{\partial x}\mathbf{a}_x + \frac{\partial(\ )}{\partial y}\mathbf{a}_y + \frac{\partial(\ )}{\partial z}\mathbf{a}_z$$

In the calculus, the differential operator D is sometimes used to represent d/dx. The symbols $\sqrt{}$ and $\int$ are also operators; standing alone, they give no indication of what they are to operate on. They look strange. And so ∇, standing alone, simply suggests the taking of certain partial derivatives, each followed by application of a unit vector in each of the three coordinates system directions. The del operator is defined only in Cartesian coordinates.

5.4   The Del Operator and Gradient

When ∇ operates on the scalar function V, the result is the gradient vector

$$\nabla V = \frac{\partial V}{\partial x}\mathbf{a}_x + \frac{\partial V}{\partial y}\mathbf{a}_y + \frac{\partial V}{\partial z}\mathbf{a}_z$$

Warning: ∇ is defined only in Cartesian coordinates. While ∇V is written for grad V in any coordinate system, it does not lead to the notion that a del operator can be defined for all these systems. For example, the gradient in cylindrical coordinates is written as

$$\nabla V = \frac{\partial V}{\partial r}\mathbf{a}_r + \frac{1}{r}\frac{\partial V}{\partial \phi}\mathbf{a}_\phi + \frac{\partial V}{\partial z}\mathbf{a}_z$$

This *does not* imply that

$$\nabla = \frac{\partial}{\partial r}\mathbf{a}_r + \frac{1}{r}\frac{\partial}{\partial \phi}\mathbf{a}_\phi + \frac{\partial}{\partial z}\mathbf{a}_z$$

in cylindrical coordinates. In fact, such a ∇ operator expression would give false results when determining $\nabla \cdot \mathbf{A}$ (the divergence, Section 5.5) or $\nabla \times \mathbf{A}$ (the curl, Section 5.10) in the same cylindrical coordinate system.

5.5   Divergence

There are two main indicators of the manner in which a vector field changes from point to point throughout space. The first of these is *divergence*, which will be examined here. It is scalar and bears a similarity to the derivative of a function. The second is *curl*, a vector which will be examined when magnetic fields are discussed in Chapter 10.

When the divergence of a vector field is nonzero, that region is said to contain *sources* or *sinks*—sources when the divergence is positive and sinks when negative. In static electric fields there is a correspondence between positive divergence, sources, and positive electric charge Q. Electric flux Ψ by definition originates on positive charges. Thus, a region which contains positive charges contains the *sources* of Ψ. The divergence of the electric flux density $\mathbf{D}$ will be positive in this region. A similar correspondence exists between negative divergence, sinks, and negative electric charge.

Divergence of the vector field $\mathbf{A}$ at the point P is defined by

$$\text{div } \mathbf{A} \equiv \lim_{\Delta v \to 0} \frac{\oint \mathbf{A} \cdot d\mathbf{S}}{\Delta v}$$

Here the integration is over the surface of an infinitesimal volume Δv that shrinks to point P.

5.6   Expressions for Divergence in Coordinate Systems

The divergence can be expressed for any vector field in any coordinate system. For the development in Cartesian coordinates, a cube is selected with edges Δx, Δy, and Δz parallel to the x, y, and z axes, respectively, as shown in Fig. 5-2. Then the vector field $\mathbf{A}$ is defined at P, the corner of the cube with the lowest values of the coordinates x, y, and z.

$$\mathbf{A} = A_x\mathbf{a}_x + A_y\mathbf{a}_y + A_z\mathbf{a}_z$$

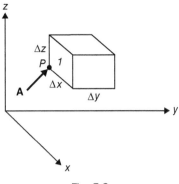

Fig. 5-2

In order to express $\oint \mathbf{A} \cdot d\mathbf{S}$ for the cube, all six faces must be covered. On each face, the direction of $d\mathbf{S}$ is outward. Since the faces are normal to the three axes, only one component of $\mathbf{A}$ will cross any two parallel faces.

In Fig. 5-3 the cube is turned such that face *1* is in full view; the *x* components of $\mathbf{A}$ over the faces to the left and right of *1* are indicated. Since the faces are small,

$$\int_{\text{left face}} \mathbf{A} \cdot d\mathbf{S} \approx - A_x(x)\, \Delta y\, \Delta z$$

$$\int_{\text{right face}} \mathbf{A} \cdot d\mathbf{S} \approx A_x(x + \Delta x)\, \Delta y\, \Delta z$$

$$\approx \left[A_x(x) + \frac{\partial A_x}{\partial x} \Delta_x \right] \Delta y\, \Delta z$$

Fig. 5-3

so that the total for these two faces is

$$\frac{\partial A_x}{\partial x} \Delta x\, \Delta y\, \Delta z$$

The same procedure is applied to the remaining two pairs of faces and the results combined.

$$\oint \mathbf{A} \cdot d\mathbf{S} \approx \left(\frac{\partial A_x}{\partial x} + \frac{\partial A_y}{\partial y} + \frac{\partial A_z}{\partial z} \right) \Delta x\, \Delta y\, \Delta z$$

Dividing by $\Delta x\, \Delta y\, \Delta z = \Delta v$ and letting $\Delta v \to 0$, one obtains

$$\text{div } \mathbf{A} = \frac{\partial A_x}{\partial x} + \frac{\partial A_y}{\partial y} + \frac{\partial A_z}{\partial z} \quad \text{(Cartesian)}$$

The same approach may be used in cylindrical (Problem 5.1) and spherical coordinates.

$$\text{div } \mathbf{A} = \frac{1}{r}\frac{\partial}{\partial r}(rA_r) + \frac{1}{r}\frac{\partial A_\phi}{\partial \phi} + \frac{\partial A_z}{\partial z} \quad \text{(cylindrical)}$$

$$\text{div } \mathbf{A} = \frac{1}{r^2}\frac{\partial}{\partial r}(r^2 A_r) + \frac{1}{r \sin \theta}\frac{\partial}{\partial \theta}(A_\theta \sin \theta) + \frac{1}{r \sin \theta}\frac{\partial A_\phi}{\partial \phi} \quad \text{(spherical)}$$

EXAMPLE 1.   Given the vector field $\mathbf{A} = 5x^2 \left(\sin \dfrac{\pi x}{2} \right) \mathbf{a}_x$, find div $\mathbf{A}$ at $x = 1$.

$$\text{div } \mathbf{A} = \frac{\partial}{\partial x} \left(5x^2 \sin \frac{\pi x}{2} \right) = 5x^2 \left(\cos \frac{\pi x}{2} \right) \frac{\pi}{2} + 10x \sin \frac{\pi x}{2} = \frac{5}{2}\pi x^2 \cos \frac{\pi x}{2} + 10x \sin \frac{\pi x}{2}$$

and div $\mathbf{A}|_{x=1} = 10$.

EXAMPLE 2.   In cylindrical coordinates a vector field is given by $\mathbf{A} = r \sin \phi \, \mathbf{a}_r + r^2 \cos \phi \, \mathbf{a}_\phi + 2re^{-5z} \mathbf{a}_z$. Find div $\mathbf{A}$ at $(\frac{1}{2}, \pi/2, 0)$.

$$\text{div } \mathbf{A} = \frac{1}{r} \frac{\partial}{\partial r} (r^2 \sin \phi) + \frac{1}{r} \frac{\partial}{\partial \phi} (r^2 \cos \phi) + \frac{\partial}{\partial z} (2re^{-5z}) = 2 \sin \phi - r \sin \phi - 10re^{-5z}$$

and
$$\text{div } \mathbf{A}\Big|_{(1/2,\, \pi/2,\, 0)} = 2 \sin \frac{\pi}{2} - \frac{1}{2} \sin \frac{\pi}{2} - 10 \left(\frac{1}{2} \right) e^0 = -\frac{7}{2}$$

EXAMPLE 3.   In spherical coordinates a vector field is given by $\mathbf{A} = (5/r^2) \sin \theta \, \mathbf{a}_r + r \cot \theta \, \mathbf{a}_\theta + r \sin \theta \cos \phi \, \mathbf{a}_\phi$. Find div $\mathbf{A}$.

$$\text{div } \mathbf{A} = \frac{1}{r^2} \frac{\partial}{\partial r} (5 \sin \theta) + \frac{1}{r \sin \theta} \frac{\partial}{\partial \theta} (r \sin \theta \cot \theta) + \frac{1}{r \sin \theta} \frac{\partial}{\partial \phi} (r \sin \theta \cos \phi) = -1 - \sin \phi$$

5.7   The Del Operator and Divergence

The del operator was defined *in Cartesian coordinates* by

$$\nabla = \frac{\partial(\ )}{\partial x} \mathbf{a}_x + \frac{\partial(\ )}{\partial y} \mathbf{a}_y + \frac{\partial(\ )}{\partial z} \mathbf{a}_z$$

When ∇ is dotted with a vector $\mathbf{A}$, the result is the divergence of $\mathbf{A}$.

$$\nabla \cdot \mathbf{A} = \left(\frac{\partial}{\partial x} \mathbf{a}_x + \frac{\partial}{\partial y} \mathbf{a}_y + \frac{\partial}{\partial z} \mathbf{a}_z \right) \cdot (A_x \mathbf{a}_x + A_y \mathbf{a}_y + A_z \mathbf{a}_z) = \text{div } \mathbf{A}$$

Hereafter, the divergence of a vector field will be written $\nabla \cdot \mathbf{A}$.

Warning: The del operator is defined only in Cartesian coordinates. When $\nabla \mathbf{A}$ is written for the divergence of $\mathbf{A}$ in other coordinates systems, it does not mean that a del operator can be defined for these systems. For example, the divergence in cylindrical coordinates will be written as

$$\nabla \cdot \mathbf{A} = \frac{1}{r} \frac{\partial}{\partial r} (rA_r) + \frac{1}{r} \frac{\partial A_\phi}{\partial \phi} + \frac{\partial A_z}{\partial z}$$

This *does not* imply that

$$\nabla = \frac{1}{r} \frac{\partial}{\partial r} (r) \mathbf{a}_r + \frac{1}{r} \frac{\partial}{\partial \phi} \mathbf{a}_\phi + \frac{\partial}{\partial z} \mathbf{a}_z$$

in cylindrical coordinates. In fact, the expression would give false results when used in determining ∇V (the gradient, Section 5.2) or $\nabla \times \mathbf{A}$ (the curl, Section 5.10).

5.8 Divergence of D

From Gauss's law (Section 4.3),

$$\frac{\oint \mathbf{D} \cdot d\mathbf{S}}{\Delta v} = \frac{Q_{enc}}{\Delta v}$$

In the limit,

$$\lim_{\Delta v \to 0} \frac{\oint \mathbf{D} \cdot d\mathbf{S}}{\Delta v} = \text{div } \mathbf{D} = \lim_{\Delta v \to 0} \frac{Q_{enc}}{\Delta v} = \rho$$

This important result is one of Maxwell's equations for static fields:

$$\text{div } \mathbf{D} = \rho \quad \text{and} \quad \text{div } \mathbf{E} = \frac{\rho}{\epsilon}$$

if ϵ is constant throughout the region under examination (if not, div $\epsilon\mathbf{E} = \rho$). Thus, both $\mathbf{E}$ and $\mathbf{D}$ fields will have a divergence of zero in any isotropic charge-free region.

EXAMPLE 4. In spherical coordinates the region $r \leq a$ contains a uniform charge density ρ, while for $r > a$ the charge density is zero. From Problem 3.54, $\mathbf{E} = E_r \mathbf{a}_r$, where $E_r = (\rho r/3\epsilon_0)$ for $r \leq a$ and $E_r = (\rho a^3/3\epsilon_0 r^2)$ for $r > a$. Then, for $r \leq a$,

$$\text{div } \mathbf{E} = \frac{1}{r^2}\frac{\partial}{\partial r}\left(r^2 \frac{\rho r}{3\epsilon_0}\right) = \frac{1}{r^2}\left(3r^2 \frac{\rho}{3\epsilon_0}\right) = \frac{\rho}{\epsilon_0}$$

and, for $r > a$,

$$\text{div } \mathbf{E} = \frac{1}{r^2}\frac{\partial}{\partial r}\left(r^2 \frac{\rho a^3}{3\epsilon_0 r^2}\right) = 0$$

5.9 The Divergence Theorem

Gauss's law states that the closed surface integral of $\mathbf{D} \cdot d\mathbf{S}$ is equal to the charge enclosed. If the charge density function ρ is known throughout the volume, then the charge enclosed may be obtained from an integration of ρ throughout the volume. Thus,

$$\oint \mathbf{D} \cdot d\mathbf{S} = \int \rho \, dv = Q_{enc}$$

But $\rho = \nabla \cdot \mathbf{D}$, and so

$$\oint \mathbf{D} \cdot d\mathbf{S} = \int (\nabla \cdot \mathbf{D}) \, dv$$

This is the *divergence theorem*, also known as *Gauss's divergence theorem*. It is a three-dimensional analog of Green's theorem for the plane. While it was arrived at from known relationships among $\mathbf{D}$, Q, and ρ, the theorem is applicable to any sufficiently regular vector field.

divergence theorem $$\oint_S \mathbf{A} \cdot d\mathbf{S} = \int_v (\nabla \cdot \mathbf{A}) \, dv$$

Of course, the volume v is that which is enclosed by the surface S.

EXAMPLE 5. The region $r \leq a$ in spherical coordinates has an electric field intensity

$$\mathbf{E} = \frac{\rho r}{3\epsilon} \mathbf{a}_r$$

Examine both sides of the divergence theorem for this vector field. For S, choose the spherical surface $r = b \leq a$.

$$\oint \mathbf{E} \cdot d\mathbf{S} \qquad\qquad \int (\nabla \cdot \mathbf{E})\, dv$$

$$\iint \left(\frac{\rho b}{3\epsilon}\, \mathbf{a}_r \right) \cdot (b^2 \sin\theta\, d\theta\, d\phi\, \mathbf{a}_r) \qquad \nabla \cdot \mathbf{E} = \frac{1}{r^2}\frac{\partial}{\partial r}\left(r^2\, \frac{\rho r}{3\epsilon} \right) = \frac{\rho}{\epsilon}$$

$$= \int_0^{2\pi} \int_0^{\pi} \frac{\rho b^3}{3\epsilon} \sin\theta\, d\theta\, d\phi \quad \text{then} \quad \int_0^{2\pi}\int_0^{\pi}\int_0^{b} \frac{\rho}{\epsilon} r^2 \sin\theta\, dr\, d\theta\, d\phi$$

$$= \frac{4\pi\rho b^3}{3\epsilon} \qquad\qquad\qquad = \frac{4\pi\rho b^3}{3\epsilon}$$

The divergence theorem applies to time-varying as well as static fields in any coordinate system. The theorem is used most often in derivations where it becomes necessary to change from a closed surface integration to a volume integration. But it may also be used to convert the volume integral of a function that can be expressed as the divergence of a vector field into a closed surface integral.

5.10 Curl

The *curl* of a vector field $\mathbf{A}$ is another vector field. Point P in Fig. 5-4 lies in a plane area ΔS bounded by a closed curve C. In the integration that defines the curl, C is traversed such that the enclosed area is on the left. The unit normal $\mathbf{a}_n$, determined by the right-hand rule, is as shown in the figure. Then the *component* of the curl of $\mathbf{A}$ in the direction $\mathbf{a}_n$ is defined as

$$(\text{curl } \mathbf{A}) \cdot \mathbf{a}_n \equiv \lim_{\Delta S \to 0} \frac{\oint \mathbf{A} \cdot d\mathbf{l}}{\Delta S}$$

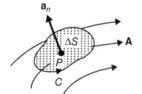

Fig. 5-4

In the various coordinate systems, curl $\mathbf{A}$ is completely specified by its components along the three unit vectors. For example, the x component in Cartesian coordinates is defined by taking as the contour C a square in the $x = \text{const.}$ plane through P, as shown in Fig. 5-5.

$$(\text{curl } \mathbf{A}) \cdot \mathbf{a}_x = \lim_{\Delta y \Delta z \to 0} \frac{\oint \mathbf{A} \cdot d\mathbf{I}}{\Delta y\, \Delta z}$$

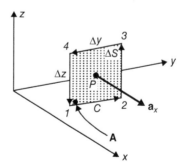

Fig. 5-5

If $\mathbf{A} = A_x\mathbf{a}_x + A_y\mathbf{a}_y + A_z\mathbf{a}_z$ at the corner of ΔS closest to the origin (point 1), then

$$\oint = \int_1^2 + \int_2^3 + \int_3^4 + \int_4^1$$

$$= A_y\,\Delta y + \left(A_z + \frac{\partial A_z}{\partial y}\,\Delta y\right)\Delta z + \left(A_y + \frac{\partial A_y}{\partial z}\,\Delta z\right)(-\Delta y) + A_z(-\Delta z)$$

$$= \left(\frac{\partial A_z}{\partial y} - \frac{\partial A_y}{\partial z}\right)\Delta y\,\Delta z$$

and

$$(\text{curl }\mathbf{A})\cdot\mathbf{a}_x = \frac{\partial A_z}{\partial y} - \frac{\partial A_y}{\partial z}$$

The y and z components can be determined in a similar fashion. Combining the three components,

$$\text{curl }\mathbf{A} = \left(\frac{\partial A_z}{\partial y} - \frac{\partial A_y}{\partial z}\right)\mathbf{a}_x + \left(\frac{\partial A_x}{\partial z} - \frac{\partial A_z}{\partial x}\right)\mathbf{a}_y + \left(\frac{\partial A_y}{\partial x} - \frac{\partial A_x}{\partial y}\right)\mathbf{a}_z \qquad \text{(Cartesian)}$$

A third-order determinant can be written, the expansion of which gives the Cartesian curl of $\mathbf{A}$.

$$\text{curl }\mathbf{A} = \begin{vmatrix} \mathbf{a}_x & \mathbf{a}_y & \mathbf{a}_z \\ \dfrac{\partial}{\partial x} & \dfrac{\partial}{\partial y} & \dfrac{\partial}{\partial z} \\ A_x & A_y & A_z \end{vmatrix}$$

The elements of the second row are the components of the del operator. This suggests (see Section 2.4) that $\nabla \times \mathbf{A}$ can be written for curl $\mathbf{A}$. As with other expressions from vector analysis, this convenient notation is used for curl $\mathbf{A}$ in other coordinate systems, even though ∇ is defined only in Cartesian coordinates.

Expressions for curl $\mathbf{A}$ in cylindrical and spherical coordinates can be derived in the same manner as above, though with more difficulty.

$$\text{curl }\mathbf{A} = \left(\frac{1}{r}\frac{\partial A_z}{\partial \phi} - \frac{\partial A_\phi}{\partial z}\right)\mathbf{a}_r + \left(\frac{\partial A_r}{\partial z} - \frac{\partial A_z}{\partial r}\right)\mathbf{a}_\phi + \frac{1}{r}\left[\frac{\partial(rA_\phi)}{\partial r} - \frac{\partial A_r}{\partial \phi}\right]\mathbf{a}_z \qquad \text{(cylindrical)}$$

$$\text{curl }\mathbf{A} = \frac{1}{r\sin\theta}\left[\frac{\partial(A_\phi\sin\theta)}{\partial \theta} - \frac{\partial A_\theta}{\partial \phi}\right]\mathbf{a}_r + \frac{1}{r}\left[\frac{1}{\sin\theta}\frac{\partial A_r}{\partial \phi} - \frac{\partial(rA_\phi)}{\partial r}\right]\mathbf{a}_\theta + \frac{1}{r}\left[\frac{\partial(rA_\theta)}{\partial r} - \frac{\partial A_r}{\partial \theta}\right]\mathbf{a}_\phi \qquad \text{(spherical)}$$

Frequently useful are two properties of the curl operator:

(1) *The divergence of a curl is the zero scalar*; that is,

$$\nabla \cdot (\nabla \times \mathbf{A}) = 0$$

for any vector field $\mathbf{A}$.

(2) *The curl of a gradient is the zero vector*; that is,

$$\nabla \times (\nabla f) = \mathbf{0}$$

for any scalar function of position f (see Problem 5.24).

Under static conditions, $\mathbf{E} = -\nabla V$, and so,

$$\nabla \times \mathbf{E} = 0$$

5.11   Laplacian

The divergence of the gradient of a scalar is called the *Laplacian*, ∇^2. In the Cartesian coordinate system,

$$\nabla^2 V \equiv \nabla \cdot (\nabla V) = \nabla \cdot \left(\frac{\partial V}{\partial x} \mathbf{a}_x + \frac{\partial V}{\partial y} \mathbf{a}_y + \frac{\partial V}{\partial z} \mathbf{a}_z \right) = \frac{\partial^2 V}{\partial x^2} + \frac{\partial^2 V}{\partial y^2} + \frac{\partial^2 V}{\partial z^2}$$

Explicit forms of the Laplacian in cylindrical and spherical coordinates are given in the next section (see also Section 9.3).

EXAMPLE 6.   In a charge-free region with uniform permittivity, $\nabla^2 V = 0$.

The Laplacian of a vector can be defined using the Laplacian of its coordinates components. For example, the Laplacian of a vector specified by its Cartesian coordinate, $\mathbf{A} = A_x \mathbf{a}_x + A_y \mathbf{a}_y + A_z \mathbf{a}_z$, is as follows

$$\nabla^2 \mathbf{A} = \left(\frac{\partial^2}{\partial x^2} + \frac{\partial^2}{\partial y^2} + \frac{\partial^2}{\partial z^2} \right) \mathbf{A} = \nabla^2 A_x \mathbf{a}_x + \nabla^2 A_y \mathbf{a}_y + \nabla^2 A_z \mathbf{a}_z$$

EXAMPLE 7.   The following identity can be verified by direct substitution

$$\nabla^2 \mathbf{A} = \nabla(\nabla \cdot \mathbf{A}) - \nabla \times (\nabla \times \mathbf{A})$$

5.12   Summary of Vector Operations

The vector operations introduced in this chapter are summarized below for three coordinate systems. Note that the del operator ∇ is defined for the Cartesian coordinate system only.

TABLE 5-1 Summary of Vector Operations

COORDINATE SYSTEM	OPERATOR	MATHEMATICAL FORMULA
Cartesian	Del operator	$\nabla = \frac{\partial(\ )}{\partial x} \mathbf{a}_x + \frac{\partial(\ )}{\partial y} \mathbf{a}_y + \frac{\partial(\ )}{\partial z} \mathbf{a}_z$
	Gradient	$\nabla V = \frac{\partial V}{\partial x} \mathbf{a}_x + \frac{\partial V}{\partial y} \mathbf{a}_y + \frac{\partial V}{\partial z} \mathbf{a}_z$
	Divergence	$\nabla \cdot \mathbf{A} = \frac{\partial A_x}{\partial x} + \frac{\partial A_y}{\partial y} + \frac{\partial A_z}{\partial z}$
	Curl	$\nabla \times \mathbf{A} = \left(\frac{\partial A_z}{\partial y} - \frac{\partial A_y}{\partial z} \right) \mathbf{a}_x + \left(\frac{\partial A_x}{\partial z} - \frac{\partial A_z}{\partial x} \right) \mathbf{a}_y + \left(\frac{\partial A_y}{\partial x} - \frac{\partial A_x}{\partial y} \right) \mathbf{a}_z$
	Laplacian	$\nabla^2 V = \frac{\partial^2 V}{\partial x^2} + \frac{\partial^2 V}{\partial y^2} + \frac{\partial^2 V}{\partial z^2}$
Cylindrical	Gradient	$\nabla V = \frac{\partial V}{\partial r} \mathbf{a}_r + \frac{\partial V}{r \partial \phi} \mathbf{a}_\phi + \frac{\partial V}{\partial z} \mathbf{a}_z$
	Divergence	$\nabla \cdot \mathbf{A} = \frac{1}{r} \frac{\partial}{\partial r} (r A_r) + \frac{1}{r} \frac{\partial A_\phi}{\partial \phi} + \frac{\partial A_z}{\partial z}$
	Curl	$\nabla \times \mathbf{A} = \left(\frac{1}{r} \frac{\partial A_z}{\partial \phi} - \frac{\partial A_\phi}{\partial z} \right) \mathbf{a}_r + \left(\frac{\partial A_r}{\partial z} - \frac{\partial A_z}{\partial r} \right) \mathbf{a}_\phi + \frac{1}{r} \left[\frac{\partial (r A_\phi)}{\partial r} - \frac{\partial A_r}{\partial \phi} \right] \mathbf{a}_z$
	Laplacian	$\nabla^2 V = \frac{1}{r} \frac{\partial}{\partial r} \left(r \frac{\partial V}{\partial r} \right) + \frac{1}{r^2} \frac{\partial^2 V}{\partial \phi^2} + \frac{\partial^2 V}{\partial z^2}$

Spherical   Gradient $\nabla V = \dfrac{\partial V}{\partial r}\mathbf{a}_r + \dfrac{1}{r}\dfrac{\partial V}{\partial \theta}\mathbf{a}_\theta + \dfrac{1}{r \sin \theta}\dfrac{\partial V}{\partial \phi}\mathbf{a}_\phi$

Divergence $\nabla \cdot \mathbf{A} = \dfrac{1}{r^2}\dfrac{\partial}{\partial r}(r^2 A_r) + \dfrac{1}{r \sin \theta}\dfrac{\partial}{\partial \theta}(A_\theta \sin \theta) + \dfrac{1}{r \sin \theta}\dfrac{\partial A_\phi}{\partial \phi}$

Curl $\nabla \times \mathbf{A} = \dfrac{1}{r \sin \theta}\left[\dfrac{\partial (A_\phi \sin \theta)}{\partial \theta} - \dfrac{\partial A_\theta}{\partial \phi}\right]\mathbf{a}_r + \dfrac{1}{r}\left[\dfrac{1}{\sin \theta}\dfrac{\partial A_r}{\partial \phi} - \dfrac{\partial (rA_\phi)}{\partial r}\right]\mathbf{a}_\theta$

$+ \dfrac{1}{r}\left[\dfrac{\partial (rA_\theta)}{\partial r} - \dfrac{\partial A_r}{\partial \theta}\right]\mathbf{a}_\phi$

Laplacian $\nabla^2 V = \dfrac{1}{r^2}\dfrac{\partial}{\partial r}\left(r^2 \dfrac{\partial V}{\partial r}\right) + \dfrac{1}{r^2 \sin \theta}\dfrac{\partial}{\partial \theta}\left(\sin \theta \dfrac{\partial V}{\partial \theta}\right) + \dfrac{1}{r^2 \sin^2 \theta}\dfrac{\partial^2 V}{\partial \phi^2}$

SOLVED PROBLEMS

5.1. Develop the expression for divergence in cylindrical coordinates.

A delta-volume is shown in Fig. 5-6 with edges Δr, $r\,\Delta\phi$, and Δz. The vector field $\mathbf{A}$ is defined at P, the corner with the lowest values of the coordinates r, ϕ, and z, as

$$\mathbf{A} = A_r \mathbf{a}_r + A_\phi \mathbf{a}_\phi + A_z \mathbf{a}_z$$

Fig. 5-6

By definition,

$$\text{div } \mathbf{A} = \lim_{\Delta v \to 0} \frac{\oint \mathbf{A} \cdot d\mathbf{S}}{\Delta v} \tag{1}$$

To express $\oint \mathbf{A} \cdot d\mathbf{S}$, all six faces of the volume must be covered. For the radial component of $\mathbf{A}$ refer to Fig. 5-7.

Fig. 5-7

Over the left face,

$$\int \mathbf{A} \cdot d\mathbf{S} \approx -A_r \, r \, \Delta\phi \, \Delta z$$

and over the right face,

$$\int \mathbf{A} \cdot d\mathbf{S} \approx A_r \, (r + \Delta r)(r + \Delta r) \, \Delta\phi \, \Delta z$$

$$\approx \left(A_r + \frac{\partial A_r}{\partial r} \Delta r \right)(r + \Delta r) \, \Delta\phi \, \Delta z$$

$$\approx A_r \, r \, \Delta\phi \, \Delta z + \left(A_r + r \frac{\partial A_r}{\partial r} \right) \Delta r \, \Delta\phi \, \Delta z$$

where the term in $(\Delta r)^2$ has been neglected. The net contribution of this pair of faces is then

$$\left(A_r + r \frac{\partial A_r}{\partial r} \right) \Delta r \, \Delta\phi \, \Delta z = \frac{\partial}{\partial r}(rA_r) \, \Delta r \, \Delta\phi \, \Delta z = \frac{1}{r} \frac{\partial}{\partial r}(rA_r) \, \Delta v \qquad (2)$$

since $\Delta v = r \, \Delta r \, \Delta\phi \, \Delta z$.

Similarly, the faces normal to $\mathbf{a}_\phi$ yield

$$A_\phi \, \Delta r \, \Delta z \qquad \text{and} \qquad \left(A_\phi + \frac{\partial A_\phi}{\partial \phi} \Delta\phi \right) \Delta r \, \Delta z$$

for a net contribution of

$$\frac{1}{r} \frac{\partial A_\phi}{\partial \phi} \, \Delta v \qquad (3)$$

and the faces normal to $\mathbf{a}_z$ yield

$$A_z r \, \Delta r \, \Delta\phi \qquad \text{and} \qquad \left(A_z + \frac{\partial A_z}{\partial z} \Delta z \right) r \, \Delta r \, \Delta\phi$$

for a net contribution of

$$\frac{\partial A_z}{\partial z} \, \Delta v \qquad (4)$$

When (2), (3), and (4) are combined to give $\oint \mathbf{A} \cdot d\mathbf{S}$, (1) yields

$$\text{div } \mathbf{A} = \frac{1}{r} \frac{\partial(rA_r)}{\partial r} + \frac{1}{r} \frac{\partial A_\phi}{\partial \phi} + \frac{\partial A_z}{\partial z}$$

5.2. Show that $\nabla \cdot \mathbf{E}$ is zero for the field of a uniform line charge.

For a line charge, in cylindrical coordinates,

$$\mathbf{E} = \frac{\rho_\ell}{2\pi \epsilon_0 r} \mathbf{a}_r$$

Then

$$\nabla \cdot \mathbf{E} = \frac{1}{r} \frac{\partial}{\partial r} \left(r \frac{\rho_\ell}{2\pi \epsilon_0 r} \right) = 0$$

The divergence of $\mathbf{E}$ for this charge configuration is zero everywhere except at $r = 0$, where the expression is indeterminate.

5.3. Show that the **D** field due to a point charge has a divergence of zero.

For a point charge, in spherical coordinates,

$$\mathbf{D} = \frac{Q}{4\pi r^2}\mathbf{a}_r$$

Then, for $r > 0$,

$$\nabla \cdot \mathbf{D} = \frac{1}{r^2}\frac{\partial}{\partial r}\left(r^2\frac{Q}{4\pi r^2}\right) = 0$$

5.4. Given $\mathbf{A} = e^{-y}(\cos x\mathbf{a}_x - \sin x\mathbf{a}_y)$, find $\nabla \cdot \mathbf{A}$.

$$\nabla \cdot \mathbf{A} = \frac{\partial}{\partial x}(e^{-y}\cos x) + \frac{\partial}{\partial y}(e^{-y}\sin x) = e^{-y}(-\sin x) + e^{-y}(\sin x) = 0$$

5.5. Given $\mathbf{A} = x^2\mathbf{a}_x + yz\mathbf{a}_y + xy\mathbf{a}_z$, find $\nabla \cdot \mathbf{A}$.

$$\nabla \cdot \mathbf{A} = \frac{\partial}{\partial x}(x^2) + \frac{\partial}{\partial y}(yz) + \frac{\partial}{\partial z}(xy) = 2x + z$$

5.6. Given $\mathbf{A} = (x^2 + y^2)^{-1/2}\mathbf{a}_x$, find $\nabla \cdot \mathbf{A}$ at $(2, 2, 0)$.

$$\nabla \cdot \mathbf{A} = -\frac{1}{2}(x^2 + y^2)^{-3/2}(2x) \quad \text{and} \quad \nabla \cdot \mathbf{A}\Big|_{(2, 2, 0)} = -8.84 \times 10^{-2}$$

5.7. Given $\mathbf{A} = r\sin\phi\,\mathbf{a}_r + 2r\cos\phi\,\mathbf{a}_\phi + 2z^2\mathbf{a}_z$, find $\nabla \cdot \mathbf{A}$.

$$\nabla \cdot \mathbf{A} = \frac{1}{r}\frac{\partial}{\partial r}(r^2\sin\phi) + \frac{1}{r}\frac{\partial}{\partial\phi}(2r\cos\phi) + \frac{\partial}{\partial z}(2z^2)$$
$$= 2\sin\phi - 2\sin\phi + 4z = 4z$$

5.8. Given $\mathbf{A} = 10\sin^2\phi\,\mathbf{a}_r + r\,\mathbf{a}_\phi + [(z^2/r)\cos^2\phi]\,\mathbf{a}_z$, find $\nabla \cdot \mathbf{A}$ at $(2, 0, 5)$.

$$\nabla \cdot \mathbf{A} = \frac{10\sin^2\phi + 2z\cos^2\phi}{r} \quad \text{and} \quad \nabla \cdot \mathbf{A}\Big|_{(2,0,5)} = 5$$

5.9. Given $\mathbf{A} = (5/r^2)\mathbf{a}_r + (10/\sin\theta)\mathbf{a}_\theta - r^2\phi\sin\theta\,\mathbf{a}_\phi$, find $\nabla \cdot \mathbf{A}$.

$$\nabla \cdot \mathbf{A} = \frac{1}{r^2}\frac{\partial}{\partial r}(5) + \frac{1}{r\sin\theta}\frac{\partial}{\partial\theta}(10) + \frac{1}{r\sin\theta}\frac{\partial}{\partial\phi}(-r^2\phi\sin\theta) = -r$$

5.10. Given $\mathbf{A} = 5\sin\theta\mathbf{a}_\theta + 5\sin\phi\mathbf{a}_\phi$, find $\nabla \cdot \mathbf{A}$ at $(0.5, \pi/4, \pi/4)$.

$$\nabla \cdot \mathbf{A} = \frac{1}{r\sin\theta}\frac{\partial}{\partial\theta}(5\sin^2\theta) + \frac{1}{r\sin\theta}\frac{\partial}{\partial\phi}(5\sin\phi) = 10\frac{\cos\theta}{r} + 5\frac{\cos\phi}{r\sin\theta}$$

and

$$\nabla \cdot \mathbf{A}\Big|_{(0.5,\pi/4,\pi/4)} = 24.14$$

5.11. Given that $\mathbf{D} = \rho_0 z\mathbf{a}_z$ in the region $-1 \le z \le 1$ in Cartesian coordinates and $\mathbf{D} = (\rho_0\, z/|z|)\mathbf{a}_z$ elsewhere, find the charge density.

$$\nabla \cdot \mathbf{D} = \rho$$

For $-1 \le z \le 1$,

$$\rho = \frac{\partial}{\partial z}(\rho_0 z) = \rho_0$$

and for $z < -1$ or $z > 1$,

$$\rho = \frac{\partial}{\partial z}(\mp \rho_0) = 0$$

The charge distribution is shown in Fig. 5-8.

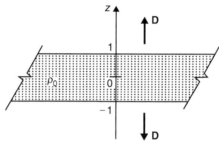

Fig. 5-8

5.12. Given that $\mathbf{D} = (10r^3/4)\mathbf{a}_r$ (C/m^2) in the region $0 < r \le 3$ m in cylindrical coordinates and $\mathbf{D} = (810/4r)\mathbf{a}_r$ (C/m^2) elsewhere, find the charge density.

For $0 < r \le 3$ m,

$$\rho = \frac{1}{r}\frac{\partial}{\partial r}\left(\frac{10r^4}{4}\right) = 10r^2 \ (\text{C/m}^3)$$

and for $r > 3$ m,

$$\rho = \frac{1}{r}\frac{\partial}{\partial r}(810/4) = 0$$

5.13. Given that

$$\mathbf{D} = \frac{Q}{\pi r^2}(1 - \cos 3r)\,\mathbf{a}_r$$

in spherical coordinates, find the charge density.

$$\rho = \frac{1}{r^2}\frac{\partial}{\partial r}\left[r^2\frac{Q}{\pi r^2}(1 - \cos 3r)\right] = \frac{3Q}{\pi r^2}\sin 3r$$

5.14. In the region $0 < r \le 1$ m, $\mathbf{D} = (-2 \times 10^{-4}/r)\mathbf{a}_r$ (C/m^2) and for $r > 1$ m, $\mathbf{D} = (-4 \times 10^{-4}/r^2)\mathbf{a}_r$ (C/m^2), in spherical coordinates. Find the charge density in both regions.

For $0 < r \le 1$ m,

$$\rho = \frac{1}{r^2}\frac{\partial}{\partial r}(-2 \times 10^{-4}\,r) = \frac{-2 \times 10^{-4}}{r^2} \quad (\text{C/m}^3)$$

and for $r > 1$ m,

$$\rho = \frac{1}{r^2}\frac{\partial}{\partial r}(-4 \times 10^{-4}) = 0$$

5.15. In the region $r \le 2$, $\mathbf{D} = (5r^2/4)\mathbf{a}_r$ and for $r > 2$, $\mathbf{D} = (20/r^2)\mathbf{a}_r$, in spherical coordinates. Find the charge density.

For $r \le 2$,

$$\rho = \frac{1}{r^2}\frac{\partial}{\partial r}(5r^4/4) = 5r$$

and for $r > 2$,

$$\rho = \frac{1}{r^2}\frac{\partial}{\partial r}(20) = 0$$

5.16. Given that $\mathbf{D} = (10x^3/3)\mathbf{a}_x$ (C/m^2), evaluate both sides of the divergence theorem for the volume of a cube, 2 m on an edge, centered at the origin and with edges parallel to the axes.

$$\oint \mathbf{D} \cdot d\mathbf{S} = \int_{\text{vol}} (\nabla \cdot \mathbf{D})\, dv$$

Since $\mathbf{D}$ has only an x component, $\mathbf{D} \cdot d\mathbf{S}$ is zero on all but the faces at $x = 1$ m and $x = -1$ m (see Fig. 5-9).

$$\oint \mathbf{D} \cdot d\mathbf{S} = \int_{-1}^{1}\int_{-1}^{1}\frac{10(1)}{3}\mathbf{a}_x \cdot dy\, dz\, \mathbf{a}_x + \int_{-1}^{1}\int_{-1}^{1}\frac{10(-1)}{3}\mathbf{a}_x \cdot dy\, dz\, (-\mathbf{a}_x)$$

$$= \frac{40}{3} + \frac{40}{3} = \frac{80}{3}\,\text{C}$$

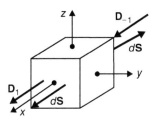

Fig. 5-9

Now for the right side of the divergence theorem. Since $\nabla \cdot \mathbf{D} = 10x^2$,

$$\int_{\text{vol}} (\nabla \cdot \mathbf{D})\, dv = \int_{-1}^{1}\int_{-1}^{1}\int_{-1}^{1}(10x^2)\, dx\, dy\, dz = \int_{-1}^{1}\int_{-1}^{1}\left[10\frac{x^3}{3}\right]_{-1}^{2} dy\, dz = \frac{80}{3}\,\text{C}$$

5.17. Given that $\mathbf{A} = 30e^{-r}\mathbf{a}_r - 2z\mathbf{a}_z$ in cylindrical coordinates, evaluate both sides of the divergence theorem for the volume enclosed by $r = 2$, $z = 0$, and $z = 5$ (Fig. 5-10).

$$\oint \mathbf{A} \cdot d\mathbf{S} = \int (\nabla \cdot \mathbf{A})\, dv$$

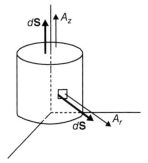

Fig. 5-10

It is noted that $A_z = 0$ for $z = 0$ and hence $\mathbf{A} \cdot d\mathbf{S}$ is zero over that part of the surface.

$$\oint \mathbf{A} \cdot d\mathbf{S} = \int_0^5 \int_0^{2\pi} 30e^{-2}\mathbf{a}_r \cdot 2 \, d\phi \, dz \, \mathbf{a}_r + \int_0^{2\pi} \int_0^2 -2(5)\mathbf{a}_z \cdot r \, dr \, d\phi \mathbf{a}_z$$
$$= 60e^{-2}(2\pi)(5) - 10(2\pi)(2) = 129.4$$

For the right side of the divergence theorem:

$$\nabla \cdot \mathbf{A} = \frac{1}{r}\frac{\partial}{\partial r}(30re^{-r}) + \frac{\partial}{\partial z}(-2z) = \frac{30e^{-r}}{r} - 30e^{-r} - 2$$

and
$$\int (\nabla \cdot \mathbf{A}) \, dv = \int_0^5 \int_0^{2\pi} \int_0^2 \left(\frac{30e^{-r}}{r} - 30e^{-r} - 2 \right) r \, dr \, d\phi \, dz = 129.4$$

5.18. Given that $\mathbf{D} = (10r^3/4)\mathbf{a}_r$ (C/m^2) in cylindrical coordinates, evaluate both sides of the divergence theorem for the volume enclosed by $r = 1$ m, $r = 2$ m, $z = 0$ and $z = 10$ m (see Fig. 5-11).

$$\oint \mathbf{D} \cdot d\mathbf{S} = \int (\nabla \cdot \mathbf{D}) \, dv$$

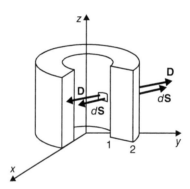

Fig. 5-11

Since $\mathbf{D}$ has no z component, $\mathbf{D} \cdot d\mathbf{S}$ is zero for the top and bottom. On the inner cylindrical surface $d\mathbf{S}$ is in the direction $-\mathbf{a}_r$.

$$\oint \mathbf{D} \cdot d\mathbf{S} = \int_0^{10} \int_0^{2\pi} \frac{10}{4}(1)^3 \mathbf{a}_r \cdot (1) \, d\phi \, dz \, (-\mathbf{a}_r)$$
$$+ \int_0^{10} \int_0^{2\pi} \frac{10}{4}(2)^3 \mathbf{a}_r \cdot (2) \, d\phi \, dz \, \mathbf{a}_r$$
$$= \frac{-200\pi}{4} + 16\frac{200\pi}{4} = 750\pi \text{ C}$$

From the right side of the divergence theorem:

$$\nabla \cdot \mathbf{D} = \frac{1}{r}\frac{\partial}{\partial r}\left(\frac{10r^4}{4} \right) = 10r^2$$

and
$$\int (\nabla \cdot \mathbf{D}) \, dv = \int_0^{10} \int_0^{2\pi} \int_1^2 (10r^2) r \, dr \, d\phi \, dz = 750\pi \text{ C}$$

5.19. Given that $\mathbf{D} = (5r^2/4)\mathbf{a}_r$ (C/m^2) in spherical coordinates, evaluate both sides of the divergence theorem for the volume enclosed by $r = 4$ m and $\theta = \pi/4$ (see Fig. 5-12).

$$\oint \mathbf{D} \cdot d\mathbf{S} = \int (\nabla \cdot \mathbf{D}) \, dv$$

Fig. 5-12

Since **D** has only a radial component, $\mathbf{D} \cdot d\mathbf{S}$ has a nonzero value only on the surface $r = 4$ m.

$$\oint \mathbf{D} \cdot d\mathbf{S} = \int_0^{2\pi} \int_0^{\pi/4} \frac{5(4)^2}{4} \mathbf{a}_r \cdot (4)^2 \sin\theta \, d\theta \, d\phi \, \mathbf{a}_r = 589.1 \, \text{C}$$

For the right side of the divergence theorem:

$$\nabla \cdot \mathbf{D} = \frac{1}{r^2} \frac{\partial}{\partial r}\left(\frac{5r^4}{4}\right) = 5r$$

and

$$\int (\nabla \cdot \mathbf{D}) \, dv = \int_0^{2\pi} \int_0^{\pi/4} \int_0^4 (5r) r^2 \sin\theta \, dr \, d\theta \, d\phi = 589.1 \, \text{C}$$

5.20. Given $\mathbf{A} = (y \cos ax)\mathbf{a}_x + (y + e^x)\mathbf{a}_z$, find $\nabla \times \mathbf{A}$ at the origin.

$$\nabla \times \mathbf{A} = \begin{vmatrix} \mathbf{a}_x & \mathbf{a}_y & \mathbf{a}_z \\ \dfrac{\partial}{\partial x} & \dfrac{\partial}{\partial y} & \dfrac{\partial}{\partial z} \\ y \cos ax & 0 & y + e^x \end{vmatrix} = \mathbf{a}_x - e^x \mathbf{a}_y - \cos ax \, \mathbf{a}_z$$

At $(0, 0, 0)$, $\nabla \times \mathbf{A} = \mathbf{a}_x - \mathbf{a}_y - \mathbf{a}_z$.

5.21. Given the general vector field $\mathbf{A} = 5r \sin\phi \, \mathbf{a}_z$ in cylindrical coordinates, find curl **A** at $(2, \pi, 0)$.

Since **A** has only a z component, only two partials in the curl expression are nonzero.

$$\nabla \times \mathbf{A} = \frac{1}{r} \frac{\partial}{\partial \phi}(5r \sin\phi)\mathbf{a}_r - \frac{\partial}{\partial r}(5r \sin\sin\phi)\mathbf{a}_\phi = 5 \cos\phi \, \mathbf{a}_r - 5 \sin\phi \, \mathbf{a}_\phi$$

Then

$$\nabla \times \mathbf{A}\big|_{(2,\pi,0)} = -5\mathbf{a}_r$$

5.22. Given the general vector field $\mathbf{A} = 5e^{-r} \cos\phi \, \mathbf{a}_r - 5 \cos\phi \, \mathbf{a}_z$ in cylindrical coordinates, find curl **A** at $(2, 3\pi/2, 0)$.

$$\nabla \times \mathbf{A} = \frac{1}{r} \frac{\partial}{\partial \phi}(-5 \cos\phi)\mathbf{a}_r + \left[\frac{d}{dz}(5e^{-r} \cos\phi) - \frac{d}{dr}(-5 \cos\phi)\right]\mathbf{a}_\phi - \frac{1}{r} \frac{\partial}{\partial \phi}(5e^{-r} \cos\phi)\mathbf{a}_z$$

$$= \left(\frac{5}{r} \sin\phi\right)\mathbf{a}_r + \left(\frac{5}{r} e^{-r} \sin\phi\right)\mathbf{a}_z$$

Then

$$\nabla \times \mathbf{A}\big|_{(2,3\pi/2,0)} = -2.50\mathbf{a}_r - 0.34\mathbf{a}_z$$

5.23. Given the general vector field $\mathbf{A} = 10 \sin \theta \mathbf{a}_\theta$ in spherical coordinates, find $\nabla \times \mathbf{A}$ at $(2, \pi/2, 0)$.

$$\nabla \times \mathbf{A} = \frac{1}{r \sin \theta}\left[-\frac{\partial}{\partial \phi}(10 \sin \theta) \right]\mathbf{a}_r + \frac{1}{r}\frac{\partial}{\partial r}(10r \sin \theta)\,\mathbf{a}_\phi = \frac{10 \sin \theta}{r}\mathbf{a}_\phi$$

Then

$$\nabla \times \mathbf{A}\Big|_{(2,\pi/2,0)} = 5\,\mathbf{a}_\phi$$

5.24. Show that the curl of a gradient is zero.

From the definition of curl $\mathbf{A}$ given in Section 5.10, it is seen that curl $\mathbf{A}$ is zero in a region if

$$\oint \mathbf{A} \cdot d\mathbf{l} = 0$$

for every closed path in the region. But if $\mathbf{A} = \nabla f$, where f is a single-valued function,

$$\oint \mathbf{A} \cdot d\mathbf{l} = \oint \nabla f \cdot d\mathbf{l} = \oint df = 0$$

(see Section 5.2).

SUPPLEMENTARY PROBLEMS

5.25. Develop the divergence in spherical coordinates. Use the delta-volume with edges Δr, $r \Delta\theta$, and $r \sin \theta \, \Delta\phi$.

5.26. Show that $\nabla \cdot \mathbf{E}$ is zero for the field of a uniform sheet charge.

5.27. The field of an electric dipole with the charges at $\pm d/2$ on the z axis is

$$\mathbf{E} = \frac{Qd}{4\pi\epsilon_0 r^3}(2 \cos \theta \mathbf{a}_r + \sin \theta \mathbf{a}_\theta)$$

Show that the divergence of this field is zero.

5.28. Given $\mathbf{A} = e^{5x}\mathbf{a}_x + 2 \cos y\mathbf{a}_y + 2 \sin z\mathbf{a}_z$, find $\nabla \cdot \mathbf{A}$ at the origin.

5.29. Given $\mathbf{A} = (3x + y^2)\mathbf{a}_x + (x - y^2)\mathbf{a}_y$, find $\nabla \cdot \mathbf{A}$.

5.30. Given $\mathbf{A} = 2xy\mathbf{a}_x + z\mathbf{a}_y + yz^2\mathbf{a}_z$, find $\nabla \cdot \mathbf{A}$ at $(2, -1, 3)$.

5.31. Given $\mathbf{A} = 4xy\mathbf{a}_x - xy^2\mathbf{a}_y + 5 \sin z\mathbf{a}_z$, find $\nabla \cdot \mathbf{A}$ at $(2, 2, 0)$.

5.32. Given $\mathbf{A} = 2r \cos^2 \phi\mathbf{a}_r + 3r^2 \sin z\mathbf{a}_\phi + 4z \sin^2 \phi\mathbf{a}_z$, find $\nabla \cdot \mathbf{A}$.

5.33. Given $\mathbf{A} = (10/r^2)\mathbf{a}_r + 5e^{-2z}\mathbf{a}_z$, find $\nabla \cdot \mathbf{A}$ at $(2, \phi, 1)$.

5.34. Given $\mathbf{A} = 5 \cos r\mathbf{a}_r + (3ze^{-2r}/r)\mathbf{a}_z$, find $\nabla \cdot \mathbf{A}$ at (π, ϕ, z).

5.35. Given $\mathbf{A} = 10\mathbf{a}_r + 5 \sin \theta\mathbf{a}_\theta$, find $\nabla \cdot \mathbf{A}$.

5.36. Given $\mathbf{A} = r\mathbf{a}_r - r^2 \cot \theta\mathbf{a}_\theta$, find $\nabla \cdot \mathbf{A}$.

5.37. Given $\mathbf{A} = [(10 \sin^2 \theta)/r]\mathbf{a}_r$ (N/m), find $\nabla \cdot \mathbf{A}$ at $(2 \text{ m}, \pi/4 \text{ rad}, \pi/2 \text{ rad})$.

5.38. Given $\mathbf{A} = r^2 \sin \theta\mathbf{a}_r + 13\phi\mathbf{a}_\theta + 2r\mathbf{a}_\phi$, find $\nabla \cdot \mathbf{A}$.

5.39. Show that the divergence of $\mathbf{E}$ is zero if $\mathbf{E} = (100/r)\mathbf{a}_\phi + 40\mathbf{a}_z$.

5.40. In the region $a \le r \le b$ (cylindrical coordinates),

$$\mathbf{D} = \rho_0\left(\frac{r^2 - a^2}{2r}\right)\mathbf{a}_r$$

and for $r > b$,

$$\mathbf{D} = \rho_0 \left(\frac{b^2 - a^2}{2r} \right) \mathbf{a}_r$$

For $r < a$, $\mathbf{D} = 0$. Find ρ in all three regions.

5.41. In the region $0 < r \leq 2$ (cylindrical coordinates), $\mathbf{D} = (4r^{-1} + 2e^{-0.5r} + 4r^{-1}e^{-0.5r})\mathbf{a}_r$, and for $r > 2$, $\mathbf{D} = (2.057/r)\mathbf{a}_r$. Find ρ in both regions.

5.42. In the region $r \leq 2$ (cylindrical coordinates), $\mathbf{D} = [10r + (r^2/3)]\mathbf{a}_r$, and for $r > 2$, $\mathbf{D} = [3/(128r)]\mathbf{a}_r$. Find ρ in both regions.

5.43. Given $\mathbf{D} = 10 \sin \theta \, \mathbf{a}_r + 2 \cos \theta \, \mathbf{a}_\theta$, find the charge density.

5.44. Given

$$\mathbf{D} = \frac{3r}{r^2 + 1} \mathbf{a}_r$$

in spherical coordinates, find the charge density.

5.45. Given

$$\mathbf{D} = \frac{10}{r^2}[1 - e^{-2r}(1 + 2r + 2r^2)]\mathbf{a}_r$$

in spherical coordinates, find the charge density.

5.46. In the region $r \leq 1$ (spherical coordinates),

$$\mathbf{D} = \left(\frac{4r}{3} - \frac{r^3}{5} \right) \mathbf{a}_r$$

and for $r > 1$, $\mathbf{D} = [5/(63r^2)]\mathbf{a}_r$. Find the charge density in both regions.

5.47. The region $r \leq 2$ m (spherical coordinates) has a field $\mathbf{E} = (5r \times 10^{-5}/\epsilon_0)\mathbf{a}_r$ (V/m). Find the net charge enclosed by the shell $r = 2$ m.

5.48. Given that $\mathbf{D} = (5r^2/4)\mathbf{a}_r$ in spherical coordinates, evaluate both sides of the divergence theorem for the volume enclosed between $r = 1$ and $r = 2$.

5.49. Given that $\mathbf{D} = (10r^3/4)\mathbf{a}_r$ in cylindrical coordinates, evaluate both sides of the divergence theorem for the volume enclosed by $r = 2$, $z = 0$, and $z = 10$.

5.50. Given that $\mathbf{D} = 10 \sin \theta \mathbf{a}_r + 2 \cos \theta \mathbf{a}_\theta$, evaluate both sides of the divergence theorem for the volume enclosed by the shell $r = 2$.

5.51. Show that the curl of $(x\mathbf{a}_x + y\mathbf{a}_y + z\mathbf{a}_z)/(x^2 + y^2 + z^2)^{3/2}$ is zero.

5.52. Given the general vector $\mathbf{A} = (-\cos x)(\cos y)\mathbf{a}_z$, find the curl of $\mathbf{A}$ at the origin.

5.53. Given the general vector $\mathbf{A} = (\cos x)(\sin y)\mathbf{a}_x + (\sin x)(\cos y)\mathbf{a}_y$, find the curl of $\mathbf{A}$ everywhere.

5.54. Given the general vector $\mathbf{A} = (\sin 2\phi)\mathbf{a}_\phi$ in cylindrical coordinates, find the curl of $\mathbf{A}$ at $(2, \pi/4, 0)$.

5.55. Given the general vector $\mathbf{A} = e^{-2z}(\sin \frac{1}{2}\phi)\mathbf{a}_\phi$ in cylindrical coordinates, find the curl of $\mathbf{A}$ at $(0.800, \pi/3, 0.500)$.

5.56. Given the general vector $\mathbf{A} = (\sin \phi)\mathbf{a}_r + (\sin \theta)\mathbf{a}_\phi$ in spherical coordinates, find the curl of $\mathbf{A}$ at the point $(2, \pi/2, 0)$.

5.57. Given the general vector $\mathbf{A} = 2.50\mathbf{a}_\theta + 5.00\mathbf{a}_\phi$ in spherical coordinates, find the curl of $\mathbf{A}$ at $(2.0, \pi/6, 0)$.

5.58. Given the general vector

$$\mathbf{A} = \frac{2\cos\theta}{r^3}\,\mathbf{a}_r + \frac{\sin\theta}{r^3}\,\mathbf{a}_\theta$$

show that the curl of **A** is everywhere zero.

ANSWERS TO SUPPLEMENTARY PROBLEMS

5.28. 7.0

5.29. $3 - 2y$

5.30. -8.0

5.31. 5.0

5.32. 4.0

5.33. -2.60

5.34. -1.59

5.35. $(2 + \cos\theta)(10/r)$

5.36. $3 - r$

5.37. 1.25 N/m^2

5.38. $4r\sin\theta + \left(\dfrac{13\phi}{r}\right)\cot\theta$

5.40. $0, \rho_0, 0$

5.41. $-e^{-0.5r}, 0$

5.42. $20 + r, 0$

5.43. $\dfrac{\sin\theta}{5}(18 + 2\cot^2\theta)$

5.44. $3(r^2 + 3)/(r^2 + 1)^2$

5.45. $40e^{-2r}$

5.46. $4 - r^2, 0$

5.47. $5.03 \times 10^{-3}\,\text{C}$

5.48. 75π

5.49. 800π

5.50. $40\pi^2$

5.51. *Hint:* $\nabla \times \mathbf{E} = \mathbf{0}$.

5.52. 0

5.53. 0

5.54. $0.5\mathbf{a}_z$

5.55. $0.368\mathbf{a}_r + 0.230\mathbf{a}_z$

5.56. 0

5.57. $4.33\mathbf{a}_r - 2.50\mathbf{a}_\theta + 1.25\mathbf{a}_\phi$

CHAPTER 6

Electrostatics: Work, Energy, and Potential

6.1 Work Done in Moving a Point Charge

A charge Q experiences a force $\mathbf{F}$ in an electric field $\mathbf{E}$. In order to maintain the charge in equilibrium, a force $\mathbf{F}_a$ must be applied in opposition (Fig. 6-1):

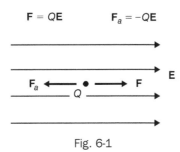

$$\mathbf{F} = Q\mathbf{E} \qquad \mathbf{F}_a = -Q\mathbf{E}$$

Fig. 6-1

Work is defined as a force acting over a distance. Therefore, a differential amount of work dW is done when the applied force $\mathbf{F}_a$ produces a differential displacement $d\mathbf{l}$ of the charge—that is, moves the charge through the distance $d\ell = |d\mathbf{l}|$. Quantitatively,

$$dW = \mathbf{F}_a \cdot d\mathbf{l} = -Q\mathbf{E} \cdot d\mathbf{l}$$

Note that when Q is positive and $d\mathbf{l}$ is in the direction of $\mathbf{E}$, $dW = -QE\,d\ell < 0$, indicating that *work was done by the electric field*. [Analogously, the gravitational field of the earth performs work on a (positive) mass M as it is moved from a higher elevation to a lower one.] On the other hand, a positive dW indicates *work done against the electric field* (cf. lifting the mass M).

Component forms of the differential displacement vector are as follows:

$$d\mathbf{l} = dx\,\mathbf{a}_x + dy\,\mathbf{a}_y + dz\,\mathbf{a}_z \qquad \text{(Cartesian)}$$

$$d\mathbf{l} = dr\,\mathbf{a}_r + r\,d\phi\,\mathbf{a}_\phi + dz\,\mathbf{a}_z \qquad \text{(cylindrical)}$$

$$d\mathbf{l} = dr\,\mathbf{a}_r + r\,d\theta\,\mathbf{a}_\theta + r\sin\theta\,d\phi\,\mathbf{a}_\phi \qquad \text{(spherical)}$$

The corresponding expressions for $d\ell$ were displayed in Section 2.6.

EXAMPLE 1.   An electrostatic field is given by $\mathbf{E} = (x/2 + 2y)\mathbf{a}_x + 2x\mathbf{a}_y$ (V/m). Find the work done in moving a point charge $Q = -20\ \mu C$ (*a*) from the origin to (4, 0, 0) m, and (*b*) from (4, 0, 0) m to (4, 2, 0) m.

(*a*)   The first path is along the *x* axis, so that $d\mathbf{l} = dx\,\mathbf{a}_x$.

$$dW = -Q\mathbf{E} \cdot d\mathbf{l} = (20 \times 10^{-6})\left(\frac{x}{2} + 2y\right)dx$$

$$W = (20 \times 10^{-6}) \int_0^4 \left(\frac{x}{2} + 2y\right)dx = 80\ \mu J$$

(*b*)   The second path is in the $\mathbf{a}_y$ direction, so that $d\mathbf{l} = dy\,\mathbf{a}_y$.

$$W = (20 \times 10^{-6}) \int_0^2 2x\,dy = 320\ \mu J$$

6.2   Conservative Property of the Electrostatic Field

The work done in moving a point charge from one location, *B*, to another, *A*, in a static electric field is independent of the path taken. Thus, in terms of Fig. 6-2,

$$\int_① \mathbf{E} \cdot d\mathbf{l} = -\int_② \mathbf{E} \cdot d\mathbf{l} \quad \text{or} \quad \oint_{①-②} \mathbf{E} \cdot d\mathbf{l} = 0$$

where the last integral is over the *closed contour* formed by ① described positively and ② described negatively.

Conversely, if a vector field $\mathbf{F}$ has the property that $\oint \mathbf{F} \cdot d\mathbf{l} = 0$ over *every* closed contour, then the value of any line integral of $\mathbf{F}$ is determined solely by the endpoints of the path. Such a field $\mathbf{F}$ is called *conservative*; it can be shown that a criterion for the conservative property is that the curl of $\mathbf{F}$ vanishes identically (see Section 5.10).

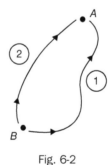

Fig. 6-2

EXAMPLE 2.   For the **E** field of Example 1, find the work done in moving the same charge from (4, 2, 0) back to (0, 0, 0) along a straight-line path.

$$W = (20 \times 10^{-6}) \int_{(4,2,0)}^{(0,0,0)} \left[\left(\frac{x}{2} + 2y\right)\mathbf{a}_x + 2x\,\mathbf{a}_y\right] \cdot (dx\,\mathbf{a}_x + dy\,\mathbf{a}_y)$$

$$= (20 \times 10^{-6}) \int_{(4,2,0)}^{(0,0,0)} \left(\frac{x}{2} + 2y\right)dx + 2x\,dy$$

The equation of the path is $y = x/2$; therefore, $dy = \frac{1}{2}\,dx$ and

$$W = (20 \times 10^{-6}) \int_4^0 \frac{5}{2}x\,dx = -400\ \mu J$$

From Example 1, $80 + 320 = 400\ \mu J$ of work was spent *against* the field along the outgoing, right-angled path. Exactly this much work was returned *by* the field along the incoming, straight-line path, for a round-trip total of zero (conservative field).

6.3   Electric Potential between Two Points

The *potential* of point A with respect to point B is defined as the work done in moving a unit positive charge, Q_u, from B to A.

$$V_{AB} = \frac{W}{Q_u} = -\int_B^A \mathbf{E} \cdot d\mathbf{l} \quad \text{(J/C or V)}$$

It should be observed that the initial, or reference, point is the lower limit of the line integral. Then, too, the minus sign must not be omitted. This sign came into the expression by way of the force $\mathbf{F}_a = -Q\mathbf{E}$, which had to be applied to put the charge in equilibrium.

Because **E** is a conservative field,

$$V_{AB} = V_{AC} - V_{BC}$$

whence V_{AB} may be considered as the *potential difference* between points A and B. When V_{AB} is positive, work must be done to move the unit positive charge from B to A, and point A is said to be at a higher potential than point B.

6.4   Potential of a Point Charge

Since the electric field due to a point charge Q is completely in the radial direction,

$$V_{AB} = -\int_B^A \mathbf{E} \cdot d\mathbf{l} = -\int_{r_B}^{r_A} E_r \, dr = -\frac{Q}{4\pi\epsilon_0} \int_{r_B}^{r_A} \frac{dr}{r^2} = \frac{Q}{4\pi\epsilon_0} \left(\frac{1}{r_A} - \frac{1}{r_B} \right)$$

For a positive charge Q, point A is at a higher potential than point B when r_A is smaller than r_B.

If the reference point B is now allowed to move out to infinity,

$$V_{A\infty} = \frac{Q}{4\pi\epsilon_0} \left(\frac{1}{r_A} - \frac{1}{\infty} \right)$$

or

$$V = \frac{Q}{4\pi\epsilon_0 r}$$

Considerable use will be made of this equation in the materials that follow. The greatest danger lies in forgetting where the reference is and attempting to apply the equation to charge distributions which themselves extend to infinity.

6.5   Potential of a Charge Distribution

If charge is distributed throughout some finite volume with a known charge density ρ (C/m³), then the potential at some external point can be determined. To do so, a differential charge at a general point within the volume is identified, as shown in Fig. 6-3. Then at P,

$$dV = \frac{dQ}{4\pi\epsilon_0 R}$$

Integration over the volume gives the total potential at P:

$$V = \int_{\text{vol}} \frac{\rho \, dv}{4\pi\epsilon_0 R}$$

where dQ is replaced by $\rho \, dv$. Now R must not be confused with r of the spherical coordinate system. And R is not a vector but the distance from dQ to the fixed point P. Finally, R almost always varies from place to place throughout the volume and so cannot be removed from the integrand.

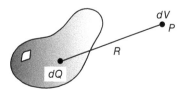

Fig. 6-3

If charge is distributed over a surface or a line, the above expression for V holds, provided that the integration is over the surface or the line and that ρ_s or ρ_ℓ is used in place of ρ. It must be emphasized that all these expressions for the potential at an external point are based upon a *zero reference at infinity*.

EXAMPLE 3.   A total charge of $\frac{40}{3}$nC is uniformly distributed in the form of a circular disk of radius 2 m. Find the potential due to this charge at a point on the axis, 2 m from the disk. Compare this potential with that which results if all of the charge is at the center of the disk.

   Using Fig. 6-4,

$$\rho_s = \frac{Q}{A} = \frac{10^{-8}}{3\pi} \, C/m^2 \qquad R = \sqrt{4+r^2} \quad (m)$$

and

$$V = \frac{30}{\pi} \int_0^{2\pi} \int_0^2 \frac{r \, dr \, d\phi}{\sqrt{4+r^2}} = 49.7 \, V$$

With the total charge at the center of the disk, the expression for the potential of a point charge applies:

$$V = \frac{Q}{4\pi\epsilon_0 z} = \frac{\dfrac{40}{3} \times 10^{-9}}{4\pi(10^{-9}/36\pi)2} = 60 \, V$$

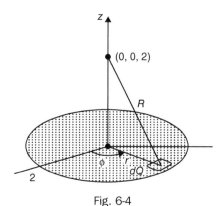

Fig. 6-4

6.6   Relationship between E and V

From the integral expression for the potential of A with respect to B, the differential of V may be written as

$$dV = -\mathbf{E} \cdot d\mathbf{l}$$

On the other hand, from the definition of the gradient of V (see Section 5.2) we have

$$dV = \nabla V \cdot d\mathbf{r}$$

Since $d\mathbf{l} = d\mathbf{r}$ is an arbitrary small displacement, it follows that

$$\mathbf{E} = -\nabla V$$

The electric field intensity **E** may be obtained when the potential function V is known by simply taking the negative of the gradient of V. The gradient was found to be a vector normal to the equipotential surfaces, directed to a positive change in V. With the negative sign here, the **E** field is found to be directed from higher to lower levels of potential V.

EXAMPLE 4. In spherical coordinates and relative to infinity, the potential in the region $r > 0$ surrounding a point charge Q is $V = Q/4\pi\epsilon_0 r$. Hence,

$$\mathbf{E} = -\nabla V = -\frac{\partial}{\partial r}\left(\frac{Q}{4\pi\epsilon_0 r}\right)\mathbf{a}_r = \frac{Q}{4\pi\epsilon_0 r^2}\mathbf{a}_r$$

in agreement with Coulomb's law. (V is obtained in principle by integrating **E**; so it is not surprising that differentiation of V gives back **E**.)

6.7 Energy in Static Electric Fields

Consider the work required to assemble, charge by charge, a distribution of $n = 3$ point charges. The region is assumed initially to be charge-free and with $\mathbf{E} = 0$ throughout.

Referring to Fig. 6-5, the work required to place the first charge, Q_1, into position 1 is zero. Then, when Q_2 is moved toward the region, work equal to the product of this charge and the potential due to Q_1 is required. The total work to position the three charges is

$$W_E = W_1 + W_2 + W_3$$
$$= 0 + (Q_2 V_{2,1}) + (Q_3 V_{3,1} + Q_3 V_{3,2})$$

The potential $V_{2,1}$ must be read "the potential at point 2 due to charge Q_1 at position 1." (This rather unusual notation will not appear again in this book.) The work W_E is the energy stored in the electric field of the charge distribution. (See Problem 6.16 for a comment on this identification.)

Now if the three charges were brought into place in reverse order, the total work would be

$$W_E = W_3 + W_2 + W_1$$
$$= 0 + (Q_2 V_{2,3}) + (Q_1 V_{1,3} + Q_1 V_{1,2})$$

When the two expressions above are added, the result is twice the stored energy:

$$2W_E = Q_1(V_{1,2} + V_{1,3}) + Q_2(V_{2,1} + V_{2,3}) + Q_3(V_{3,1} + V_{3,2})$$

The term $Q_1(V_{1,2} + V_{1,3})$ was the work done against the fields of Q_2 and Q_3, the only other charges in the region. Hence, $V_{1,2} + V_{1,3} = V_1$, the potential at position 1. Then

$$2W_E = Q_1 V_1 + Q_2 V_2 + Q_3 V_3$$

and

$$W_E = \frac{1}{2}\sum_{m=1}^{n} Q_m V_m$$

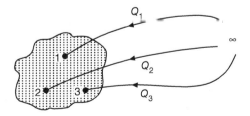

Fig. 6-5

for a region containing n point charges. For a region with a charge density ρ (C/m³) the summation becomes an integration,

$$W_E = \frac{1}{2}\int \rho V \, dv$$

Other forms (see Problem 6.11) of the expression for stored energy are

$$W_E = \frac{1}{2}\int \mathbf{D}\cdot\mathbf{E}\,dv \qquad W_E = \frac{1}{2}\int \epsilon E^2\,dv \qquad W_E = \frac{1}{2}\int \frac{D^2}{\epsilon}\,dv$$

In an electric circuit, the energy stored in the field of a capacitor is given by

$$W_E = \frac{1}{2}QV = \frac{1}{2}CV^2$$

where C is the capacitance (in farads), V is the voltage difference between the two conductors making up the capacitor, and Q is the magnitude of the total charge on one of the conductors.

EXAMPLE 5.   A parallel-plate capacitor, for which $C = \epsilon A/d$, has a constant voltage V applied across the plates (Fig. 6-6). Find the stored energy in the electric field.

Fig. 6-6

With fringing neglected, the field is $\mathbf{E} = (V/d)\mathbf{a}_n$ between the plates and $\mathbf{E} = 0$ elsewhere.

$$W_E = \frac{1}{2}\int \epsilon E^2 dv$$

$$= \frac{\epsilon}{2}\left(\frac{V}{d}\right)^2 \int dv$$

$$= \frac{\epsilon A V^2}{2d}$$

$$= \frac{1}{2}CV^2$$

As an alternate approach, the total charge on one conductor may be found from $\mathbf{D}$ at the surface via Gauss's law (Section 4.3).

$$\mathbf{D} = \frac{\epsilon V}{d}\mathbf{a}_n$$

$$Q = |\mathbf{D}|A = \frac{\epsilon V A}{d}$$

Then

$$W = \frac{1}{2}QV = \frac{1}{2}\left(\frac{\epsilon A V^2}{d}\right) = \frac{1}{2}CV^2$$

SOLVED PROBLEMS

6.1. Given the electric field $\mathbf{E} = 2x\mathbf{a}_x - 4y\mathbf{a}_y$ (V/m), find the work done in moving a point charge $+2$ C
(*a*) from $(2, 0, 0)$ m to $(0, 0, 0)$ m and then from $(0, 0, 0)$ m to $(0, 2, 0)$ m; (*b*) from $(2, 0, 0)$ m to $(0, 2, 0)$ m along the straight-line path joining the two points. (See Fig. 6-7.)

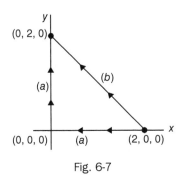

Fig. 6-7

(*a*) Along the *x* axis, $y = dy = dz = 0$, and

$$dW = -2(2x\mathbf{a}_x) \cdot (dx\,\mathbf{a}_x) = -4x\,dx$$

Along the *y* axis, $x = dx = dz = 0$, and

$$dW = -2(-4y\mathbf{a}_y) \cdot (dy\mathbf{a}_y) = 8y\,dy$$

Thus,
$$W = -4\int_{2}^{0} x\,dx + 8\int_{0}^{2} y\,dy = 24\text{ J}$$

(*b*) The straight-line path has the parametric equations

$$x = 2 - 2t \qquad y = 2t \qquad z = 0$$

where $0 \le t \le 1$. Hence,

$$dW = -2[2(2 - 2t)\mathbf{a}_x - 4(2t)\mathbf{a}_y] \cdot [(-2\,dt)\mathbf{a}_x + (2\,dt)\mathbf{a}_y]$$
$$= 16(1 + t)\,dt$$

and
$$W = 16\int_{0}^{1} (1 + t)\,dt = 24\text{ J}$$

6.2. Given the field $\mathbf{E} = (k/r)\mathbf{a}_r$ (V/m) in cylindrical coordinates, show that the work needed to move a point charge Q from any radial distance r to a point at twice that radial distance is independent of r.

Since the field has only a radial component,

$$dW = -Q\mathbf{E} \cdot d\mathbf{l} = -QE_r\ dr = \frac{-kQ}{r}\,dr$$

For the limits of integration use r_1 and $2r_1$.

$$W = -kQ\int_{r_1}^{2r_1} \frac{dr}{r} = -kQ\ln 2$$

which is independent of r_1.

6.3. For a line charge $\rho_\ell = (10^{-9}/2)$ C/m on the z axis, find V_{AB}, where A is (2 m, $\pi/2$, 0) and B is (4 m, π, 5 m).

$$V_{AB} = -\int_B^A \mathbf{E} \cdot d\mathbf{l} \quad \text{where} \quad \mathbf{E} = \frac{\rho_\ell}{2\pi\epsilon_0 r}\mathbf{a}_r$$

Since the field due to the line charge is completely in the radial direction, the dot product with $d\mathbf{l}$ results in $E_r \, dr$.

$$V_{AB} = -\int_B^A \frac{10^{-9}}{2(2\pi\epsilon_0 r)} \, dr = -9[\ln r]_4^2 = 6.24 \text{ V}$$

6.4. In the field of Problem 6.3, find V_{BC}, where $r_B = 4$ m and $r_C = 10$ m. Then find V_{AC} and compare with the sum of V_{AB} and V_{BC}.

$$V_{BC} = -9[\ln r]_{r_C}^{r_B} = -9(\ln 4 - \ln 10) = 8.25 \text{ V}$$
$$V_{AC} = -9[\ln r]_{r_C}^{r_A} = -9(\ln 2 - \ln 10) = 14.49 \text{ V}$$
$$V_{AB} + V_{BC} = 6.24 \text{ V} + 8.25 \text{ V} = 14.49 \text{ V} = V_{AC}$$

6.5. Given the field $\mathbf{E} = (-16/r^2)\mathbf{a}_r$ (V/m) in spherical coordinates, find the potential of point (2m, π, $\pi/2$) with respect to (4m, 0, π).

The equipotential surfaces are concentric spherical shells. Let $r = 2$ m be A and $r = 4$ m, B. Then

$$V_{AB} = -\int_4^2 \left(\frac{-16}{r^2}\right) dr = -4 \text{ V}$$

6.6. A line charge $\rho_\ell = 400$ pC/m lies along the x axis and the surface of zero potential passes through the point (0, 5, 12) m in Cartesian coordinates (see Fig. 6-8). Find the potential at (2, 3, −4) m.

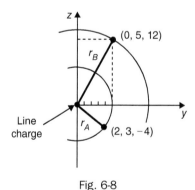

Fig. 6-8

With the line charge along the x axis, the x coordinates of the two points may be ignored

$$r_A = \sqrt{9 + 16} = 5 \text{ m} \qquad r_B = \sqrt{25 + 144} = 13 \text{ m}$$

Then

$$V_{AB} = -\int_{r_B}^{r_A} \frac{\rho_\ell}{2\pi\epsilon_0 r} \, dr = -\frac{\rho_\ell}{2\pi\epsilon_0} \ln \frac{r_A}{r_B} = 6.88 \text{ V}$$

6.7. Find the potential at $r_A = 5$ m with respect to $r_B = 15$ m due to a point charge $Q = 500$ pC at the origin and zero reference at infinity.

Due to a point charge,

$$V_{AB} = \frac{Q}{4\pi\epsilon_0}\left(\frac{1}{r_A} - \frac{1}{r_B}\right)$$

To find the potential difference, the zero reference is not needed.

$$V_{AB} = \frac{500 \times 10^{-12}}{4\pi(10^{-9}/36\pi)}\left(\frac{1}{5} - \frac{1}{15}\right) = 0.60 \text{ V}$$

The zero reference at infinity may be used to find V_5 and V_{15}.

$$V_5 = \frac{Q}{4\pi\epsilon_0}\left(\frac{1}{5}\right) = 0.90 \text{ V} \qquad V_{15} = \frac{Q}{4\pi\epsilon_0}\left(\frac{1}{15}\right) = 0.30 \text{ V}$$

Then

$$V_{AB} = V_5 - V_{15} = 0.60 \text{ V}$$

6.8. Forty nanocoulombs of charge is uniformly distributed around a circular ring of radius 2 m. Find the potential at a point on the axis 5 m from the plane of the ring. Compare with the result where all the charge is at the origin in the form of a point charge.

With the charge in a line,

$$V = \int \frac{\rho_\ell \, d\ell}{4\pi\epsilon_0 R}$$

Here

$$\rho_\ell = \frac{40 \times 10^{-9}}{2\pi(2)} = \frac{10^{-8}}{\pi} \text{ C/m}$$

and (see Fig. 6-9) $R = \sqrt{29}$ m, $d\ell = (2 \text{ m}) \, d\phi$.

$$V = \int_0^{2\pi} \frac{(10^{-8}/\pi)(2) \, d\phi}{4\pi(10^{-9}/36\pi)\sqrt{29}} = 66.9 \text{ V}$$

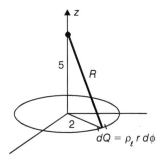

Fig. 6-9

If the charge is concentrated at the origin,

$$V = \frac{40 \times 10^{-9}}{4\pi\epsilon_0(5)} = 72.0 \text{ V}$$

6.9. Five equal point charges, $Q = 20$ nC, are located at $x = 2, 3, 4, 5,$ and 6 m. Find the potential at the origin.

$$V = \frac{1}{4\pi\epsilon_0}\sum_{m=1}^{n}\frac{Q_m}{R_m} = \frac{20 \times 10^{-9}}{4\pi\epsilon_0}\left(\frac{1}{2} + \frac{1}{3} + \frac{1}{4} + \frac{1}{5} + \frac{1}{6}\right) = 261 \text{ V}$$

6.10. Charge is distributed uniformly along a straight line of finite length $2L$ (Fig. 6-10). Show that for two external points near the midpoint, such that r_1 and r_2 are small compared to the length, the potential V_{12} is the same as for an infinite line charge.

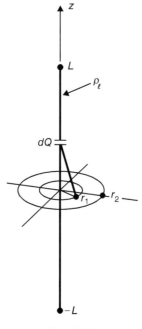

Fig. 6-10

The potential at point 1 with zero reference at infinity is

$$V_1 = 2\int_0^L \frac{\rho_\ell \, dz}{4\pi\epsilon_0(z^2 + r_1^2)^{1/2}}$$

$$= \frac{2\rho_\ell}{4\pi\epsilon_0}[\ln(z + \sqrt{z^2 + r_1^2})]_0^L$$

$$= \frac{\rho_\ell}{4\pi\epsilon_0}[\ln(L + \sqrt{L^2 + r_1^2}) - \ln r_1]$$

Similarly, the potential at point 2 is

$$V_2 = \frac{\rho_\ell}{2\pi\epsilon_0}[\ln(L + \sqrt{L^2 + r_2^2}) - \ln r_2]$$

Now if $L \gg r_1$ and $L \gg r_2$,

$$V_1 \approx \frac{\rho_\ell}{2\pi\epsilon_0}(\ln 2L - \ln r_1)$$

$$V_2 \approx \frac{\rho_\ell}{2\pi\epsilon_0}(\ln 2L - \ln r_2)$$

Then

$$V_{12} = V_1 - V_2 \approx \frac{\rho_\ell}{2\pi\epsilon_0}\ln\frac{r_2}{r_1}$$

which agrees with the expression found in Problem 6.6 for the infinite line.

6.11. Charge distributed throughout a volume v with density ρ gives rise to an electric field with energy content

$$W_E = \frac{1}{2}\int_v \rho V \, dv$$

Show that an equivalent expression for the stored energy is

$$W_E = \frac{1}{2}\int \epsilon E^2\, dv$$

Fig. 6-11 shows the charge-containing volume v enclosed within a large sphere of radius R. Since ρ vanishes outside v,

$$W_E = \frac{1}{2}\int_v \rho V\, dv = \frac{1}{2}\int_{\substack{\text{spherical}\\\text{volume}}} \rho V\, dv = \frac{1}{2}\int_{\substack{\text{spherical}\\\text{volume}}} (\nabla \cdot \mathbf{D})\, V\, dv$$

The vector identity $\nabla \cdot V\mathbf{A} = \mathbf{A}\cdot\nabla V + V(\nabla \cdot \mathbf{A})$, applied to the integrand, gives

$$W_E = \frac{1}{2}\int_{\substack{\text{spherical}\\\text{volume}}} (\nabla \cdot V\mathbf{D})\, dv - \frac{1}{2}\int_{\substack{\text{spherical}\\\text{volume}}} (\nabla \cdot V\mathbf{D})\, dv$$

This expression holds for an arbitrarily large radius R; the plan is to let $R \to \infty$.

The first integral on the right equals, by the divergence theorem,

$$\frac{1}{2}\oint_{\substack{\text{spherical}\\\text{surface}}} V\mathbf{D}\cdot d\mathbf{S}$$

Now, as the enclosing sphere becomes very large, the enclosed volume charge looks like a point charge. Thus, at the surface, D appears as k_1/R^2 and V appears as k_2/R. So the integrand is decreasing as $1/R^3$. Since the surface area increases only as R^2, it follows that

$$\lim_{R \to \infty} \oint_{\substack{\text{spherical}\\\text{surface}}} V\mathbf{D}\cdot d\mathbf{S} = 0$$

The remaining integral gives, in the limit,

$$W_E = \frac{1}{2}\int (\mathbf{D}\cdot\nabla V)\, dv = \frac{1}{2}\int (\mathbf{D}\cdot\mathbf{E})\, dv$$

And since $\mathbf{D} = \epsilon\mathbf{E}$, the stored energy is also given by

$$W_E = \frac{1}{2}\int \epsilon E^2\, dv \quad \text{or} \quad W_E = \frac{1}{2}\int \frac{D^2}{\epsilon}\, dv$$

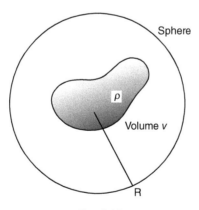

Fig. 6-11

6.12. Given the potential function $V = 2x + 4y$ (V) in free space, find the stored energy in a 1-m³ volume centered at the origin. Examine other 1-m³ volumes.

$$\mathbf{E} = -\nabla V = -\left(\frac{\partial V}{\partial x}\mathbf{a}_x + \frac{\partial V}{\partial y}\mathbf{a}_y + \frac{\partial V}{\partial z}\mathbf{a}_z\right) = -2\mathbf{a}_x - 4\mathbf{a}_y \quad \text{(V/m)}$$

This field is constant in magnitude ($E = \sqrt{20}$ V/m) and direction over all space, and so the total stored energy is infinite. (The field could be that within an infinite parallel-plate capacitor. It would take an infinite amount of work to charge such a capacitor.)

Nevertheless, it is possible to speak of an *energy density* for this and other fields. The expression

$$W_E = \frac{1}{2} \int \epsilon E^2 \, dv$$

suggests that each tiny volume dv be assigned the energy content $w \, dv$, where

$$w = \frac{1}{2} \epsilon E^2$$

For the present field, the energy density is constant:

$$w = \frac{1}{2} \epsilon_0 (20) = \frac{10^{-8}}{36\pi} \text{ J/m}^3$$

and so every 1-m^3 volume contains $(10^{-8}/36\pi)$ J of energy.

6.13. Two thin conducting half planes, at $\phi = 0$ and $\phi = \pi/6$, are insulated from each other along the z axis. Given that the potential function for $0 \le \phi \le \pi/6$ is $V = (-60\phi/\pi)$ V, find the energy stored between the half planes for $0.1 \le r \le 0.6$ m and $0 \le z \le 1$ m. Assume free space.

To find the energy, W'_E, stored in a limited region of space, one must integrate the energy density (see Problem 6.12) through the region. Between the half planes,

$$\mathbf{E} = -\nabla V = -\frac{1}{r}\frac{\partial}{\partial \phi}\left(\frac{-60\phi}{\pi}\right)\mathbf{a}_\phi = \frac{60}{\pi r}\mathbf{a}_\phi \quad \text{(V/m)}$$

and so

$$W'_E = \frac{\epsilon_0}{2} \int_0^1 \int_0^{\pi/6} \int_{0.1}^{0.6} \left(\frac{60}{\pi r}\right)^2 r \, dr \, d\phi \, dz = \frac{300\epsilon_0}{\pi} \ln 6 = 1.51 \text{ nJ}$$

6.14. The electric field between two concentric cylindrical conductors at $r = 0.01$ m and $r = 0.05$ m is given by $\mathbf{E} = (10^5/r)\mathbf{a}_r$ (V/m), fringing neglected. Find the energy stored in a 0.5-m length. Assume free space.

$$W'_E = \frac{1}{2}\int \epsilon_0 E^2 \, dv = \frac{\epsilon_0}{2}\int_h^{h+0.5}\int_0^{2\pi}\int_{0.01}^{0.05}\left(\frac{10^5}{r}\right)^2 r \, dr \, d\phi \, dz = 0.224 \text{ J}$$

6.15. Find the stored energy in a system of four identical point charges, $Q = 4$ nC, at the corners of a square 1 m on a side. What is the stored energy in the system when only two charges at opposite corners are in place?

$$2W_E = Q_1 V_1 + Q_2 V_2 + Q_3 V_3 + Q_4 V_4 = 4Q_1 V_1$$

where the last equality follows from the symmetry of the system.

$$V_1 = \frac{Q_2}{4\pi\epsilon_0 R_{12}} + \frac{Q_3}{4\pi\epsilon_0 R_{13}} + \frac{Q_4}{4\pi\epsilon_0 R_{14}} = \frac{4\times 10^{-9}}{4\pi\epsilon_0}\left(\frac{1}{1}+\frac{1}{1}+\frac{1}{\sqrt{2}}\right) = 97.5 \text{ V}$$

Then

$$W_E = 2Q_1 V_1 = 2(4\times 10^{-9})(97.5) = 780 \text{ nJ}$$

For only two charges in place,

$$2W_E = Q_1 V_1 = (4\times 10^{-9})\left(\frac{4\times 10^{-9}}{4\pi\epsilon_0\sqrt{2}}\right) = 102 \text{ nJ}$$

6.16. What energy is stored in the system of two point charges, $Q_1 = 3$ nC and $Q_2 = -3$ nC, separated by a distance of $d = 0.2$ m?

$$2W_E = Q_1 V_1 + Q_2 V_2 = Q_1 \left(\frac{Q_2}{4\pi\epsilon_0 d} \right) + Q_2 \left(\frac{Q_1}{4\pi\epsilon_0 d} \right)$$

whence
$$W_E = \frac{Q_1 Q_2}{4\pi\epsilon_0 d} = -\frac{(3 \times 10^{-9})^2}{4\pi(10^{-9}/36\pi)(0.2)} = -405 \text{ nJ}$$

It may seem paradoxical that the stored energy turns out to be negative here, whereas $\frac{1}{2}\epsilon E^2$, and hence

$$W_E = \frac{1}{2} \int_{\text{all space}} \epsilon E^2 \, dv$$

is necessarily positive. The reason for the discrepancy is that in equating the work done in assembling a system of point charges to the energy stored in the field, one neglects the infinite energy already in the field when the charges were at infinity. (It took an infinite amount of work to create the separate charges at infinity.) Thus, the above result, $W_E = -405$ nJ, may be taken to mean that the energy is 405 nJ below the (infinite) reference level at infinity. Since only energy *differences* have physical significance, the reference level may properly be disregarded.

6.17. A spherical conducting shell of radius a, centered at the origin, has a potential field

$$V = \begin{cases} V_0 & r \leq a \\ V_0 a/r & r > a \end{cases}$$

with the zero reference at infinity. Find an expression for the stored energy that this potential represents.

$$\mathbf{E} = -\nabla V = \begin{cases} 0 & r \leq a \\ (V_0 a/r^2) \mathbf{a}_r & r > a \end{cases}$$

$$W_E = \frac{1}{2} \int \epsilon_0 E^2 \, dv = 0 + \frac{\epsilon_0}{2} \int_0^{2\pi} \int_0^{\pi} \int_0^{\infty} \left(\frac{V_0 a}{r^2} \right)^2 r^2 \sin\theta \, dr \, d\theta \, d\phi = 2\pi\epsilon_0 V_0^2 a$$

Note that the total charge on the shell is, from Gauss's law,

$$Q = DA = \left(\frac{\epsilon_0 V_0 a}{a^2} \right)(4\pi a^2) = 4\pi\epsilon_0 V_0 a$$

while the potential at the shell is $V = V_0$. Thus, $W_E = \frac{1}{2} QV$, the familiar result for the energy stored in a capacitor (in this case, a spherical capacitor with the other plate of infinite radius).

SUPPLEMENTARY PROBLEMS

6.18. Find the work done in moving a point charge $Q = -20\mu C$ from the origin to $(4, 2, 0)$ m in the field

$$\mathbf{E} = 2(x + 4y)\mathbf{a}_x + 8x\mathbf{a}_y \text{ (V/m)}$$

along the path $x^2 = 8y$.

6.19. Find the work done in moving a point charge $Q = 3 \ \mu C$ from $(4 \text{ m}, \pi, 0)$ to $(2 \text{ m}, \pi/2, 2 \text{ m})$, cylindrical coordinates, in the field $\mathbf{E} = (10^5/r)\mathbf{a}_r + 10^5 z\mathbf{a}_z$ (V/m).

6.20. Find the difference in the amounts of work required to bring a point charge $Q = 2$ nC from infinity to $r = 2$ m and from infinity to $r = 4$ m, in the field $\mathbf{E} = (10^5/r)\mathbf{a}_r$ (V/m).

6.21. A uniform line charge of density $\rho_\ell = 1$ nC/m is arranged in the form of a square 6 m on a side, as shown in Fig. 6-12. Find the potential at $(0, 0, 5)$ m.

Fig. 6-12

6.22. Develop an expression for the potential at a point d meters radially outward from the midpoint of a finite line charge L meters long and of uniform density ρ_ℓ (C/m). Apply this result to Problem 6.21 as a check.

6.23. Show that the potential at the origin due to a uniform surface charge density ρ_s over the ring $z = 0$, $R \le r \le R + 1$ is independent of R.

6.24. A total charge of 160 nC is first separated into four equal point charges spaced at 90° intervals around a circle of 3 m radius. Find the potential at a point on the axis, 5 m from the plane of the circle. Separate the total charge into eight equal parts and repeat with the charges at 45° intervals. What would be the answer in the limit $\rho_\ell = (160/6\pi)$ nC/m?

6.25. In spherical coordinates, point A is at a radius 2 m while B is at 4 m. Given the field $\mathbf{E} = (-16/r^2)\mathbf{a}_r$ (V/m), find the potential of point A, zero reference at infinity. Repeat for point B. Now express the potential difference $V_A - V_B$ and compare the result with Problem 6.5.

6.26. If the zero potential reference is at $r = 10$ m and a point charge $Q = 0.5$ nC is at the origin, find the potentials at $r = 5$ m and $r = 15$ m. At what radius is the potential the same in magnitude as that at $r = 5$ m but opposite in sign?

6.27. A point charge $Q = 0.4$ nC is located at (2, 3, 3) m in Cartesian coordinates. Find the potential difference V_{AB}, where point A is (2, 2, 3) m and B is (−2, 3, 3) m.

6.28. Find the potential in spherical coordinates due to two equal but opposite point charges on the y axis at $y = \pm d/2$. Assume $r \gg d$.

6.29. Repeat Problem 6.28 with the charges on the z axis.

6.30. Find the charge densities on the conductors in Problem 6.13.

6.31. A uniform line charge $\rho_\ell = 2$ nC/m lies in the $z = 0$ plane parallel to the x axis at $y = 3$ m. Find the potential difference V_{AB} for the points $A(2, 0, 4)$ m and $B(0, 0, 0)$ m.

6.32. A uniform sheet of charge, $\rho_s = (1/6\pi)$ nC/m², is at $x = 0$ and a second sheet, $\rho_s = (-1/6\pi)$ nC/m², is at $x = 10$ m. Find V_{AB}, V_{BC}, and V_{AC} for $A(10$ m, 0, 0), $B(4$ m, 0, 0), and $C(0, 0, 0)$ m.

6.33. Given the cylindrical coordinate electric fields $\mathbf{E} = (5/r)\mathbf{a}_r$ (V/m) for $0 \le r \le 2$ m and $\mathbf{E} = 2.5\mathbf{a}_r$ V/m for $r > 2$ m, find the potential difference V_{AB} for $A(1$ m, 0, 0) and $B(4$ m, 0, 0).

6.34. A parallel-plate capacitor 0.5 m by 1.0 m, has a separation distance of 2 cm and a voltage difference of 10 V. Find the stored energy, assuming that $\epsilon = \epsilon_0$.

6.35. The capacitor described in Problem 6.34 has an applied voltage of 200 V.

    (*a*)   Find the stored energy.

    (*b*)   Hold d_1 (Fig. 6-13) at 2 cm and the voltage difference at 200 V, while increasing d_2 to 2.2 cm. Find the final stored energy.

Fig. 6-13

6.36. Find the energy stored in a system of three equal point charges, $Q = 2$ nC, arranged in a line with 0.5 m separation between them.

6.37. Repeat Problem 6.36 if the charge in the center is −2 nC.

6.38. Four equal point charges, $Q = 2$ nC, are to be placed at the corners of a square $\frac{1}{3}$ m on a side, one at a time. Find the energy in the system after each charge is positioned.

6.39. Given the electric field $\mathbf{E} = -5e^{-r/a}\mathbf{a}_r$ in cylindrical coordinates, find the energy stored in the volume described by $r \le 2a$ and $0 \le z \le 5a$.

6.40. Given a potential $V = 3x^2 + 4y^2$ (V), find the energy stored in the volume described by $0 \le x \le 1$ m, $0 \le y \le 1$ m, and $0 \le z \le 1$ m.

ANSWERS TO SUPPLEMENTARY PROBLEMS

6.18. 1.60 mJ

6.19. −0.392 J

6.20. 1.39×10^{-4} J

6.21. 35.6 V

6.22. $\dfrac{\rho_\ell}{2\pi\epsilon_0}\ln\dfrac{L/2+\sqrt{d^2+L^2/4}}{d}$ (V)

6.24. 247 V

6.25. $V_A = 2V_B = -8$ V

6.26. 0.45 V, −0.15 V, ∞

6.27. 2.70 V

6.28. $(Qd\sin\theta)/(4\pi\epsilon_0 r^2)$

6.29. $(Qd\cos\theta)/(4\pi\epsilon_0 r^2)$

6.30. $\dfrac{+60\epsilon_0}{\pi r}$ (C/m^2) on $\phi = 0$, $\dfrac{-60\epsilon_0}{\pi r}$ (C/m^2) on $\phi = \dfrac{\pi}{6}$

6.31. -18.4 V

6.32. -36 V, -24 V, -60 V

6.33. 8.47 V

6.34. 11.1 nJ

6.35. *Hint:*　$\Delta W_E = \frac{1}{2}(\Delta C)V^2$
　　　　(a) 4.4 μJ;　　(b) 4.2 μJ

6.36. 180 nJ

6.37. -108 nJ

6.38. 0, 108 nJ, 292 nJ, 585 nJ

6.39. $7.89 \times 10^{-10} a^3$

6.40. 147 pJ

CHAPTER 7

Electric Current

7.1 Introduction

Electric current is the rate of transport of electric charge past a specified point or across a specified surface. The symbol I is generally used for constant currents and i for time-variable currents. The unit of current is the *ampere* (1 A = 1 C/s; in the SI system, the ampere is the basic unit and the coulomb is the derived unit).

Ohm's law relates current to voltage and resistance. For simple dc circuits, $I = V/R$. However, when charges are suspended in a liquid or a gas, or where both positive and negative charge carriers are present with different characteristics, the simple form of Ohm's law is insufficient. Consequently, the current density $\mathbf{J}$ (A/m^2) receives more attention in electromagnetics than does current I.

7.2 Charges in Motion

Consider the force on a positively charged particle in an electric field in vacuum, as shown in Fig. 7-1(*a*). This force, $\mathbf{F} = +Q\mathbf{E}$, is unopposed and results in constant acceleration. Thus, the charge moves in the direction of $\mathbf{E}$ with a velocity $\mathbf{U}$ that increases as long as the particle is in the $\mathbf{E}$ field. When the charge is in a liquid or gas, as shown in Fig. 7-1(*b*), it collides repeatedly with particles in the medium, resulting in random changes in direction. But for constant $\mathbf{E}$ and a homogeneous medium, the random velocity components cancel out, leaving a constant average velocity, known as the *drift velocity* $\mathbf{U}$, along the direction of $\mathbf{E}$. Conduction in metals takes place by movement of the electrons in the outermost shells of the atoms making up the crystalline structure. According to the *electron-gas theory*, these electrons reach an average drift velocity in much the same way as a charged particle moving through a liquid or gas. The drift velocity is directly proportional to the electric field intensity,

$$\mathbf{U} = \mu\mathbf{E}$$

where μ, the *mobility*, has the units m^2/ V · s. Each cubic meter of a conductor contains on the order of 10^{28} atoms. Good conductors have one or two electrons from each atom free to move upon application of the field. The mobility μ varies with temperature and the crystalline structure of the solid. The particles in the solid have a vibratory motion which increases with temperature. This makes it more difficult for the charges to move. Thus, at higher temperatures the mobility μ is reduced, resulting in a smaller drift velocity (or current) for a given $\mathbf{E}$. In circuit analysis this phenomenon is accounted for by stating a *resistivity* for each material and specifying an increase in this resistivity with increasing temperature.

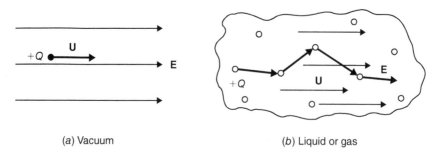

(a) Vacuum   (b) Liquid or gas

Fig. 7-1

7.3   Convection Current Density J

A set of charged particles giving rise to a charge density ρ in a volume v is shown in Fig. 7-2 to have a velocity U to the right. The particles are assumed to maintain their relative positions within the volume. As this charge configuration passes a surface S, it constitutes a *convection current,* with density

$$\mathbf{J} = \rho \mathbf{U} \quad (\text{A}/\text{m}^2)$$

Of course, if the cross section of v varies or if the density ρ is not constant throughout v, then $\mathbf{J}$ will not be constant with time. Further, $\mathbf{J}$ will be zero when the last portion of the volume crosses S. Nevertheless, the concept of a current density caused by a cloud of charged particles in motion is at times useful in the study of electromagnetic field theory.

Fig. 7-2

7.4   Conduction Current Density J

Of more interest is the *conduction current* that occurs in the presence of an electric field within a conductor of fixed cross section. The current density is again given by

$$\mathbf{J} = \rho \mathbf{U} \quad (\text{A}/\text{m}^2)$$

which, in view of the relation $\mathbf{U} = \mu \mathbf{E}$, can be written

$$\mathbf{J} = \sigma \mathbf{E}$$

where $\sigma = \rho \mu$ is the *conductivity* of the material, in *siemens per meter* (S/m). In metallic conductors the charge carriers are electrons, which drift in a direction opposite to that of the electric field (Fig. 7-3). Hence, for electrons, both ρ and μ are negative, which results in a positive conductivity σ, just as in the case of positive charge carriers. It follows that $\mathbf{J}$ and $\mathbf{E}$ have the same direction regardless of the sign of the charge carriers. It is conventional to treat electrons moving to the left as positive charges moving to the right, and always to report ρ and μ as positive.

The relation $\mathbf{J} = \sigma \mathbf{E}$ is often referred to as the *point form of Ohm's law*. The factor σ takes into account the density of the electrons free to move (ρ) and the relative ease with which they move through the crystalline structure (μ). As might be expected, σ is a function of temperature.

Fig. 7-3

EXAMPLE 1. What electric field intensity and current density correspond to a drift velocity of 6.0×10^{-4} m/s in a silver conductor?

For silver $\sigma = 61.7$ MS/m and $\mu = 5.6 \times 10^{-3}$ m²/V · s.

$$E = \frac{U}{\mu} = \frac{6.0 \times 10^{-4}}{5.6 \times 10^{-3}} = 1.07 \times 10^{-1} \text{ V/m}$$

$$J = \sigma E = 6.61 \times 10^6 \text{ A /m}^2$$

7.5   Conductivity σ

In a liquid or gas there are generally present both positive and negative ions, some singly charged and others doubly charged, and possibly of different masses. A conductivity expression would include all such factors. However, if it is assumed that all the negative ions are alike and so too the positive ions, then the conductivity contains two terms as shown in Fig. 7-4 (*a*). In a metallic conductor, only the valence electrons are free to move. In Fig. 7-4(*b*) they are shown in motion to the left. The conductivity then contains only one term, the product of the charge density of the electrons free to move, ρ_e, and their mobility, μ_e.

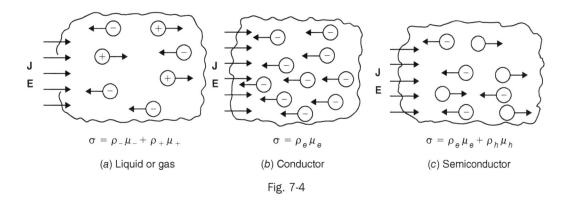

$\sigma = \rho_- \mu_- + \rho_+ \mu_+$ $\sigma = \rho_e \mu_e$ $\sigma = \rho_e \mu_e + \rho_h \mu_h$

(a) Liquid or gas   (b) Conductor   (c) Semiconductor

Fig. 7-4

A somewhat more complex conduction occurs in semiconductors such as germanium and silicon. In the crystal structure each atom has four covalent bonds with adjacent atoms. However, at room temperature, and upon influx of energy from some external source such as light, electrons can move out of the position called for by the covalent bonding. This creates an *electron-hole pair* available for conduction. Such materials are called *intrinsic* semiconductors. Electron-hole pairs have a short lifetime, disappearing by recombination. However, others are constantly being formed and at all times some are available for conduction. As shown in Fig. 7-4(*c*), the conductivity σ consists of two terms, one for the electrons and another for the holes. In practice, impurities, in the form of valence-three or valence-five elements, are added to create *p*-type and *n-type* semiconductor materials. The intrinsic behavior just described continues but is far overshadowed by the presence of extra electrons in *n*-type, or holes in *p*-type, materials. Then, in the conductivity σ, one of the densities, ρ_e or ρ_h, will far exceed the other.

EXAMPLE 2.   Determine the conductivity of intrinsic germanium at room temperature.

At 300 K there are 2.5×10^{19} electron-hole pairs per cubic meter. The electron mobility is $\mu_e = 0.38 \ \text{m}^2/\text{V} \cdot \text{s}$ and the hole mobility is $\mu_h = 0.18 \ \text{m}^2/\text{V} \cdot \text{s}$. Since the material is not doped, the numbers of electrons and holes are equal.

$$\sigma = N_e e(\mu_e + \mu_h) = (2.5 \times 10^{19})(1.6 \times 10^{-19})(0.38 + 0.18) = 2.24 \ \text{S/m}$$

7.6   Current *I*

Where current density **J** crosses a surface *S*, as in Fig. 7-5, the current *I* is obtained by integrating the dot product of **J** and *d***S**.

$$dI = \mathbf{J} \cdot d\mathbf{S} \qquad I = \int_S \mathbf{J} \cdot d\mathbf{S}$$

Of course, **J** need not be uniform over *S* and *S* need not be a plane surface.

Fig. 7-5

EXAMPLE 3.   Find the current in the circular wire shown in Fig. 7-6 if the current density is $\mathbf{J} = 15(1 - e^{-1000r}) \ \mathbf{a}_z \ (\text{A}/\text{m}^2)$. The radius of the wire is 2 mm.

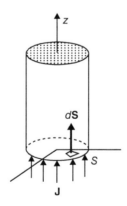

Fig. 7-6

A cross section of the wire is chosen for *S*. Then

$$dI = \mathbf{J} \cdot d\mathbf{S}$$
$$= 15(1 - e^{-1000r}) \mathbf{a}_z \cdot r \, dr \, d\phi \, \mathbf{a}_z$$

and

$$I = \int_0^{2\pi} \int_0^{0.002} 15(1 - e^{-1000r}) r \, dr \, d\phi$$
$$= 1.33 \times 10^{-4} \, \text{A} = 0.133 \ \text{mA}$$

Any surface S which has a perimeter that meets the outer surface of the conductor all the way around will have the same total current, $I = 0.133$ mA, crossing it.

7.7   Resistance *R*

If a conductor of uniform cross-sectional area A and length ℓ, as shown in Fig. 7-7, has a voltage difference V between its ends, then

$$E = \frac{V}{\ell} \quad \text{and} \quad J = \frac{\sigma V}{\ell}$$

assuming that the current is uniformly distributed over the area A. The total current is then

$$I = JA = \frac{\sigma A V}{\ell}$$

Since Ohm's law states that $V = IR$, the resistance is

$$R = \frac{\ell}{\sigma A} \quad (\Omega)$$

(Note that $1\ \mathrm{S}^{-1} = 1\ \Omega$; the siemens was formerly known as the *mho*.) This expression for resistance is generally applied to all conductors where the cross section remains constant over the length ℓ. However, if the current density is greater along the surface area of the conductor than in the center, then the expression is not valid. For such nonuniform current distributions the resistance is given by

$$R = \frac{V}{\displaystyle\int \mathbf{J} \cdot d\mathbf{S}} = \frac{V}{\displaystyle\int \sigma \mathbf{E} \cdot d\mathbf{S}}$$

If $\mathbf{E}$ is known rather than the voltage difference between the two faces, the resistance is given by

$$R = \frac{\displaystyle\int \mathbf{E} \cdot d\mathbf{l}}{\displaystyle\int \sigma \mathbf{E} \cdot d\mathbf{S}}$$

The numerator gives the voltage drop across the sample, while the denominator gives the total current I.

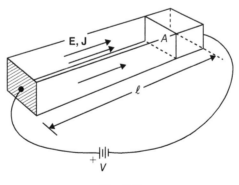

Fig. 7-7

EXAMPLE 4.   Find the resistance between the inner and outer curved surfaces of the block shown in Fig. 7-8, where the material is silver for which $\sigma = 6.17 \times 10^7$ S/m.
    If the same current I crosses both the inner and outer curved surfaces,

$$\mathbf{J} = \frac{k}{r}\mathbf{a}_r \quad \text{and} \quad \mathbf{E} = \frac{k}{\sigma r}\mathbf{a}_r$$

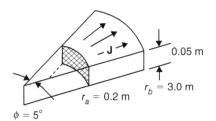

Fig. 7-8

Then ($5° = 0.0873$ rad),

$$R = \frac{\displaystyle\int_{0.2}^{3.0} \frac{k}{\sigma r}\, \mathbf{a}_r \cdot dr\, \mathbf{a}_r}{\displaystyle\int_0^{0.05}\int_0^{0.0873} \frac{k}{r}\, \mathbf{a}_r \cdot r\, d\phi\, dz\, \mathbf{a}_r}$$

$$= \frac{\ln 15}{\sigma(0,05)(0.0873)} = 1.01 \times 10^{-5}\,\Omega = 10.1\,\mu\Omega$$

7.8   Current Sheet Density K

At times current is confined to the surface of a conductor, such as the inside walls of a waveguide. For such a *current sheet* it is helpful to define the density vector **K** (in A/m), which gives the rate of charge transport per unit transverse length. (Some books use the notation $\mathbf{J}_s$.) Fig. 7-9 shows a total current of **I**, in the form of a cylindrical sheet of radius r, flowing in the positive z direction. In this case,

$$\mathbf{K} = \frac{1}{2\pi r}\, \mathbf{a}_z$$

at each point of the sheet. For other sheets, **K** might vary from point to point.

Fig. 7-9

In general, the current flowing through a contour C within a current sheet is obtained by integrating the *normal* component of **K** along the contour.

$$I = \int_C K_n\, d\ell$$

EXAMPLE 5.   A thin conducting sheet lies in the $z = 0$ plane for $0 < x < 0.05$ m. An $\mathbf{a}_y$ directed current of 25 A is sinusoidally distributed across the sheet, with linear density zero for $x = 0$ and $x = 0.05$ m and maximum at $x = 0.025$ m (see Fig. 7-10). Obtain an expression for **K**.

The data give $\mathbf{K} = (k \sin 20\pi x)\mathbf{a}_y$ (A/m), for an unknown constant k. Then

$$I = 25 = \int K_y\, dx = k\int_0^{0.05} \sin 20\pi x\, dx$$

or

$$25 = k/10\pi \quad \text{or} \quad k = 250\pi \text{ A/m}.$$

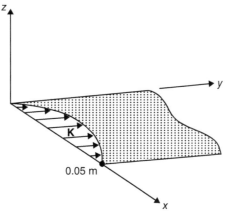

Fig. 7-10

7.9 Continuity of Current

Current I crossing a general surface S has been examined where $\mathbf{J}$ at the surface was known. Now, if the surface is *closed*, in order for net current to come out, there must be a decrease of positive charge within:

$$\oint \mathbf{J} \cdot d\mathbf{S} = I = -\frac{dQ}{dt} = -\frac{\partial}{\partial t} \int \rho \, dv$$

where the unit normal in $d\mathbf{S}$ is the outward-directed normal. Dividing by Δv,

$$\frac{\oint \mathbf{J} \cdot d\mathbf{S}}{\Delta v} = -\frac{\partial}{\partial t} \frac{\int \rho \, dv}{\Delta v}$$

As $\Delta v \to 0$, the left side by definition approaches $\nabla \cdot \mathbf{J}$, the divergence of the current density, while the right side approaches $-\partial \rho / \partial t$. Thus,

$$\nabla \cdot \mathbf{J} = -\frac{\partial \rho}{\partial t}$$

This is the *equation of continuity* for current. In it ρ stands for the *net charge* density, not just the density of mobile charge. As will be shown below, $\partial \rho / \partial t$ can be nonzero within a conductor only transiently. Then the continuity equation, $\nabla \cdot \mathbf{J} = 0$, becomes the field equivalent of Kirchhoff's current law, which states that the net current leaving a junction of several conductors is zero.

   In the process of conduction, valence electrons are free to move upon the application of an electric field. So, to the extent that these electrons are in motion, static conditions no longer exist. However, these electrons should not be confused with *net charge,* for each conduction electron is balanced by a proton in the nucleus such that there is zero net charge in every Δv of the material. Suppose, however, that through a temporary imbalance a region within a solid conductor has a *net* charge density ρ_0 at time $t = 0$. Then, since $\mathbf{J} = \sigma \mathbf{E} = (\sigma/\epsilon)\mathbf{D}$,

$$\nabla \cdot \frac{\sigma}{\epsilon} \mathbf{D} = -\frac{\partial \rho}{\partial t}$$

Now, the divergence operation consists of partial derivatives with respect to the spatial coordinates. If σ and ϵ are constants, as they would be in a homogeneous sample, then they may be removed from the partial derivatives.

$$\frac{\sigma}{\epsilon} (\nabla \cdot \mathbf{D}) = -\frac{\partial \rho}{\partial t}$$

$$\frac{\sigma}{\epsilon} \rho = -\frac{\partial \rho}{\partial t}$$

or

$$\frac{\partial \rho}{\partial t} + \frac{\sigma}{\epsilon} \rho = 0$$

The solution to this equation is

$$\rho = \rho_0 e^{-(\sigma/\epsilon)t}$$

Thus, ρ decays exponentially, with a *time constant* $\tau = \epsilon/\sigma$, also known as the *relaxation time*. At $t = \tau$, ρ has decayed to 36.8% of its initial value. For a conductor τ is extremely small, on the order of 10^{-19} seconds. This confirms that *free charge* cannot remain within a conductor and instead is distributed evenly over the conductor surface.

EXAMPLE 6.   Determine the relaxation time for silver, given that $\sigma = 6.17 \times 10^7$ S/m. If charge of density ρ_0 is placed within a silver block, find ρ after one, and also after five, time constants.

Since $\epsilon \approx \epsilon_0$,

$$\tau = \frac{\epsilon}{\sigma} = \frac{10^{-9}36\pi}{6.17 \times 10^7} = 1.43 \times 10^{-19}\,\text{s}$$

Therefore,

$$\text{at}\quad t = \tau: \qquad \rho = \rho_0 e^{-1} = 0.368\rho_0$$

$$\text{at}\quad t = 5\tau: \qquad \rho = \rho_0 e^{-5} = 6.74 \times 10^{-3}\rho_0$$

7.10 Conductor-Dielectric Boundary Conditions

Under static conditions all net charge will be on the outer surfaces of a conductor and both **E** and **D** are therefore zero within the conductor. Because the electric field is a conservative field, the line integral of $\mathbf{E} \cdot d\mathbf{l}$ is zero for any closed path. A rectangular path with corners *1, 2, 3, 4* is shown in Fig. 7-11. For this path,

$$\int_1^2 \mathbf{E} \cdot d\mathbf{l} + \int_2^3 \mathbf{E} \cdot d\mathbf{l} + \int_3^4 \mathbf{E} \cdot d\mathbf{l} + \int_4^1 \mathbf{E} \cdot d\mathbf{l} = 0$$

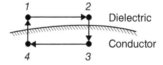

Fig. 7-11

If the path lengths *2* to *3* and *4* to *1* are now permitted to approach zero, keeping the interface between them, then the second and fourth integrals are zero. The path from *3* to *4* is within the conductor where **E** must be zero. This leaves

$$\int_1^2 \mathbf{E} \cdot d\mathbf{l} = \int_1^2 E_t\, d\ell = 0$$

where E_t is the tangential component of **E** at the surface of the dielectric. Since the interval *1* to *2* can be chosen arbitrarily,

$$E_t = D_t = 0$$

at each point of the surface.

To discover the conditions on the normal components, a small, closed, right circular cylinder is placed across the interface as shown in Fig. 7-12. Gauss's law applied to this surface gives

$$\oint \mathbf{D} \cdot d\mathbf{S} = Q_{\text{enc}}$$

or

$$\int_{\text{top}} \mathbf{D} \cdot d\mathbf{S} + \int_{\text{bottom}} \mathbf{D} \cdot d\mathbf{S} + \int_{\text{side}} \mathbf{D} \cdot d\mathbf{S} = \int_A \rho_s\, dS$$

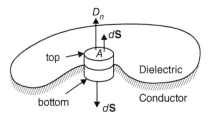

Fig. 7-12

The third integral is zero since, as just determined, $D_t = 0$ on either side of the interface. The second integral is also zero, since the bottom of the cylinder is within the conductor, where **D** and **E** are zero. Then,

$$\int_{top} \mathbf{D} \cdot d\mathbf{S} = \int_{top} D_n \, dS = \oint_A \rho_s \, dS$$

which can hold only if

$$D_n = \rho_s \quad \text{and} \quad E_n = \frac{\rho_s}{\epsilon}$$

EXAMPLE 7. The electric field intensity at a point on the surface of a conductor is given by $\mathbf{E} = 0.2\mathbf{a}_x - 0.3\mathbf{a}_y - 0.2\mathbf{a}_z$ (V/m). Find the surface charge density at the point.

Supposing the conductor to be surrounded by free space,

$$D_n = \epsilon_o E_n = \rho_s$$
$$E_n = \pm|\mathbf{E}| = \pm 0.412 \text{ V/m}$$
$$\rho_s = \left(\frac{10^{-9}}{36\pi}\right)(\pm 0.412) = \pm 3.64 \text{ pC/m}^2$$

The ambiguity in sign arises from that in the direction of the outer normal to the surface at the given point.

In short, under static conditions the field just outside a conductor is zero (both tangential and normal components) unless there exists a surface charge distribution. A surface charge does not imply a *net* charge in the conductor, however. To illustrate this, consider a positive charge at the origin of spherical coordinates. Now if this point charge is enclosed by an *uncharged* conducting spherical shell of finite thickness, as shown in Fig. 7-13(*a*), then the field is still given by

$$\mathbf{E} = \frac{+Q}{4\pi\epsilon r^2}\mathbf{a}_r$$

except within the conductor itself, where **E** must be zero. The coulomb forces caused by $+Q$ attract the conduction electrons to the inner surface, where they create a ρ_{s1} of negative sign. Then the deficiency of electrons on the outer surface constitutes a positive surface charge density ρ_{s2}. The electric flux lines Ψ, leaving the point charge $+Q$, terminate at the electrons on the inner surface of the conductor, as shown in Fig. 7-13(*b*). Then electric flux lines Ψ originate once again on the positive charges on the outer surface of the conductor. It should be noted that the flux does not pass through the conductor and the *net* charge on the conductor remains zero.

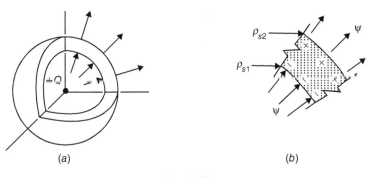

(a)   (b)

Fig. 7-13

SOLVED PROBLEMS

7.1. An AWG #12 copper conductor has an 80.8-mil diameter. A 50-foot long conductor of this type carries a current of 20 A. Find the electric field intensity E, drift velocity U, the voltage drop, and the resistance for the 50-foot length.

Since a mil is $\frac{1}{1000}$ inch, the cross-sectional area is

$$A = \pi \left[\left(\frac{0.0808 \text{ in}}{2} \right) \left(\frac{2.54 \times 10^{-2} \text{ m}}{1 \text{ in}} \right) \right]^2 = 3.31 \times 10^{-6} \text{ m}^2$$

Then

$$J = \frac{1}{A} = \frac{20}{3.31 \times 10^{-6}} = 6.04 \times 10^6 \text{ A/m}^2$$

For copper, $\sigma = 5.8 \times 10^7$ S/m. Then

$$E = \frac{J}{\sigma} = \frac{6.04 \times 10^6}{5.8 \times 10^7} = 1.04 \times 10^{-1} \text{ V/m}$$

$$V = E\ell = (1.04 \times 10^{-1})(50)(12)(0.0254) = 1.59 \text{ V}$$

$$R = \frac{V}{I} = \frac{1.59}{20} = 7.95 \times 10^{-2} \text{ } \Omega$$

The electron mobility in copper is $\mu = 0.0032$ m²/V · s, and since $\sigma = \rho\mu$, the charge density is

$$\rho = \frac{\sigma}{\mu} = \frac{5.8 \times 10^7}{0.0032} = 1.81 \times 10^{10} \text{ C/m}^3$$

From $J = \rho U$ the drift velocity is now found as

$$U = \frac{J}{\rho} = \frac{6.05 \times 10^6}{1.81 \times 10^{10}} = 3.34 \times 10^{-4} \text{ m/s}$$

With this drift velocity, an electron takes approximately 30 seconds to move a distance of 1 centimeter in the #12 copper conductor.

7.2. What current density and electric field intensity correspond to a drift velocity of 5.3×10^{-4} m/s in aluminum?

For aluminum, the conductivity is $\sigma = 3.82 \times 10^7$ S/m and the mobility is $\mu = 0.0014$ m²/V · s.

$$J = \rho U = \frac{\sigma}{\mu} U = \frac{3.83 \times 10^7}{0.0014} (5.3 \times 10^{-4}) = 1.45 \times 10^7 \text{ A/m}^2$$

$$E = \frac{J}{\sigma} = \frac{U}{\mu} = 3.79 \times 10^{-1} \text{ V/m}$$

7.3. A long copper conductor has a circular cross section of diameter 3.0 mm and carries a current of 10 A. Each second, what percent of the conduction electrons must leave (to be replaced by others) a 100-mm length?

Avogadro's number is $N = 6.02 \times 10^{26}$ atoms/kmol. The specific gravity of copper is 8.96 and the atomic weight is 63.54. Assuming one conduction electron per atom, the number of electrons per unit volume is

$$N_e = \left(6.02 \times 10^{26} \frac{\text{atoms}}{\text{kmol}} \right) \left(\frac{1 \text{ kmol}}{63.54 \text{ kg}} \right) \left(8.96 \times 10^3 \frac{\text{kg}}{\text{m}^3} \right) \left(1 \frac{\text{electron}}{\text{atom}} \right)$$

$$= 8.49 \times 10^{28} \text{ electrons/m}^3$$

The number of electrons in a 100 mm length is

$$N = \pi \left(\frac{3 \times 10^{-3}}{2} \right)^2 (0.100)(8.49 \times 10^{28}) = 6.00 \times 10^{22}$$

A 10-A current requires that

$$\left(10 \frac{C}{s} \right) \left(\frac{1}{1.6 \times 10^{-19}} \frac{electron}{C} \right) = 6.25 \times 10^{19} \, electrons/s$$

pass a fixed point. Then the percent leaving the 100 mm length per second is

$$\frac{6.25 \times 10^{19}}{6.00 \times 10^{22}} (100) = 0.104\%$$

7.4. What current would result if all the conduction electrons in a 1-centimeter cube of aluminum passed a specified point in 2.0s? Assume one conduction electron per atom.

The density of aluminum is 2.70×10^3 kg/m^3 and the atomic weight is 26.98 kg/kmol. Then

$$N_e = (6.02 \times 10^{26}) \left(\frac{1}{26.98} \right) (2.70 \times 10^3) = 6.02 \times 10^{28} \, electrons/m^3$$

and

$$I = \frac{\Delta Q}{\Delta t} = \frac{(6.02 \times 10^{28} \, electrons/m^3)(10^{-2} m)^3 (1.6 \times 10^{-19} C/electron)}{2s} = 4.82 \, kA$$

7.5. What is the density of free electrons in a metal for a mobility of 0.0046 m^2/V · s and a conductivity of 29.1 MS/m?

Since $\sigma = \mu \rho$,

$$\rho = \frac{\sigma}{\mu} = \frac{29.1 \times 10^6}{0.0046} = 6.33 \times 10^9 \, C/m^3$$

and

$$N_e = \frac{6.33 \times 10^9}{1.6 \times 10^{-19}} = 3.96 \times 10^{28} \, electrons/m^3$$

7.6. Find the conductivity of *n*-type germanium (Ge) at 300 K, assuming one donor atom in each 10^8 atoms. The density of Ge is 5.32×10^3 kg/m^3 and the atomic weight is 72.6 kg/kmol.

The carriers in an *n*-type semiconductor material are electrons. Since 1 kmol of a substance contains 6.02×10^{26} atoms, the carrier density is given by

$$N_e = \left(6.02 \times 10^{26} \frac{atoms}{kmol} \right) \left(\frac{1 \, kmol}{72.6 \, kg} \right) \left(5.32 \times 10^3 \frac{kg}{m^3} \right) \left(\frac{electrons}{10^8 \, atoms} \right)$$
$$= 4.41 \times 10^{20} \, electrons/m^3$$

The intrinsic concentration n_i for Ge at 300 K is 2.5×10^{19} m^{-3}. The *mass-action law*, $N_e N_h = n_i^2$, then gives the density of holes:

$$N_h = \frac{(2.5 \times 10^{19})^2}{4.41 \times 10^{20}} = 1.42 \times 10^{18} \, holes/m^3$$

Because $N_e \gg N_h$, conductivity will be controlled by the donated electrons, whose mobility at 300 K is

$$\sigma \approx N_e e \mu_e = (4.41 \times 10^{20})(1.6 \times 10^{-19})(0.38) = 26.8 \, S/m$$

7.7. A conductor of uniform cross section and 150 m long has a voltage drop of 1.3 V and a current density of 4.65×10^5 A/m^2. What is the conductivity of the material in the conductor?

Since $E = V/\ell$ and $J = \sigma E$,

$$4.65 \times 10^5 = \sigma \left(\frac{1.3}{150} \right) \quad \text{or} \quad \sigma = 5.37 \times 10^7 \text{ S/m}$$

7.8. A table of resistivities gives 10.4 ohm · circular mils per foot for annealed copper. What is the corresponding conductivity in siemens per meter?

A *circular mil* is the area of a circle with a diameter of one mil (10^{-3} in).

$$1 \text{ cir mil} = \pi \left[\left(\frac{10^{-3} \text{in}}{2} \right) \left(0.0254 \frac{\text{m}}{\text{in}} \right) \right]^2 = 5.07 \times 10^{-10} \text{ m}^2$$

The conductivity is the reciprocal of the resistivity.

$$\sigma = \left(\frac{1}{10.4} \frac{\text{ft}}{\Omega \cdot \text{cir mil}} \right) \left(12 \frac{\text{in}}{\text{ft}} \right) \left(0.0254 \frac{\text{m}}{\text{in}} \right) \left(\frac{1 \text{ cir mil}}{5.07 \times 10^{-10} \text{m}^2} \right) = 5.78 \times 10^7 \text{ S/m}$$

7.9. An AWG #20 aluminum wire has a resistance of 16.7 ohms per 1000 feet. What conductivity does this imply for aluminum?

From wire tables, a #20 wire has a diameter of 32 mils.

$$A = \pi \left[\frac{32 \times 10^{-3}}{2} (0.0254) \right]^2 = 5.19 \times 10^{-7} \text{ m}^2$$

$$\ell = (1000 \text{ ft})(12 \text{ in/ft})(0.0254 \text{ m/in}) = 3.05 \times 10^2 \text{ m}$$

Then from $R = \ell/\sigma A$,

$$\sigma = \frac{3.05 \times 10^2}{(16.7)(5.19 \times 10^{-7})} = 35.2 \text{ MS/m}$$

7.10. In a cylindrical conductor of radius 2 mm, the current density varies with the distance from the axis according to

$$J = 10^3 e^{-400r} \text{ (A/m}^2)$$

Find the total current I.

$$I = \int \mathbf{J} \cdot d\mathbf{S} = \int J \, dS = \int_0^{2\pi} \int_0^{0.002} 10^3 e^{-400r} r \, dr \, d\phi$$

$$= 2\pi(10^3) \left[\frac{e^{-400r}}{(-400)^2} (-400r - 1) \right]_0^{0.002} = 7.51 \text{ mA}$$

7.11. Find the current crossing the portion of the $y = 0$ plane defined by $-0.1 \le x \le 0.1$ m and $-0.002 \le z \le 0.002$ m if

$$\mathbf{J} = 10^2 |x| \mathbf{a}_y \quad \text{(A/m}^2)$$

$$I = \int \mathbf{J} \cdot d\mathbf{S} = \int_{-0.002}^{0.002} \int_{-0.1}^{0.1} 10^2 |x| \mathbf{a}_y \cdot dx \, dz \mathbf{a}_y = 4 \text{ mA}$$

7.12. Find the current crossing the portion of the $x = 0$ plane defined by $-\pi/4 \le y \le \pi/4$ m and $-0.01 \le z \le 0.01$ m if

$$\mathbf{J} = 100 \cos 2y \, \mathbf{a}_x \quad \text{(A/m}^2)$$

$$I = \int \mathbf{J} \cdot d\mathbf{S} = \int_{-0.01}^{0.01} \int_{-\pi/4}^{\pi/4} 100 \cos 2y \, \mathbf{a}_x \cdot dy \, dz \mathbf{a}_x = 2.0 \text{ A}$$

7.13. Given $\mathbf{J} = 10^3 \sin \theta \mathbf{a}_r$ A/m² in spherical coordinates, find the current crossing the spherical shell $r = 0.02$ m.

Since $\mathbf{J}$ and

$$dS = r^2 \sin \theta \, d\theta \, d\phi \, \mathbf{a}_r$$

are radial,

$$I = \int_0^{2\pi} \int_0^{\pi} 10^3 (0.02)^2 \sin^2 \theta \, d\theta \, d\phi = 3.95 \text{ A}$$

7.14. Show that the resistance of any conductor of constant cross-sectional area A and length ℓ is given by $R = \ell/\sigma A$, assuming uniform current distribution.

A constant cross section along the length ℓ results in constant E, and the voltage drop is

$$V = \int \mathbf{E} \cdot d\mathbf{l} = E\ell$$

If the current is uniformly distributed over the area A,

$$I = \int \mathbf{J} \cdot d\mathbf{S} = JA = \sigma E A$$

where σ is the conductivity. Then, since $R = V/I$,

$$R = \frac{\ell}{\sigma A}$$

7.15. Determine the resistance of the insulation in a length ℓ of coaxial cable, as shown in Fig. 7-14.

Fig. 7-14

Assume a total current I from the inner conductor to the outer conductor. Then, at a radial distance r,

$$J = \frac{I}{A} = \frac{I}{2\pi r \ell}$$

and so

$$E = \frac{I}{2\pi \sigma r \ell}$$

The voltage difference between the conductors is then

$$V_{ab} = -\int_b^a \frac{I}{2\pi \sigma r \ell} \, dr = \frac{I}{2\pi \sigma \ell} \ln \frac{b}{a}$$

and the resistance is

$$R = \frac{V}{I} = \frac{I}{2\pi \sigma r \ell} \ln \frac{b}{a}$$

7.16. A current sheet of width 4 m lies in the $z = 0$ plane and contains a total current of 10 A in a direction from the origin to (1, 3, 0) m. Find an expression for $\mathbf{K}$.

At each point of the sheet, the direction of $\mathbf{K}$ is the unit vector

$$\frac{\mathbf{a}_x + 3\mathbf{a}_y}{\sqrt{10}}$$

and the magnitude of **K** is $\frac{10}{4}$ A /m. Thus,

$$\mathbf{K} = \frac{10}{4}\left(\frac{\mathbf{a}_x + 3\mathbf{a}_y}{\sqrt{10}}\right) \text{A/m}$$

7.17. As shown in Fig. 7-15, a current I_T follows a filament down the z axis and enters a thin conducting sheet at $z = 0$. Express **K** for this sheet.

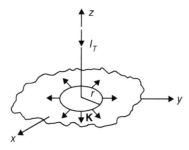

Fig. 7-15

Consider a circle in the $z = 0$ plane. The current I_T on the sheet spreads out uniformly over the circumference $2\pi r$. The direction of **K** is $\mathbf{a}_r$. Then

$$\mathbf{K} = \frac{I_T}{2\pi r}\mathbf{a}_r$$

7.18. For the current sheet of Problem 7.17 find the current in a 30° section of the plane (Fig. 7-16).

$$I = \int K_n \, d\ell = \int_0^{\pi/6} \frac{I_T}{2\pi r} r \, d\phi = \frac{I_T}{12}$$

Fig. 7-16

However, integration is not necessary, since for uniformly distributed current a 30° segment will contain 30°/360°, or 1/12 of the total.

7.19. A current I(A) enters a thin right circular cylinder at the top, as shown in Fig. 7-17. Express **K** if the radius of the cylinder is 2 cm.

Fig. 7-17

On the top, the current is uniformly distributed over any circumference $2\pi r$, so that

$$\mathbf{K} = \frac{I}{2\pi r}\mathbf{a}_r \quad (\mathrm{A/m})$$

Down the side, the current is uniformly distributed over the circumference $2\pi\,(0.02\ \mathrm{m})$, so that

$$\mathbf{K} = \frac{I}{0.04\pi}(-\mathbf{a}_z) \quad (\mathrm{A/m})$$

7.20. A cylindrical conductor of radius 0.05 m with its axis along the z axis has a surface charge density $\rho_s = \rho_0/z$ (C/m²). Write an expression for **E** at the surface.

Since $D_n = \rho_s$, $E_n = \rho_s/\epsilon_0$. At $(0.05, \phi, z)$,

$$\mathbf{E} = E_n\mathbf{a}_r = \frac{\rho_0}{\epsilon_0 z}\mathbf{a}_r \quad (\mathrm{V/m})$$

7.21. A conductor occupying the region $x \geq 5$ has a surface charge density

$$\rho_s = \frac{\rho_0}{\sqrt{y^2 + z^2}}$$

Write expressions for **E** and **D** just outside the conductor.

The outer normal is $-\mathbf{a}_x$. Then, just outside the conductor,

$$\mathbf{D} = D_n(-\mathbf{a}_x) = \rho_s(-\mathbf{a}_x) = \frac{\rho_0}{\sqrt{y^2 + z^2}}(-\mathbf{a}_x)$$

and

$$\mathbf{E} = \frac{\rho_0}{\epsilon_0\sqrt{y^2 + z^2}}(-\mathbf{a}_x)$$

7.22. Two concentric cylindrical conductors, $r_a = 0.01$ m and $r_b = 0.08$ m, have charge densities $\rho_{sa} = 40$ pC/m² and ρ_{sb}, such that **D** and **E** fields exist between the two cylinders but are zero elsewhere. See Fig. 7-18. Find ρ_{sb} and write expressions for **D** and **E** between the cylinders.

Fig. 7-18

By symmetry, the field between the cylinders must be radial and a function of r only. Then, for $r_a < r < r_b$,

$$\nabla \cdot \mathbf{D} = \frac{1}{r}\frac{d}{dr}(rD_r) = 0 \quad \text{or} \quad rD_r = c$$

To evaluate the constant c, use the fact that $D_n = D_r = \rho_{sa}$ at $r = r_a + 0$.

$$c = (0.01)(40 \times 10^{-12}) = 4 \times 10^{-13}\ \mathrm{C/m}$$

and so

$$\mathbf{D} = \frac{4 \times 10^{-13}}{r} \, \mathbf{a}_r \, (\mathrm{C/m^2}) \qquad \text{and} \qquad \mathbf{E} = \frac{\mathbf{D}}{\epsilon_0} = \frac{4.52 \times 10^{-2}}{r} \, \mathbf{a}_r \, (\mathrm{V/m})$$

The density ρ_{sb} is now found from

$$\rho_{sb} = D_n\big|_{r=r_b-0} = -D_r\big|_{r=r_b-0} = -\frac{4 \times 10^{-13}}{0.08} = -5 \, \mathrm{pC/m^2}$$

SUPPLEMENTARY PROBLEMS

7.23. Find the mobility of the conduction electrons in aluminum, given a conductivity 38.2 MS/m and conduction electron density 1.70×10^{29} m^{-3}.

7.24. Repeat Problem 7.23 (*a*) for copper, where $\sigma = 58.0$ MS/m and $N_e = 1.13 \times 10^{29}$ m^{-3}; (*b*) for silver, where $\sigma = 61.7$ MS/m and $N_e = 7.44 \times 10^{28}$ m^{-3}.

7.25. Find the concentration of holes, N_h, in *p*-type germanium, where $\sigma = 10^4$ S/m and the hole mobility is $\mu_h = 0.18$ m^2/V · s.

7.26. Using the data of Problem 7.25, find the concentration of electrons, N_e, if the intrinsic concentration is $n_i = 2.5 \times 10^{19}$ m^{-3}.

7.27. Find the electron and hole concentrations in *n*-type silicon for which $\sigma = 10.0$ S/m, $\mu_e = 0.13$ m^2/V · s, and $n_i = 1.5 \times 10^{16}$ m^{-3}.

7.28. Determine the number of conduction electrons in a 1-meter cube of tungsten, of which the density is 18.8×10^3 kg/m^3 and the atomic weight is 184.0. Assume two conduction electrons per atom.

7.29. Find the number of conduction electrons in a 1-meter cube of copper if $\sigma = 58$ MS/m and $\mu = 3.2 \times 10^{-3}$ m^2/ V · s. On the average, how many electrons is this per atom? The atomic weight is 63.54 and the density is 8.96×10^3 kg/m^3.

7.30. A copper bar of rectangular cross section 0.02 m by 0.08 m and length 2.0 m has a voltage drop of 50 mV. Find the resistance, current, current density, electric field intensity, and conduction electron drift velocity.

7.31. An aluminum bus bar 0.01 m by 0.07 m in cross section and of length 3 m carries a current of 300 A. Find the electric field intensity, current density, and conduction electron drift velocity.

7.32. A wire table gives for AWG #20 copper wire at 20°C the resistance 33.31 Ω/km. What conductivity (in S/m) does this imply for copper? The diameter of AWG #20 is 32 mils.

7.33. A wire table gives for AWG #18 platinum wire the resistance 1.21×10^{-3} Ω/cm. What conductivity (in S/m) does this imply for platinum? The diameter of AWG #18 is 40 mils.

7.34. What is the conductivity of AWG #32 tungsten wire with a resistance of 0.0172 Ω/cm? The diameter of AWG #32 is 8.0 mils.

7.35. Determine the resistance per meter of a hollow cylindrical aluminum conductor with an outer diameter of 32 mm and wall thickness of 6 mm.

7.36. Find the resistance of an aluminum foil 1.0 mil thick and 5.0 cm square (*a*) between opposite edges on a square face, (*b*) between the two square faces.

7.37. Find the resistance of 100 ft of AWG #4/0 conductor in both copper and aluminum. An AWG #4/0 has a diameter of 460 mils.

7.38. Determine the resistance of a copper conductor 2 m long with a circular cross section and a radius of 1 mm at one end increasing linearly to a radius of 5 mm at the other.

7.39. Determine the resistance of a copper conductor 1 m long with a square cross section and a side 1 mm at one end increasing linearly to 3 mm at the other.

7.40. Develop an expression for the resistance of a conductor of length ℓ if the cross section retains the same shape and the area increases linearly from A to kA over ℓ.

7.41. Find the current density in an AWG #12 conductor when it is carrying its rated current of 30 A. A #12 wire has a diameter of 81 mils.

7.42. Find the total current in a circular conductor of radius 2 mm if the current density varies with r according to $J = 10^3/r$ (A/m²).

7.43. In cylindrical coordinates, $\mathbf{J} = 10e^{-100r}\mathbf{a}_\phi$ (A/m²) for the region $0.01 \le r \le 0.02$ m, $0 < z \le 1$ m. Find the total current crossing the intersection of this region with the plane $\phi = $ const.

7.44. Given a current density

$$\mathbf{J} = \left(\frac{10^3}{r^2} \cos\theta\right)\mathbf{a}_\theta \quad (\text{A/m}^2)$$

in spherical coordinates, find the current crossing the conical strip $\theta = \pi/4$, $0.001 \le r \le 0.080$ m.

7.45. Find the total current directed outward from a 1-meter cube with one corner at the origin and edges parallel to the coordinate axes if $\mathbf{J} = 2x^2\mathbf{a}_x + 2xy^3\mathbf{a}_y + 2xy\mathbf{a}_z$ (A/m²).

7.46. As shown in Fig. 7-19, a current of 50 A passes down the z axis, enters a thin spherical shell of radius 0.03 m, and at $\theta = \pi/2$ enters a plane sheet. Write expressions for the current sheet densities $\mathbf{K}$ in the spherical shell and in the plane.

Fig. 7-19

7.47. A filamentary current of I(A) passes down the z axis to $z = 5 \times 10^{-2}$ m, where it enters the portion $0 \le \phi \le \pi/4$ of a spherical shell of radius 5×10^{-2} m. Find $\mathbf{K}$ for this current sheet.

7.48. A current sheet of density $\mathbf{K} = 20\mathbf{a}_z$ (A/m) lies in the plane $x = 0$ and a current density $\mathbf{J} = 10\,\mathbf{a}_z$ (A/m²) also exists throughout space. (*a*) Find the current crossing the area enclosed by a circle of radius 0.5 m centered at the origin in the $z = 0$ plane. (*b*) Find the current crossing the square $|x| \le 0.25$ m, $|y| \le 0.25$ m, $z = 0$.

7.49. A hollow, thin-walled, rectangular conductor 0.01 m by 0.02 m carries a current of 10 A in the positive x direction. Express $\mathbf{K}$.

7.50. A solid conductor has a surface described by $x + y = 3$ m and extends toward the origin. At the surface the electric field intensity is 0.35 (V/m). Express $\mathbf{E}$ and $\mathbf{D}$ at the surface and find ρ_s.

7.51. A conductor that extends into the region $z < 0$ has one face in the plane $z = 0$, over which there is a surface charge density

$$\rho_s = 5 \times 10^{-10}e^{-10r}\sin^2\phi \quad (\text{C/m}^2)$$

in cylindrical coordinates. Find the electric field intensity at $(0.15\text{ m}, \pi/3, 0)$.

7.52. A spherical conductor centered at the origin and of radius 3 has a surface charge density $\rho_s = \rho_0 \cos^2\theta$. Find $\mathbf{E}$ at the surface.

7.53. The electric field intensity at a point on a conductor surface is given by $\mathbf{E} = 0.2\mathbf{a}_x - 0.3\mathbf{a}_y - 0.2\mathbf{a}_z$ (V/m). What is the surface charge density at the point?

7.54. A spherical conductor centered at the origin has an electric field intensity at its surface $\mathbf{E} = 0.53(\sin^2 \phi)\mathbf{a}_r$ (V/m) in spherical coordinates. What is the charge density where the sphere meets the y axis?

ANSWERS TO SUPPLEMENTARY PROBLEMS

7.23. 1.40×10^{-3} m²/V · s

7.24. (a) 3.21×10^{-3} m²/V · s;
   (b) 5.18×10^{-3} m²/V · s

7.25. 3.47×10^{23} m⁻³

7.26. 1.80×10^{15} m⁻³

7.27. 4.81×10^{20} m⁻³, 4.68×10^{11} m⁻³

7.28. 1.23×10^{29}

7.29. 1.13×10^{29}, 1.33

7.30. 21.6 $\mu\Omega$, 2.32 kA, 1.45 MA/m²,
   25 mV/m, 0.08 mm/s

7.31. 1.12×10^{-2} V/m, 4.28×10^{5} A/m²,
   1.57×10^{-5} m/s

7.32. 5.8×10^{7} S/m

7.33. 1.00×10^{7} S/m

7.34. 17.9 MS/m

7.35. 53.4 $\mu\Omega$/m

7.36. (a)   1.03 mΩ;   (b)   266 pΩ

7.37. 4.91 mΩ, 7.46 mΩ

7.38. 2.20 mΩ

7.39. 5.75 mΩ

7.40. $\dfrac{\ell}{\sigma A}\left(\dfrac{\ln k}{k-1}\right)$

7.41. 9.09×10^{6} A/m²

7.42. 4π A

7.43. 2.33×10^{-2} A

7.44. 1.38×10^{4} A

7.45. 3.0 A

7.46. $\dfrac{265}{\sin \theta}\mathbf{a}_\theta$ (A/m), $\dfrac{7.96}{r}\mathbf{a}_r$ (A/m)

7.47. $\dfrac{80I}{\pi \sin \theta}\mathbf{a}_\theta$ (A/m)

7.48. (a)   27.9 A;   (b)   12.5 A

7.49. $167\mathbf{a}_x$ A/m

7.50. $\pm 0.247(\mathbf{a}_x + \mathbf{a}_y)$ V/m, $\pm 2.19 \times 10^{-12}(\mathbf{a}_x + \mathbf{a}_y)$ C/m²,
   $\pm 3.10 \times 10^{-12}$ C/m²

7.51. $9.45\mathbf{a}_z$ V/m

7.52. $\dfrac{\rho_0}{\epsilon_0} \cos^2 \theta\, \mathbf{a}_r$

7.53. ± 3.65 pC/m²

7.54. 4.69 pC/m²

CHAPTER 8

Capacitance and Dielectric Materials

8.1 Polarization P and Relative Permittivity ϵ_r

Dielectric materials become *polarized* in an electric field, with the result that the electric flux density **D** is greater than it would be under free-space conditions with the same field intensity. A simplified but satisfactory theory of polarization can be obtained by treating an atom of the dielectric as two superimposed positive and negative charge regions, as shown in Fig. 8-1(*a*). Upon application of an **E** field, the positive charge region moves in the direction of the applied field and the negative charge region moves in the opposite direction. This displacement can be represented by an *electric dipole moment*, **p** = Q**d**, as shown in Fig. 8-1(*c*).

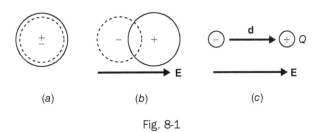

(*a*)   (*b*)   (*c*)

Fig. 8-1

For most materials, the charge regions will return to their original superimposed positions when the applied field is removed. As with a spring obeying Hooke's law, the work done in the distortion is recoverable when the system is permitted to go back to its original state. Energy storage takes place in this distortion in the same manner as with the spring.

A region Δv of a polarized dielectric will contain N dipole moments **p**. Polarization **P** is defined as the dipole moment per unit volume:

$$\mathbf{P} = \lim_{\Delta v \to 0} \frac{N\mathbf{p}}{\Delta v} \quad (\text{C/m}^2)$$

This suggests a smooth and continuous distribution of electric dipole moments throughout the volume, which, of course, is not the case. In the macroscopic view, however, polarization **P** can account for the increase in the electric flux density, the equation being

$$\mathbf{D} = \epsilon_0 \mathbf{E} + \mathbf{P}$$

This equation permits **E** and **P** to have different directions, as they do in certain crystalline dielectrics. In an isotropic, linear material, **E** and **P** are parallel at each point, which is expressed by

$$\mathbf{P} = \chi_e \epsilon_0 \mathbf{E} \quad \text{(isotropic material)}$$

where the *electric susceptibility* χ_e is a dimensionless constant. Then,

$$\mathbf{D} = \epsilon_0 (1 + \chi_e)\mathbf{E} = \epsilon_0 \epsilon_r \mathbf{E} \quad \text{(isotropic material)}$$

where $\epsilon_r \equiv 1 + \chi_e$ is also a pure number. Since $\mathbf{D} = \epsilon \mathbf{E}$ (Section 4.4),

$$\epsilon_r = \frac{\epsilon}{\epsilon_0}$$

whence ϵ_r is called the *relative permittivity*. (Compare Section 1.6.)

EXAMPLE 1.   Find the magnitudes of **D** and **P** for a dielectric material in which $E = 0.15$ MV/m and $\chi_e = 4.25$. Since $\epsilon_r = \chi_e + 1 = 5.25$,

$$D = \epsilon_0 \epsilon_r E = \frac{10^{-9}}{36\pi}(5.25)(0.15 \times 10^6) = 6.96 \ \mu C/m^2$$

$$P = \chi_e \epsilon_0 E = \frac{10^{-9}}{36\pi}(4.25)(0.15 \times 10^6) = 5.64 \ \mu C/m^2$$

8.2   Capacitance

Any two conducting bodies separated by free space or a dielectric material have a *capacitance* between them. A voltage difference applied results in a charge $+Q$ on one conductor and $-Q$ on the other. The ratio of the absolute value of the charge to the absolute value of the voltage difference is defined as the capacitance of the system:

$$C = \frac{Q}{V} \quad \text{(F)}$$

where 1 farad(F) = 1 C/V.

The capacitance depends only on the geometry of the system and the properties of the dielectric(s) involved. In Fig. 8-2, charge $+Q$ placed on conductor 1 and $-Q$ on conductor 2 creates a flux field as shown. The **D** and **E** fields are therefore also established. Doubling the charges would simply double **D** and **E**, and therefore double the voltage difference. Hence, the ratio Q/V would remain fixed.

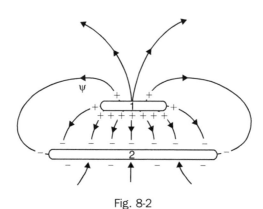

Fig. 8-2

EXAMPLE 2. Find the capacitance of the parallel plates in Fig. 8-3, neglecting fringing.

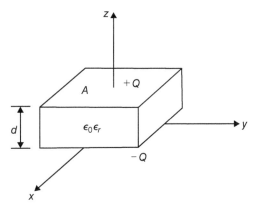

Fig. 8-3

Assume a total charge $+Q$ on the upper plate and $-Q$ on the lower plate. This charge would normally be distributed over the plates with a higher density at the edges. By *neglecting fringing*, the problem is simplified and uniform densities $\rho_s = \pm Q/A$ may be assumed on the plates. Between the plates $\mathbf{D}$ is uniform, directed from $+\rho_s$ to $-\rho_s$.

$$\mathbf{D} = \frac{Q}{A}(-\mathbf{a}_z) \quad \text{and} \quad \mathbf{E} = \frac{Q}{\epsilon_0 \epsilon_r A}(-\mathbf{a}_z)$$

The potential of the upper plate with respect to the lower plate is obtained as in Section 6.3.

$$V = -\int_0^d \frac{Q}{\epsilon_0 \epsilon_r A}(-\mathbf{a}_z) \cdot (dz\,\mathbf{a}_z) = \frac{Qd}{\epsilon_0 \epsilon_r A}$$

Then $C = Q/V = \epsilon_0 \epsilon_r A/d$. Notice that the result does not depend upon the shape of the plates but rather the area, the separation distance, and the dielectric material between the plates.

8.3 Multiple-Dielectric Capacitors

When two dielectrics are present in a capacitor with the interface *parallel to* $\mathbf{E}$ and $\mathbf{D}$, as shown in Fig. 8-4(*a*), the equivalent capacitance can be obtained by treating the arrangement as two capacitors in parallel [Fig. 8-4(*b*)].

$$C_1 = \frac{\epsilon_0 \epsilon_{r1} A_1}{d} \quad C_2 = \frac{\epsilon_0 \epsilon_{r2} A_2}{d}$$

$$C_{eq} = C_1 + C_2 = \frac{\epsilon_0}{d}(\epsilon_{r1} A_1 + \epsilon_{r2} A_2)$$

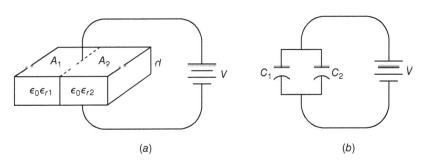

(a)   (b)

Fig. 8-4

When two dielectrics are present such that the interface is *normal to* **D** and **E**, as shown in Fig. 8-5(*a*), the equivalent capacitance can be obtained by treating the arrangement as two capacitors in series [Fig. 8-5(*b*)].

$$C_1 = \frac{\epsilon_0 \epsilon_{r1} A_1}{d_1} \qquad C_2 = \frac{\epsilon_0 \epsilon_{r2} A}{d_2}$$

$$\frac{1}{C_{eq}} = \frac{1}{C_1} + \frac{1}{C_2} = \frac{\epsilon_{r2} d_1 + \epsilon_{r1} d_2}{\epsilon_0 \epsilon_{r1} \epsilon_{r2} A}$$

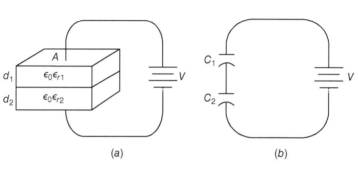

(*a*)   (*b*)

Fig. 8-5

The result can be extended to any number of dielectrics such that the interfaces are all normal to **D** and **E**: *The reciprocal of the equivalent capacitance is the sum of the reciprocals of the individual capacitances.*

EXAMPLE 3.   A parallel-plate capacitor with area 0.30 m² and separation 5.5 mm contains three dielectrics with interfaces normal to **E** and **D**, as follows: $\epsilon_{r1} = 3.0$, $d_1 = 1.0$ mm; $\epsilon_{r2} = 4.0$, $d_2 = 2.0$ mm; $\epsilon_{r3} = 6.0$, $d_3 = 2.5$ mm. Find the capacitance.

Each dielectric is treated as making up one capacitor in a set of three capacitors in series.

$$C_1 = \frac{\epsilon_0 \epsilon_{r1} A}{d_1} = \frac{\epsilon_0 (3.0)(0.30)}{10^{-3}} = 7.96\,\text{nF}$$

Similarly, $C_2 = 5.31$ nF and $C_3 = 6.37$ nF; whence

$$\frac{1}{C_{eq}} = \frac{1}{7.96 \times 10^{-9}} + \frac{1}{5.31 \times 10^{-9}} + \frac{1}{6.37 \times 10^{-9}} \qquad \text{or} \quad C_{eq} = 2.12\,\text{nF}$$

8.4   Energy Stored in a Capacitor

By Section 6.7, the energy stored in the electric field of a capacitor is given by

$$W_E = \frac{1}{2} \int \mathbf{D} \cdot \mathbf{E}\, dv$$

where the integration may be taken over the space between the conductors with fringing neglected. If this space is occupied by a dielectric of relative permittivity ϵ_r, then $\mathbf{D} = \epsilon_0 \epsilon_r \mathbf{E}$, giving

$$W_E = \frac{1}{2} \int \epsilon_0 \epsilon_r E^2\, dv$$

It is seen that, *for the same* **E** *field as in free space*, the presence of a dielectric results in an increase in stored energy by the factor $\epsilon_r > 1$. In terms of the capacitance C and the voltage V, this stored energy is given by

$$W_E = \frac{1}{2} CV^2$$

and the energy increase relative to free space is reflected in C, which is directly proportional to ϵ_r.

8.5 Fixed-Voltage D and E

A parallel-plate capacitor with free space between the plates and a constant applied voltage V, as shown in Fig. 8-6, has a constant electric field intensity $\mathbf{E}$. With fringing neglected,

$$\mathbf{E}_0 = \frac{V}{d}\,\mathbf{a}_n \qquad \mathbf{D}_0 = \epsilon_0\mathbf{E}_0 = \frac{\epsilon_0 V}{d}\,\mathbf{a}_n$$

Fig. 8-6

Now, when a dielectric with relative permittivity ϵ_r fills the space between the plates,

$$\mathbf{E} = \mathbf{E}_0 \qquad \mathbf{D} = \epsilon_r\mathbf{D}_0$$

because the voltage remains fixed, whereas the permittivity increases by the factor ϵ_r.

EXAMPLE 4. A parallel-plate capacitor with free space between the plates is connected to a constant source of voltage. Determine how W_E, C, Q, and ρ_s change as a dielectric of $\epsilon_r = 2$ is inserted between the plates.

Relationship	Explanation
$W_E = 2W_{E0}$	Section 8.4
$C = 2C_0$	$C = 2W_E/V^2$
$\rho_s = 2\rho_{s0}$	$\rho_s = D_n$
$Q = 2Q_0$	$Q = \rho_s A$

Insertion of the dielectric causes additional charge in the amount Q_0 to be pulled from the constant-voltage source.

8.6 Fixed-Charge D and E

The parallel-plate capacitor in Fig. 8-7 has a charge $+Q$ on the upper plate and $-Q$ on the lower plate. This charge could have resulted from the connection of a voltage source V which was subsequently removed. With free space between the plates and fringing neglected,

$$\mathbf{D}_0 = \frac{Q}{A}\,\mathbf{a}_n \qquad \mathbf{E}_0 = \frac{1}{\epsilon_0}\mathbf{D}_0 = \frac{Q}{\epsilon_0 A}\,\mathbf{a}_n$$

In this arrangement there is no way for the charge to increase or decrease, since there is no conducting path to the plates. Thus, when a dielectric material is inserted between the plates,

$$\mathbf{D} = \mathbf{D}_0 \qquad \mathbf{E} = \frac{1}{\epsilon_r}\mathbf{E}_0$$

Fig. 8-7

EXAMPLE 5.   A charged parallel-plate capacitor in free space is kept electrically insulated as a dielectric of relative permittivity 2 is inserted between the plates. Determine the changes in W_E, C, and V.

Relationship	Explanation
$W_E = \dfrac{1}{2} W_{E0}$	$\mathbf{D} \cdot \mathbf{E} = \dfrac{1}{2} \mathbf{D}_0 \cdot \mathbf{E}_0$
$V = \dfrac{1}{2} V_0$	$V = Ed$
$C = 2C_0$	$C = Q/V$

(See Problem 8.20.)

8.7   Boundary Conditions at the Interface of Two Dielectrics

If the conductor in Figs. 7-11 and 7-12 is replaced by a second, different, dielectric, then the same argument as was made in Section 7.10 establishes the following two boundary conditions:

(1) *The tangential component of* $\mathbf{E}$ *is continuous across a dielectric interface.* Symbolically,

$$E_{t1} = E_{t2} \quad \text{and} \quad \frac{D_{t1}}{\epsilon_{r1}} = \frac{D_{t2}}{\epsilon_{r2}}$$

(2) *The normal component of* $\mathbf{D}$ *has a discontinuity of magnitude* $|\rho_s|$ *across a dielectric interface.* If the unit normal vector is chosen to point into dielectric 2, then this condition can be written

$$D_{n1} - D_{n2} = -\rho_s \quad \text{and} \quad \epsilon_{r1}E_{n1} - \epsilon_{r2}E_{n2} = -\frac{\rho_s}{\epsilon_0}$$

Generally the interface will have no free charges ($\rho_s = 0$), so that

$$D_{n1} = D_{n2} \quad \text{and} \quad \epsilon_{r1}E_{n1} = \epsilon_{r2}E_{n2}$$

EXAMPLE 6.   Given that $\mathbf{E}_1 = 2\mathbf{a}_x - 3\mathbf{a}_y + 5\mathbf{a}_z$ (V/m) at the charge-free dielectric interface of Fig. 8-8, find $\mathbf{D}_2$ and the angles θ_1 and θ_2.

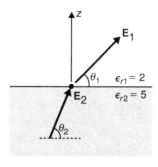

Fig. 8-8

The interface is a $z = $ const. plane. The x and y components are tangential, and the z components are normal. By continuity of the tangential component of $\mathbf{E}$ and the normal component of $\mathbf{D}$:

$$E_1 = 2a_x - 3a_y + 5a_z$$
$$E_2 = 2a_x - 3a_y + E_{z2}a_z$$
$$D_1 = \epsilon_0\epsilon_{r1}E_1 = 4\epsilon_0 a_x - 6\epsilon_0 a_y + 10\epsilon_0 a_z$$
$$D_2 = D_{x2}a_x + D_{y2}a_y + 10\epsilon_0 a_z$$

The unknown components are now found from the relation $D_2 = \epsilon_0\epsilon_{r2}E_2$.

$$D_{x2}a_x + D_{y2}a_y + 10\epsilon_0 a_x = 2\epsilon_0\epsilon_{r2}a_x - 3\epsilon_0\epsilon_{r2}a_y + \epsilon_0\epsilon_{r2}E_{z2}a_z$$

from which

$$D_{x2} = 2\epsilon_0\epsilon_{r2} = 10\epsilon_2 \qquad D_{y2} = -3\epsilon_0\epsilon_{r2} = -15\epsilon_0 \qquad E_{z2} = \frac{10}{\epsilon_{r2}} = 2$$

The angles made with the plane of the interface are easiest found from

$$E_1 \cdot a_z = |E_1| \cos(90° - \theta_1) \qquad E_2 \cdot a_z = |E_2| \cos(90° - \theta_2)$$
$$5 = \sqrt{38} \sin\theta_1 \qquad\qquad 2 = \sqrt{17} \sin\theta_2$$
$$\theta_1 = 54.2° \qquad\qquad\qquad \theta_2 = 29.0°$$

A useful relation can be obtained from

$$\tan\theta_1 = \frac{E_{z1}}{\sqrt{E_{x1}^2 + E_{y1}^2}} = \frac{D_{z1}/\epsilon_0\epsilon_{r1}}{\sqrt{E_{x1}^2 + E_{y1}^2}}$$

$$\tan\theta_2 = \frac{E_{z2}}{\sqrt{E_{x2}^2 + E_{y2}^2}} = \frac{D_{z2}/\epsilon_0\epsilon_{r2}}{\sqrt{E_{x2}^2 + E_{y2}^2}}$$

in view of the continuity relations, division of these two equations gives

$$\frac{\tan\theta_1}{\tan\theta_2} = \frac{\epsilon_{r2}}{\epsilon_{r1}}$$

8.8 Method of Images

Consider the electric field due to a pair of $\pm Q$ point charges at $z = \pm d$ in the Cartesian coordinate system. Electric potential on the plane at $z = 0$ is zero, and the vector E is normal to the plane. Now consider the field due to a point charge Q above a grounded conducting infinite plane placed at $z = 0$. The grounded plane forms an equipotential surface at $V = 0$, with the vector E normal to it, and the same boundary conditions as for the dipole. The two fields are equivalent in the space above the grounded plane. The electric field of the single charge above the conducting plane may be found by adding its mirror image and removing the conducting plane. This procedure is called the *method of images* and can be used for any charge configuration above an infinite grounded plane. See Problem 8.22.

SOLVED PROBLEMS

8.1. Find the polarization P in a dielectric material with $\epsilon_r = 2.8$ if $D = 3.0 \times 10^{-7}a$ C/m^2.

Assuming the material to be homogeneous and isotropic,

$$P = \chi_e\epsilon_0 E$$

Since $D = \epsilon_0\epsilon_r E$ and $\chi_e = \epsilon_r - 1$,

$$P = \left(\frac{\epsilon_p - 1}{\epsilon_r}\right)D = 1.93 \times 10^{-7}a \text{ C/m}^2$$

8.2. Determine the value of **E** in a material for which the electric susceptibility is 3.5 and $\mathbf{P} = 2.3 \times 10^{-7}\mathbf{a}$ C/m².

Assuming that **P** and **E** are in the same direction,

$$\mathbf{E} = \frac{1}{\chi_e \epsilon_0}\mathbf{P} = 7.42 \times 10^3 \mathbf{a} \text{ V/m}$$

8.3. Two point charges in a dielectric medium where $\epsilon_r = 5.2$ interact with a force of 8.6×10^{-3} N. What force could be expected if the charges were in free space?

Coulomb's law, $F = Q_1 Q_2 / (4\pi\epsilon_0 \epsilon_r d^2)$, shows that the force is inversely proportional to ϵ_r. In free space the force will have its maximum value.

$$F_{\max} = \frac{5.2}{1}(8.6 \times 10^{-3}) = 4.47 \times 10^{-2}\text{ N}$$

8.4. Region 1, defined by $x < 0$, is free space, while region 2, $x > 0$, is a dielectric material for which $\epsilon_{r2} = 2.4$. See Fig. 8-9. Given

$$\mathbf{D}_1 = 3\mathbf{a}_x - 4\mathbf{a}_y + 6\mathbf{a}_z \quad \text{C/m}^2$$

find $\mathbf{E}_2$ and the angles θ_1 and θ_2.

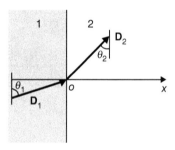

Fig. 8-9

The x components are normal to the interface: D_n and E_t are continuous.

$$\mathbf{D}_1 = 3\mathbf{a}_x - 4\mathbf{a}_y + 6\mathbf{a}_z \qquad\qquad \mathbf{E}_1 = \frac{3}{\epsilon_0}\mathbf{a}_x - \frac{4}{\epsilon_0}\mathbf{a}_y + \frac{6}{\epsilon_0}\mathbf{a}_z$$

$$\mathbf{D}_2 = 3\mathbf{a}_x + D_{y2}\mathbf{a}_y + D_{z2}\mathbf{a}_z \qquad\qquad \mathbf{E}_2 = E_{x2}\mathbf{a}_x - \frac{4}{\epsilon_0}\mathbf{a}_y + \frac{6}{\epsilon_0}\mathbf{a}_z$$

Then $\mathbf{D}_2 = \epsilon_0 \epsilon_{r2}\mathbf{E}_2$ gives

$$3\mathbf{a}_x + D_{y2}\mathbf{a}_y + D_{z2}\mathbf{a}_z = \epsilon_0 \epsilon_{r2}E_{x2}\mathbf{a}_x - 4\epsilon_{r2}\mathbf{a}_y + 6\epsilon_{r2}\mathbf{a}_z$$

whence $\qquad\qquad E_{x2} = \dfrac{3}{\epsilon_0 \epsilon_{r2}} = \dfrac{1.25}{\epsilon_0} \quad D_{y2} = -4\epsilon_{r2} = -9.6 \quad D_{z2} = 6\epsilon_{r2} = 14.4$

To find the angles:

$$\mathbf{D}_1 \cdot \mathbf{a}_x = |\mathbf{D}_1|\cos(90° - \theta_1)$$
$$3 = \sqrt{61}\sin\theta_1$$
$$\theta_1 = 22.6°$$

Similarly, $\theta_2 = 9.83°$.

8.5. In the free-space region $x < 0$ the electric field intensity is $\mathbf{E}_1 = 3\mathbf{a}_x + 5\mathbf{a}_y - 3\mathbf{a}_z$ V/m. The region $x > 0$ is a dielectric for which $\epsilon_{r2} = 3.6$. Find the angle θ_2 that the field in the dielectric makes with the $x = 0$ plane.

The angle made by $\mathbf{E}_1$ is found from

$$\mathbf{E}_1 \cdot \mathbf{a}_x = |\mathbf{E}_1| \cos(90° - \theta_1)$$
$$3 = \sqrt{43} \sin \theta_1$$
$$\theta_1 = 27.2°$$

Then, by the formula developed in Example 6,

$$\tan \theta_2 = \frac{1}{\epsilon_{r2}} \tan \theta_1 = 0.1428$$

and $\theta_2 = 8.13°$.

8.6. A dielectric free-space interface has the equation $3x + 2y + z = 12$ m. The origin side of the interface has $\epsilon_{r1} = 3.0$ and $\mathbf{E}_1 = 2\mathbf{a}_x + 5\mathbf{a}_z$ V/m. Find $\mathbf{E}_2$.

The interface is indicated in Fig. 8-10 by its intersections with the axes. The unit normal vector on the free-space side is

$$\mathbf{a}_n = \frac{3\mathbf{a}_x + 2\mathbf{a}_y + \mathbf{a}_z}{\sqrt{14}}$$

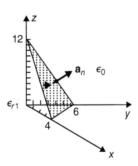

Fig. 8-10

The projection of $\mathbf{E}_1$ on $\mathbf{a}_n$ is the normal component of $\mathbf{E}$ at the interface.

$$\mathbf{E}_1 \cdot \mathbf{a}_n = \frac{11}{\sqrt{14}}$$

Then

$$\mathbf{E}_{n1} = \frac{11}{\sqrt{14}} \mathbf{a}_n = 2.36\mathbf{a}_x + 1.57\mathbf{a}_y + 0.79\mathbf{a}_z$$
$$\mathbf{E}_{t1} = \mathbf{E}_1 - \mathbf{E}_{n1} = -0.36\mathbf{a}_x - 1.57\mathbf{a}_y + 4.21\mathbf{a}_z = \mathbf{E}_{t2}$$
$$\mathbf{D}_{n1} = \epsilon_0 \epsilon_{r1} \mathbf{E}_{n1} = \epsilon_0 (7.08\mathbf{a}_x + 4.71\mathbf{a}_y + 2.37\mathbf{a}_z) = \mathbf{D}_{n2}$$
$$\mathbf{E}_{n2} = \frac{1}{\epsilon_0} \mathbf{D}_{n2} = 7.08\mathbf{a}_x + 4.71\mathbf{a}_y + 2.37\mathbf{a}_z$$

and finally

$$\mathbf{E}_2 = \mathbf{E}_{n2} + \mathbf{E}_{t2} = 6.72\mathbf{a}_x + 3.14\mathbf{a}_y + 6.58\mathbf{a}_z \quad \text{V/m}$$

8.7. Fig. 8-11 shows a planar dielectric slab with free space on either side. Assuming a constant field $\mathbf{E}_2$ within the slab, show that $\mathbf{E}_3 = \mathbf{E}_1$.

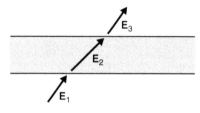

Fig. 8-11

By continuity of E_t across the two interfaces,

$$E_{t3} = E_{t1}$$

By continuity of D_n across the two interfaces (no surface charges),

$$D_{n3} = D_{n1} \quad \text{and so} \quad E_{n3} = E_{n1}$$

Consequently, $\mathbf{E}_3 = \mathbf{E}_1$.

8.8. (*a*) Show that the capacitor of Fig. 8-4(*a*) has capacitance

$$C_{eq} = \frac{\epsilon_0 \epsilon_{r1} A_1}{d} + \frac{\epsilon_0 \epsilon_{r2} A_2}{d} = C_1 + C_2$$

(*b*) Show that the capacitor of Fig. 8-5(*a*) has reciprocal capacitance

$$\frac{1}{C_{eq}} = \frac{1}{\epsilon_0 \epsilon_{r1} A/d_1} + \frac{1}{\epsilon_0 \epsilon_{r2} A/d_2} = \frac{1}{C_1} + \frac{1}{C_2}$$

(*a*) Because the voltage difference V is common to the two dielectrics,

$$\mathbf{E}_1 = \mathbf{E}_2 = \frac{V}{d}\, \mathbf{a}_n \quad \text{and} \quad \frac{\mathbf{D}_1}{\epsilon_0 \epsilon_{r1}} = \frac{\mathbf{D}_2}{\epsilon_0 \epsilon_{r2}} = \frac{V}{d}\, \mathbf{a}_n$$

where $\mathbf{a}_n$ is the downward normal to the upper plate. Since $D_n = \rho_s$, the charge densities on the two sections of the upper plate are

$$\rho_{s1} = \frac{V}{d}\, \epsilon_0 \epsilon_{r1} \qquad \rho_{s2} = \frac{V}{d}\, \epsilon_0 \epsilon_{r2}$$

and the total charge is

$$Q = \rho_{s1} A_1 + \rho_{s2} A_2 = V\left(\frac{\epsilon_0 \epsilon_{r1} A_1}{d} + \frac{\epsilon_0 \epsilon_{r2} A_2}{d} \right)$$

Thus, the capacitance of the system, $C_{eq} = Q/V$, has the asserted form.

(*b*) Let $+Q$ be the charge on the upper plate. Then

$$\mathbf{D} = \frac{Q}{A}\, \mathbf{a}_n$$

everywhere between the plates, so that

$$\mathbf{E}_1 = \frac{Q}{\epsilon_0 \epsilon_{r1} A}\, \mathbf{a}_n \qquad \mathbf{E}_2 = \frac{Q}{\epsilon_0 \epsilon_{r2} A}\, \mathbf{a}_n$$

The voltage differences across the two dielectrics are then

$$V_1 = E_1 d_1 = \frac{Qd_1}{\epsilon_0 \epsilon_{r1} A} \qquad V_2 = E_2 d_2 = \frac{Qd_2}{\epsilon_0 \epsilon_{r2} A}$$

and

$$V = V_1 + V_2 = Q\left(\frac{1}{\epsilon_0 \epsilon_{r1} A/d_1} + \frac{1}{\epsilon_0 \epsilon_{r2} A/d_2}\right)$$

From this it is seen that $1/C_{eq} = V/Q$ has the asserted form.

8.9. Find the capacitance of a coaxial capacitor of length L, where the inner conductor has radius a and the outer has radius b. See Fig. 8-12.

Fig. 8-12

With fringing neglected, Gauss's law requires that $D \propto 1/r$ between the conductors (see Problem 7.22). At $r = a$, $D = \rho_s$, where ρ_s is the (assumed positive) surface charge density on the inner conductor. Therefore,

$$\mathbf{D} = \rho_s \frac{a}{r}\mathbf{a}_r \qquad \mathbf{E} = \frac{\rho_s a}{\epsilon_0 \epsilon_r r}\mathbf{a}_r$$

and the voltage difference between the conductors is

$$V_{ab} = -\int_b^a \left(\frac{\rho_s a}{\epsilon_0 \epsilon_r r}\mathbf{a}_r\right)\cdot d r\mathbf{a}_r = \frac{\rho_s a}{\epsilon_0 \epsilon_r}\ln\frac{b}{a}$$

The total charge on the inner conductor is $Q = \rho_s(2\pi a L)$, and so

$$C = \frac{Q}{V} = \frac{2\pi\epsilon_0 \epsilon_r L}{\ln(b/a)}$$

8.10. In the capacitor shown in Fig. 8-13, the region between the plates is filled with a dielectric having $\epsilon_r = 4.5$. Find the capacitance.

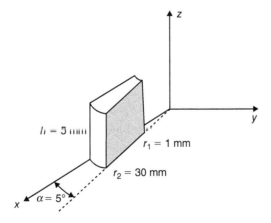

$h = 5$ mm

$r_1 = 1$ mm

$r_2 = 30$ mm

$\alpha = 5°$

Fig. 8-13

With fringing neglected, the $\mathbf{D}$ field between the plates should, in cylindrical coordinates, be of the form $\mathbf{D} = D_\phi \mathbf{a}_\phi$, where D_ϕ depends only or r. Then, if the voltage of the plate $\phi = \alpha$ with respect to the plate $\phi = 0$ is V_0,

$$V_0 = -\int \mathbf{E} \cdot d\mathbf{l} = -\int_0^a \left(\frac{D_\phi}{\epsilon_0 \epsilon_r} \mathbf{a}_\phi\right) \cdot (r \, d\phi \mathbf{a}_\phi) = -\frac{D_\phi r}{\epsilon_0 \epsilon_r} \int_0^a d\phi = -\frac{D_\phi r \alpha}{\epsilon_0 \epsilon_r}$$

Thus, $D_\phi = -\epsilon_0 \epsilon_r V_0 / r\alpha$, and the charge density on the plate $\phi = \alpha$ is

$$\rho_s = D_n = -D_\phi = \frac{\epsilon_0 \epsilon_r V_0}{r\alpha}$$

The total charge on the plate is then given by

$$Q = \int \rho_s \, dS = \int_0^h \int_{r_1}^{r_2} dr \, dz$$
$$= \frac{\epsilon_0 \epsilon_r V_0 h}{a} \ln \frac{r_2}{r_1}$$

Hence,

$$C = \frac{Q}{V_0} = \frac{\epsilon_0 \epsilon_r h}{\alpha} \ln \frac{r_2}{r_1}$$

When the numerical values are substituted (with α converted to radians), one obtains $C = 7.76$ pF.

8.11. Referring to Problem 8.10, find the separation d which results in the same capacitance when the plates are brought into parallel arrangement, with the same dielectric in between.

With the plates parallel

$$C = \frac{\epsilon_0 \epsilon_r A}{d}$$

so that

$$d = \frac{\epsilon_0 \epsilon_r A}{C} = \frac{\epsilon_0 \epsilon_r h (r_2 - r_1)}{(\epsilon_0 \epsilon_r h / \alpha)[\ln (r_2 / r_1)]} = \frac{\alpha (r_2 - r_1)}{\ln (r_2 / r_1)}$$

Notice that the numerator on the right is the difference of the arc lengths at the two ends of the capacitor, while the denominator is the logarithm of the ratio of these arc lengths. For the data of Problem 8.10, $\alpha r_1 = 0.087$ mm, $\alpha r_2 = 2.62$ mm, and $d = 0.74$ mm.

8.12. Find the capacitance of an isolated spherical shell of radius a.

The potential of such a conductor with a zero reference at infinity is (see Problem 3.34)

$$V = \frac{Q}{2\pi \epsilon_0 a}$$

Then

$$C = \frac{Q}{V} = 4\pi \epsilon_0 a$$

8.13. Find the capacitance due to two spherical shells of radius a separated by a distance $d \gg a$.

As an approximation, the result of Problem 8.12 for the capacitance of a single spherical shell, $4\pi \epsilon_0 a$, may be used. From Fig. 8-14 two such identical capacitors appear to be in series.

$$\frac{1}{C} = \frac{1}{C_1} + \frac{1}{C_2}$$
$$C = \frac{C_1 C_2}{C_1 + C_2} = 2\pi \epsilon_0 a$$

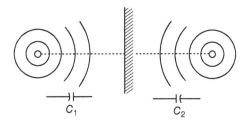

Fig. 8-14

8.14. Find the capacitance of a parallel-plate capacitor containing two dielectrics, $\epsilon_{r1} = 1.5$ and $\epsilon_{r2} = 3.5$, each composing one-half the volume, as shown in Fig. 8-15. Here, $A = 2 \text{ m}^2$ and $d = 10^{-3} \text{ m}$.

$$C_1 = \frac{\epsilon_0 \epsilon_{r1} A_1}{d} = \frac{(8.854 \times 10^{-12})}{10^{-3}} = 13.3 \text{ nF}$$

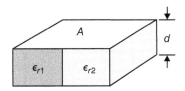

Fig. 8-15

Similarly, $C_2 = 31.0 \text{ nF}$. Then

$$C = C_1 + C_2 = 44.3 \text{ nF}$$

8.15. Repeat Problem 8.14 if the two dielectrics each occupy one-half of the space between the plates but the interface is parallel to the plates.

$$C_1 = \frac{\epsilon_0 \epsilon_r A}{d_1} = \frac{\epsilon_0 \epsilon_r A}{d/2} = \frac{(8.854 \times 10^{-12})(1.5)}{10^{-3}/2} = 53.1 \text{ nF}$$

Similarly, $C_2 = 124 \text{ nF}$. Then

$$C = \frac{C_1 C_2}{C_1 + C_2} = 37.2 \text{ nF}$$

8.16. In the cylindrical capacitor shown in Fig. 8-16, each dielectric occupies one-half the volume. Find the capacitance.

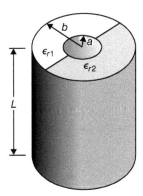

Fig. 8-16

The dielectric interface is parallel to **D** and **E**, so the configuration may be treated as two capacitors in parallel. Since each capacitor carries half as much charge as a full cylinder would carry, the result of Problem 8.9 gives

$$C = C_1 + C_2 = \frac{\pi \epsilon_0 \epsilon_{r1} L}{\ln (b/a)} + \frac{\pi \epsilon_0 \epsilon_{r2} L}{\ln (b/a)} = \frac{2 \pi \epsilon_0 \epsilon_{r\,avg} L}{\ln (b/a)}$$

where $\epsilon_{ravg} = \frac{1}{2}(\epsilon_{r1} + \epsilon_{r2})$. The two dielectrics act like a single dielectric having the average relative permittivity.

8.17. Find the voltage across each dielectric in the capacitor shown in Fig. 8-17 when the applied voltage is 200 V.

$$C_1 = \frac{\epsilon_0 5(1)}{10^{-3}} = 5000 \epsilon_0$$

$$C_2 = \frac{1000 \epsilon_0}{3}$$

and

$$C = \frac{C_1 C_2}{C_1 + C_2} = 312.5 \epsilon_0 = 2.77 \times 10^{-9} \text{ F}$$

1 m²

3 mm

1 mm

ϵ_0

2

1

$\epsilon_{r1} = 5$

Fig. 8-17

The **D** field within the capacitor is now found from

$$D_n = \rho_s = \frac{Q}{A} = \frac{CV}{A} = \frac{(2.77 \times 10^{-9})(200)}{1} = 5.54 \times 10^{-7} \text{ C/m}^2$$

Then,

$$E_1 = \frac{D}{\epsilon_0 \epsilon_{r1}} = 12.5 \times 10^4 \text{ V/m} \qquad E_2 = \frac{D}{\epsilon_0} = 6.25 \times 10^4 \text{ V/m}$$

from which

$$V_1 = E_1 d_1 = 12.5 \text{ V} \qquad V_2 = E_2 d_2 = 187.5 \text{ V}$$

8.18. Find the voltage drop across each dielectric in Fig. 8-18, where $\epsilon_{r1} = 2.0$ and $\epsilon_{r2} = 5.0$. The inner conductor is at $r_1 = 2$ cm and the outer at $r_2 = 2.5$ cm, with the dielectric interface halfway between.

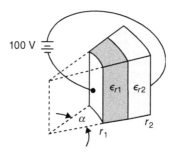

100 V

ϵ_{r1} ϵ_{r2}

α

r_1

r_2

Fig. 8-18

The voltage division is the same as it would be for full right circular cylinders. The segment shown, with angle α, will have a capacitance $\alpha/2\pi$ times that of the complete coaxial capacitor. From Problem 8.9,

$$C_1 = \left(\frac{a}{2\pi}\right)\frac{2\pi\epsilon_0\epsilon_{r1}L}{\ln(2.25/2.0)} = \alpha L(1.5\times10^{-10}) \quad (F)$$
$$C_2 = \alpha L(4.2\times10^{-10}) \quad (F)$$

Since $Q = C_1V_1 = C_2V_2$ and $V_1 + V_2 = V$, it follows that

$$V_1 = \frac{C_2}{C_1+C_2}V = \frac{4.2}{1.5+4.2}(100) = 74 \text{ V}$$
$$V_2 = \frac{C}{C_1+C_2}V = \frac{1.5}{1.5+4.2}(100) = 26 \text{ V}$$

8.19. A free-space parallel-plate capacitor is charged by momentary connection to a voltage source V, which is then removed. Determine how W_E, D, E, C, and V change as the plates are moved apart to a separation distance $d_2 = 2d_1$ without disturbing the charge.

Relationship	Explanation
$D_2 = D$	$D = Q/A$
$E_2 = E_1$	$E = D/\epsilon_0$
$W_{E2} = 2W_{E1}$	$W_E = \frac{1}{2}\int\epsilon_0E^2\,dv$, and the volume is doubled
$C_2 = \frac{1}{2}C_1$	$C = \epsilon_A/d$
$V_2 = 2V_1$	$V = Q/C$

8.20. Explain physically the energy changes found in (*a*) Problem 8.19, (*b*) Example 5.

(*a*)   External work (in the amount W_{E1}) is done *on* the system in forcing apart the oppositely charged plates. This work shows up as an increase in internal energy (stored in the **E** field).

(*b*)   The charged plates *draw* the dielectric slab into the gap. Thus, the system *performs* work (in the amount $\frac{1}{2}W_{E0}$) on the surroundings—specifically, on whatever is guiding the slab into position. The internal energy suffers a corresponding *decrease*.

8.21. A parallel-plate capacitor with a separation $d = 1.0$ cm has 29 kV applied when free space is the only dielectric. Assume that air has a dielectric strength of 30 kV/cm. Show why the air breaks down when a thin piece of glass ($\epsilon_r = 6.5$) with a dielectric strength of 290 kV/cm and thicknesses $d_2 = 0.20$ cm is inserted as shown in Fig. 8-19.

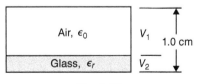

Fig. 8-19

The problem becomes one of two capacitors in series,

$$C_1 = \frac{\epsilon_0 A}{8\times10^{-3}} = 125\epsilon_0 A$$
$$C_2 = \frac{\epsilon_0\epsilon_r A}{2\times10^{-3}} = 3250\epsilon_0 A$$

Then, as in Problem 8.18,

$$V_1 = \frac{3250}{125 + 3250}(29) = 27.93 \text{ kV}$$

so that

$$E_1 = \frac{27.93 \text{ kV}}{0.80 \text{ cm}} = 34.9 \text{ kV/cm}$$

which exceeds the dielectric strength of air.

8.22. Find the capacitance per unit length between a cylindrical conductor of radius $a = 2.5$ cm and a ground plane parallel to the conductor axis and a distance $h = 6.0$ m from it.

A useful technique in problems of this kind is the *method of images*. Take the mirror image of the conductor in the ground plane, and let this image conductor carry the negative of the charge distribution on the actual conductor. Now suppose the ground plane is removed. It is clear that the electric field of the two conductors obeys the right boundary condition at the actual conductor, and, by symmetry, has an equipotential surface (Section 5.2) where the ground plane was. Thus, this field is *the* field in the region between the actual conductor and the ground plane.

Approximating the actual and image charge distributions by line charges $+\rho_\ell$ and $-\rho_\ell$, respectively, at the conductor centers, one has (see Fig. 8-20):

$$\text{Potential at radius } a \text{ due to} +\rho_\ell = -\left(\frac{+\rho_\ell}{2\pi\epsilon_0}\right)\ln a$$

$$\text{Potential at point } P \text{ due to} -\rho_\ell = -\left(\frac{-\rho_\ell}{2\pi\epsilon_0}\right)\ln (2h - a)$$

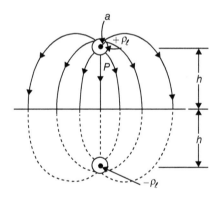

Fig. 8-20

The potential due to $-\rho_\ell$ is *not* constant over $r = a$, the surface of the actual conductor. But it is very nearly so if $a \ll h$. To this approximation, then, the total potential of the actual conductor is

$$V_a = \frac{\rho_\ell}{2\pi\epsilon_0}\ln a + \frac{\rho_\ell}{2\pi\epsilon_0}\ln (2h - a) \approx -\frac{\rho_\ell}{2\pi\epsilon_0}\ln a + \frac{\rho_\ell}{2\pi\epsilon_0}\ln 2h = \frac{\rho_\ell}{2\pi\epsilon_0}\ln \frac{2h}{a}$$

Similarly, the potential of the image conductor is $-V_a$. Thus, the potential difference between the conductors is $2V_a$, so that the potential difference between the actual conductor and the ground plane is $\frac{1}{2}(2V_a) = V_a$. The desired capacitance per unit length is then

$$\frac{C}{L} = \frac{Q/L}{V_a} = \frac{\rho_\ell}{V_a} = \frac{2\pi\epsilon_0}{\ln (2h/a)}$$

For the given values of a and h, $C/L = 9.0$ pF/m.

The above expression for C/L is not exact, but it provides a good approximation when $a \ll h$ (the practical case). An exact solution gives

$$\left(\frac{C}{L}\right)_{\text{exact}} = \frac{2\pi\epsilon_0}{\ln\left(\dfrac{h + \sqrt{h^2 - a^2}}{z}\right)}$$

Observe that C/L for the source–image system (more generally, for any pair of parallel cylindrical conductors with center-to-center separation $2h$) is one-half the value found above (same charge, twice the voltage). That is, with $d = 2h$,

$$\frac{C}{L} = \frac{\pi\epsilon_0}{\ln\left(\dfrac{d + \sqrt{d^2 - 4a^2}}{2a}\right)} \approx \frac{\pi\epsilon_0}{\ln(d/a)}$$

SUPPLEMENTARY PROBLEMS

8.23. Find the magnitudes of **D**, **P**, and ϵ_r, for a dielectric material in which $E = 0.15$ MV/m and $\chi_e = 4.25$.

8.24. In a dielectric material with $\epsilon_r = 3.6$, $D = 285$ nC/m². Find the magnitudes of **E**, **P**, and χ_e.

8.25. Given $\mathbf{E} = -3\mathbf{a}_x + 4\mathbf{a}_y - 2\mathbf{a}_z$ V/m in the region $z < 0$, where $\epsilon_r = 2.0$, find **E** in the region $z > 0$, for which $\epsilon_r = 6.5$.

8.26. Given that $\mathbf{D} = 2\mathbf{a}_x - 4\mathbf{a}_y + 1.5\mathbf{a}_z$ C/m² in the region $x > 0$, which is free space, find **P** in the region $x < 0$, which is a dielectric with $\epsilon_r = 5.0$.

8.27. Region 1, $z < 0$ m, is free space where $\mathbf{D} = 5\mathbf{a}_y + 7\mathbf{a}_z$ C/m². Region 2, $0 < z \le 1$ m, has $\epsilon_r = 2.5$. And region 3, $z > 1$ m, has $\epsilon_r = 3.0$. Find $\mathbf{E}_2$, $\mathbf{P}_2$, and θ_3.

8.28. The plane interface between two dielectrics is given by $3x + z = 5$. On the side including the origin, $\mathbf{D}_1 = (4.5\mathbf{a}_x + 3.2\mathbf{a}_z)10^{-7}$ and $\epsilon_{r1} = 4.3$, while on the other side, $\epsilon_{r2} = 1.80$. Find E_1, E_2, D_2, and θ_2.

8.29. A dielectric interface is described by $4y + 3z = 12$ m. The side including the origin is free space where $\mathbf{D}_1 = \mathbf{a}_x + 3\mathbf{a}_y + 2\mathbf{a}_z$ μC/m². On the other side, $\epsilon_{r2} = 3.6$. Find D_2 and θ_2.

8.30. Find the capacitance of a parallel-plate capacitor with a dielectric of $\epsilon_r = 3.0$, area 0.92 m², and separation 4.5 mm.

8.31. A parallel-plate capacitor of 8.0 nF has an area 1.51 m² and separation 10 mm. What separation would be required to obtain the same capacitance with free space between the plates?

8.32. Find the capacitance between the inner and outer curved conductor surfaces shown in Fig. 8-21. Neglect fringing.

Fig. 8-21

8.33. Find the capacitance per unit length between a cylindrical conductor 2.75 inches in diameter and a parallel plane 28 ft from the conductor axis.

8.34. Double the conductor diameter in Problem 8.33 and find the capacitance per unit length.

8.35. Find the capacitance per unit length between two parallel cylindrical conductors in air, of radius 1.5 cm and with a center-to-center separation of 85 cm.

8.36. A parallel-plate capacitor with area 0.30 m^2 and separation 5.5 mm contains three dielectrics with interfaces normal to **E** and **D**, as follows: $\epsilon_{r1} = 3.0$, $d_1 = 1.0$ mm; $\epsilon_{r2} = 4.0$, $d_2 = 2.0$ mm; $\epsilon_{r3} = 6.0$, $d_3 = 2.5$ mm. Find the capacitance.

8.37. With a potential of 1000 V applied to the capacitor of Problem 8.36, find the potential difference and potential gradient (electric field intensity) in each dielectric.

8.38. Find the capacitance per unit length of a coaxial conductor with outer radius 4 mm and inner radius 0.5 mm if the dielectric has $\epsilon_r = 5.2$.

8.39. Find the capacitance per unit length of a cable with an inside conductor of radius 0.75 cm and a cylindrical shield of radius 2.25 cm if the dielectric has $\epsilon_r = 2.70$.

8.40. The coaxial cable in Fig. 8-22 has an inner conductor radius of 0.5 mm and an outer conductor radius of 5 mm. Find the capacitance per unit length with spacers as shown.

$\epsilon_r = 5.5$ ϵ_0

10 mm

50 mm

Fig. 8-22

8.41. A parallel-plate capacitor with free space between the plates is charged by momentarily connecting it to a constant 200-V source. After removal from the source, a dielectric of $\epsilon_r = 2.0$ is inserted, completely filling the space. Compare the values of W_E, D, E, ρ_s, V, and C after insertion of the dielectric to the values before.

8.42. A parallel-plate capacitor has its dielectric changed from $\epsilon_{r1} = 2.0$ to $\epsilon_{r2} = 6.0$. It is noted that the stored energy remains fixed: $W_2 = W_1$. Examine the changes, if any, in V, C, D, E, Q, and ρ_s.

8.43. A parallel-plate capacitor with free space between the plates remains connected to a constant voltage source while the plates are moved closer together, from separation d to $\frac{1}{2}d$. Examine the changes in Q, ρ_s, C, D, E, and W_E.

8.44. A parallel-plate capacitor with free space between the plates remains connected to a constant voltage source while the plates are moved farther apart, from separation d to $2d$. Express the changes in D, E, Q, ρ_s, C, and W_E.

8.45. A parallel-plate capacitor has free space as the dielectric and a separation d. Without disturbing the charge Q, the plates are moved closer together, to $d/2$, with a dielectric of $\epsilon_r = 3$ completely filling the space between the plates. Express the changes in D, E, V, C, and W_E.

8.46. A parallel-plate capacitor has free space between the plates. Compare the voltage gradient in this free space to that in the free space when a sheet of mica, $\epsilon_r = 5.4$, fills 20% of the distance between the plates. Assume the same applied voltage in each case.

8.47. A shielded power cable operates at a voltage of 12.5 kV on the inner conductor with respect to the cylindrical shield. There are two insulations; the first has $\epsilon_{r1} = 6.0$ and is from the inner conductor at $r = 0.8$ cm to $r = 1.0$ cm, while the second has $\epsilon_{r2} = 3.0$ and is from $r = 1.0$ cm to $r = 3.0$ cm, the inside surface of the shield. Find the maximum voltage gradient in each insulation.

8.48. A shielded power cable has a polyethylene insulation for which $\epsilon_r = 2.26$ and the dielectric strength is 18.1 MV/m. What is the upper limit of voltage on the inner conductor with respect to the shield when the inner conductor has a radius 1 cm and the inner side of the concentric shield is at a radius of 8 cm?

8.49. For the coaxial capacitor of Fig. 8-16, $a = 3$ cm, $b = 12$ cm, $\epsilon_{r1} = 2.50$, $\epsilon_{r2} = 4.0$. Find $\mathbf{E}_1$, $\mathbf{E}_2$, $\mathbf{D}_1$, and $\mathbf{D}_2$ if the voltage difference is 50 V.

8.50. In Fig 8-23, the center conductor, $r_1 = 1$ mm, is at 100 V with respect to the outer conductor at $r_3 = 100$ mm. The region $1 < r < 50$ mm is free space, while $50 < r < 100$ mm is a dielectric with $\epsilon_r = 2.0$. Find the voltage across each region.

Fig. 8-23

8.51. Find the stored energy per unit length in the two regions of Problem 8.50.

ANSWERS TO SUPPLEMENTARY PROBLEMS

8.23. 6.97 μC/m², 5.64 μC/m², 5.25

8.24. 8.94 kV/m, 206 nC/m², 2.6

8.25. $-3\mathbf{a}_x + 4\mathbf{a}_y - \dfrac{4}{6.5}\mathbf{a}_z$ V/m

8.26. $1.6\mathbf{a}_x - 16\mathbf{a}_y + 6\mathbf{a}_z$ C/m²

8.27. $\dfrac{1}{\epsilon_0}\left(5\mathbf{a}_y + \dfrac{7}{2.5}\mathbf{a}_z\right)$ (V/m), $7.5\mathbf{a}_y + 4.2\mathbf{a}_z$ C/m², 25.02°

8.28. 1.45×10^4, 3.37×10^4, 5.37×10^{-7}, 83.06°

8.29. 5.14 μC/m², 44.4°

8.30. 5.43 nF

8.31. 1.67 mm

8.32. 6.86 pF

8.33. 8.99 pF/m (note units)

8.34. 10.1 pF/m

8.35. 6.92 pF/m

8.36. 2.12 nF

8.37. 267V, 267 kV/m; 400 V, 200 kV/m; 333 V, 133 kV/m

8.38. 139 pF/m

8.39. 137 pF/m

8.40. 45.9 pF/m

8.41. *Partial Ans.* $V_2 = \frac{1}{2}V_1$

8.42. *Partial Ans.* $\rho_{s2} = \sqrt{3}\rho_{s1}$

8.43. *Partial Ans.* $D_2 = 2D_1$

8.44. *Partial Ans.* $D_2 = \frac{1}{2}D_1$

8.45. *Partial Ans.* $V_2 = \frac{1}{6}V_1$

8.46. 0.84

8.47. 0.645 MV/m, 1.03 MV/m

8.48. 0.376 MV

8.49. *Partial Ans.* $\mathbf{E}_2 = \pm(36.1/r)\mathbf{a}_r$ (V/m)

8.50. 91.8 V, 8.2 V

8.51. 59.9 nJ/m, 5.30 nJ/m

CHAPTER 9

Laplace's Equation

9.1 Introduction

Electric field intensity **E** was determined in Chapter 3 by summation or integration of point charges, line charges, and other charge configurations. In Chapter 4, Gauss's law was used to obtain **D**, which then gave **E**. While these two approaches are of value to an understanding of electromagnetic field theory, they both tend to be impractical because charge distributions are not usually known. The method of Chapter 6, where **E** was found to be the negative of the gradient of V, requires that the potential function throughout the region be known. But it is generally not known. Instead, conducting materials in the form of planes, curved surfaces, or lines are usually specified and the voltage on one is known with respect to some reference, often one of the other conductors. Laplace's equation then provides a method whereby the potential function V can be obtained subject to the conditions on the bounding conductors.

9.2 Poisson's Equation and Laplace's Equation

In Section 5.8 one of Maxwell's equations, $\nabla \cdot \mathbf{D} = \rho$, was developed. substituting $\epsilon\mathbf{E} = \mathbf{D}$ and $-\nabla V = \mathbf{E}$,

$$\nabla \cdot \epsilon(-\nabla V) = \rho$$

If throughout the region of interest the medium is homogeneous, then ϵ may be removed from the partial derivatives involved in the divergence, giving

$$\nabla \cdot \nabla V = -\frac{\rho}{\epsilon} \qquad \text{or} \qquad \nabla^2 V = -\frac{\rho}{\epsilon}$$

which is *Poisson's equation.*

When the region of interest contains charges in a known distribution ρ, Poisson's equation can be used to determine the potential function. Very often the region is charge-free (as well as being of uniform permittivity). Poisson's equation then becomes

$$\nabla^2 V = 0$$

which is *Laplace's equation.*

9.3 Explicit Forms of Laplace's Equation

Since the left side of Laplace's equation is the *divergence of the gradient* of V, these two operations can be used to arrive at the form of the equation in a particular coordinate system.

Cartesian Coordinates.

$$\nabla V = \frac{\partial V}{\partial x}\mathbf{a}_x + \frac{\partial V}{\partial y}\mathbf{a}_y + \frac{\partial V}{\partial z}\mathbf{a}_z$$

and, for a general vector field $\mathbf{A}$,

$$\nabla \cdot \mathbf{A} = \frac{\partial A_x}{\partial x} + \frac{\partial A_y}{\partial y} + \frac{\partial A_z}{\partial z}$$

Hence, Laplace's equation is

$$\nabla^2 V = \frac{\partial^2 V}{\partial x^2} + \frac{\partial^2 V}{\partial y^2} + \frac{\partial^2 V}{\partial z^2} = 0$$

Cylindrical Coordinates.

$$\nabla V = \frac{\partial V}{\partial r}\mathbf{a}_r + \frac{1}{r}\frac{\partial V}{\partial \phi}\mathbf{a}_\phi + \frac{\partial V}{\partial z}\mathbf{a}_z$$

and

$$\nabla \cdot \mathbf{A} = \frac{1}{r}\frac{\partial}{\partial r}(rA_r) + \frac{1}{r}\frac{\partial A_\phi}{\partial \phi} + \frac{\partial A_z}{\partial z}$$

so that Laplace's equation is

$$\nabla^2 V = \frac{1}{r}\frac{\partial}{\partial r}\left(r\frac{\partial V}{\partial r}\right) + \frac{1}{r^2}\frac{\partial^2 V}{\partial \phi^2} + \frac{\partial^2 V}{\partial z^2} = 0$$

Spherical Coordinates.

$$\nabla V = \frac{\partial V}{\partial r}\mathbf{a}_r + \frac{1}{r}\frac{\partial V}{\partial \theta}\mathbf{a}_\theta + \frac{1}{r \sin \theta}\frac{\partial V}{\partial \phi}\mathbf{a}_\phi$$

and

$$\nabla \cdot \mathbf{A} = \frac{1}{r^2}\frac{\partial}{\partial r}(r^2 A_r) - \frac{1}{r \sin \theta}\frac{\partial}{\partial \theta}(A_\theta \sin \theta) + \frac{1}{r \sin \theta}\frac{\partial A_\phi}{\partial \phi}$$

so that Laplace's equation is

$$\nabla^2 V = \frac{1}{r^2}\frac{\partial}{\partial r}\left(r^2\frac{\partial V}{\partial r}\right) + \frac{1}{r^2 \sin \theta}\frac{\partial}{\partial \theta}\left(\sin \theta \frac{\partial V}{\partial \theta}\right) + \frac{1}{r^2 \sin^2 \theta}\frac{\partial^2 V}{\partial \phi^2} = 0$$

9.4   Uniqueness Theorem

Any solution to Laplace's equation or Poisson's equation which also satisfies the boundary conditions must be the only solution that exists; it is *unique*. At times there is some confusion on this point due to incomplete boundaries. As an example, consider the conducting plane at $z = 0$, as shown in Fig. 9-1, with a voltage of 100 V. It is clear that both

$$V_1 = 5z + 100$$

and
$$V_2 = 100$$

satisfy Laplace's equations and the requirement that $V = 100$ when $Z = 0$. The answer is that a single conducting surface with a voltage specified and no reference given does not form the complete boundary of a properly defined region. Even two finite parallel conducting planes do not form a complete boundary, since the fringing of the field around the edges cannot be determined. However, when parallel planes are specified and it is also stated to *neglect fringing*, then the region between the planes has proper boundaries.

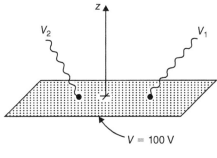

Fig. 9-1

9.5   Mean Value and Maximum Value Theorems

Two important properties of the potential in a charge-free region can be obtained from Laplace's equation:

(1) At the center of an included circle or sphere, the potential V is equal to the average of the values it assumes on the circle or sphere. (See Problems 9.1 and 9.2.)

(2) The potential V cannot have a maximum (or a minimum) within the region. (See Problem 9.3.)

It follows from (2) that any maximum of V must occur on the boundary of the region. Now, since V obeys Laplace's equation,

$$\frac{\partial^2 V}{\partial x^2} + \frac{\partial^2 V}{\partial y^2} + \frac{\partial^2 V}{\partial z^2} = 0$$

so do $\partial V/\partial x$, $\partial V/\partial y$, and $\partial V/\partial z$. Thus, *the Cartesian components of the electric field intensity take their maximum values on the boundary.*

9.6   Cartesian Solution in One Variable

Consider the parallel conductors of Fig. 9-2, where $V = 0$ at $z = 0$ and $V = 100\,\text{V}$ at $z = d$. Assuming the region between the plates is charge-free,

$$\nabla^2 V = \frac{\partial^2 V}{\partial x^2} + \frac{\partial^2 V}{\partial y^2} + \frac{\partial^2 V}{\partial z^2} = 0$$

With fringing neglected, the potential can vary only with z. Then

$$\frac{d^2 V}{dz^2} = 0$$

Integrating,

$$V = Az + B$$

Fig. 9-2

The boundary condition $V = 0$ at $z = 0$ requires that $B = 0$. And $V = 100$ at $z = d$ gives $A = 100/d$. Thus,

$$V = 100\left(\frac{z}{d}\right) \quad (\text{V})$$

The electric field intensity $\mathbf{E}$ can now be obtained from

$$\mathbf{E} = -\nabla V = -\left(\frac{\partial V}{\partial x}\mathbf{a}_x + \frac{\partial V}{\partial y}\mathbf{a}_y + \frac{\partial V}{\partial z}\mathbf{a}_z\right) = -\frac{\partial}{\partial z}\left(100\frac{z}{d}\right)\mathbf{a}_z = -\frac{100}{d}\mathbf{a}_z \quad (\text{V/m})$$

Then
$$\mathbf{D} = -\frac{\epsilon 100}{d}\mathbf{a}_z \quad (\text{C/m}^2)$$

At the conductors,

$$\rho_s = D_n = \pm\frac{\epsilon 100}{d} \quad (\text{C/m}^2)$$

where the plus sign applies at $z = d$ and the minus at $z = 0$.

9.7 Cartesian Product Solution

When the potential in Cartesian coordinates varies in more that one direction, Laplace's equation will contain more than one term. Suppose that V is a function of both x and y and has the special form $V = X(x)Y(y)$. This will make possible the separation of the variables.

$$\frac{\partial^2(XY)}{\partial x^2} + \frac{\partial^2(XY)}{\partial y^2} = 0$$

becomes

$$Y\frac{d^2X}{dx^2} + X\frac{d^2Y}{dy^2} = 0 \quad \text{or} \quad \frac{1}{X}\frac{d^2X}{dx^2} + \frac{1}{Y}\frac{d^2Y}{dy^2} = 0$$

Since the first term is independent of y, and the second of x, each may be set equal to a constant. However, the constant for one must be the negative of that for the other. Let the constant be a^2.

$$\frac{1}{X}\frac{d^2X}{dx^2} = a^2 \qquad \frac{1}{Y}\frac{d^2Y}{dy^2} = -a^2$$

The general solution for X (for a given a) is

$$X = A_1 e^{ax} + A_2 e^{-ax}$$

or, equivalently,

$$X = A_3 \cosh ax + A_4 \sinh ax$$

and the general solution for Y (for a given a) is

$$Y = B_1 e^{jay} + B_2 e^{-jay}$$

or, equivalently,

$$Y = B_3 \cos ay + B_4 \sin ay$$

Therefore, the potential function in the variables x and y can be written

$$V = (A_1 e^{ax} + A_2 e^{-ax})(B_1 e^{jay} + B_2 e^{-jay})$$

or

$$V = (A_3 \cosh ax + A_4 \sinh ax)(B_3 \cos ay + B_4 \sin ay)$$

Because Laplace's equation is a linear, homogeneous equation, a sum of products of the above form—each product corresponding to a different value of a—is also a solution. The most general solution can be generated in this fashion.

Three-dimensional solutions, $V = X(x)Y(y)Z(z)$, of similar form can be obtained, but now there are two separation constants.

9.8   Cylindrical Product Solution

If a solution of the form $V = R(r)\Phi(\phi)Z(z)$ is assumed, Laplace's equation becomes

$$\frac{\Phi Z}{r}\frac{d}{dr}\left(r\frac{dR}{dr}\right) + \frac{RZ}{r^2}\frac{d^2\Phi}{d\phi^2} + R\Phi\frac{d^2Z}{dz^2} = 0$$

Dividing by $R\,\Phi\,Z$ and expanding the r-derivative,

$$\frac{1}{R}\frac{d^2R}{dr^2} + \frac{1}{Rr}\frac{dR}{dr} + \frac{1}{r^2\Phi}\frac{d^2\Phi}{d\phi^2} = -\frac{1}{Z}\frac{d^2Z}{dz^2} = -b^2$$

The r and ϕ terms contain no z and the z term contains neither r nor ϕ. They may be set equal to a constant, $-b^2$, as above. Then

$$\frac{1}{Z}\frac{d^2Z}{dz^2} = b^2$$

This equation was encountered in the Cartesian product solution. The solution is

$$Z = C_1 \cosh bz + C_2 \sinh bz$$

Now the equation in r and ϕ may be further separated as follows:

$$\frac{r^2}{R}\frac{d^2R}{dr^2} + \frac{r}{R}\frac{dR}{dr} + b^2r^2 = -\frac{1}{\Phi}\frac{d^2\Phi}{d\phi^2} = a^2$$

The resulting equation in ϕ,

$$\frac{1}{\Phi}\frac{d^2\Phi}{d\phi^2} = -a^2$$

has solution

$$\Phi = C_3 \cos a\phi + C_4 \sin a\phi$$

The equation in r,

$$\frac{d^2R}{dr^2} + \frac{1}{r}\frac{dR}{dr} + \left(b^2 - \frac{a^2}{r^2}\right)R = 0$$

is a form of *Bessel's differential equation*. Its solutions are in the form of power series called *Bessel functions*.

$$R = C_5 J_a(br) + C_6 N_a(br)$$

where

$$J_a(br) = \sum_{m=0}^{\infty} \frac{(-1)^m (br/2)^{a+2m}}{m!\,\Gamma(a+m+1)}$$

and

$$N_a(br) = \frac{(\cos a\pi)J_a(br) - J_{-a}(br)}{\sin a\pi}$$

The series $J_a(br)$ is known as a Bessel function of the *first kind, order* a; if $a = n$, an integer, the gamma function in the power series may be replaced by $(n + m)!$. $N_a(br)$ is a Bessel function of the *second kind, order* a; if $a = n$, an integer, $N_n(br)$ is defined as the limit of the above quotient as $a \to n$.

The function $N_a(br)$ behaves like $\ln r$ near $r = 0$ (see Fig. 9-3). Therefore, it is not involved in the solution ($C_6 = 0$) whenever the potential is known to be finite at $r = 0$.

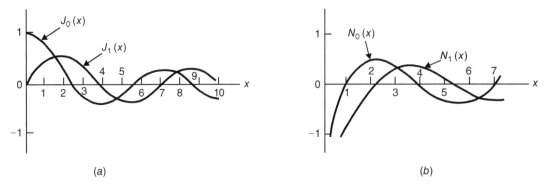

Fig. 9-3

For integral order n and large argument x, the Bessel functions behave like damped sine waves:

$$J_n(x) \approx \sqrt{\frac{2}{\pi x}} \cos\left(x - \frac{\pi}{4} - \frac{n\pi}{2}\right) \qquad N_n(x) \approx \sqrt{\frac{2}{\pi x}} \sin\left(x - \frac{\pi}{4} - \frac{n\pi}{2}\right)$$

See Fig. 9-3.

9.9　Spherical Product Solution

Of particular interest in spherical coordinates are those problems in which V may vary with r and θ but not with ϕ. For product solution $V = R(r)\Theta(\theta)$, Laplace's equation becomes

$$\left(\frac{r^2}{R}\frac{d^2R}{dr^2} + \frac{2r}{R}\frac{dR}{dr}\right) + \left(\frac{1}{\Theta}\frac{d^2\Theta}{d\theta^2} + \frac{1}{\Theta\tan\theta}\frac{d\Theta}{d\theta}\right) = 0$$

The separation constant is chosen as $n(n + 1)$, where n is an integer, for reasons which will become apparent. The two separated equations are

$$r^2\frac{d^2R}{dr^2} + 2r\frac{dR}{dr} - n(n+1)R = 0$$

and

$$\frac{d^2\Theta}{d\theta^2} + \frac{1}{\tan\theta}\frac{d\Theta}{d\theta} + n(n+1)\Theta = 0$$

The equation in r has the solution

$$R = C_1 r^n + C_2 r^{-(n+1)}$$

The equation in θ possesses (unlike Bessel's equation) a polynomial solution of degree n in the variable $\xi = \cos\theta$, given by

$$P_n(\xi) = \frac{1}{2^n n!}\frac{d^n}{d\xi^n}(\xi^2 - 1)^n \qquad n = 0, 1, 2, \dots.$$

The polynomial $P_n(\xi)$ is the *Legendre polynomial of order n*. There is a second, independent solution, $Q_n(\xi)$, which is logarithmically infinite at $\xi = \pm1$ (i.e., $\theta = 0, \pi$).

SOLVED PROBLEMS

9.1. As shown in Fig. 9-4(a), the potential has the value V_1 on $1/n$ of the circle, and the value 0 on the rest of the circle. Find the potential at the center of the circle. The entire region is charge-free.

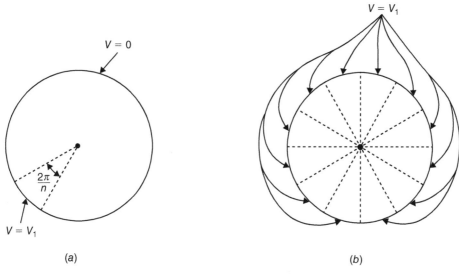

(a)   (b)

Fig. 9-4

Call the potential at the center V_c. Laplace's equation allows superposition of solutions. If n problems of the type of Fig. 9-4(a) are superposed, the result is the problem shown in Fig. 9-4(b). Because of the rotational symmetry, each subproblem in Fig. 9-4(b) gives the same potential, V_c, at the center of the circle. The total potential at the center is therefore nV_c. But, clearly, the unique solution for Fig. 9-4(b) is $V = V_1$ everywhere inside the circle, in particular at the center. Hence,

$$nV_c = V_1 \quad \text{or} \quad V_c = \frac{V_1}{n}$$

9.2. Show how the mean value theorem follows from the result of Problem 9.1.

Consider first the special case shown in Fig. 9-5, where the potential assumes n different values on n equal segments of a circle. A superposition of the solutions found in Problem 9.1 gives for the potential at the center

$$V_c = \frac{V_1}{n} + \frac{V_2}{n} + \cdots + \frac{V_n}{n} = \frac{V_1 + V_2 + \cdots + V_n}{n}$$

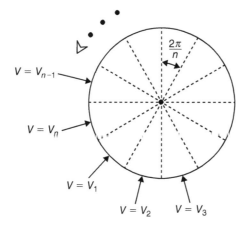

Fig. 9-5

which is the mean value theorem in this special case. With $\Delta\phi = 2\pi/n$,

$$V_c = \frac{1}{2\pi}(V_1\Delta\phi + V_2\Delta\phi + \cdots + V_n\Delta\phi)$$

Now, letting $n \to \infty$,

$$V_c = \frac{1}{2\pi}\int_0^{2\pi} V(\phi)\,d\phi$$

which is the general mean value theorem for a circle.

Exactly the same reasoning, but with solid angles in place of plane angles, establishes the mean value theorem for a sphere.

9.3. Prove that within a charge-free region the potential cannot attain a maximum value

Suppose that a maximum were attained at an interior point P. Then a very small sphere could be centered on P, such that the potential V_c at P exceeded the potential at each point on the sphere. Then V_c would also exceed the average value of the potential over the sphere. But that would contradict the mean value theorem.

9.4. Find the potential function for the region between the parallel circular disks of Fig. 9-6. Neglect fringing.

Since V is not a function of r or ϕ, Laplace's equation reduces to

$$\frac{d^2V}{dz^2} = 0$$

and the solution is $V = Az + B$.

The parallel circular disks have a potential function identical to that for any pair of parallel planes. For another choice of axes, the linear potential function might be $Ay + B$ or $Ax + B$.

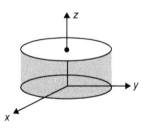

Fig. 9-6

9.5. Two parallel conducting planes in free space are at $y = 0$ and $y = 0.02$ m, and the zero voltage reference is at $y = 0.01$ m. If $\mathbf{D} = 253\mathbf{a}_y$ nC/m^2 between the conductors, determine the conductor voltages.

From Problem 9.4, $V = Ay + B$. Then

$$\mathbf{E} = \frac{\mathbf{D}}{\epsilon_0} = -\nabla V = -A\mathbf{a}_y$$

$$\frac{253\times10^{-9}}{8.854\times10^{-12}}\mathbf{a}_y = -A\mathbf{a}_y$$

whence $A = -2.86 \times 10^4$ V/m. Then,

$$0 = (-2.86\times10^4)(0.01) + B \qquad \text{or} \qquad B = 2.86\times10^2 \text{ V}$$

and $\qquad\qquad\qquad V = -2.86\times10^4 y + 2.86\times10^2 \qquad \text{(V)}$

Then, for $y = 0$, $V = 286$ V and for $y = 0.02$, $V = -286$ V.

9.6. The parallel conducting disks in Fig. 9-7 are separated by 5 mm and contain a dielectric for which $\epsilon_r = 2.2$. Determine the charge densities on the disks.

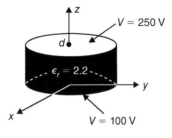

Fig. 9-7

Since $V = Az + B$,

$$A = \frac{\Delta V}{\Delta z} = \frac{250 - 100}{5 \times 10^{-3}} = 3 \times 10^4 \text{ V/m}$$

and
$$\mathbf{E} = -\nabla V = -3 \times 10^4 \mathbf{a}_z \text{ V/m}$$
$$\mathbf{D} = \epsilon_0 \epsilon_r \mathbf{E} = -5.84 \times 10^{-7} \mathbf{a}_z \text{ C/m}^2$$

Since $\mathbf{D}$ is constant between the disks, and $D_n = \rho_s$ at a conductor surface,

$$\rho_s = \pm 5.84 \times 10^{-7} \text{ C/m}^2$$

+ on the upper plate, and − on the lower plate.

9.7. Find the potential function and the electric field intensity for the region between two concentric right circular cylinders, where $V = 0$ at $r = 1$ mm and $V = 150$ V at $r = 20$ mm. Neglect fringing. See Fig. 9-8.

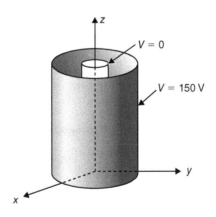

Fig. 9-8

The potential is constant with ϕ and z. Then Laplace's equation reduces to

$$\frac{1}{r} \frac{d}{dr} \left(r \frac{dV}{dr} \right) = 0$$

Integrating once,

$$r \frac{dV}{dr} = A$$

and again, $V = A \ln r + B$. Applying the boundary conditions,

$$0 = A \ln 0.001 + B \qquad 150 = A \ln 0.020 + B$$

gives $A = 50.1$, $B = 345.9$. Thus,

$$V = 50.1 \ln r + 345.9 \text{ (V)}$$

and

$$\mathbf{E} = \frac{50.1}{r}(-\mathbf{a}_r) \quad (\text{V}/\text{m})$$

9.8. In cylindrical coordinates two $\phi = $ const. planes are insulated along the z axis, as shown in Fig. 9-9. Neglect fringing and find the expression for $\mathbf{E}$ between the planes, assuming a potential of 100 V for $\phi = \alpha$ and a zero reference at $\phi = 0$.

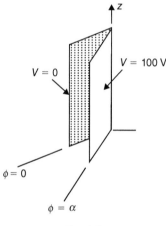

$V = 0$

$V = 100$ V

$\phi = 0$

$\phi = \alpha$

Fig. 9-9

This problem has already been solved in Problem 8.10; here Laplace's equation will be used to obtain the same result.

Since the potential is constant with r and z, Laplace's equation is

$$\frac{1}{r}\frac{d^2V}{d\phi^2} = 0$$

Integrating, $V = A\phi + B$. Applying the boundary conditions,

$$0 = A(0) + B \qquad 100 = A(\alpha) + B$$

whence

$$A = \frac{100}{\alpha} \qquad B = 0$$

Thus,

$$V = 100\frac{\phi}{\alpha}$$

and

$$\mathbf{E} = -\nabla V = -\frac{1}{r}\frac{d}{d\phi}\left(100\frac{\phi}{\alpha}\right)\mathbf{a}_\phi = -\frac{100}{r\alpha}\mathbf{a}_\phi \quad (\text{V}/\text{m})$$

9.9. In spherical coordinates, $V = 0$ for $r = 0.10$ m and $V = 100$ V for $r = 2.0$ m. Assuming free space between these concentric spherical shells, find $\mathbf{E}$ and $\mathbf{D}$.

Since V is not a function of θ or ϕ, Laplace's equation reduces to

$$\frac{1}{r^2}\frac{d}{dr}\left(r^2\frac{dV}{dr}\right) = 0$$

Integrating gives

$$r^2 \frac{dV}{dr} = A$$

and a second integration gives

$$V = \frac{-A}{r} + B$$

The boundary conditions give

$$0 = \frac{-A}{0.10} + B \quad \text{and} \quad 100 = \frac{-A}{2.00} + B$$

whence $A = 10.53$ V $\cdot$ m, $B = 105.3$ V. Then

$$V = \frac{-10.53}{r} + 105.3 \quad (V)$$

$$\mathbf{E} = -\nabla V = -\frac{dV}{dr} \mathbf{a}_r = -\frac{10.53}{r^2} \mathbf{a}_r \quad (V/m)$$

$$\mathbf{D} = \epsilon_0 \mathbf{E} = \frac{-9.32 \times 10^{-11}}{r^2} \mathbf{a}_r \quad (C/m^2)$$

9.10. In spherical coordinates, $V = -25$ V on a conductor at $r = 2$ cm and $V = 150$ V at $r = 35$ cm. The space between the conductors is a dielectric for which $\varepsilon_r = 3.12$. Find the surface charge densities on the conductors.

From Problem 9.9,

$$V = \frac{-A}{r} + B$$

The constants are determined from the boundary conditions

$$-25 = \frac{-A}{0.02} + B \qquad 150 = \frac{-A}{0.35} + B$$

giving

$$V = \frac{-3.71}{r} + 160.61 \quad (V)$$

$$\mathbf{E} = -\nabla V = -\frac{d}{dr}\left(\frac{-3.71}{r} + 160.61\right)\mathbf{a}_r = \frac{-3.71}{r^2}\mathbf{a}_r \quad (V/m)$$

$$\mathbf{D} = \epsilon_0 \epsilon_r \mathbf{E} = \frac{-0.103}{r^2}\mathbf{a}_r \quad (nC/m^2)$$

On a conductor surface, $D_n = \rho_s$

at $r = 0.02$ m: $\rho_s = \frac{-0.103}{(0.02)^2} = -256 \text{ nC/m}^2$

at $r = 0.35$ m: $\rho_s = \frac{+0.103}{(0.35)^2} = +0.837 \text{ nC/m}^2$

9.11. Solve Laplace's equation for the region between coaxial cones, as shown in Fig. 9-10. A potential V_1 is assumed at θ_1, and $V = 0$ at θ_2. The cone vertices are insulated at $r = 0$.

The potential is constant with r and ϕ. Laplace's equation reduces to

$$\frac{1}{r^2 \sin\theta} \frac{d}{d\theta}\left(\sin\theta \frac{dV}{d\theta}\right) = 0$$

Integrating

$$\sin\theta\left(\frac{dV}{d\theta}\right) = A$$

and

$$V = A \ln\left(\tan\frac{\theta}{2}\right) + B$$

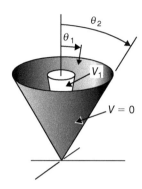

Fig. 9-10

The constants are found from

$$V_1 = A \ln\left(\tan\frac{\theta_1}{2}\right) + B \qquad 0 = A \ln\left(\tan\frac{\theta_2}{2}\right) + B$$

Hence,

$$V = V_1 \frac{\ln\left(\tan\dfrac{\theta}{2}\right) - \ln\left(\tan\dfrac{\theta_2}{2}\right)}{\ln\left(\tan\dfrac{\theta_1}{2}\right) - \ln\left(\tan\dfrac{\theta_2}{2}\right)}$$

9.12. In Problem 9.11, let $\theta_1 = 10°$, $\theta_2 = 30°$, and $V_1 = 100$ V. Find the voltage at $\theta = 20°$. At what angle θ is the voltage 50 V?

Substituting the values in the general potential expression gives

$$V = -89.34\left[\ln\left(\tan\frac{\theta}{2}\right) - \ln 0.268\right] = -89.34 \ln\left(\frac{\tan\dfrac{\theta}{2}}{0.268}\right)$$

Then, at $\theta = 20°$, $\qquad V = -89.34 \ln\left(\dfrac{\tan 10°}{0.268}\right) = 37.40$ V

For $V = 50$ V, $\qquad 50 = -89.34 \ln\left(\dfrac{\tan \theta/2}{0.268}\right)$

Solving gives $\theta = 17.41°$.

9.13. With reference to Problems 9.11 and 9.12 and Fig. 9-11, find the charge distribution on the conducting plane at $\theta_2 = 90°$.

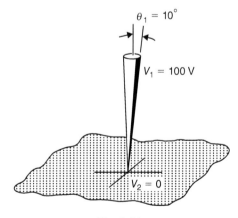

Fig. 9-11

The potential is obtained by substituting $\theta_2 = 90°$, $\theta_1 = 10°$, and $V_1 = 100$ V in the expression of Problem 9.11. Thus,

$$V = 100 \frac{\ln\left(\dfrac{\tan\theta}{2}\right)}{\ln(\tan 5°)}$$

Then

$$\mathbf{E} = -\frac{1}{r}\frac{dV}{d\theta}\mathbf{a}_\theta = \frac{-100}{(r\sin\theta)\ln(\tan 5°)}\mathbf{a}_\theta = \frac{41.05}{r\sin\theta}\mathbf{a}_\theta$$

$$\mathbf{D} = \epsilon_0\mathbf{E} = \frac{3.63\times 10^{-10}}{r\sin\theta}\mathbf{a}_\theta \qquad (C/m^2)$$

On the plane $\theta = 90°$, $\sin\theta = 1$, and the direction of $\mathbf{D}$ requires that the surface charge on the plane be negative in sign. Hence,

$$\rho_s = -\frac{3.63\times 10^{-10}}{r} \qquad (C/m^2)$$

9.14. Find the capacitance between the two cones of Fig. 9-12. Assume free space.

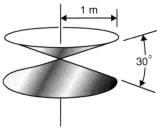

1 m

30°

Fig. 9-12

If fringing is neglected, the potential function is given by the expression of Problem 9.11 with $\theta_1 = 75°$, $\theta_2 = 105°$. Thus,

$$V = V_1 \frac{\ln\left(\tan\dfrac{\theta}{2}\right) - \ln(\tan 52.5°)}{\ln(\tan 37.5°) - \ln(\tan 52.5°)}$$

$$= (-1.89 V_1)\ln\left(\tan\frac{\theta}{2}\right) + \text{const.}$$

from which

$$\mathbf{D} = \epsilon_0\mathbf{E} = \epsilon_0\left(-\frac{1}{r}\frac{dV}{d\theta}\mathbf{a}_\theta\right) = \frac{1.89\,\epsilon_0 V_1}{r\sin\theta}\mathbf{a}_\theta$$

The charge density on the upper plate is then

$$\rho_r = D_n = \frac{1.89\epsilon_0 V_1}{r\sin 75°}$$

so that the total charge on the upper plate is

$$Q = \int \rho_s\, dS = \int_0^{2\pi}\int_0^{\csc 75°}\frac{1.89\epsilon_0 V_1}{r\sin 75°} r\sin 75°\, dr\, d\phi = 12.28\epsilon_0 V_1$$

and the capacitance is $C = Q/V_1 = 12.28\epsilon_0$.

9.15. The region between two concentric right circular cylinders contains a uniform charge density ρ. Use Poisson's equation to find V.

Neglecting fringing, Poisson's equation reduces to

$$\frac{1}{r}\frac{d}{dr}\left(r\frac{dV}{dr}\right) = -\frac{\rho}{\epsilon}$$

$$\frac{d}{dr}\left(r\frac{dV}{dr}\right) = -\frac{\rho r}{\epsilon}$$

Integrating,

$$r\frac{dV}{dr} = -\frac{\rho r^2}{2\epsilon} + A$$

$$\frac{dV}{dr} = -\frac{\rho r}{2\epsilon} + \frac{A}{r}$$

$$V = -\frac{\rho r^2}{4\epsilon} + A\ln r + B$$

Note that static problems involving charge distributions in space are theoretical exercises, since no means exist to hold the charges in position against the coulomb forces.

9.16. The region

$$-\frac{\pi}{2} < \frac{z}{z_0} < \frac{\pi}{2}$$

has a charge density $\rho = 10^{-8}\cos(z/z_0)$ (C/m³). Elsewhere, the charge density is zero. Find V and $\mathbf{E}$ from Poisson's equation, and compare with the results given by Gauss's law.

Since V is not a function of x or y, Poisson's equation is

$$\frac{d^2V}{dz^2} = -\frac{\rho}{\epsilon} = -\frac{10^{-8}\cos(z/z_0)}{\epsilon}$$

Integrating twice,

$$V = \frac{10^{-8}z_0^2\cos(z/z_0)}{\epsilon} + Az + B \qquad \text{(V)}$$

and

$$\mathbf{E} = -\nabla V = \left(\frac{10^{-8}z_0\sin(z/z_0)}{\epsilon} - A\right)\mathbf{a}_z \qquad \text{(V/m)}$$

But by the symmetry of the charge distribution, the field must vanish on the plane $z = 0$. Therefore, $A = 0$ and

$$\mathbf{E} = \frac{10^{-8}z_0\sin(z/z_0)}{\epsilon}\mathbf{a}_z \qquad \text{(V/m)}$$

A special Gaussian surface centered about $z = 0$ is shown in Fig. 9-13. $\mathbf{D}$ cuts only the top and bottom surfaces, each of area A. Furthermore, since the charge distribution is symmetrical about $z = 0$, $\mathbf{D}$ must be antisymmetrical about $z = 0$, so that $\mathbf{D}_{\text{top}} = D\mathbf{a}_z$, $\mathbf{D}_{\text{bottom}} = D(-\mathbf{a}_z)$.

Fig. 9-13

$$D\int_{\text{top}} dS + D\int_{\text{bottom}} dS = \int_{-z}^{z}\iint 10^{-8}\cos(z/z_0)\,dx\,dy\,dz$$

$$2DA = 2z_0 A 10^{-8}\sin(z/z_0)$$

or
$$D = z_0 10^{-8}\sin(z/z_0) \qquad \text{for} \qquad 0 < z < \pi z_0/2$$

Then, for $-\pi z_0/2 < z < \pi z_0/2$,

$$\mathbf{D} = z_0 10^{-8}\sin(z/z_0)\,\mathbf{a}_z \qquad (\text{C/m}^2)$$

and $\mathbf{E} = \mathbf{D}/\epsilon$ agrees with the result from Poisson's equation.

9.17. A potential in cylindrical coordinates is a function of r and ϕ but not z. Obtain the separated differential equations for R and Φ, where $V = R(r)\Phi(\phi)$, and solve them. The region is charge-free.

Laplace's equation becomes

$$\Phi\frac{d^2R}{dr^2} + \frac{\Phi}{r}\frac{dR}{dr} + \frac{R}{r^2}\frac{d^2\Phi}{d\phi^2} = 0$$

or
$$\frac{r^2}{R}\frac{d^2R}{dr^2} + \frac{r}{R}\frac{dR}{dr} = -\frac{1}{\Phi}\frac{d^2\Phi}{d\phi^2}$$

The left side is a function of r only, while the right side is a function of ϕ only; therefore, both sides are equal to a constant, a^2.

$$\frac{r^2}{R}\frac{d^2R}{dr^2} + \frac{r}{R}\frac{dR}{dr} = a^2$$

or
$$\frac{d^2R}{dr^2} + \frac{1}{r}\frac{dR}{dr} - \frac{a^2R}{r^2} = 0$$

with solution $R = C_1 r^a + C_2 r^{-a}$. Also,

$$-\frac{1}{\Phi}\frac{d^2\Phi}{d\phi^2} = a^2$$

with solution $\Phi = C_3\cos a\phi + C_4\sin a\phi$.

9.18. Given the potential function $V = V_0(\sinh ax)(\sin az)$ (see Section 9.7), determine the shape and location of the surfaces on which $V = 0$ and $V = V_0$. Assume that $a > 0$.

Since the potential is not a function of y, the equipotential surfaces extend to $\pm\infty$ in the y direction. Because $\sin az = 0$ for $z = n\pi/a$, where $n = 0, 1, 2, \ldots$, the planes $z = 0$ and $z = \pi/a$ are at zero potential. Because $\sinh ax = 0$ for $x = 0$, the plane $x = 0$ is also at zero potential. The $V = 0$ equipotential is shown in Fig. 9-14.

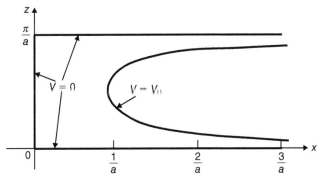

Fig. 9-14

The potential function is then

$$V = \sum_{n\,\mathrm{odd}} \frac{4V_0}{n\pi} \frac{\sinh(n\pi z/c)}{\sinh(n\pi d/c)} \sin \frac{n\pi x}{c}$$

for $0 < x < c, 0 < z < d$.

9.20. Identify the spherical product solution

$$V = \frac{C_2}{r^2} P_1(\cos\theta) = \frac{C_2 \cos\theta}{r^2}$$

(Section 9.9, with $C_1 = 0$, $n = 1$) with a point dipole at the origin.

Fig. 9-16 shows a finite dipole along the z axis, consisting of a point charge $+Q$ at $z = +d/2$ and a point charge $-Q$ at $z = -d/2$. The quantity $p = Qd$ is the dipole moment (Section 8.1). The potential at point P is

$$V = \frac{Q}{4\pi\epsilon_0 r_1} - \frac{Q}{4\pi\epsilon_0 r_2} = \frac{P}{4\pi\epsilon_0 d}\left(\frac{r_2 - r_1}{r_1 r_2}\right)$$

A point dipole at the origin is obtained in the limit as $d \to 0$. For small d,

$$r_2 - r_1 \approx d\cos\theta_2 \approx d\cos\theta \quad \text{and} \quad r_1 r_2 \approx r^2$$

Therefore, in the limit,

$$V = \frac{p}{4\pi\epsilon_0} \frac{\cos\theta}{r^2}$$

which is the spherical product solution with $C_2 = p/4\pi\epsilon_0$.

Similarly, the higher-order Legendre polynomials correspond to point quadrupoles, octupoles, and so on.

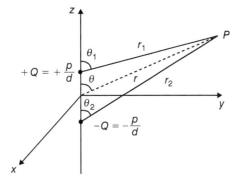

Fig. 9-16

SUPPLEMENTARY PROBLEMS

9.21. In Cartesian coordinates, a potential is a function of x only. At $x = -2.0$ cm, $V = 25.0$ V and $\mathbf{E} = 1.5 \times 10^3(-\mathbf{a}_x)$ V/m throughout the region. Find V at $x = 3.0$ cm.

9.22. In Cartesian coordinates, a plane at $z = 3.0$ cm is the voltage reference. Find the voltage and the charge density on the conductor $z = 0$ if $\mathbf{E} = 6.67 \times 10^3 \mathbf{a}_z$ V/m for $z > 0$ and the region contains a dielectric for which $\epsilon_r = 4.5$.

9.23. In cylindrical coordinates, $V = 75.0$ V at $r = 5$ mm and $V = 0$ at $r = 60$ mm. Find the voltage at $r = 130$ mm if the potential depends only on r.

9.24. Concentric, right circular, conducting cylinders in free space at $r = 5$ mm and $r = 25$ mm have voltages of zero and V_0, respectively. If $\mathbf{E} = -8.28 \times 10^3 \mathbf{a}_r$ V/m at $r = 15$ mm, find V_0 and the charge density on the outer conductor.

9.25. For concentric conducting cylinders, $V = 75$ V at $r = 1$ mm and $V = 0$ at $r = 20$ mm. Find $\mathbf{D}$ in the region between the cylinders, where $\epsilon_r = 3.6$.

9.26. Conducting planes at $\phi = 10°$ and $\phi = 0°$ in cylindrical coordinates have voltages of 75 V and zero, respectively. Obtain $\mathbf{D}$ in the region between the planes, which contains a material for which $\epsilon_r = 1.65$.

9.27. Two square conducting planes 50 cm on a side are separated by 2.0 cm along one side and 2.5 cm along the other (Fig. 9-17). Assume a voltage difference and compare the charge density at the center of one plane to that on an identical pair with a uniform separation of 2.0 cm.

Fig. 9-17

9.28. The voltage reference is at $r = 15$ mm in spherical coordinates and the voltage is V_0 at $r = 200$ mm. Given $\mathbf{E} = -334.7\mathbf{a}_r$ V/m at $r = 110$ mm, find V_0. The potential is a function of r only.

9.29. In spherical coordinates, $V = 865$ V at $r = 50$ cm and $\mathbf{E} = 748.2\mathbf{a}_r$ V/m at $r = 85$ cm. Determine the location of the voltage reference if the potential depends only on r.

9.30. With a zero reference at infinity and $V = 45.0$ V at $r = 0.22$ m in spherical coordinates, a dielectric of $\epsilon_r = 1.72$ occupies the region $0.22 < r < 1.00$ m and free space occupies $r > 1.00$ m. Determine E at $r = 1.00 \pm 0$ m.

9.31. In Fig. 9-18 the cone at $\theta = 45°$ has a voltage V with respect to the reference at $\theta = 30°$. At $r = 0.25$ m and $\theta = 30°$, $\mathbf{E} = -2.30 \times 10^3 \mathbf{a}_\theta$ V/m. Determine the voltage difference V.

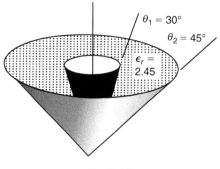

Fig. 9-18

9.32. In Problem 9.31 determine the surface charge densities on the conducting cones at 30° and 45°, if $\epsilon_r = 2.45$ between the cones.

9.33. Find E in the region between the two cones shown in Fig. 9-19.

$\theta = 20°$

$V = V_1 > 0$

$V = 0$

$\theta = 160°$

Fig. 9-19

9.34. In cylindrical coordinates, $\rho = 111/r$ (pC/m^3). Given that $V = 0$ at $r = 1.0$ m and $V = 50$ V at $r = 3.0$ m due to this charge configuration, find the expression for E.

9.35. Determine E in spherical coordinates from Poisson's equation, assuming a uniform charge density ρ.

9.36. Specialize the solution found in Problem 9.35 to the case of a uniformly charged sphere.

9.37. Assume that a potential in cylindrical coordinates is a function of r and z but not ϕ, $V = R(r)Z(z)$. Write Laplace's equation and obtain the separated differential equations in r and z. Show that the solutions to the equation in r are Bessel functions and that the solutions in z are exponentials or hyperbolic functions.

9.38. Verify that the first five Legendre polynomials are

$$P_0(\cos\theta) = 1$$
$$P_1(\cos\theta) = \cos\theta$$
$$P_2(\cos\theta) = \frac{1}{2}(3\cos^2\theta - 1)$$
$$P_3(\cos\theta) = \frac{1}{2}(5\cos^3\theta - 3\cos\theta)$$
$$P_4(\cos\theta) = \frac{1}{8}(35\cos^4\theta - 30\cos^2\theta + 3)$$

and graph them against $\zeta = \cos\theta$.

9.39. Obtain E for Problem 9.18 and plot several values on Fig. 9-14. Note the orthogonality of E and the equipotential surfaces.

9.40. Given $V = V_0(\cosh ax)(\sin ay)$, where $a > 0$, determine the shape and location of the surfaces on which $V = 0$ and $V = V_0$. Make a sketch similar to Fig. 9-14.

9.41. From the potential function of Problem 9.40, obtain E and plot several values on the sketch of the equipotential surfaces, Fig. 9-20.

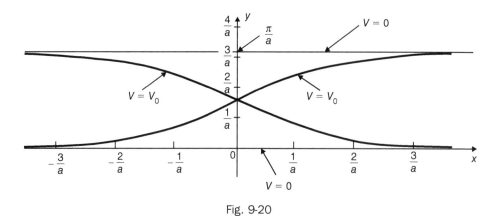

Fig. 9-20

9.42. Use a superposition of the product solutions found in Problem 9.17 to obtain the potential function for the semicircular strip shown in Fig. 9-21.

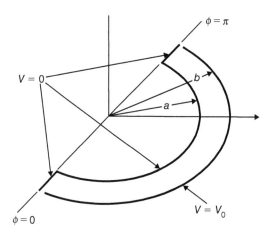

Fig. 9-21

ANSWERS TO SUPPLEMENTARY PROBLEMS

9.21. 100 V

9.22. 200 V, 266 nC/m^2

9.23. −23.34 V

9.24. 200 V, +44 nC/m^2

9.25. $(798/r)\mathbf{a}_r$ (pC/m^2)

9.26. $(-6.28/r)\mathbf{a}_r$ (nC/m^2)

9.27. 0.89

9.28. 250 V

9.29. $r = 250$ cm

9.30. 8.55 V/m, 14.7 V/m

9.31. 125.5 V

9.32. $\dfrac{-12.5}{r}$ (nC/m^2), $\dfrac{8.84}{r}$ (nC/m^2)

9.33. $\dfrac{0.288V_1}{r\sin\theta}$ (V/m)

9.34. $\left(12.5 - \dfrac{68.3}{r}\right)\mathbf{a}_r$ (V/m)

9.35. $\left(\dfrac{\rho r}{3\epsilon} - \dfrac{A}{r^2}\right)\mathbf{a}_r$

9.36. See Problem 3.54.

9.38. See Fig. 9-22.

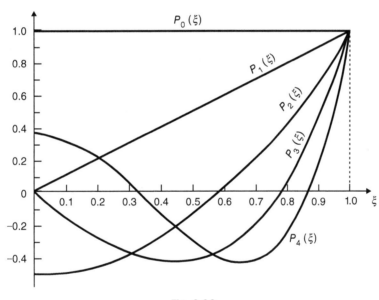

Fig. 9-22

9.39. $\mathbf{E} = -V_0 a[(\cosh ax)(\sin az)\mathbf{a}_x + (\sinh ax)(\cos az)\mathbf{a}_z]$

9.40. See Fig. 9-20.

9.41. $\mathbf{E} = -V_0 a[(\sinh ax)(\sin ay)\mathbf{a}_x + (\cosh ax)(\cos ay)\mathbf{a}_y]$

9.42. $V = \displaystyle\sum_{n\,\text{odd}} \dfrac{4V_0}{n\pi}\, \dfrac{r^n - (a^2/r)^n}{b^n - (a^2/b)^n}\sin n\phi$

CHAPTER 10

Magnetic Field and Boundary Conditions

10.1 Introduction

A static magnetic field can originate from either a constant current or a permanent magnet. This chapter will treat the magnetic fields of constant currents. (Time-varying magnetic fields, which coexist with time-varying electric fields, will be examined in Chapter 13.) It will also treat the behavior of the magnetic field strength **H** and the magnetic flux density **B** across the interface of two different material. The treatment uses the static magnetic field as the vehicle to develop boundary conditions, but the results apply to both static and time-varying magnetic fields.

10.2 Biot-Savart Law

A differential *magnetic field strength*, $d\mathbf{H}$, results from a differential current element $I\,d\mathbf{l}$. The field varies inversely with the distance squared, is independent of the surrounding medium, and has a direction given by the cross product of $I\,d\mathbf{l}$ and $\mathbf{a}_R$. This relationship is known as the *Biot-Savart law*:

$$d\mathbf{H} = \frac{I\,d\mathbf{l} \times \mathbf{a}_R}{4\pi R^2} \quad (\text{A}/\text{m})$$

The direction of **R** must be from the current element to the point at which $d\mathbf{H}$ is to be determined, as shown in Fig. 10-1.

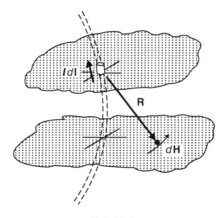

Fig. 10-1

Current elements have no separate existence. All elements making up the complete current filament contribute to **H** and must be included. The summation leads to the integral form of the Biot-Savart law:

$$\mathbf{H} = \oint \frac{I\, d\mathbf{l} \times \mathbf{a}_R}{4\pi R^2}$$

A *closed* line integral is required to ensure that *all* current elements are included (the contour may close at ∞).

EXAMPLE 1. An infinitely long, straight, filamentary current I along the z axis in cylindrical coordinates is shown in Fig. 10-2. A point in the $z = 0$ plane is selected with no loss in generality. In differential form,

$$dH = \frac{I\, dz\, \mathbf{a}_z \times (r\mathbf{a}_r - z\mathbf{a}_z)}{4\pi(r^2 + z^2)^{3/2}}$$

$$= \frac{I\, dz\, r\mathbf{a}_\phi}{4\pi(r^2 + z^2)^{3/2}}$$

The variable of integration is z. Since $\mathbf{a}_\phi$ does not change with z, it may be removed from the integrand before integrating.

$$\mathbf{H} = \left[\int_{-\infty}^{\infty} \frac{Ir\, dz}{4\pi(r^2 + z^2)^{3/2}}\right] \mathbf{a}_\phi = \frac{1}{2\pi r}\mathbf{a}_\phi$$

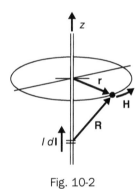

Fig. 10-2

This important result shows that **H** is inversely proportional to the radial distance. The direction is seen to be in agreement with the "right-hand rule" whereby the fingers of the right hand point in the direction of the field when the conductor is grasped such that the right thumb points in the direction of the current.

EXAMPLE 2. An infinite current sheet lies in the $z = 0$ plane with $\mathbf{K} = K\mathbf{a}_y$, as shown in Fig. 10-3. Find **H**.

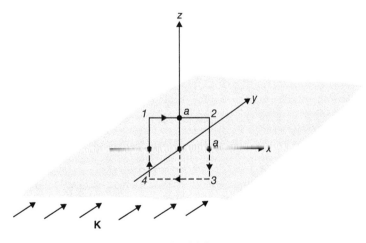

Fig. 10-3

The Biot-Savart law and considerations of symmetry show that **H** has only an *x* component and is not a function of *x* or *y*. Applying Ampère's law to the square contour *12341*, and using the fact that **H** must be antisymmetric in *z*,

$$\oint \mathbf{H} \cdot d\mathbf{l} = (H)(2a) + 0 + (H)(2a) + 0 = (K)(2a) \qquad \text{or} \qquad H = \frac{K}{2}$$

Thus, for all $z > 0$, $\mathbf{H} = (K/2)\mathbf{a}_x$. More generally, for an arbitrary orientation of the current sheet,

$$\mathbf{H} = \frac{1}{2}\mathbf{K} \times \mathbf{a}_n$$

Observe that **H** is independent of the distance from the sheet. Furthermore, the directions of **H** above and below the sheet can be found by applying the *right-hand rule* to a few of the current elements in the sheet.

10.3   Ampère's Law

The line integral of the tangential component of the magnetic field strength around a closed path is equal to the current enclosed by the path:

$$\oint \mathbf{H} \cdot d\mathbf{l} = I_{\text{enc}}$$

At first glance one would think that the law is used to determine the current *I* by an integration. Instead, the current is usually known and the law provides a method of finding **H**. This is quite similar to the use of Gauss's law to find **D** given the charge distribution.

In order to utilize Ampère's law to determine **H**, there must be a considerable degree of symmetry in the problem. Two conditions must be met:

1.   At each point of the closed path **H** is either tangential or normal to the path.
2.   *H* has the same value at all points of the path where **H** is tangential.

The Biot-Savart law can be used to aid in selecting a path which meets the above conditions. In most cases a proper path will be evident.

EXAMPLE 3.   Use Ampère's law to obtain **H** due to an infinitely long, straight filament of current *I*.

The Biot-Savart law shows that at each point of the circle in Fig. 10-2 **H** is tangential and of the same magnitude. Then

$$\oint \mathbf{H} \cdot d\mathbf{l} = H(2\pi r) = I$$

so that

$$\mathbf{H} = \frac{1}{2\pi r}\mathbf{a}_\phi$$

10.4   Relationship of J and H

In view of Ampère's law, the defining equation for (curl **H**)$_x$ (see Section 5.10) may be rewritten as

$$(\text{curl } \mathbf{H}) \cdot \mathbf{a}_x = \lim_{\Delta y \Delta z \to 0} \frac{I_x}{\Delta y \, \Delta z} \equiv J_x$$

where $J_x = dI_x/dS$ is the area density of *x*-directed current. Thus, the *x* components of curl **H** and the *current density* **J** are equal at any point. Similarly for the *y* and *z* components, so that

$$\nabla \times \mathbf{H} = \mathbf{J}$$

This is one of Maxwell's equations for static fields. If **H** is known throughout a region, then $\nabla \times \mathbf{H}$ will produce **J** for that region.

EXAMPLE 4.   A long, straight conductor cross section with radius *a* has a magnetic field strength $\mathbf{H} = (Ir/2\pi a^2)\mathbf{a}_\phi$ within the conductor $(r < a)$ and $\mathbf{H} = (I/2\pi r)\mathbf{a}_\phi$ for $r > a$. Find **J** in both regions.

Within the conductor,

$$\mathbf{J} = \nabla \times \mathbf{H} = -\frac{\partial}{\partial z}\left(\frac{Ir}{2\pi a^2}\right)\mathbf{a}_r + \frac{1}{r}\frac{\partial}{\partial r}\left(\frac{Ir^2}{2\pi a^2}\right)\mathbf{a}_z = \frac{I}{\pi a^2}\mathbf{a}_z$$

which corresponds to a current of magnitude I in the $+z$ direction which is distributed uniformly over the cross-sectional area πa^2.

Outside the conductor,

$$\mathbf{J} = \nabla \times \mathbf{H} = -\frac{\partial}{\partial z}\left(\frac{I}{2\pi r}\right)\mathbf{a}_r + \frac{1}{r}\frac{\partial}{\partial r}\left(\frac{I}{2\pi}\right)\mathbf{a}_z = \mathbf{0}$$

10.5 Magnetic Flux Density B

Like $\mathbf{D}$, the magnetic field strength $\mathbf{H}$ depends only on (moving) charges and is independent of the medium. The force field associated with $\mathbf{H}$ is the *magnetic flux density* $\mathbf{B}$, which is given by

$$\mathbf{B} = \mu\mathbf{H}$$

where $\mu = \mu_0\mu_r$ is the *permeability* of the medium. The unit of $\mathbf{B}$ is the *tesla*,

$$1\,\text{T} = 1\frac{\text{N}}{\text{A}\cdot\text{m}}$$

The free-space permeability μ_0 has a numerical value of $4\pi \times 10^{-7}$ and has the units *henries per meter*, H/m; μ_r, the *relative permeability* of the medium, is a pure number very near unity, except for a small group of *ferromagnetic* materials, which will be treated in Chapter 12.

Magnetic flux, Φ, through a surface is defined as

$$\Phi = \int_S \mathbf{B} \cdot d\mathbf{S}$$

The sign on Φ may be positive or negative depending upon the choice of the surface normal in $d\mathbf{S}$. The unit of magnetic flux is the *weber*, Wb. The various magnetic units are related by

$$1\,\text{T} = 1\,\text{Wb/m}^2 \qquad 1\,\text{H} = 1\,\text{Wb/A}$$

EXAMPLE 5. Find the flux crossing the portion of the plane $\phi = \pi/4$ defined by $0.01 < r < 0.05$ m and $0 < z < 2$ m (see Fig. 10-4). A current filament of 2.50 A along the z axis is in the $\mathbf{a}_z$ direction.

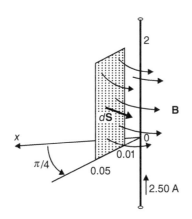

Fig. 10-4

$$\mathbf{B} = \mu_0\mathbf{H} = \frac{\mu_0 I}{2\pi r}\mathbf{a}_\phi$$

$$d\mathbf{S} = dr\,dz\,\mathbf{a}_\phi$$

$$\Phi = \int_0^2 \int_{0.01}^{0.05} \frac{\mu_0 I}{2\pi r}\mathbf{a}_\phi \cdot dr\,dz\,\mathbf{a}_\phi$$

$$= \frac{2\mu_0 I}{2\pi}\ln\frac{0.05}{0.01}$$

$$= 1.61 \times 10^{-6}\,\text{Wb} \quad \text{or} \quad 1.61\,\mu\text{Wb}$$

It should be observed that the lines of magnetic flux Φ are closed curves, with no starting point or termination point. This is in contrast with electric flux Ψ, which originates on positive charge and terminates on negative charge. In Fig. 10-5 all of the magnetic flux Φ that enters the closed surface must leave the surface. Thus, **B** fields have no sources or sinks, which is mathematically expressed by

$$\nabla \cdot \mathbf{B} = 0$$

(see Section 5.5).

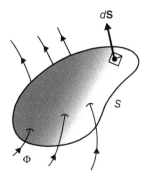

Fig. 10-5

10.6   Boundary Relations for Magnetic Fields

When **H** and **B** are examined at the interface between two different materials, abrupt changes can be expected, similar to those noted in **E** and **D** at the interface between two different dielectrics (see Section 8.7).

In Fig. 10-6 an interface is shown separating material *1*, with properties σ_1 and μ_{r1}, from *2*, with σ_2 and μ_{r2}. The behavior of **B** can be determined by use of a small right circular cylinder positioned across the interface as shown. Since magnetic flux lines are continuous,

$$\oint \mathbf{B} \cdot d\mathbf{S} = \int_{\text{end 1}} \mathbf{B}_1 \cdot d\mathbf{S}_1 + \int_{\text{cyl}} \mathbf{B} \cdot d\mathbf{S} + \int_{\text{end 2}} \mathbf{B}_2 \cdot d\mathbf{S}_2 = 0$$

Now if the two planes are allowed to approach one another, keeping the interface between them, the area of the curved surface will approach zero, giving

$$\int_{\text{end 1}} \mathbf{B}_1 \cdot d\mathbf{S}_1 + \int_{\text{end 2}} \mathbf{B}_2 \cdot d\mathbf{S}_2 = 0$$

or

$$-B_{n1} \int_{\text{end 1}} d\mathbf{S}_1 + B_{n2} \int_{\text{end 2}} d\mathbf{S}_2 = 0$$

from which

$$B_{n1} = B_{n2}$$

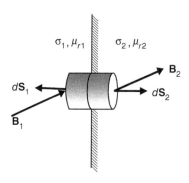

Fig. 10-6

In words, *the normal component of* **B** *is continuous across an interface.* Note that *either* normal to the interface may be used in calculating B_{n1} and B_{n2}.

The variation in **H** across an interface is obtained by the application of Ampère's law around a closed rectangular path, as shown in Fig. 10-7. Assuming no current at the interface, and letting the rectangle shrink to zero in the usual way,

$$0 = \oint \mathbf{H} \cdot d\mathbf{l} \rightarrow H_{\ell 1} \Delta \ell_1 - H_{\ell 2} \Delta \ell_2$$

whence

$$H_{\ell 1} = H_{\ell 2}$$

Thus, tangential **H** has the same projection along the two sides of the rectangle. Since the rectangle can be rotated 90° and the argument repeated, it follows that

$$H_{t1} = H_{t2}$$

In words, *the tangential component of* **H** *is continuous across a current-free interface.*

The relation

$$\frac{\tan \theta_1}{\tan \theta_2} = \frac{\mu_{r2}}{\mu_{r1}}$$

between the angles made by $\mathbf{H}_1$ and $\mathbf{H}_2$ with a current-free interface (see Fig. 10-7) is obtained by analogy with Example 6, Section 8.7.

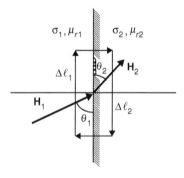

Fig. 10-7

10.7 Current Sheet at the Boundary

If one material at the interface has a nonzero conductivity, a current may be present. This could be a current throughout the material; however, of more interest is the case of a current sheet at the interface.

Fig. 10-8 shows a uniform current sheet. In the indicated coordinate system, the current sheet has density $\mathbf{K} = K_0 \mathbf{a}_y$ and is located at the interface $x = 0$ between regions *1* and *2*. The magnetic field $\mathbf{H}'$ produced by this current sheet is given by Example 2, Section 10.2,

$$\mathbf{H}_1' = \frac{1}{2} \mathbf{K} \times \mathbf{a}_{n1} = \frac{1}{2} K_0 \mathbf{a}_z \qquad \mathbf{H}_2' = \frac{1}{2} \mathbf{K} \times \mathbf{a}_{n2} = \frac{1}{2} K_0 (-\mathbf{a}_z)$$

Thus, $\mathbf{H}'$ has a tangential discontinuity of magnitude $|K_0|$ at the interface. If a second magnetic field, $\mathbf{H}''$, arising from some other source, is present, its tangential component will be continuous at the interface. The resultant magnetic field,

$$\mathbf{H} = \mathbf{H}' + \mathbf{H}''$$

will then have a discontinuity of magnitude $|K_0|$ in its tangential component. This is expressed by the vector formula

$$(\mathbf{H}_1 - \mathbf{H}_2) \times \mathbf{a}_{n12} = \mathbf{K}$$

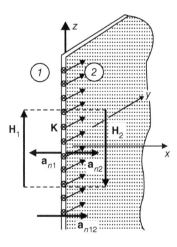

Fig. 10-8

where $\mathbf{a}_{n12}$ is the unit normal from region *1* to region *2*. The vector relation, which is independent of the choice of coordinate system, also holds for a nonuniform current sheet, where $\mathbf{K}$ is the value of the current density at the considered point of the interface.

10.8   Summary of Boundary Conditions

For reference purposes, the relationships for $\mathbf{E}$ and $\mathbf{D}$ across the interface of two dielectrics are shown below along with the relationships for $\mathbf{H}$ and $\mathbf{B}$.

Magnetic Fields	**Electric Fields**

$$B_{n1} = B_{n2}$$

$$\begin{cases} D_{n1} = D_{n2} & \text{(charge-free)} \\ (\mathbf{D}_1 - \mathbf{D}_2) \cdot \mathbf{a}_{n12} = -\rho_s & \text{(with surface charge)} \end{cases}$$

$$\begin{cases} H_{r1} = H_{r2} & \text{(current-free)} \\ (\mathbf{H}_1 - \mathbf{H}_2) \times \mathbf{a}_{n12} = \mathbf{K} & \text{(with current sheet)} \end{cases}$$

$$E_{t1} = E_{t2}$$

$$\frac{\tan \theta_1}{\tan \theta_2} = \frac{\mu_{r2}}{\mu_{r1}} \quad \text{(current-free)}$$

$$\frac{\tan \theta_1}{\tan \theta_2} = \frac{\epsilon_{r2}}{\epsilon_{r1}} \quad \text{(charge-free)}$$

These relationships were obtained assuming static conditions. However, in Chapter 14 they will be found to apply equally well to time-variable fields.

10.9   Vector Magnetic Potential A

Electric field intensity $\mathbf{E}$ was first obtained from known charge configurations. Later, electric potential V was developed and it was found that $\mathbf{E}$ could be obtained as the negative gradient of V, i.e., $\mathbf{E} = -\nabla V$. Laplace's equation provided a method of obtaining V from known potentials on the boundary conductors. Similarly, a *vector magnetic potential*, $\mathbf{A}$, defined such that

$$\nabla \times \mathbf{A} = \mathbf{B}$$

serves as an intermediate quantity, from which $\mathbf{B}$, and hence $\mathbf{H}$, can be calculated. Note that the definition of $\mathbf{A}$ is consistent with the requirement that $\nabla \cdot \mathbf{B} = 0$. The units of $\mathbf{A}$ are Wb/m or T · m.

If the additional condition

$$\nabla \cdot \mathbf{A} = 0$$

is imposed, then vector magnetic potential $\mathbf{A}$ can be determined from the known currents in the region of interest. For the three standard current configurations the expressions are as follows.

current filament: $\mathbf{A} = \oint \dfrac{\mu I \, d\mathbf{l}}{4\pi R}$

sheet current: $\mathbf{A} = \displaystyle\int_S \dfrac{\mu \mathbf{K} \, dS}{4\pi R}$

volume current: $\mathbf{A} = \displaystyle\int_v \dfrac{\mu \mathbf{J} \, dv}{4\pi R}$

Here, R is the distance from the current element to the point at which the vector magnetic potential is being calculated. Like the analogous integral for the electric potential (see Section 6.5), the above expressions for $\mathbf{A}$ presuppose a zero level at infinity; they cannot be applied if the current distribution itself extends to infinity.

EXAMPLE 6.   Investigate the vector magnetic potential for the infinite, straight, current filament I in free space.
    In Fig. 10-9 the current filament is along the z axis and the observation point is (x, y, z). The particular current element

$$I \, d\mathbf{l} = I \, d\ell \, \mathbf{a}_z$$

at $\ell = 0$ is shown, where ℓ is the running variable along the z axis. It is clear that the integral

$$\mathbf{A} = \int_{-\infty}^{\infty} \frac{\mu_0 I \, d\ell}{4\pi R} \, \mathbf{a}_z$$

does not exist, since, when ℓ is large, $R \approx \ell$. This is a case of a current distribution that extends to infinity.
    It is possible, however, to consider the *differential* vector potential

$$d\mathbf{A} = \frac{\mu_0 I \, d\ell}{4\pi R} \, \mathbf{a}_z$$

and to obtain from it the *differential* $\mathbf{B}$. Thus, for the particular current element at $\ell = 0$,

$$d\mathbf{A} = \frac{\mu_0 I \, d\ell}{4\pi (x^2 + y^2 + z^2)^{1/2}} \, \mathbf{a}_z$$

and $$d\mathbf{B} = \nabla \times d\mathbf{A} = \frac{\mu_0 I \, d\ell}{4\pi} \left[\frac{-y}{(x^2 + y^2 + z^3)^{3/2}} \, \mathbf{a}_x + \frac{x}{(x^2 + y^2 + z^2)^{3/2}} \, \mathbf{a}_y \right]$$

This result agrees with that for $d\mathbf{H} = (1/\mu_0) \, d\mathbf{B}$ given by the Biot-Savart law.
    For a way of defining $\mathbf{A}$ for the infinite current filament, see Problem 10.20.

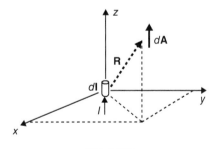

Fig. 10-9

10.10 Stokes' Theorem

Consider an open surface S whose boundary is a closed curve C. *Stokes' theorem* states that the integral of the tangential component of a vector field $\mathbf{F}$ around C is equal to the integral of the normal component of curl $\mathbf{F}$ over S:

$$\oint \mathbf{F} \cdot d\mathbf{l} = \int_S (\nabla \times \mathbf{F}) \cdot d\mathbf{S}$$

If **F** is chosen to be the vector magnetic potential **A**, Stokes' theorem gives

$$\oint \mathbf{A} \cdot d\mathbf{l} = \int_{S} \mathbf{B} \cdot d\mathbf{S} = \Phi$$

SOLVED PROBLEMS

10.1. Find **H** at the center of a square current loop of side L.

Choose a Cartesian coordinate system such that the loop is located as shown in Fig. 10-10. By symmetry, each half-side contributes the same amount to **H** at the center. For the half-side $0 \le x \le L/2$, $y = -L/2$, the Biot-Savart law gives for the field at the origin

$$d\mathbf{H} = \frac{(I \, dx \, \mathbf{a}_x) \times [-x\mathbf{a}_x + (L/2)\mathbf{a}_y]}{4\pi \, [x^2 + (L/2)^2]^{3/2}}$$

$$= \frac{I \, dx \, (L/2)\mathbf{a}_z}{4\pi \, [x^2 + (L/2)^2]^{3/2}}$$

Therefore, the total field at the origin is

$$\mathbf{H} = 8 \int_{0}^{L/2} \frac{I \, dx \, (L/2)\mathbf{a}_z}{4\pi \, [x^2 + (L/2)^2]^{3/2}}$$

$$= \frac{2\sqrt{2}\,I}{\pi L} \mathbf{a}_z = \frac{2\sqrt{2}\,I}{\pi L} \mathbf{a}_n$$

where $\mathbf{a}_n$ is the unit normal to the plane of the loop as given by the usual right-hand rule.

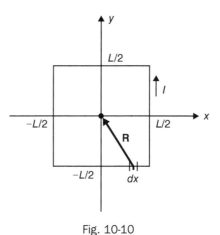

Fig. 10-10

10.2. A current filament of 5.0 A in the $\mathbf{a}_y$ direction is parallel to the y axis at $x = 2$ m, $z = -2$ m (Fig. 10-11). Find **H** at the origin.

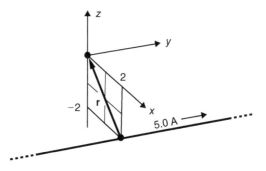

Fig. 10-11

The expression for **H** due to a straight current filament applies,

$$\mathbf{H} = \frac{I}{2\pi r} \mathbf{a}_\phi$$

where $r = 2\sqrt{2}$ and (use the right-hand rule)

$$\mathbf{a}_\phi = \frac{\mathbf{a}_x + \mathbf{a}_z}{\sqrt{2}}$$

Thus,
$$\mathbf{H} = \frac{5.0}{2\pi(2\sqrt{2})}\left(\frac{\mathbf{a}_x + \mathbf{a}_z}{\sqrt{2}}\right) = (0.281)\left(\frac{\mathbf{a}_x + \mathbf{a}_z}{\sqrt{2}}\right) \text{A/m}$$

10.3. A current sheet, $\mathbf{K} = 10\mathbf{a}_z$ A/m, lies in the $x = 5$ m plane and a second sheet, $\mathbf{K} = -10\mathbf{a}_z$ A/m, is at $x = -5$ m. Find **H** at all points.

In Fig. 10-12 it is apparent that at any point between the sheets, $\mathbf{K} \times \mathbf{a}_n = -K\mathbf{a}_y$ for each sheet. Then, for $-5 < x < 5$, $\mathbf{H} = 10(-\mathbf{a}_y)$ A/m. Elsewhere, $\mathbf{H} = \mathbf{0}$.

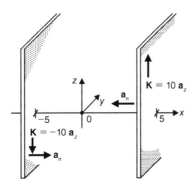

Fig. 10-12

10.4. A thin cylindrical conductor of radius a, infinite in length, carries a current I. Find **H** at all points using Ampère's law.

The Biot-Savart law shows that **H** has only a ϕ component. Furthermore, H_ϕ is a function of r only. Proper paths for Ampère's law are concentric circles. For path *1* shown in Fig. 10-13,

$$\oint \mathbf{H} \cdot d\mathbf{l} = 2\pi r H_\phi = I_{\text{enc}} = 0$$

and for path 2,
$$\oint \mathbf{H} \cdot d\mathbf{l} = 2\pi r H_\phi = I$$

Thus, for points within the cylindrical conducting shell, $\mathbf{H} = \mathbf{0}$, and for external points, $\mathbf{H} = (I/2\pi r)\mathbf{a}_\phi$, the same field as that of a current filament I along the axis.

Fig. 10-13

10.5. Determine **H** for a solid cylindrical conductor of radius a, where the current I is uniformly distributed over the cross section.

Applying Ampère's law to contour l in Fig. 10-14,

$$\oint \mathbf{H} \cdot d\mathbf{l} = I_{enc}$$

$$H(2\pi r) = I\left(\frac{\pi r^2}{\pi a^2}\right)$$

$$\mathbf{H} = \frac{Ir}{2\pi a^2}\,\mathbf{a}_\phi$$

For external points, $\mathbf{H} = (I/2\pi r)\,\mathbf{a}_\phi$.

Fig. 10-14

10.6. In the region $0 < r < 0.5$ m, in cylindrical coordinates, the current density is

$$\mathbf{J} = 4.5e^{-2r}\mathbf{a}_z \qquad (\text{A/m}^2)$$

and $\mathbf{J} = 0$ elsewhere. Use Ampère's law to find **H**.

Because the current density is symmetrical about the origin, a circular path may be used in Ampère's law, with the enclosed current given by $\oint \mathbf{J} \cdot d\mathbf{S}$. Thus, for $r < 0.5$ m,

$$H_\phi(2\pi r) = \int_0^{2\pi}\int_0^r 4.5e^{-2r}r\,dr\,d\phi$$

$$\mathbf{H} = \frac{1.125}{r}(1 - e^{-2r} - 2re^{-2r})\mathbf{a}_\phi \quad (\text{A/m})$$

For any $r \ge 0.5$ m, the enclosed current is the same, 0.594π A. Then,

$$H_\phi(2\pi r) = 0.594\pi \quad \text{or} \quad \mathbf{H} = \frac{0.297}{r}\mathbf{a}_\phi \quad (\text{A/m})$$

10.7. Find **H** on the axis of a circular current loop of radius a. Specialize the result to the center of the loop.

For the point shown in Fig. 10-15,

$$\mathbf{R} = -a\mathbf{a}_r + h\mathbf{a}_z$$

$$d\mathbf{H} = \frac{(Ia\,d\phi\,\mathbf{a}_\phi)\times(-a\mathbf{a}_r + h\mathbf{a}_z)}{4\pi(a^2 + h^2)^{3/2}} = \frac{(Ia\,d\phi)(a\mathbf{a}_z + h\mathbf{a}_r)}{4\pi(a^2 + h^2)^{3/2}}$$

Inspection shows that diametrically opposite current elements produce r components which cancel each other. Then,

$$\mathbf{H} = \int_0^{2\pi}\frac{Ia^2\,d\phi}{4\pi\,(a^2 + h^2)^{3/2}}\mathbf{a}_z = \frac{Ia^2}{2\,(a^2 + h^2)^{3/2}}\mathbf{a}_z$$

At $h = 0$, $\mathbf{H} = (I/2a)\mathbf{a}_z$.

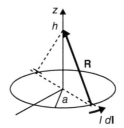

Fig. 10-15

10.8. A current sheet, $\mathbf{K} = 6.0\mathbf{a}_x$ A/m, lies in the $z = 0$ plane and a current filament is located at $y = 0$, $z = 4$ m, as shown in Fig. 10-16. Determine I and its direction if $\mathbf{H} = \mathbf{0}$ at $(0, 0, 1.5)$ m.

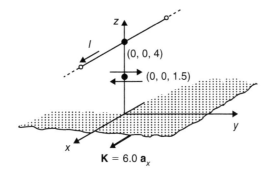

Fig. 10-16

Due to the current sheet,

$$\mathbf{H} = \frac{1}{2}\mathbf{K} \times \mathbf{a}_n = \frac{6.0}{2}(-\mathbf{a}_y) \text{ A/m}$$

For the field to vanish at $(0, 0, 1.5)$ m, $|\mathbf{H}|$ due to the filament must be 3.0 A/m.

$$|\mathbf{H}| = \frac{1}{2\pi r}$$

$$3.0 = \frac{1}{2\pi(2.5)}$$

$$I = 47.1 \text{ A}$$

To cancel the $\mathbf{H}$ from the sheet, this current must be in the $\mathbf{a}_x$ direction, as shown in Fig. 10-16.

10.9. Calculate the curl of $\mathbf{H}$ in Cartesian coordinates due to a current filament along the z axis with current I in the $\mathbf{a}_z$ direction.

From Example 1,

$$\mathbf{H} = \frac{1}{2\pi r}\mathbf{a}_\phi = \frac{1}{2\pi}\left(\frac{-y\mathbf{a}_x + x\mathbf{a}_y}{x^2 + y^2}\right)$$

and so

$$\nabla \times \mathbf{H} = \begin{vmatrix} \mathbf{a}_x & \mathbf{a}_y & \mathbf{a}_z \\ \dfrac{\partial}{\partial x} & \dfrac{\partial}{\partial y} & \dfrac{\partial}{\partial z} \\ \dfrac{-y}{x^2 + y^2} & \dfrac{x}{x^2 + y^2} & 0 \end{vmatrix}$$

$$\nabla \times \mathbf{H} = \left[\frac{\partial}{\partial x}\left(\frac{x}{x^2 + y^2}\right) - \frac{\partial}{\partial y}\left(\frac{-y}{x^2 + y^2}\right)\right]\mathbf{a}_z$$

$$= 0$$

except at $x = y = 0$. This is consistent with $\nabla \times \mathbf{H} = \mathbf{J}$.

10.10. A circular conductor of radius $r_0 = 1$ cm has an internal field

$$\mathbf{H} = \frac{10^4}{r}\left(\frac{1}{a^2}\sin ar - \frac{r}{a}\cos ar\right)\mathbf{a}_\phi \quad (\text{A/m})$$

where $a = \pi/2r_0$. Find the total current in the conductor.

There are two methods: (1) to calculate $\mathbf{J} = \nabla \times \mathbf{H}$ and then integrate; (2) to use Ampère's law. The second is simpler here.

$$I_{enc} = \oint_{r=r_0} \mathbf{H} \cdot d\mathbf{l} = \int_0^{2\pi} \frac{10^4}{r_0}\left(\frac{4r_0^2}{\pi^2}\sin\frac{\pi}{2} - \frac{2r_0^2}{\pi}\cos\frac{\pi}{2}\right)r_0\, d\phi$$

$$= \frac{8\times 10^4 r_0^2}{\pi} = \frac{8}{\pi}\ \text{A}$$

10.11. A radial field

$$\mathbf{H} = \frac{2.39\times 10^6}{r}\cos\phi\ \mathbf{a}_r\ \text{A/m}$$

exists in free space. Find the magnetic flux Φ crossing the surface defined by $-\pi/4 \le \phi \le \pi/4$, $0 \le z \le 1$ m. See Fig. 10-17.

$$\mathbf{B} = \mu_0\mathbf{H} = \frac{3.00}{r}\cos\phi\mathbf{a}_r\quad (\text{T})$$

$$\Phi = \int_0^1 \int_{-\pi/4}^{\pi/4}\left(\frac{3.00}{r}\cos\phi\right)\mathbf{a}_r \cdot r\, d\phi\, dz\, \mathbf{a}_r$$

$$= 4.24\ \text{Wb}$$

Fig. 10-17

Since $\mathbf{B}$ is inversely proportional to r (as required by $\nabla \cdot \mathbf{B} = 0$), it makes no difference what radial distance is chosen. The total flux will be the same.

10.12. In cylindrical coordinates, $\mathbf{B} = (2.0/r)\mathbf{a}_\phi$ (T). Determine the magnetic flux Φ crossing the plane surface defined by $0.5 \le r \le 2.5$ m and $0 \le z \le 2.0$ m. See Fig. 10-18.

$$\Phi = \int \mathbf{B} \cdot d\mathbf{S}$$

$$= \int_0^{2.0}\int_{0.5}^{2.5}\frac{2.0}{r}\mathbf{a}_\phi \cdot dr\, dz\, \mathbf{a}_\phi$$

$$= 4.0\left(\ln\frac{2.5}{0.5}\right) = 6.44\ \text{Wb}$$

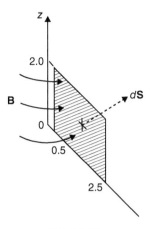

Fig. 10-18

10.13. In region *1* of Fig. 10-19, $\mathbf{B}_1 = 1.2\mathbf{a}_x + 0.8\mathbf{a}_y + 0.4\mathbf{a}_z$ (T). Find $\mathbf{H}_2$ (i.e., $\mathbf{H}$ at $z = +0$) and the angles between the field vectors and a tangent to the interface.

Fig. 10-19

Write $\mathbf{H}_1$ directly below $\mathbf{B}_1$. Then write those components of $\mathbf{H}_2$ and $\mathbf{B}_2$ which follow directly from the two rules: **B** *normal is continuous* and **H** *tangential is continuous* across a current-free interface.

$$\mathbf{B}_1 = 1.2\mathbf{a}_x + 0.8\mathbf{a}_y + 0.4\mathbf{a}_z \qquad\qquad \text{(T)}$$

$$\mathbf{H}_1 = \frac{1}{\mu_0}(8.0\mathbf{a}_x + 5.33\mathbf{a}_y + 2.67\mathbf{a}_z)10^{-2} \qquad \text{(A/m)}$$

$$\mathbf{H}_2 = \frac{1}{\mu_0}(8.0\mathbf{a}_x + 5.33\mathbf{a}_y + 10^2\mu_0 H_{z2}\mathbf{a}_z)10^{-2} \qquad \text{(A/m)}$$

$$\mathbf{B}_2 = B_{x2}\mathbf{a}_x + B_{y2}\mathbf{a}_y + 0.4\mathbf{a}_z \qquad\qquad \text{(T)}$$

Now the remaining terms follow directly:

$$B_{x2} = \mu_0\mu_{r2}H_{x2} = 8.0 \times 10^{-2} \text{ (T)} \qquad B_{y2} = 5.33 \times 10^{-2} \text{ (T)} \qquad H_{z2} = \frac{B_{z2}}{\mu_0\mu_{r2}} = \frac{0.4}{\mu_0} \text{ (A/m)}$$

Angle θ_1 is $90° - \alpha_1$, where α_1 is the angle between $\mathbf{B}_1$ and the normal, $\mathbf{a}_z$.

$$\cos\alpha_1 = \frac{\mathbf{B}_1 \cdot \mathbf{a}_z}{|\mathbf{B}_1|} = 0.27$$

whence $\alpha_1 = 74.5°$ and $\theta_1 = 15.5°$ Similarly, $\theta_2 = 76.5°$.

Check: $(\tan\theta_1)/(\tan\theta_2) = \mu_{r2}/\mu_{r1}$.

10.14. Region *1*, for which $\mu_{r1} = 3$, is defined by $x < 0$ and region 2, $x > 0$, has $\mu_{r2} = 5$. Given

$$\mathbf{H}_1 = 4.0\mathbf{a}_x + 3.0\mathbf{a}_y - 6.0\mathbf{a}_z \text{ (A/m)}$$

show that $\theta_2 = 19.7°$ and $H_2 = 7.12$ A/m.

Proceed as in Problem 10.13.

$$\mathbf{H}_1 = 4.0\mathbf{a}_x + 3.0\mathbf{a}_y - 6.0\mathbf{a}_z \qquad \text{(A/m)}$$
$$\mathbf{B}_1 = \mu_0(12.0\mathbf{a}_x + 9.0\mathbf{a}_y - 18.0\mathbf{a}_z) \qquad \text{(T)}$$
$$\mathbf{B}_2 = \mu_0(12.0\mathbf{a}_x + 15.0\mathbf{a}_y - 30.0\mathbf{a}_z) \qquad \text{(T)}$$
$$\mathbf{H}_2 = 2.40\mathbf{a}_x + 3.0\mathbf{a}_y - 6.0\mathbf{a}_z \qquad \text{(A/m)}$$

Now
$$H_2 = \sqrt{(2.40)^2 + (3.0)^2 + (-6.0)^2} = 7.12 \text{ A/m}$$

The angle α_2 between $\mathbf{H}_2$ and the normal is given by

$$\cos\alpha_2 = \frac{H_{x2}}{H_2} = 0.34 \quad \text{or} \quad \alpha_2 = 70.3°$$

Then $\theta_2 = 90° - \alpha_2 = 19.7°$.

10.15. Region *1*, where $\mu_{r1} = 4$, is the side of the plane $y + z = 1$ containing the origin (see Fig. 10-20). In region 2, $\mu_{r2} = 6$. $\mathbf{B}_1 = 2.0\mathbf{a}_x + 1.0\mathbf{a}_y$ (T). Find $\mathbf{B}_2$ and $\mathbf{H}_2$.

Fig. 10-20

Choosing the unit normal $\mathbf{a}_n = (\mathbf{a}_y + \mathbf{a}_z)/\sqrt{2}$,

$$\mathbf{B}_{n1} = \frac{(2.0\mathbf{a}_x + 1.0\mathbf{a}_y)\cdot(\mathbf{a}_y + \mathbf{a}_z)}{\sqrt{2}} = \frac{1}{\sqrt{2}}$$

$$\mathbf{B}_{n1} = \left(\frac{1}{\sqrt{2}}\right)\mathbf{a}_n = 0.5\mathbf{a}_y + 0.5\mathbf{a}_z = \mathbf{B}_{n2}$$

$$\mathbf{B}_{t1} = \mathbf{B}_1 - \mathbf{B}_{n1} = 2.0\mathbf{a}_x + 0.5\mathbf{a}_y - 0.5\mathbf{a}_z$$

$$\mathbf{H}_{t1} = \frac{1}{\mu_0}(0.5\mathbf{a}_x + 0.125\mathbf{a}_y - 0.125\mathbf{a}_z) = \mathbf{H}_{t2}$$

$$\mathbf{B}_{t2} = \mu_0\mu_{r2}\mathbf{H}_{t2} = 3.0\mathbf{a}_x \; 0.75\mathbf{a}_y - 0.75\mathbf{a}_z$$

Now the normal and tangential parts of $\mathbf{B}_2$ are combined.

$$\mathbf{B}_2 = 3.0\mathbf{a}_x + 1.25\mathbf{a}_y - 0.25\mathbf{a}_z \quad \text{(T)}$$

$$\mathbf{H}_2 = \frac{1}{\mu_0}(0.50\mathbf{a}_x + 0.21\mathbf{a}_y - 0.04\mathbf{a}_z) \quad \text{(A/m)}$$

10.16. In region *1*, defined by $z < 0$, $\mu_{r1} = 3$ and

$$\mathbf{H}_1 = \frac{1}{\mu_0}(0.2\mathbf{a}_x + 0.5\mathbf{a}_y - 1.0\mathbf{a}_z) \quad \text{(A/m)}$$

Find $\mathbf{H}_2$ if it is known that $\theta_2 = 45°$.

$$\cos\alpha_1 = \frac{\mathbf{H}_1 \cdot \mathbf{a}_z}{|\mathbf{H}_1|} = 0.88 \quad \text{or} \quad \alpha_1 = 28.3°$$

Then, $\theta_1 = 61.7°$ and

$$\frac{\tan 61.7°}{\tan 45°} = \frac{\mu_{r2}}{3} \quad \text{or} \quad \mu_{r2} = 5.57$$

From the continuity of the normal component of **B**, $\mu_{r1}H_{z1} = \mu_{r2}H_{z2}$, and so

$$\mathbf{H}_2 = \frac{1}{\mu_0}\left(0.2\mathbf{a}_x + 0.5\mathbf{a}_y + \frac{\mu_{r1}}{\mu_{r2}}1.0\mathbf{a}_z\right) = \frac{1}{\mu_0}(0.2\mathbf{a}_x + 0.5\mathbf{a}_y + 0.54\mathbf{a}_z) \quad \text{(A/m)}$$

10.17. A current sheet, $\mathbf{K} = 6.5\mathbf{a}_z$ A/m, at $x = 0$ separates region *1*, $x < 0$, where $\mathbf{H}_1 = 10\mathbf{a}_y$ A/m and region 2, $x > 0$. Find $\mathbf{H}_2$ at $x = +0$.

Nothing is said about the permeabilities of the two regions; however, since $\mathbf{H}_1$ is entirely tangential, a change in permeability would have no effect. Since $B_{n1} = 0$, $B_{n2} = 0$ and therefore $H_{n2} = 0$,

$$(\mathbf{H}_1 - \mathbf{H}_2) \times \mathbf{a}_{n12} = \mathbf{K}$$
$$(10\mathbf{a}_y - H_{y2}\mathbf{a}_y) \times \mathbf{a}_x = 6.5\mathbf{a}_z$$
$$(10 - H_{y2})(-\mathbf{a}_z) = 6.5\mathbf{a}_z$$
$$H_{y2} = 16.5 \quad \text{(A/m)}$$

Thus, $\mathbf{H}_2 = 16.5\mathbf{a}_y$ (A/m).

10.18. A current sheet, $\mathbf{K} = 9.0\mathbf{a}_y$ A/m, is located at $z = 0$, the interface between region *1*, $z < 0$, with $\mu_{r1} = 4$, and region 2, $z > 0$, $\mu_{r2} = 3$. Given that $\mathbf{H}_2 = 14.5\mathbf{a}_x + 8.0\mathbf{a}_z$ (A/m), find $\mathbf{H}_1$.

The current sheet shown in Fig. 10-21 is first examined alone.

$$\mathbf{H}'_1 = \frac{1}{2}(9.0)\mathbf{a}_y \times (-\mathbf{a}_z) = 4.5(-\mathbf{a}_x)$$

$$\mathbf{H}'_2 = \frac{1}{2}(9.0)\,\mathbf{a}_y \times \mathbf{a}_z = 4.5\mathbf{a}_x$$

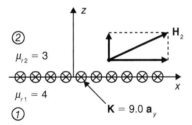

Fig. 10-21

From region *1* to region 2, H_x will increase by 9.0 A/m due to the current sheet.

Now the complete **H** and **B** fields are examined:

$$\begin{array}{ll} \mathbf{H}_2 = 14.5\mathbf{a}_x + 8.0\mathbf{a}_z & \text{(A/m)} \\ \mathbf{B}_2 = \mu_0(43.5\mathbf{a}_x + 24.0\mathbf{a}_z) & \text{(T)} \\ \mathbf{B}_1 = \mu_0(22.0\mathbf{a}_x + 24.0\mathbf{a}_x) & \text{(T)} \\ \mathbf{H}_1 = 5.5\mathbf{a}_x + 6.0\mathbf{a}_z & \text{(A/m)} \end{array}$$

Note that H_{x1} must be 9.0 A/m less than H_{x2} because of the current sheet. B_{n1} is obtained as $\mu_0\mu_{r1}H_{z1}$

An alternate method is to apply $(\mathbf{H}_1 - \mathbf{H}_2) \times \mathbf{a}_{n12} = \mathbf{K}$:

$$(H_{x1}\mathbf{a}_x + H_{y1}\mathbf{a}_y + H_{z1}\mathbf{a}_z) \times \mathbf{a}_z = \mathbf{K} + (14.5\mathbf{a}_x + 8.0\mathbf{a}_z) \times \mathbf{a}_z$$
$$-H_{x1}\mathbf{a}_y + H_{y1}\mathbf{a}_x = -5.5\mathbf{a}_y$$

from which $H_{x1} = 5.5$ A/m and $H_{y1} = 0$. This method deals exclusively with tangential **H**; any normal component must be determined by the previous methods.

10.19. Region *1*, $z < 0$, has $\mu_{r1} = 1.5$, while region 2, $z > 0$, has $\mu_{r2} = 5$. Near $(0, 0, 0)$,

$$\mathbf{B}_1 = 2.40\mathbf{a}_x + 10.0\mathbf{a}_z \text{ (T)} \qquad \mathbf{B}_2 = 25.75\mathbf{a}_x - 17.7\mathbf{a}_y + 10.0\mathbf{a}_z \text{ (T)}$$

If the interface carries a sheet current, what is its density at the origin?

Near the origin,

$$\mathbf{H}_1 = \frac{1}{\mu_0 \mu_{r1}} \mathbf{B}_1 = \frac{1}{\mu_0}(1.60\mathbf{a}_x + 6.67\mathbf{a}_z) \text{ (A/m)}$$

$$\mathbf{H}_2 = \frac{1}{\mu_0}(5.15\mathbf{a}_x - 3.54\mathbf{a}_y + 2.0\mathbf{a}_z) \text{ (A/m)}$$

Then the local value of **K** is given by

$$\mathbf{K} = (\mathbf{H}_1 - \mathbf{H}_2) \times \mathbf{a}_{n12} = \frac{1}{\mu_0}(-3.55\mathbf{a}_x + 3.54\mathbf{a}_y + 4.67\mathbf{a}_z) \times \mathbf{a}_z = \frac{5.0}{\mu_0}\left(\frac{\mathbf{a}_x + \mathbf{a}_y}{\sqrt{2}}\right) \text{ (A/m)}$$

10.20. Obtain the vector magnetic potential **A** in the region surrounding an infinitely long, straight, filamentary current *I*.

As shown in Example 6, the direct expression for **A** as an integral cannot be used. However, the relation

$$\nabla \times \mathbf{A} = \mathbf{B} = \frac{\mu_0 I}{2\pi r}\mathbf{a}_\phi$$

may be treated as a vector differential equation for **A**. Since **B** possesses only a ϕ component, only the ϕ component of the cylindrical curl is needed.

$$\frac{\partial A_r}{\partial z} - \frac{\partial A_r}{\partial r} = \frac{\mu_0 I}{2\pi r}$$

It is evident that **A** cannot be a function of *z*, since the filament is uniform with *z*. Then

$$-\frac{dA_z}{dr} = \frac{\mu_0 I}{2\pi r} \qquad \text{or} \qquad A_z = -\frac{\mu_0 I}{2\pi}\ln r + C$$

The constant of integration permits the location of a zero reference. With $A_z = 0$ at $r = r_0$, the expression becomes

$$\mathbf{A} = \frac{\mu_0 I}{2\pi}\left(\ln\frac{r_0}{r}\right)\mathbf{a}_z$$

10.21. Obtain the vector magnetic potential **A** for the current sheet of Example 2.

For $z > 0$,

$$\nabla \times \mathbf{A} = \mathbf{B} = \frac{\mu_0 K}{2}\mathbf{a}_x$$

whence

$$\frac{\partial A_z}{\partial y} - \frac{\partial A_y}{\partial z} = \frac{\mu_0 K}{2}$$

As **A** must be independent of *x* and *y*,

$$-\frac{dA_y}{dz} = \frac{\mu_0 K}{2} \qquad \text{or} \qquad A_y = -\frac{\mu_0 K}{2}(z - z_0)$$

Thus, for $z > 0$,

$$\mathbf{A} = -\frac{\mu_0 K}{2}(z - z_0)\mathbf{a}_y = -\frac{\mu_0}{2}(z - z_0)\mathbf{K}$$

For $z < 0$, change the sign of the above expression.

10.22. Using the vector magnetic potential found in Problem 10.21, find the magnetic flux crossing the rectangular area shown in Fig. 10-22.

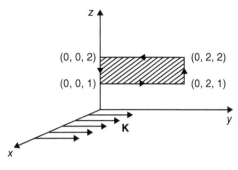

Fig. 10-22

Let the zero reference be at $z_0 = 2$, so that

$$\mathbf{A} = -\frac{\mu_0}{2}(z-2)\mathbf{K}$$

In the line integral

$$\Phi = \oint \mathbf{A} \cdot d\mathbf{l}$$

A is perpendicular to the contour on two sides and vanishes on the third ($z = 2$). Thus,

$$\Phi = \int_{y=0}^{y=2} \mathbf{A} \cdot d\mathbf{l} = -\frac{\mu_0}{2}(1-2)\int_0^2 K\,dy = \mu_0 K$$

Note how the choice of zero reference simplified the computation. By Stokes' theorem it is $\nabla \times \mathbf{A}$, and not **A** itself, that determines Φ; hence the zero reference may be chosen at pleasure.

SUPPLEMENTARY PROBLEMS

10.23. Show that the magnetic field due to the finite current element shown in Fig. 10-23 is given by

$$\mathbf{H} = \frac{1}{4\pi r}(\sin \alpha_1 - \sin \alpha_2)\,\mathbf{a}_\phi$$

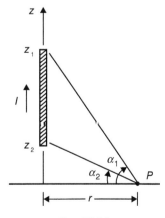

Fig. 10-23

10.24. Obtain $d\mathbf{H}$ at a general point (r, θ, ϕ) in spherical coordinates, due to a differential current element $I\,d\mathbf{I}$ at the origin in the positive z direction.

10.25. Currents in the inner and outer conductors of Fig. 10-24 are uniformly distributed. Use Ampère's law to show that for $b \le r \le c$,

$$\mathbf{H} = \frac{I}{2\pi r}\left(\frac{c^2 - r^2}{c^2 - b^2}\right)\mathbf{a}_\phi$$

Fig. 10-24

10.26. Two identical circular current loops of radius $r = 3$ m and $I = 20$ A are in parallel planes, separated on their common axis by 10 m. Find $\mathbf{H}$ at a point midway between the two loops.

10.27. A current filament of 10 A in the $+y$ direction lies along the y axis, and a current sheet, $\mathbf{K} = 2.0\mathbf{a}_x$ A/m, is located at $z = 4$ m. Determine $\mathbf{H}$ at the point $(2, 2, 2)$ m.

10.28. A cylindrical conductor of radius 10^{-2} m has an internal magnetic field

$$\mathbf{H} = (4.77 \times 10^4)\left(\frac{r}{2} - \frac{r^2}{3 \times 10^{-2}}\right)\mathbf{a}_\phi \quad \text{(A/m)}$$

What is the total current in the conductor?

10.29. In cylindrical coordinates, $\mathbf{J} = 10^5(\cos^2 2r)\mathbf{a}_z$ in a certain region. Obtain $\mathbf{H}$ from this current density and then take the curl of $\mathbf{H}$ and compare with $\mathbf{J}$.

10.30. In Cartesian coordinates, a constant current density, $\mathbf{J} = J_0\mathbf{a}_y$, exists in the region $-a \le z \le a$. See Fig. 10-25. Use Ampère's law to find $\mathbf{H}$ in all regions. Obtain the curl of $\mathbf{H}$ and compare with $\mathbf{J}$.

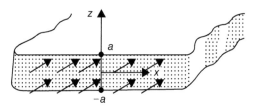

Fig. 10-25

10.31. Compute the total magnetic flux Φ crossing the $z = 0$ plane in cylindrical coordinates for $r \le 5 \times 10^{-2}$ m if

$$\mathbf{B} = \frac{0.2}{r}(\sin^2 \phi)\mathbf{a}_z \quad \text{(T)}$$

10.32. Given that

$$\mathbf{B} = 2.50 \left(\sin \frac{\pi x}{2} \right) e^{-2y} \mathbf{a}_z \quad (\text{T})$$

find the total magnetic flux crossing the strip $z = 0$, $y \geq 0$, $0 \leq x \leq 2$ m.

10.33. A coaxial conductor with an inner conductor of radius a and an outer conductor of inner and outer radii b and c, respectively, carries current I in the inner conductor. Find the magnetic flux per unit length crossing a plane $\phi = $ const. between the conductors.

10.34. Region *1*, where $\mu_{r1} = 5$, is on the side of the plane $6x + 4y + 3z = 12$ that includes the origin. In region 2, $\mu_{r2} = 3$. Given

$$\mathbf{H}_1 = \frac{1}{\mu_0} (3.0\mathbf{a}_x - 0.5\mathbf{a}_y) \quad (\text{A/m})$$

find $\mathbf{B}_2$ and θ_2.

10.35. The interface between two different regions is normal to one of the three Cartesian axes. If

$$\mathbf{B}_1 = \mu_0(43.5\mathbf{a}_x + 24.0\mathbf{a}_z) \qquad \mathbf{B}_2 = \mu_0(22.0\mathbf{a}_x + 24.0\mathbf{a}_z)$$

what is the ratio $(\tan \theta_1)/(\tan \theta_2)$?

10.36. Inside a right circular cylinder, $\mu_{r1} = 1000$. The exterior is free space. If $\mathbf{B}_1 = 2.5\mathbf{a}_\phi$ (T) inside the cylinder, determine $\mathbf{B}_2$ just outside.

10.37. In spherical coordinates, region *1* is $r < a$, region 2 is $a < r < b$ and region *3* is $r > b$. Regions *1* and *3* are free space, while $\mu_{r2} = 500$. Given $\mathbf{B}_1 = 0.20\mathbf{a}_r$ (T), find $\mathbf{H}$ in each region.

10.38. A current sheet, $\mathbf{K} = (8.0/\mu_0)\mathbf{a}_y$ (A/m), at $x = 0$ separates region *1*, $x < 0$ and $\mu_{r1} = 3$, from region 2, $x > 0$ and $\mu_{r2} = 1$. Given $\mathbf{H}_1 = (10.0/\mu_0)(\mathbf{a}_y + \mathbf{a}_z)$ (A/m), find $\mathbf{H}_2$.

10.39. The $x = 0$ plane contains a current sheet of density $\mathbf{K}$ which separates region *1*, $x < 0$ and $\mu_{r1} = 2$, from region 2, $x < 0$ and $\mu_{r2} = 7$. Given

$$\mathbf{B}_1 = 6.0\mathbf{a}_x + 4.0\mathbf{a}_y + 10.0\mathbf{a}_z \ (\text{T}) \qquad \mathbf{B}_2 = 6.0\mathbf{a}_x - 50.96\mathbf{a}_y + 8.96\mathbf{a}_z \ (\text{T})$$

find $\mathbf{K}$.

10.40. One uniform current sheet, $\mathbf{K} = K_0\mathbf{a}_y$, is at $z = b > 2$ and another, $\mathbf{K} = K_0(-\mathbf{a}_y)$, is at $z = -b$. Find the magnetic flux crossing the area defined by $x = $ const., $-2 \leq x \leq 2$, $0 \leq y \leq L$. Assume free space.

10.41. Use the vector magnetic potential from Problem 10.20 to obtain the flux crossing the rectangle $\phi = $ const., $r_1 \leq r \leq r_0$, $0 \leq z \leq L$, due to a current filament I on the z axis.

10.42. Given that the vector magnetic potential within a cylindrical conductor of radius a is

$$\mathbf{A} = -\frac{\mu_0 I r^2}{4\pi a^2} \mathbf{a}_z$$

find the corresponding $\mathbf{H}$.

10.43. One uniform current sheet, $\mathbf{K} = K_0(-\mathbf{a}_y)$, is located at $x = 0$ and another, $\mathbf{K} = K_0\mathbf{a}_y$, is at $x = a$. Find the vector magnetic potential between the sheets.

10.44. Between the current sheets of Problem 10.43 a portion of a $z = $ const. plane is defined by $0 \leq x \leq b$ and $0 \leq y \leq a$. Find the flux Φ crossing this portion, both from $\int \mathbf{B} \cdot d\mathbf{S}$ and from $\oint \mathbf{A} \cdot d\mathbf{l}$.

ANSWERS TO SUPPLEMENTARY PROBLEMS

10.24. $\dfrac{I\,d\ell\,\sin\theta}{4\pi r^2}\,\mathbf{a}_\phi$

10.26. $0.908\mathbf{a}_n$ A/m

10.27. $0.398\mathbf{a}_x + 1.0\mathbf{a}_y - 0.398\mathbf{a}_z$ A/m

10.28. 5.0 A

10.29. $\mathbf{H}=10^5\left(\dfrac{r}{4}+\dfrac{\sin 4r}{8}+\dfrac{\cos 4r}{32r}-\dfrac{1}{32r}\right)\mathbf{a}_\phi$

10.30. $\mathbf{H}=\begin{cases} J_0 a\mathbf{a}_x & z>a \\ J_0 z\mathbf{a}_x & -a\le z\le a \\ -J_0 a\mathbf{a}_x & z<-a \end{cases}$

curl $\mathbf{H}=\mathbf{J}$

10.31. 3.14×10^{-2} Wb

10.32. 1.59 Wb

10.33. $\dfrac{\mu_0 I}{2\pi}\ln\dfrac{b}{n}$

10.34. $12.15\mathbf{a}_x + 0.60\mathbf{a}_y + 1.58\mathbf{a}_z$ (T), $56.6°$

10.35. 0.506

10.36. $2.5\mathbf{a}_\phi$ (mT)

10.37. $\dfrac{0.20}{\mu_0}$ (A/m), $\dfrac{4\times 10^{-4}}{\mu_0}$ (A/m), $\dfrac{0.20}{\mu_0}$ (A/m)

10.38. $\dfrac{1}{\mu_0}(10.0\,\mathbf{a}_y + 2.0\mathbf{a}_z)$ (A/m)

10.39. $\dfrac{1}{\mu_0}(3.72\mathbf{a}_y - 9.28\mathbf{a}_z)$ (A/m)

10.40. $4\mu_0 K_0 L$

10.41. $\dfrac{\mu_0 IL}{2\pi}\ln\dfrac{r_0}{r_1}$

10.42. $\mu_0\mathbf{H}=\text{curl }\mathbf{A}$

10.43. $(\mu_0 K_0 x + C)\mathbf{a}_y$

10.44. $ab\mu_0 K_0$

CHAPTER 11

Forces and Torques in Magnetic Fields

11.1 Magnetic Force on Particles

A charged particle *in motion* in a magnetic field experiences a force at right angles to its velocity, with a magnitude proportional to the charge, the velocity, and the magnetic flux density. The complete expression is given by the cross product

$$\mathbf{F} = Q\mathbf{U} \times \mathbf{B}$$

Therefore, the direction of a particle in motion can be changed by a magnetic field. The magnitude of the velocity, U, and consequently the kinetic energy, will remain the same. This is in contrast to an electric field, where the force $\mathbf{F} = Q\mathbf{E}$ does work on the particle and therefore changes its kinetic energy.

If the field $\mathbf{B}$ is uniform throughout a region and the particle has an initial velocity normal to the field, the path of the particle is a circle of a certain radius r. The force of the field is of magnitude $F = |Q|\,UB$ and is directed toward the center of the circle. The centripetal acceleration is of magnitude $\omega^2 r = U^2/r$. Then, by Newton's second law,

$$|Q|\,UB = m\,\frac{U^2}{r} \quad \text{or} \quad r = \frac{mU}{|Q|\,B}$$

Observe that r is a measure of the particle's linear momentum, mU.

EXAMPLE 1.   Find the force on a particle of mass 1.70×10^{-27} kg and charge 1.60×10^{-19} C if it enters a field $B = 5$ mT with an initial speed of 83.5 km/s.

Unless directions are known for $\mathbf{B}$ and $\mathbf{U}_0$, the particle's initial velocity, the force cannot be calculated. Assuming that $\mathbf{U}_0$ and $\mathbf{B}$ are perpendicular, as shown in Fig. 11-1,

$$F = |Q|\,UB$$
$$= (1.60 \times 10^{-19})\,(83.5 \times 10^3)\,(5 \times 10^{-3})$$
$$= 6.68 \times 10^{-17}\ \mathbf{N}$$

$$
\begin{array}{cccc}
\times & \times & \times & \times \\
\times & \times & \times & \times \\
\times & \times & \times & \times \\
\times & \times & \times & \times \\
\end{array}
$$

(**B** into page)

Fig. 11-1

EXAMPLE 2. For the particle of Example 1, find the radius of the circular path and the time required for one revolution.

$$
r = \frac{mU}{|Q|B} = \frac{(1.70 \times 10^{-27})(83.5 \times 10^3)}{(1.60 \times 10^{-19})(5 \times 10^{-3})} = 0.177 \text{ m}
$$

$$
T = \frac{2\pi r}{U} = 13.3 \ \mu s
$$

11.2 Electric and Magnetic Fields Combined

When both fields are present in a region at the same time, the force on a particle is given by

$$
\mathbf{F} = Q(\mathbf{E} + \mathbf{U} \times \mathbf{B})
$$

This *Lorentz force*, together with the initial conditions, determines the path of the particle.

EXAMPLE 3. In a certain region surrounding the origin of coordinates, $\mathbf{B} = 5.0 \times 10^{-4}\mathbf{a}_z$ T and $\mathbf{E} = 5.0\mathbf{a}_z$ V/m. A proton ($Q_p = 1.602 \times 10^{-19}$ C, $m_p = 1.673 \times 10^{-27}$kg) enters the fields at the origin with an initial velocity $\mathbf{U}_0 = 2.5 \times 10^5\mathbf{a}_x$ m/s. Describe the proton's motion and give its position after three complete revolutions.

The initial force on the particle is

$$
\mathbf{F}_0 = Q(\mathbf{E} + \mathbf{U}_0 \times \mathbf{B}) = Q_p(E\mathbf{a}_z - U_0 B\mathbf{a}_y)
$$

The z component (electric component) of the force is constant and produces a constant acceleration in the z direction. Thus, the equation of motion in the z direction is

$$
z = \frac{1}{2}at^2 = \frac{1}{2}\left(\frac{Q_p E}{m_p}\right)t^2
$$

The other (magnetic) component, which changes into $-Q_p UB\mathbf{a}_r$, produces circular motion perpendicular to the z axis, with period

$$
T = \frac{2\pi r}{U} = \frac{2\pi m_p}{Q_p B}
$$

The resultant motion is helical, as shown in Fig. 11-2.

Fig. 11-2

After three revolutions, $x = y = 0$ and

$$z = \frac{1}{2}\left(\frac{Q_p E}{m_p}\right)(3T)^2 = \frac{18\pi^2 E m_p}{Q_p B^2} = 37.0 \text{ m}$$

11.3   Magnetic Force on a Current Element

A frequently encountered situation is that of a current-carrying conductor in an external magnetic field. Since $I = dQ/dt$, the differential force equation may be written

$$d\mathbf{F} = dQ(\mathbf{U} \times \mathbf{B}) = (I\,dt)(\mathbf{U} \times \mathbf{B}) = I(d\mathbf{I} \times \mathbf{B})$$

where $d\mathbf{I} = \mathbf{U}\,dt$ is the elementary length in the direction of the conventional current I. If the conductor is straight and the field is constant along it, the differential force may be integrated to give

$$F = ILB \sin \theta$$

The magnetic force is actually exerted on the electrons that make up the current I. However, since the electrons are confined to the conductor, the force is effectively transferred to the heavy lattice; this transferred force can do work on the conductor as a whole. While this fact provides a reasonable introduction to the behavior of current-carrying conductors in electric machines, certain essential considerations have been omitted. No mention was made, nor will be made in Section 11.4, of the current source and the energy that would be required to maintain a constant current I. Faraday's law of induction (Section 13.3) was not applied. In electric machine theory the result will be modified by these considerations. Conductors in motion in magnetic fields are treated again in Chapter 13; see particularly Problems 13.10 and 13.13.

EXAMPLE 4.   Find the force on a straight conductor of length 0.30 m carrying a current of 5.0 A in the $-\mathbf{a}_z$ direction, where the field is $\mathbf{B} = 3.50 \times 10^{-3}(\mathbf{a}_x - \mathbf{a}_y)$ T.

$$\mathbf{F} = I(\mathbf{L} \times \mathbf{B})$$
$$= (5.0)[(0.30)(-\mathbf{a}_z) \times 3.50 \times 10^{-3}(\mathbf{a}_x - \mathbf{a}_y)]$$
$$= 7.42 \times 10^{-3}\left(\frac{-\mathbf{a}_x - \mathbf{a}_y}{\sqrt{2}}\right) \text{ N}$$

The force, of magnitude 7.42 mN, is at right angles to both the field $\mathbf{B}$ and the current direction, as shown in Fig. 11-3.

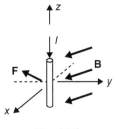

Fig. 11-3

11.4   Work and Power

The magnetic forces on the charged particles and current-carrying conductors examined above result from the field. To counter these forces and establish equilibrium, equal and opposite forces, $\mathbf{F}_a$, would have to be applied. If motion occurs, the work done on the system by the outside agent applying the force is given by the integral

$$W = \int_{\text{initial } \mathbf{l}}^{\text{final } \mathbf{l}} \mathbf{F}_a \cdot d\mathbf{l}$$

A positive result from the integration indicates that work was done by the agent on the system to move the particles or conductor from the initial to the final location and against the field. Because the magnetic force, and hence $\mathbf{F}_a$, is generally nonconservative, the entire path of integration joining the initial and final locations of the conductor must be specified.

EXAMPLE 5.   Find the work and power required to move the conductor shown in Fig. 11-4 one full revolution in the direction shown in 0.02 s, if $\mathbf{B} = 2.50 \times 10^{-3}\mathbf{a}_r$ T and the current is 45.0 A.

$$\mathbf{F} = I(\mathbf{l} \times \mathbf{B}) = 1.13 \times 10^{-2}\mathbf{a}_\phi \text{ N}$$

and so $\mathbf{F}_a = -1.13 \times 10^{-2}\mathbf{a}_\phi$ N.

$$W = \int \mathbf{F}_a \cdot d\mathbf{l}$$
$$= \int_0^{2\pi} (-1.13 \times 10^{-2})\mathbf{a}_\phi \cdot r\,d\phi\mathbf{a}_\phi$$
$$= -2.13 \times 10^{-3} \text{ J}$$

and $P = W/t = -0.107$ W.

0.10 m

x $r = 0.03$ m

Fig. 11-4

The negative sign means that work is done by the magnetic field in moving the conductor in the direction shown. For motion in the opposite direction, the reversed limits will provide the change of sign, and no attempt to place a sign on $r\,d\phi\mathbf{a}_\phi$ should be made.

11.5   Torque

The *moment of a force* or *torque* about a specified point is the cross product of the *lever arm* about that point and the force. The lever arm, $\mathbf{r}$, is directed from the point about which the torque is to be obtained to the point of application of the force. In Fig. 11-5 the force at P has a torque about O given by

$$\mathbf{T} = \mathbf{r} \times \mathbf{F}$$

where $\mathbf{T}$ has the units N $\cdot$ m. (The units N $\cdot$ m/rad have been suggested, in order to distinguish torque from energy.)

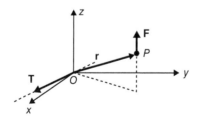

Fig. 11-5

In Fig. 11-5, **T** lies along an axis (in the *xy* plane) through *O*. If *P* were joined to *O* by a rigid rod freely pivoted at *O*, then the applied force would tend to rotate *P* about that axis. The torque **T** would then be said to be *about the axis*, rather than *about point O*.

EXAMPLE 6. A conductor located at $x = 0.4$ m, $y = 0$ and $0 < z < 2.0$ m carries a current of 5.0 A in the $\mathbf{a}_x$ direction. Along the length of the conductor $\mathbf{B} = 2.5\mathbf{a}_z$ T. Find the torque about the *z* axis.

$$\mathbf{F} = I(\mathbf{L} \times \mathbf{B}) = 5.0(2.0\mathbf{a}_z \times 2.5\mathbf{a}_x) = 25.0\mathbf{a}_y \text{ N}$$
$$\mathbf{T} = \mathbf{r} \times \mathbf{F} = 0.4\mathbf{a}_x \times 25.0\mathbf{a}_y = 10.0\mathbf{a}_z \text{ N} \cdot \text{m}$$

11.6 Magnetic Moment of a Planar Coil

Consider the single-turn coil in the $z = 0$ plane shown in Fig. 11-6, of width *w* in the *x* direction and length ℓ along *y*. The field **B** is uniform and in the +*x* direction. Only the

Fig. 11-6

$\pm y$ -directed currents give rise to forces. For the side on the left,

$$\mathbf{F} = I(\ell\mathbf{a}_y \times B\mathbf{a}_x) = -BI\,\ell\mathbf{a}_z$$

and for the side on the right,

$$\mathbf{F} = BI\,\ell\mathbf{a}_z$$

The torque about the *y* axis from the left current element requires a lever arm $\mathbf{r} = -(w/2)\mathbf{a}_x$; the sign will change for the lever arm of the right current element. The torque from both elements is

$$\mathbf{T} = \left(-\frac{w}{2}\right)\mathbf{a}_x \times (-BI\,\ell)\,\mathbf{a}_z + \left(\frac{w}{2}\right)\mathbf{a}_x \times BI\,\ell\mathbf{a}_z = BI\ell w\,(-\mathbf{a}_y) = BI\,A(-\mathbf{a}_y)$$

where *A* is the area of the coil. It can be shown that this expression for the torque holds for a flat coil of arbitrary shape (and for any axis parallel to the *y* axis).

The *magnetic moment* **m** of a planar current loop is defined as $IA\mathbf{a}_n$, where the unit normal $\mathbf{a}_n$ is determined by the right-hand rule. (The right thumb gives the direction of $\mathbf{a}_n$ when the fingers point in the direction of the current.) It is seen that the torque on a planar coil is related to the applied field by

$$\mathbf{T} = \mathbf{m} \times \mathbf{B}$$

This concept of magnetic moment is essential to an understanding of the behavior of orbiting charged particles. For example, a positive charge *Q* moving in a circular orbit at a velocity *U*, or an angular velocity ω, is equivalent to a current $I = (\omega/2\pi)Q$, and so gives rise to a magnetic moment

$$\mathbf{m} = \frac{\omega}{2\pi} Q A \mathbf{a}_n$$

as shown in Fig. 11-7. More important to the present discussion is that in the presence of a magnetic field **B** there will be a torque **T** = **m** × **B** which tends to turn the current loop until **m** and **B** are in the same direction, in which orientation the torque will be zero.

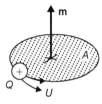

Fig. 11-7

SOLVED PROBLEMS

11.1. A conductor 4 m long lies along the y axis with a current of 10.0 A in the $\mathbf{a}_y$ direction. Find the force on the conductor if the field in the region is **B** = $0.05\mathbf{a}_x$ T.

$$\mathbf{F} = I\mathbf{L} \times \mathbf{B} = 10.0(4\mathbf{a}_y \times 0.05\mathbf{a}_x) = -2.0\mathbf{a}_z \text{ N}$$

11.2. A conductor of length 2.5 m located at $z = 0$, $x = 4$ m carries a current of 12.0 A in the $-\mathbf{a}_y$ direction. Find the uniform **B** in the region if the force on the conductor is 1.20×10^{-2} N in the direction $(-\mathbf{a}_x + \mathbf{a}_z)/\sqrt{2}$.

From **F** = $I\mathbf{L} \times \mathbf{B}$,

$$(1.20 \times 10^{-2})\left(\frac{-\mathbf{a}_x + \mathbf{a}_z}{\sqrt{2}}\right) = \begin{vmatrix} \mathbf{a}_x & \mathbf{a}_y & \mathbf{a}_z \\ 0 & -(12.0)(2.5) & 0 \\ B_x & B_y & B_z \end{vmatrix} = -30B_z\mathbf{a}_x + 30B_x\mathbf{a}_z$$

whence
$$B_z = B_x = \frac{4 \times 10^{-4}}{\sqrt{2}}\text{T}$$

The y component of **B** may have any value.

11.3. A current strip 2 cm wide carries a current of 15.0 A in the $\mathbf{a}_x$ direction, as shown in Fig. 11-8. Find the force on the strip per unit length if the uniform field is **B** = $0.20\mathbf{a}_y$ T.

Fig. 11-8

In the expression for $d\mathbf{F}$, $I\,d\mathbf{l}$ may be replaced by **K** dS.

$$d\mathbf{F} = (\mathbf{K}\,dS) \times \mathbf{B}$$
$$= \left(\frac{15.0}{0.02}\right) dx\,dy\,(0.20)\,\mathbf{a}_z$$
$$\mathbf{F} = \int_{-0.01}^{0.01}\int_0^L 150.0\,dx\,dy\,\mathbf{a}_z$$
$$\frac{\mathbf{F}}{L} = 3.0\mathbf{a}_z \text{ N/m}$$

11.4. Find the forces per unit length on two long, straight, parallel conductors if each carries a current of 10.0 A in the same direction and the separation distance is 0.20 m.

Consider the arrangement in Cartesian coordinates shown in Fig. 11-9. The conductor on the left creates a field whose magnitude at the right-hand conductor is

$$B = \frac{\mu_0 I}{2\pi r} = \frac{(4\pi \times 10^{-7})(10.0)}{2\pi(0.20)} = 10^{-5}\,\text{T}$$

Fig. 11-9

and whose direction is $-\mathbf{a}_z$. Then the force on the right conductor is

$$\mathbf{F} = IL\mathbf{a}_y \times B(-\mathbf{a}_z) = ILB(-\mathbf{a}_x)$$

and

$$\frac{\mathbf{F}}{L} = 10^{-4}(-\mathbf{a}_x)\,\text{N/m}$$

An equal but opposite force acts on the left-hand conductor. The force is seen to be one of attraction. Two parallel conductors carrying current in the same direction will have forces tending to pull them together.

11.5. A conductor carries current I parallel to a current strip of density K_0 and width w, as shown in Fig. 11-10. Find an expression for the force per unit length on the conductor. What is the result when the width w approaches infinity?

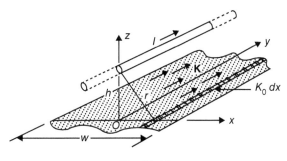

Fig. 11-10

From Problem 11.4, the filament $K_0\,dx$ shown in Fig. 11-10 exerts an attractive force

$$\frac{d\mathbf{F}}{L} = IB\mathbf{a} = I\frac{\mu_0(K_0\,dx)}{2\pi r}\mathbf{a}_r$$

on the conductor. Adding to this the force due to the similar filament at $-x$, the components in the x direction cancel, giving a resultant

$$\frac{d\mathbf{F}}{L} = I\frac{\mu_0(K_0\,dx)}{2\pi r}\left(2\frac{h}{r}\right)(-\mathbf{a}_z) = \frac{\mu_0 I K_0 h}{\pi}\frac{dx}{h^2 + x^2}(-\mathbf{a}_z)$$

Integrating over the half-width of the strip,

$$\frac{\mathbf{F}}{L} = \frac{\mu_0 I K_0 h}{\pi}(-\mathbf{a}_z)\int_0^{w/2}\frac{dx}{h^2+x^2} = \left(\frac{\mu_0 I K_0}{\pi}\arctan\frac{w}{2h}\right)(-\mathbf{a}_z)$$

The force is one of attraction, as expected.

As the strip width approaches infinity, $\mathbf{F}/L \to (\mu_0 I K_0/2)(-\mathbf{a}_z)$.

11.6. Find the torque about the *y* axis for the two conductors of length ℓ, separated by a fixed distance *w*, in the uniform field **B** shown in Fig. 11-11.

Fig. 11-11

The conductor on the left experiences the force

$$\mathbf{F}_1 = I\,\ell\mathbf{a}_y \times B\mathbf{a}_x = BI\ell(-\mathbf{a}_z)$$

the torque of which is

$$\mathbf{T}_1 = \frac{w}{2}(-\mathbf{a}_x) \times BI\ell(-\mathbf{a}_z) = BI\ell\frac{w}{2}(-\mathbf{a}_y)$$

The force on the conductor on the right results in the same torque. The sum is, therefore,

$$\mathbf{T} = BI\ell w(-\mathbf{a}_y)$$

11.7. A D'Arsonval meter movement has a uniform radial field of $B = 0.10$ T and a restoring spring with a torque $T = 5.87 \times 10^{-5}\theta$ (N · m), where the angle of rotation is in radians. The coil contains 35 turns and measures 23 mm by 17 mm. What angle of rotation results from a coil current of 15 mA?

The shaped pole pieces shown in Fig. 11-12 result in a uniform radial field over a limited range of deflection. Assuming that the entire coil length is in the field, the torque produced is

$$T = nBI\ell w = 35(0.10)(15 \times 10^{-3})(23 \times 10^{-3})(17 \times 10^{-3})$$
$$= 2.05 \times 10^{-5} \text{ N · m}$$

This coil turns until this torque equals the spring torque.

$$2.05 \times 10^{-5} = 5.87 \times 10^{-5}\theta$$
$$\theta = 0.349 \text{ rad or } 20°$$

Fig. 11-12

11.8. The rectangular coil in Fig. 11-13 is in a field

$$\mathbf{B} = 0.05 \frac{\mathbf{a}_x + \mathbf{a}_y}{\sqrt{2}} \, \text{T}$$

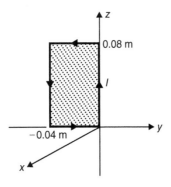

Fig. 11-13

Find the torque about the z axis when the coil is in the position shown and carries a current of 5.0 A.

$$\mathbf{m} = I A \mathbf{a}_n = 1.60 \times 10^{-2} \mathbf{a}_x$$

$$\mathbf{T} = \mathbf{m} \times \mathbf{B} = 1.60 \times 10^{-2} \mathbf{a}_x \times 0.05 \frac{\mathbf{a}_x + \mathbf{a}_y}{\sqrt{2}}$$

$$= 5.66 \times 10^{-4} \mathbf{a}_z \, \text{N} \cdot \text{m}$$

If the coil turns through 45°, the direction of $\mathbf{m}$ will be $(\mathbf{a}_x + \mathbf{a}_y)/\sqrt{2}$ and the torque will be zero.

11.9. Find the maximum torque on an 85-turn, rectangular coil, 0.2 m by 0.3 m, carrying a current of 2.0 A in a field $B = 6.5$ T.

$$T_{\text{max}} = nBI\ell w = 85(6.5)(2.0)(0.2)(0.3) = 66.3 \, \text{N} \cdot \text{m}$$

11.10. Find the maximum torque on an orbiting charged particle if the charge is 1.602×10^{-19} C, the circular path has a radius of 0.5×10^{-10} m, the angular velocity is 4.0×10^{16} rad/s, and $B = 0.4 \times 10^{-3}$ T.

The orbiting charge has a magnetic moment

$$\mathbf{m} = \frac{\omega}{2\pi} Q A \mathbf{a}_n = \frac{4 \times 10^{16}}{2\pi} (1.602 \times 10^{-19}) \pi (0.5 \times 10^{-10})^2 \mathbf{a}_n = 8.01 \times 10^{-24} \mathbf{a}_n \quad \text{A} \cdot \text{m}^2$$

Then the maximum torque results when $\mathbf{a}_n$ is normal to $\mathbf{B}$.

$$T_{\text{max}} = mB = 3.20 \times 10^{-27} \, \text{N} \cdot \text{m}$$

11.11. A conductor of length 4 m, with current held at 10 A in the $\mathbf{a}_y$ direction, lies along the y axis between $y = \pm 2$ m. If the field is $\mathbf{B} = 0.05\mathbf{a}_x$ T, find the work done in moving the conductor parallel to itself at constant speed to $x = z = 2$ m.

For the entire motion,

$$\mathbf{F} = I\mathbf{L} \times \mathbf{B} = -2.0\mathbf{a}_z$$

The applied force is equal and opposite,

$$\mathbf{F}_a = 2.0\mathbf{a}_z$$

Because this force is constant, and therefore conservative, the conductor may be moved first along z, then in the x direction, as shown in Fig. 11-14. Since $\mathbf{F}_a$ is completely in the z direction, no work is done in moving along x. Then,

$$W = \int_0^2 (2.0\,\mathbf{a}_z) \cdot dz\,\mathbf{a}_z = 4.0\,\text{J}$$

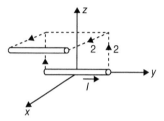

Fig. 11-14

11.12. A conductor lies along the z axis at $-1.5 \leq z \leq 1.5$ m and carries a fixed current of 10.0 A in the $-\mathbf{a}_z$ direction. See Fig. 11-15. For a field

$$\mathbf{B} = 3.0 \times 10^{-4} e^{-0.2x}\mathbf{a}_y \quad (\text{T})$$

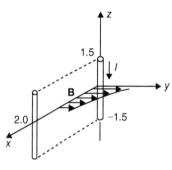

Fig. 11-15

find the work and power required to move the conductor at constant speed to $x = 2.0$ m, $y = 0$ in 5×10^{-3} s. Assume parallel motion along the x axis.

$$\mathbf{F} = I\mathbf{L} \times \mathbf{B} = 9.0 \times 10^{-3} e^{-0.2x}\mathbf{a}_x$$

Then $\mathbf{F}_a = -9.0 \times 10^{-3} e^{-0.2x}\mathbf{a}_x$ and

$$W = \int_0^2 (-9.0 \times 10^{-3}\, e^{-0.2x}\mathbf{a}_x) \cdot dx\,\mathbf{a}_x$$
$$= -1.48 \times 10^{-2}\,\text{J}$$

The field moves the conductor, and therefore the work is negative. The power is given by

$$P = \frac{W}{t} = \frac{-1.48 \times 10^{-2}}{5 \times 10^{-3}} = -2.97\,\text{W}$$

11.13. Find the work and power required to move the conductor shown in Fig. 11-16 one full turn in the positive direction at a rotational frequency of N revolutions per minute, if $\mathbf{B} = B_0\mathbf{a}_r$ (B_0 a positive constant).

Fig. 11-16

The force on the conductor is

$$\mathbf{F} = I\mathbf{L} \times \mathbf{B} = IL\mathbf{a}_z \times B_0\mathbf{a}_r = B_0IL\mathbf{a}_\phi$$

so that the applied force is

$$\mathbf{F}_a = B_0\, IL(-\mathbf{a}_\phi)$$

The conductor is to be turned in the $\mathbf{a}_\phi$ direction. Therefore, the work required for one full revolution is

$$W = \int_0^{2\pi} B_0IL(-\mathbf{a}_\phi) \cdot r\, d\phi \mathbf{a}_\phi = -2\pi r\, B_0IL$$

For a rotational frequency of N revolutions per 60 seconds, the power is

$$P = -\frac{2\pi r\, B_0\, I\, LN}{60}$$

The negative signs on work and power indicate that the field does the work. The fact that work is done around a closed path shows that the force is nonconservative in this case.

11.14. In the configuration shown in Fig. 11-16 the conductor is 100 mm long and carries a constant 5.0 A in the $\mathbf{a}_z$ direction. If the field is

$$\mathbf{B} = -3.5 \sin \phi \mathbf{a}_r \quad \text{mT}$$

and $r = 25$ mm, find the work done in moving the conductor at constant speed from $\phi = 0$ to $\phi = \pi$, in the direction shown. If the current direction is reversed for $\pi < \phi < 2\pi$, what is the total work required for one full revolution?

$$\mathbf{F} = I\mathbf{L} \times \mathbf{B} = -1.75 \times 10^{-3} \sin \phi\, \mathbf{a}_\phi \quad \text{N}$$
$$\mathbf{F}_a = 1.75 \times 10^{-3} \sin \phi\, \mathbf{a}_\phi \quad \text{N}$$

Then

$$W = \int_0^\pi 1.75 \times 10^{-3} \sin \phi \mathbf{a}_\phi \cdot r\, d\phi \mathbf{a}_\phi = 87.5\, \mu\text{J}$$

If the current direction changes when the conductor is between π and 2π, the work will be the same. The total work is 175 μJ.

11.15. Compute the centripetal force necessary to hold an electron ($m_e = 9.107 \times 10^{-31}$ kg) in a circular orbit of radius 0.35×10^{-10} m with an angular velocity of 2×10^{16} rad/s.

$$F = m_e\omega^2 r = (9.107 \times 10^{-31})\, (2 \times 10^{16})^2\, (0.35 \times 10^{-10}) = 1.27 \times 10^{-8}\, \text{N}$$

11.16. A uniform magnetic field $\mathbf{B} = 85.3\mathbf{a}_z\ \mu$T exists in the region $x \geq 0$. If an electron enters this field at the origin with a velocity $\mathbf{U}_0 = 450\mathbf{a}_x$ km/s, find the position where it exits the field. Where would a proton with the same initial velocity exit?

$$r_e = \frac{m_e U_0}{|Q|B} = 3.00 \times 10^{-2}\,\text{m}$$

The electron experiences an initial force in the $\mathbf{a}_y$ direction and it exits the field at $x = z = 0$, $y = 6$ cm.

A proton would turn the other way. Part of the circular path is shown at P in Fig. 11-17. With $m_p = 1840m_e$,

$$r_p = \frac{m_p}{m_e}r_e = 55\,\text{m}$$

and the proton exits at $x = z = 0$, $y = -110$ m.

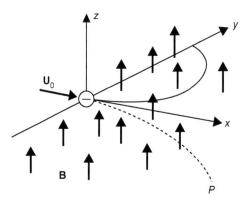

Fig. 11-17

11.17. If a proton is fixed in position and an electron revolves about it in a circular path of radius 0.35×10^{-10} m, what is the magnetic field at the proton?

The proton and electron are attracted by the coulomb force,

$$F = \frac{Q^2}{4\pi\epsilon_0 r^2}$$

which furnishes the centripetal force for the circular motion. Thus,

$$\frac{Q^2}{4\pi\epsilon_0 r^2} = m_e\omega^2 r \qquad \text{or} \qquad \omega^2 = \frac{Q^2}{4\pi\epsilon_0 m_e r^3}$$

Now, the electron is equivalent to a current loop $I = (\omega/2\pi)Q$. The field at the center of such a loop is, from Problem 10.7,

$$B = \mu_0 H = \frac{\mu_0 I}{2r} = \frac{\mu_0 \omega Q}{4\pi r}$$

Substituting the value of ω found above,

$$B = \frac{(\mu_0/4\pi)Q^2}{r^2\sqrt{4\pi\epsilon_0 m_e r}} = \frac{(10^{-7})(1.6\times10^{-19})^2}{(0.35\times10^{-10})2\sqrt{\left(\frac{1}{9}\times10^{-9}\right)(9.1\times10^{-31})(0.35\times10^{-10})}} = 35\,\text{T}$$

SUPPLEMENTARY PROBLEMS

11.18. A current element 2 m in length lies along the y axis centered at the origin. The current is 5.0 A in the $\mathbf{a}_y$ direction. If it experiences a force $1.50(\mathbf{a}_x + \mathbf{a}_z)/\sqrt{2}$ N due to a uniform field $\mathbf{B}$, determine $\mathbf{B}$.

11.19. A magnetic field, $\mathbf{B} = 3.5 \times 10^{-2}\mathbf{a}_z$ T, exerts a force on a 0.30-m conductor along the x axis. If the conductor current is 5.0 A in the $-\mathbf{a}_x$ direction, what force must be applied to hold the conductor in position?

11.20. A current sheet, $\mathbf{K} = 30.0\mathbf{a}_y$ A/m, lies in the plane $z = -5$ m and a filamentary conductor is on the y axis with a current of 5.0 A in the $\mathbf{a}_y$ direction. Find the force per unit length.

11.21. A conductor with current I pierces a plane current sheet $\mathbf{K}$ orthogonally, as shown in Fig. 11-18. Find the force per unit length on the conductor above and below the sheet.

Fig. 11-18

11.22. Find the force on a 2-m conductor on the z axis with a current of 5.0 A in the $\mathbf{a}_z$ direction, if

$$\mathbf{B} = 2.0\mathbf{a}_x + 6.0\mathbf{a}_y \text{ T}$$

11.23. Two infinite current sheets, each of constant density K_0, are parallel and have their currents oppositely directed. Find the force per unit area on the sheets. Is the force one of repulsion or attraction?

11.24. The circular current loop shown in Fig. 11-19 is in the plane $z = h$, parallel to a uniform current sheet, $\mathbf{K} = K_0\mathbf{a}_y$, at $z = 0$. Express the force on a differential length of the loop. Integrate and show that the total force is zero.

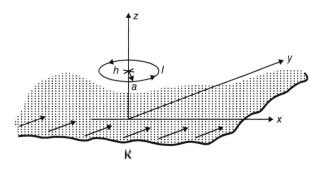

Fig. 11-19

11.25. Two conductors of length ℓ normal to $\mathbf{B}$ are shown in Fig. 11-20; they have a fixed separation w. Show that the torque about any axis parallel to the conductors is given by $BI\ell w \cos \theta$.

Fig. 11-20

11.26. A circular current loop of radius r and current I lies in the $z = 0$ plane. Find the torque which results if the current is in the $\mathbf{a}_\phi$ direction and there is a uniform field $\mathbf{B} = B_0(\mathbf{a}_x + \mathbf{a}_z)/\sqrt{2}$.

11.27. A current loop of radius $r = 0.35$ m is centered about the x axis in the plane $x = 0$, and at $(0, 0, 0.35)$ m the current is in the $-\mathbf{a}_y$ direction at a magnitude of 5.0 A. Find the torque if the uniform field is $\mathbf{B} = 88.4(\mathbf{a}_x + \mathbf{a}_z)\,\mu$T.

11.28. A current of 2.5 A is directed generally in the $\mathbf{a}_\phi$ direction about a square-conducting loop centered at the origin in the $z = 0$ plane with 0.60 m sides parallel to the x and y axes. Find the forces and the torque on the loop if $\mathbf{B} = 15\mathbf{a}_y$ mT. Would the torque be different if the loop were rotated through 45° in the $z = 0$ plane?

11.29. A 200-turn, rectangular coil, 0.30 m by 0.15 m with a current of 5.0 A, is in a uniform field $B = 0.2$ T. Find the magnetic moment m and the maximum torque.

11.30. Two conductors of length 4.0 m are on a cylindrical shell of radius 2.0 m centered on the z axis, as shown in Fig. 11-21. Currents of 10.0 A are directed as shown and there is an external field $\mathbf{B} = 0.5\mathbf{a}_x$ T at $\phi = 0$ and $\mathbf{B} = -0.5\mathbf{a}_x$ T at $\phi = \pi$. Find the sum of the forces and the torque about the axis.

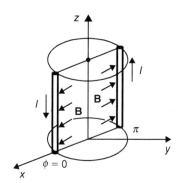

Fig. 11-21

11.31. A right circular cylinder contains 550 conductors on the curved surface and each has a current of constant magnitude 7.5 A. The magnetic field is $\mathbf{B} = 38 \sin \phi\, \mathbf{a}_r$ mT. The current direction is $\mathbf{a}_z$ for $0 < \phi < \pi$ and $-\mathbf{a}_z$ for $\pi < \phi < 2\pi$ (Fig. 11-22). Find the mechanical power required if the cylinder turns at 1600 revolutions per minute in the $-\mathbf{a}_\phi$ direction.

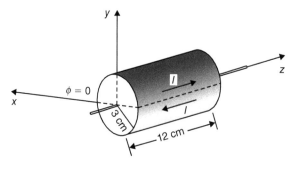

Fig. 11-22

11.32. Obtain an expression for the power required to turn a cylindrical set of n conductors (see Fig. 11-22) against the field at N revolutions per minute, if $\mathbf{B} = B_0 \sin 2\phi \, \mathbf{a}_r$ and the currents change direction in each quadrant where the sign of $\mathbf{B}$ changes.

11.33. A conductor of length ℓ lies along the x axis with current I in the $\mathbf{a}_x$ direction. Find the work done in turning it at constant speed, as shown in Fig. 11-23, if the uniform field is $\mathbf{B} = B_0 \mathbf{a}_z$.

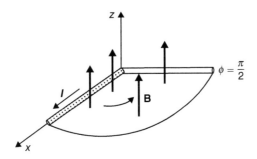

Fig. 11-23

11.34. A rectangular current loop, of length ℓ along the y axis, is in a uniform field $\mathbf{B} = B_0 \mathbf{a}_z$, as shown in Fig. 11-24. Show that the work done in moving the loop along the x axis at constant speed is zero.

Fig. 11-24

11.35. For the configuration shown in Fig. 11-24, the magnetic field is

$$\mathbf{B} = B_0 \left(\sin \frac{\pi x}{w} \right) \mathbf{a}_z$$

Find the work done in moving the coil a distance w along the x axis at constant speed, starting from the location shown.

11.36. A conductor of length 0.25 m lies along the y axis and carries a current of 25.0 A in the $\mathbf{a}_y$ direction. Find the power needed for parallel translation of the conductor to $x = 5.0$ m at constant speed in 3.0 s if the uniform field is $\mathbf{B} = 0.06\mathbf{a}_z$ T.

11.37. Find the tangential velocity of a proton in a field $B = 30 \ \mu T$ if the circular path has a diameter of 1 cm.

11.38. An alpha particle and a proton ($Q_a = 2Q_p$) enter a magnetic field $B = 1 \ \mu T$ with an initial speed $U_0 = 8.5$ m/s. Given the masses 6.68×10^{-27} kg and 1.673×10^{-27} kg for the alpha particle and the proton, respectively, find the radii of the circular paths.

11.39. If a proton in a magnetic field completes one circular orbit in 2.35 μs, what is the magnitude of $\mathbf{B}$?

11.40. An electron in a field $B = 4.0 \times 10^{-2}$ T has a circular path with radius 0.35×10^{-10} m and a maximum torque of 7.85×10^{-26} N · m. Determine the angular velocity.

11.41. A region contains uniform **B** and **E** fields in the same direction, with $B = 650 \ \mu$T. An electron follows a helical path, where the circle has a radius of 35 mm. If the electron has zero initial velocity in the axial direction and advances 431 mm along the axis in the time required for one full circle, find the magnitude of **E**.

ANSWERS TO SUPPLEMENTARY PROBLEMS

11.18. $0.106(-\mathbf{a}_x + \mathbf{a}_z)$ T

11.19. $-5.25 \times 10^{-2}\mathbf{a}_y$ N

11.20. 94.2 μN/m (attraction)

11.21. $\pm\mu_0 KI/2$

11.22. $-60\mathbf{a}_x + 20\mathbf{a}_y$ N

11.23. $\mu_0 K_0^2/2$ (repulsion)

11.24. $d\mathbf{F} = \frac{1}{2}Ia\mu_0 K_0 \cos \phi \, d\phi \, (-\mathbf{a}_z)$

11.25. Use magnetic moment, section 11.6.

11.26. $(\pi r^2 B_0 I \sqrt{2})\mathbf{a}_y$

11.27. $1.70 \times 10^{-4}(-\mathbf{a}_y)$ N $\cdot$ m

11.28. $1.35 \times 10^{-2}(-\mathbf{a}_z)$ N $\cdot$ m; $\mathbf{T} = \mathbf{m} \times \mathbf{B}$

11.29. 45.0 A $\cdot$ m^2, 9.0 N $\cdot$ m

11.30. $-40\mathbf{a}_y$ N, 0

11.31. 60.2 W

11.32. $\dfrac{B_0 n \, I\ell r N}{60}$ (W)

11.33. $\pi B_0 \ell^2 I/4$

11.34. Elements parallel to the *y*-axis experience work components which cancel each other.

11.35. $-4B_0 I\ell w/\pi$

11.36. -0.625 W

11.37. 14.4 m/s

11.38. 177 mm, 88.8 mm

11.39. $2.79 \times 10^{-2}T$

11.40. 2.0×10^{16} rad/s

11.41. 1.62 kV/m

CHAPTER 12

Inductance and Magnetic Circuits

12.1 Inductance

The *inductance L* of a conductor system may be defined as *the ratio of the linking magnetic flux to the current producing the flux*. For static (or, at most, low-frequency) current I and a coil containing N turns, as shown in Fig. 12-1,

$$L = \frac{N\,\Phi}{I}$$

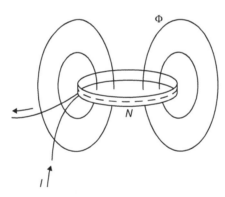

Fig. 12-1

The units on L are *henries*, where 1 H = 1 Wb/A. Inductance is also given by $L = \lambda/I$, where λ, the *flux linkage*, is $N\Phi$ for coils with N turns or simply Φ for other conductor arrangements.

It should be noted that L will always be the product of the permeability μ of the medium (units on μ are H/m) and a geometrical factor having the units of length. Compare the expressions for resistance R (Chapter 7) and capacitance C (Chapter 8).

EXAMPLE 1. Find the inductance per unit length of a coaxial conductor such as that shown in Fig.12-2. Between the conductors,

$$\mathbf{H} = \frac{I}{2\pi r}\,\mathbf{a}_\phi$$

$$\mathbf{B} = \frac{\mu_0 I}{2\pi r}\,\mathbf{a}_\phi$$

Fig. 12-2

The currents in the two conductors are linked by the flux across the surface $\phi =$ const. For a length ℓ,

$$\lambda = \int_0^\ell \int_a^b \frac{\mu_0 I}{2\pi r} \, dr \, dz = \frac{\mu_0 I \ell}{2\pi} \ln \frac{b}{a}$$

and

$$\frac{L}{\ell} = \frac{\mu_0}{2\pi} \ln \frac{b}{a} \quad \text{(H/m)}$$

EXAMPLE 2. Find the inductance of an ideal solenoid with 300 turns, $\ell = 0.50$ m, and a circular cross section of radius 0.02 m.

The turns per unit length is $n = 300/0.50 = 600$, so that the axial field is

$$B = \mu_0 H = \mu_0 600 I \quad \text{(Wb/m}^2\text{)}$$

Then

$$\frac{L}{\ell} = \frac{N\Phi}{I} = N\left(\frac{B}{I}\right) A = 300(600\mu_0)\pi(4 \times 10^{-4})$$

$$= 568 \ \mu\text{H/m}$$

or $L = 284 \ \mu\text{H}$.

In Section 6.7 an imagined bringing-in of point charges from infinity was used to derive the energy content of an electric field:

$$W_E = \frac{1}{2} \int_{\text{vol}} \mathbf{D} \cdot \mathbf{E} \, dv$$

There is no equivalent in a magnetic field to the point charge, and consequently no parallel development for its stored energy. However, a more sophisticated approach yields the completely analogous expression

$$W_H = \frac{1}{2} \int_{\text{vol}} \mathbf{B} \cdot \mathbf{H} \, dv$$

Comparing this with the formula $W_H = \frac{1}{2} L I^2$ from circuit analysis yields

$$L = \int_{\text{vol}} \frac{\mathbf{B} \cdot \mathbf{H}}{I^2} \, dv$$

EXAMPLE 3.   Checking Example 1,

$$L = \int_{vol} \frac{\mathbf{B} \cdot \mathbf{H}}{I^2}\, dv = \frac{\mu_0}{I^2} \int_0^\ell \int_0^{2\pi} \int_a^b \left(\frac{I^2}{4\pi^2 r^2}\right) r\, dr\, d\phi\, dz = \frac{\mu_0 \ell}{2\pi} \ln \frac{b}{a}$$

12.2   Standard Conductor Configurations

Figs. 12-3 through 12-7 give exact or approximate inductances of some common noncoaxial arrangements.

$$L = \frac{\mu_0 N^2 a}{2\pi} \ln \frac{r_2}{r_1} \quad (\text{H})$$

Fig. 12-3 Toroid, square cross section.

$$L \approx \frac{\mu_0 N^2 S}{2\pi r} \quad (\text{H})$$
(assuming average flux density at average radius r)

Fig. 12-4 Toroid, general cross section S.

$$\frac{L}{\ell} = \frac{\mu_0}{\pi} \cosh^{-1} \frac{d}{2a} \quad (\text{H/m})$$

For $d \gg a$,

$$\frac{L}{\ell} \approx \frac{\mu_0}{\pi} \ln \frac{d}{a} \quad (\text{H/m})$$

Fig. 12-5 Parallel conductors of radius *a*.

$$\frac{L}{\ell} = \frac{\mu_0}{2\pi} \cosh^{-1} \frac{d}{2a} \quad (\text{H/m})$$

$$\approx \frac{\mu_0}{2\pi} \ln \frac{d}{a} \quad (\text{H/m})$$

Fig. 12-6 Cylindrical conductor parallel to a ground plane.

$$L = \frac{\mu_0 N^2 S}{\ell} \quad (\text{H})$$

Fig. 12-7 Long solenoid of small cross-sectional area S.

12.3   Faraday's Law and Self-Inductance

Consider an open surface S bounded by a closed contour C. If the magnetic flux ϕ linking S varies with time, then a *voltage v around C* exists; by *Faraday's law*,

$$v = -\frac{d\phi}{dt}$$

As was shown in Chapter 6, the electrostatic potential or voltage, V, is well-defined in space and is associated with a conservative electric field. By contrast, the *induced* voltage v given by Faraday's law is a multivalued function of position and is associated with a nonconservative field (*electromotive force*). More about this in Chapter 13.

Faraday's law holds in particular when the flux through a circuit element is changing *because the current in that same element is changing*:

$$v = -\frac{d\phi}{di}\frac{di}{dt} = -L\frac{di}{dt}$$

In circuit theory, L is called the *self-inductance* of the element and v is called the *voltage of self-inductance* or the back-voltage *in the inductor*.

12.4   Internal Inductance

Magnetic flux occurs within a conductor cross section as well as external to the conductor. This internal flux gives rise to an *internal inductance*, which is often small compared to the external inductance and frequently ignored. In Fig. 12-8(*a*) a conductor of circular cross section is shown, with a current I assumed to be uniformly distributed over the area. (This assumption is valid only at low frequencies, since *skin effect* at higher frequencies forces the current to be concentrated at the outer surface.) Within the conductor of radius a, Ampère's law gives

$$\mathbf{H} = \frac{Ir}{2\pi a^2}\,\mathbf{a}_\phi \quad \text{and} \quad \mathbf{B} = \frac{\mu_0 Ir}{2\pi a^2}\,\mathbf{a}_\phi$$

(a)   (b)

Fig. 12-8

The straight piece of conductor shown in Fig. 12-8(*a*) must be imagined as a short section of an infinite torus, as suggested in Fig. 12-8(*b*). The current filaments become circles of infinite radius. The lines of flux $d\Phi$ through the strip $\ell\,dr$ encircle only those filaments whose distance from the conductor axis is smaller than r. Thus, an open surface bounded by one of those filaments is cut once (or an odd number of times) by the lines of $d\Phi$; whereas, for a filament such as *1* or *2*, the surface is cut zero times (or an even number of times). It follows that $d\Phi$ links only with the fraction $\pi r^2/\pi a^2$ of the total current, so that the total flux linkage is given by the weighted "sum"

$$\lambda = \int \left(\frac{\pi r^2}{\pi a^2}\right) d\Phi = \int_0^a \left(\frac{\pi r^2}{\pi a^2}\right) \frac{\mu_0 I r}{2\pi a^2} \ell \, dr = \frac{\mu_0 I \ell}{8\pi}$$

and

$$\frac{L}{\ell} = \frac{\lambda/I}{\ell} = \frac{\mu_0}{8\pi} = \frac{1}{2} \times 10^{-7} \text{ H/m}$$

This result is independent of the conductor radius. The total inductance is the sum of the external and internal inductances. If the external inductance is of the order of $\frac{1}{2} \times 10^{-7}$ H/m, the internal inductance should not be ignored.

12.5 Mutual Inductance

In Fig. 12-9 a part ϕ_{12} of the magnetic flux produced by the current i_1 through coil 1 links the N_2 turns of coil 2. The voltage of *mutual induction* in coil 2 is given by

$$v_2 = N_2 \frac{d\phi_{12}}{dt} \quad \text{(negative sign omitted)}$$

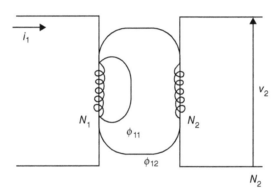

Fig. 12-9

In terms of the *mutual inductance* $M_{12} \equiv N_2 \phi_{12}/I_1$,

$$v_2 = N_2 \frac{d\phi_{12}}{di_1} \frac{di_1}{dt} = M_{12} \frac{di_1}{dt}$$

This mutual inductance will be a product of the permeability μ of the region between the coils and a geometrical length, just like inductance L. If the roles of coils 1 and 2 are reversed,

$$v_1 = M_{21} \frac{di_2}{dt}$$

The following reciprocity relation can be established: $M_{12} = M_{21}$.

EXAMPLE 4. A solenoid with $N_1 = 1000$, $r_1 = 1.0$ cm, and $\ell_1 = 50$ cm is concentric within a second coil of $N_2 = 2000$, $r_2 = 2.0$ cm, and $\ell_2 = 50$ cm. Find the mutual inductance assuming free-space conditions.

For long coils of small cross sections, H may be assumed constant inside the coil and zero for points just outside the coil. With the first coil carrying a current I_1,

$$H = \left(\frac{1000}{0.50}\right) I_1 \quad \text{(A/m)} \qquad \text{(in the axial direction)}$$

$$B = \mu_0 2000 I_1 \quad \text{(Wb/m}^2)$$

$$\Phi = BA = (\mu_0 2000 I_1)(\pi \times 10^{-4}) \quad \text{(Wb)}$$

Since H and B are zero outside the coils, this is the only flux linking the second coil.

$$M_{12} = N_2 \left(\frac{\Phi}{I_1} \right) = (2000)(4\pi \times 10^{-7})(2000)(\pi \times 10^{-4}) = 1.58 \, \text{mH}$$

12.6   Magnetic Circuits

In Chapter 10, magnetic field intensity $\mathbf{H}$, flux Φ, and magnetic flux density $\mathbf{B}$ were examined and various problems were solved where the medium was free space. For example, when Ampère's law is applied to the closed path C through the long, air-core coil shown in Fig. 12-10, the result is

$$\oint \mathbf{H} \cdot d\mathbf{I} = NI$$

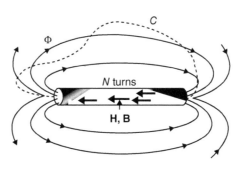

Fig. 12-10

But since the flux lines are widely spread outside of the coil, B is small there. The flux is effectively restricted to the inside of the coil, where

$$H \approx \frac{NI}{\ell}$$

Ferromagnetic materials have relative permeabilities μ_r in the order of thousands. Consequently, the flux density $B = \mu_0 \mu_r H$ is, for a given H, much greater than would result in free space. In Fig. 12-11, the coil is not distributed over the iron core. Even so, the NI of the coil causes a flux Φ which follows the core. It might be said that the flux prefers the core to the surrounding space by a ratio of several thousand to one. This is so different from the free-space magnetics of Chapter 10 that an entire subject area, known as *iron-core magnetics* or *magnetic circuits*, has developed. This brief introduction to the subject assumes that *all* of the flux is within the core. It is further assumed that the flux is uniformly distributed over the cross section of the core. Core lengths required for calculation of NI drops are mean lengths.

Fig. 12-11

12.7 The *B-H* Curve

A sample of ferromagnetic material could be tested by applying increasing values of H and measuring the corresponding values of flux density B. *Magnetization curves*, or simply *B-H curves*, for some common ferromagnetic materials are given in Figs. 12-12 and 12-13. The relative permeability can be computed from the *B-H* curve by use of $\mu_r = B/\mu_0 H$. Fig. 12-14 shows the extreme nonlinearity of μ_r versus H for silicon steel. This nonlinearity requires that problems be solved graphically.

Fig. 12-12 *B-H* curves, $H < 400$ A/m.

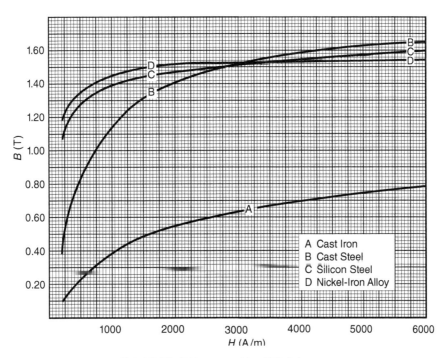

Fig. 12-13 *B-H* curves, $H > 400$ A/m.

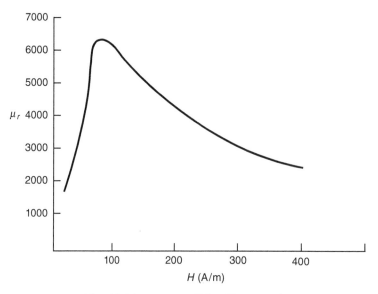

Fig. 12-14 μ_r versus H for silicon steel.

12.8 Ampère's Law for Magnetic Circuits

A coil of N turns and current I around a ferromagnetic core produces a *magnetomotive force* (mmf) given by NI. The symbol F is sometimes used for this mmf; the units are amperes or *ampere turns*. Ampère's law, applied around the path in the center of the core shown in Fig. 12-15(a), gives

$$F = NI = \oint \mathbf{H} \cdot d\mathbf{l}$$

$$= \int_1 \mathbf{H} \cdot d\mathbf{l} + \int_2 \mathbf{H} \cdot d\mathbf{l} + \int_3 \mathbf{H} \cdot d\mathbf{l}$$

$$= H_1 \ell_1 + H_2 \ell_2 + H_3 \ell_3$$

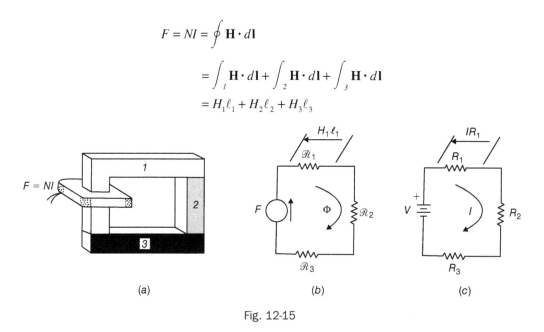

(a)   (b)   (c)

Fig. 12-15

Comparison with Kirchhoff's law around a single closed loop with three resistors and an emf V,

$$V = V_1 + V_2 + V_3$$

suggests that F can be viewed as an *NI rise* and the $H\ell$ terms considered *NI drops*, in analogy to the voltage rise V and voltage drops V_1, V_2 and V_3. The analogy is developed in Fig. 12-15(b) and (c). Flux Φ in Fig. 12-15(b) is analogous to current I, and *reluctance* $\mathcal{R}$ is analogous to resistance R. An expression for reluctance can be developed as follows.

$$NI \text{ drop} = H\ell = BA\left(\frac{\ell}{\mu A}\right) = \Phi \mathcal{R}$$

Hence,
$$\mathcal{R} = \frac{\ell}{\mu A} \ \ (\text{H}^{-1})$$

If the reluctances are known, then the equation

$$F = NI = \Phi(\mathcal{R}_1 + \mathcal{R}_2 + \mathcal{R}_3)$$

can be written for the magnetic circuit of Fig. 12-15(*b*). However, μ_r must be known for each material before its reluctance can be calculated. And only after B or H is known will the value of μ_r be known. This is in contrast to the relation

$$R = \frac{\ell}{\sigma A}$$

(Section 7.7), in which the conductivity σ is independent of the current.

12.9   Cores with Air Gaps

Magnetic circuits with small air gaps are very common. The gaps are generally kept as small as possible, since the *NI* drop of the air gap is often much greater than the drop in the core. The flux fringes outward at the gap, so that the area at the gap exceeds the area of the adjacent core. Provided that the gap length ℓ_a is less than $\frac{1}{10}$ the smaller dimension of the core, an *apparent area*, S_a, of the air gap can be calculated. For a rectangular core of dimensions a and b,

$$S_a = (a + \ell_a)(b + \ell_a)$$

If the total flux in the air gap is known, H_a and $H_a\ell_a$ can be computed directly.

$$H_a = \frac{1}{\mu_0}\left(\frac{\Phi}{S_a}\right) \qquad H_a\ell_a = \frac{\ell_a \Phi}{\mu_0 S_a}$$

For a uniform iron core of length ℓ_i with a single air gap, Ampère's law reads

$$NI = H_i\ell_i + H_a\ell_a = H_i\ell_i + \frac{\ell_a \Phi}{\mu_0 S_a}$$

If the flux Φ is known, it is not difficult to compute the *NI* drop across the air gap, obtain B_i, take H_i from the appropriate *B-H* curve and compute the *NI* drop in the core, $H_i\ell_i$. The sum is the *NI* required to establish the flux Φ. However, with *NI* given, it is a matter of trial and error to obtain B_i and Φ, as will be seen in the problems. Graphical methods of solution are also available.

12.10   Multiple Coils

Two or more coils on a core could be wound such that their mmfs either aid or oppose one another. Consequently, a method of indicating polarity is given in Fig. 12-16. An assumed direction for the resulting flux Φ could be incorrect, just as an assumed current in a dc circuit with two or more voltage sources may be incorrect. A negative result simply means that the flux is in the opposite direction.

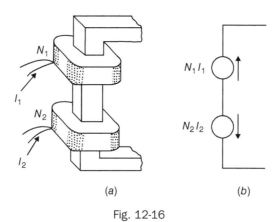

(a)   (b)

Fig. 12-16

12.11 Parallel Magnetic Circuits

The method of solving a parallel magnetic circuit is suggested by the two-loop equivalent circuit shown in Fig. 12-17(b). The leg on the left contains an *NI* rise and an *NI* drop. The *NI* drop between the junctions *a* and *b* can be written for each leg as follows:

$$F - H_1\ell_1 = H_2\ell_2 = H_3\ell_3$$

and the fluxes satisfy

$$\Phi_1 = \Phi_2 + \Phi_3$$

Different materials for the core parts will necessitate working with several *B-H* curves. An air gap in one of the legs would lead to $H_i\ell_i + H_a\ell_a$ for the mmf between the junctions for that leg.

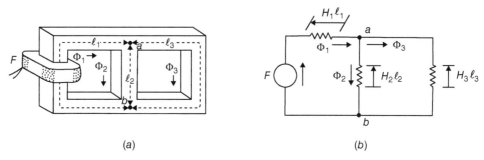

(a)   (b)

Fig. 12-17

The equivalent magnetic circuit should be drawn for parallel magnetic circuit problems. It is good practice to mark the material types, cross-sectional areas, and mean lengths directly on the diagram. In more complex problems a scheme like Table 12-1 can be helpful. The data are inserted directly into the table, and the remaining quantities are then calculated or taken from the appropriate *B-H* curve.

TABLE 12-1

PART	MATERIAL	AREA	ℓ	Φ	B	H	$H\ell$
1							
2							
3							

SOLVED PROBLEMS

12.1. Find the inductance per unit length of the coaxial cable in Fig. 12-2 if $a = 1$ mm and $b = 3$ mm. Assume $\mu_r = 1$ and omit internal inductance.

$$\frac{L}{\ell} = \frac{\mu}{2\pi} \ln \frac{b}{a} = \frac{4\pi \times 10^{-7}}{2\pi} \ln 3 = 0.22 \; \mu\text{H}/\text{m}$$

12.2. Find the inductance per unit length of the parallel cylindrical conductors shown in Fig. 12-5, where $d = 25$ ft, $a = 0.803$ in.

$$\frac{L}{\ell} = \frac{\mu_0}{\pi} \cosh^{-1} \frac{d}{2a} = (4 \times 10^{-7}) \cosh^{-1} \frac{25(12)}{2(0.803)} = 2.37 \mu\text{H}/\text{m}$$

The approximate formula gives

$$\frac{L}{\ell} = \frac{\mu_0}{\pi} \ln \frac{d}{a} = 2.37 \; \mu\text{H}/\text{m}$$

When $d/a \geq 10$, the approximate formula may be used with an error of less than 0.5%.

12.3. A circular conductor with the same radius as in Problem 12.2 is 12.5 ft from an infinite conducting plane. Find the inductance.

$$\frac{L}{\ell} = \frac{\mu_0}{2\pi} \ln \frac{d}{a} = (2 \times 10^{-7}) \ln \frac{25(12)}{0.803} = 1.18 \; \mu\text{H}/\text{m}$$

This result is $\frac{1}{2}$ that of Problem 12.2. A conducting plane may be inserted midway between the two conductors of Fig. 12-5. The inductance between each conductor and the plane is 1.18 μH/m. Since they are in series, the total inductance is the sum, 2.37 μH/m.

12.4. Assume that the air-core toroid shown in Fig. 12-4 has a circular cross section of radius 4 mm. Find the inductance if there are 2500 turns and the mean radius is $r = 20$ mm.

$$L = \frac{\mu N^2 S}{2\pi r} = \frac{(4\pi \times 10^{-7})(2500)^2 \pi (0.004)^2}{2\pi(0.020)} = 3.14 \; \text{mH}$$

12.5. Assume that the air-core toroid in Fig. 12-3 has 700 turns, an inner radius of 1 cm, an outer radius of 2 cm, and height $a = 1.5$ cm. Find L using (a) the formula for square cross-section toroids; (b) the approximate formula for a general toroid, which assumes a uniform H at a mean radius.

(a)
$$L = \frac{\mu_0 N^2 a}{2\pi} \ln \frac{r_2}{r_1} = \frac{(4\pi \times 10^{-7})(700)^2(0.015)}{2\pi} \ln 2 = 1.02 \; \text{mH}$$

(b)
$$L = \frac{\mu_0 N^2 S}{2\pi r} = \frac{(4\pi \times 10^{-7})(700)^2(0.01)(0.015)}{2\pi(0.015)} = 0.98 \; \text{mH}$$

With a radius that is larger compared to the cross section, the two formulas yield the same result. See Problem 12.26.

12.6 Use the energy integral to find the internal inductance per unit length of a cylindrical conductor of radius a.

At a distance $r \leq a$ from the conductor axis,

$$\mathbf{H} = \frac{Ir}{2\pi a^2} \mathbf{a}_\phi \qquad \mathbf{B} = \frac{\mu_0 Ir}{2\pi a^2} \mathbf{a}_\phi$$

whence
$$\mathbf{B} \cdot \mathbf{H} = \frac{\mu_0 I^2}{4\pi^2 a^4} r^2$$

The inductance corresponding to energy storage within a length ℓ of the conductor is then

$$L = \int \frac{(\mathbf{B} \cdot \mathbf{H}) \, dv}{I^2} = \frac{\mu_0}{4\pi^2 a^4} \int_0^a r^2 2\pi r \ell \, dr = \frac{\mu_0 \ell}{8\pi}$$

or $L/\ell = \mu_0/8\pi$. This agrees with the result of Section 12.4.

12.7. The cast-iron core shown in Fig. 12-18 has an inner radius of 7 cm and an outer radius of 9 cm. Find the flux Φ if the coil mmf is 500 A.

$$\ell = 2\pi(0.08) = 0.503 \text{ m}$$

$$H = \frac{F}{\ell} = \frac{500}{0.503} = 995 \text{ A/m}$$

From the *B-H* curve for cast iron in Fig. 12-13, $B = 0.40$ T.

$$\Phi = BS = (0.40)(0.02)^2 = 0.16 \text{ m Wb}$$

Fig. 12-18

12.8. The magnetic circuit shown in Fig. 12-19 has a C-shaped cast-steel part, *1*, and a cast-iron part, *2*. Find the current required in the 150-turn coil if the flux density in the cast iron is $B_2 = 0.45$ T.

Fig. 12-19

The calculated areas are $S_1 = 4 \times 10^{-4}$ m^2 and $S_2 = 3.6 \times 10^{-4}$ m^2. The mean lengths are

$$\ell_1 = 0.11 + 0.11 + 0.12 = 0.34 \text{ m}$$
$$\ell_2 = 0.12 + 0.009 + 0.009 = 0.138 \text{ m}$$

From the *B-H* curve for cast iron in Fig. 12-13, $H_2 = 1270$ A/m.

$$\Phi = B_2 S_2 = (0.45)(3.6 \times 10^{-4}) = 1.62 \times 10^{-4} \text{ Wb}$$

$$B_1 = \frac{\Phi}{S_1} = 0.41 \text{ T}$$

Then, from the cast-steel curve in Fig. 12-12, $H_1 = 233$ A/m.

The equivalent circuit, Fig. 12-20, suggests the equation

$$F = NI = H_1\ell_1 + H_2\ell_2$$
$$150I = 233(0.34) + 1270(0.138)$$
$$I = 1.70 \text{ A}$$

Fig. 12-20

12.9. The magnetic circuit shown in Fig. 12-21 is cast-iron with a mean length $\ell_1 = 0.44$ m and square cross section 0.02×0.02 m. The air-gap length is $\ell_a = 2$ mm and the coil contains 400 turns. Find the current I required to establish an air-gap flux of 0.141 mWb.

Fig. 12-21

The flux Φ in the air gap is also the flux in the core.

$$B_i = \frac{\Phi}{S_i} = \frac{0.141 \times 10^{-3}}{4 \times 10^{-4}} = 0.35 \text{ T}$$

From Fig. 12-13, $H_i = 850$ A/m. Then

$$H_i\ell_i = 850(0.44) = 374 \text{ A}$$

For the air gap, $S_a = (0.02 + 0.002)^2 = 4.84 \times 10^{-4}$ m², and so

$$H_a\ell_a = \frac{\Phi}{\mu_0 S_a}\ell_a = \frac{0.141 \times 10^{-3}}{(4\pi \times 10^{-7})(4.84 \times 10^{-4})}(2 \times 10^{-3}) = 464 \text{ A}$$

Therefore, $F = H_i\ell_i + H_a\ell_a = 838$ A and

$$I = \frac{F}{N} = \frac{838}{400} = 2.09 \text{ A}$$

12.10. Determine the reluctance of an air gap in a dc machine where the apparent area is $S_a = 4.26 \times 10^{-2}$ m² and the gap length $\ell_a = 5.6$ mm.

$$\mathcal{R} = \frac{\ell_a}{\mu_0 S_a} = \frac{5.6 \times 10^{-3}}{(4\pi \times 10^{-7})(4.26 \times 10^{-2})} = 1.05 \times 10^5 \text{ H}^{-1}$$

12.11. The cast-iron magnetic core shown in Fig. 12-22 has an area $S_i = 4$ cm^2 and a mean length 0.438 m. The 2-mm air gap has an apparent area $S_a = 4.84$ cm^2. Determine the air-gap flux Φ.

Fig. 12-22

The core is quite long compared to the length of the air gap, and cast iron is not a particularly good magnetic material. As a first estimate, therefore, assume that 600 of the total ampere turns are dropped at the air gap, i.e., $H_a \ell_a = 600$ A.

$$H_a \ell_a = \frac{\Phi}{\mu_0 S_a} \ell_a$$

$$\Phi = \frac{600(4\pi \times 10^{-7})(4.84 \times 10^{-4})}{2 \times 10^{-3}} = 1.82 \times 10^{-4} \text{ Wb}$$

Then $B_i = \Phi/S_i = 0.46$ T, and from Fig. 12-13, $H_i = 1340$ A/m. The core drop is then

$$H_i \ell_i = 1340(0.438) = 587 \text{ A}$$

so that

$$H_i \ell_i + H_a \ell_a = 1187 \text{ A}$$

This sum exceeds the 1000 A mmf of the coil. Consequently, values of B_i lower than 0.46 T should be tried until the sum of $H_i \ell_i$ and $H_a \ell_a$ is 1000 A. The values $B_i = 0.41$ T and $\Phi = 1.64 \times 10^{-4}$ Wb will result in a sum very close to 1000 A.

12.12. Solve Problem 12.11 using reluctances and the equivalent magnetic circuit, Fig. 12-23.

Fig. 12-23

From the values of B_i and H_i obtained in Problem 12.11,

$$\mu_0 \mu_r = \frac{B_i}{H_i} = 3.83 \times 10^{-4} \text{ H/m}$$

Then, for the core,

$$\mathcal{R}_i = \frac{\ell_i}{\mu_0 \mu_r S_i} = \frac{0.438}{(3.83 \times 10^{-4})(4 \times 10^{-4})} = 2.86 \times 10^6 \text{ H}^{-1}$$

and for the air gap,

$$\mathcal{R}_a = \frac{\ell_a}{\mu_0 S_a} = \frac{2 \times 10^{-3}}{(4\pi \times 10^{-7})(4.84 \times 10^{-4})} = 3.29 \times 10^6 \, \text{H}^{-1}$$

The circuit equation,

$$F = \Phi(\mathcal{R}_i + \mathcal{R}_a)$$

gives

$$\Phi = \frac{1000}{2.86 \times 10^6 + 3.29 \times 10^6} = 1.63 \times 10^{-4} \, \text{Wb}$$

The corresponding flux density in the iron is 0.41 T, in agreement with the results of Problem 12.11. While the air-gap reluctance can be calculated from the dimensions and μ_0, the same is not true for the reluctance of the iron. The reason is that μ_r for the iron depends on the values of B_i and H_i.

12.13. Solve Problem 12.11 graphically with a plot of Φ versus F.

Values of H_i from 700 through 1100 A/m are listed in the first column of Table 12-2; the corresponding values of B_i are found from the cast-iron curve, Fig. 12-13. The values of Φ and $H_i \ell_i$ are computed, and $H_a \ell_a$ is obtained from $\Phi \ell_a / \mu_0 S_a$. Then F is given as the sum of $H_i \ell_i$ and $H_a \ell_a$. Since the air gap is linear, only two points are required. The flux Φ for $F = 1000$ A is seen from Fig. 12-24 to be approximately 1.65×10^{-4} Wb.

This method is simply a plot of the trial and error data used in Problem 12.11. However, it is helpful if several different coils or coil currents are to be examined.

TABLE 12-2

H_i (A/m)	B_i (T)	Φ (Wb)	$H_i \ell_i$ (A)	$H_a \ell_a$ (A)	F (A)
700	0.295	1.18×10^{-4}	307	388	695
800	0.335	1.34×10^{-4}	350	441	791
900	0.365	1.46×10^{-4}	395	480	874
1000	0.400	1.60×10^{-4}	438	526	964
1100	0.420	1.68×10^{-4}	482	552	1034

Fig. 12-24

12.14. Determine the fluxes Φ in the core of Problem 12.11 for coil mmfs of 800 and 1200 A. Use a graphical approach and the *negative air-gap line*.

The Φ versus $H_i\ell_i$ data for the cast-iron core, developed in Problem 12.13, are plotted in Fig. 12-25. The air-gap Φ versus F is linear. One end of the negative air-gap line for the coil mmf of 800 A is at $\Phi = 0$, $F = 800$ A. The other end assumes $H_a\ell_a = 800$ A, from which

$$\Phi = \frac{\mu_0 S_a (H_a \ell_a)}{\ell_a} = 2.43 \times 10^{-4}\,\text{Wb}$$

which locates this end at $\Phi = 2.43 \times 10^{-4}$ Wb, $F = 0$.

The intersection of the $F = 800$ A negative air-gap line with the nonlinear Φ versus F curve for the cast-iron core gives $\Phi = 1.34 \times 10^{-4}$ Wb. Other negative air-gap lines have the same negative slope. For a coil mmf of 1000 A, $\Phi = 1.63 \times 10^{-4}$ Wb and for 1200 A, $\Phi = 1.85 \times 10^{-4}$ Wb.

Fig. 12-25

12.15. Solve Problem 12.11 for a coil mmf of 1000 A using the *B-H* curve for cast iron.

This method avoids the construction of an additional curve such as the Φ versus F curves of Problems 12.13 and 12.14. Now, in order to plot the air-gap line on the *B-H* curve of iron, adjustments must be made for the different areas and the different lengths. Table 12-3 suggests the necessary calculations.

$$\frac{F}{\ell_i} = \frac{1000}{0.438} = 2283 \text{ A/m}$$

TABLE 12-3

B_a (T)	H_a (A/m)	$B_a\left(\dfrac{S_a}{S_i}\right)$ (T)	$H_a\left(\dfrac{\ell_a}{\ell_i}\right)$ (A/m)	$\dfrac{F}{\ell_i} - H_a\left(\dfrac{\ell_a}{\ell_i}\right)$ (A/m)
0.10	0.80×10^5	0.12	363	1920
0.30	2.39×10^5	0.36	1091	1192
0.50	3.98×10^5	0.61	1817	466

The data from the third and fifth columns may be plotted directly on the cast-iron *B-H* curve, as shown in Fig. 12-26. The air gap is linear and only two points are needed. The answer is seen to be $B_i = 0.41$ T. The method can be used with two nonlinear core parts as well (see Problem 12.16).

Fig. 12-26

12.16. The magnetic circuit shown in Fig. 12-27 consists of nickel-iron alloy in part *1*, where $\ell_1 = 10$ cm and $S_1 = 2.25$ cm^2, and cast-steel for part *2*, where $\ell_2 = 8$ cm and $S_2 = 3$ cm^2. Find the flux densities B_1 and B_2.

Fig. 12-27

The data for part *2* of cast-steel will be converted and plotted on the *B-H* curve for part *1* of nickel-iron alloy ($F/\ell_1 = 400$ A/m). Table 12-4 suggests the necessary calculations.

TABLE 12-4

B_2 (T)	H_2 (A/m)	$B_2\left(\dfrac{S_2}{S_1}\right)$ (T)	$H_2\left(\dfrac{\ell_2}{\ell_1}\right)$ (A/m)	$\dfrac{F}{\ell_1} - H_2\left(\dfrac{\ell_2}{\ell_1}\right)$ (A/m)
0.33	200	0.44	160	240
0.44	250	0.59	200	200
0.55	300	0.73	240	160
0.65	350	0.87	280	120
0.73	400	0.97	320	80
0.78	450	1.04	360	40
0.83	500	1.11	400	0

From the graph, Fig. 12-28, $B_1 = 1.01$ T. Then, since $B_1 S_1 = B_2 S_2$,

$$B_2 = 1.01 \left(\frac{2.25 \times 10^{-4}}{3 \times 10^{-4}} \right) = 0.76 \text{ T}$$

These values can be checked by obtaining the corresponding H_1 and H_2 from the appropriate *B-H* curves and substituting in

$$F = H_1 \ell_1 + H_2 \ell_2$$

Fig. 12-28

12.17. The cast-steel parallel magnetic circuit in Fig. 12-29(*a*) has a coil with 500 turns. The mean lengths are $\ell_2 = \ell_3 = 10$ cm, $\ell_1 = 4$ cm. Find the coil current if $\Phi_3 = 0.173$ mWb.

$$\Phi_1 = \Phi_2 + \Phi_3$$

Since the cross-sectional area of the center leg is twice that of the two side legs, the flux density is the same throughout the core, i.e.,

$$B_1 = B_2 = B_3 = \frac{0.173 \times 10^{-3}}{1.5 \times 10^{-4}} = 1.15 \text{ T}$$

Corresponding to $B = 1.15$ T, Fig. 12-13 gives $H = 1030$ A/m. The *NI* drop between points *a* and *b* is now used to write the following equation [see Fig. 12-29(*b*)]:

$$F - H\ell_1 = H\ell_2 = H\ell_3 \qquad \text{or} \qquad F = H(\ell_1 + \ell_2) = 1030(0.14) = 144.2 \text{ A}$$

Then
$$I = \frac{F}{N} = \frac{144.2}{500} = 0.29 \text{ A}$$

Fig. 12-29

12.18. The same cast-steel core as in Problem 12.17 has identical 500-turn coils on the outer legs, with the winding sense as shown in Fig. 12-30(a). If again $\Phi_3 = 0.173$ m Wb, find the coil currents.

The flux densities are the same throughout the core and consequently H is the same. The equivalent circuit in Fig. 12-30(b) suggests that the problem can be solved on a *per pole* basis.

$$B = \frac{\Phi_3}{S_3} = 1.15\,\text{T} \quad \text{and} \quad H = 1030\,\text{A/m} \quad (\text{from Fig. 12-13})$$

$$F_3 = H(\ell_1 + \ell_3) = 1030(0.14) = 144.2\,\text{A} \qquad I = 0.29\,\text{A}$$

Each coil must have a current of 0.29 A.

Fig. 12-30

12.19. The parallel magnetic circuit shown in Fig. 12-31(a) is silicon steel with the same cross-sectional area throughout, $S = 1.30$ cm². The mean lengths are $\ell_1 = \ell_3 = 25$ cm, $\ell_2 = 5$ cm. The coils have 50 turns each. Given that $\Phi_1 = 90\ \mu$ Wb and $\Phi_3 = 120\ \mu$ Wb, find the coil currents.

$$\Phi_2 = \Phi_3 - \Phi_1 = 0.30 \times 10^{-4}\ \text{Wb}$$

$$B_1 = \frac{90 \times 10^{-6}}{1.30 \times 10^{-4}} = 0.69\ \text{T}$$

From Fig. 12-12, $H_1 = 87$ A/m. Then, $H_1\ell_1 = 21.8$ A. Similarly, $B_2 = 0.23$ T, $H_2 = 49$ A/m, $H_2\ell_2 = 2.5$ A and $B_3 = 0.92$ T, $H_3 = 140$ A/m, $H_3\ell_3 = 35.0$ A. The equivalent circuit in Fig. 12-31(b) suggests the following equations for the NI drop between points a and b:

$$H_1\ell_1 - F_1 = H_2\ell_2 = F_3 - H_3\ell_3$$
$$21.8 - F_1 = 2.5 = F_3 - 35.0$$

from which $F_1 = 19.3$ A and $F_3 = 37.5$ A. The currents are $I_1 = 0.39$ A and $I_3 = 0.75$ A.

(a)   (b)

Fig. 12-31

12.20. Obtain the equivalent magnetic circuit for Problem 12.19 using reluctances for three legs, and calculate the flux in the core using $F_1 = 19.3$ A and $F_3 = 37.5$ A.

$$\mathcal{R} = \frac{\ell}{\mu_0 \mu_r S}$$

From the values of B and H found in Problem 12.19,

$$\mu_0 \mu_{r1} = 7.93 \times 10^{-3} \text{ H/m} \qquad \mu_0 \mu_{r2} = 4.69 \times 10^{-3} \text{ H/m} \qquad \mu_0 \mu_{r3} = 6.57 \times 10^{-3} \text{ H/m}$$

Now the reluctances are calculated:

$$\mathcal{R}_1 = \frac{\ell_1}{\mu_0 \mu_{r1} S_1} = 2.43 \times 10^5 \text{ H}^{-1}$$

$\mathcal{R}_2 = 8.20 \times 10^4 \text{ H}^{-1}$, $\mathcal{R}_3 = 2.93 \times 10^5 \text{ H}^{-1}$. From Fig. 12-32,

$$F_3 = \Phi_3 \mathcal{R}_3 + \Phi_2 \mathcal{R}_2 \tag{1}$$
$$F_1 = \Phi_1 \mathcal{R}_1 - \Phi_2 \mathcal{R}_2 \tag{2}$$
$$\Phi_1 + \Phi_2 = \Phi_3 \tag{3}$$

Fig. 12-32

Substituting Φ_2 from (3) into (1) and (2) results in the following set of simultaneous equations in Φ_1 and Φ_3:

$$F_1 = \Phi_1(\mathcal{R}_1 + \mathcal{R}_2) - \Phi_3 \mathcal{R}_2$$
$$F_3 = -\Phi_1 \mathcal{R}_2 \quad\quad + \Phi_3(\mathcal{R}_2 + \mathcal{R}_3)$$

or

$$19.3 = \Phi_1(3.25 \times 10^5) - \Phi_3(0.82 \times 10^5)$$
$$37.5 = -\Phi_1(0.82 \times 10^5) + \Phi_3(3.75 \times 10^5)$$

Solving, $\Phi_1 = 89.7 \ \mu$Wb, $\Phi_2 = 30.3 \ \mu$Wb, $\Phi_3 = 120 \ \mu$Wb.

Although the simultaneous equations above and the similarity to a two-mesh circuit problem may be interesting, it should be noted that the flux densities B_1, B_2, and B_3 had to be known before the relative permeabilities and reluctances could be computed. But if B is known, why not find the flux directly from $\Phi = BS$? Reluctance is simply not of much help in solving problems of this type.

SUPPLEMENTARY PROBLEMS

12.21. Find the inductance per unit length of a coaxial conductor with an inner radius $a = 2$ mm and an outer conductor at $b = 9$ mm. Assume $\mu_r = 1$.

12.22. Find the inductance per unit length of two parallel cylindrical conductors, where the conductor radius is 1 mm and the center-to-center separation is 12 mm.

12.23. Two parallel cylindrical conductors separated by 1 m have an inductance per unit length of 2.12 μH/m. What is the conductor radius?

12.24. An air-core solenoid with 2500 evenly spaced turns has a length of 1.5 m and a radius of 2×10^{-2} m. Find the inductance L.

12.25. A square-cross-section, air-core toroid such as that in Fig. 12-3 has inner radius 5 cm, outer radius 7 cm, and height 1.5 cm. If the inductance is 495 μH, how many turns are there in the toroid? Examine the approximate formula and compare the result.

12.26. A square-cross-section toroid such as that in Fig. 12-3 has $r_1 = 80$ cm, $r_2 = 82$ cm, $a = 1.5$ cm, and 700 turns. Find L using both formulas and compare the results. (See Problem 12.5.)

12.27. A coil with 5000 turns, $r_1 = 1.25$ cm, and $\ell_1 = 1.0$ m has a core with $\mu_r = 50$. A second coil of 500 turns, $r_2 = 2.0$ cm, and $\ell_2 = 10.0$ cm is concentric with the first coil, and in the space between the coils $\mu \approx \mu_0$. Find the mutual inductance.

12.28. Determine the relative permeabilities of cast-iron, cast-steel, silicon steel, and nickel-iron alloy at a flux density of 0.4 T. Use Figs. 12-12 and 12-13.

12.29. An air gap of length $\ell_a = 2$ mm has a flux density of 0.4 T. Determine the length of a magnetic core with the same NI drop if the core is of (*a*) cast-iron, (*b*) cast-steel, (*c*) silicon steel.

12.30. A magnetic circuit consists of two parts of the same ferromagnetic material ($\mu_r = 4000$). Part *1* has $\ell_1 = 50$ mm, $S_1 = 104$ mm^2; part 2 has $\ell_2 = 30$ mm, $S_2 = 120$ mm^2. The material is at a part of the curve where the relative permeability is proportional to the flux density. Find the flux Φ if the mmf is 4.0 A.

12.31. A toroid with a circular cross section of radius 20 mm has a mean length 280 mm and a flux $\Phi = 1.50$ mWb. Find the required mmf if the core is silicon steel.

12.32. Both parts of the magnetic circuit in Fig. 12-33 are cast-steel. Part *1* has $\ell_1 = 34$ cm and $S_1 = 6$ cm^2; part 2 has $\ell_2 = 16$ cm and $S_2 = 4$ cm^2. Determine the coil current I_1, if $I_2 = 0.5$ A, $N_1 = 200$ turns, $N_2 = 100$ turns, and $\Phi = 120$ μWb.

Fig. 12-33

12.33. The silicon steel core shown in Fig. 12-34 has a rectangular cross section 10 mm by 8 mm and a mean length 150 mm. The air-gap length is 0.8 mm and the air-gap flux is 80 μWb. Find the mmf.

Fig. 12-34

12.34. Solve Problem 12.33 in reverse: the coil mmf is known to be 561.2 A and the air-gap flux is to be determined. Use the trial and error method, starting with the assumption that 90% of the *NI* drop is across the air gap.

12.35. The silicon steel magnetic circuit of Problem 12.33 has an mmf of 600 A. Determine the air-gap flux.

12.36. For the silicon steel magnetic circuit of Problem 12.33, calculate the reluctance of the iron, $\mathcal{R}_i$, and the reluctance of the air gap, $\mathcal{R}_a$. Assume the flux is $\Phi = 80\ \mu\text{Wb}$ and solve for *F*. See Fig. 12-35.

Fig. 12-35

12.37. A silicon steel core such as shown in Fig. 12-34 has a rectangular cross section of area $S_i = 80\ \text{mm}^2$ and an air gap of length $\ell_a = 0.8\ \text{mm}$ with area $S_a = 95\ \text{mm}^2$. The mean length of the core is 150 mm and the mmf is 600 A. Solve graphically for the flux by plotting Φ versus *F* in the manner of Problem 12.13.

12.38. Solve Problem 12.37 graphically using the negative air-gap line for an mmf of 600 A.

12.39. Solve Problem 12.37 graphically in the manner of Problem 12.15, obtaining the flux density in the core.

12.40. A rectangular ferromagnetic core 40×60 mm has a flux $\Phi = 1.44$ mWb. An air gap in the core is of length $\ell_a = 2.5$ mm. Find the *NI* drop across the air gap.

12.41. A toroid with cross section of radius 2 cm has a silicon steel core of mean length 28 cm and an air gap of length 1 mm. Assume the air-gap area, S_a, is 10% greater than the adjacent core and find the mmf required to establish an air-gap flux of 1.5 mWb.

12.42. The magnetic circuit shown in Fig. 12-36 has an mmf of 500 A. Part *1* is cast-steel with $\ell_1 = 340$ mm and $S_1 = 400\ \text{mm}^2$; part *2* is cast-iron with $\ell_2 = 138$ mm and $S_2 = 360\ \text{mm}^2$. Determine the flux Φ.

Fig. 12-36

12.43. Solve Problem 12.42 graphically in the manner of Problem 12.16.

12.44. A toroid of square cross section, with $r_1 = 2$ cm, $r_2 = 3$ cm, and height $a = 1$ cm, has a two-part core. Part *1* is silicon steel of mean length 7.9 cm; part *2* is nickel-iron alloy of mean length 7.9 cm. Find the flux that results from an mmf of 17.38 A.

12.45. Solve Problem 12.44 by the graphical method of Problem 12.15. Why is it that the plotting of the second reverse *B-H* curve on the first is not as difficult as might be expected?

12.46. The cast-steel parallel magnetic circuit in Fig. 12-37 has a 500-turn coil in the center leg, where the cross-sectional area is twice that of the remainder of the core. The dimensions are $\ell_a = 1$ mm, $S_2 = S_3 = 150$ mm^2, $S_1 = 300$ mm^2, $\ell_1 = 40$ mm, $\ell_2 = 110$ mm, and $\ell_3 = 109$ mm. Find the coil current required to produce an air-gap flux of 125 μWb. Assume that S_a exceeds S_3 by 17%.

Fig. 12-37

12.47. The cast-iron parallel circuit core in Fig. 12-38 has a 500-turn coil and a uniform cross section of 1.5 cm^2 throughout. The mean lengths are $\ell_1 = \ell_3 = 10$ cm and $\ell_2 = 4$ cm. Determine the coil current necessary to result in a flux density of 0.25 T in leg *3*.

Fig. 12-38

12.48. Two identical 500-turn coils have equal currents and are wound as indicated in Fig. 12-39. The cast-steel core has a flux in leg *3* of 120 μWb. Determine the coil currents and the flux in leg *1*.

Fig. 12-39

12.49. Two identical coils are wound as indicated in Fig. 12-40. The silicon steel core has a cross section of 6 cm^2 throughout. The mean lengths are $\ell_1 = \ell_3 = 14$ cm and $\ell_2 = 4$ cm. Find the coil mmfs if the flux in leg *1* is 0.7 mWb.

Fig. 12-40

ANSWERS TO SUPPLEMENTARY PROBLEMS

12.21. 0.301 μH/m

12.22. 0.992 μH/m

12.23. 5 mm

12.24. 6.58 mH

12.25. 700, 704

12.26. 36.3 μH (both formulas)

12.27. 7.71 mH

12.28. 318, 1384, 5305, 42, 440

12.29. (*a*) 0.64 cm; (*b*) 2.77 m; (*c*) 10.6 m

12.30. 26.3 μWb

12.31. 83.2 A

12.32. 0.65 A

12.33. 561.2 A

12.34. 80 μWb

12.35. 85.2 μWb

12.36. $\mathscr{R}_1 = 0.313$ μH^{-1}, $\mathscr{R}_a = 6.70$ μH^{-1}, $F = 561$ A

12.37. 85 μWb

12.38. 85 μWb

12.39. 1.06 T

12.40. 1079 A

12.41. 952 A

12.42. 229 μWb

12.43. 229 μWb

12.44. 10^{-4} Wb

12.45. 10^{-4} Wb. The mean lengths and cross-sectional areas are the same.

12.46. 1.34 A

12.47. 1.05 A

12.48. 0.41 A, 0 Wb

12.49. 38.5 A

Time-Varying Fields and Maxwell's Equations

13.1 Introduction

Static electric and magnetic fields were treated separately in the previous chapters. Our first observation on a time-varying field was Faraday's law introduced briefly in Chapter 12 in order to explain self- and mutual-inductance. The present chapter starts with electromagnetic induction and the electromotive force (emf) due to a changing magnetic field. It then introduces the *displacement current* proposed by Maxwell to remove the contradiction in Ampère's law when applied to time-varying electric fields. The collection of Faraday's law, Ampère's law, and Gauss's laws (both for the electric and magnetic fields) are called Maxwell's equations. They govern electrostatic, magnetostatic, and time-varying (also called dynamic) electromagnetic fields.

13.2 Maxwell's Equations for Static Fields

Static electric and magnetic fields are not interconnected. They are treated separately by two sets of uncoupled vector equations as follows:

Electric field: $\nabla \times \mathbf{E} = 0$ (Faraday's law) $\nabla \cdot \mathbf{D} = \rho$ (Gauss's law for the electric field)

Magnetic field: $\nabla \times \mathbf{H} = \mathbf{J}$ (Ampère's law) $\nabla \cdot \mathbf{B} = 0$ (Gauss's law for the magnetic field)

Here ρ is charge density and $\mathbf{J}$ is current density.

13.3 Faraday's Law and Lenz's Law

The minus sign in Faraday's law (Section 12.3) implicitly gives the polarity of the induced voltage v. To make this explicit, consider the case of a plane area S, bounded by a closed curve C, where S is cut perpendicularly by a time-variable flux density $\mathbf{B}$ (Fig. 13-1). Faraday's law here takes the integral form

$$\oint_C \mathbf{E} \cdot d\mathbf{l} = -\frac{d}{dt}\int_S \mathbf{B} \cdot d\mathbf{S}$$

in which the positive sense around C and the direction of the normal, $d\mathbf{S}$, are corrected by the usual right-hand rule [Fig. 13-1(a)]. Now if $\mathbf{B}$ is increasing with time, the time derivative will be positive and, thus, the right side of the above equation will be negative. In order for the left integral to be negative, the direction of $\mathbf{E}$ must be opposite to that of the contour, Fig. 13-1(b). A conducting filament in place of the contour would carry a current i_c, also in the direction of $\mathbf{E}$. As shown in Fig. 13-1(c), such a current loop generates a flux ϕ' which opposes the increase in $\mathbf{B}$. *Lenz's law* summarizes this discussion: *The voltage induced by a changing flux has a polarity such that the current established in a closed path gives rise to a flux which opposes the change in flux.*

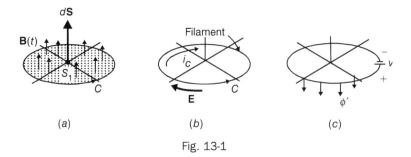

Fig. 13-1

In the special case of a conductor moving through a time-independent magnetic field, the polarity predicted by Lenz's law is yielded by two other methods. (1) The polarity is such that the conductor experiences magnetic forces which *oppose* its motion. (2) As indicated in Fig. 13-2, a moving conductor appears to distort the flux, pushing the flux lines in front of it as it moves. This same distortion is suggested by the counterclockwise flux lines shown around the conductor. By the right-hand rule, the current which would result if a closed path were provided would have the direction shown, and the polarity of the induced voltage is + at the end of the conductor where the current would *leave*. Fig. 13-3 confirms this by comparing the moving conductor and its resulting current to a voltage source connected to a similar external circuit.

Fig. 13-2

Fig. 13-3

13.4   Conductors' Motion in Time-Independent Fields

The force $\mathbf{F}$ on a charge Q in a magnetic field $\mathbf{B}$, where the charge is moving with velocity $\mathbf{U}$, was examined in Chapter 11.

$$\mathbf{F} = Q(\mathbf{U} \times \mathbf{B})$$

A *motional* electric field intensity, $\mathbf{E}_m$, can be defined as the force per unit charge:

$$\mathbf{E}_m = \frac{\mathbf{F}}{Q} = \mathbf{U} \times \mathbf{B}$$

When a conductor with a great number of free charges moves through a field $\mathbf{B}$, the impressed $\mathbf{E}_m$ creates a voltage difference between the two ends of the conductor, the magnitude of which depends on how $\mathbf{E}_m$ is oriented with respect to the conductor. With conductor ends a and b, the voltage of a with respect to b is

$$v_{ab} = \int_b^a \mathbf{E}_m \cdot d\mathbf{l} = \int_b^a (\mathbf{U} \times \mathbf{B}) \cdot d\mathbf{l}$$

If the velocity **U** and the field **B** are at right angles, and the conductor is normal to both, then a conductor of length ℓ will have a voltage

$$v = B\ell U$$

For a closed loop the line integral must be taken around the entire loop:

$$v = \oint (\mathbf{U} \times \mathbf{B}) \cdot d\mathbf{l}$$

Of course, if only part of the complete loop is in motion, it is necessary only that the integral cover this part, since $\mathbf{E}_m$ will be zero elsewhere.

EXAMPLE 1.   In Fig. 13-4, two conducting bars move outward with velocities $\mathbf{U}_1 = 12.5(-\mathbf{a}_y)$ m/s and $\mathbf{U}_2 = 8.0\mathbf{a}_y$ m/s in the field $\mathbf{B} = 0.35\mathbf{a}_z$ T. Find the voltage of b with respect to c.
   At the two conductors,

$$\mathbf{E}_{m1} = \mathbf{U}_1 \times \mathbf{B} = 4.38(-\mathbf{a}_x) \quad \text{V/m}$$
$$\mathbf{E}_{m2} = \mathbf{U}_2 \times \mathbf{B} = 2.80\mathbf{a}_x \quad \text{V/m}$$

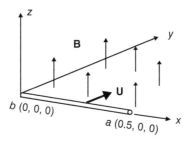

Fig. 13-4

and so

$$v_{ab} = \int_0^{0.50} 4.38(-\mathbf{a}_x) \cdot dx\,\mathbf{a}_x = -2.19\text{V} \quad v_{dc} = \int_0^{0.50} 2.80\mathbf{a}_x \cdot dx\,\mathbf{a}_x = 1.40\,\text{V}$$

$$v_{bc} = v_{ba} + v_{ad} + v_{dc} = 2.19 + 0 + 1.40 = 3.59\ \text{V}$$

Since b is positive with respect to c, current through the meter will be in the $\mathbf{a}_y$ direction. This clockwise current in the circuit gives rise to flux in the $-\mathbf{a}_z$ direction, which, in accordance with Lenz's law, counters the increase in the flux in the $+\mathbf{a}_z$ direction due to the expansion of the circuit. Moreover, the forces that **B** exerts on the moving conductors are directed opposite to their velocities.

13.5   Conductors' Motion in Time-Dependent Fields

When a closed conducting loop is in motion (this includes changes in shape) and also the field **B** is a function of time (as well as of position), then the total induced voltage is made up of a contribution from each of the two sources of flux change. Faraday's law becomes

$$v = -\frac{d}{dt}\int_S \mathbf{B} \cdot d\mathbf{S} = -\int_S \frac{\partial \mathbf{B}}{\partial t} \cdot d\mathbf{S} + \oint (\mathbf{U} \times \mathbf{B}) \cdot d\mathbf{l}$$

The first term on the right is the voltage due to the change in **B**, with the loop held fixed; the second term is the voltage arising from the motion of the loop, with **B** held fixed. The polarity of each term is found from the appropriate form of Lenz's law, and the two terms are then added with regard to those polarities.

EXAMPLE 2.   As shown in Fig. 13-5(a), a planar conducting loop rotates with angular velocity ω about the x axis; at $t = 0$ it is in the xy plane. A time-varying magnetic field, $\mathbf{B} = B(t)\mathbf{a}_z$, is present. Find the voltage induced in the loop by using the two-term form of Faraday's law.

Fig. 13-5

Let the area of the loop be A. The contribution to v due to the variation of $\mathbf{B}$ is

$$v_1 = -\int_S \frac{\partial \mathbf{B}}{\partial t} \cdot d\mathbf{S} = -\int_S \frac{dB}{dt} \mathbf{a}_z \cdot dS\, \mathbf{a}_n = -\frac{dB}{dt} A \cos \omega t$$

since $\mathbf{a}_z \cdot \mathbf{a}_n = \cos \omega t$.

To calculate the second, motional contribution to v, the velocity $\mathbf{U}$ of a point on the loop is needed. From Fig. 13-5(b) it is seen that

$$\mathbf{U} = r\omega \mathbf{a}_n = \frac{y}{\cos \omega t} \omega \mathbf{a}_n$$

so that

$$\mathbf{U} \times \mathbf{B} = \frac{y}{\cos \omega t} \omega \mathbf{a}_n \times B\mathbf{a}_z = \frac{y}{\cos \omega t} \omega B \sin \omega t(-\mathbf{a}_x)$$

since $\mathbf{a}_n \times \mathbf{a}_z = \sin \omega t(-\mathbf{a}_x)$. Consequently,

$$v_2 = \oint (\mathbf{U} \times \mathbf{B}) \cdot d\mathbf{l} = -\frac{\omega B \sin \omega t}{\cos \omega t} \oint y\mathbf{a}_x \cdot d\mathbf{l}$$

Stokes' theorem (Section 10.10) can be used to evaluate the last integral. Since $\nabla \times y\mathbf{a}_x = -\mathbf{a}_z$,

$$\oint y\mathbf{a}_x \cdot d\mathbf{l} = \int_S (\nabla \times y\mathbf{a}_x) \cdot d\mathbf{S} = \int_S (-\mathbf{a}_z) \cdot dS\, \mathbf{a}_n = -A \cos \omega t$$

Therefore, $$v_2 = -\frac{\omega B \sin \omega t}{\cos \omega t}(-A \cos \omega t) = BA\omega \sin \omega t$$

13.6   Displacement Current

In static fields the curl of $\mathbf{H}$ was found to be pointwise equal to the current density $\mathbf{J}_c$. This is *conduction* current density; the subscript c has been added to emphasize that moving charges—electrons, photons, or ions— compose the current. If $\nabla \times \mathbf{H} = \mathbf{J}_c$ were valid where the fields and charges are variable with time, then the continuity equation would be $\nabla \cdot \mathbf{J}_c = \nabla \cdot (\nabla \times H) = 0$, instead of the correct

$$\nabla \cdot \mathbf{J}_c = -\frac{\partial \rho}{\partial t}$$

Hence, James Clerk Maxwell postulated that

$$\nabla \times \mathbf{H} = \mathbf{J}_c + \mathbf{J}_D \quad \text{where} \quad \mathbf{J}_D \equiv \frac{\partial \mathbf{D}}{\partial t}$$

With the inclusion of the *displacement* current density $\mathbf{J}_D$, the continuity equation is satisfied:

$$\nabla \cdot \mathbf{J}_c = -\nabla \cdot \mathbf{J}_D = -\nabla \cdot \frac{\partial \mathbf{D}}{\partial t} = -\frac{\partial}{\partial t}(\nabla \cdot \mathbf{D}) = -\frac{\partial \rho}{\partial t}$$

The displacement current i_D through a specified surface is obtained by integration of the normal component of $\mathbf{J}_D$ over the surface (just as i_c is obtained from $\mathbf{J}_c$).

$$i_D = \int_S \mathbf{J}_D \cdot d\mathbf{S} = \int_S \frac{\partial \mathbf{D}}{\partial t} \cdot d\mathbf{S} = \frac{d}{dt}\int_S \mathbf{D} \cdot d\mathbf{S}$$

Here, the last expression assumes that the surface S is fixed in space.

EXAMPLE 3.   Use Stokes' theorem (Section 10.10) to show that $i_c = i_D$ in the circuit of Fig. 13-6.

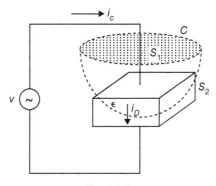

Fig. 13-6

Since the two surfaces S_1 and S_2 have the common contour C,

$$\oint_C \mathbf{H} \cdot d\mathbf{l} = \int_{S_1} (\nabla \times \mathbf{H}) \cdot d\mathbf{S} = \int_{S_2} (\nabla \times \mathbf{H}) \cdot d\mathbf{S}$$

$$= \int_{S_1}\left(\mathbf{J}_c + \frac{\partial \mathbf{D}}{\partial t}\right) \cdot d\mathbf{S} = \int_{S_2}\left(\mathbf{J}_c + \frac{\partial \mathbf{D}}{\partial t}\right) \cdot d\mathbf{S}$$

Assuming the flux is confined to the dielectric between the conducting plates, $\mathbf{D} = \mathbf{0}$ over S_1. And since no free charges are in motion within the dielectric, $\mathbf{J}_c = \mathbf{0}$ over S_2. Therefore,

$$\int_{S_1} \mathbf{J}_c \cdot d\mathbf{S} = \int_{S_2} \frac{\partial \mathbf{D}}{\partial t} \cdot d\mathbf{S} \quad \text{or} \quad i_c = i_D$$

It should be noted that $\partial \mathbf{D}/\partial t$ is nonzero only over that part of S_2 that lies within the dielectric.

EXAMPLE 4.   Repeat Example 3, this time using circuit analysis.
   Refer to Fig. 13-6. The capacitance of the capacitor is

$$C = \frac{\epsilon A}{d}$$

where A is the plate area and d is the separation. The conduction current is then

$$i_c = C\frac{dv}{dt} = \frac{\epsilon A}{d}\frac{dv}{dt}$$

On the other hand, the electric field in the dielectric is, neglecting fringing, $E = v/d$. Hence,

$$D = \epsilon E = \frac{\epsilon}{d}v \qquad \frac{\partial D}{\partial t} = \frac{\epsilon}{d}\frac{dv}{dt}$$

and the displacement current is ($\mathbf{D}$ is normal to the plates)

$$i_D = \int_A \frac{\partial \mathbf{D}}{\partial t}\cdot d\mathbf{S} = \int_A \frac{\epsilon}{d}\frac{dv}{dt}\,dS = \frac{\epsilon A}{d}\frac{dv}{dt} = i_c$$

13.7   Ratio of J_c to J_D

Some materials are neither good conductors nor perfect dielectrics, so that both conduction current and displacement current exist. A model for the poor conductor or lossy dielectric is shown in Fig. 13-7. Assuming the time dependence $e^{j\omega t}$ for $\mathbf{E}$, the total current density is

$$\mathbf{J}_t = \mathbf{J}_c + \mathbf{J}_D = \sigma\mathbf{E} + \frac{\partial}{\partial t}(\epsilon\mathbf{E}) = \sigma\mathbf{E} + j\omega\epsilon\mathbf{E}$$

from which

$$\frac{J_c}{J_D} = \frac{\sigma}{\omega\epsilon}$$

As expected, the displacement current becomes increasingly important as the frequency increases.

Fig. 13-7

EXAMPLE 5.   A circular-cross-section conductor of radius 1.5 mm carries a current $i_c = 5.5 \sin(4\times 10^{10}t)$ (μA). What is the amplitude of the displacement current density, if $\sigma = 35$ MS/m and $\epsilon_r = 1$?

$$\frac{J_c}{J_D} = \frac{\sigma}{\omega\epsilon} = \frac{3.50\times 10^7}{(4\times 10^{10})(10^{-9}/36\pi)} = 9.90\times 10^7$$

Then
$$J_D = \frac{(5.5\times 10^{-6})/[\pi(1.5\times 10^{-3})^2]}{9.90\times 10^7} = 7.86\times 10^{-3}\ \mu\text{A}/\text{m}^2$$

13.8   Maxwell's Equations for Time-Varying Fields

A static $\mathbf{E}$ field can exist in the absence of a magnetic field $\mathbf{H}$; a capacitor with a static charge Q furnishes an example. Likewise, a conductor with a constant current I has a magnetic field $\mathbf{H}$ without an $\mathbf{E}$ field. When fields are time-variable, however, $\mathbf{H}$ cannot exist without an $\mathbf{E}$ field nor can $\mathbf{E}$ exist without a corresponding $\mathbf{H}$ field. While much valuable information can be derived from static field theory, only with time-variable fields can the full value of electromagnetic field theory be demonstrated. The experiments of Faraday and Hertz and the theoretical analyses of Maxwell all involved time-variable fields.

The equations grouped below, called *Maxwell's equations*, were separately developed and examined in earlier chapters. In Table 13-1, the most general form is presented, where charges and conduction current may be present in the region. Note that the point and integral forms of the first two equations are equivalent under Stokes' theorem, while the point and integral forms of the last two equations are equivalent under the divergence theorem.

TABLE 13-1 Maxwell's Equations, General Set

POINT FORM	INTEGRAL FORM
$\nabla \times \mathbf{H} = \mathbf{J}_c + \dfrac{\partial \mathbf{D}}{\partial t}$	$\oint \mathbf{H} \cdot d\mathbf{l} = \int_S \left(\mathbf{J}_c + \dfrac{\partial \mathbf{D}}{\partial t} \right) \cdot d\mathbf{S}$ (Ampère's law)
$\nabla \times \mathbf{E} = -\dfrac{\partial \mathbf{B}}{\partial t}$	$\oint \mathbf{E} \cdot d\mathbf{l} = \int_S \left(-\dfrac{\partial \mathbf{B}}{\partial t} \right) \cdot d\mathbf{S}$ (Faraday's law; S fixed)
$\nabla \cdot \mathbf{D} = \rho$	$\oint_S \mathbf{D} \cdot d\mathbf{S} = \int_v \rho \, dv$ (Gauss's law)
$\nabla \cdot \mathbf{B} = 0$	$\oint_S \mathbf{B} \cdot d\mathbf{S} = 0$ (nonexistence of monopole)

For free space, where there are no charges ($\rho = 0$) and no conduction currents ($\mathbf{J}_c = 0$), Maxwell's equations take the form shown in Table 13-2.

TABLE 13-2 Maxwell's Equations, Free-Space Set

POINT FORM	INTEGRAL FORM
$\nabla \times \mathbf{H} = \dfrac{\partial \mathbf{D}}{\partial t}$	$\oint \mathbf{H} \cdot d\mathbf{l} = \int_S \left(\dfrac{\partial \mathbf{D}}{\partial t} \right) \cdot d\mathbf{S}$
$\nabla \times \mathbf{E} = -\dfrac{\partial \mathbf{B}}{\partial t}$	$\oint \mathbf{E} \cdot d\mathbf{l} = \int_S \left(-\dfrac{\partial \mathbf{B}}{\partial t} \right) \cdot d\mathbf{S}$
$\nabla \cdot \mathbf{D} = 0$	$\oint_S \mathbf{D} \cdot d\mathbf{S} = 0$
$\nabla \cdot \mathbf{B} = 0$	$\oint_S \mathbf{B} \cdot d\mathbf{S} = 0$

The first and second point-form equations in the free-space set can be used to show that time-variable $\mathbf{E}$ and $\mathbf{H}$ fields cannot exist independently. For example, if $\mathbf{E}$ is a function of time, then $\mathbf{D} = \epsilon_0 \mathbf{E}$ will also be a function of time, so that $\partial \mathbf{D}/\partial t$ will be nonzero. Consequently, $\nabla \times \mathbf{H}$ is nonzero, and so a nonzero $\mathbf{H}$ must exist. In a similar way, the second equation can be used to show that if $\mathbf{H}$ is a function of time, then there must be an $\mathbf{E}$ field present.

The point form of Maxwell's equations is used most frequently in the problems. However, the integral form is important in that it better displays the underlying physical laws.

SOLVED PROBLEMS

13.1. In a material for which $\sigma = 5.0$ S/m and $\epsilon_r = 1$ the electric field intensity is $E = 250 \sin 10^{10}t$ (V/m). Find the conduction and displacement current densities, and the frequency at which they have equal magnitudes.

$$J_c = \sigma E = 1250 \sin 10^{10}t \quad (\text{A/m}^2)$$

On the assumption that the field direction does not vary with time,

$$J_D = \frac{\partial D}{\partial t} = \frac{\partial}{\partial t}(\epsilon_0 \epsilon_r \, 250 \sin 10^{10} t) = 22.1 \cos 10^{10} t \quad (A/m^2)$$

For $J_c = J_D$,

$$\sigma = \omega \epsilon \quad \text{or} \quad \omega = \frac{5.0}{8.854 \times 10^{-12}} = 5.65 \times 10^{11} \text{ rad/s}$$

which is equivalent to a frequency $f = 8.99 \times 10^{10}$ Hz $= 89.9$ GHz.

13.2. A coaxial capacitor with inner radius 5 mm, outer radius 6 mm, and length 500 mm has a dielectric for which $\epsilon_r = 6.7$ and an applied voltage $250 \sin 377t$ (V). Determine the displacement current i_D and compare with the conduction current i_c.

Assume the inner conductor to be at $v = 0$. Then, from Problem 9.7, the potential at $0.005 \le r \le 0.006$ m is

$$v = \left[\frac{250}{\ln\left(\frac{6}{5}\right)} \sin 377t \right] \left(\ln \frac{r}{0.005} \right) \quad (V)$$

From this,

$$\mathbf{E} = -\nabla v = -\frac{1.37 \times 10^3}{r} \sin 377t \, \mathbf{a}_r \quad (V/m)$$

$$\mathbf{D} = \epsilon_0 \epsilon_r \mathbf{E} = -\frac{8.13 \times 10^{-8}}{r} \sin 377t \, \mathbf{a}_r \quad (C/m^2)$$

$$\mathbf{J}_D = \frac{\partial \mathbf{D}}{\partial t} = -\frac{3.07 \times 10^{-5}}{r} \cos 377t \, \mathbf{a}_r \quad (A/m^2)$$

$$i_D = J_D(2\pi r L) = 9.63 \times 10^{-5} \cos 377t \quad (A)$$

The circuit analysis method for i_c requires the capacitance,

$$C = \frac{2\pi \epsilon_0 \epsilon_r L}{\ln\left(\frac{6}{5}\right)} = 1.02 \text{ nF}$$

Then $i_c = C \dfrac{dv}{dt} = (1.02 \times 10^{-9})(250)(377)(\cos 377t) = 9.63 \times 10^{-5} \cos 377t$ (A)

It is seen that $i_c = i_D$.

13.3. Moist soil has a conductivity of 10^{-3} S/m and $\epsilon_r = 2.5$. Find J_c and J_D where

$$E = 6.0 \times 10^{-6} \sin 9.0 \times 10^9 t \quad (V/m)$$

First, $J_c = \sigma E = 6.0 \times 10^{-9} \sin 9.0 \times 10^9 t$ (A/m^2). Then, since $D = \epsilon_0 \epsilon_r E$,

$$J_D = \frac{\partial D}{\partial t} = \epsilon_0 \epsilon_r \frac{\partial E}{\partial t} = 1.20 \times 10^{-6} \cos 9.0 \times 10^9 t \quad (A/m^2)$$

13.4. Find the induced voltage in the conductor of Fig. 13-8 where $\mathbf{B} = 0.04\mathbf{a}_y$ T and

$$\mathbf{U} = 2.5 \sin 10^3 t \mathbf{a}_z \quad (m/s)$$

$$\mathbf{E}_m = \mathbf{U} \times \mathbf{B} = 0.10 \sin 10^3 t (-\mathbf{a}_x) \quad (V/m)$$

$$v = \int_0^{0.20} 0.10 \sin 10^3 t (-\mathbf{a}_x) \cdot dx \mathbf{a}_x$$

$$= -0.02 \sin 10^3 t \quad (V)$$

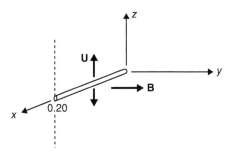

Fig. 13-8

The conductor first moves in the $\mathbf{a}_z$ direction. The $x = 0.20$ end is negative with respect to the end at the z axis for this half cycle.

13.5. Rework Problem 13.4 if the magnetic field is changed to $\mathbf{B} = 0.04\mathbf{a}_x$ (T).

Because the conductor cuts no field lines, the induced voltage must be zero. This may be verified analytically by use of Problem 2.8.

$$v = \int (\mathbf{U} \times \mathbf{B}) \cdot d\mathbf{l} = \int \mathbf{U} \cdot (\mathbf{B} \times d\mathbf{l}) = 0$$

since $\mathbf{B}$ and $d\mathbf{l}$ are always parallel.

13.6. An area of 0.65 m² in the $z = 0$ plane is enclosed by a filamentary conductor. Find the induced voltage, given that

$$\mathbf{B} = 0.05 \cos 10^3 t \left(\frac{\mathbf{a}_y + \mathbf{a}_z}{\sqrt{2}} \right) \quad (\text{T})$$

See Fig. 13-9.

$$v = -\int_s \frac{\partial \mathbf{B}}{\partial t} \cdot dS\,\mathbf{a}_z$$

$$= \int_s 50 \sin 10^3 t \left(\frac{\mathbf{a}_y + \mathbf{a}_z}{\sqrt{2}} \right) \cdot dS\,\mathbf{a}_z$$

$$= 23.0 \sin 10^3 t \quad (\text{V})$$

The field is decreasing in the first half cycle of the cosine function. The direction of i in a closed circuit must be such as to oppose this decrease. Thus the conventional current must have the direction shown in Fig. 13-9.

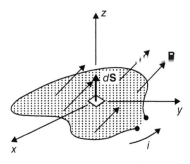

Fig. 13-9

13.7. The circular loop conductor shown in Fig. 13-10 lies in the $z = 0$ plane, has a radius of 0.10 m and a resistance of 5.0 Ω. Given $\mathbf{B} = 0.20 \sin 10^3 t\, \mathbf{a}_z$ (T), determine the current.

$$\phi = \mathbf{B} \cdot \mathbf{S} = 2 \times 10^{-3} \pi \sin 10^3 t \quad \text{(Wb)}$$

$$v = -\frac{d\phi}{dt} = -2\pi \cos 10^3 t \quad \text{(V)}$$

$$i = \frac{v}{R} = -0.4\pi \cos 10^3 t \quad \text{(A)}$$

At $t = 0+$ the flux is increasing. In order to oppose this increase, current in the loop must have an instantaneous direction $-\mathbf{a}_y$ where the loop crosses the positive x axis.

Fig. 13-10

13.8. The rectangular loop shown in Fig. 13-11 moves toward the origin at a velocity $\mathbf{U} = -250\mathbf{a}_y$ m/s in a field

$$\mathbf{B} = 0.80e^{-0.50y}\mathbf{a}_z \quad \text{(T)}$$

Find the current at the instant the coil sides are at $y = 0.50$ m and 0.60 m, if $R = 2.5$ Ω.

Fig. 13-11

Only the 1.0-m sides have induced voltages. Let the side at $y = 0.50$ m be *1*.

$$v_1 = B_1 \ell U = 0.80e^{-0.25}(1)(250) = 155.8 \text{ V} \qquad v_2 = B_2 \ell U = 148.2 \text{ V}$$

The voltages are of the polarity shown. The instantaneous current is

$$i = \frac{155.8 - 148.2}{2.5} = 3.04 \text{ A}$$

13.9. A conductor 1 cm in length is parallel to the z axis and rotates at a radius of 25 cm at 1200 rev/min (see Fig. 13-12). Find the induced voltage if the radial field is given by $\mathbf{B} = 0.5\mathbf{a}_r$ T.

Fig. 13-12

The angular velocity is

$$\left(1200\ \frac{rev}{min}\right)\left(\frac{1}{60}\ \frac{min}{s}\right)\left(2\pi\ \frac{rad}{rev}\right) = 40\pi\ \frac{rad}{s}$$

Hence,
$$U = r\omega = (0.25)(40\pi)\ m/s$$

$$\mathbf{E}_m = 10\pi\mathbf{a}_\phi \times 0.5\mathbf{a}_r = 5.0\pi\ (-\mathbf{a}_z)\ V/m$$

$$v = \int_0^{0.01} 5.0\pi(-\mathbf{a}_z)\cdot dz\mathbf{a}_z = -5.0\times10^{-2}\pi\ V$$

The negative sign indicates that the lower end of the conductor is positive with respect to the upper end.

13.10. A conducting cylinder of radius 7 cm and height 15 cm rotates at 600 rev/min in a radial field $\mathbf{B} = 0.20\mathbf{a}_r$ T. Sliding contacts at the top and bottom connect to a voltmeter as shown in Fig. 13-13. Find the induced voltage.

$$\omega = (600)\left(\tfrac{1}{60}\right)(2\pi) = 20\pi\ rad/s$$

$$\mathbf{U} = (20\pi)(0.07)\mathbf{a}_\phi\ m/s$$

$$\mathbf{E}_m = \mathbf{U}\times\mathbf{B} = 0.88(-\mathbf{a}_z)\ V/m$$

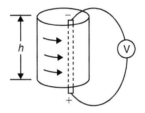

Fig. 13-13

Each vertical element of the curved surface cuts the same flux and has the same induced voltage. These elements are effectively in a parallel connection and the induced voltage of any element is the same as the total.

$$v = \int_0^{0.15} 0.88\,(-\mathbf{a}_z)\cdot dz\mathbf{a}_z = -0.13\ V \quad (+\text{ at the bottom})$$

13.11. In Fig. 13-14 a rectangular conducting loop with resistance $R = 0.20\ \Omega$ turns at 500 rev/min. The vertical conductor at $r_1 = 0.03$ m is in a field $\mathbf{B}_1 = 0.25\mathbf{a}_r$ T, and the conductor at $r_2 = 0.05$ m is in a field $\mathbf{B}_2 = 0.80\mathbf{a}_r$ T. Find the current in the loop.

Fig. 13-14

$$\mathbf{U}_1 = (500)\left(\tfrac{1}{60}\right)(2\pi)(0.03)\mathbf{a}_\phi = 0.50\pi\mathbf{a}_\phi\ m/s$$

$$v_1 = \int_0^{0.50} (0.50\pi\mathbf{a}_\phi \times 0.25\mathbf{a}_r)\cdot dz\mathbf{a}_z = -0.20\ V$$

Similarly, $\mathbf{U}_2 = 0.83\pi\mathbf{a}_\phi$ m/s and $v_2 = -1.04$ V. Then

$$i = \frac{1.04 - 0.20}{0.20} = 4.20 \text{ A}$$

in the direction shown on the diagram.

13.12. The circular disk shown in Fig. 13-15 rotates at ω (rad/s) in a uniform flux density $\mathbf{B} = B\mathbf{a}_z$. Sliding contacts connect a voltmeter to the disk. What voltage is indicated on the meter from this *Faraday homopolar generator*?

Fig. 13-15

One radial element is examined. A general point on this radial element has velocity $\mathbf{U} = \omega r\mathbf{a}_\phi$, so that

$$\mathbf{E}_m = \mathbf{U} \times \mathbf{B} = \omega r B\mathbf{a}_r$$

and

$$v = \int_0^a \omega r B\mathbf{a}_r \cdot d r\mathbf{a}_r = \frac{\omega a^2 B}{2}$$

where a is the radius of the disk. The positive result indicates that the outer point is positive with respect to the center for the directions of $\mathbf{B}$ and ω shown.

13.13. A square coil, 0.60 m on a side, rotates about the x axis at $\omega = 60\pi$ rad/s in a field $\mathbf{B} = 0.80\mathbf{a}_z$ T, as shown in Fig. 13-16(a). Find the induced voltage.

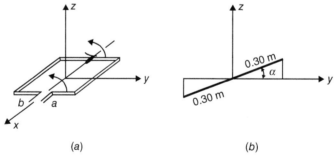

(a)   (b)

Fig. 13-16

Assuming that the coil is initially in the xy plane,

$$\alpha = \omega t = 60\pi t \text{ (rad)}$$

The projected area on the xy plane becomes [see Fig. 13-16(b)]:

$$A = (0.6)(0.6 \cos 60\pi t) \text{ (m}^2)$$

Then $\phi = BA = 0.288 \cos 60\pi t$ (Wb) and

$$v = -\frac{d\phi}{dt} = 54.3 \sin 60\pi t \quad \text{(V)}$$

Lenz's law shows that this is the voltage of a with respect to b.

Alternate Method

Each side parallel to the x axis has a y component of velocity whose magnitude is

$$|U_y| = |r\omega \sin \alpha| = |18.0\pi \sin 60\pi t| \quad \text{(m/s)}$$

The voltages $B\ell|U_y|$ for the two sides add, giving

$$|v| = 2(B\ell|U_y|) = |54.3 \sin 60\pi t| \quad \text{(V)}$$

Lenz's law again determines the proper sign.

13.14. Check Example 2 by means of the original, differential form of Faraday's law.

From Fig. 13-5(b) the projected loop area normal to the field is $A \cos \omega t$, whence

$$\phi = B(t) (A \cos \omega t)$$

and

$$v = -\frac{d\phi}{dt} = -\frac{dB}{dt} A \cos \omega t + BA\omega \sin \omega t = v_1 + v_2$$

(It is almost always simpler to use the differential form.)

13.15. Find the electric power generated in the loop of Problem 13.11. Check the result by calculating the rate at which mechanical work is done on the loop.

The electric power is the power loss in the resistor:

$$P_e = i^2 R = (4.20)^2(0.20) = 3.53 \text{ W}$$

The forces exerted by the field on the two vertical conductors are

$$\mathbf{F}_1 = i(\mathbf{l}_1 \times \mathbf{B}_1) = (4.20)(0.50)(0.25) \, (\mathbf{a}_z \times \mathbf{a}_r) = 0.525\mathbf{a}_\phi \text{ N}$$
$$\mathbf{F}_2 = i(\mathbf{l}_2 \times \mathbf{B}_2) = (4.20)(0.50)(0.80)(-\mathbf{a}_z \times \mathbf{a}_r) = -1.68\mathbf{a}_\phi \text{ N}$$

To turn the loop, forces $-\mathbf{F}_1$ and $-\mathbf{F}_2$ must be applied; these do work at the rate

$$P = (-\mathbf{F}_1) \cdot \mathbf{U}_1 + (-\mathbf{F}_2) \cdot \mathbf{U}_2 = (-0.525)(0.50\pi) + (1.68)(0.83\pi) = 3.55 \text{ W}$$

To within rounding errors, $P = P_e$.

13.16. Given $\mathbf{E} = E_m \sin(\omega t - \beta z) \, \mathbf{a}_y$ in free space, find $\mathbf{D}$, $\mathbf{B}$, and $\mathbf{H}$. Sketch $\mathbf{E}$ and $\mathbf{H}$ at $t = 0$.

$$\mathbf{D} = \epsilon_0 \mathbf{E} = \epsilon_0 E_m \sin(\omega t - \beta z)\mathbf{a}_y$$

The Maxwell equation $\nabla \times \mathbf{E} = -\partial \mathbf{B}/\partial t$ gives

$$\begin{vmatrix} \mathbf{a}_x & \mathbf{a}_y & \mathbf{a}_z \\ \dfrac{\partial}{\partial x} & \dfrac{\partial}{\partial y} & \dfrac{\partial}{\partial z} \\ 0 & E_m \sin(\omega t - \beta z) & 0 \end{vmatrix} = -\frac{\partial \mathbf{B}}{\partial t}$$

or

$$-\frac{\partial \mathbf{B}}{\partial t} = \beta E_m \cos(\omega t - \beta z)\mathbf{a}_x$$

Integrating,

$$\mathbf{B} = -\frac{\beta E_m}{\omega} \sin(\omega t - \beta z)\mathbf{a}_x$$

where the "constant" of integration, which is a static field, has been neglected. Then,

$$\mathbf{H} = -\frac{\beta E_m}{\omega \mu_0} \sin(\omega t - \beta z)\mathbf{a}_x$$

Note that $\mathbf{E}$ and $\mathbf{H}$ are mutually perpendicular. At $t = 0$, $\sin(\omega t - \beta z) = -\sin \beta z$. Fig. 13-17 shows the two fields along the z axis, on the assumption that E_m and β are positive.

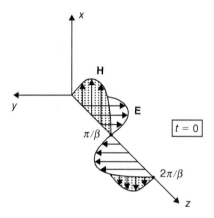

Fig. 13-17

13.17. Show that the $\mathbf{E}$ and $\mathbf{H}$ fields of Problem 13.16 constitute a wave traveling in the z direction. Verify that the wave speed and E/H depend only on the properties of free space.

$\mathbf{E}$ and $\mathbf{H}$ together vary as $\sin(\omega t - \beta z)$. A given state of $\mathbf{E}$ and $\mathbf{H}$ is then characterized by

$$\omega t - \beta z = \text{const.} = \omega t_0 \quad \text{or} \quad z = \frac{\omega}{\beta}(t - t_0)$$

But this is the equation of a plane moving with speed

$$c = \frac{\omega}{\beta}$$

in the direction of its normal, $\mathbf{a}_z$. (It is assumed that β, as well as ω, is positive; for a negative β, the direction of motion would be $-\mathbf{a}_z$.) Thus, the entire pattern of Fig. 13-17 moves down the z axis with speed c.

The Maxwell equation $\nabla \times \mathbf{H} = \partial \mathbf{D}/\partial t$ gives

$$\begin{vmatrix} \mathbf{a}_x & \mathbf{a}_y & \mathbf{a}_z \\ \dfrac{\partial}{\partial x} & \dfrac{\partial}{\partial y} & \dfrac{\partial}{\partial z} \\ \dfrac{-\beta E_m}{\omega \mu_0}\sin(\omega t - \beta z) & 0 & 0 \end{vmatrix} = \frac{\partial}{\partial t}\epsilon_0 E_m \sin(\omega t - \beta z)\mathbf{a}_y$$

$$\frac{\beta^2 E_m}{\omega \mu_0}\cos(\omega t - \beta z)\mathbf{a}_y = \epsilon_0 E_m \omega \cos(\omega t - \beta z)\mathbf{a}_y$$

$$\frac{1}{\epsilon_0 \mu_0} = \frac{\omega^2}{\beta^2}$$

Consequently,

$$c = \sqrt{\frac{1}{\epsilon_0 \mu_0}} \approx \sqrt{\frac{1}{(10^{-9}/36\pi)(4\pi \times 10^{-7})}} = 3 \times 10^8 \text{ (m/s)}$$

Moreover,

$$\frac{E}{H} = \frac{\omega \mu_0}{\beta} = \sqrt{\frac{\mu_0}{\epsilon_0}} \approx 120\pi \text{ (V/A)} = 120\pi \ \Omega$$

13.18. Given $\mathbf{H} = H_m e^{j(\omega t + \beta z)}\mathbf{a}_x$ in free space, find $\mathbf{E}$.

$$\nabla \times \mathbf{H} = \frac{\partial \mathbf{D}}{\partial t}$$

$$\frac{\partial}{\partial z} H_m e^{j(\omega t + \beta z)}\mathbf{a}_y = \frac{\partial \mathbf{D}}{\partial t}$$

$$j\beta H_m e^{j(\omega t + \beta z)}\mathbf{a}_y = \frac{\partial \mathbf{D}}{\partial t}$$

$$\mathbf{D} = \frac{\beta H_m}{\omega} e^{j(\omega t + \beta z)}\mathbf{a}_y$$

and $\mathbf{E} = \mathbf{D}/\epsilon_0$.

13.19. Given

$$\mathbf{E} = 30\pi e^{j(10^8 t + \beta z)}\mathbf{a}_x \quad (\text{V/m}) \qquad \mathbf{H} = H_m e^{j(10^8 t + \beta z)}\mathbf{a}_y \quad (\text{A/m})$$

in free space, find H_m and β ($\beta > 0$).

This is a plane wave, essentially the same as that in Problems 13.16 and 13.17 (except that, there $\mathbf{E}$ was in the y direction and $\mathbf{H}$ in the x direction). The results of Problem 13.17 hold for any such wave in free space:

$$\frac{\omega}{\beta} = \frac{1}{\sqrt{\epsilon_0 \mu_0}} = 3 \times 10^8 \ (\text{m/s}) \qquad \frac{E}{H} = \sqrt{\frac{\mu_0}{\epsilon_0}} = 120\pi \ \Omega$$

Thus, for the given wave,

$$\beta = \frac{10^8}{3 \times 10^8} = \frac{1}{3} \ (\text{rad/m}) \qquad H_m = \pm \frac{30\pi}{120\pi} = \pm \frac{1}{4} \ (\text{A/m})$$

To fix the sign of H_m, apply $\nabla \times \mathbf{E} = -\partial \mathbf{B}/\partial t$:

$$j\beta \, 30\pi e^{j(10^8 t + \beta z)}\mathbf{a}_y = -j10^8 \mu_0 H_m e^{j(10^8 t + \beta z)}\mathbf{a}_y$$

which shows that H_m must be negative.

13.20. In a homogeneous nonconducting region where $\mu_r = 1$, find ϵ_r and ω if

$$\mathbf{E} = 30\pi e^{j[\omega t - (4/3)y]}\mathbf{a}_z \ (\text{V/m}) \qquad \mathbf{H} = 1.0 e^{j[\omega t - (4/3)y]}\mathbf{a}_x \ (\text{A/m})$$

Here, by analogy to Problem 13.17,

$$\frac{\omega}{\beta} = \frac{1}{\sqrt{\epsilon \mu}} = \frac{3 \times 10^8}{\sqrt{\epsilon_r \mu_r}} \quad (\text{m/s}) \qquad \frac{E}{H} = \sqrt{\frac{\mu}{\epsilon}} = 120\pi \sqrt{\frac{\mu_r}{\epsilon_r}} \quad (\Omega)$$

Thus, since $\mu_r = 1$,

$$\frac{\omega}{\frac{4}{3}} = \frac{3 \times 10^8}{\sqrt{\epsilon_r}} \qquad 30\pi = 120\pi \frac{1}{\sqrt{\epsilon_r}}$$

which yield $\epsilon_r = 16$, $\omega = 10^8$ rad/s. In this medium the speed of light is $c/4$.

SUPPLEMENTARY PROBLEMS

13.21. Given the conduction current density in a lossy dielectric as $J_c = 0.02 \sin 10^9 t$ (A/m²), find the displacement current density if $\sigma = 10^3$ S/m and $\epsilon_r = 6.5$.

13.22. A circular-cross-section conductor of radius 1.5 mm carries a current $i_c = 5.5 \sin 4 \times 10^{10} t$ (μA). What is the amplitude of the displacement current density, if $\sigma = 35$ MS/m and $\epsilon_r = 1$?

13.23. Find the frequency at which conduction current density and displacement current density are equal in (a) distilled water, where $\sigma = 2.0 \times 10^{-4}$ S/m and $\epsilon_r = 81$; (b) seawater, where $\sigma = 4.0$ S/m and $\epsilon_r = 1$.

13.24. Concentric spherical conducting shells at $r_1 = 0.5$ mm and $r_2 = 1$ mm are separated by a dielectric for which $\epsilon_r = 8.5$. Find the capacitance and calculate i_c, given an applied voltage $v = 150 \sin 5000t$ (V). Obtain the displacement current i_D and compare it with i_c.

13.25. Two parallel conducting plates of area 0.05 m² are separated by 2 mm of a lossy dielectric for which $\epsilon_r = 8.3$ and $\sigma = 8.0 \times 10^{-4}$ S/m. Given an applied voltage $v = 10 \sin 10^7 t$ (V), find the total rms current.

13.26. A parallel-plate capacitor of separation 0.6 mm and with a dielectric of $\epsilon_r = 15.3$ has an applied rms voltage of 25 V at a frequency of 15 GHz. Find the rms displacement current density. Neglect fringing.

13.27 A conductor on the x axis between $x = 0$ and $x = 0.2$ m has a velocity $\mathbf{U} = 6.0\mathbf{a}_z$ m/s in a field $\mathbf{B} = 0.04\mathbf{a}_y$ T. Find the induced voltage by using (a) the motional electric field intensity, (b) $d\phi/dt$, and (c) $B\ell U$. Determine the polarity and discuss Lenz's law if the conductor was connected to a closed loop.

13.28. Repeat Problem 13.27 for $\mathbf{B} = 0.04 \sin kz\mathbf{a}_y$ (T). Discuss Lenz's law as the conductor moves from flux in one direction to the reverse direction.

13.29. The bar conductor parallel to the y axis shown in Fig. 13-18 completes a loop by sliding contact with the conductors at $y = 0$ and $y = 0.05$ m. (a) Find the induced voltage when the bar is stationary at $x = 0.05$ m and $\mathbf{B} = 0.30 \sin 10^4 t\mathbf{a}_z$ (T). (b) Repeat for a velocity of the bar $\mathbf{U} = 150\mathbf{a}_x$ m/s. Discuss the polarity.

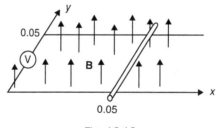

Fig. 13-18

13.30. The rectangular coil in Fig. 13-19 moves to the right at speed $U = 2.5$ m/s. The left side cuts flux at right angles, where $B_1 = 0.30$ T, while the right side cuts equal flux in the opposite direction. Find the instantaneous current in the coil and discuss its direction by use of Lenz's law.

Fig. 13-19

13.31. A rectangular conducting loop in the $z = 0$ plane with sides parallel to the axes has y dimension 1 cm and x dimension 2 cm. Its resistance is 5.0 Ω. At a time when the coil sides are at $x = 20$ cm and $x = 22$ cm it is moving toward the origin at a velocity of 2.5 m/s along the x axis. Find the current if $\mathbf{B} = 5.0e^{-10x}\mathbf{a}_z$ (T). Repeat for the coil sides at $x = 5$ cm and $x = 7$ cm.

13.32. The 2.0-m conductor shown in Fig. 13-20 rotates at 1200 rev/min in the radial field $\mathbf{B} = 0.10 \sin \phi \, \mathbf{a}_r$ (T). Find the current in the closed loop with a resistance of 100 Ω. Discuss the polarity and the current direction.

Fig. 13-20

13.33. In a radial field $\mathbf{B} = 0.50\mathbf{a}_r$ (T), two conductors at $r = 0.23$ m and $r = 0.25$ m are parallel to the z axis and are 0.01 m in length. If both conductors are in the plane $\phi = 40\pi t$, what voltage is available to circulate a current when the two conductors are connected by radial conductors?

13.34. In Fig. 13-21 a radial conductor, $3 \le r \le 6$ cm, is shown embedded in a rotating glass disk. Two 11.2 mΩ resistors complete two circuits. The disk turns at 12 rev/min. If the field at the disk is $\mathbf{B} = 0.30\mathbf{a}_n$ (T), calculate the electric power generated. What is the effect of this on the rotation? Discuss Lenz's law as it applies to this problem.

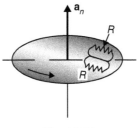

Fig. 13-21

13.35. What voltage is developed by a Faraday disk generator (Problem 13.12) with the meter connections at $r_1 = 1$ mm and $r_2 = 100$ mm when the disk turns at 500 rev/min in a flux density of 0.80 T?

13.36. A coil such as that shown in Fig. 13-16(a) is 75 mm wide (y dimension) and 100 mm long (x dimension). What is the speed of rotation if an rms voltage of 0.25 V is developed in the uniform field $\mathbf{B} = 0.45\mathbf{a}_y$ (T)?

13.37. In free space, $\mathbf{D} = D_m \sin(\omega t + \beta z)\mathbf{a}_x$. Using Maxwell's equations, show that

$$\mathbf{B} = \frac{-\omega\mu_0 D_m}{\beta} \sin(\omega t + \beta z)\mathbf{a}_y$$

Sketch the fields at $t = 0$ along the z axis, assuming that $D_m > 0$, $\beta > 0$.

13.38. In free space,

$$\mathbf{B} = B_m e^{j(\omega t + \beta z)} \mathbf{a}_y$$

Show that

$$\mathbf{E} = -\frac{\omega B_m}{\beta} e^{j(\omega t + \beta z)} \mathbf{a}_x$$

13.39. In a homogeneous region where $\mu_r = 1$ and $\epsilon_r = 50$,

$$\mathbf{E} = 20\pi\, e^{j(\omega t - \beta z)} \mathbf{a}_x \ (\text{V/m}) \qquad \mathbf{B} = \mu_0 H_m e^{j(\omega t - \beta z)} \mathbf{a}_y \ (\text{T})$$

Find ω and H_m if the wavelength is 1.78 m.

ANSWERS TO SUPPLEMENTARY PROBLEMS

13.21. $1.15 \times 10^{-6} \cos 10^9 t \ (\text{A/m}^2)$

13.22. $7.87 \times 10^{-3} \ \mu \text{A/m}^2$

13.23. (*a*) 4.44×10^4 Hz; (*b*) 7.19×10^{10} Hz

13.24. $i_c = i_D = 7.09 \times 10^{-7} \cos 5000t \ (\text{A})$

13.25. 0.192 A

13.26. $5.32 \times 10^5 \ \text{A/m}^2$

13.27. 0.048 V ($x = 0$ end is positive)

13.28. $0.048 \sin kz$ (V)

13.29. (*a*) $-7.5 \cos 10^4 t$ (V);
(*b*) $-7.5 \cos 10^4 t - 2.25 \sin 10^4 t$ (V)

13.30. 15 mA (counterclockwise)

13.31. 0.613 mA, 2.75 mA

13.32. $5.03 \times 10^{-2} \sin 40\pi t$ (A)

13.33. 12.6 mV

13.34. 46.3 μW

13.35. 0.209 V

13.36. 1000 rev/min

13.37. See Fig. 13-22.

13.38. See problem 13.16.

13.39. 1.5×10^8 rad/s, 1.18 A/m

Fig. 13-22

Electromagnetic Waves

14.1 Introduction

Some wave solutions to Maxwell's equations have already been encountered in the Solved Problems of Chapter 13. The present chapter will extend the treatment of electromagnetic waves. Since most regions of interest are free of charge, it will be assumed that charge density $\rho = 0$. Moreover, linear isotropic materials will be assumed, with $\mathbf{D} = \epsilon\mathbf{E}$, $\mathbf{B} = \mu\mathbf{H}$, and $\mathbf{J} = \sigma\mathbf{E}$.

14.2 Wave Equations

With the above assumptions and with time dependence $e^{j\omega t}$ for both $\mathbf{E}$ and $\mathbf{H}$, Maxwell's equations (Table 13-1) become

$$\nabla \times \mathbf{H} = (\sigma + j\omega\epsilon)\mathbf{E} \tag{1}$$

$$\nabla \times \mathbf{E} = -j\omega\mu\mathbf{H} \tag{2}$$

$$\nabla \cdot \mathbf{E} = 0 \tag{3}$$

$$\nabla \cdot \mathbf{H} = 0 \tag{4}$$

Taking the curl of (1) and (2),

$$\nabla \times (\nabla \times \mathbf{H}) = (\sigma + j\omega\epsilon)(\nabla \times \mathbf{E})$$

$$\nabla \times (\nabla \times \mathbf{E}) = -j\omega\mu(\nabla \times \mathbf{H})$$

Now, *in Cartesian coordinates only*, the Laplacian of a vector

$$\nabla^2\mathbf{A} \equiv (\nabla^2 A_x)\mathbf{a}_x + (\nabla^2 A_y)\mathbf{a}_y + (\nabla^2 A_z)\mathbf{a}_z$$

satisfies the identity

$$\nabla \times (\nabla \times \mathbf{A}) = \nabla(\nabla \cdot \mathbf{A}) - \nabla^2\mathbf{A}$$

Substitution for the "curl curls" and use of (3) and (4) yields the *vector wave equations*

$$\nabla^2\mathbf{H} = j\omega\mu(\sigma + j\omega\epsilon)\mathbf{H} \equiv \gamma^2\mathbf{H}$$

$$\nabla^2\mathbf{E} = j\omega\mu(\sigma + j\omega\epsilon)\mathbf{E} \equiv \gamma^2\mathbf{E}$$

The *propagation constant* γ is that square root of γ^2 whose real and imaginary parts are positive:

$$\gamma = \alpha + j\beta$$

with

$$\alpha = \omega \sqrt{\frac{\mu\epsilon}{2} \left(\sqrt{1 + \left(\frac{\sigma}{\omega\epsilon}\right)^2} - 1 \right)} \qquad (5)$$

$$\beta = \omega \sqrt{\frac{\mu\epsilon}{2} \left(\sqrt{1 + \left(\frac{\sigma}{\omega\epsilon}\right)^2} + 1 \right)} \qquad (6)$$

14.3   Solutions in Cartesian Coordinates

The familiar scalar wave equation in one dimension,

$$\frac{\partial^2 F}{\partial z^2} = \frac{1}{u^2} \frac{\partial^2 F}{\partial t^2}$$

has solutions of the form $F = f(z - ut)$ and $F = g(z + ut)$, where f and g are arbitrary functions. These represent waves traveling with speed u in the $+z$ and $-z$ directions, respectively. In Fig. 14-1 the first solution is shown at $t = 0$ and $t = t_1$; the wave has advanced in the $+z$ direction a distance of ut_1 in the time interval t_1. For the particular choices

$$f(x) = Ce^{-j\omega x/u} \qquad \text{and} \qquad g(x) = De^{+j\omega x/u}$$

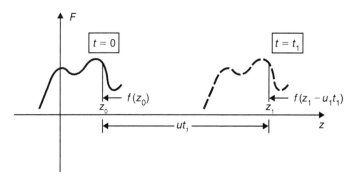

Fig. 14-1

harmonic waves of angular frequency ω are obtained:

$$F = Ce^{j(\omega t - \beta z)} \qquad \text{and} \qquad F = De^{j(\omega t + \beta z)}$$

in which $\beta \equiv \omega/u$. Of course, the real and imaginary parts are also solutions to the wave equation. One of these solutions, $F = C \sin(\omega t - \beta z)$, is shown in Fig. 14-2 at $t = 0$ and $t = \pi/2\omega$. In this interval the wave has advanced in the *positive* z direction a distance $d = u(\pi/2\omega) = \pi/2\beta$. At any fixed t, the waveform repeats itself when x changes by $2\pi/\beta$; the distance

$$\lambda \equiv \frac{2\pi}{\beta}$$

is called the *wavelength*. The wavelength and the *frequency* $f \equiv \omega/2\pi$ enjoy the relation

$$\lambda f = u \qquad \text{or} \qquad \lambda = Tu$$

where $T \equiv 1/f = 2\pi/\omega$ is the *period* of the harmonic wave.

The vector wave equations of Section 14.2 have solutions similar to those just discussed. Because the unit vectors $\mathbf{a}_x$, $\mathbf{a}_y$, and $\mathbf{a}_z$ in Cartesian coordinates have fixed directions, the wave equation for $\mathbf{H}$ can be rewritten in the form

$$\frac{\partial^2 \mathbf{H}}{\partial x^2} + \frac{\partial^2 \mathbf{H}}{\partial y^2} + \frac{\partial^2 \mathbf{H}}{\partial z^2} = \gamma^2 \mathbf{H}$$

Fig. 14-2

14.4 Plane Waves

Of particular interest are solutions (*plane waves*) that depend on only one spatial coordinate, say z. Then the equation becomes

$$\frac{d^2 \mathbf{H}}{dz^2} = \gamma^2 \mathbf{H}$$

which, for an assumed time dependence $e^{j\omega t}$, is the vector analog of the one-dimensional scalar wave equation. Solutions are as above, in terms of the propagation constant γ.

$$\mathbf{H}(z, t) = \mathbf{H}_0 e^{\pm \gamma z} e^{j\omega t} \mathbf{a}_H$$

The corresponding solutions for the electric field are

$$\mathbf{E}(z, t) = E_0 e^{\pm \gamma z} e^{j\omega t} \mathbf{a}_E$$

The fixed unit vectors $\mathbf{a}_H$ and $\mathbf{a}_E$ are orthogonal and neither field has a component in the direction of propagation. This being the case, one can rotate the axes to put one of the fields, say $\mathbf{E}$, along the x axis. Then from Maxwell's equation (2) it follows that $\mathbf{H}$ will lie along the $\pm y$ axis for propagation in the $\pm z$ direction.

EXAMPLE 1. Given the field $\mathbf{E} = E_0 e^{-\gamma z} \mathbf{a}_E$ (time dependence suppressed), show that $\mathbf{E}$ can have no component in the propagation direction, $+\mathbf{a}_z$.
The Cartesian components of $\mathbf{a}_E$ are found by projection:

$$\mathbf{E} = E_0 e^{-\gamma z}[(\mathbf{a}_E \cdot \mathbf{a}_x)\mathbf{a}_x + (\mathbf{a}_E \cdot \mathbf{a}_y)\mathbf{a}_y + (\mathbf{a}_E \cdot \mathbf{a}_z)\mathbf{a}_z]$$

From $\nabla \cdot \mathbf{E} = 0$,

$$\frac{\partial}{\partial z} E_0 e^{-\gamma z}(\mathbf{a}_E \cdot \mathbf{a}_z) = 0$$

which can hold only if $\mathbf{a}_E \cdot \mathbf{a}_z = 0$. Consequently, E has no component in $\mathbf{a}_z$.
The plane wave solutions obtained above depend on the properties μ, ϵ, and σ of the medium, because these properties are involved in the propagation constant γ.

14.5   Solutions for Partially Conducting Media

For a region in which there is some but not much conductivity (e.g., moist earth, seawater), the solution to the wave equation in **E** is taken to be

$$\mathbf{E} = E_0 e^{-\gamma z} \mathbf{a}_x$$

Then, from (2) of Section 14.2,

$$\mathbf{H} = \sqrt{\frac{\sigma + j\omega\epsilon}{j\omega\mu}} E_0 e^{-\gamma z} \mathbf{a}_y$$

The ratio E/H is characteristic of the medium (it is also frequency-dependent). More specifically for waves $\mathbf{E} = E_x \mathbf{a}_x$, $\mathbf{H} = H_y \mathbf{a}_y$ which propagate in the $+z$ direction, the *intrinsic impedance*, η, of the medium is defined by

$$\eta = \frac{E_x}{H_y}$$

Thus,

$$\eta = \sqrt{\frac{j\omega\mu}{\sigma + j\omega\epsilon}}$$

where the correct square root may be written in polar form, $|\eta|\underline{/\theta}$, with

$$|\eta| = \frac{\sqrt{\mu/\epsilon}}{\sqrt[4]{1 + \left(\frac{\sigma}{\omega\epsilon}\right)^2}}, \qquad \tan 2\theta = \frac{\sigma}{\omega\epsilon} \qquad \text{and} \qquad 0° < \theta < 45°$$

(If the wave propagates in the $-z$ direction, $E_x/H_y = -\eta$. In effect, γ is replaced by $-\gamma$ and the other square root used.)

Inserting the time factor $e^{j\omega t}$ and writing $\gamma = \alpha + j\beta$ results in the following equations for the fields in a partially conducting region:

$$\mathbf{E}(z,t) = E_0 e^{-\alpha z} e^{j(\omega t - \beta z)} \mathbf{a}_x$$

$$\mathbf{H}(z,t) = \frac{E_0}{|\eta|} e^{-\alpha z} e^{j(\omega t - \beta z - \theta)} \mathbf{a}_y$$

The factor $e^{-\alpha z}$ attenuates the magnitudes of both **E** and **H** as they propagate in the $+z$ direction. The expression for α, (5) of Section 14.2, shows that there will be some attenuation unless the conductivity σ is zero, which would be the case only for perfect dielectrics or free space. Likewise, the phase difference θ between $\mathbf{E}(z,t)$ and $\mathbf{H}(z,t)$ vanishes only when σ is zero.

The velocity of propagation and the wavelength are given by

$$u = \frac{\omega}{\beta} = \frac{1}{\sqrt{\frac{\mu\epsilon}{2}\left(\sqrt{1 + \left(\frac{\sigma}{\omega\epsilon}\right)^2} + 1\right)}}$$

$$\lambda = \frac{2\pi}{\beta} = \frac{2\pi}{\omega\sqrt{\frac{\mu\epsilon}{2}\left(\sqrt{1 + \left(\frac{\sigma}{\omega\epsilon}\right)^2} + 1\right)}}$$

If the propagation velocity is known, $\lambda f = u$ may be used to determine the wavelength λ. The term $(\sigma/\omega\epsilon)^2$ has the effect of reducing both the velocity and the wavelength from what they would be in either free space or perfect dielectrics, where $\sigma = 0$. Observe that the medium is *dispersive*: waves with different frequencies ω have different velocities u.

14.6 Solutions for Perfect Dielectrics

For a perfect dielectric, $\sigma = 0$, and so

$$\alpha = 0 \qquad \beta = \omega\sqrt{\mu\epsilon} \qquad \eta = \sqrt{\frac{\mu}{\epsilon}}\ \underline{/0°}$$

Since $\alpha = 0$, there is no attenuation of the **E** and **H** waves. The zero angle on η results in **H** being in time phase with **E** at each fixed location. Assuming **E** in $\mathbf{a}_x$ and propagation in $\mathbf{a}_z$, the field equations may be obtained as the limits of those in Section 14.5

$$\mathbf{E}(z, t) = E_0 e^{j(\omega t - \beta z)}\mathbf{a}_x$$

$$\mathbf{H}(z, t) = \frac{E_0}{\eta}\ e^{j(\omega t - \beta z)}\mathbf{a}_y$$

The velocity and the wavelength are

$$u = \frac{\omega}{\beta} = \frac{1}{\sqrt{\mu\epsilon}} \qquad \lambda = \frac{2\pi}{\beta} = \frac{2\pi}{\omega\sqrt{\mu\epsilon}}$$

Solutions in Free Space.

Free space is nothing more than the perfect dielectric for which

$$\mu = \mu_0 = 4\pi \times 10^{-7}\ \text{H/m} \qquad \epsilon = \epsilon_0 = 8.854 \times 10^{-12}\ \text{F/m} \approx \frac{10^{-9}}{36\pi}\ \text{F/m}$$

For free space, $\eta = \eta_0 \approx 120\pi\ \Omega$ and $u = c \approx 3 \times 10^8$ m/s.

14.7 Solutions for Good Conductors; Skin Depth

Materials are ordinarily classified as good conductors if $\sigma \gg \omega\epsilon$ in the range of practical frequencies. Therefore, the propagation constant and the intrinsic impedance are

$$\gamma = \alpha + j\beta \qquad \alpha = \beta = \sqrt{\frac{\omega\mu\sigma}{2}} = \sqrt{\pi f\mu\sigma} = \eta = \sqrt{\frac{\omega\mu}{\sigma}}\ \underline{/45°}$$

It is seen that for all conductors the **E** and **H** waves are attenuated. Numerical examples will show that this is a very rapid attenuation. α will always be equal to β. At each fixed location **H** is out of time phase with **E** by 45° or $\pi/4$ rad. Once again assuming **E** in $\mathbf{a}_x$ and propagation in $\mathbf{a}_z$, the field equations are, from Section 14.5,

$$\mathbf{E}(z, t) = E_0 e^{-\alpha z}e^{j(\omega t - \beta z)}\ \mathbf{a}_x \qquad \mathbf{H}(z, t) = \frac{E_0}{|\eta|}e^{-\alpha z}e^{j(\omega t - \beta z - \pi/4)}\mathbf{a}_y$$

Moreover,

$$u = \frac{\omega}{\beta} = \sqrt{\frac{2\omega}{\mu\sigma}} = \omega\delta \qquad \lambda = \frac{2\pi}{\beta} = \frac{2\pi}{\sqrt{\pi f\mu\sigma}} = 2\pi\delta$$

The velocity and wavelength in a conducting medium are written here in terms of the *skin depth* or *depth of penetration*,

$$\delta \equiv \frac{1}{\sqrt{\pi f \mu \sigma}}$$

EXAMPLE 2.   Assume a field $\mathbf{E} = 1.0e^{-\alpha z}e^{j(\omega t - \beta z)}\mathbf{a}_x$ (V/m), with $f = \omega/2\pi = 100$ MHz, at the surface of a copper conductor, $\sigma = 58$ MS/m, located at $z > 0$, as shown in Fig. 14-3. Examine the attenuation as the wave propagates into the conductor.

Fig. 14-3

At depth z the magnitude of the field is

$$|\mathbf{E}| = 1.0e^{-\alpha z} = 1.0e^{-z/\delta}$$

where

$$\delta = \frac{1}{\sqrt{\pi f \mu \sigma}} = 6.61 \quad \mu\text{m}$$

Thus, after just 6.61 micrometers the field is attenuated to $e^{-1} = 36.8\%$ of its initial value. At 5δ or 33 micrometers, the magnitude is 0.67% of its initial value—practically zero.

14.8   Interface Conditions at Normal Incidence

When a traveling wave reaches an interface between two different regions, it is partly reflected and partly transmitted, with the magnitudes of the two parts determined by the constants of the two regions. In Fig. 14-4, a traveling $\mathbf{E}$ wave approaches the interface $z = 0$ from region *1*, $z < 0$. $\mathbf{E}^i$ and $\mathbf{E}^r$ are at $z = -0$, while $\mathbf{E}^t$ is at $z = +0$ (in region 2). Here, *i* signifies "incident," *r* "reflected" and *t* "transmitted." Normal incidence is assumed. The equations for $\mathbf{E}$ and $\mathbf{H}$ can be written as

$$\mathbf{E}^i(z,t) = E_0^i e^{-\gamma_1 z}e^{j\omega t}\mathbf{a}_x$$

$$\mathbf{E}^r(z,t) = E_0^r e^{-\gamma_1 z}e^{j\omega t}\mathbf{a}_x$$

$$\mathbf{E}^t(z,t) = E_0^t e^{-\gamma_2 z}e^{j\omega t}\mathbf{a}_x$$

$$\mathbf{H}^i(z,t) = H_0^i e^{-\gamma_1 z}e^{j\omega t}\mathbf{a}_y$$

$$\mathbf{H}^r(z,t) = H_0^r e^{\gamma_1 z}e^{j\omega t}\mathbf{a}_y$$

$$\mathbf{H}^t(z,t) = H_0^t e^{-\gamma_2 z}e^{j\omega t}\mathbf{a}_y$$

One of the six constants—it is almost always E_0^i—may be taken as real. Under the interface conditions about to be derived, one or more of the remaining five may turn out to be complex.

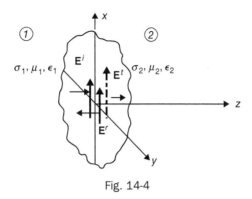

Fig. 14-4

With normal incidence, **E** and **H** are entirely tangential to the interface, and thus are continuous across it. At $z = 0$ this implies

$$E_0^i + E_0^r = E_0^t \qquad H_0^i + H_0^r = H_0^t$$

Furthermore, the intrinsic impedance in either region is equal to $\pm E_x/H_y$ (see Section 14.5).

$$\frac{\mathbf{E}_0^i}{H_0^i} = \eta_1 \qquad \frac{\mathbf{E}_0^r}{H_0^r} = -\eta_1 \qquad \frac{\mathbf{E}_0^t}{H_0^t} = \eta_2$$

The five equations above can be combined to produce the following ratios in terms of the intrinsic impedances:

$$\frac{E_0^r}{E_0^i} = \frac{\eta_2 - \eta_1}{\eta_1 + \eta_2} \qquad \frac{H_0^r}{H_0^i} = \frac{\eta_1 - \eta_2}{\eta_1 + \eta_2}$$

$$\frac{E_0^t}{E_0^i} = \frac{2\eta_2}{\eta_1 + \eta_2} \qquad \frac{H_0^t}{H_0^i} = \frac{2\eta_1}{\eta_1 + \eta_2}$$

The intrinsic impedances for various materials were examined earlier. They are repeated here for reference.

$$\text{partially conducting medium:} \qquad \eta = \sqrt{\frac{j\omega\mu}{\sigma + j\omega\epsilon}}$$

$$\text{conducting medium:} \qquad \eta = \sqrt{\frac{\omega\mu}{\sigma}} \; \underline{/45^\circ}$$

$$\text{perfect dielectric:} \qquad \eta = \sqrt{\frac{\mu}{\epsilon}}$$

$$\text{free space:} \qquad \eta_0 = \sqrt{\frac{\mu_0}{\epsilon_0}} \approx 120\pi \; \Omega$$

EXAMPLE 3. Traveling **E** and **H** waves in free space (region *1*) are normally incident on the interface with a perfect dielectric (region *2*) for which $\epsilon_r = 3.0$. Compare the magnitudes of the incident, reflected, and transmitted **E** and **H** waves at the interface.

$$\eta_1 = \eta_0 = 120\pi \; \Omega \qquad\qquad \eta_2 = \sqrt{\frac{\mu}{\epsilon}} = \frac{120\pi}{\sqrt{\epsilon_r}} = 217.7 \; \Omega$$

$$\frac{E_0^r}{E_0^i} = \frac{\eta_2 - \eta_1}{\eta_1 + \eta_2} = -0.268 \qquad \frac{H_0^r}{H_0^i} = \frac{\eta_1 - \eta_2}{\eta_1 + \eta_2} = 0.268$$

$$\frac{E_0^t}{E_0^i} = \frac{2\eta_2}{\eta_1 + \eta_2} = 0.732 \qquad \frac{H_0^t}{H_0^i} = \frac{2\eta_1}{\eta_1 + \eta_2} = 1.268$$

14.9   Oblique Incidence and Snell's Laws

An incident wave that approaches a plane interface between two different media generally will result in a transmitted wave in the second medium and a reflected wave in the first. The *plane of incidence* is the plane containing the incident wave normal and the local normal to the interface; in Fig. 14-5 this is the *xz* plane. The normals to the reflected and transmitted waves also lie in the plane of incidence. The *angle of incidence* θ_i, the *angle of reflection* θ_r, and the *angle of transmission* θ_t—all defined as in Fig. 14-5—obey *Snell's law of reflection*,

$$\theta_i = \theta_r$$

and *Snell's law of refraction*,

$$\frac{\sin \theta_i}{\sin \theta_t} = \sqrt{\frac{\mu_2 \epsilon_2}{\mu_1 \epsilon_1}}$$

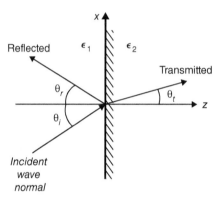

Fig. 14-5

EXAMPLE 4.   A wave is incident at an angle of 30° from air to Teflon, $\epsilon_r = 2.1$. Calculate the angle of transmission, and repeat with an interchange of the regions.
   Since $\mu_1 = \mu_2$,

$$\frac{\sin \theta_i}{\sin \theta_t} = \frac{\sin 30°}{\sin \theta_t} = \sqrt{\frac{\epsilon_{r2}}{\epsilon_{r1}}} = \sqrt{2.1} \quad \text{or} \quad \theta_t = 20.18°$$

From Teflon to air,

$$\frac{\sin 30°}{\sin \theta_t} = \frac{1}{\sqrt{2.1}} \quad \text{or} \quad \theta_t = 46.43°$$

Supposing both media of the same permeability, propagation from the optically denser medium ($\epsilon_1 > \epsilon_2$) results in $\theta_t > \theta_i$. As θ_i increases, an angle of incidence will be reached that results in $\theta_t = 90°$. At this *critical angle* of incidence, instead of a wave being transmitted into the second medium there will be a wave that propagates along the surface. The critical angle is given by

$$\theta_c = \sin^{-1} \sqrt{\frac{\epsilon_{r2}}{\epsilon_{r1}}}$$

EXAMPLE 5.   The critical angle for a wave propagating from Teflon into free space is

$$\theta_c = \sin^{-1} \frac{1}{\sqrt{2.1}} = 43.64°$$

14.10   Perpendicular Polarization

The orientation of the electric field **E** with respect to the plane of incidence determines the *polarization* of a wave at the interface between two different regions. In *perpendicular* polarization, **E** is perpendicular to the plane of incidence (the *xz* plane in Fig. 14-6) and is thus parallel to the (planar) interface. At the interface,

$$\frac{E_0^r}{E_0^i} = \frac{\eta_2 \cos \theta_i - \eta_1 \cos \theta_t}{\eta_2 \cos \theta_i + \eta_1 \cos \theta_t}$$

and

$$\frac{E_0^t}{E_0^i} = \frac{2\eta_2 \cos \theta_i}{\eta_2 \cos \theta_i + \eta_1 \cos \theta_t}$$

Note that for normal incidence, $\theta_i = \theta_t = 0°$ and the expressions reduce to those found in Section 14.9.

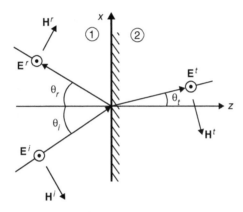

Fig. 14-6

It is not difficult to show that if $\mu_1 = \mu_2$,

$$\eta_2 \cos \theta_i - \eta_1 \cos \theta_t \neq 0 \qquad \text{for any } \theta_i$$

Hence, a perpendicularly polarized incident wave suffers either partial or total reflection.

14.11   Parallel Polarization

For *parallel* polarization, the electric field vector **E** lies entirely within the plane of incidence, the *xz* plane as shown in Fig. 14-7. (Thus **E** assumes the role played by **H** in perpendicular polarization.) At the interface,

$$\frac{E_0^r}{E_0^i} = \frac{\eta_2 \cos \theta_t - \eta_1 \cos \theta_i}{\eta_1 \cos \theta_i + \eta_2 \cos \theta_t}$$

and

$$\frac{E_0^t}{E_0^i} = \frac{2\eta_2 \cos \theta_i}{\eta_1 \cos \theta_i - \eta_2 \cos \theta_t}$$

In contrast to perpendicular polarizations, if $\mu_1 = \mu_2$ there will be a particular angle of incidence for which there is no reflected wave. This *Brewster angle* is given by

$$\theta_B = \tan^{-1} \sqrt{\frac{\epsilon_2}{\epsilon_1}}$$

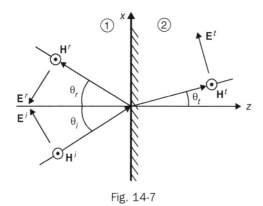

Fig. 14-7

EXAMPLE 6.   The Brewster angle for a parallel-polarized wave traveling from air into glass for which $\epsilon_r = 5.0$ is

$$\theta_B = \tan^{-1} \sqrt{5.0} = 65.91°$$

14.12   Standing Waves

When waves traveling in a perfect dielectric ($\sigma_1 = \alpha_1 = 0$) are normally incident on the interface with a perfect conductor ($\sigma_2 = \infty$, $\eta_2 = 0$), the reflected wave in combination with the incident wave produces a *standing wave*. In such a wave, which is readily demonstrated on a clamped taut string, the oscillations at all points of a half-wavelength interval are in time phase. The combination of incident and reflected waves may be written

$$\mathbf{E}(z, t) = [E_0^i e^{j(\omega t - \beta z)} + E_0^r e^{j(\omega t - \beta z)}]\mathbf{a}_x = e^{j\omega t}(E_0^i e^{-j\beta z} + E_0^r e^{j\beta z})\mathbf{a}_x$$

Since $\eta_2 = 0$, $E_0^r / E_0^i = -1$ and

$$\mathbf{E}(z, t) = e^{j\omega t}(E_0^i e^{-j\beta z} - E_0^i e^{j\beta z})\mathbf{a}_x = -2jE_0^i \sin \beta z\, e^{j\omega t}\mathbf{a}_x$$

Taking the real part,

$$\mathbf{E}(z, t) = 2E_0^i \sin \beta z \sin \omega t\, \mathbf{a}_x$$

The standing wave is shown in Fig. 14-8 at time intervals of $T/8$, where $T = 2\pi/\omega$ is the period. At $t = 0$, $\mathbf{E} = \mathbf{0}$ everywhere; at $t = 1(T/8)$, the endpoints of the $\mathbf{E}$ vectors lie on sine curve *1*; at $t = 2(T/8)$, they lie on sine curve *2*; and so forth. Sine curves *2* and *6* form an envelope for the oscillations; the amplitude of this envelope is twice the amplitude of the incident wave. Note that adjacent half-wavelength segments are 180° out of phase with each other.

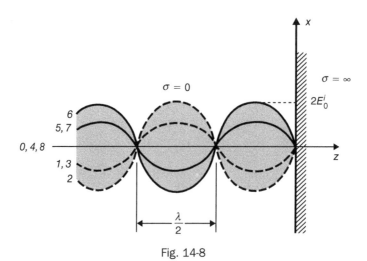

Fig. 14-8

14.13 Power and the Poynting Vector

Maxwell's first equation for a region with conductivity σ is written and then $\mathbf{E}$ is dotted with each term

$$\nabla \times \mathbf{H} = \sigma \mathbf{E} + \epsilon \frac{\partial \mathbf{E}}{\partial t}$$

$$\mathbf{E} \cdot (\nabla \times \mathbf{H}) = \sigma E^2 + \mathbf{E} \cdot \epsilon \frac{\partial \mathbf{E}}{\partial t}$$

where, as usual, $E^2 = \mathbf{E} \cdot \mathbf{E}$. The vector identity $\nabla \cdot (\mathbf{A} \times \mathbf{B}) = \mathbf{B} \cdot (\nabla \times \mathbf{A}) - \mathbf{A} \cdot (\nabla \times \mathbf{B})$ is employed to change the left side of the equation.

$$\mathbf{H} \cdot (\nabla \times \mathbf{E}) - \nabla \cdot (\mathbf{E} \times \mathbf{H}) = \sigma E^2 + \mathbf{E} \cdot \epsilon \frac{\partial \mathbf{E}}{\partial t}$$

By Maxwell's second equation,

$$\mathbf{H} \cdot (\nabla \times \mathbf{E}) = \mathbf{H} \cdot \left(-\mu \frac{\partial \mathbf{H}}{\partial t} \right) = -\frac{\mu}{2} \frac{\partial H^2}{\partial t}$$

Similarly,

$$\mathbf{E} \cdot \epsilon \frac{\partial \mathbf{E}}{\partial t} = \frac{\epsilon}{2} \frac{\partial E^2}{\partial t}$$

Substituting and rearranging terms,

$$\sigma E^2 = -\frac{\epsilon}{2} \frac{\partial E^2}{\partial t} - \frac{\mu}{2} \frac{\partial H^2}{\partial t} - \nabla \cdot (\mathbf{E} \times \mathbf{H})$$

Integration of this equation throughout an arbitrary volume v gives

$$\int_v \sigma E^2 \, dv = -\int_v \left(\frac{\epsilon}{2} \frac{\partial E^2}{\partial t} + \frac{\mu}{2} \frac{\partial H^2}{\partial t} \right) dv - \oint_S (\mathbf{E} \times \mathbf{H}) \cdot d\mathbf{S}$$

where the last term has been converted to an integral over the surface of v by use of the divergence theorem.

The integral on the left has the units of watts and is the usual ohmic term representing energy dissipated per unit time as heat. This dissipated energy has its source in the integrals on the right. Because $\epsilon E^2/2$ and $\mu H^2/2$ are the densities of energy stored in the electric and magnetic fields, respectively, the volume integral (including the minus sign) gives the decrease in this stored energy. Consequently, the surface integral (including the minus sign) must be the rate of energy entering the volume from outside. A change of sign then produces the *instantaneous rate of energy leaving the volume*:

$$P(t) = \oint_S (\mathbf{E} \times \mathbf{H}) \cdot d\mathbf{S} = \oint_S \mathcal{P} \cdot d\mathbf{S}$$

where $\mathcal{P} = \mathbf{E} \times \mathbf{H}$ is the *Poynting vector*, the instantaneous rate of energy flow per unit area at a point.

In the cross product that defines the Poynting vector, the fields are supposed to be in real form. If, instead, $\mathbf{E}$ and $\mathbf{H}$ are expressed in complex form and have the common time-dependence $e^{j\omega t}$, then the time-average of $\mathcal{P}$ is given by

$$\mathcal{P}_{\text{avg}} = \frac{1}{2} \operatorname{Re} (\mathbf{E} \times \mathbf{H}^*)$$

where $\mathbf{H}^*$ is the complex conjugate of $\mathbf{H}$. This follows the *complex power* of circuit analysis, $\mathbf{S} = \frac{1}{2} \mathbf{V} \mathbf{I}^*$, of which the power is the real part, $P = \frac{1}{2} \operatorname{Re} \mathbf{V} \mathbf{I}^*$.

For plane waves, the direction of energy flow is the direction of propagation. Thus, the Poynting vector offers a useful, coordinate-free way of specifying the direction of propagation, or of determining the directions of the fields if the direction of propagation is known. This can be particularly valuable where incident, transmitted, and reflected waves are being examined.

SOLVED PROBLEMS

14.1. A traveling wave is described by $y = 10 \sin(\beta z - \omega t)$. Sketch the wave at $t = 0$ and at $t = t_1$, when it has advanced $\lambda/8$, if the velocity is 3×10^8 m/s and the angular frequency $\omega = 10^6$ rad/s. Repeat for $\omega = 2 \times 10^6$ rad/s and the same t_1.

The wave advances λ in one period, $T = 2\pi/\omega$. Hence,

$$t_1 = \frac{T}{8} = \frac{\pi}{4\omega}$$

$$\frac{\lambda}{8} = ct_1 = (3 \times 10^8)\frac{\pi}{4(10^6)} = 236 \text{ m}$$

The wave is shown at $t = 0$ and $t = t_1$ in Fig. 14-9(*a*). At twice the frequency, the wavelength λ is one-half, and the phase shift constant β is twice the former value. See Fig. 14-9(*b*). At t_1 the wave has also advanced 236 m, but this distance is now $\lambda/4$.

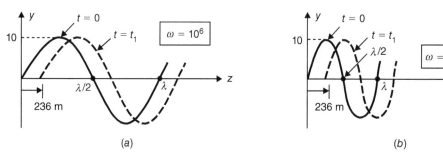

(a)   (b)

Fig. 14-9

14.2. In free space, $\mathbf{E}(z, t) = 10^3 \sin(\omega t - \beta z)\mathbf{a}_y$ (V/m). Obtain $\mathbf{H}(z, t)$.

Examination of the phase, $\omega t - \beta z$, shows that the direction of propagation is $+z$. Since $\mathbf{E} \times \mathbf{H}$ must also be in the $+z$ direction, $\mathbf{H}$ must have the direction $-\mathbf{a}_x$. Consequently,

$$\frac{E_y}{-H_x} = \eta_0 = 120\pi \ \ \Omega \quad \text{or} \quad H_x = -\frac{10^3}{120\pi}\sin(\omega t - \beta z) \quad \text{(A/m)}$$

and

$$\mathbf{H}(z, t) = -\frac{10^3}{120\pi}\sin(\omega t - \beta z)\mathbf{a}_x \quad \text{(A/m)}$$

14.3. For the wave of Problem 14.2 determine the propagation constant γ, given that the frequency is $f = 95.5$ MHz.

In general, $\gamma = \sqrt{j\omega\mu(\sigma + j\omega\epsilon)}$. In free space, $\sigma = 0$ so that

$$\gamma = j\omega\sqrt{\mu_0\epsilon_0} = j\left(\frac{2\pi f}{c}\right) = j\frac{2\pi(95.5 \times 10^6)}{3 \times 10^8} = j(2.0)\text{m}^{-1}$$

Note that this result shows that the attenuation factor is $\alpha = 0$ and the phase-shift constant is $\beta = 2.0$ rad/m.

14.4. Examine the field

$$\mathbf{E}(z, t) = 10 \sin(\omega t + \beta z)\mathbf{a}_x + 10 \cos(\omega t + \beta z)\mathbf{a}_y$$

in the $z = 0$ plane, for $\omega t = 0$, $\pi/4$, $\pi/2$, $3\pi/4$, and π.

The computations are presented in Table 14-1.

TABLE 14-1

ωt	$E_x = 10 \sin \omega t$	$E_y = \cos \omega t$	$\mathbf{E} = E_x \mathbf{a}_x + E_y \mathbf{a}_y$
0	0	10	$10\mathbf{a}_y$
$\dfrac{\pi}{4}$	$\dfrac{10}{\sqrt{2}}$	$\dfrac{10}{\sqrt{2}}$	$10\left(\dfrac{\mathbf{a}_x + \mathbf{a}_y}{\sqrt{2}}\right)$
$\dfrac{\pi}{2}$	10	0	$10\mathbf{a}_x$
$\dfrac{3\pi}{4}$	$\dfrac{10}{\sqrt{2}}$	$\dfrac{-10}{\sqrt{2}}$	$10\left(\dfrac{\mathbf{a}_x - \mathbf{a}_y}{\sqrt{2}}\right)$
π	0	-10	$10(-\mathbf{a}_y)$

As shown in Fig. 14-10, $\mathbf{E}(x, t)$ is circularly polarized. In addition, the wave travels in the $-\mathbf{a}_z$ direction.

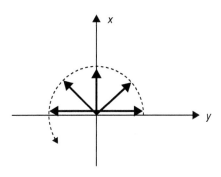

Fig. 14-10

14.5. An $\mathbf{H}$ field travels in the $-\mathbf{a}_z$ direction in free space with a phase-shift constant of 30.0 rad/m and an amplitude of $(1/3\pi)$ A/m. If the field has the direction $-\mathbf{a}_y$ when $t = 0$ and $z = 0$, write suitable expressions for $\mathbf{E}$ and $\mathbf{H}$. Determine the frequency and wavelength.

In a medium of conductivity σ, the intrinsic impedance η, which relates E and H, would be complex, and so the phase of $\mathbf{E}$ and $\mathbf{H}$ would have to be written in complex form. In free space this restriction is unnecessary. Using cosines,

$$\mathbf{H}(z, t) = -\frac{1}{3\pi} \cos{(\omega t + \beta z)} \mathbf{a}_y$$

For propagation in the $-z$ direction,

$$\frac{E_x}{H_y} = -\eta_0 = -120\pi \quad \Omega \qquad \text{or} \qquad E_x = +40 \cos{(\omega t + \beta z)} \quad \text{(V/m)}$$

Thus, $$\mathbf{E}(z, t) = 40 \cos(\omega t + \beta z) \mathbf{a}_x \quad \text{(V/m)}$$

Since $\beta = 30$ rad/m,

$$\lambda = \frac{2\pi}{\beta} = \frac{\pi}{15} \text{m} \qquad \text{or} \qquad f = \frac{c}{\lambda} = \frac{3 \times 10^8}{\pi/15} = \frac{45}{\pi} \times 10^8 \text{ Hz}$$

14.6. Determine the propagation constant γ for a material having $\mu_r = 1$, $\epsilon_r = 8$, and $\sigma = 0.25$ pS/m, if the wave frequency is 1.6 MHz.

In this case,

$$\frac{\sigma}{\omega\epsilon} = \frac{0.25\times10^{-12}}{2\pi(1.6\times10^6)(8)(10^{-9}/36\pi)} \approx 10^{-9} \approx 0$$

so that

$$\alpha \approx 0 \quad \beta \approx \omega\sqrt{\mu\epsilon} = 2\pi f\frac{\sqrt{\mu_r\epsilon_r}}{c} = 9.48\times10^{-2} \text{ rad/m}$$

and $\gamma = \alpha + j\beta \approx j9.48\times10^{-2}$ m^{-1}. The material behaves like a perfect dielectric at the given frequency. Conductivity of the order of 1 pS/m indicates that the material is more like an insulator than a conductor.

14.7. Determine the conversion factor between the neper and the decibel.

Consider a plane wave traveling in the $+z$ direction whose amplitude decays according to

$$E = E_0 e^{-\alpha z}$$

From Section 14.13, the power carried by the wave is proportional to E^2, so that

$$P = P_0 e^{-2\alpha z}$$

Then, by definition of the decibel, the power drop over the distance z is $10\log_{10}(P_0/P)$ dB. But

$$10\log_{10}\frac{P_0}{P} = \frac{10}{2.3026}\ln\frac{P_0}{P} = \frac{20}{2.3026}(\alpha z) = 8.686(\alpha z)$$

Thus, αz nepers is equivalent to $8.686(\alpha z)$ decibels; i.e.,

$$1 \text{ Np} = 8.686 \text{ dB}$$

14.8. At what frequencies may the earth be considered a perfect dielectric, if $\sigma = 5\times10^{-3}$ S/m, $\mu_r = 1$, and $\epsilon_r = 8$? Can α be assumed zero at these frequencies?

Assume arbitrarily that

$$\frac{\sigma}{\omega\epsilon} \leq \frac{1}{100}$$

marks the cutoff. Then

$$f = \frac{\omega}{2\pi} \geq \frac{100\sigma}{2\pi\epsilon} = 1.13 \text{ GHz}$$

For small $\sigma/\omega\epsilon$,

$$\alpha = \omega\sqrt{\frac{\mu\epsilon}{2}\left(\sqrt{1+\left(\frac{\sigma}{\omega\epsilon}\right)^2}-1\right)}$$

$$\approx \omega\sqrt{\frac{\mu\epsilon}{2}\left[\frac{1}{2}\left(\frac{\sigma}{\omega\epsilon}\right)^2\right]} = \frac{\sigma}{2}\sqrt{\frac{\mu}{\epsilon}} = \frac{\sigma}{2}\sqrt{\frac{\mu_r}{\epsilon_r}}(120\pi) = 0.333 \text{ Np/m}$$

Thus, no matter how high the frequency, α will be about 0.333 Np/m, or almost 3 db/m (see Problem 14.7); α cannot be assumed zero.

14.9. Find the skin depth δ at a frequency of 1.6 MHz in aluminum, where $\sigma = 38.2$ MS/m and $\mu_r = 1$. Also find γ and the wave velocity u.

$$\delta = \frac{1}{\sqrt{\pi f \mu \sigma}} = 6.44 \times 10^{-5}\,\text{m} = 64.4\ \mu\text{m}$$

Because $\alpha = \beta = \delta^{-1}$,

$$\gamma = 1.55 \times 10^4 + j1.55 \times 10^4 = 2.20 \times 10^4 \angle 45°\ (\text{m}^{-1})$$

and

$$u = \frac{\omega}{\beta} = \omega \delta = 647\ (\text{m/s})$$

14.10. A perpendicularly polarized wave propagates from region *1* ($\epsilon_{r1} = 8.5$, $\mu_{r1} = 1$, $\sigma_1 = 0$) to region 2, free space, with an angle of incidence of 15°. Given $E_0^i = 1.0\ \mu$V/m, find: E_0^r, E_0^t, H_0^i, H_0^r, and H_0^t.

The intrinsic impedances are

$$\eta_1 = \frac{\eta_0}{\sqrt{\epsilon_{r1}}} = \frac{120}{\sqrt{8.5}} = 129\ \ \Omega \qquad \text{and} \qquad \eta_2 = \eta_0 = 120\pi\ \ \Omega$$

and the angle of transmission is given by

$$\frac{\sin 15°}{\sin \theta_t} = \sqrt{\frac{\epsilon}{8.5 \epsilon_0}} \quad \text{or} \quad \theta_t = 48.99°$$

Then

$$\frac{E_0^r}{E_0^i} = \frac{\eta_2 \cos \theta_i - \eta_1 \cos \theta_t}{\eta_2 \cos \theta_i + \eta_1 \cos \theta_t} = 0.623 \quad \text{or} \quad E_0^r = 0.623\ \mu\text{V/m}$$

$$\frac{E_0^t}{E_0^i} = \frac{2\eta_2 \cos \theta_i}{\eta_2 \cos \theta_i + \eta_1 \cos \theta_t} = 1.623 \quad \text{or} \quad E_0^t = 1.623\ \mu\text{V/m}$$

Finally, $H_0^i = E_0^i/\eta_1 = 7.75$ n A/m, $H_{0^r} = 4.83$ nA/m, and $H_0^t = 4.31$ nA/m.

14.11. Calculate the intrinsic impedance η, the propagation constant γ, and the wave velocity u at a frequency $f = 100$ MHz for a conducting medium in which $\sigma = 58$ MS/m and $\mu_r = 1$

$$\gamma = \sqrt{\omega \mu \sigma}\ \underline{|45°} = 2.14 \times 10^5\ \underline{|45°}\ \text{m}^{-1}$$

$$\eta = \sqrt{\frac{\omega \mu}{\sigma}}\ \underline{|45°} = 3.69 \times 10^{-3}\ \underline{|45°}\ \Omega^{-1}$$

$$\alpha = \beta = 1.51 \times 10^5 \qquad \delta = \frac{1}{\alpha} = 6.61\ \mu\text{m} \qquad u = \omega \delta = 4.15 \times 10^3\ \text{m/s}$$

14.12. A plane wave traveling in the +z direction in free space ($z < 0$) is normally incident at $z = 0$ on a conductor ($z > 0$) for which $\sigma = 61.7$ MS/m, $\mu_r = 1$. The free-space **E** wave has a frequency $f = 1.5$ MHz and an amplitude of 1.0 V/m; at the interface it is given by

$$\mathbf{E}(0, t) = 1.0 \sin 2\pi f t\, \mathbf{a}_y\ \ (\text{V/m})$$

Find $\mathbf{H}(z, t)$ for $z > 0$.

For $z > 0$, in complex form,

$$\mathbf{E}(z, t) = 1.0 e^{-\alpha z}\, e^{j(2\pi f t - \beta z)} \mathbf{a}_y\ \ (\text{V/m})$$

where the imaginary part will ultimately be taken. In the conductor,

$$\alpha = \beta = \sqrt{\pi f \sigma} = \sqrt{\pi(1.5\times10^6)(4\pi\times10^{-7})(61.7\times10^6)} = 1.91\times10^4$$

$$\eta = \sqrt{\frac{\omega\mu}{\sigma}}\underline{|45°} = 4.38\times10^{-4}e^{j\pi/4}$$

Then, since $E_y/(-H_x) = \eta$,

$$\mathbf{H}(z,t) = -2.28\times10^3 e^{-\alpha z}\,e^{j(2\pi ft-\beta z-\pi/4)}\mathbf{a}_x \quad (\text{A/m})$$

or, taking the imaginary part,

$$\mathbf{H}(z,t) = -2.28\times10^3 e^{-\alpha z}\sin(2\pi ft-\beta z-\pi/4)\,\mathbf{a}_x\ (\text{A/m})$$

where f, α, and β are as given above.

14.13. In free space, $\mathbf{E}(z,t) = 50\cos(\omega t - \beta z)\mathbf{a}_x$ (V/m). Find the average power crossing a circular area of radius 2.5 m in the plane z = const.

In complex form,

$$\mathbf{E} = 50e^{j(\omega t-\beta z)}\mathbf{a}_x \quad (\text{V/m})$$

and since $\eta = 120\pi\,\Omega$ and propagation is in the $+z$ direction,

$$\mathbf{H} = \frac{5}{12\pi}e^{j(\omega t-\beta z)}\mathbf{a}_y \quad (\text{A/m})$$

Then,

$$\mathcal{P}_{avg} = \frac{1}{2}\text{Re}(\mathbf{E}\times\mathbf{H}^*) = \frac{1}{2}(50)\left(\frac{5}{12\pi}\right)\mathbf{a}_z \ \text{W/m}^2$$

The flow is normal to the area, and so

$$P_{avg} = \frac{1}{2}(50)\left(\frac{5}{12\pi}\right)\pi(2.5)^2 = 65.1 \ \text{W}$$

14.14 A voltage source, v, is connected to a pure resistor R by a length of coaxial cable, as shown in Fig. 14-11(a). Show that use of the Poynting vector $\mathcal{P}$ in the dielectric leads to the same instantaneous power in the resistor as methods of circuit analysis.

Fig. 14-11

From Problem 8.9 and Ampère's law,

$$E = \frac{v}{r \ln (b/a)} \mathbf{a}_r \quad \text{and} \quad H = \frac{i}{2\pi r} \mathbf{a}_\phi$$

where a and b are the radii of the inner and outer conductors, as shown in Fig. 14-11 (b). Then

$$\mathcal{P} = \mathbf{E} \times \mathbf{H} = \frac{vi}{2\pi r^2 \ln (b/a)} \mathbf{a}_z$$

This is the instantaneous power density. The total instantaneous power over the cross section of the dielectric is

$$P(t) = \int_0^{2\pi} \int_a^b \frac{vi}{2\pi r^2 \ln (b/a)} \mathbf{a}_z \cdot r\, dr\, d\phi \, \mathbf{a}_z = vi$$

which is also the circuit-theory result for the instantaneous power loss in the resistor.

14.15. Determine the amplitudes of the reflected and transmitted **E** and **H** fields at the interface shown in Fig. 14-12, if $E_0^i = 1.5 \times 10^{-3}$ V/m in region 1, in which $\epsilon_{r1} = 8.5$, $\mu_{r1} = 1$, and $\sigma_1 = 0$. Region 2 is free space. Assume normal incidence.

$$\eta_1 = \sqrt{\frac{\mu_0 \mu_{r1}}{\epsilon_0 \epsilon_{r1}}} = 129\ \Omega \qquad \eta_2 = 120\pi\ \Omega = 377\ \Omega$$

$$E_0^r = \frac{\eta_2 - \eta_1}{\eta_2 + \eta_1} E_0^i = 7.35 \times 10^{-4}\ \text{V/m}$$

$$E_0^t = \frac{2\eta_2}{\eta_2 + \eta_1} E_0^i = 2.24 \times 10^{-3}\ \text{V/m}$$

$$H_0^i = \frac{E_0^i}{\eta_1} = 1.16 \times 10^{-5}\ \text{A/m}$$

$$H_0^r = \frac{\eta_1 - \eta_2}{\eta_1 + \eta_2} H_0^i = -5.69 \times 10^{-6}\ \text{A/m}$$

$$H_0^t = \frac{2\eta_1}{\eta_1 + \eta_2} H_0^i = 5.91 \times 10^{-6}\ \text{A/m}$$

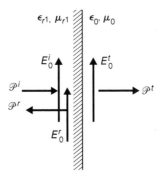

Fig. 14-12

14.16. The amplitude of $\mathbf{E}^i$ in free space (region 1) at the interface with region 2 is 1.0 V/m. If $H_0^r = -1.41 \times 10^{-3}$ A/m, $\epsilon_{r2} = 18.5$, and $\sigma_2 = 0$, find μ_{r2}.

From

$$\frac{E_0^r}{H_0^r} = -120\pi\ \Omega = -377\ \Omega \quad \text{and} \quad \frac{E_0^r}{E_0^i} = \frac{\eta_2 - 377}{377 + \eta_2}$$

$$\frac{E_0^i}{H_0^r} = \frac{1.0}{-1.41 \times 10^{-3}} = \frac{-377\,(377 + \eta_2)}{\eta_2 - 377} \quad \text{or} \quad \eta_2 = 1234\ \Omega$$

Then
$$1234 = \sqrt{\frac{\mu_0 \mu_{r2}}{\epsilon_0 (18.5)}} \quad \text{or} \quad \mu_{r2} = 198.4$$

14.17. A normally incident **E** field has amplitude $E_0^i = 1.0$ V/m in free space just outside of seawater in which $\epsilon_r = 80$, $\mu_r = 1$, and $\sigma = 2.5$ S/m. For a frequency of 30 MHz, at what depth will the amplitude of **E** be 1.0 m V/m?

Let the free space be region *1* and the seawater be region *2*.

$$\eta_1 = 377\ \Omega \qquad \eta_2 = 9.73\underline{/43.5^\circ}\ \Omega$$

Then the amplitude of **E** just inside the seawater is E_0^t.

$$\frac{E_0^t}{E_0^i} = \frac{2\eta_2}{\eta_1 + \eta_2} \quad \text{or} \quad E_0^t = 5.07 \times 10^{-2}\ \text{V/m}$$

From
$$\gamma = \sqrt{j\omega\mu(\sigma + j\omega\epsilon)} = 24.36\ \underline{/46.53^\circ}\ \text{m}^{-1}$$
$$a = 24.36 \cos 46.53^\circ = 16.76\ \text{Np/m}$$

Then, from

$$10^{-3} = (5.07 \times 10^{-2}) e^{-16.76z}$$

$z = 0.234$ m.

14.18. A traveling **E** field in free space, of amplitude 100 V/m, strikes a sheet of silver of thickness 5 μm, as shown in Fig. 14-13. Assuming $\sigma = 61.7$ MS/m and a frequency $f = 200$ MHz, find the amplitudes $|E_2|$, $|E_3|$, and $|E_4|$.

Fig. 14-13

For the silver sheet at 200 MHz, $\eta = 5.06 \times 10^{-3}\underline{/45^\circ}\ \Omega$.

$$\frac{E_2}{E_1} = \frac{2(5.06 \times 10^{-3}\ \underline{/45^\circ})}{377 + 5.06 \times 10^{-3}\ \underline{/45^\circ}} \quad \text{whence} \quad |E_2| \approx 2.68 \times 10^{-3}\,\text{V/m}$$

Within the conductor,

$$\alpha = \beta = \sqrt{\pi f \mu \sigma} = 2.21 \times 10^5$$

Thus, in addition to attenuation there is phase shift as the wave travels through the conductor. Since $|E_3|$ and $|E_4|$ represent maximum values of the sinusoidally varying wave, this phase shift is not involved.

$$|E_3| = |E_2| e^{-\alpha z} = (2.68 \times 10^{-3})e^{-(2.21 \times 10^5)(5 \times 10^{-6})} = 8.88 \times 10^{-4} \text{ V/m}$$

and $\quad \dfrac{E_4}{E_3} = \dfrac{2(377)}{377 + 5.06 \times 10^{-3} \, \underline{/45°}} \quad$ whence $\quad |E_4| \approx 1.78 \times 10^{-3}$ V/m

SUPPLEMENTARY PROBLEMS

14.19. Given

$$\mathbf{E}(z, t) = 10^3 \sin(6 \times 10^8 t - \beta z) \, \mathbf{a}_y \text{ (V/m)}$$

in free space, sketch the wave at $t = 0$ and at time t_1 when it has traveled $\lambda/4$ along the z axis. Find t_1, β, and λ.

14.20. In free space,

$$\mathbf{H}(z, t) = 1.0e^{j(1.5 \times 10^8 t + \beta z)}\mathbf{a}_x \quad \text{(A/m)}$$

Obtain an expression for $\mathbf{E}(z, t)$ and determine the propagation direction.

14.21. In free space,

$$\mathbf{H}(z, t) = 1.33 \times 10^{-1} \cos(4 \times 10^7 t - \beta z)\mathbf{a}_x \text{(A/m)}$$

Obtain an expression for $\mathbf{E}(z, t)$. Find β and λ.

14.22. A traveling wave has a velocity of 10^6 m/s and is described by

$$y = 10 \cos(2.5z + \omega t)$$

Sketch the wave as a function of z at $t = 0$ and $t = t_1 = 0.838 \ \mu s$. What fraction of a wavelength is traveled between these two times?

14.23. Find the magnitude and direction of

$$\mathbf{E}(z, t) = 10 \sin(\omega t - \beta z)\mathbf{a}_x - 15 \sin(\omega t - \beta z)\mathbf{a}_y \text{ (V/m)}$$

at $t = 0$, $z = 3\lambda/4$.

14.24. Determine γ at 500 kHz for a medium in which $\mu_r = 1$, $\epsilon_r = 15$, $\sigma = 0$. At what velocity will an electromagnetic wave travel in this medium?

14.25. An electromagnetic wave in free space has a wavelength of 0.20 m. When this same wave enters a perfect dielectric, the wavelength changes to 0.09 m. Assuming that $\mu_r = 1$, determine ϵ_r and the wave velocity in the dielectric.

14.26. An electromagnetic wave in free space has a phase-shift constant of 0.524 rad/m. The same wave has a phase-shift constant of 1.81 rad/m upon entering a perfect dielectric. Assuming that $\mu_r = 1$, find ϵ_r and the velocity of propagation.

14.27. Find the propagation constant at 400 MHz for a medium in which $\epsilon_r = 16$, $\mu_r = 4.5$, and $\sigma = 0.6$ S/m. Find the ratio of the velocity u to the free-space velocity c.

14.28. In a partially conducting medium, $\epsilon_r = 18.5$, $\mu_r = 800$, and $\sigma = 1$ S/m. Find α, β, η, and the velocity u, for a frequency of 10^9 Hz. Determine $\mathbf{H}(z, t)$, given

$$\mathbf{E}(z, t) = 50.0e^{-\alpha z} \cos(\omega t - \beta z)\mathbf{a}_y \text{ (V/m)}$$

14.29. For silver, $\sigma = 3.0$ MS/m. At what frequency will the depth of penetration δ be 1 mm?

14.30. At a certain frequency in copper ($\sigma = 58.0$ MS/m) the phase-shift constant is 3.71×10^5 rad/m. Determine the frequency.

14.31. The amplitude of **E** just inside a liquid is 10.0 V/m and the constants are $\mu_r = 1$, $\epsilon_r = 20$, and $\sigma = 0.50$ S/m. Determine the amplitude of **E** at a distance of 10 cm inside the medium for frequencies of (*a*) 5 MHz, (*b*) 50 MHz, and (*c*) 500 MHz.

14.32. In free space, $\mathbf{E}(z, t) = 1.0 \sin (\omega t - \beta z)\mathbf{a}_x$ (V/m). Show that the average power crossing a circular disk of radius 15.5 m in a $z = $ const. plane is 1 W.

14.33. In spherical coordinates, the *spherical wave*

$$\mathbf{E} = \frac{100}{r} \sin \theta \cos (\omega t - \beta r)\mathbf{a}_\theta \quad \text{(V/m)} \qquad \mathbf{H} = \frac{0.265}{r} \sin \theta \cos (\omega t - \beta r) \, \mathbf{a}_\phi \quad \text{(A/m)}$$

represents the electromagnetic field at large distances r from a certain dipole antenna in free space. Find the average power crossing the hemispherical shell $r = 1$ km, $0 \le \theta \le \pi/2$.

14.34. In free space, $\mathbf{E}(z, t) = 150 \sin (\omega t - \beta z)\mathbf{a}_x$ (V/m). Find the total power passing through a rectangular area, of sides 30 mm and 15 mm, in the $z = 0$ plane.

14.35. A free space-silver interface has $E_0^i = 100$ V/m on the free-space side. The frequency is 15 MHz and the silver constants are $\epsilon_r = \mu_r = 1$ and $\sigma = 61.7$ MS/m. Determine E_0^r and E_0^t at the interface.

14.36. A free space-conductor interface has $H_0^i = 1.0$ A/m on the free-space side. The frequency is 31.8 MHz and the conductor constants are $\epsilon_r = \mu_r = 1$ and $\sigma = 1.26$ MS/m. Determine H_0^r and H_0^t and the depth of penetration of $\mathbf{H}^t$.

14.37. A traveling **H** field in free space, of amplitude 1.0 A/m and frequency 200 MHz, strikes a sheet of silver of thickness 5 μm with $\sigma = 61.7$ MS/m, as shown in Fig. 14-14. Find H_0^t just beyond the sheet.

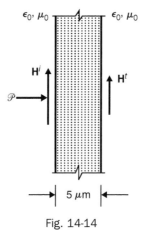

Fig. 14-14

14.38. A traveling **E** field in free space, of amplitude 100 V/m, strikes a perfect dielectric, as shown in Fig. 14-15. Determine E_0^t.

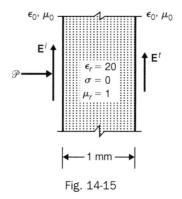

Fig. 14-15

14.39. A traveling **E** field in free space strikes a partially conducting medium, as shown in Fig. 14-16. Given a frequency of 500 MHz and $E_0^i = 100$ V/m, determine E_0^t and H_0^t.

Fig. 14-16

14.40. A wave propagates from a dielectric medium to the interface with free space. If the angle of incidence is the critical angle of 20°, find the relative permittivity.

14.41. Compute the ratios E_0^r/E_0^i and E_0^t/E_0^i for normal incidence and for oblique incidence at $\theta_i = 10°$. For region 1, assume $\epsilon_{r1} = 8.5$, $\mu_{r1} = 1$, and $\sigma_1 = 0$. Region 2 is free space.

14.42. A parallel-polarized wave propagates from air into a dielectric at a Brewster's angle of 75°. Find ϵ_r.

ANSWERS TO SUPPLEMENTARY PROBLEMS

14.19. $t_1 = 2.62$ *ns*, $\beta = 2$ rad/m, $\lambda = \pi$m. See Fig. 14-17.

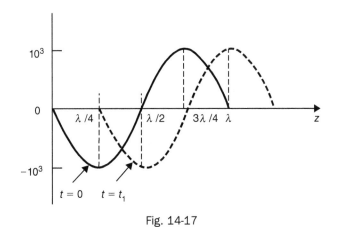

Fig. 14-17

14.20. $E_0 = 377$ V/m, $-\mathbf{u}_z$

14.21. $E_0 = 50$V/m, $\left(\dfrac{4}{30}\right)$ rad/m, 15π m

14.22. $\dfrac{1}{3}$. See Fig. 14.18.

Fig. 14-18

14.23. 18.03 V/m, $0.555\mathbf{a}_x - 0.832\mathbf{a}_y$

14.24. $j4.06 \times 10^{-2}$ m^{-1}, 7.74×10^7 m/s

14.25. 4.94, 1.35×10^8 m/s

14.26. 11.9, 8.69×10^7 m/s

14.27. 99.58 $\underline{/60.34°}$ m^{-1}, 0.097

14.28. 1130 Np/m, 2790 rad/m, 2100 $\underline{/22.1°}$ Ω, 2.25×10^6 m/s, $2.38 \times 10^{-2} e^{-\alpha z} \cos{(\omega t - 0.386 - \beta z)} (-\mathbf{a}_x)$ (A/m)

14.29. 84.4 kHz

14.30. 601 MHz

14.31. (*a*)   7.32 V/m;   (*b*)   3.91 V/m;   (*c*)   1.42 V/m

14.33. 55.5 W

14.34. 13.4 mW

14.35. -100 V/m, $7.35 \times 10^{-4} \underline{/45°}$ V/m

14.36. 1.0 A/m, 2.0 A/m, 80 μm

14.37. 1.78×10^{-5} A/m

14.38. 59.7 V/m

14.39. 19.0 V/m, 0.0504 A/m

14.40. 8.55

14.41. For normal incidence, $E_0^i/E_0^r = 0.490$ and $E_0^t/E_0^i = 1.490$. At 10°, $E_0^r/E_0^i = 0.539$ and $E_0^t/E_0^i = 1.539$.

14.42. 13.93

CHAPTER 15

Transmission Lines

(with contributions by Milton L. Kult)

15.1 Introduction

Unguided propagation of electromagnetic energy was investigated in Chapter 14. In this chapter the transmission of energy will be studied when the waves are guided by two conductors in a dielectric medium. Exact analysis of this two-conductor *transmission line* requires field theory. However, the performance of the system can be predicted by modeling the transmission line with distributed parameters and using voltages and currents associated with the electric and magnetic fields.

Only *uniform* transmission lines will be considered; that is, the incremental distributed parameters shall be assumed constant along the line.

15.2 Distributed Parameters

The incremental distributed parameters per unit length of line are inductance and capacitance as determined in Chapters 8 and 12, the resistance of the conductors, and the conductance of the dielectric medium. It was seen that the parameters depend on the geometry of the configuration, the characteristics of the materials, and in some cases the frequency. In the following summary list the dependence on geometry is represented by a *geometrical factor* GF.

Capacitance.

$$C = \pi \epsilon_d (\text{GFC}) \quad \text{(F/m)} \qquad [\epsilon_d = \text{permittivity of dielectric}]$$

Conductance.

$$G = \frac{C}{\epsilon_d} \sigma_d \quad \text{(S/m)} \qquad [\sigma_d = \text{conductivity of dielectric}]$$

Inductance (external).

$$L_e = \frac{\mu_d}{\pi} (\text{GFL}) \quad \text{(H/m)} \qquad [\mu_d = \text{permeability of dielectric} \approx \mu_0]$$

DC Resistance (useful for operation up to 10 kHz).

$$R_d = \frac{1}{\sigma_c \pi} (\text{GFR}_d) \quad (\Omega/\text{m}) \qquad [\sigma_c = \text{conductivity of conductors}]$$

AC Resistance (for frequencies above 10 kHz).

$$R_a = \frac{1}{2\pi\sigma_c\delta}(\text{GFR}_a) \quad (\Omega/\text{m}) \quad \left[\delta = \frac{2}{\sqrt{\pi f \mu_c \sigma_c}} \equiv \text{skin depth}\right]$$

Inductance (internal).

$$L_i = \begin{cases} R_a/2\pi f & (\text{H/m}) & \text{for } f > 10 \text{ kHz} \\ \mu_0/4\pi & (\text{H/m}) & \text{for } f < 10 \text{ kHz} \end{cases}$$

Inductance (total).

$$L_t = L_e + L_i \approx L_e$$

For three common line configurations the geometrical factors are as follows:

Coaxial Line (inner radius a, outer radius b, outer thickness t).

$$\text{GFC} = \frac{2}{\ln(b/a)} \qquad\qquad \text{GFL} = \frac{1}{\text{GFC}}$$

$$\text{GFR}_d = \frac{1}{a^2} + \frac{1}{t(b+t)} \qquad \text{GFR}_a = \frac{1}{a} + \frac{1}{b} \quad \text{for } t \gg \delta$$

Parallel Wires (radius a, separation d).

$$\text{GFC} = \frac{1}{\text{GFL}} \qquad\qquad \text{GFL} = \cosh^{-1}\frac{d}{2a} \approx \ln\frac{d}{a} \quad \text{for } d \gg a$$

$$\text{GFR}_d = \frac{2}{a^2} \qquad\qquad \text{GFR}_a = \frac{2}{a}$$

Parallel Plates (width w, thickness t, separation d).

$$\text{GFC} = \frac{w}{\pi d} \qquad\qquad \text{GFL} = \frac{1}{\text{GFC}}$$

$$\text{GFR}_d = \frac{2\pi}{wt} \qquad\qquad \text{GFR}_a = \frac{4\pi}{w} \quad \text{for } t \gg \delta$$

15.3   Incremental Models

The model in Fig. 15-1, where R, L, G, and C are as given in Section 15.2, is the simplest incremental model of a two-conductor transmission line. It permits analysis of the line using voltages and currents at each cell in the model. For within a cell of length Δx, the voltages across the line at points a and b differ by

$$\Delta v(x,t) = (R\Delta x)i(x,t) + (L\Delta x)\frac{\partial i(x,t)}{\partial t} \tag{1-a}$$

Fig. 15-1

Likewise, the current at point c differs from that at b by

$$\Delta i(x,t) = (G\Delta x)v(x,t) + (C\Delta x)\frac{\partial v(x,t)}{\partial t} \qquad (1-b)$$

Other incremental models may also be used. They lead to the same transmission line equation as the one obtained in the next section.

15.4 Transmission Line Equation

The incremental equations for the model of Fig. 15–1 can be written as the following:

$$\frac{\Delta v(x,t)}{\Delta x} = Ri(x,t) + L\frac{\partial i(x,t)}{\partial t} \qquad (1-a)$$

$$\frac{\Delta i(x,t)}{\Delta x} = Gv(x,t) + C\frac{\partial v(x,t)}{\partial t} \qquad (1-b)$$

In the limit as $\Delta x \to 0$, the equations become first-order partial differential equations

$$\frac{\partial v(x,t)}{\partial x} = Ri(x,t) + L\frac{\partial i(x,t)}{\partial t} \qquad (2-a)$$

$$\frac{\partial i(x,t)}{\partial x} = Gv(x,t) + C\frac{\partial v(x,t)}{\partial t} \qquad (2-b)$$

The above two first-order partial differential equations imply a single second-order partial differential equation

$$\frac{\partial^2 f(x,t)}{\partial x^2} = RG\,f(x,t) + (RC+LG)\frac{\partial f(x,t)}{\partial t} + LC\frac{\partial^2 f(x,t)}{\partial t^2} \qquad (3)$$

whose $f(x,t)$ can be either $v(x,t)$ or $i(x,t)$. Equation (3) describes the behavior of the current and voltage at any point on the line. It is an equation of the hyperbolic type and very similar to the wave equation studied in Chapter 14. Thus, it is known in advance that the transmission lines support voltage and current waves which can be reflected and/or transmitted at discontinuities (sites of abrupt parameter changes) in the line. However, propagation of signals along the above transmission line is associated with i) attenuation (due to energy loss by R and G), and ii) dispersion (due to variation of wave velocity with frequency). A pulse propagating along the line becomes smaller and, as its frequency components travel at different velocities, the pulse shape stretches. On a line with multiple pulses each pulse interferes with its neighbors.

15.5 Impedance, Admittance, and Other Features of Interest

A transmission line system is a uniform medium that guides the propagation of electromagnetic waves and its equations may be derived from wave equations such as those in Chapter 14. The line supports the propagation of a wave in one direction and its possible reflection. From that point of view, one is concerned with features such as attenuation, phase, reflection, traveling and standing waves, propagation speed, dispersion, and power. From a second point of view, the line equation may be derived, as was done in the previous section, from element models (line characteristics R, L, G, and C), electrical variables (voltage and current), and circuit laws (KVL and KCL). In that sense one deals with features such as impedance, admittance, power transfer and loss, and open- and short-circuit conditions. These two groups of features are manifestations of the same physical phenomenon. They are interrelated and both are used in the analysis and design of transmission line systems. The features are most conveniently defined for the steady-state condition. Of particular interest are the following:

i)   Characteristic impedance of the line, which is $Z_0 \equiv \dfrac{\hat{V}^+}{\hat{I}^+} = \sqrt{\dfrac{R + j\omega L}{G + j\omega C}}$, where $\hat{V}^+$ and $\hat{I}^+$ are phasors representing voltage and current traveling in the + direction of the line. The inverse of Z_0 is the line's characteristic admittance. For a lossless line, $Z_0 = \sqrt{\dfrac{L}{C}} \equiv R_0$ is a constant, independent of operating frequency.

ii) Propagation constant, the exponent that specifies propagation in time and along the line, which is $\gamma = \sqrt{(R + jL\omega)(G + jC\omega)}$.

iii) Reflection coefficient at a point on the line, which is $\Gamma \equiv \dfrac{V_{\text{refl}}}{V_{\text{inc}}}$, where V_{refl} and V_{inc} are phasor representations of the reflected and incident voltages, respectively, at that point. The reflection coefficient at the receiving end of a line terminating on an impedance Z_R is $\Gamma_R = \dfrac{\hat{V}^-}{\hat{V}^+} = \dfrac{Z_R - Z_0}{Z_R + Z_0}$.

iv) Voltage standing-wave ratio, which is $VSWR \equiv \dfrac{\left|\hat{V}\right|_{\text{max}}}{\left|\hat{V}\right|_{\text{min}}}$ along the length of the line.

v)   Input impedance, which is $Z_{\text{in}} \equiv \dfrac{\hat{V}}{\hat{I}}$, where $\hat{V}$ and $\hat{I}$ are phasor representations of the voltage and current at the input terminal of the line.

These will be discussed in detail in sections that follow.

15.6 Sinusoidal Steady-State Excitation

When the transmission line of Fig. 15-1 is driven for a long time by a sinusoidal source (angular frequency ω), the voltage and current also become sinusoidal, with the same frequency:

$$v(x, t) = \text{Re}\,[\hat{V}(x)e^{j\omega t}] \qquad i(x, t) = \text{Re}\,[\hat{I}(x)e^{j\omega t}]$$

Here, the *phasors* $\hat{V}(x)$ and $\hat{I}(x)$ are generally complex-valued; often they are indicated in *polar form* (with the x-dependence suppressed) as

$$\hat{V} = \left|\hat{V}\right| \underline{/\phi_V} \qquad \hat{I} = \left|\hat{I}\right| \underline{/\phi_I}$$

where ϕ denotes the angle between the complex vector and the real axis. Steady-state analysis of the transmission line is much simplified when all voltages and currents are replaced by their phasor representations.

Fig. 15-2 models in the phasor domain a uniform line of length ℓ that is terminated in a (complex) load Z_R at the receiving end and is driven at the sending end by a generator with internal impedance Z_g and voltage $\hat{V}_g = V_{gm} \underline{/\theta}$. The per-unit-length series impedance and shunt admittance of the line are given by

$$Z = R + j\omega L \qquad Y = G + j\omega C$$

Distance from the receiving end is measured by the variable x; from the sending end, by d.

Fig. 15-2

Equations (2) and (3) of Section 4 become ODEs for the phasors $\hat{V}(x)$ and $\hat{I}(x)$.

$$\frac{d\hat{V}(x)}{dx} = (R + jL\omega)\hat{I}(x) = Z\hat{I}(x) \tag{2-a bis}$$

$$\frac{d\hat{I}(x)}{dx} = (G + jC\omega)\hat{V}(x) = Y\hat{V}(x) \tag{2-b bis}$$

$$\frac{d^2\hat{F}(x)}{dx^2} = \gamma^2\hat{F}(x) \tag{3 bis}$$

where $Z = R + jL\omega$, $Y = G + jC\omega$, and $\gamma = \sqrt{ZY} = \sqrt{(R + jL\omega)(G + jC\omega)} = \alpha + j\beta$ is called the propagation constant. The square root is chosen to make α and β both non-negative. Equation (3 *bis*) is identical in form to the equation of plane waves (Section 14.4); it has the following traveling-wave solutions

$$\hat{V}(x) = \hat{V}^+ e^{-\gamma x} + \hat{V}^- e^{\gamma x} = \hat{V}_{inc} + \hat{V}_{refl}$$

$$\hat{I}(x) = \hat{I}^+ e^{-\gamma x} + \hat{I}^- e^{\gamma x} = \hat{I}_{inc} + \hat{I}_{refl}$$

The coefficients $\hat{V}^+$, etc., are phasors independent of x that are interrelated by the *characteristic impedance* Z_0 and the *boundary reflection coefficient* Γ_R, defined as

$$Z_0 \equiv \frac{\hat{V}^+}{\hat{I}^+} = -\frac{\hat{V}^-}{\hat{I}^-} = \sqrt{\frac{Z}{Y}}$$

$$\Gamma_R \equiv \frac{\hat{V}^-}{\hat{V}^+} = -\frac{\hat{I}^-}{\hat{I}^+} = \frac{\hat{V}_{refl}(0)}{\hat{V}_{inc}(0)}$$

It is easy to express Γ_R in terms of the characteristic and load impedance:

$$\Gamma_R = \frac{Z_R - Z_0}{Z_R + Z_0}$$

Then, if a pointwise reflection coefficient is defined by

$$\Gamma(x) \equiv \frac{\hat{V}_{refl}(x)}{\hat{V}_{inc}(x)}$$

it follows that

$$\Gamma(x) = \Gamma_R e^{-2\gamma x} = \frac{Z_R - Z_0}{Z_R + Z_0} e^{-2\gamma x}$$

Similarly, if $Z(x) \equiv \hat{V}(x)/\hat{I}(x)$ is the pointwise impedance looking back to the receiving end ($x = 0$), then

$$Z(x) = Z_0 \frac{1 + \Gamma(x)}{1 - \Gamma(x)}$$

The conditions at the sending end [rerotate $\Gamma(\ell)$, etc., as Γ_S, etc.] are

$$Z_S = Z_0 \frac{1 + \Gamma_S}{1 - \Gamma_S}$$

$$\hat{V}_S = \hat{V}_g \frac{Z_S}{Z_S + Z_g}$$

$$\hat{I}_S = \frac{\hat{V}_S}{Z_S}$$

Average power received at the load and average power supplied to the sending end are calculated as

$$P_R = \frac{1}{2}\,\mathrm{Re}\,(\hat{V}_R\,\hat{I}_R^*) = \frac{1}{2}\left|\hat{I}_R\right|^2\,\mathrm{Re}\,(Z_R)$$

$$= P_{\mathrm{inc}}(x=0) - P_{\mathrm{refl}}(x=0)$$

$$P_S = \frac{1}{2}\,\mathrm{Re}\,(\hat{V}_S\,\hat{I}_S^*) = \frac{1}{2}\left|\hat{I}_S\right|^2\,\mathrm{Re}\,(Z_S)$$

15.7 Lossless Lines

A line is ideally lossless only when $R = G = 0$. In practice, at high frequencies for which $R \ll \omega L$ and $G \ll \omega C$ (e.g., above 1 MHz), the line is approximately lossless and (2) becomes

$$\frac{\partial v(x,t)}{\partial x} = L\frac{\partial i(x,t)}{\partial t} \qquad\qquad (4-a)$$

$$\frac{\partial i(x,t)}{\partial x} = C\frac{\partial v(x,t)}{\partial t} \qquad\qquad (4-b)$$

Combining the above two equations we obtain the following equation for the lossless transmission line:

$$\frac{\partial^2 f(x,t)}{\partial x^2} = LC\frac{\partial^2 f(x,t)}{\partial t^2} \qquad\qquad (5)$$

in which $f(x, t)$ can be either $v(x, t)$ or $i(x, t)$. This equation is precisely the one-dimensional scalar wave equation studied in Section 14.3.

In the sinusoidal steady-state parameters of the lossless line and propagation along it are simplified to

$$Z_0 = \sqrt{\frac{Z}{Y}} = \sqrt{\frac{R+j\omega L}{G+j\omega C}}\bigg|_{R=G=0} = \sqrt{\frac{L}{C}} = R_0$$

$$\gamma = \sqrt{ZY} = \sqrt{(R+j\omega L)(G+j\omega C)}\bigg|_{R=G=0} = j\omega\sqrt{LC} = j\beta,$$

$$u_p = \frac{\omega}{\beta} = \frac{1}{\sqrt{LC}} \quad\text{and}\quad \lambda = \frac{2\pi}{\beta} = \frac{1}{f\sqrt{LC}}$$

where, as always, u_p and λ denote phase velocity and wavelength.

For the ideal lossless line with $R = 0$ and $G = 0$, the reflection coefficient is of constant magnitude.

$$\Gamma(x) = \Gamma_R e^{-j2\beta x} = \left|\frac{Z_R - R_0}{Z_R + R_0}\right|\,\underline{/\phi_R - 2\beta x}$$

where ϕ_R is the polar angle of Γ_R. The voltage is given by

$$\hat{V}(x) = \hat{V}^+(1 + \Gamma_R\,\underline{/-2\beta x})$$

which implies

$$\left|\hat{V}\right|_{\max} = \left|\hat{V}^+\right|(1+|\Gamma_R|) \qquad \left|\hat{V}\right|_{\min} = \left|\hat{V}^+\right|(1-|\Gamma_R|)$$

Adjacent maxima and minima are separated by $\beta x = 90°$, or one-quarter wavelength. For the resulting wave the *voltage standing-wave ratio*, VSWR, is defined as

$$\mathrm{VSWR} \equiv \frac{\left|\hat{V}\right|_{\max}}{\left|\hat{V}\right|_{\min}} = \frac{1+|\Gamma_R|}{1-|\Gamma_R|}$$

For the small-dissipation line the VSWR can still be used if a correction is made for the attenuation.

Some other parameters of lossless transmission are also discussed in Section 1.15.

15.8 The Smith Chart

Analysis and design of transmission line systems involve working with inter-related parameters such as imped-ance, admittance, voltage reflection coefficient, voltage standing wave ratio, propagation constant, and power. These parameters are in general complex numbers and entail lengthy calculations if an analytic solution is used.

The Smith Chart (Fig. 15-3) is a graphical tool that circumvents analytic solutions, thus saving much labor and time. At its core is the graphical mapping from the complex z-plane onto the Gamma-plane using the follow-ing transformation:

$$\Gamma(x) = \frac{z(x)-1}{z(x)+1} \quad \text{where} \quad z(x) \equiv r(x) + j\chi(x)$$

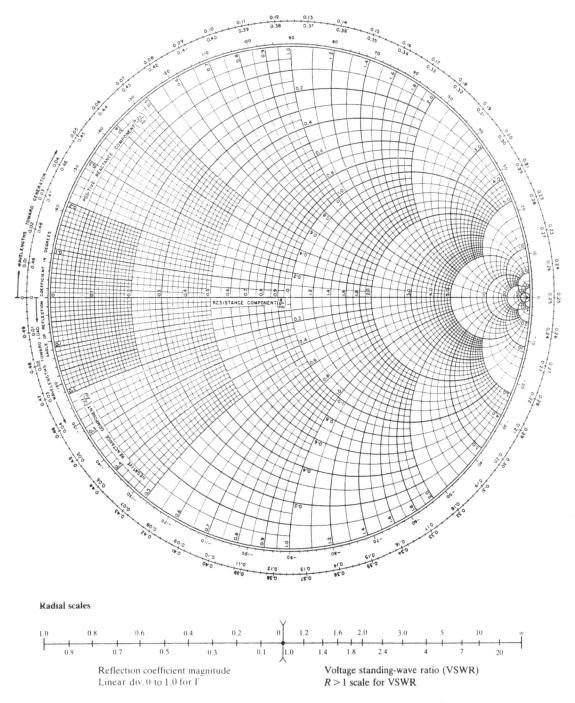

Radial scales

Reflection coefficient magnitude
Linear div. 0 to 1.0 for Γ

Voltage standing-wave ratio (VSWR)
$R > 1$ scale for VSWR

Fig. 15-3 Smith Chart: normalized resistance and reactance coordinates.

Lines of constant r in the z domain get mapped onto circles centered on the real axis in the Γ domain [Fig. 15-4(b)]. Similarly, lines of constant χ get mapped onto circles centered on the imaginary axis [Fig. 15-4(c)]. The Smith Chart is used mainly for solving lossless transmission lines ($\alpha = 0$), or lines at high frequencies with $R \ll L\omega$ and $G \ll C\omega$ (where $\alpha \approx 0$). The characteristic impedance of such a line is shown by a positive real number R_0. When solving transmission line problems $z(x)$ is the point-wise impedance of a line looking back toward the receiving end, normalized by the line characteristic impedance and is related to $\Gamma(x)$ by

$$z(x) = \frac{Z(x)}{R_0} \equiv r(x) + j\chi(x) = \frac{1+\Gamma(x)}{1-\Gamma(x)}$$

The reflection coefficient at a point x along the line is $\Gamma(x) = \Gamma_R e^{-j2\beta x}$. The input impedance of the line (at the sending end in Fig. 15-2, $x = \ell$) is

$$Z_{in} = R_0 \frac{1+\Gamma_R e^{-j2\beta\ell}}{1-\Gamma_R e^{-j2\beta\ell}}$$

The complete Smith Chart of Fig. 15-3 is obtained by superposing Figs. 15-4(b) and (c). The circles of constant $|\Gamma|$ are not included; instead the value of $|\Gamma|$ corresponding to a point (r, χ) is read off the left-hand external scale. The value of the VSWR is read from the right-hand scale. The two circumferential distance scales are in fractions of a wavelength. From $r = 0$, $\chi = 0$, the outer scale goes clockwise *toward the generator* (i.e., measures

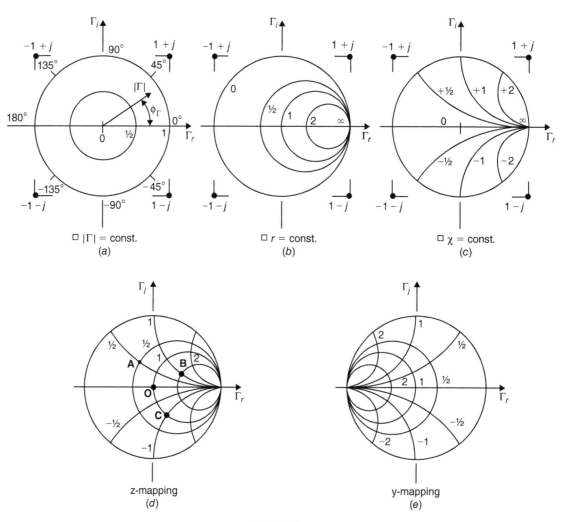

Fig. 15-4

TABLE **15-1**

CONDITION	Γ	r	χ
Open-circuit	$1\underline{/0°}$	∞ (arbitrary)	arbitrary (∞)
Short-circuit	$1\underline{/180°}$	0	0
Pure reactance	$1\underline{/\pm90°}$	0	±1
Matched line	0	1	1

x/λ), and the inner one counterclockwise *toward the load* (i.e., measures d/λ). Once around the chart is one-half wavelength. The third circumferential scale gives $\phi_\Gamma = \phi_R - 2\beta x$.

The chart can be used for normalized admittances,

$$\frac{Y(x)}{G_0} \equiv y(x) \equiv g(x) + jb(x)$$

where r-circles are used for g, χ-arcs are used for b, the angle of Γ for a given y is $180° + \phi_\Gamma$, and the point $y = 0 + j0$ is an open-circuit.

EXAMPLE 1. Consider a lossless line with $R_0 = 50\,\Omega$ feeding a load $Z_R = 25 + j25$. The line is 25 cm long and operates at $\lambda = 2$ m. Find the input impedance of the line (at the sending end) and its reflection coefficient.

Solution. The normalized load impedance is $z_R = 0.5 + j0.5$. On the chart we first locate the intersection point of the curves of $r = 0.5$ and $\chi = 0.5$. The intersection is shown by point A on Fig. 15-4(d). The vector OA represents the reflection coefficient at the load. From the chart we read its magnitude and phase to obtain $\Gamma_R = 0.44\angle 116°$. The reflection coefficient at the sending end of the line is

$$\Gamma_S = \Gamma_R e^{-j2\beta\ell}, \quad 2\beta\ell = 2\frac{2\pi}{\lambda}\ell = \frac{\pi}{2}, \quad \Gamma_S = 0.44\angle 116 - 90° = 0.44\angle 26°$$

Γ_S is obtained by a 90° clockwise rotation of Γ_R. The result is shown by point B on the chart. The vector OB is $\Gamma_S = 0.44\angle 26°$. Point B is also the intersection of constant resistance and reactance curves representing input impedance, from which we find $r = 2$ and $\chi = 1$. The input impedance of the line is therefore $Z_{in} = R_0(r + j\chi) = 100 + j50$.

Analytical solution:

$$\Gamma_R = \frac{z_R - 1}{z_R + 1} = \frac{-0.5 + j0.5}{1.5 + j0.5} = \frac{-1 + j}{3 + j} = 0.447\angle 116.56$$

$$\Gamma_S = \Gamma_R e^{-j\frac{\pi}{2}} = -j\frac{-1 + j}{3 + j} = \frac{1 + j}{3 + j} = 0.447\angle 26.56$$

$$Z_{in} = R_0 \frac{1 + \Gamma_S}{1 - \Gamma_S} = 50(2 + j) = 100 + j50$$

EXAMPLE 2. Repeat Example 1 for a line that is 50 cm long.

Solution. The reflection coefficient at the load is the same as in Example 1. It is $\Gamma_R = 0.44\angle 116°$ at point A on Fig. 15-4(d). Rotate it in the clockwise direction by $2\beta\ell = \pi$ to obtain $\Gamma_S = -\Gamma_R = 0.44\angle -64°$, as represented by point C on the chart of Fig. 15-4(d) with $r = 1$ and $\chi = -1$. The input impedance of the line is therefore $Z_{in} = 50 - j50$.

Analytical solution:

$$\Gamma_R = \frac{z_R - 1}{z_R + 1} = \frac{-0.5 + j0.5}{1.5 + j0.5} = \frac{-1 + j}{3 + j} = 0.447\angle 116.56°$$

$$\Gamma_S = \Gamma_R e^{-j\pi} = \frac{1 - j}{3 + j} = 0.447\angle -63.44°$$

$$Z_{in} = 50(1 - j) = 50 - j50$$

15.9   Admittance Plane

Admittance is the inverse of impedance. The characteristic admittance of a line is the inverse of its characteristic impedance, $Y_0 = \dfrac{1}{Z_0}$. The admittance of a load Y normalized by the characteristic admittance of the line is

$$y \equiv \frac{Y}{Y_0} = \frac{Z_0}{Z} = \frac{1}{z},\ \text{where } z \text{ is the normalized load impedance.}$$

It is a complex number shown by $y = g + jb$. g is called the normalized conductance (always non-negative) and b is called the normalized susceptance (positive if capacitive, and negative if inductive).

When loads, and networks, are in parallel, it is convenient to work with their admittances. The Smith Chart can be used to solve transmission line equations that employ admittances. The Smith Chart is based on this relationship:

$$\Gamma = \frac{z-1}{z+1} = \frac{\frac{1}{y}-1}{\frac{1}{y}+1} = -\frac{y-1}{y+1}$$

The chart may be looked at as a mapping from the z-plane or y-plane onto the Γ-plane. (We will call them separately a z-mapping or a y-mapping.) The y-mapping, shown in Fig. 15-4(e), produces the mirror image, with respect to the center, of the z-mapping. Some charts combine the mappings from both the z and y planes into a single graph. A z-y chart is a powerful tool but may look confusing at first.

Admittance problems, however, may be solved using the z-plane chart of Fig. 15-3 only. Constant r curves become constant g curves; constant χ curves become constant b curves; $\Gamma(z)$ becomes $-\Gamma(y)$.

EXAMPLE 3.   Consider a lossless line with characteristic impedance $R_0 = 50\,\Omega$ feeding a load characterized by the admittance $Y_R = 0.01 + j0.01$. The line is 50 cm long and operates at $\lambda = 2\,\text{m}$. Find the input admittance of the line (at the sending end) and its reflection coefficient.

Solution.   The normalized load admittance is $y_R = R_0 Y_R = 50(0.01 + j0.01) = 0.5 + j0.5$. On the chart of Fig. 15-4(d) change r to g and χ to b. The constant-conductance curves are now shown by circles centered on the real axis and constant susceptance curves are circles centered on the imaginary axis. We first locate the intersection point of the curves of $g = 0.5$ and $b = 0.5$. The intersection is shown by point A on Fig. 15-4(d). The vector OA represents $-\Gamma_R = 0.44\angle 116°$. Rotate it in the clockwise rotation by $2\beta\ell = \pi$ to obtain $\Gamma_s = -\Gamma_R = 0.44\angle -64°$, shown by point C on the chart. Point C is the intersection of $g = 1$ and $b = -1$. This gives us $y_{in} = 1 - j$, the normalized input admittance of the line. The normalized input impedance is $\dfrac{1}{y} = \dfrac{1}{1-j} = 0.5 + j0.5$. The input admittance and impedance of the line are

$$Y_{in} = 0.02 - j0.02\ S \quad \text{and} \quad Z_{in} = 25 + j25\ \Omega$$

Analytical solution:

$$\Gamma_R = -\frac{y_R - 1}{y_R + 1} = \frac{-0.5 + j0.5}{1.5 + j0.5} = \frac{-1 + j}{3 + j} = 0.447\angle 116.56°$$

$$\Gamma_s = \Gamma_R e^{-j\pi} = \frac{1-j}{3+j} = 0.447\angle -63.44°$$

$$y_{in} = 1 - j,\ z_{in} = \frac{1}{1-j} = \frac{1+j}{1-j} = 0.5 + j0.5 \quad Z_{in} = 25 + j25\ \Omega$$

15.10   Quarter-Wave Transformer

The input impedance of a lossless line with characteristic impedance R_0 and terminating on an impedance Z_R is

$$Z_{in} = R_0 \frac{Z_R \cos\beta\ell + jR_0 \sin\beta\ell}{R_0 \cos\beta\ell + jZ_R \sin\beta\ell}$$

For a quarter-wave line,

$$\ell = \frac{\lambda}{4}, \ \beta\ell = \frac{2\pi}{\lambda}\frac{\lambda}{4} = \frac{\pi}{2}, \ Z_{in} = \frac{R_0^2}{Z_R}$$

The quarter-wave line transforms the load impedance Z_R into a new value $\dfrac{R_0^2}{Z_R}$. This may be used in matching a line to a load or joining line segments together.

EXAMPLE 4. A 50-Ω line is to feed a 200-Ω load. To match the load to the line we insert, between the 50-Ω line and the load, a lossless quarter-wave line whose characteristic impedance is R_0. Find R_0 so that the 50-Ω line terminates on 50 Ω.

Solution. $\dfrac{R_0^2}{200} = 50, R_0 = 100 \ \Omega$

EXAMPLE 5. A lossless line a with characteristic impedance R_a terminates on a second line b with characteristic impedance $R_b \neq R_a$. Insert a quarter-wave line with characteristic impedance R_c between lines a and b. Determine R_c so that line a effectively feeds a load with impedance R_a.

Solution. $\dfrac{R_c^2}{R_b} = R_a, R_c = \sqrt{R_a R_b}$

15.11 Impedance Matching

At high frequencies it is essential to operate at minimum VSWR (ideally, at VSWR = 1). Several methods are used to match a load Z_R to the line, or to match cascaded lines with different characteristic impedances. Matching networks can be placed at the load ($x = 0$) or at some position $x = x_1$ along the line, as in Fig. 15-5. The two sets of normalized conditions are as follows:

(a) Before match: $\quad z(0) = z_R = r_0 + jx_0;\quad y(0) = g_0 + jb_0;\quad$ VSWR > 1

   After match: $\quad z(0) = 1 + j0;\quad y(0) = 1 + j0;\quad$ VSWR = 1

Fig. 15-5

(b) At load: $\quad\quad\quad z(0) = r_0 + jx_0;\quad y(0) = g_0 + jb_0;\quad$ VSWR(0) > 1

   Before match: $\quad z(x_1) = r_1 + jx_1;\quad y(x_1) = g_1 + jb_1;\quad$ VSWR = VSWR(0)

   After match: $\quad z(x_1) = 1 + j0;\quad y(x_1) = 1 + j0;\quad$ VSWR = 1

The matching networks at lower (radio) frequencies can be made with lumped low-loss reactive components; one lumped L-C network is shown in Fig. 15-6. If Z_R has a reactive component, a reactance of opposite sign is added in series so that $Z_R' = R + j0$. Then, for a match,

$$Y_{in} = j\omega C_2 + \frac{1}{R + j\omega L_1} = \frac{1}{R_0}$$

Fig. 15-6

or
$$L_1 = \frac{1}{\omega}\sqrt{R(R_0 - R)} \quad \text{and} \quad C_2 = \frac{L_1}{RR_0}$$

If $R > R_0$, the capacitor should be connected to the other end of the inductor.

To minimize dissipation losses at higher frequencies a length of open- or short-circuited line is used for matching, in either a *single-stub* or *double-stub* configuration.

15.12 Single-Stub Matching

The configuration shown in Fig. 15-7 uses one shorted stub, of length ℓ_s, placed at a distance x_1 from the load. To accomplish matching:

(1) Determine x_1 such that $y(x_1) = 1 + jb_1$.
(2) Determine ℓ_s such that $y(\ell_s) = 0 - jb_1$.

After matching, $y(x_1) = 1 + j0$ and VSWR $= 1$ from x_1 to ℓ.

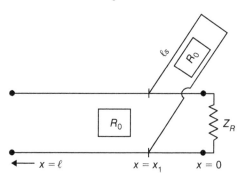

Fig. 15-7

EXAMPLE 6. The above two steps may be accomplished on the Smith Chart (Fig. 15-8).

(a) Plot y_R and trace the $|\Gamma_R|$ [or VSWR(0)] circle.
(b) Mark the intersections of the $|\Gamma_R|$ circle and the circle $g = 1$.
(c) From y_R move *toward the generator* to the first intersection, read $y_1 = 1 + jb_1$, and note the distance x_1 as a fraction of λ (or read off angle $2\beta x_1$).
(d) Mark the point $y = 0 - jb_1$ on the $|\Gamma| = 1$ circle. From the short-circuit position $y = \infty$, move *toward the generator* to the point $y = -jb_1$. Note the distance ℓ_s as a fraction of λ. If the first intersection is not accessible, the second one can be used by readjusting the stub length for the susceptance at the new position.

For matching two cascaded lines with different characteristic impedances, the above procedure is used at the connection point where the equivalent load is the input impedance to the second line.

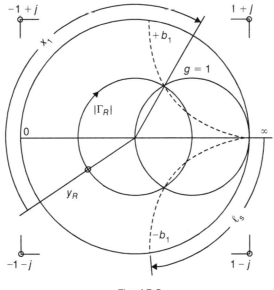

Fig. 15-8

15.13   Double-Stub Matching

A double stub "tuner" has two shorted stub lines separated by a distance d_s on the main line, as shown in Fig. 15-9. Stub 1 is nearest the load and frequently is connected at the load ($x = 0$). Common separations for the two stubs are $\lambda/4$ and $3\lambda/8$, hence the names "quarter-wavelength tuner," etc. The Smith Chart solution for the two-stub matching problem involves the construction of the *tuner circle* for the given d_s. This is the circle $g_T \equiv g(d_s) = 1$, which plays the same role for stub 2 as the $g = 1$ circle plays for the main line. The tuner circle is obtained by clockwise rotation of $g = 1$, about the center of the chart, $1 + j0$: a rotation of $180°$ gives the $\lambda/4$ tuner circle, rotation of $90°$ gives the $3\lambda/8$ tuner circle, etc. See Fig. 15-10.

EXAMPLE 7.   Assuming that $d_s = \lambda/4$, a five-step sequence is used for two-stub matching, as shown in Fig. 15-11.

1. Plot the $\lambda/4$ tuner circle.
2. Mark the intersection(s) of the tuner circle and the g_R circle through the entry point $y_R = g_R + jb_R$. Read b_T at this point, which may be either intersection.
3. Stub 1 at $x = 0$ is used to change the susceptance b_R to b_T.
4. From $y_T = g_R + jb_T$ move on the $\left|\Gamma_R\right|$ circle a distance $d_s = \lambda/4$ *toward the generator* onto the $g = 1$ circle and read $y = 1 + jb_2$.
5. Cancel the susceptance b_2 by adjusting stub 2 to produce $y = 1 + j0$, the matched condition.

Fig. 15-9

Fig. 15-10

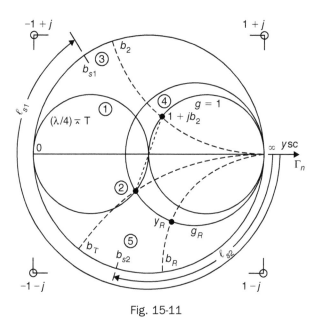

Fig. 15-11

A problem arises when using the $\lambda/4$ tuner to match a load with $g_R > 1$, since the conductance circle does not intersect the tuner circle. The $3\lambda/8$ tuner works for some values of $g_R > 1$. In any case, a tuner can be displaced from the load by a distance x_1 to put g in the range for matching. Should $g = 1$ at the displaced position, the single-stub condition holds and stub 2 must be set for $b = 0$.

Note the standing waves on the various sections of line. The shorted stubs each have VSWR $= \infty$. For $d_s < x < \ell$, VSWR $= 1$; for $0 < x < d_s$, VSWR is determined by $y = g_R + jb_T$; and if a line is added between the load and stub 1, the VSWR is determined by y_R.

15.14 Impedance Measurement

A *slotted line* is used with high-frequency coaxial lines to measure VSWR and to locate voltage minima on the line. With the aid of the Smith Chart, the impedance of an unknown termination can be easily found from the VSWR and the shift of a voltage minimum from a short-circuit reference position.

In Fig. 15-12 the slotted line is inserted at a convenient terminal. With the Z_R in place, a probe is moved along the line to locate and measure maximum and minimum voltages. A suitable amplifier/indicator converts the probe output to a VSWR reading. Z_R is replaced by a short circuit, and the reference minima are located for the high-VSWR condition. As would be expected, maxima and minima alternate at intervals of $\lambda/4$.

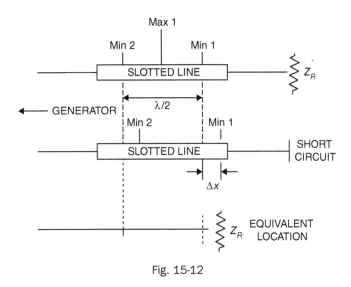

Fig. 15-12

To find Z_R with the Smith Chart, draw the measured VSWR circle as in Fig. 15-13 and locate the voltage-minimum line (from 0 to 1 on the $\chi = 0$ line). Convert the measured Δx to wavelengths, and mark the points on the VSWR circle that are Δx from the V_{min} line. The correct Z_r is capacitive; a rotation through Δx *toward the generator* takes it into a V_{min} point. (If Z_R were inductive, Δx would be greater than a quarter wavelength and a V_{max} point would occur before the V_{min} point.)

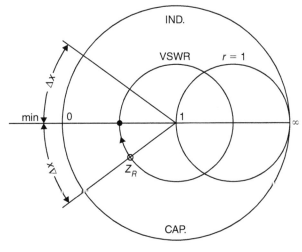

Fig. 15-13

15.15 Transients in Lossless Lines

In switching applications and pulse operation, a change in voltage is suddenly applied to the line. An analysis of this transient condition generally requires recourse to the time PDEs of Section 15.4 or to their Laplace transforms. However, in the special case of a lossless line ($R = G = 0$, $R_0 = \sqrt{L/C}$, $u_p = 1/\sqrt{L/C}$), a simple graphical method is available, based on superposition of multiple reflected waves.

Fig. 15-14 shows a model for the lossless system, in which the exciting voltage $v_g(t)$ is switched on at $t = 0$ and where R_g is the source resistance. Now, an abrupt change at one end of the line has an effect at the other end only after one *delay time*, $t_D = \ell/u_p$, has elapsed. Reflection will occur at the receiving end if the load is not matched to the line ($R_R \neq R_0$); at the sending end if the source is not matched ($R_g \neq R_0$).

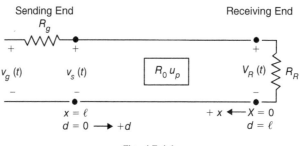

Fig. 15-14

EXAMPLE 8. For the case where $v_g(t)$ is a 10-V step at $t = 0$ (i.e., a DC voltage), and where the line is matched at both ends ($R_R = R_g = R_0$), the transient voltage conditions are displayed in the *time-distance plots* of Fig. 15-15. Because the source voltage is constant and there is no reflection at the receiving end, the system reaches a steady state, $v(d, t) = 5$ V, after only one delay time. In Fig. 15-15(a) and (b) different boldface numerals indicate different space-time combinations corresponding to the steady-state condition. For instance, **5** signals $v(0.5\ell, 0.5t_D) = 5$ V.

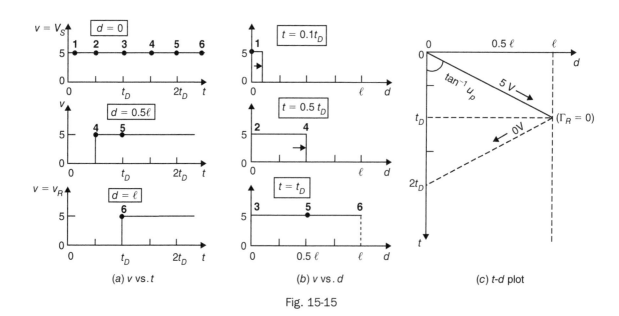

(a) v vs. t (b) v vs. d (c) t-d plot

Fig. 15-15

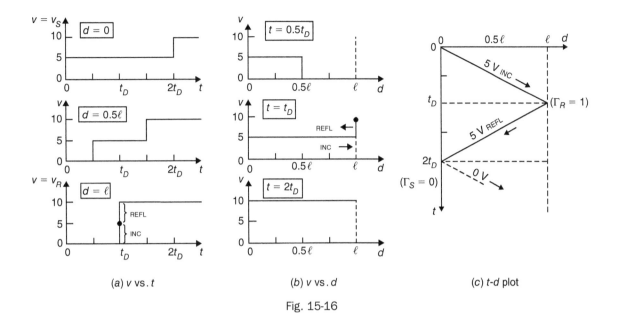

(a) v vs. t (b) v vs. d (c) t-d plot

Fig. 15-16

EXAMPLE 9. Assume that everything is as in Example 8, with the exception of the load, which is now an open-circuit ($R_R = \infty$). Fig. 15-16 gives the time-distance plots. Because of the single reflection at the load, a uniform steady state of 10 V is attained after $2t_D$.

EXAMPLE 10. A line is excited as in Examples 8 and 9; parameter values are

$$V_g = 20 \text{ V dc} \qquad R_g = 3R_0 \qquad \Gamma_g = \frac{1}{2} \qquad \Gamma_R = 1 \text{ (open-circuit)}$$

The voltage transient is described in Fig. 15-17. With reflections occurring at both ends of the line, an infinite time is needed for the attainment of a uniform steady state of 20 V.

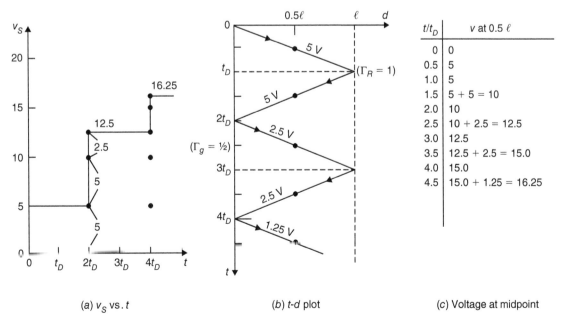

(a) v_S vs. t (b) t-d plot   (c) Voltage at midpoint

Fig. 15-17

SOLVED PROBLEMS

15.1. A parallel-wire transmission line is constructed of #6 AWG copper wire (dia. = 0.162 in., $\sigma_x = 58$ MS/m) with a 12-inch separation in air. Neglecting internal inductance, find the per-meter values of L, C, G, the dc resistance, and the ac resistance at 1 MHz.

The four geometrical factors for the parallel-wire line involve the conductor radius, $a = 2.06 \times 10^{-3}$ m, and the separation $d = 0.305$ m. Since $d \gg a$

$$\mathrm{GFL} = \ln\left(\frac{d}{a}\right) = 5.0 \qquad\qquad \mathrm{GFC} = \frac{1}{\mathrm{GFL}} = 0.20$$

$$\mathrm{GFR}_d = \frac{2}{a^2} = 4.72 \times 10^5 \text{ m}^{-2} \qquad \mathrm{GFR}_a = \frac{2}{a} = 971 \text{ m}^{-1}$$

For air dielectric, $\mu_d = \mu_0$ and $\epsilon_d = \epsilon_0$; for copper, $\mu_c \approx \mu_0$. Hence:

$$L = \frac{\mu_d}{\pi}(\mathrm{GFL}) = 2.0 \ \mu\mathrm{H/m} \qquad R_d = \frac{1}{\pi\sigma_c}(\mathrm{GFR}_d) = 2.59 \times 10^{-3} \ \Omega/\mathrm{m}$$

$$C = \pi\epsilon_d(\mathrm{GFC}) = 5.56 \ \mathrm{pF/m} \qquad \delta = \frac{1}{\sqrt{\pi f \mu_c \sigma_c}} = 66 \ \mu\mathrm{m}$$

$$G = 0 \ \mathrm{S/m} \qquad R_a = \frac{1}{2\pi\delta_c\sigma_c}(\mathrm{GFR}_a) = 4.04 \times 10^{22} \ \Omega/\mathrm{m}$$

15.2. The specifications for a rigid air-dielectric coaxial line used in a radar set operating at 3 GHz are: copper material, stub-supported at intervals to maintain the air dielectric; outside diameter, $\frac{7}{8}$ inch; wall thickness, 0.032 inch; inner-conductor diameter, 0.375 inch; characteristic impedance, 46.4 Ω; attenuation, 0.066 dB/m; maximum peak power, 1.31 kW; operating peak power, 200 kW; lowest safe wavelength, 5.28 cm. Determine the per-meter values of L, C, G, and R_a for the line, neglecting internal inductance.

The inner radius a is 4.76 mm and the outer radius b is 10.3 mm. Then $\ln(b/a) = 0.771$, GFL = 0.386, GFC = 2.59.

$$L = \frac{\mu_0}{\pi}(\mathrm{GFL}) = 0.154 \ \mu\mathrm{H/m} \qquad C = \pi\epsilon_0(\mathrm{GFC}) = 71.9 \ \mathrm{pF/m}$$

For copper and a frequency of 3 GHz, $\delta = 1.2 \ \mu$m. Then,

$$\mathrm{GFR}_a = \frac{1}{a} + \frac{1}{b} = 307 \,\mathrm{m}^{-1} \qquad \text{and} \qquad R_a = \frac{1}{2\pi\sigma_c\delta}(\mathrm{GFR}_a) = 0.702 \ \Omega/\mathrm{m}$$

For air dielectric, $G = 0$ S/m.

15.3. Show that the voltage $v(x, t) = A \cos(\omega t + \theta)e^{j\beta x}$ satisfies the transmission line equation (3), for a uniform lossless line, if $\beta = \omega\sqrt{LC}$.

For the lossless line, $R = G = 0$, so that the equation reduces to

$$\frac{\partial^2 v(x,t)}{\partial x^2} = LC\frac{\partial^2 v(x,t)}{\partial t^2}$$

For the given voltage, this requires

$$-\beta^2 v = LC(-\omega^2 v) \qquad \text{or} \qquad \beta = \omega\sqrt{LC}$$

15.4. For the parallel-wire line of Problem 15.1, find the characteristic impedance, propagation constant (attenuation and phase shift), velocity of propagation, and wavelength, for operation at 5 kHz.

At 5 kHz the dc resistance may be used.

$$Z = R_d + j\omega L = 2.59 \times 10^{-3} + j2\pi(5 \times 10^3)(2 \times 10^{-6}) = 6.289 \times 10^{-2} \underline{/87.6°}\ \Omega/\text{m}$$

$$Y = G + j\omega C = j2\pi(5 \times 10^3)(5.56 \times 10^{-12}) = 1.747 \times 10^{-7} \underline{/90°}\ \text{S/m}$$

$$Z_0 = \sqrt{\frac{Z}{Y}} = 600\underline{/-1.2°}\ \Omega$$

$$\gamma = \sqrt{ZY} = 1.048 \times 10^{-4} \underline{/88.8°} = (2.19 \times 10^{-6}) + j(1.048 \times 10^{-4})\ \text{m}^{-1}$$

Then $\alpha = 2.19 \times 10^{-6}$ N/m, $\beta = 1.048 \times 10^{-4}$ rad/m, $u_p = \omega/\beta = 2.998 \times 10^8$ m/s, $\lambda = 2\pi/\beta = 59.96$ km.

15.5. A 10-km parallel-wire line operating at 100 kHz has $Z_0 = 557\Omega$, $\alpha = 2.4 \times 10^{-5}$ Np/m, and $\beta = 2.12 \times 10^{-3}$ rad/m. For a matched termination at $x = 0$ and $\hat{V}_R = 10\underline{/0°}$ V, evaluate $\hat{V}(x)$ at x-increments of $\lambda/4$ and plot the phasors.

The line is matched at the receiving end, so that $\Gamma_R = 0$ and $\hat{V}(x) = \hat{V}^+ e^{\alpha x}\underline{/\beta x}$. But

$$\hat{V}(0) = \hat{V}^+ = \hat{V}_R = \underline{/0°}\ \text{V}$$

whence
$$\hat{V}(x) = 10e^{\alpha x}\underline{/\beta x}\quad\text{(V)}$$

For $x = n(\lambda/4)$ ($n = 0, 1, 2, \ldots, 13, 13.48$), where $n = 13.48$ corresponds to the 10-km length,

$$\beta x = n\left(\frac{\pi}{2}\ \text{rad}\right) = n(90°)$$

$$\alpha x = \frac{\alpha}{\beta}(\beta x) = n\,0.0178\ \text{Np}$$

By use of these increments, Table 15-2 is generated. A polar plot of the tabulated results is given in Fig. 15-18.

TABLE **15-2**

QUARTER WAVELENGTHS FROM LOAD	$\beta x = \phi_v$, deg.	αx, Np	$|\hat{V}(x)|$, V
0	0	0.0	10.00
1	90	0.0178	10.18
2	180	0.0356	10.36
3	270	0.0534	10.55
4	360	0.0711	10.74
5	450	0.0889	10.93
6	540	0.1067	11.13
7	630	0.1245	11.33
8	720	0.1423	11.53
9	810	0.1601	11.74
10	900	0.1779	11.95
11	990	0.1956	12.16
12	1080	0.2134	12.38
13	1170	0.2312	12.60
13.48	1215	0.24	12.71

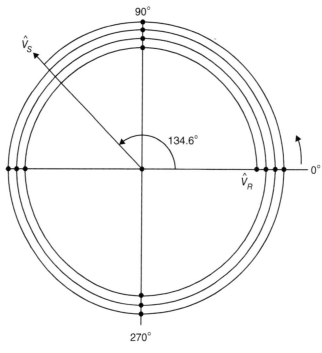

Fig. 15-18

15.6. Repeat Problem 15.5 if a mismatched load results in $\Gamma_R = 0.4 \,\underline{/0°}$; all other data remain the same.

In contrast to Problem 15.5, the voltage is now given by the superposition of an incident and a reflected wave:

$$\hat{V}(x) = \hat{V}_{inc}(x) + \hat{V}_{refl}(x) = \hat{V}^+ e^{\alpha x} \,\underline{/\beta x} + \Gamma_R \hat{V}^+ e^{-\alpha x} \,\underline{/-\beta x}$$

The boundary condition at $x = 0$ gives (omitting physical units)

$$10 \,\underline{/0°} = 1.4 \hat{V}^+ \,\underline{/0°} \qquad \text{or} \qquad \hat{V}^+ = 7.14 \,\underline{/0°}$$

Thus, $\qquad\qquad \hat{V}(x) = 7.14 e^{\alpha x} \,\underline{/\beta x} + 2.86 e^{-\alpha x} \,\underline{/-\beta x}$

where α and β are as specified in Problem 15.5. The required calculations are presented in Table 15-3 and Fig. 15-19.

TABLE **15-3**

λ/4 FROM LOAD	αx, Np	$e^{\alpha x}$	βx	$V_{inc}(x)$	$V_{ref}(x)$	$|V(x)|$
0	0.0	1.0	0°	$7.14\underline{/0°}$	$2.86\underline{/0°}$	$10.00\underline{/0°}$
1	0.0178	1.018	90°	$7.27\underline{/90°}$	$2.81\underline{/-90°}$	$4.46\underline{/90°}$
2	0.0356	1.036	180°	$7.40\underline{/180°}$	$2.76\underline{/-180°}$	$10.16\underline{/180°}$
3	0.0534	1.055	270°	$7.53\underline{/270°}$	$2.71\underline{/-270°}$	$4.82\underline{/-90°}$
4	0.0711	1.074	360°	$7.67\underline{/360°}$	$2.66\underline{/-360°}$	$10.33\underline{/0°}$
5	0.0889	1.093	450°	$7.80\underline{/450°}$	$2.62\underline{/-450°}$	$5.18\underline{/90°}$
6	0.1067	1.113	540°	$7.94\underline{/540°}$	$2.57\underline{/-540°}$	$10.51\underline{/180°}$
7	0.1245	1.133	630°	$8.09\underline{/630°}$	$2.52\underline{/-630°}$	$5.57\underline{/-90°}$
8	0.1423	1.153	720°	$8.23\underline{/720°}$	$2.48\underline{/-720°}$	$10.71\underline{/0°}$
9	0.1601	1.174	810°	$8.38\underline{/810°}$	$2.44\underline{/-810°}$	$5.94\underline{/90°}$
10	0.1779	1.195	900°	$8.53\underline{/900°}$	$2.39\underline{/-900°}$	$10.92\underline{/180°}$
11	0.1956	1.216	990°	$8.68\underline{/990°}$	$2.35\underline{/-990°}$	$6.33\underline{/-90°}$
12	0.2134	1.238	1080°	$8.84\underline{/1080°}$	$2.31\underline{/-1080°}$	$11.15\underline{/0°}$
13	0.2312	1.260	1170°	$9.00\underline{/1170°}$	$2.27\underline{/-1170°}$	$6.73\underline{/90°}$
13.48	0.24	1.271	1215°	$9.08\underline{/1215°}$	$2.25\underline{/-1215°}$	$9.34\underline{/148.5°}$

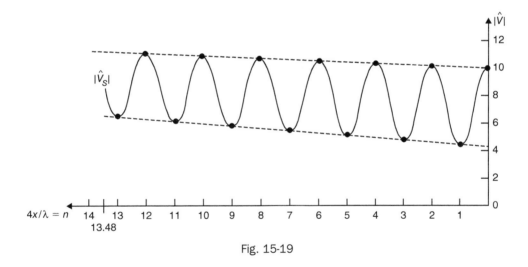

Fig. 15-19

15.7. Measurements are made at 5 kHz on a 0.5-mile-long transmission line. The results show that the characteristic impedance is $94\underline{/-23.2°}$ Ω, the total attenuation is 0.06 Np, and the phase shift between input and output is 8°. Find the R, L, G, and C per mile for the line; the phase velocity on the line; and the power lost on the line when the sending-end power is 3 W and the load is matched.

The measured attenuation is $\alpha\ell = 0.06$ Np, whence $\alpha = 0.12$ Np/mi, the phase shift is $\beta\ell = 8° = 0.14$ rad, so that $\beta = 0.28$ rad/mi. Hence,

$$\sqrt{ZY} = \gamma = 0.12 + j0.28 = 0.305\underline{/66.8°} \text{ mi}^{-1} \qquad \text{or} \qquad ZY = 0.093\underline{/133.6°} \text{ mi}^{-2}$$

From this and the measured value $\sqrt{Z/Y} = 94\underline{/-23.2°}$ Ω:

$$Z = 28.67\underline{/43.6°} = 20.8 + j19.8 \text{ Ω/mi} = R + j2\pi fL$$
$$Y = 3.24 \times 10^{-3}\underline{/90°} = j3.24 \times 10^{-3} \text{ S/mi} = G + j2\pi fC$$

which imply: $R = 20.8$ Ω/mi; $L = 630$ μH/mi; $G = 0$; $C = 0.103$ μF/mi.

The phase velocity is $u_p = 2\pi f/\beta = 2\pi(5 \times 10^3)/0.28 = 1.12 \times 10^5$ mi/s.

For a matched load (no reflections), the received power is given by

$$P_R = P_S e^{-2\alpha \ell} = 3e^{-0.12} = 2.66 \text{ W}$$

and the power lost as the result of attenuation is 0.34 W.

15.8. A 600-Ω transmission line is 150 m long, operates at 400 kHz with $\alpha = 2.4 \times 10^{-3}$ Np/m and $\beta = 0.0212$ rad/m, and supplies a load impedance $Z_R = 424.3 \underline{/45°}$ Ω. Find the length of line in wavelengths, Γ_R, Γ_S, and Z_s. For a received voltage $\hat{V}_R = 50\underline{/0°}$ V, find $\hat{V}_S$, the position on the line where the voltage is a maximum, and the value of $|\hat{V}|_{max}$.

Because $\lambda = 2\pi/\beta = 296.4$ m, $\ell = 150$ m $= 0.51 \lambda$. At $x = 0$,

$$\Gamma_R = \frac{Z_R - Z_0}{Z_R + Z_0} = \frac{300 + j300 - 600}{300 + j300 + 600} = 0.45\underline{/116.6°} = -0.2 + j0.4$$

Therefore, at $x = \ell$,

$$\Gamma_S = |\Gamma_R| e^{-2\alpha \ell} \underline{/\phi_R - 2\beta \ell} = 0.45e^{-0.72}\underline{/116.6° - 363°}$$
$$= 0.22\underline{/113.6°} = -0.09 + j0.20$$

and

$$Z_S = Z_0 \left(\frac{1 + \Gamma_S}{1 - \Gamma_S}\right) = 600 \left(\frac{0.91 + j0.2}{1.09 - j0.2}\right) 502.7 \underline{/22.8°} \ \Omega$$

From $\hat{V}_R = 50\underline{/0°} = \hat{V}^+ (1 + \Gamma_R)$, $\hat{V}^+ = 56.2\underline{/-26.6°}$ V. Then,

$$\hat{V}_S = (\hat{V}^+ e^{\alpha \ell}\underline{/\beta \ell})[1 + \Gamma_S] = (56.2e^{0.36}\underline{/-26.6° + 181.5°})[0.91 + j0.2] = 75.0\underline{/167.3°} \text{ V}$$

To find x where the voltage is a maximum, construct the phasor diagram Fig. 15-20. At $x = 0$ the incident and reflected voltages are separated by an angle of 116.6°. When $\hat{V}_{inc}$ rotates 58.3° counterclockwise and $\hat{V}_{refl}$ rotates the same angle clockwise, the two phasors add together. The distance x for which $\beta x = 58.3°$ is 48.2 m, the position of the maximum. The magnitude is

$$|\hat{V}|_{max} = 56.2e^{0.116} + (0.45)(56.2)e^{-0.116} = 85.5 \text{ V}$$

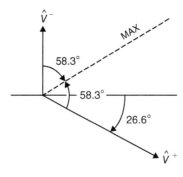

Fig. 15-20

15.9. For the coaxial line specified in Problem 15.2, determine the actual characteristic impedance and attenuation, and compare the values with the specifications. Determine the length of the shorted stub required to support the center conductor at the operating frequency of 3 GHz and calculate the highest "safe" frequency of operation for this line from the specifications.

The characteristic impedance for the high-frequency low-loss line is

$$R_0 = \sqrt{\frac{L}{C}} = \sqrt{\frac{1.54 \times 10^{-7}}{7.19 \times 10^{-11}}} = 46.33\ \Omega \quad \text{(specification is 46.4 }\Omega\text{)}$$

The per-meter attenuation is

$$\alpha = \frac{R_a}{2R_0} = \frac{0.702}{2(46.33)} = 7.58 \times 10^{-3}\ \text{Np/m} = 0.0658\ \text{dB/m} \quad \text{(specification is 0.066 dB/m)}$$

where the conversion 1 Np = 8.686 dB has been used.

A stub to support the center conductor must be $\lambda/4$ long so that the short circuit reflects to an open circuit at the point of connection to the main line. At 3 GHz the length should be

$$\ell_s = \frac{1}{4}\frac{u_p}{f} = \frac{1}{4}\left(\frac{3 \times 10^8}{3 \times 10^9}\right) = 0.025\ \text{m} \quad \text{or} \quad 2.5\ \text{cm}$$

The "safe" highest frequency of operation is determined by the specification for lowest "safe" wavelength.

$$f_{\text{hi}} = \frac{u_p}{\lambda_{\text{low}}} = \frac{3 \times 10^8}{5.28 \times 10^{-2}} = 5.68\ \text{GHz}$$

At frequencies above this value, propagation modes other than the TEM could exist.

15.10. A 70-Ω high-frequency lossless line is used at a frequency where $\lambda = 80$ cm with a load at $x = 0$ of $(140 + j91)\ \Omega$. Use the Smith Chart to find the following: Γ_R, VSWR, distance to the first voltage maximum from the load, distance to the first voltage minimum from the load, the impedance at V_{max}, the impedance at V_{min}, the input impedance for a section of line that is 54 cm long, and the input admittance.

On the Smith Chart, plot the normalized load $Z_R/R_0 = 2 + j1.3$, as shown in Fig. 15-21. Draw a radial line from the center through this point to the outer λ-circle. Read the angle of Γ_R on the angle scale: $\phi_R = 29°$. Measure the distance from the center to the z-point and determine the magnitudes of Γ_R and VSWR from the scales at the bottom of the chart.

$$|\Gamma_R| = 0.50 \qquad \text{VSWR} = 3.0 \qquad \text{and} \qquad \Gamma_R = 0.5\underline{/29°}$$

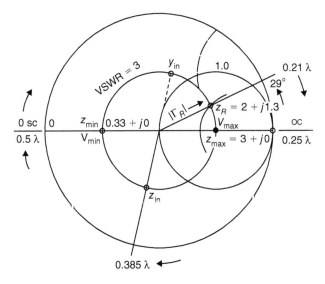

Fig. 15-21

Draw a circle at the center passing through the plotted normalized impedance. Note that this circle intersects the horizontal line at $3 + j0$. This point of intersection could be used to determine the VSWR instead of the bottom scale, because the circle represents a constant VSWR. Locate the intersection of the VSWR circle and the radial line from the center to the open-circuit point at the right of the z-chart. This intersection is the point where the voltage is a maximum (the current is a minimum) and the impedance is a maximum. The normalized impedance at this point is $3 + j0$, whence $Z_{max} = 210 + j0 \ \Omega$. To find the distance from the load to the first V_{max}, use the outer scale (*wavelengths toward the generator*). The reference position is at 0.21λ and the max. line is at $0.25 \ \lambda$; so the distance is 0.04λ toward the generator, or 3.2 cm from the load.

From the V_{max} point move 0.25λ toward the generator and locate the V_{min} point. The normalized impedance is $0.33 + j0$, and $Z_{min} = 23.1 + j0 \ \Omega$. The distance from the load to the first minimum is

$$0.25\lambda + 0.04\lambda = 0.29\lambda = 23.2 \text{ cm}$$

To find the input impedance, move $\frac{54}{80} = 0.675$ wavelengths from the load toward the generator, and read the normalized impedance. Once around the circle is 0.5λ, so locate the point that is 0.175λ from the load on the outer scale. The point is at $0.21\lambda + 0.175\lambda = 0.385\lambda$. Through this point draw a radial line and locate the intersection with the VSWR circle. The normal impedance is $0.56 - j0.71$ and $Z_{in} = 39.2 - j49.7 \ \Omega$.

The normalized input admittance is located a diameter across on the chart, which corresponds to the inversion of a complex number. For $z = 0.56 - j0.71$, $y = 0.68 + j0.87$; therefore,

$$Y_{in} = \frac{y}{R_0} = (9.71 + j12.4) \text{ mS}$$

15.11. The high-frequency lossless transmission system shown in Fig. 15-22 operates at 700 MHz with a phase velocity for each line section of 2.1×10^8 m/s. Use the Smith Chart to find the VSWR on each section of line and the input impedance to line #1 at the drive point. (There are three distinct transmission line problems to be solved.)

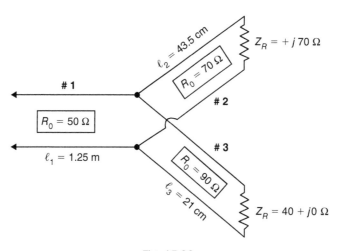

Fig. 15-22

For the three lines the wavelength is $\lambda = (2.1 \times 10^8)/(7 \times 10^8) = 30$ cm. For line #2 the length is $(43.5/30)\lambda = 1.45\lambda$ and the normalized load is $(0 + j70)/70 = j1$. Plot this value as point **1** in Fig. 15-23. Note the reference position, 0.125λ and VSWR $= \infty$. Move on the VSWR circle 1.45λ *toward the generator* to point **2** and read the value $z_{in} = 0 + j0.51$. The input impedance to line #2,

$$Z_{in2} = z_{in}R_{02} = 0 + j35.7 \ \Omega$$

is one part of the load on line #1.

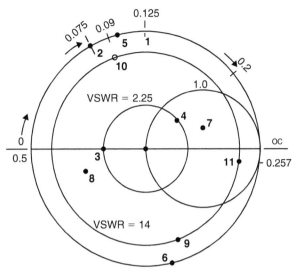

Fig. 15-23

For line #3 the length is $\frac{21}{30} = 0.7\lambda$ and the normalized load is $(40 + j0)/90 = 0.44 + j0$. Plot this value as point **3** and note the reference position of 0λ and the VSWR = 2.25. Move on the VSWR circle 0.7λ *toward the generator* to point **4**, and read off

$$z_{in} = 1.62 + j0.86 \quad \text{or} \quad Z_{in3} = z_{in}R_{03} = 145.8 + j77.4 \ \Omega$$

This is the second part of the load on line #1.

For line #1: the length is $1.25/0.30 = 4.167\lambda$ and the load is the parallel combination of Z_{in2} and Z_{in3}. Normalize each impedance to the 50-Ω line, find each admittance, add the admittances for y_R, and then find z_R.

$$z_2 = j\left(\frac{35.7}{50}\right) = 0 + j0.714 \quad \text{(point 5)} \quad \text{and} \quad y_2 = 0 - j1.41 \quad \text{(point 6)}$$

$$z_3 = \frac{145.8 + j77.4}{50} = 2.92 + j1.55 \quad \text{(point 7)} \quad \text{and} \quad y_3 = 0.27 - j0.14 \quad \text{(point 8)}$$

$$y_R = 0.27 - j1.55 \quad \text{(point 9)} \quad \text{with} \quad \text{VSWR} = 14$$

Invert by moving a diameter across to point **10** for $z_R = 0.1 + j0.63$ at the reference position 0.09λ. Now move 4.167λ *toward the generator* from z_R on the VSWR = 14 circle to point **11**, and read $z_{in} = 9.5 - j6.3$. The input impedance to line #1 is

$$50(9.5 - j6.3) = 475 - j315 \ \Omega$$

15.12. (*a*) A high-frequency 50-Ω lossless line is 141.6 cm long, with a relative dielectric constant $\epsilon_r = 2.49$. At 500 MHz the input impedance of the terminated line is measured as $Z_{in} = (20 + j25) \ \Omega$. Use the Smith Chart to find the value of the terminating load. (*b*) After the impedance measurement an 8-pF lossless capacitor is connected in parallel with the line at a distance of 8.5 cm from the load. Find the VSWR on the main line.

(*a*) For $\epsilon_r = 2.49$,

$$u_p = \frac{3 \times 10^8}{\sqrt{2.49}} = 1.9 \times 10^8 \ \text{m/s} \qquad \lambda = \frac{u_p}{f} = \frac{1.9 \times 10^8}{5 \times 10^8} = 38 \ \text{cm}$$

and the length of line is $(141.6/38)\lambda = 3.726\lambda$. The normalized input impedance is $z_{in} = (20 + j25)/50 = 0.4 + j0.5$. Plot this value on Fig. 15-24 as point **1**, measure the VSWR, draw the VSWR = 3.2 circle, and note the reference position at 0.418λ *toward the load*. From z_{in} move 3.726λ toward the load on the VSWR circle (a net change of 0.226λ) and read the normalized load impedance $z_R = 0.72 - j0.98$ at point **2**. The load impedance is $Z_R = (36 - j49)$ Ω at 500 MHz.

(*b*)   Since the capacitor is connected in parallel it is convenient to work on the *y*-chart, Fig. 15-25. In Fig. 15-24 read the value diametrically opposite z_R: $y_R = 0.48 + j0.67$. Plot y_R as point **3** in Fig. 15-25 and draw the VSWR = 3.2 circle. The reference position is 0.105λ *toward the generator*, corresponding to $x = 0$. Move 8.5 cm, or $(8.5/38)\lambda = 0.224\lambda$ toward the generator on the VSWR circle and read $y(x_1)$ at point **4**. Before the capacitor is added, $y(x_1) = 1.04 - j1.22$. The normalized admittance of the capacitor is

$$y_c = (j2\pi fC)R_0 = j2\pi(5 \times 10^8)(8 \times 10^{-12})(50) = 0 + j1.26$$

and the new admittance at x_1 is $y_c + y(x_1) = 1.04 + j0.04$. Plot this new admittance as point **5** and measure VSWR = 1.04 (a significant reduction from 3.2).

Fig. 15-24

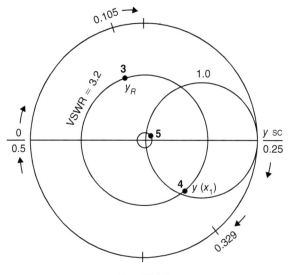

Fig. 15-25

15.13. A 4-m-long, stub-supported, lossless, 300 Ω, air-dielectric line (Fig. 15-26) was designed for operation at 300 MHz with a 300-Ω resistive load, using shorted ($\lambda/4$)-supports. With no changes in dimensions or load, the line is operated at 400 MHz. Use the Smith Chart to find the VSWR on each section of line, including the supports, and the input impedance at the new frequency.

Fig. 15-26

The wavelength is $\lambda = u_p/f = (3 \times 10^8)/(4 \times 10^8) = 75$ cm and distances in terms of λ are

Total length = 4 m = 5.333λ

Load to stub 1 = 50 cm = 0.667λ

Stub length = 25 cm = 0.333λ

Stub separation = 2.5 m = 3.333λ

Stub 2 to input = 1 m = 1.33λ

Since the stubs are in parallel, use a y-chart, Fig. 15-27, for the solution. At $x = 0$, $y_R = R_0/Z_R = 1 + j0$ (point **1**) and VSWR = 1. The line is flat to the point of connection of the first stub, $0.667\ \lambda$ from the load, with $y(x_1) = 1 + j0$ in the absence of stubs.

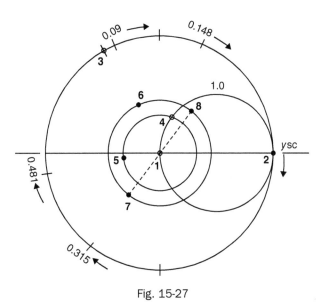

Fig. 15-27

To find the admittance of the shorted stubs, plot y_{sc} at point **2**, move 0.333λ *toward the generator* on the VSWR = ∞ circle to point **3**, and read $y = 0 + j0.58$. This value must be added to $y = 1 + j0$ to get the admittance at x_1 with stub 1 connected; thus, $y(x_1) = 1 + j0.58$ (point **4**), VSWR = 1.75, and the reference position is 0.148λ *toward the generator*. Draw the VSWR circle through point **4**; move 3.333λ toward the generator from **4** to **5**; and read the admittance at x_2 without stub 2 in place: $y(x_2) = 0.57 - j0.08$. At this point add the second stub to get $y(x_2) = 0.57 + j0.50$ (point **6**) draw the VSWR = 2.3 circle. The reference position is 0.092λ *toward the generator*. From point **6** move 1.333λ toward the generator on the VSWR = 2.3 circle to point **7** and read the normalized input admittance $y_{in} = 0.52 - j0.38$. Invert this value by moving across a diameter and read $z_{in} = 1.23 + j0.92$ (point **8**). The input impedance to the line at 400 MHz is $z_{in}R_0 = (369 + j276)\ \Omega$.

15.14. The lossless lumped-parameter network shown in Fig. 15-28 is used to match a 50-Ω line to the input of an RF transistor operating at 1 GHz. The input reflection coefficient for the transistor is $\Gamma = 0.6\underline{/-150°}$, measured for a 50-$\Omega$ system. Find the values of L and C for the conjugate matched condition.

Fig. 15-28

Normalizing the reactances of the matching network to the 50-Ω line gives $\chi = \omega L/50$ and $b = 50\omega C$. The normalized impedance looking back to the network from the transistor is

$$z_m = j\chi + \frac{1}{1 + jb} \qquad (1)$$

Now, the matching criterion is $\Gamma_R = \Gamma^*$, or

$$z_m = \frac{1 + \Gamma^*}{1 - \Gamma^*} = 0.27 + j0.25 \qquad (2)$$

together (1) and (2) yield $b = \pm 1.64$. For $b = +1.64$, $x = +0.70$, where the positive sign on b corresponds to a capacitance. Then

$$C = \frac{b}{\omega R_0} = 5.2\ \text{pF} \qquad \text{and} \qquad L = \frac{\chi R_0}{\omega} = 5.6\ \text{nH}$$

15.15. A 15-m length of 300-Ω line must be connected to a 3-m length of 150-Ω line that is terminated in a 150-Ω resistor. Assuming the lossless condition for the air-dielectric lines and operation at a fixed frequency of 50 MHz, find the R_0 and the length for a quarter-wave section of line (*quarter-wave transformer*) to match the two lines for a VSWR = 1 on the main line. If no transformer is used, what is the VSWR on the main line?

A model for the system is shown in Fig. 15-29. For $f = 50$ MHz and $u_p = 3 \times 10^8$ m/s, the wavelength is $\lambda = 6$ m; a $\lambda/4$ section of line must be 1.5 m long.

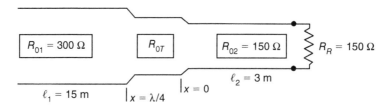

Fig. 15-29

With no transformer in place, the termination of the 300-Ω line is 150 Ω, since line 2 is R_0-terminated. The reflection coefficient on line 1 is

$$\Gamma = \frac{150-300}{150+300} = -\frac{1}{3} \quad \text{and} \quad \text{VSWR} = \frac{1+\left(\frac{1}{3}\right)}{1-\left(\frac{1}{3}\right)} = 2$$

With the transformer inserted as shown, the reflection coefficient at the load R_R is

$$\Gamma_R = \frac{R_R - R_{0T}}{R_R + R_{0T}} \tag{1}$$

and the input impedance at $\beta x = 90°$, which, as the load on line 1, must be 300 Ω, is

$$Z_{\text{in}} = 300\ \Omega = R_{0T} \frac{1+\Gamma_R\underline{/-180°}}{1-\Gamma_R\underline{/-180°}} = R_{0T}\frac{1-\Gamma_R}{1+\Gamma_R} \tag{2}$$

Substitution of (1), with $R_R = 150\ \Omega$, in (2) gives

$$300(150 + R_{0T} + 150 - R_{0T}) = R_{0T}(150 + R_{0T} - 150 + R_{0T})$$

or $R_{0T} = \sqrt{300\times150} = \sqrt{R_{01}R_{02}} = 212.1\ \Omega.$

15.16. A generator at 150 MHz drives a 10-m-long, 75-Ω coaxial line terminated in a composite load consisting of the parallel connection of two 50-Ω lines of lengths 0.5 m and 1 m, each terminated in a 50-Ω resistance. All lines are lossless with $\epsilon_R = 2.2$. With reference to Fig. 15-30, determine the length ℓ_s and connection point x_1 of a parallel-connected 75-Ω stub that will produce minimum VSWR on the feed line. The stub should be as close as possible to the load.

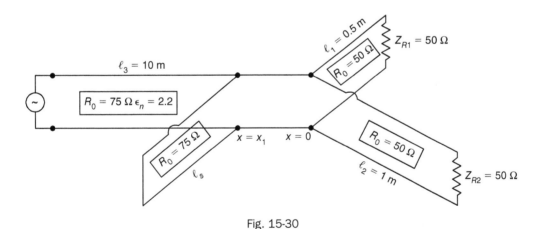

Fig. 15-30

Phase velocity, $u_p = 3 \times 10^8/\sqrt{2.2} = 2.02 \times 10^8$ m/s; wavelength, $\lambda = u_p/f = 1.35$ m. The input impedance to each of the 50-Ω lines is 50 Ω for R_0-termination, the composite load on the 75-Ω line is 25 Ω or, when normalized, $z_R = 0.333 + j0$. Plot z_R on the Smith Chart and through this point draw the $|\Gamma_R|$ circle and the radial line to the angle scale, as shown in Fig. 15-31. Read $\phi_R = 180°$ and measure

$$|\Gamma| = 0.5 \quad \text{and} \quad \text{VSWR} = 3$$

Since the matching stub is in parallel, locate $y_R = 3 + j0$ by projecting a diameter across from z_R. Locate the intersections of the $g = 1$ and VSWR $= 3$ circles and note the distances from the load at $x = 0$:

$$y = 1 + j \quad 1.15 \text{ at a distance} \quad 0.25 + 0.166 = 0.416\lambda \quad \text{toward the generator}$$
$$y = 1 - j \quad 1.15 \text{ at a distance} \quad 0.3335 - 0.25 = 0.0835\lambda \quad \text{toward the generator}$$

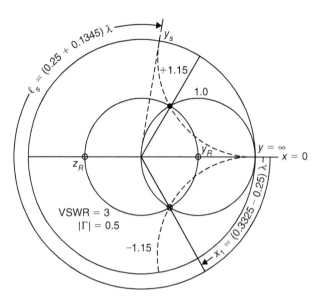

Fig. 15-31

Locate the 75-Ω stub at $x_1 = 0.0835\lambda = 11.3$ cm. The stub length ℓ_s is that which makes $y_s = 0 + j1.15$, for a net $y = 1 + j0$, (matched condition). Thus, plot y_s and determine the distance from the short-circuit condition $y = \infty$ to this point. The length of stub is $(0.25 + 0.1345)\lambda = 51.9$ cm.

The VSWR on lines ℓ_1 and ℓ_2 is 1.0 for the matched loads. On the shorted stub the VSWR is infinite. From $x = 0$ on the main line to $x = x_1$ the VSWR is 3.0 and from $x = x_1$ to $x = \ell_3$ the VSWR is 1.0.

15.17. Find the shortest distance from the load and the length (both in centimeter) of a shorted stub connected in parallel to a 300-Ω lossless air-dielectric line in order to match a load $Z_R = (600 + j300)$ Ω at 600 MHz. The matching stub is the same type of line as the main line.

For both the line and the stub, $u_p = 3 \times 10^8$ m/s and $\lambda = 0.5$ m. Plot $z_R = (600 + j300)/300 = 2 + j1$ on the y-chart, Fig. 15-32. Draw the VSWR = 2.6 circle, move diametrically across to $y_R = 0.4 - j0.2$, and read the reference position 0.464λ *toward the generator*. Move from y_R on the VSWR circle to the first intersection with the $g = 1$ circle, and read $y(x_1) = 1 + j1$ at the reference position 0.162λ. The stub location is

$$x_1 = [(0.5 - 0.464) + 0.162]\lambda = 0.198\lambda = 9.9 \text{ cm}$$

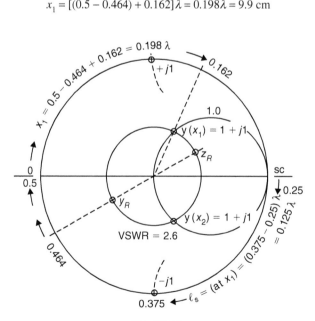

Fig. 15-32

from the load. To match the line for VSWR = 1, the admittance of the shorted stub must be $y_s = 0 - j1$ to cancel the susceptance at point x_1. The required length of stub is $0.125\lambda = 6.25$ cm.

If this position is not accessible, the second intersection with the $g = 1$ circle may be used, where $y(x_2) = 1 - j1$ and

$$x_2 = [(0.05 - 0.464) + 0.338]\lambda = 0.374\lambda = 18.7 \text{ cm}$$

The stub would have to be adjusted to give $y_s = +j1$, for a length of $0.375\lambda = 18.75$ cm.

15.18. A high-frequency lossless 70-Ω line, with $\epsilon_r = 2.1$, is terminated in $Z_R = 50\underline{/30°}$ Ω at 320 MHz. The load is to be matched with a shorted section of 50-Ω line, with $\epsilon_r = 2.3$, connected in parallel; the stub must be at least 5 cm from the load. If such matching is possible, find the distance from the load and the length of the stub.

For the main line, $u_p = 3 \times 10^8/\sqrt{2.1} = 2.07 \times 10^8$ m/s, $\lambda = u_p/f = 64.7$ cm; for the stub line, $u_{ps} = 3 \times 10^8/\sqrt{2.3} = 1.98 \times 10^8$ m/s, $\lambda_s = 61.9$ cm. The normalized load is $z_R = (50\underline{/30°})/70 = 0.62 + j0.36$, with VSWR = 1.92, and the admittance is $y_R = 1.20 - j0.70$ at reference position $0.327\lambda_m$ *toward the generator*; see Fig. 15-33. Move on the VSWR circle from y_R toward the generator to the first intersection, $y(x_1) = 1 - j0.66$, at 0.350λ, or a distance of $0.023\lambda = 1.49$ cm. This point cannot be used due to the 5-cm limitation. Continue on the VSWR circle to $y(x_2) = 1 + j0.66$ at position $0.151\lambda_m$; the distance

$$x_2 = (0.5 - 0.327) + 0.151 = 0.324\lambda_m = 21.0 \text{ cm}$$

gives the point of connection for the stub.

As the stub has a different R_0, it is necessary first to "denormalize" $y(x_2)$:

$$y(x_2) = \frac{1 + j0.66}{70} = (1.4 + j0.94) \times 10^{-2} \text{ S}$$

which shows that for cancellation of susceptance we must have

$$y_s = (-j0.94 \times 10^{-2})(50) = -j0.47$$

The length of shorted stub is then $(0.43 - 0.25)\lambda_s = 0.18\lambda_s = 11.1$ cm.

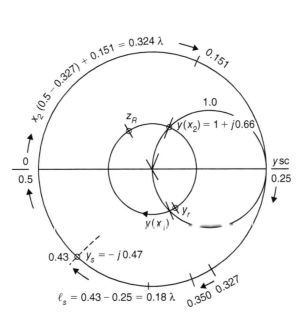

Fig. 15-33

15.19. A complex load is measured with a VHF bridge at 500 MHz; the impedance is $29\underline{/30°}$ Ω. This load is connected to a 50-Ω air-dielectric line, with a 50-Ω $3\lambda/8$ tuner between the load and line. Find the lengths of each shorted stub to produce a VSWR of 1.0 on the main line. Show both solutions if they exist.

The model for the system is shown in Fig. 15-9. For the air line, $u_p = 3 \times 10^8$ m/s and $\lambda = u_p/f = 60$ cm. The normalized load impedance is

$$z_R = \frac{Z_R}{R_0} = 0.58\underline{/30°} = 0.5 + j0.29$$

On the Smith Chart draw the $3\lambda/8$ tuner circle, plot z_R, draw the VSWR = 2.25 circle, locate $y_R = 1.52 - j0.88$, and find the intersections of the tuner circle and the $g_R = 1.52$ circle. There is a solution for each intersection; first consider $y = 1.52 - j1.82$ (Fig. 15-34a). Here, the first stub must be adjusted to change the susceptance from −0.88 to −1.82 (point **1**); thus, $y_{s1} = 0 - j0.94$ at point **2**. The stub length for this b is read on λ scale from $y = \infty$ *toward the generator*:

$$\ell_{s1} = (0.380 - 0.25)\lambda = 7.8 \text{ cm}$$

From point **1** move $3\lambda/8$ toward the generator to point **3**, where $y = 1 + j1.53$. Stub 2 must add $y = 0 - j1.53$ (point **4**); and the stub length is

$$\ell_{s2} = (0.342 - 0.25)\lambda = 5.52 \text{ cm}$$

Fig. 15-34b presents the second solution, which follows the same pattern.

At 1′: $y = 1.52 - j0.16$

At 2′: $y_{s1} = 0 + j0.72$ and

         $\ell_{s1} = (0.25 + 0.099)\lambda = 21.6$ cm

At 3′: $y = 1 + j0.45$

At 4′: $y_{s2} = 0 - j0.45$ and

         $\ell_{s2} = (0.433 - 0.25)\lambda = 11.4$ cm

The first solution is preferred because the total length of the stubs with infinite VSWR is 12.63 cm, which will introduce lower losses in a practical system.

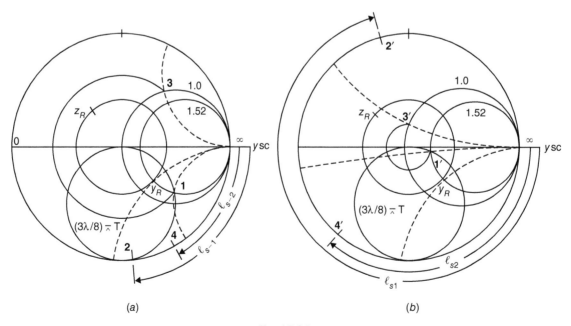

(a)   (b)

Fig. 15-34

15.20. Use a two-stub quarter-wave tuner (50-Ω, shorted stubs) located 7.2 cm from the load of Problem 15.19 in order to match the load to the line.

The normalized load admittance in Problem 15.19 is $y_R = 1/z_R = 1.52 - j0.88$, and the wavelength is $\lambda = 60$ cm. At 7.2 cm or 0.12λ from the load, $y_1 = 0.54 - j0.36$; this value is to be matched to the line with the tuner. Two solutions exist:

Solution 1 (Fig. 15-35)

$$y_1 = 0.54 - j0.36$$

1: $\quad y_T = 0.54 - j0.50$

2: $\quad y_{s1} = -j0.14$

$\quad \ell_{s1} = (0.478 - 0.25)\lambda = 13.68$ cm

3: Move $\lambda/4$ to $y = 1 + j0.95$

4: $\quad y_{s2} = -j0.95$

$\quad \ell_{s2} = (0.3795 - 0.25)\lambda = 7.77$ cm

Total stub length = 21.45 cm (preferred)

Solution 2 (Fig. 15-36)

$$y_2 = 0.54 - j0.36$$

1′: $\quad y_T = 0.54 + j0.50$

2′: $\quad y_{s1} + j0.86$

$\quad \ell_{s1} = (0.25 + 0.113)\lambda = 21.78$ cm

3′: Move $\lambda/4$ to $y = 1 - j0.95$

4′: $\quad y_{s2} = +j0.95$

$\quad \ell_{s2} = (0.25 + 0.1205)\lambda = 22.23$ cm

Total stub length = 44.01 cm

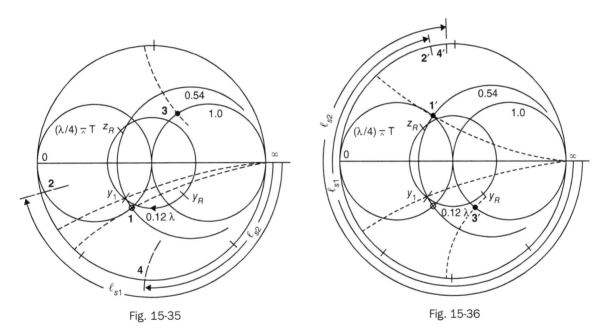

Fig. 15-35   Fig. 15-36

15.21. A 70-Ω double-stub tuner is used to match a load $Y_R = (4.76 + j1.43)$ mS at 600 MHz to a 70-Ω lossless air-dielectric line. The first stub is located at the load and the separation between the stubs is 10 cm. Find the shorted-stub lengths for the matched condition.

For the air line, $\lambda = (3 \times 10^8)/(6 \times 10^8) = 0.50$ m and the stub separation is 10 cm = $\lambda/5$. Draw the $\lambda/5$ tuner circle as shown in Fig. 15-37. Plot the normalized load $y_R = Y_R R_0 = 0.33 + j0.10$, which determines the VSWR = 3.0 circle. Two solutions exist, one for the intersection with the tuner circle at $y_1 = 0.333 - j0.18$ (VSWR = 3.2) and the other at $y_2 = 0.333 + j0.84$ (VSWR = 4.9).

First solution. $y_{s1} = -j0.28$ to change y_R to y_1, for a length of $0.207\lambda = 10.35$ cm. Move on the VSWR = 3.2 circle 0.2λ *toward the generator* from y_R, to $y = 1.0 + j1.23$. The second stub must be adjusted to give $y_{s2} = -j1.23$ for a net $y = 1 + j0$, the matched condition. The length is $0.109\lambda = 5.45$ cm.

Second solution. $y'_{s1} = +j0.74$, for $y_2 = 0.33 + j0.84$ and a length $0.351\lambda = 17.55$ cm. Move on the VSWR = 4.9 circle 0.2λ *toward the generator* from y_R, to $y' = 1.0 - j1.75$. The second stub must be adjusted for $y'_{s2} = -j1.75$ to produce $1 + j0$, the matched condition. The length is $0.417\lambda = 20.85$ cm.

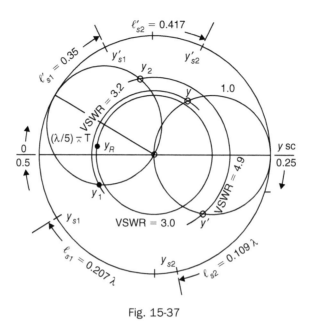

Fig. 15-37

15.22. A 50-Ω slotted line that is 40 cm long is inserted in a 50-Ω lossless line feeding an antenna at 600 MHz. Standing-wave measurements with a short-circuit termination and with the antenna in place yield the data of Fig. 15-38; the scale on the slotted line has the lowest number on the load side. Find the impedance of the antenna, the reflection coefficient due to the load, and the velocity of propagation on the line.

Fig. 15-38

For the short circuit, minima are separated by a half-wavelength, so $\lambda = 50$ cm. For a frequency of 600 MHz the phase velocity is $u_p = f\lambda = 3 \times 10^8$ m/s (air dielectric). With the antenna in place the minimum shifts 5 cm = 0.1λ toward the generator. On the Smith Chart draw the VSWR = 2.2 circle and identify the voltage minimum line as in Fig. 15-39. Locate z_R on the VSWR circle 0.1λ *toward the load* from the V_{min} position:

$$z_R = 0.64 - j0.52 \quad \text{and} \quad Z_R = R_0 z_R = (32 - j26)\ \Omega$$

The load Γ_R is read from the chart: $\phi_R = -108°$ and $|\Gamma_R| = 0.375$ is the distance from the center to z_R, as read off the external scale.

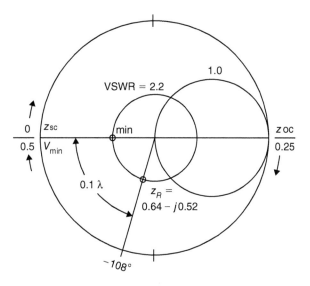

Fig. 15-39

15.23. A 40-m length of lossless 50-Ω coaxial cable with a phase velocity of 2×10^8 m/s is connected at $t = 0$ to a source with $v_g(t) = 18$ V dc and $R_g = 100\ \Omega$. If the receiving end is short-circuit terminated, sketch the sending-end voltage $v_S(t)$ from $t = 0$ to $t = 2.5\ \mu s$.

The delay time of the line is

$$t_D = \frac{\ell}{u_p} = \frac{40}{2 \times 10^8} = 0.2\ \mu s$$

The incident voltage at the sending end at $t = 0$ is

$$v_S(0) = \frac{v_g R_0}{R_g + R_0} = \frac{18 \times 50}{100 + 50} = 6\ \text{V}$$

The reflection coefficients at the two ends are

$$\Gamma_g = \frac{R_g - R_0}{R_g + R_0} = \frac{100 - 50}{100 + 50} = +\frac{1}{3} \qquad \Gamma_R = \frac{R_R - R_0}{R_R + R_0} = \frac{0 - 50}{0 + 50} = -1$$

Fig. 15-40 shows the $t = d$ plot over a total time of 2.5 $\mu s = 12.5 t_D$. From this, the desired $v_s = t$ plot, Fig. 15-41, is easily derived. At any time v_s is the sum of all incident and reflected waves present at $d = a$, up to and including the last-created incident wave. For example,

$$v_s(4.01 t_D) = 6 - 6 - 2 + 2 + \frac{2}{3} = \frac{2}{3}$$

On account of $\Gamma_R = -1$ the waves preceding the last incident wave cancel in pairs.

Fig. 15-40

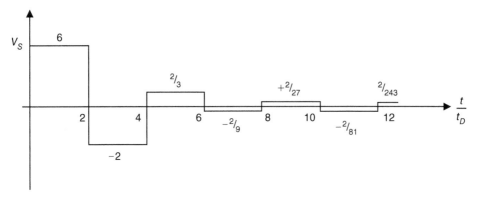

Fig. 15-41

15.24. A well-designed, lossless, 100-Ω, 100-μs delay line produces a good 10-μs pulse at the output 100 μs after it is driven at the input, at $t = 0$, by a 10-μs rectangular pulse recurring with a period of 2 ms. The generator has a 9-V peak open-circuit output and an internal resistance of 50 Ω. Sketch $v_S(t)$ and $v_R(t)$ from $t = 0$ to $t = 650$ μs if the termination is a 50-Ω resistor.

At $t = 0$ the sending-end incident voltage is pulse of 10-μs duration with a peak value of

$$V_{inc} = \frac{(9)(100)}{50 + 100} = 6 \text{V}$$

The sending-end and receiving-end reflection coefficients are

$$\Gamma_g = \frac{R_g - R_0}{R_g + R_0} = \frac{50 - 100}{50 + 100} = -\frac{1}{3} \qquad \Gamma_R = \frac{R_R - R_0}{R_R + R_0} = \frac{50 - 100}{50 + 100} = -\frac{1}{3}$$

Since the pulse period is 2000 μs, only the pulse sent out at $t = 0$ need be considered in the $t = d$ plot of Fig. 15-42, which covers only the first 650 μs. Applying to Fig. 15-42 the summation technique described in Problem 15.23, one obtains the required voltage plots, Fig. 15-43.

For proper operation the delay line must be terminated in $R_0 = 100$ Ω.

Fig. 15-42

Fig. 15-43

SUPPLEMENTARY PROBLEMS

15.25. A coaxial cable with the dimensions $a = 0.5$ mm, $b = 3$ mm, and $t = 0.4$ mm is filled with a dielectric material having $\epsilon_r = 2.0$, $\sigma_d = 10\ \mu S/m$. The conductors have $\sigma_c = 50$ MS/m. Calculate the per-meter values of L, C, G, R_d, and R_a at 50 MHz. Neglect internal inductance.

15.26. Find the per-meter values of L, C, G, and R for a parallel-wire line constructed in air of #12 AWG copper wire (dia. = 0.081 in., $\sigma_c = 52.8$ MS/m) with a 4-inch separation. Operation is at 100 kHz.

15.27. In a "twin-lead" transmission line, two parallel copper wires ($\sigma_c = 50$ MS/m) are embedded 0.625 in. apart in a low-loss dielectric with $\epsilon_r = 2.4$. Neglecting losses, determine the diameter of the conductors for a characteristic impedance of 300 Ω. For this size of conductor, find the dc resistance and the ac resistance at 100 MHz.

15.28. A high-frequency application uses a coaxial cable with copper conductors, where the diameter of the inner conductor is 0.8 mm and the inside diameter of the outer conductor is 8.0 mm. The dielectric material has $\epsilon_r = 2.35$, and the thickness of the outer conductor is much greater than the depth of penetration at the operating frequency. The engineer wants to use a new cable having the same R_0, but with a larger outer conductor such that $b_2 - a = 1.5(b_1 - a)$. Find ϵ_r for the new cable and calculate R_0 and the capacitance per meter for each cable.

15.29. For the coaxial cable of Problem 15.28, calculate the line characteristics Z_0, α, β, u_p, λ for operation at 10 kHz.

15.30. Find the characteristic impedance, propagation constant, velocity of propagation, and wavelength for the parallel-wire line of Problem 15.26.

15.31. A transmission line is 2 miles long, operates at 10 kHz, and has parameters $R = 30\ \Omega/mi$, $C = 80$ nF/mi, $L = 2.2$ mH/mi, and $G = 20$ nS/mi. Find the characteristic impedance, attenuation per mile, phase shift per mile, phase velocity, and wavelength. What is the received power to a matched load when the sending-end power is 1.2 W?

15.32. A transmission line 250 m long operates at 2 MHz with a load impedance of 200 Ω. The line characteristics are $Z_0 = 300\ \underline{/0°}\ \Omega$, $\alpha = 4 \times 10^{-4}$ Np/m, $\beta = 0.06$ rad/m. If the sending-end voltage is $30\ \underline{/0°}$ V, find the receiving-end voltage, power to the load, sending-end current and power, and the reflected power from the load.

15.33. One method of determining the characteristics of a line is to measure the input impedance at $x = \ell$ (line disconnected from source) when the receiving end is opened for Z_{oc}, and when it is shorted for Z_{sc}. From the product $Z_{oc}Z_{sc}$ and the ratio Z_{oc}/Z_{sc} the characteristic impedance and the propagation constant per unit length can be calculated. If measured values at 5 kHz are $Z_{oc} = 141.9\underline{/-84.1°}\ \Omega$ and $Z_{sc} = 62.0\underline{/37.7°}\ \Omega$ for a 2-mile length of line, use the equation for Z_S to find Z_0, α (per mile), and β (per mile).

15.34. A 200-m length of 300-Ω transmission line has $\alpha = 2.5 \times 10^{-3}$ Np/m and $\beta = 0.02$ rad/m when operating at 200 kHz. If $\hat{V}_R = 20 \,\underline{/0°}$ V and $Z_R = 350 \,\underline{/20°}\,\Omega$, find the distance from the receiving end to the first impedance minimum. What is the value of this Z_{min}?

15.35. A 500-Ω line is connected to a 10-kHz generator rated at $80 \,\underline{/0°}$ V open-circuit with an internal resistance of 600 Ω. The line is 3 miles long, with $\alpha = 0.05$ Np/mi and $\beta = 0.9$ rad/mi at 10 kHz. For a matched load at $x = 0$, find the sending-end power, the receiving-end power, and $\hat{V}_R$. If the line is opened at the receiving end, what is the sending-end power?

15.36. For the line of Problem 15.35, find the receiving-end current and the sending-end power if the line is shorted at $x = 0$.

15.37. The rigid coaxial line of Problems 15.2 and 15.9 would be classified as a low-loss line. (*a*) What are the reflection coefficients at the load and VSWR if the load is a 40-Ω resistor? (*b*) Determine the maximum and minimum load resistance for VSWR = 1.5. (*c*) Calculate the reflection coefficient 3 cm from the load, if $Z_R = (55 + j0)\,\Omega$ (consider attenuation).

15.38. A 90-Ω, lossless, high-frequency, coaxial line, with $\epsilon_r = 2.1$, operates at 150 MHz. Of interest is the sensitivity of the VSWR to small changes in terminating resistance. (*a*) Tabulate Γ_R and VSWR against $R_R = (90 \pm 2n)\,\Omega$, for integral values of n from 0 to 5. (*b*) If the specifications for an application limit the maximum VSWR to 1.025, find the maximum and minimum values of terminating resistance.

15.39. For the transmission line of Problem 15.38, (*a*) find the phase velocity, wavelength, and the phase shift per meter. (*b*) If the terminating resistance is 100 Ω, find the input impedances for line lengths $\lambda/2$, $\lambda/4$, and $\lambda/8$.

15.40. Use the Smith Chart to find (*a*) Γ_R, (*b*) VSWR, and (*c*) y_r for the following (Z_R, R_0)-pairs, in ohms: $(100 + j150, 50)$; $(28 - j35, 70)$; $90\,\underline{/-30°}, 90)$; $(120 \,\underline{/90°}, 50)$; $(0, 70)$; $(50 + j5, 50)$.

15.41. Find (*a*) y_R, (*b*) VSWR, and (*c*) Y_R (in mS) for the following (Γ_R, R_0)-pairs: $(0.5 \,\underline{/60°}, 50\,\Omega)$; $(1\,\underline{/-80°}, 90\,\Omega)$; $(0.1 \,\underline{/0°}, 70\,\Omega)$; $(-0.6\,\underline{/-30°}, 50\,\Omega)$; $(0.8 + j0.4, 70\,\Omega)$.

15.42. A lossless high-frequency line 3 m long, with $R_0 = 50\,\Omega$ and $\epsilon_r = 1.9$, is operated at 350 MHz. The VSWR on the line is 2.4 and the first voltage maximum is located 7 cm from the load. Use the Smith Chart to find the load impedance, the reflection coefficient at the receiving end, the location of the first voltage minimum, and the input impedance.

15.43. A 70-Ω lossless line, with $\epsilon_r = 2.2$, is 2.5 m long and operates at 625 MHz. The VSWR on the line is 1.7 and the first voltage minimum is located 5 cm from the load. Use the Smith Chart to find the load admittance, the reflection coefficient at $x = 0$, and the input admittance to the line.

15.44. An air-dielectric line with $R_0 = 150\,\Omega$ is terminated in a load of $(150 - j150)\,\Omega$ at the operating frequency, 75 MHz. (*a*) Use the Smith Chart to find the shortest length of line for which the input impedance is $(150 + j150)\,\Omega$. (*b*) What are the VSWR on the line and the reflection coefficient at the load? What is the shortest length of line for which $Z_{in} = R + j0$, and what is the value of R?

15.45. Two lines are connected in parallel at the input to a 250-MHz source. Each line is 2 m long and is terminated in a 70-Ω resistance. Line #1 has $R_0 = 50\,\Omega$, $\epsilon_r = 1.9$, line #2 has $R_0 = 90\,\Omega$, $\epsilon_r = 2.3$. Use the Smith Chart to find the input impedance to the parallel combination. (Be careful in combining the two input impedances/admittances.)

15.46. A lossless 50-Ω line, with a phase velocity 2.5×10^8 m/s, is 105 cm long and is terminated in a load $Y_R = (20 - j16)$ mS at 500 MHz. A short-circuited line, 17.85 cm long and also having $R_0 = 50\,\Omega$, is connected across Y, as shown in Fig. 15-44. Use the Smith Chart to find the VSWR on the main line and the input impedance. What is the equivalent capacitance (or inductance) of the short-circuited line?

Fig. 15-44

15.47. In the line of Problem 15.46, the short circuit on line two is inadvertently changed to an open circuit. Use the Smith Chart to find the VSWR on the main line and the input impedance.

15.48. A parallel-wire line of the type in Problem 15.1 is operated at 20 MHz to supply a resistive load of 500 Ω through a quarter-wave matching transformer connected at the load. Neglect losses on the main line and the transformer section. (*a*) For the transformer calculate the length of line and characteristic impedance required for matching. (*b*) If the same sized wire is used for the main line and the transformer, find the separation *d* (in inches) required for matching.

15.49. A lossless 70-Ω line is terminated in $Z_R = 60.3\underline{/-30.7°}$ Ω at 280 MHz. Use the Smith Chart to find the value of the inductance or capacitance to connect in parallel with the load for minimum VSWR on the line. What length (in centimeter) of shorted line would give the desired value, if $\epsilon_r = 2.1$?

15.50. A 200-Ω air-dielectric line is terminated in $Y_R = (3.3 - j1.0)$ mS at 200 MHz. (*a*) Find the VSWR and the position nearest the load where the real part of the normalized admittance is unity, using the Smith Chart. (*b*) What value of susceptance (in millisiemens) should be connected at this point to make VSWR = 1 on the line?

15.51. Two 72-Ω resistive loads are connected in parallel as the termination for a 120-Ω air-dielectric lossless line at 150 MHz. Find the location nearest the load and the length (both in centimeters) of a single shorted parallel-connected stub to match the line for a VSWR = 1.0.

15.52. (*a*) In Problem 15.51, if the maximum length of the adjustable shorted stub is 50 cm, can the load be matched to the line? (*b*) If the answer to (*a*) is Yes, find the position and length of the stub for the matched condition. (*c*) If the stub were left at its original position and set to the 50-cm maximum, what would be the VSWR on the line?

15.53. A 90-Ω lossless line with $\epsilon_r = 1.8$ operates at 280 MHz and is matched to the termination with a single shorted stub that produces VSWR = 1.0. The stub is located 15.8 cm from the load and is of length 10 cm. Find the ohmic value of the terminating impedance.

15.54. A 50-Ω air-dielectric lossless line has $Z_R = (25 - j30)$ Ω at 120 MHz. An adjustable shorted stub is located 45 cm from the load (fixed in position). Find the length of stub for the best match on the line. What is the minimum VSWR on the line?

15.55. (*a*) An air-dielectric lossless 70-Ω line is matched at 200 MHz to a 140-Ω load by means of a shorted parallel stub. Find the position nearest the load and the length of the stub (both in centimeter) for the matched condition. (*b*) The line is now used at 220 MHz without changing the position or length of the stub. Find the VSWR on the main line at the new frequency.

15.56. The termination on a 90-Ω lossless air-dielectric line is $Z_R = (270 + j0)$ Ω at 600 MHz. A double-stub 0.25λ tuner is connected with the first stub at the load for matching. Find the lengths for the shorted stubs (both solutions). Which solution is preferred?

15.57. A $3\lambda/8$ tuner is connected at the load to match $Z_R = (50 - j50)$ Ω at 400 MHz to a 50-Ω lossless air-dielectric line. Find the lengths of the shorted stubs for both solutions and indicate the preferred solution.

15.58. A 50-Ω air-dielectric line, with a load $Y_R = (0.024 - j0.02)$ S at 470 MHz, has a $\lambda/4$ tuner with the first stub located 7 cm from the load. Find both solutions for the lengths of the shorted stubs to match the load to the line. Indicate the preferred solution.

15.59. A two-stub $3\lambda/8$ tuner is constructed of 70-Ω line with $\epsilon_r = 2.0$ for use at 272 MHz on the same type of line and a certain load. For the matched condition the shorted stub at the load is 4.76 cm long and the other shorted stub is 4.60 cm long. Find the ohmic impedance of the load at the operating frequency.

15.60. A 225-Ω resistive load is matched to a 90-Ω air-dielectric line at 300 MHz. The matching is via two shorted stubs separated by 30 cm, with the first stub connected at the load. Find the lengths of the stubs (both solutions) and indicate the preferred solution.

15.61. A 50-Ω slotted line is used to determine the load impedance at 750 MHz on a lossless 50-Ω line. When the line is terminated in a short circuit, the high VSWR has adjacent minima at 30 cm and 10 cm (the scale has the low numbers on the load side). With Z_R connected, the VSWR is 3.2, a minimum is located at 13.2 cm, and the adjacent maximum is at 23.2 cm. Find the ohmic value of Z_R at the operating frequency.

15.62. Find the load impedance and the operating frequency for a 90-Ω air-dielectric system that has the following slotted-line measurements:

With load: VSWR = 1.6 and a voltage minimum at 10 cm (high numbers on load side).

With short circuit: VSWR > 100, minimum at 40 cm, maximum at 10 cm.

15.63. A 50-Ω slotted line is used to measure the load impedance at 625 MHz on a 50-Ω lossless coaxial line. Adjacent voltage minima are found at 10 mm and 250 mm (high numbers at the load side) when the termination is a short circuit. With the load connected, VSWR > 100 and a minimum occurs at 172.7 mm. Find the ohmic value of the load impedance.

15.64. A tuner is connected at the load to match the load to a 50-Ω lossless air-dielectric line at 517 MHz. To check the quality of the matching, a slotted line is inserted in the system. With the tuner and load connected, VSWR = 1.15, with a V_{min} at 253.4 mm. When the tuner and load are both removed and replaced by a short circuit, adjacent minima are found at 40 mm and 330 mm (low numbers on the scale are at load side). Find the residual normalized admittance on the line that results from the "best match."

15.65. A 60 m-long, lossless, 50-Ω coaxial cable, with a phase velocity of 2×10^8 m/s, is terminated with a short circuit. The line is connected at $t = 0$ to a 30-V dc source having internal resistance 25 Ω. Plot the sending-end voltage from $t = 0$ up to the time when the voltage drops below 0.1 V.

15.66. A 90-Ω lossless line, with $\epsilon_r = 2.78$, is connected at $t = 0$ to a 70-V dc source with an internal resistance of 120 Ω. If the line is 135 m long, find the time when the open-circuit voltage at the receiving end is 97% of the steady-state value. When is the voltage 99.95% of the steady-state value?

15.67. A pulse generator with internal resistance 150 Ω produces a 20-μs pulse with an open-circuit amplitude of +8 V. The generator is connected to a 50-Ω, lossless, 200-μs delay line that is terminated in a 100-Ω resistance. If the period of the recurring pulses is 4 ms, sketch the voltage at the input to the delay line from pulse onset at $t = 0$ to $t = 1.4$ ms.

15.68. Sketch v_S and v_R versus time, from $t = 0^+$ to $t = 300$ μs, when a 70-Ω, lossless, 50-μs delay line is terminated with a 30-Ω resistor and driven by a pulse generator. The generator has an internal resistance of 70 Ω and produces a 2-μs pulse with a peak open-circuit voltage of +10 V at a repetition rate of 1000 pulses per second.

15.69. In Fig. 15-45 a line is used to produce a short rectangular pulse of width 12 ns and peak value 800 V. With S-2 open, S-1 is closed to charge the line to V_{dc}; after charging, S-1 is opened. Then, at $t = 0$, S-2 is closed to discharge the line through R_R and form the pulse. Find the length of line and V_{dc}.

Fig. 15-45

15.70. Sketch v_S and v_R versus time, from $t = 0^+$ to $t = 30$ μs, when a 220-m-long, 90-Ω, lossless line, with $\epsilon_r = 3.65$, is terminated in a 50-Ω resistance and driven by a pulse generator. The generator has an internal resistance of 90 Ω and produces a 5-μs pulse with open-circuit peak value +140 V, at a repetition rate of 100 pulses per second.

15.71. Use the Laplace transform to solve (5) for a very long lossless transmission line connected at $x = 0$ to a voltage source $v(t)$. Show and describe the steps in the solution. The equation and boundary conditions are the following:

$$\frac{\partial^2 f(x,t)}{\partial t^2} = u^2 \frac{\partial^2 f(x,t)}{\partial x^2}, \quad u = \frac{1}{\sqrt{LC}} \qquad\qquad x > 0, t > 0 \qquad (5\ bis)$$

$$f(x,0) = \frac{\partial f(x,t)}{\partial t}\bigg|_{t=0} = 0 \qquad\qquad x > 0 \qquad (5a)$$

$$f(0,t) = v(t), \ \lim_{x \to \infty} f(x,t) = 0 \qquad\qquad t \geq 0 \qquad (5b)$$

Step 1. Take the Laplace transform of both sides of (5) with respect to t.

By definitions: $$F(x, s) = \mathcal{L}\{f(x, t)\} = \int_0^\infty f(x, t)e^{-st}\, dt$$

From the left side of (5): $$\mathcal{L}\left\{\frac{\partial^2 f(x, t)}{\partial t^2}\right\} = s^2 F(x, s)$$

From the right side of (5): $$\mathcal{L}\left\{\frac{\partial^2 f(x, t)}{\partial t^2}\right\} = \int_0^\infty \frac{\partial^2 f(x, t)}{\partial x^2}e^{-st}\, dt = \frac{\partial^2}{\partial x^2}\int_0^\infty f(x, t)e^{-st}\, dt = \frac{\partial^2 F(x, s)}{\partial x^2}$$

Transform of (5): $$\frac{\partial^2 F(x, s)}{\partial x^2} - \frac{s^2}{u^2}F(x, s) = 0 \qquad (5c)$$

Step 2. Because s is a parameter, (5c) may be written as the ordinary differential equation (6a) with the boundary conditions given by (6b).

Differential equation for $F(x, s)$: $$\frac{d^2 F(x, s)}{\partial x^2} - \frac{s^2}{u^2}F(x, s) = 0 \qquad (6a)$$

Boundary conditions: $$F(0, s) = \mathcal{L}\{v(t)\} = \int_0^\infty v(t)e^{-st}\, dt, \quad \text{and} \quad \lim_{x \to \infty} F(x, s) = 0 \qquad (6b)$$

Step 3. Solve for $F(x, s)$ in (6a) and using the boundary conditions determine the constants of integration.

General solution of (6a): $\qquad\qquad F(x, s) = C_1 e^{-sx/u} + C_2 e^{sx/u}$

But $C_2 = 0$ because in the Laplace transform $s > 0$ and $\lim_{x \to \infty} F(x, s) = 0$. Therefore, $\quad F(x, s) = C_1 e^{-sx/u}$

From the first condition in (6b) we find $C_1 = V(s)$ (transform of the voltage source) $\quad F(x, s) = V(s)e^{-sx/u}$

From the shift property of the Laplace transform

$$f(x, t) = \begin{cases} v\left(t - \dfrac{x}{u}\right) & \text{for } t \geq \dfrac{x}{u} \\ 0 & \text{for } t < \dfrac{x}{u} \end{cases}$$

ANSWERS TO SUPPLEMENTARY PROBLEMS

15.25. $0.358\ \mu\text{H/m}$, $62.0\ \text{pF/m}$, $35.1\ \mu\text{S/m}$, $0.030\ \Omega/\text{m}$, $0.743\ \Omega/\text{m}$

15.26. $1.84\ \mu\text{H/m}$, $6.05\ \text{pF/m}$, 0, $R_a = 0.0268\ \Omega/\text{m}$

15.27. $0.026\ \text{in.} = 0.66\ \text{mm}$, $0.117\ \Omega/\text{m}$, $2.72\ \Omega/\text{m}$

15.28. 3.18, $90\ \Omega$, $56.8\ \text{pF/m}$ (old), $66.1\ \text{pF/m}$ (new)

15.29. $32.7\underline{/15.2°}\ \Omega$, $1.04 \times 10^{-3}\ \text{Np/m}$; $4.2 \times 10^{-4}\ \text{rad/m}$, $1.49 \times 10^8\ \text{m/s}$, $14.9\ \text{km}$

15.30. $552.5\underline{/-0.65°}\ \Omega$, $(2.4 + j210)10^{-5}\ \text{m}^{-1}$, $2.99 \times 10^8\ \text{m/s}$, $2.99\ \text{km}$

15.31. $167.7\underline{/-6.1°}\ \Omega$, $0.0896\ \text{Np/mi}$, $0.838\ \text{rad/mi}$, $7.5 \times 10^4\ \text{mi/s}$, $7.5\ \text{mi}$; $838.6\ \text{mW}$

15.32. $22\underline{/-130°}\ \text{V}$; $1.21\ \text{W}$; $105.4\underline{/18.3°}\ \text{mA}$, $1.5\ \text{W}$; $50\ \text{mW}$

15.33. $93.8\underline{/-23.2°}\ \Omega$, $0.12\ \text{Np/mi}$, $0.28\ \text{rad/mi}$

15.34. $107.2\ \text{m}$, $239.4\ \Omega$

15.35. $1.32\ \text{W}$, $0.98\ \text{W}$, $31.3\underline{/-154.7°}\ \text{V}$; $0.65\ \text{W}$

15.36. $0.12\underline{/-157.6°}\ \text{A}$, $0.55\ \text{W}$

15.37. (a) -0.073, 1.16; (b) $69.45\ \Omega$, $30.89\ \Omega$; (c) $0.0856\underline{/-216°}$

15.38. (a) See Table 15-4. (b) $92.24\ \Omega$, $87.81\ \Omega$

TABLE 15-4

N	R_R	Γ_R	VSWR
0	90	0.0	1.0
1	92	0.0110	1.022
	88	−0.0112	1.023
2	94	0.0217	1.044
	86	−0.0227	1.046
3	96	0.0323	1.067
	84	−0.0345	1.071
4	98	0.0426	1.089
	82	−0.0465	1.098
5	100	0.0526	1.111
	80	−0.0588	1.125

15.39. (a) 2.07×10^8 m/s, 1.38 m, 4.55 rad/m; (b) $100\underline{/\text{−}0°}$ Ω, $81\underline{/\text{−}0°}$ Ω, $90\underline{/\text{−}6°}$ Ω

15.40. (a) $0.75\underline{/26.5°}$, $0.53\underline{/\text{−}121°}$, $0.27\underline{/\text{−}90}$, $1.0\underline{/45°}$, −1.0, $0.05\underline{/90°}$

     (b) 7, 3.3, 1.75, ∞, ∞, 1.1

     (c) $0.16 - j0.225$, $0.97 + j1.23$, $0.87 + j0.52$, $-j0.415$, ∞, $1 - j0.1$

15.41. (a) $0.44 - j0.495$, $0 + j0.84$, $0.83 + j0$, $2.0 - j1.85$, $0.06 - j0.238$

     (b) 3.0, ∞, 1.2, 4.0, 17

     (c) $8.8 - j9.9$, $0 + j9.3$, $11.9 + j0$, $40 - j37$, $0.86 - j3.4$

15.42. $(40 + j39)$ Ω, $0.42\underline{/\,81°}$, 22.6 cm, $(22.3 - j11)$ Ω

15.43. $(10.4 + j5.4)$ mS, $0.27\underline{/\text{−}68°}$, $(16 - j7.9)$ mS

15.44. (a) 1.3 m; (b) 2.6, $0.47\underline{/\text{−}64°}$; (c) 64.8 cm, 57 Ω

15.45. $(24.6 + j3.5)$ Ω

15.46. 1.0, 50 Ω; 5.1 pF

15.47. 6.2, $(26.5 + j72.5)$ Ω

15.48. (a) $\ell_T = 3.75$ m, $R_{0T} = 547.7$ Ω; (b) $d_T = 7.77$ in.

15.49. $C = 4.8$ pF (VSWR$_{\min}$ = 1.0); 24.8 cm

15.50. (a) 1.65, 29.3 cm; (b) −2.55 (inductive)

15.51. 16 cm, 78.6 cm

15.52. (a) Yes; (b) 83.8 cm, 21.4 cm; (c) 3.3.

15.53. *Hint:* Remove y_s, find the VSWR, and move back toward the load.

     $201.2\underline{/26.6°}$ Ω

15.54. 96 cm, 1.08

15.55. (a) 22.65 cm, 22.80 cm; (b) 1.22

15.56. 9 cm and 4.95 cm (preferred); otherwise, 16 cm and 20.05 cm.

15.57. 4.5 cm and 4.3 cm (preferred); otherwise, 12.1 cm and 26.1 cm.

15.58. 14.5 cm and 7.6 cm (preferred); otherwise, 23.1 cm and 24.3 cm.

15.59. $(58.1 - j58.1)\ \Omega$

15.60. 13.6 cm and 8.5 cm (preferred); otherwise, 28.1 cm and 37.5 cm.

15.61. $31.24\underline{/-50.2°}\ \Omega$

15.62. 144 Ω; 250 MHz

15.63. 80 Ω (capacitative)

15.64. $0.98 - j0.14$

15.65. See Fig. 15-46.

15.66. 2.25 μs, 5.25 μs

15.67. See Fig. 15-47.

15.68. See Fig. 15-48.

15.69. 1.2 m, 1600 V

15.70. See Fig. 15-49.

15.71. $f(x,t) = \begin{cases} v\left(t - \dfrac{x}{u}\right) & \text{for } t \geq \dfrac{x}{u} \\ 0 & \text{for } t < \dfrac{x}{u} \end{cases}$

Fig. 15-46

Fig. 15-47

Fig. 15-48

Fig. 15-49

Waveguides

(by Milton L. Kult)

16.1 Introduction

The electromagnetic waves of Chapter 14 can be guided in a given direction of propagation using several different methods. For instance, the two-conductor transmission line, supporting what are essentially plane waves at megahertz frequencies, was considered in Chapter 15. The present chapter is restricted to single-conductor (hollow-pipe) *waveguides*, of rectangular or circular cross section, which operate in the gigahertz (microwave) range. These devices too support "plane waves"—in the sense that the wavefronts are planes perpendicular to the direction of propagation. However, the boundary conditions at the inner surface of the pipe force the fields to vary over a wavefront.

16.2 Transverse and Axial Fields

The waveguide is positioned with the longitudinal direction along the z axis. In general, the guide walls have $\sigma_c = \infty$ (perfect conductor) and the dielectric-filled hollow has $\sigma = 0$ (perfect dielectric), $\mu = \mu_0 \mu_r$, and $\epsilon = \epsilon_0 \epsilon_r$. It is further supposed that $\rho = 0$ (no free charge) in the dielectric. The dimensions for the cross section are inside dimensions. In Fig. 16-1(a) the $a \times b$ rectangular waveguide is shown in a Cartesian coordinate system, Fig. 16-1(b) shows the circular or cylindrical waveguide of radius a in a cylindrical coordinate system.

(a)

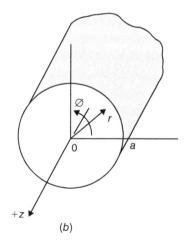

(b)

Fig. 16-1

As in Chapter 14 the time dependence $e^{j\omega t}$ will be assumed for the electromagnetic field in the dielectric core; this time factor will be suppressed everywhere in the analysis (as in phasor notation). Thus we have the following expressions for the field vector **F** (which stands for either **E** or **H**), assuming wave propagation in the $+z$ direction.

Rectangular coordinates. $\quad \mathbf{F} = \mathbf{F}(x, y)e^{-jkz}$ where

$$\mathbf{F}(x, y) = F_x(x, y)\mathbf{a}_x + F_y(x, y)\mathbf{a}_y + F_z(x, y)\mathbf{a}_z$$
$$\equiv \mathbf{F}_T(x, y) + F_z(x, y)\mathbf{a}_z$$

Cylindrical coordinates. $\quad \mathbf{F} = \mathbf{F}(r, \phi)e^{-jkz}$ where

$$\mathbf{F}(r, \phi) = F_r(r, \phi)\mathbf{a}_r + F_\phi(r, \phi)\mathbf{a}_\phi + F_z(r, \phi)\mathbf{a}_z$$
$$\equiv \mathbf{F}_T(r, \phi) + F_z(r, \phi)\mathbf{a}_z$$

Because the dielectric is lossless ($\sigma = 0$), the wave propagates without attenuation; hence, the *wave number* $k = 2\pi/\lambda$ (in rad/m) is constrained to be real and positive.

Note: In the other chapters of this book, unbounded dielectric media are considered, for which the wave number, notated β, depends on frequency and dielectric properties only. However, as will soon appear, the wave number in a bounded dielectric depends additionally on the geometry of the boundary. This important distinction is emphasized by the employment of a new symbol, k, in the present chapter.

The reason for decomposing the field vector into a transverse vector component $\mathbf{F}_T$ and an axial vector component $F_z\mathbf{a}_z$ is two-fold. On the one hand, the boundary conditions apply to $\mathbf{E}_T$ and $\mathbf{H}_T$ alone (see Problems 16.1 and 16.2). On the other hand, as will now be shown, the complete **E** and **H** fields in the waveguide are known once *either Cartesian component D_z or H_z is known.*

Transverse Components from Axial Components.

Assume a rectangular coordinate system. Maxwell's equation (2) of Section 14.2 yields the three scalar equations

$$-j\omega\mu H_x = jkE_y + \frac{\partial E_z}{\partial y} \tag{1a}$$

$$-j\omega\mu H_y = -jkE_x - \frac{\partial E_z}{\partial x} \tag{1b}$$

$$-j\omega\mu H_z = \frac{\partial E_y}{\partial x} - \frac{\partial E_x}{\partial y} \tag{1c}$$

Maxwell's equation (1) of Section 14.2, with $\sigma = 0$, gives three additional scalar equations:

$$j\omega\epsilon E_x = jkH_y + \frac{\partial H_z}{\partial y} \tag{2a}$$

$$j\omega\epsilon E_y = -jkH_x - \frac{\partial H_z}{\partial x} \tag{2b}$$

$$j\omega\epsilon E_z = \frac{\partial H_y}{\partial x} - \frac{\partial H_x}{\partial y} \tag{2c}$$

Now eliminate H_x between (1a) and (2b), and H_y between (1b) and (2a), to obtain

$$E_y = -\frac{jk}{k_c^2}\frac{\partial E_z}{\partial y} + \frac{j\omega\mu}{k_c^2}\frac{\partial H_z}{\partial x} \tag{3a}$$

$$E_x = -\frac{jk}{k_c^2}\frac{\partial E_z}{\partial x} - \frac{j\omega\mu}{k_c^2}\frac{\partial H_z}{\partial y} \tag{3b}$$

in which $k_c^2 \equiv \omega^2 \mu \epsilon - k^2$. The parameter k_c (also in rad/m) functions as a *critical wave number*; see Problem 16.3. Finally, slide (3b) and (3a) back into (2a) and (2b), to find

$$H_y = -\frac{jk}{k_c^2}\frac{\partial H_z}{\partial y} - \frac{j\omega\epsilon}{k_c^2}\frac{\partial E_z}{\partial x} \tag{3c}$$

$$H_x = -\frac{jk}{k_c^2}\frac{\partial H_z}{\partial x} + \frac{j\omega\epsilon}{k_c^2}\frac{\partial E_z}{\partial y} \tag{3d}$$

By exciting the waveguide in suitable fashion it is possible to force either E_z or H_z (but not both) to vanish identically. The nonvanishing axial component will then determine all other components via Equations (3).

See Problems 16.4 and 16.5 for the analogous results in cylindrical coordinates.

16.3 TE and TM Modes; Wave Impedances

The two types of waves found in Section 16.2 are referred to as *transverse electric* (TE) or *transverse magnetic* (TM) waves, according as $E_z \equiv 0$ or $H_z \equiv 0$. When carrying such waves, the guide is said to operate in a TE or TM *mode*.

For any transverse electromagnetic wave, the *wave impedance* (in ohms) is defined as

$$\eta \equiv \frac{|\mathbf{E}_T|}{|\mathbf{H}_T|} \tag{4}$$

(compare Chapter 14). For a waveguide in a TE mode, (1a) and (1b) imply

$$|\mathbf{E}_T|^2 = |E_x|^2 + |E_y|^2 = \left(\frac{\omega\mu}{k_{TE}}\right)^2 \left(|H_y|^2 + |H_x|^2\right) = \left(\frac{\omega\mu}{k_{TE}}\right)^2 |\mathbf{H}_T|^2$$

or

$$\eta_{TE} = \frac{\omega\mu}{k_{TE}} \tag{5}$$

Because (4) only involves lengths of two-dimensional vectors, η must be independent of the coordinate system. Problem 16.6 confirms the value of η_{TE} by recalculating it in cylindrical coordinates. In Problem 16.7 it is shown (using rectangular coordinates) that

$$\eta_{TM} = \frac{k_{TM}}{\omega\epsilon} \tag{6}$$

16.4 Determination of the Axial Fields

All that remains for a complete description of the TE and TM modes is the determination of the respective axial fields: $F_z = H_z$ for TE; $F_z = E_z$ for TM. The good word is that $F_z e^{-jkz}$, being a *Cartesian* component of $\mathbf{F}$ (in either rectangular or cylindrical coordinates), must satisfy the scalar wave equation found in Section 14.2,

$$\nabla^2(F_z e^{-jkz}) = -\omega^2 \mu \epsilon (F_z e^{-jkz}) \tag{7}$$

together with appropriate boundary conditions which are inferred from the boundary conditions on the components of $\mathbf{F}_T$. [*Warning*: Transverse components such as $H_\phi e^{-jkz}$ are not Cartesian components and *do not obey* a scalar wave equation.]

Explicit Solutions for TE Modes of a Rectangular Guide.

The wave equation (7) becomes

$$\frac{\partial^2 H_z}{\partial x^2} + \frac{\partial^2 H_z}{\partial y^2} + k_{cTE}^2 H_z = 0$$

where, as previously defined, $k^2_{c\,TE} = \omega^2\mu\epsilon - k^2_{TE}$. Solving by separation of variables (Section 9.7),

$$H_z(x, y) = (A_x \cos k_x x + B_x \sin k_x x)(A_y \cos k_y y + B_y \sin k_y y) \tag{8}$$

where $k^2_x + k^2_y = k^2_{cTE}$. The separation constants k_x and k_y are determined by the boundary conditions (review Problem 9.19). Consider first the x-conditions $E_y(0, y) = E_y(a, y) = 0$; in view of (3a) and $E_z \equiv 0$ these translate into

$$\left.\frac{\partial H_z}{\partial x}\right|_{x=0} = \left.\frac{\partial H_z}{\partial x}\right|_{x=a} = 0$$

Applying these conditions to (8) gives $B_x = 0$ and

$$\sin k_x a = 0 \qquad \text{or} \qquad k_x = \frac{m\pi}{a} \quad (m = 0, 1, 2, \ldots)$$

By symmetry, the boundary conditions in y force $B_y = 0$ and

$$k_y = \frac{n\pi}{b} \quad (n = 0, 1, 2, \ldots)$$

Each pair of nonnegative integers (m, n)—with the exception of $(0, 0)$ which gives a trivial solution—identifies a distinct TE mode, indicated as TE_{mn}. This mode has the axial field

$$H_{zmn}(x, y) = H_{mn} \cos \frac{m\pi x}{a} \cos \frac{n\pi y}{b} \tag{9}$$

from which the transverse field is obtained through (3). The critical wave number for TE_{mn} is

$$k_{c\,TE\,mn} = \sqrt{\left(\frac{m\pi}{a}\right)^2 + \left(\frac{n\pi}{b}\right)^2}$$

in terms of which the wave number and wave impedance for TE_{mn} are

$$k_{TE\,mn} = \sqrt{\omega^2\mu\epsilon - k^2_{cTE\,mn}} \tag{11}$$

$$\eta_{TE\,mn} = \frac{\omega\mu}{\sqrt{\omega^2\mu\epsilon - k^2_{cTE\,mn}}} \tag{12}$$

See Problem 16.9 for the TM_{mn} modes of a rectangular waveguide; it is shown there that $k_{cTM\,mn} = k_{cTE\,mn}$. Consequently, the subscripts TE and TM can be dropped from all modal parameters of *rectangular* guides save the wave impedance. This is not the case with cylindrical guides; see Problem 16.12.

16.5 Mode Cutoff Frequencies

In practice, one deals with frequencies, not wave numbers; it is then desirable to replace the concept of critical wave number (k_c) by one of *cutoff frequency* (f_c). This is accomplished in the definition (see Problem 16.3)

$$f_c \equiv \frac{u_0}{2\pi} k_c = \frac{1}{2\pi\sqrt{\mu\epsilon}} k_c \tag{13}$$

In terms of the cutoff frequency f_c and the operating frequency $f = \omega/2\pi > f_c$ (10), (11), and (12) become

$$f_{cmn} = \frac{u_0}{2}\sqrt{\left(\frac{m}{a}\right)^2 + \left(\frac{n}{b}\right)^2} \quad (\textit{rectangular waveguide}) \qquad (10\ bis)$$

$$k_{mn} = \frac{2\pi}{u_0}\sqrt{f^2 - f_{cmn}^2} \quad \text{or} \quad \lambda_{mn} = \frac{\lambda_0}{\sqrt{1-(f_{cmn}/f)^2}} \qquad (11\ bis)$$

$$\eta_{\text{TE}mn} = \frac{\eta_0}{\sqrt{1-(f_{cmn}/f)^2}} \qquad (12\ bis)$$

where $\lambda_0 = u_0/f$ is the wavelength of an imaginary uniform plane wave at the operating frequency and where $\eta_0 = \sqrt{\mu/\epsilon}$ is the plane-wave impedance of the lossless dielectric. The second form of (11 *bis*) exhibits the relation between the *operating wavelength* λ_0 and the actual *guide wavelength* λ_{mn}. For TM$_{mn}$ waves, (12 *bis*) is replaced by [see (6)]

$$\eta_{\text{TM}mn} = \eta_0\sqrt{1 - \left(\frac{f_{cmn}}{f}\right)^2} \qquad (14)$$

The phase velocity of a TE$_{mn}$ or TM$_{mn}$ wave is given by

$$u_{mn} = \lambda_{mn} f = \frac{u_0}{\sqrt{1 - \left(\dfrac{f_{cmn}}{f}\right)^2}} \qquad (15)$$

If (10 *bis*) is replaced by a similar expression involving a Bessel function (see Problems 16.10 and 16.11), all formulas remain valid for cylindrical guides.

    The meaning of cutoff is made particularly clear in (15). As the operating frequency drops down to the cutoff frequency, the velocity becomes infinite—which is characteristic, not of wave propagation, but of *diffusion* (instantaneous spread of exponentially small disturbances).

16.6   Dominant Mode

The *dominant mode* of any waveguide is that of lowest cutoff frequency. Now, for a rectangular guide, the coordinate system may always be oriented to make $a \geq b$. Since (Problem 16.9)

$$f_{cmn} = \frac{u_0}{2}\sqrt{\left(\frac{m}{a}\right)^2 + \left(\frac{n}{b}\right)^2}$$

for either TE or TM, but neither m nor n can vanish in TM, the dominant mode of a rectangular guide is invariably TE$_{10}$, with

$$f_{c10} = \frac{u_0}{2a} \qquad \lambda_{10} = \frac{\lambda_0}{\sqrt{1 - (\lambda_0/2a)^2}} \equiv \frac{2\pi}{k_{10}} \qquad u_{10} = \lambda_{10}f \qquad \eta_{10} = \frac{\lambda_{10}}{\lambda_0}\eta_0$$

From (9), $E_{z10} \equiv 0$, and the equations of Section 16.2:

$$H_{z10} = H_{10}\cos\frac{\pi x}{a} \qquad\qquad E_{x10} = 0$$

$$H_{x10} = j\left(\frac{2a}{\lambda_{10}}\right)H_{10}\sin\frac{\pi x}{a} \qquad E_{y10} = -\eta_{10}H_{x10} = -j\eta_0\left(\frac{2a}{\lambda_0}\right)H_{10}\sin\frac{\pi x}{a} \qquad (16)$$

$$H_{y10} = 0$$

For H_{10} real, the three nonzero field components have the time-domain expressions

$$H_{z10} = H_{10} \cos\left(\frac{\pi x}{a}\right) \cos(\omega t - k_{10} z)$$

$$H_{x10} = -\left(\frac{2a}{\lambda_{10}}\right) H_{10} \sin\left(\frac{\pi x}{a}\right) \sin(\omega t - k_{10} z) \qquad (17)$$

$$E_{y10} = \eta_0 \left(\frac{2a}{\lambda_0}\right) H_{10} \sin\left(\frac{\pi x}{a}\right) \sin(\omega t - k_{10} z)$$

Plot of the dominant-mode fields (17) at $t = 0$ are given in Figs. 16-2 and 16-3. Both $|E_y|$ and $|H_x|$ vary as $\sin(\pi x/a)$. This is indicated in Fig. 16-2 by drawing the lines of **E** close together near $x = a/2$ and far apart near $x = 0$ and $x = a$. The lines of **H** are shown evenly spaced because there is no variation with y. This same line-density convention is used to indicate the local value of $|\mathbf{E}| = |E_y|$ in Fig. 16-3(*a*) and of

$$|\mathbf{H}| = \sqrt{H_x^2 + H_z^2}$$

in Fig. 16-3(*b*). Observe that the lines of **H** are closed curves (div $\mathbf{H} = 0$); the **H** field may be considered as circulating about the perpendicular displacement current density $\mathbf{J}_D$ (Section 13.6).

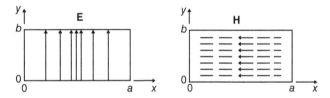

Fig. 16-2   Transverse cross section $z = -\lambda_{10}/4$, $(-k_{10} z = \pi/2)$.

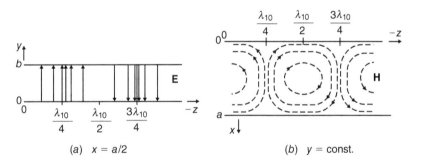

(a) $x = a/2$ (b) $y = $ const.

Fig. 16-3   Longitudinal cross sections.

Fig. 16-4 illustrates how the TE_{10} mode can be initiated in a rectangular waveguide by inserting a probe halfway across the top wall ($y = b$, $x = a/2$), at a distance $z = \lambda_{10}/4$ from the end of the guide. Higher-order modes are present in the vicinity of the probe, but they will not propagate if the frequency-size condition is selected correctly.

See Problem 16.13 for the dominant mode of a cylindrical waveguide.

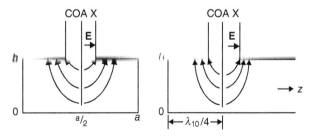

Fig. 16-4

16.7   Power Transmitted in a Lossless Waveguide

The time-average power transmitted in the $+z$ direction is calculated by integration of the z component of the complex Poynting vector over a transverse cross section of the guide (cf. Section 14.13):

$$\bar{P}_z = \frac{1}{2}\text{Re}\iint_{\substack{\text{cross}\\\text{section}}} \mathbf{E}_T \times \mathbf{H}_T^* \cdot \mathbf{a}_z \, dS \tag{18}$$

Substituting the field components from (16) and writing $A_g = ab$, we obtain for the dominant mode of a lossless rectangular waveguide:

$$\bar{P}_{z10} = \frac{\eta_0}{4}|H_{10}|^2\left(\frac{2a}{\lambda_0}\right)\left(\frac{2a}{\lambda_{10}}\right)A_g = \frac{\eta_0}{4}|H_{10}|^2 A_g\left(\frac{f}{f_{c10}}\right)^2\sqrt{1-\left(\frac{f_{c10}}{f}\right)^2} \tag{19}$$

As expected for a lossless system, $\bar{P}_{z10}$ is independent of z; moreover, the power is proportional to the square of the field amplitude and to the cross-sectional area of the guide. Since the excitation of a guide is commonly specified through the electric field amplitude,

$$|E_{10}| = \eta_0\left(\frac{2a}{\lambda_0}\right)|H_{10}|$$

it is useful to rewrite (19) as

$$\bar{P}_{z10} = \frac{|E_{10}|^2 A_g}{4\eta_0}\sqrt{1-\left(\frac{f_{c10}}{f}\right)^2} = \frac{|E_{10}|^2 A_g}{4\eta_{\text{TE}10}} \quad \text{(W)} \tag{19 bis}$$

Relations similar to (19) and (19 bis) exist for the higher-order modes.

For the lossless cylindrical guide, see Problem 16.15.

16.8   Power Dissipation in a Lossy Waveguide

When the conductivity of the guide dielectric is nonzero (but small) and/or the conductivity of the guide walls is noninfinite, the wave in any propagating mode will be attenuated and transmitted power will decrease exponentially with z. An approximate treatment of these *dielectric* and *wall losses* is possible on the assumptions that the two types may be analyzed separately and that the fields which interact with the walls are those which would be present if the dielectric were lossless. To keep the mathematics as simple as possible, only the TE_{10} mode of a rectangular waveguide will be treated.

Dielectric Loss.

Maxwell's equations (1)–(4) of Section 14.2 are unchanged if $\sigma = \sigma_d$, the dielectric conductivity, is replaced by zero and $\epsilon = \epsilon_d$, the dielectric permittivity, is replaced by its *complex permittivity*

$$\hat{\epsilon} \equiv \epsilon_d - \frac{j\sigma_d}{\omega}$$

Therefore, the field equations for the lossy dielectric may be obtained from those for the lossless dielectric by formal substitution of $\hat{\epsilon}$ for ϵ_d. In particular, the z dependence of the field vectors in the lossy TE_{10} mode is $\exp(-\gamma_{10}z)$, where, by (11),

$$\gamma_{10} = jk_{10}(\hat{\epsilon}) = j\sqrt{\omega^2\mu_d\hat{\epsilon} - k_{c10}^2} = j\sqrt{(\omega^2\mu_d\epsilon_d - k_{c10}^2) - j\omega\mu_d\sigma_d}$$

$$\equiv j\beta_{10}\left(1-\frac{j\omega\mu_d\sigma_d}{\beta_{10}^2}\right)^{1/2} \approx \left(\frac{\omega\mu_d\sigma_d}{2\beta_{10}}\right)+j\beta_{10} \tag{20}$$

In (20),

$$\beta_{10} \equiv \sqrt{\omega^2 \mu_d \epsilon_d - k_{c10}^2} = k_{10}(\epsilon_d) = \frac{2\pi}{\lambda_0}\sqrt{1-(f_{c10}/f)^2} \tag{21}$$

and the binomial approximation presumes that σ_d and ω are small enough to make $\omega\mu_d\sigma_d \ll \beta_{10}^2$. *To this order of approximation*, then, the wave number—the imaginary part of γ_{10}—in the lossy dielectric equals the wave number in the perfect dielectric; while the *attenuation factor*, $\alpha_d = \text{Re } \gamma_{10}$, which governs the power loss in the dielectric, is given by

$$\alpha_d \approx \frac{\omega\mu_d\sigma_d}{2\beta_{10}} = \frac{\left(\sqrt{\mu_d/\epsilon_d}\right)\sigma_d}{2\sqrt{1-(f_{c10}/f)^2}} = \frac{1}{2}\eta_{\text{TE}10}\sigma_d \quad \text{(Np/m)} \tag{22}$$

Wall Loss.

The attenuation factor α_w governing the wall loss may be determined indirectly, as follows. Because power varies as the square of the field strength, the time-average transmitted power in the TE_{10} mode must obey

$$P_{\text{av}}(z) = \overline{P}_{z10}e^{-2\alpha_w z}$$

where the entrance power $\overline{P}_{z10}$ is as given in (19). The power dissipated in the walls per unit z-length is thus

$$P_{\text{loss}}(z) = -P'_{\text{av}}(z) = 2\alpha_w P_{\text{av}}(z)$$

whence
$$\alpha_w = \frac{P_{\text{loss}}(z)}{2P_{\text{av}}(z)} = \frac{P_{\text{loss}}(0)}{2\overline{P}_{z10}} \tag{23}$$

All that remains is to calculate $P_{\text{loss}}(0)$, the power flowing into the first 1 m of wall inner surface. Now, it is not hard to show that, at a wall surface, tangential **H**—which by hypothesis can be obtained from (16)—sets up a Poynting vector, of time-average magnitude

$$\overline{S}_{\text{loss}} = \frac{1}{2}R_s\left|\mathbf{H}_{\text{tang}}\right|^2 \tag{24}$$

and directed into the wall. Here, $R_s = \text{Re } \eta_w = \sqrt{\pi f \mu_w/\sigma_w}$ (Section 14.7) is the *surface resistance* (Ω) of the wall material at the given frequency f. Integrating the appropriate expression (24) over the first 1 m of each wall surface and adding the results yields finally

$$P_{\text{loss}}(0) = R_s\left|H_{10}\right|^2\left[b+\frac{a}{2}(f/f_{c10})^2\right] \quad \text{(W/m)} \tag{25}$$

From (23), (19), and (25),

$$\alpha_w = \frac{R_{sc10}}{\eta_0}\left(\sqrt{\frac{f}{f_{c10}}}\right)\frac{a+2b(f_{c10}/f)^2}{ab\sqrt{1-(f_{c10}/f)^2}} \quad \text{(Np/m)} \tag{26}$$

in which R_{sc10} is the surface resistance at the cutoff frequency of TE_{10} and $\eta_0 = \sqrt{\mu_d/\epsilon_d}$ is the plane-wave impedance of the (lossless) dielectric.

Combined Losses.

The total attenuation factor is $\alpha_{\text{tot}} = \alpha_w + \alpha_d$. To convert from Np/m to the more usual dB/m, see Problem 14.7.

SOLVED PROBLEMS

16.1. Give the boundary conditions on **E** and **H** at each perfectly conducting wall of the waveguide of Fig. 16-1(*a*).

At a perfect conductor tangential **E** and normal **H** must vanish. Therefore:

Top wall $E_z(x, b) = E_x(x, b) = 0$ and $H_y(x, b) = 0$

Left wall $E_z(0, y) = E_y(0, y) = 0$ and $H_x(0, y) = 0$

Right wall $E_z(a, y) = E_y(a, y) = 0$ and $H_x(a, y) = 0$

Bottom wall $E_z(x, 0) = E_x(x, 0) = 0$ and $H_y(x, 0) = 0$

16.2. Repeat Problem 16.1 for the guide of Fig. 16-1(*b*).

At the single cylindrical wall,

$$E_z(a, \phi) = E_\phi(a, \phi) = 0 \quad \text{and} \quad H_r(a, \phi) = 0$$

16.3. What is "critical" about the number k_c?

For propagation through a lossless dielectric, the wave number k must be real. But

$$k = \sqrt{\omega^2 \mu \epsilon - k_c^2} = \sqrt{k_0^2 - k_c^2}$$

where k_0 is the wave number of a *uniform* plane wave in the *unbounded* dielectric at the given ω. Thus, k_c is a critical wave number in the sense that a guided wave's same-frequency "twin" must have a wave number exceeding k_c. Stated otherwise, the frequency f of the guided wave must exceed the quantity $(u_0/2\pi)k_c$, where $u_0 = 1/\sqrt{\mu\epsilon}$ is the wave velocity in the unbounded dielectric.

16.4. Express Maxwell's equations (1) and (2) of Section 14.2 in scalar form in a cylindrical coordinate system.

For the curl in cylindrical coordinates, see the Appendix. Equation (1) yields ($\sigma = 0$):

$$j\omega\epsilon E_r = \frac{1}{r}\frac{\partial H_z}{\partial \phi} + jkH_\phi \tag{i}$$

$$j\omega\epsilon E_\phi = -jkH_r - \frac{\partial H_z}{\partial r} \tag{ii}$$

$$j\omega\epsilon E_z = \frac{1}{r}\frac{\partial}{\partial r}(rH_\phi) - \frac{1}{r}\frac{\partial H_r}{\partial \phi} \tag{iii}$$

Equation (2) yields:

$$-j\omega\mu H_r = \frac{1}{r}\frac{\partial E_z}{\partial \phi} + jkE_\phi \tag{iv}$$

$$-j\omega\mu H_\phi = -jkE_r - \frac{\partial E_z}{\partial r} \tag{v}$$

$$-j\omega\mu H_z = \frac{1}{r}\frac{\partial}{\partial r}(rE_\phi) - \frac{1}{r}\frac{\partial E_r}{\partial \phi} \tag{vi}$$

16.5. Using the equations of Problem 16.4, find all cylindrical field components in terms of E_z and H_z.

From (i) and (v), with k_c as previously defined,

$$E_r = -\frac{j\omega\mu}{k_c^2}\frac{1}{r}\frac{\partial H_z}{\partial \phi} - \frac{jk}{k_c^2}\frac{\partial E_z}{\partial r} \tag{1}$$

From (ii) and (iv),

$$H_r = \frac{j\omega\epsilon}{k_c^2}\frac{1}{r}\frac{\partial E_z}{\partial \phi} - \frac{jk}{k_c^2}\frac{\partial H_z}{\partial r}$$

(2)

From (1) and (i),

$$H_\phi = -\frac{j\omega\epsilon}{k_c^2}\frac{\partial E_z}{\partial r} - \frac{jk}{k_c^2}\frac{1}{r}\frac{\partial H_z}{\partial \phi}$$

(3)

From (2) and (ii),

$$E_\phi = -\frac{jk}{k_c^2}\frac{1}{r}\frac{\partial E_z}{\partial \phi} + \frac{j\omega\mu}{k_c^2}\frac{\partial H_z}{\partial r}$$

(4)

16.6. Calculate η_{TE} from the field components in cylindrical coordinates.

With $E_z \equiv 0$, (iv) and (v) of Problem 16.4 yield

$$|\mathbf{H}_T| = \sqrt{|H_r|^2 + |H_\phi|^2} = \sqrt{\left(\frac{k_{TE}}{\omega\mu}\right)^2 |E_\phi|^2 + \left(\frac{k_{TE}}{\omega\mu}\right)^2 |E_r|^2} = \frac{k_{TE}}{\omega\mu}|\mathbf{E}_T|$$

whence

$$\eta_{TE} \equiv \frac{|\mathbf{E}_T|}{|\mathbf{H}_T|} = \frac{\omega\mu}{k_{TE}}$$

16.7. Calculate η_{TM} from the field components in rectangular coordinates.

With $H_z \equiv 0$, (2a) and (2b) give

$$|E_z|^2 + |E_y|^2 = \left(\frac{k_{TM}}{\omega\epsilon}\right)^2 \left(|H_y|^2 + |H_x|^2\right) \quad \text{or} \quad |\mathbf{E}_T| = \frac{k_{TM}}{\omega\epsilon}|\mathbf{H}_T|$$

whence

$$\eta_{TM} \equiv \frac{|\mathbf{E}_T|}{|\mathbf{H}_T|} = \frac{k_{TM}}{\omega\epsilon}$$

16.8. Show that **E** and **H** are mutually perpendicular in any TE or TM wave (as with ordinary plane waves).

For either type of wave $E_x = \eta H_y$ and $E_y = -\eta H_x$; therefore, since η is real,

$$\mathbf{E}_T \cdot \mathbf{H}_T = \text{Re }(E_x H_x^* + E_y H_y^*) = \text{Re }(\eta H_y H_x^* - \eta H_x H_y^*)$$
$$= \eta \text{ Re }(H_y H_x^* - H_x H_y^*) = 0$$

Because $E_z H_z^*$ also vanishes, $\mathbf{E} \cdot \mathbf{H} = 0$.

16.9. Obtain the analogues of (9)–(12) for TM_{mn}.

Analogous to (8),

$$E_z(x, y) = (C_x \cos k_x x + D_x \sin k_x x)(C_y \cos k_y y + D_y \sin k_y y)$$

where

$$k_x^2 + k_y^2 = k_{cTM}^2 \equiv \omega^2 \mu\epsilon - k_{TM}^2$$

But now the boundary conditions,

$$E_z(0, y) = E_z(a, y) = 0 \qquad \text{and} \qquad E_z(x, 0) = E_z(x, b) = 0$$

require that

$$C_x = 0 \qquad k_x = \frac{m\pi}{a} \qquad C_y = 0 \qquad k_y = \frac{n\pi}{b}$$

where $m, n = 1, 2, 3, \dots$. Note that neither m nor n is zero in a TM mode.

The required formulas are

$$E_{zmn}(x, y) = E_{mn} \sin \frac{m\pi x}{a} \sin \frac{n\pi y}{b} \tag{1}$$

$$k_{cTMmn} = \sqrt{\left(\frac{m\pi}{a}\right)^2 + \left(\frac{n\pi}{b}\right)^2} = k_{cTEmn} \tag{2}$$

$$k_{TMmn} = k_{TEmn} \tag{3}$$

$$\eta_{TMmn} = \frac{k_{TM}}{\omega\epsilon} \tag{4}$$

16.10. Determine the TM modes of a lossless cylindrical waveguide.

The Laplacian in cylindrical coordinates is given in the Appendix; the wave equation (7) for $E_z(r, \phi)$ becomes

$$\frac{\partial^2 E_z}{\partial r^2} + \frac{1}{r}\frac{\partial E_z}{\partial r} + \frac{1}{r^2}\frac{\partial^2 E_z}{\partial \phi^2} + k_{cTM}^2 E_z = 0 \quad (k_{cTM}^2 = \omega^2\mu\epsilon - k_{TM}^2)$$

subject to the boundary conditions (i) $E_z(r, \phi + 2\pi) = E_z(r, \phi)$; (ii) $E_z(0, \phi)$ bounded; (iii) $E_z(a, \phi) = 0$.

Following Section 9.8, one solves by separation of variables to find

$$E_{znp}(r, \phi) = E_{np} J_n(k_{cTMnp}r) \cos n\phi \tag{1}$$

where $n = 0, 1, 2, \ldots$ and where $x_{np} \equiv k_{cTMnp}a$ is the pth positive root $(p = 1, 2, \ldots)$ *of* $J_n(x) = 0$. (The first few such roots are listed in Table 16-1.)

TABLE 16-1   Roots x_{np} of $J_n(x) = 0$

	$n = 0$	$n = 1$	$n = 2$	$n = 3$
$p = 1$	2.405	3.832	5.136	6.380
$p = 2$	5.520	7.016	8.417	9.761
$p = 3$	8.645	10.173	11.620	12.015

The expression (1), together with $H_z \equiv 0$, determines all transverse field components in TM via Problem 16.5. The cutoff frequency of TM_{np} is given by

$$f_{cTMnp} = \frac{u_0}{2\pi a} x_{np} \tag{2}$$

When (2) is used, all rectangular-guide formulas also apply to cylindrical guides; for example,

$$\eta_{TMnp} = \eta_0 \sqrt{1 - \left(\frac{\lambda_0 x_{np}}{2\pi a}\right)^2} \tag{3}$$

16.11. Determine the TE modes of a lossless cylindrical waveguide.

In a TE mode the axial field $H_z(r, \phi)$ obeys the wave equation and the conditions (i) and (ii) of Problem 16.10. As a consequence of (2) of Problem 16.5, condition (iii) must be replaced by

$$(iii)' \quad \left.\frac{\partial H_z}{\partial r}\right|_{r=a} = 0$$

The solution by separation is therefore:

$$H_{znp}(r, \phi) = H_{np} J_n(k_{cTEnp}r) \cos n\phi \tag{1}$$

where $n = 0, 1, 2, \ldots$ and where $x'_{np} \equiv k_{cTEnp}$ is the pth positive root $(p = 1, 2, \ldots)$ of $J'_n(x) = 0$. See Table 16-2.

TABLE 16-2   Roots x'_{np} of $J'_n(x) = 0$

	$n = 0$	$n = 1$	$n = 2$	$n = 3$
$p = 1$	3.832	1.841	3.054	4.201
$p = 2$	7.016	5.331	6.706	8.015
$p = 3$	10.173	8.536	9.969	11.346

The analogues of (2) and (3) of Problem 16.10 are

$$f_{cTEnp} = \frac{u_0}{2\pi a} x'_{np} \tag{2}$$

$$\eta_{TEnp} = \frac{\eta_0}{\sqrt{1 - \left(\dfrac{\lambda_0 x'_{np}}{2\pi a}\right)^2}}$$

16.12. Discuss the relative magnitudes of f_{cTEnp} and f_{cTMnp}.

For each fixed n, the zeros x_{np} of $J_n(x)$ and the stationary points x'_{np}—where $J_n(x)$ is a maximum or a minimum—alternate along the x axis; this sine-wave-like behavior is clear in Fig. 9-3(a). For $n > 0$, the function starts at 0, and the first stationary point precedes the first *positive* zero; thus, $x'_{np} < x_{np}$, whence

$$k_{cTEnp} < k_{cTMnp} \qquad \text{and} \qquad f_{cTEnp} < f_{cTMnp}$$

For $n = 0$, the function starts at a maximum, and the ordering is reversed:

$$k_{cTE0p} > k_{cTM0p} \qquad \text{and} \qquad f_{cTE0p} > f_{cTM0p}$$

16.13. (a)   What is the dominant mode of a lossless cylindrical waveguide? (b) List the first five modes in order of increasing cutoff frequency.

(a)   By Problem 16.12, the dominant mode is either TM_{01} or the TE_{n1} with the lowest cutoff. Tables 16-1 and 16-2 indicate (and analysis establishes) that the winner is TE_{11}.

(b) TE_{11}, TM_{01}, TE_{21}, TE_{01}, and TM_{11} (a tie). [The first column of Table 16-2 is identical to the second column of Table 16-1 because $J'_0(x) = -J_1(x)$.]

16.14. Obtain the transverse fields for the TE_{11} (dominant) mode of a cylindrical waveguide.

For $m = p = 1$, Equation (1) of Problem 16.11, $E_z \equiv 0$, and (1)–(4) of Problem 16.5 yield

$$E_{r11} = \frac{j\omega\mu H_{11}}{k_{cTE11}^2 r} J_1(k_{cTE11}r)\sin\phi \tag{1}$$

$$H_{r11} = \frac{-jk_{TE11}H_{11}}{k_{cTE11}} J'_1(k_{cTE11}r)\cos\phi \tag{2}$$

$$H_{\phi 11} = \frac{jk_{TE11}H_{11}}{k_{cTE11}^2 r} J_1(k_{cTE11}r)\sin\phi \tag{3}$$

$$E_{\phi 11} = \frac{j\omega\mu H_{11}}{k_{cTE11}} J'_1(k_{cTE11}r)\cos\phi \tag{4}$$

in which $k_{cTE11} = x'_{11}/a$ and $k_{TE11} = \sqrt{\omega^2\mu\epsilon - (x'_{11}/a^2)}$.

16.15. Calculate the time-average power transmission in the TE_{11} mode of a lossless cylindrical guide.

Follow Section 16.7, with the transverse fields as given by Problem 16.14.

$$\frac{1}{2}\mathbf{E}_T \times \mathbf{H}_T^* \cdot \mathbf{a}_z = \frac{1}{2}(E_{r11}H_{\phi 11}^* - E_{\phi 11}H_{r11}^*)$$

$$= \frac{\omega \mu k_{TE11}|H_{11}|^2}{2k_{cTE11}^2}\left\{\left[\frac{J_1(v)}{v}\right]^2 \sin^2\phi + [J_1'(v)]^2 \cos^2\phi\right\} \tag{1}$$

which the integration variable $v = k_{cTE11}r$ has been introduced. In the integration of (1) over the cross section $0 \le \phi \le 2\pi$ and $0 \le v \le x_{11}'$, the $\sin^2$ and $\cos^2$ both integrate to π; therefore,

$$\bar{P}_{z11} = \frac{\pi \omega \mu k_{TE11}|H_{11}|^2}{2k_{cTE11}^4}\int_0^{x_{11}'}\left\{[J_1'(v)]^2 + \left[\frac{J_1(v)}{v}\right]^2\right\}v\,dv \tag{2}$$

There is a general rule for evaluating an integral like the one in (2): Go back to the ordinary differential equation arising from the separation of variables. In this case that equation is (see Section 9.8)

$$J_1'' + \frac{1}{v}J_1' + \left(1 - \frac{1}{v^2}\right)J_1 = 0 \tag{3}$$

Thus, using integration by parts, (3), and the end conditions $J_1(0) = J_1'(x_{11}') = 0$, we have

$$\int_0^{x_{11}'}[(J_1')^2 + (J_1/v)^2]v\,dv = \int_0^{x_{11}'}\left[J_1' + \left(\frac{J_1}{v}\right)\right]^2 v\,dv - \int_0^{x_{11}'}d(J_1^2)$$

$$= \int_0^{x_{11}'}\left[J_1' + \left(\frac{J_1}{v}\right)\right]^2 d\left(\frac{v^2}{2}\right) - J_1^2(x_{11}')$$

$$= \frac{1}{2}(vJ_1' + J_1)^2\Big|_0^{x_{11}'} - \int_0^{x_{11}'}v^2\left[J_1' + \frac{J_1}{v}\right]$$

$$\times \left(J_1'' + \frac{1}{v}J_1' - \frac{1}{v^2}J_1\right)dv - J_1^2(x_{11}')$$

$$= -\frac{1}{2}J_1^2(x_{11}') - \int_0^{x_{11}'}v^2\left[J_1' + \frac{J_1}{v}\right](-J_1)\,dv$$

$$= -\frac{1}{2}J_1^2(x_{11}') + \int_0^{x_{11}'}v^2 d\left(\frac{J_1^2}{2}\right) + \int_0^{x_{11}'}vJ_1^2\,dv$$

$$= -\frac{1}{2}J_1^2(x_{11}') + \frac{1}{2}v^2 J_1^2\Big|_0^{x_{11}'} = \frac{(x_{11}')^2 - 1}{2}J_1^2(x_{11}')$$

Substituting this result in (2), and replacing k_{TE11} and k_{cTE11} by their respective expressions in $x_{11}' = (2\pi a/u_0)f_{cTE11}$, one finds after some algebra:

$$\bar{P}_{z11} = \frac{\eta_0}{4}|H_{11}|^2 A_g\left(\frac{f}{f_{cTE11}}\right)^2\sqrt{1 - \left(\frac{f_{cTE11}}{f}\right)^2}\left[\frac{(x_{11}')^2 - 1}{(x_{11}')^2}J_1^2(x_{11}')\right] \tag{4}$$

in which $A_g = \pi a^2$ is the cross-sectional area.

16.16. Compare the rectangular and cylindrical waveguides as power transmitters when each operates in its dominant mode.

The two power formulas, (19) of Section 16.7 and (4) of Problem 16.15, show identical dependence on H-amplitude, cross-sectional area, and normalized frequency. The only difference lies in a geometrical factor, which has the value 1.0 for the rectangular guide and the value

$$\frac{(1.841)^2 - 1}{(1.841)^2}(0.5814)^2 = 0.239$$

for the cylindrical guide.

16.17. (*a*) Define the notion of *cutoff wavelength*. (*b*) Is the cutoff wavelength an upper limit on the guide wavelength, just as the cutoff frequency is a lower limit on the guide frequency?

(*a*) The cutoff wavelength λ_c is the wavelength of an unguided plane wave whose frequency is the cutoff frequency; i.e., $\lambda_c f_c = u_0$.

(*b*) No; in fact, the formula

$$\lambda_{mn} = \frac{u_0}{\sqrt{f^2 - f_{cmn}^2}}$$

shows that an (*m, n*) mode can propagate with *any* guide wavelength greater than λ.

16.18. A lossless air-dielectric waveguide for an S-band radar has inside dimensions $a = 7.214$ cm and $b = 3.404$ cm. For the TM_{11} mode propagating at an operating frequency that is 1.1 times the cutoff frequency of the mode, calculate (*a*) critical wave number, (*b*) cutoff frequency, (*c*) operating frequency, (*d*) propagation constant, (*e*) cutoff wavelength, (*f*) operating wavelength, (*g*) guide wavelength, (*h*) phase velocity, (*i*) wave impedance.

(*a*) By (10), $k_{c11} = \sqrt{(\pi/0.07214)^2 + (\pi/0.03404)^2} = 102.05$ rad/m.

(*b*) By (13), $f_{c11} = [(3 \times 10^8)/2\pi)] (102.05) = 4.87$ GHz.

(*c*) $f = 1.1 f_{c11} = 5.36$ GHz.

(*d*) By (11 *bis*),

$$\gamma_{11} = jk_{11} = j\frac{2\pi}{3 \times 10^8} \sqrt{(5.36)^2 - (4.87)^2}\,(10^9) = j46.8 \text{ m}^{-1}$$

(*e*) $\lambda_{c11} = u_0/f_{c11} = (3 \times 10^8)/(4.87 \times 10^9) = 6.16$ cm.

(*f*) $\lambda_0 = u_0/f = (3 \times 10^8)/(5.36 \times 10^9) = 5.60$ cm.

(*g*) $\lambda_{11} = 2\pi/k_{11} = 2\pi/46.8 = 13.4$ cm.

(*h*) By (15), $u_{11} = (0.134)(5.36 \times 10^9) = 7.18 \times 10^8$ m/s.

(*i*) For air, $\eta_0 = 120\pi\ \Omega$ and (14) gives

$$\eta_{TM11} = 120\pi\sqrt{1 - \left(\frac{1}{1.1}\right)^2} = 157.5\ \Omega$$

16.19. A lossless, air-dielectric cylindrical waveguide, of inside diameter 3 cm, is operated at 14 GHz. For the TM_{11} mode propagating in the +*z* direction, find the cutoff frequency, guide wavelength, and wave impedance.

By (2) of Problem 16.10, along with Table 16-1,

$$f_{cTM11} = \frac{u_0}{2\pi a} x_{11} = \frac{3 \times 10^8}{\pi(3 \times 10^{-2})}(3.832) = 12.2 \text{ GHz}$$

Then, by (11 *bis*) and (14),

$$\lambda_{11} = \frac{u_0}{\sqrt{f^2 - f_{cTM11}^2}} = \frac{3 \times 10^8}{\sqrt{(14)^2 - (12.2)^2}\,(10^9)} = 4.36 \text{ cm}$$

$$\eta_{TM11} = \eta_0\sqrt{1 - \left(\frac{f_{cTM11}}{f}\right)^2} = 120\pi\sqrt{1 - \left(\frac{12.2}{14}\right)^2} = 185\ \Omega$$

16.20 Find the inside diameter of a lossless air dielectric cylindrical waveguide so that a TE_{11} mode propagates at a frequency of 10 GHz, with the cutoff wavelength of the mode being 1.3 times the operating wavelength.

The condition is $\lambda_c 11 = 1.3\lambda_0$, or

$$\frac{u_0}{f_{cTE11}} = 1.3\frac{u_0}{f} \quad \text{or} \quad f_{cTE11} = \frac{f}{1.3} = 7.692 \text{ GHz}$$

But, by Problem 16.11,

$$f_{cTE11} = \frac{u_0}{2\pi a} x'_{11} = \frac{0.3}{\pi d}(1.841) \quad \text{(GHz)}$$

Equating the two expressions yields $d = 2.28$ cm.

16.21. Represent the **E** field of Problem 16.14 in the time domain, using as space variables $\rho \equiv r/a$, ϕ, and $\zeta \equiv k_{TE11}z$.

In terms of the lumped constants

$$K_\rho \equiv \frac{\omega\mu H_{11}}{k_{cTE11}^2 a} \qquad K_\phi \equiv \frac{\omega\mu H_{11}}{k_{cTE11}}$$

which are presumed real, we have ($x'_{11} = 1.841$):

$$E_\rho(\rho,\phi,\zeta,t) = \text{Re}\,[E_{r11}e^{j(\omega t - \zeta)}] = -\frac{K_\rho}{\rho}J_1(1.841\rho)\sin\phi\sin(\omega t - \zeta)$$

$$E_\phi(\rho,\phi,\zeta,t) = \text{Re}\,[E_{\phi11}e^{j(\omega t - \zeta)}] = -K_\phi J'_1(1.841\rho)\cos\phi\sin(\omega t - \zeta)$$

16.22. For the **E** field obtained in Problem 16.21, calculate and plot the *field lines*. Also plot (without calculation) the lines of the transverse **H** field.

The lines of any vector field are a family of space curves such that, at each point of space, the vector is tangent to the curve through that point. Thus the differential equation of the lines of **E** in a cross-sectional plane is $dy/dx = E_y/E_x$, in Cartesian coordinates (x, y), or

$$\frac{1}{\rho}\frac{d\rho}{d\phi} = \frac{E_\rho}{E_\phi} \tag{1}$$

in polar coordinates (ρ, ϕ). Substitution in (1) of the components of **E** from Problem 16.21 gives

$$\frac{d\rho}{d\phi} = K_1 \frac{J_1(1.841\rho)}{J'_1(1.841\rho)}\tan\phi \tag{2}$$

It is seen that the TE_{11} mode of a cylindrical waveguide has the special property that the field pattern does not change with time or with distance ζ along the guide.

Normally, the field lines are found by a numerical integration of the differential equation; but in this case an analytic solution is simply obtained:

$$\ln\frac{J_1(1.841\rho)}{J_1(1.841\rho_0)} = K_2\ln\left|\sec\phi\right| \quad (K_2 > 0) \tag{3}$$

This is a one-parameter family of curves, where the parameter ρ_0 gives the radius at which a curve cuts the horizontal axis $\sin\phi = 0$. Note that the right side of (3) does not change when ϕ is replaced by $-\phi$ or by $\phi + \pi$; hence the field pattern is symmetric about both the horizontal and vertical axes, and only the quadrant $0 \le \phi \le \pi/2$ need be considered. As one moves along a field line through increasingly positive ϕ-values, the right side of (3) increases through positive values. Consequently [see Fig. 9-3(a)], ρ/ρ_0 increases through values greater than 1. This, together with the constraint that the field line hit the boundary $\rho = 1$ orthogonally, shows that the field line must bend away from the origin, as shown in Fig. 16-5. The line $\rho_0 = 1$ degenerates into a single point.

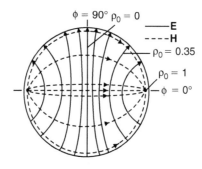

Fig. 16-5

The lines of **H** are plotted as the orthogonal trajectories of the **E** lines; see Problem 16.8. By Problem 16.14 both H_ρ and H_ϕ vanish at the points $\rho = 1$, $\phi = 0$, π; hence the direction of **H** is indeterminate there.

16.23. A lossless air-dielectric waveguide for an S-band radar system has the dimensions $a = 7.214$ cm and $b = 3.404$ cm. The dominant mode propagates in the $+z$ direction at 3 GHz. Find the average power transmitted if the excitation level of the **E** field is 10 kV/m.

The cutoff frequency for TE_{10} is

$$f_{c10} = \frac{u_0}{2a} = \frac{3 \times 10^8}{2(0.07214)} = 2.08 \text{ GHz}$$

and (19 *bis*) yields

$$\bar{P}_{z10} = \frac{(10^4)^2(7.214)(3.404)10^{-4}}{4(377)} \sqrt{1 - \left(\frac{2.08}{3}\right)^2} = 117.4 \text{ W}$$

16.24. In a lossless air-dielectric cylindrical waveguide with a 1 cm radius the transmitted power in the dominant mode at 15 GHz is 2 W. Find the level of excitation for the magnetic field.

The cutoff frequency for TE_{11} is (see Table 16-2):

$$f_{cTE11} = \frac{u_0}{2\pi a} x'_{11} = \frac{3 \times 10^8}{2\pi(1 \times 10^{-2})}(1.841) = 8.79 \text{ GHz}$$

so that (4) of Problem 16.15 becomes (see also Problem 16.16):

$$2 = \frac{377}{4}|H_{11}|^2 (\pi 10^{-4})(15/8.79)^2 \sqrt{1 - (8.79/15)^2} \, [0.239]$$

Solving, $|H_{11}| = 0.11$ A/cm.

16.25. A section of X-band waveguide with dimensions $a = 2.286$ cm and $b = 1.016$ cm has perfectly conducting walls and is filled with a lossy dielectric ($\sigma_d = 367.5$ μS/m, $\epsilon_r = 2.1$, $\mu_r = 1$). Find the attenuation factor, in dB/m, for the dominant mode of propagation at a frequency of 9 GHz.

The cutoff frequency of TE_{10} is

$$f_{c10} = \frac{u_0}{2a} = \frac{(3 \times 10^8)/\sqrt{2.1}}{2(0.02286)} = 4.53 \text{ GHz}$$

and (22) gives (second form):

$$\alpha_d(dB/m) \approx \frac{(377/\sqrt{2.1})(367.5 \times 10^{-6})}{2\sqrt{1 - (4.53/9)^2}} \times 8.69 = 0.48$$

The reader should verify that the underlying approximation, $\omega\mu_d\sigma_d \ll \beta^2_{10}$, holds for the data.

16.26. An X-band air-dielectric rectangular waveguide has brass walls ($\mu_w = \mu_0$, $\sigma_w = 16$ MS/m) with $a = 2.286$ cm and $b = 1.016$ cm. Find the dB/m of attenuation due to wall loss when the dominant mode is propagating at 9.6 GHz.

At the cutoff frequency of the dominant mode,

$$f_{c10} = \frac{u_0}{2a} = \frac{3 \times 10^8}{4.572 \times 10^{-2}} = 6.56 \text{ GHz}$$

the surface resistance of the brass is

$$R_{sc10} = \sqrt{\frac{\pi(6.56 \times 10^9)(4\pi \times 10^{-7})}{16 \times 10^6}} = 40.24 \text{ m}\Omega$$

and, by (26),

$$\alpha_w(\text{dB/m}) = \frac{0.04024}{377}\left(\sqrt{\frac{9.6}{6.56}}\right)\frac{0.02286 + 2(0.01016)(6.56/9.6)^2}{(0.02286)(0.01016)\sqrt{1-(6.56/9.6)^2}} \times 8.69 = 0.214$$

16.27. An air-dielectric cylindrical waveguide ($a = 5$ mm) operates in the TM_{01} mode at frequency $f = 1.3\,f_{c\text{TM01}}$. Find the dB/m of attenuation due to wall loss in a short section of copper ($\sigma_w = 58$ MS/m).

First derive an expression for $P_{\text{loss}}(0)$, following Section 16.8. By (1) of Problem 16.10, $E_{z01}(r,\phi) = E_{01}J_0(x_{01}r/a)$. Then (3) of Problem 16.5 gives the tangential magnetic field at the wall as $[J_0'(v) = -J_1(v)]$:

$$H_{\phi 01}(a,\phi) = \frac{j\omega\epsilon_0 x_{01}E_{01}J_1(x_{01})}{k_{c\text{TM01}}^2 a} = \frac{jE_{01}J_1(x_{01})}{\eta_0}\left(\frac{f}{f_{c\text{TM01}}}\right)$$

and, since $H_{\phi 01}$ is constant, (24) gives

$$P_{\text{loss}}(0) = \frac{1}{2}R_s\left[\frac{|E_{01}|^2 J_1^2(x_{01})}{\eta_0^2}\left(\frac{f}{f_{c\text{TM01}}}\right)^2\right](2\pi a) \tag{1}$$

Next find $P_{z\text{TM01}}$ by the method of Problem 16.15. By Problem 16.15,

$$E_{r01} = \frac{jk_{\text{TM01}}E_{01}}{k_{c\text{TM01}}}J_1\left(\frac{x_{01}r}{a}\right) = jE_{01}\left(\frac{f}{f_{c\text{TM01}}}\right)\left(\sqrt{1-\left(\frac{f_{c\text{TM01}}}{f}\right)^2}\right)J_1\left(\frac{x_{01}r}{a}\right)$$

$$H_{\phi 01} = \frac{jE_{01}(f/f_{c\text{TM01}})}{\eta_0}J_1\left(\frac{x_{01}r}{a}\right)$$

while $H_{r01} = E_{\phi 01} = 0$. Thus the time-average Poynting vector is

$$\bar{S} = \frac{1}{2}E_{r01}H_{\phi 01}^* = \frac{|E_{01}|^2(f/f_{c\text{TM01}})^2\sqrt{1-(f_{c\text{TM01}}/f)^2}}{2\eta_0}J_1^2\left(\frac{x_{01}r}{a}\right)$$

Integrating over a cross section,

$$\int_0^a\int_0^{2\pi}J_1^2\left(\frac{x_{01}r}{a}\right)r\,dr\,d\phi = \frac{2A_g}{x_{01}^2}\int_0^{x_{01}}J_1^2(v)v\,dv = A_g J_1^2(x_{01})$$

Combining these results,

$$\alpha_w = \frac{P_{\text{loss}}(0)}{2\bar{P}_{z\text{TM01}}} = \frac{R_s}{\eta_0 a\sqrt{1-(f_{c\text{TM01}}/f)^2}} \tag{2}$$

For the data,

$$f_{c\text{TM01}} = \frac{u_0}{2\pi a}x_{01} = \frac{3\times10^8}{2\pi(5\times10^{-3})}(2.405) = 22.99 \text{ GHz}$$

$$f = (1.3)(22.99) = 29.89 \text{ GHz}$$

$$R_s = \sqrt{\frac{\pi f\mu_w}{\sigma_w}} = \sqrt{\frac{\pi(29.89\times10^9)(4\pi\times10^{-7})}{58\times10^6}} = 0.0451\,\Omega$$

$$\alpha_w = \frac{0.0451}{(377)(5\times10^{-3})\sqrt{1-(1/1.3)^2}} = 0.0374 \text{ Np/m} = 0.325 \text{ dB/m}$$

SUPPLEMENTARY PROBLEMS

16.28. Determine the condition(s) under which a magnetic field with

$$H_z(x, y, z, t) = K \cos 87.3x \cos 92.4y \cos (2\pi ft - 109.1z)$$

can exist in free space.

16.29. Obtain the critical wave number for a 4-GHz wave propagating in a medium with $\mu_r = 1$ and $\epsilon_r = 2.2$, if the phase shift constant (wave number) is $54°$ per cm.

16.30. If $H_z(x, y, z, t)$ in Problem 16.28 represents the axial field of a TE_{21} wave in a rectangular waveguide, find (*a*) the guide size, (*b*) the critical wave number, (*c*) the guide wavelength.

16.31. The S-band waveguide of Problem 16.18 is used in the X-band at 9 GHz. Identify the modes that could propagate in the guide.

16.32. In Problem 16.19, what other modes could propagate at the given frequency?

16.33. A C-band waveguide for use between 3.95 and 5.85 GHz measures 4.755 cm by 2.215 cm. For air dielectric, calculate the dominant mode cutoff frequency and the guide wavelength when the operating frequency is 4.2 GHz.

16.34. The WC-50 cylindrical waveguide with air dielectric is used in the frequency range 15.9–21.8 GHz for dominant-mode propagation. Calculate the cutoff frequency for an inside diameter of 1.270 cm. Also obtain the cutoff frequency for the TM_{01} mode.

16.35. An air-dielectric L-band rectangular waveguide has $a/b = 2$ and a dominant-mode cutoff frequency of 0.908 GHz. If the measured guide wavelength is 40 cm, find the operating frequency, the guide dimensions, and the wave number.

16.36. For the waveguide in Problem 16.35 find the lowest frequency at which a TE_{21} mode would propagate.

16.37. A V-band waveguide for use between 26.5 and 40 GHz has inside dimensions 0.711 cm by 0.356 cm. (*a*) Calculate the dominant-mode critical wave number for air dielectric. (*b*) If the measured guide wavelength is 1.41 cm, what is the operating frequency?

16.38. The WC-19 air-dielectric cylindrical waveguide is used for dominant-mode operation in the 42.4–58.10 GHz range. Find the inside diameter for the specified cutoff frequency of 36.776 GHz.

16.39. A Ku-band air-dielectric guide with $a/b = 2$ is used in the 12.4–18.8 GHz range for dominant-mode operation with a cutoff frequency of 9.49 GHz. What are the inside dimensions?

16.40. Find the radius and guide wavelength in an air-dielectric cylindrical waveguide for the dominant mode at $f = 30$ GHz $= 1.5 f_{cTE11}$. Will the TM_{11} mode propagate under these conditions?

16.41. Solve Problem 16.40 for the guide with a lossless dielectric of $\epsilon_r = 2.2$.

16.42. A K-band rectangular waveguide with dimensions 1.067 cm and 0.432 cm operates in the dominant mode at 18 GHz. Find the cutoff frequency, guide wavelength, phase velocity, and wave impedance, if the dielectric is air.

16.43. Solve Problem 16.42 if the guide is filled with a lossless dielectric of $\epsilon_r = 2.0$.

16.44. Calculate the radius and guide wavelength for a TM_{11} mode at $f = 30$ GHz $= 1.5 f_{cTM11}$ in an air-dielectric cylindrical waveguide. [Compare Problem 16.40.]

16.45. For an (m, n) mode operated below its cutoff frequency, the *cutoff attenuation factor* is defined as $\alpha_{cmn} = -jk_{mn}$. Calculate α_{cTE11}, in dB/cm when a lossless air-dielectric guide, 2.286 cm by 1.016 cm is operated at 9.4 GHz.

16.46. In a certain cross section of a rectangular waveguide the instantaneous components of **E** are

$$E_y = -A \sin\left(\frac{\pi x}{a}\right) \cos\left(\frac{\pi y}{b}\right) \qquad E_x = B \cos\left(\frac{\pi x}{a}\right) \sin\left(\frac{\pi y}{b}\right) \qquad E_z = 0$$

Sketch this **E** field and identify the mode of operation.

16.47. The air-dielectric waveguide of Problem 16.23 transports 200 W of average power at 2.6 GHz. Find the excitation level of the field.

16.48. If a lossless dielectric having $\epsilon_r = 1.8$ is inserted in the waveguide of Problem 16.47, calculate the excitation level for the transport of 200 W.

16.49. The air-dielectric waveguide of Problem 16.24 is filled with a lossless dielectric having $\epsilon_r = 2.1$. Find the power transported in the dominant mode, if the excitation level and frequency are unchanged.

16.50. Show that result (2) of Problem 16.27 can be rewritten as $\alpha_w = \dfrac{1}{\sigma_w a\, \delta_w \eta_{\text{TM01}}}$, where δ_w is the (frequency dependent) skin depth.

ANSWERS TO SUPPLEMENTARY PROBLEMS

16.28. $f = 8.0$ GHz

16.29. 81.1 rad/m

16.30. (a) 7.2 cm by 3.4 cm; (b) 127.1 rad/m; (c) 5.76 cm

16.31. TE_{01}, TE_{02}, TE_{10}, TE_{11}, TE_{20}, TE_{21}, TE_{30}, TE_{31}, TE_{40}; TM_{11}, TM_{21}, TM_{31}

16.32. TE_{01}, TE_{11}, TE_{21}, TE_{31}; TM_{01}

16.33. 3.155 GHz, 10.82 cm

16.34. 13.84 GHz, 18.08 GHz

16.35. 1.18 GHz, 16.52 cm by 8.26 cm, 15.7 rad/m

16.36. $f > 2.569$ GHz

16.37. (a) 441.86 rad/m; (b) 29.98 GHz

16.38. 0.478 cm

16.39. 1.58 cm by 0.79 cm

16.40. 0.44 cm, 1.34 cm; No

16.41. 0.296 cm, 0.903 cm; No

16.42. 14.06 GHz, 2.67 cm, 4.81×10^8 m/s, 604.2 Ω

16.43. 9.93 GHz, 1.44 cm, 2.54×10^8 m/s, 319.6 Ω

16.44. 0.915 cm, 1.342 cm

16.45. 23.9

16.46. See Fig. 16-6; TE_{11}

16.47. 143 V/cm

16.48. 106.8 V/cm

16.49. 0.09 A/cmm

Fig. 16-6

Antennas

(by Kai-Fong Lee)

17.1 Introduction

Maxwell's equations as examined in Chapter 14 predict propagating plane waves in an unbounded source-free region. In this chapter the propagating waves produced by current sources or antennas are examined; in general, these waves have spherical wavefronts and direction-dependent amplitudes. Because free-space conditions are exclusively assumed throughout the chapter, the notation for the permittivity, permeability, propagation speed, and characteristic impedance of the medium can omit the subscript 0; likewise the wave number (phase shift constant) of the radiation will be written $\beta = \omega\sqrt{\mu\epsilon} = \omega/u$.

17.2 Current Source and the E and H Fields

The vector magnetic potential $\mathbf{A}$ defined in Section 10.9 gives the phasor fields in the region outside of the current source as

$$\mathbf{H} = \frac{1}{\mu}\nabla\times\mathbf{A} = \frac{\mu}{\eta}\nabla\times\mathbf{A}$$

$$\mathbf{E} = \frac{1}{j\omega\epsilon}\nabla\times\mathbf{H} = \frac{1}{j\omega\mu\epsilon}\nabla\times\nabla\times\mathbf{A} = \frac{\mu}{j\beta}\nabla\times\nabla\times\mathbf{A}$$

(1)

in which $u = 3\times 10^8$ m/s and $\eta = 120\pi\ \Omega$.

The phasor $\mathbf{A}$ is itself given by

$$\mathbf{A} = \int_{vol}\frac{\mu(\mathbf{J}_s e^{-j\beta r})}{4\pi r}\,dv$$

(2)

In (2), r is the distance between the observation point and the source current element $\mathbf{J}_s\,dv$. The significance of the factor $e^{-j\beta r}$ becomes clear when $\mathbf{A}$ is transformed to the time domain:

$$\mathbf{A} = \int_{vol}\frac{\mu\mathbf{J}_s\cos\omega(t - r/u)}{4\pi r}\,dv$$

Thus, $\mathbf{A}$ at the observation point properly reflects conditions at the source at earlier times—the lag for any given ꞏꞏꞏ ꞏ ꞏꞏꞏꞏꞏꞏ bꞏꞏꞏꞏ ꞏꞏꞏꞏꞏꞏꞏ ꞏꞏꞏ ꞏꞏꞏꞏ ꞏ/ꞏ ꞏꞏꞏꞏꞏ ꞏꞏꞏ ꞏꞏ ꞏꞏꞏꞏꞏꞏꞏꞏ ꞏꞏ propagate to the observation point.

17.3 Electric (Hertzian) Dipole Antenna

The vector potential set up by the infinitesimal current element of Fig. 17-1 is, by (2),

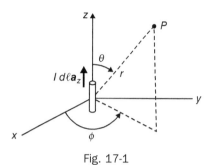

Fig. 17-1

$$\mathbf{A}(P) = \frac{\mu e^{-j\beta r}}{4\pi r}(I\,d\ell)\mathbf{a}_z$$

In spherical coordinates, $\mathbf{a}_z = \cos\theta\mathbf{a}_r - \sin\theta\mathbf{a}_\theta$; relations (1) yield

$$H_\phi = \frac{I\,d\ell}{4\pi}\beta^2\sin\theta e^{-j\beta r}\left[\frac{j}{\beta r} + \frac{1}{\beta^2 r^2}\right]$$

$$E_r = \eta\frac{2I\,d\ell}{4\pi}\beta^2\cos\theta e^{-j\beta r}\left[\frac{1}{\beta^2 r^2} - j\frac{1}{\beta^3 r^3}\right]$$

$$E_\theta = \eta\frac{I\,d\ell}{4\pi}\beta^2\sin\theta e^{-j\beta r}\left[j\frac{1}{\beta r} + \frac{1}{\beta^2 r^2} - j\frac{1}{\beta^3 r^3}\right]$$

All other components are zero. Attention will be restricted to the *far field*, in which terms in $1/r^2$ or $1/r^3$ are neglected.

Far field $$H_\phi = \frac{jI\,d\ell\beta}{4\pi r}\sin\theta e^{-j\beta r}$$

$$E_\theta = \eta\frac{jI\,d\ell\beta}{4\pi r}\sin\theta e^{-j\beta r} = \eta H_\phi \qquad (3)$$

It is clear that (3) represents a diverging spherical wave which at any point is traveling in the $+\mathbf{a}_r$ direction with an amplitude that falls off as $1/r$.

The power radiated of the Hertzian dipole is obtained by integrating the time-averaged Poynting vector,

$$\mathcal{P}_{avg} = \frac{1}{2}\mathrm{Re}\,(\mathbf{E}\times\mathbf{H}^*)$$

(Section 14.13), of the far field over the surface of a (large) sphere.

$$P_{rad} = \int_0^{2\pi}\int_0^\pi \mathcal{P}_{avg}\cdot r^2\sin\theta\,d\theta\,d\phi\,\mathbf{a}_r$$

$$= \int_0^{2\pi}\int_0^\pi\left[\frac{1}{2}\mathrm{Re}\,(E_\theta H_\phi^*)\right]r^2\sin\theta\,d\theta\,d\phi$$

$$= \frac{\eta(\beta I\,d\ell)^2}{12\pi} = \frac{\eta\pi I^2}{3}\left(\frac{d\ell}{\lambda}\right)^2 \qquad (4)$$

17.4 Antenna Parameters

The *radiation resistance* R_{rad} is defined as the value of a hypothetical resistor that would dissipate a power equal to the power radiated by the antenna when fed by the same current, thus, $P_{rad} = \frac{1}{2}I_0^2 R_{rad}$ or $R_{rad} = 2P_{rad}/I_0^2$, where I_0 is the peak value of the feed point current. For the Hertzian dipole, from (4),

$$R_{rad} = \frac{2\pi\eta}{3}\left(\frac{d\ell}{\lambda}\right)^2 \approx 790\left(\frac{d\ell}{\lambda}\right)^2 \quad (\Omega)$$

The *pattern function* $F(\theta, \phi)$ gives the variation of the far-zone electric or magnetic field magnitude with direction. For the Hertzian dipole this reduces to $F(\theta) = \sin\theta$, since $|\mathbf{E}|$ and $|\mathbf{H}|$ are independent of ϕ.

The *radiation intensity* $U(\theta, \phi)$ is another measure of antenna performance; it is defined as the time-averaged radiated power per unit solid angle. From Fig. 17-2,

$$U(\theta, \phi) \equiv \frac{dP_{rad}}{d\Omega} = \frac{|\mathscr{P}_{avg}| \, dS'}{dS'/r^2} = r^2 |\mathscr{P}_{avg}|$$

Fig. 17-2

Because U is independent of r (by energy conservation), the far field may be used in its evaluation. For the Hertzian dipole,

$$U(\theta) = \frac{\eta}{8}\left(\frac{I \, d\ell}{\lambda}\right)^2 \sin^2\theta \tag{5}$$

Polar plots of the pattern function and radiation intensity distribution for the Hertzian dipole are given in Fig. 17-3.

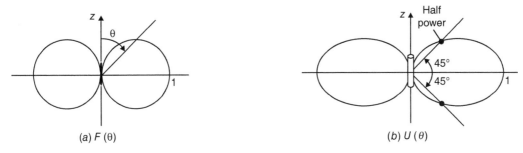

(a) $F(\theta)$ (b) $U(\theta)$

Fig. 17-3

In Fig. 17-3(b), the *half-power points* are at $\theta = 45°$ and $\theta = 135°$ and the *half-power beamwidth* is therefore $90°$. In general, the smaller the beamwidth (about the direction of U_{max}), the more directive the antenna.

Directive gain $D(\theta, \phi)$ of an antenna is defined as the ratio of the radiation intensity $U(\theta, \phi)$ to that of a hypothetical *isotropic* radiator that radiates the same total power U_0. For the isotropic radiator,

$$U_0 = \frac{P_{rad}}{4\pi}$$

Then
$$D(\theta, \phi) = \frac{U(\theta, \phi)}{U_0} = \frac{4\pi U(\theta, \phi)}{P_{rad}}$$

The *directivity* of an antenna is the maximum value of its directive gain:

$$D_{max} = \frac{4\pi U_{max}}{P_{rad}}$$

For the Hertzian dipole, (4) and (5) give

$$D(\theta, \phi) = \frac{(4\pi)\frac{\eta}{8}\left(\frac{I\,d\ell}{\lambda}\right)^2 \sin^2\theta}{\left(\frac{\eta\pi}{3}\right)\left(\frac{I\,d\ell}{\lambda}\right)^2} = 1.5\sin^2\theta \quad \text{and} \quad D_{\max} = 1.5 \tag{6}$$

The *radiation efficiency* of an antenna is $\epsilon_{\mathrm{rad}} \equiv P_{\mathrm{rad}}/P_{\mathrm{in}}$, where P_{in} is the time-averaged power that the antenna accepts from the feed. The (*power*) *gain* $G(\theta, \phi)$ is defined as the efficiency times the directive gain:

$$G(\theta, \phi) \equiv \epsilon_{\mathrm{rad}}D(\theta, \phi) = \frac{4\pi U(\theta, \phi)}{P_{\mathrm{in}}} = \frac{4\pi U(\theta, \phi)}{P_{\mathrm{rad}} + P_L}$$

where P_L is the ohmic loss of the antenna. A lossless isotropic radiator has a power gain $G_0 = 1$. At times the power gain of an antenna is expressed in decibels, where

$$G_{\mathrm{dB}} = 10\log_{10}\frac{G}{G_0} = 10\log_{10}G$$

17.5 Small Circular-Loop Antenna

Also known as the *magnetic dipole*, a small loop in the $z = 0$ plane, shown in Fig. 17-4, carrying a phasor current $I\mathbf{a}_\phi$, produces radiating $\mathbf{E}$ and $\mathbf{H}$ fields with characteristics similar to those of the Hertzian dipole, but with the directions of $\mathbf{E}$ and $\mathbf{H}$ interchanged. In the far zone,

$$H_\theta = -\frac{(\beta^2\pi a^2)Ie^{-j\beta r}}{4\pi r}\sin\theta$$

$$E_\phi = -\eta H_\theta$$

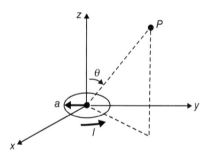

Fig. 17-4

The radiation resistance of the small loop antenna is found as part of Problem 17.6: $R_{\mathrm{rad}} = (20\,\Omega)(\beta^2\pi a^2)^2$.

17.6 Finite-Length Dipole

The expression (4) for the radiated power of the Hertzian dipole contains the term $(d\ell/\lambda)^2$, which suggests that the length should be comparable to the wavelength. The open-circuited two-wire transmission line shown in Fig. 17-5(*a*) has currents in the conductors that are out of phase, so that the far field nearly cancels out. An efficient antenna results when the line is opened out as shown in Fig. 17-5(*b*), producing current phasors

$$I_1(z') = I_m\sin\beta\left(\frac{L}{2} - z'\right) \qquad (0 < z' < L/2)$$

and

$$I_2(z') = I_m\sin\beta\left(\frac{L}{2} + z'\right) \qquad (-L/2 < z' < 0)$$

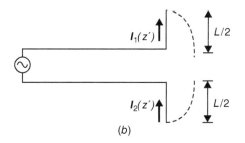

Fig. 17-5

The two currents are exactly in phase at mirror-image points in the y axis, and they vanish at the endpoints $z' = \pm L/2$. The two legs form a single dipole antenna of finite length L. Note that the current at the feed point ($z' = 0$) is related to the maximum current by $I_0 = I_m \sin \frac{\beta L}{2}$.

The far field is calculated by means of (2) and (1), under the assumption $r \gg L$ and $r \gg \lambda$.

$$H_\phi = \frac{jI_m e^{-j\beta r}}{2\pi r} F(\theta) \qquad E_\theta = \eta H_\phi$$

where the pattern function is given by

$$F(\theta) = \frac{\cos\left(\beta \frac{L}{2} \cos\theta\right) - \cos\left(\beta \frac{L}{2}\right)}{\sin\theta}$$

The antenna can also be assigned an *effective length* [write $I(z') = I_m \sin \beta(L/2 - |z'|)$]:

$$h_e(\theta) = \frac{\sin\theta}{I_0} \int_{-L/2}^{L/2} I(z') e^{j\beta z' \cos\theta} dz' = \frac{2I_m}{\beta I_0} F(\theta)$$

which has the units of length and contains all the pattern information.

For L up to about 1.2λ the antenna patterns resemble the figure eight, becoming sharper as L approaches 1.2λ. In the other limit, as $L \ll \lambda$, the pattern is that of the Hertzian dipole shown in Fig. 17-3(a). As L becomes greater than 1.2λ, the patterns become multilobed. See Fig. 17-6.

(a) $L = \lambda/2$ (b) $L = \lambda$ (c) $L = 3\lambda/2$

Fig. 17-6

The radiation resistance of a finite dipole of length $(2n - 1)\lambda/2$ ($n = 1, 2, 3, \ldots$) can be shown to be $R_{rad} = (30\ \Omega) \text{Cin}\,[(4n - 2)\pi]$, where

$$\text{Cin}\,(x) \equiv \int_0^x \frac{1 - \cos y}{y} dy$$

is a tabulated function. For $n = 1$ (*half-wave dipole*), $R_{rad} = 30(2.438) = 73\ \Omega$ and $D_{max} = 1.64$ (see Problem 17.8).

17.7 Monopole Antenna

A conductor of length $L/2$ normal to an infinite conducting plane [Fig. 17-7(a)] forms a monopole antenna. When fed at the base, the resulting **E** and **H** fields are identical to the dipole's. This is evident when the *image* of the monopole is positioned below the conducting plane as shown in Fig. 17-7(b).

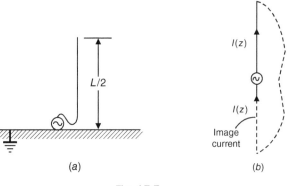

Fig. 17-7

As the monopole radiates power only in the region above the conducting plane, the total radiated power is one-half that of the corresponding dipole. From $R_{\mathrm{rad}} = 2P_{\mathrm{rad}}/I_0^2$, it follows that the radiation resistance is one-half the value for the dipole. Thus, for $L/2 = \lambda/4$ (*quarter-wave monopole*), $R_{\mathrm{rad}} = 36.5\ \Omega$.

17.8   Self- and Mutual Impedances

With respect to its feed, an antenna is equivalent to a load impedance $Z_a = R_a + jX_a$, where $R_a = R_{\mathrm{rad}} + R_L$, and R_L is ohmic resistance. The reactance X_a is not easily calculated; it is a function of the radius ρ of the conductors for dipoles and monopoles. Fig. 17-8 illustrates the variation of both R_a and X_a for monopoles of length $L/2$; the figure also applies to dipoles of length L if vertical scale values are doubled. Thus, the half-wave dipole has $R_a = 73\ \Omega$ and, roughly independent of ρ, $X_a \approx 40\ \Omega$. (It can be shown that as $\rho \to 0$, $X_a \to 42.5\ \Omega$.)

    When a second antenna is placed adjacent to a first antenna, a current in one will induce a voltage in the other. Consequently, a mutual impedance $Z_{21} = V_{21}/I_1 = R_{21} + jX_{21}$ exists in the system. For two side-by-side half-wave dipoles with very small conductor size, R_{21} and X_{21} vary with the separation d as shown in Fig. 17-9.

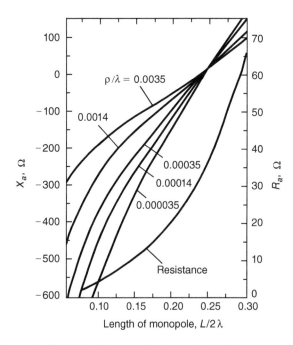

Fig. 17-8 (Source: Edward C. Jordan/Keith G. Balmain, *Electromagnetic Waves and Radiating Systems*, 2nd ed., © 1968, p. 548. Reprinted by permission of Prentice-Hall, Inc., Englewood Cliffs, N.J.).

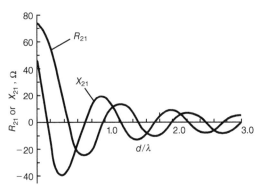

Fig. 17-9 (Source: Weeks (1968), *Antenna Engineering*. Reproduced by permission of McGraw-Hill, Inc.).

17.9 The Receiving Antenna

An antenna in the far field of a transmitter extracts energy from what is essentially a plane wave and delivers it to a load impedance Z_l. In Fig. 17-10(a) the dipole antenna lies along the z axis and the incident wave has a Poynting vector $\mathcal{P}$. The open-circuit voltage is equal to the product of the effective length $h_e(\theta)$ and the magnitude E of the projection of **E** onto the plane of incidence. [For the coordinate system of Fig. 17-10(a), $E = \sqrt{E_y^2 + E_z^2}$.]

$$V_{oc} = h_e(\theta)E$$

The pattern for the receiving antenna is identical to that of a similar transmitting antenna. The *available power* P_a is the maximum power which the receiving antenna can deliver to a load, which occurs when $Z_l = Z_a^*$. From the equivalent circuit of Fig. 17-10(b),

$$P_a = \frac{h_e(\theta)^2 E^2}{8R_a}$$

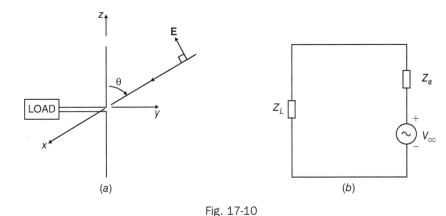

(a)   (b)

Fig. 17-10

The *effective area* $A_e(\theta)$ for an antenna is a hypothetical area such that when multiplied by the power density of the incident wave, $E^2/2\eta$, it results in the available power.

$$A_e(\theta)\left(\frac{E^2}{2\eta}\right) = P_a = \frac{h_e(\theta)^2 E^2}{8R_a} \quad \text{or} \quad A_e(\theta) = h_e(\theta)^2\left(\frac{\eta}{4R_a}\right)$$

It can be shown that the effective area is related to the directive gain by

$$\frac{A_e(\theta, \phi)}{D(\theta, \phi)} = \frac{\lambda^2}{4\pi}$$

When both a transmitting and a receiving antenna are considered, the power $P_{rad\ 1}$ radiated by antenna 1 and the available power P_{a2} at the receiving antenna 2 are related by the *Friss transmission formula*,

$$\frac{P_{a2}}{P_{rad1}} = \frac{D_1(\theta_1, \phi_1) A_{e2}(\theta_2, \phi_2)}{4\pi r^2}$$

Here, r is the separation of the two antennas. Angles θ_1 and ϕ_1 specify the direction of the receiving antenna as seen from the coordinate system of antenna 1. Similarly, θ_2 and ϕ_2 specify the direction of the transmitting antenna as viewed from the coordinate system of antenna 2.

17.10　Linear Arrays

A far-field pattern with a narrow beamwidth and high gain can be achieved by forming an array of identical antenna elements, each with the same orientation as shown in Fig. 17-11. The pattern function of the array is equal to the pattern function of an individual element multiplied by an *array factor* $f(\chi)$. In Problem 17.15 it is shown that, for a uniformly spaced array of N elements where d is the spacing

$$f(\chi) = \sum_{n=0}^{N-1} a_n e^{j\beta nd \cos \chi}$$

Fig. 17-11

The angle χ is the angle between the array axis and the line OP; by geometry, $\cos \chi = \sin \theta \cos \phi$. If the elements are progressively phased so that $I_n = a_n e^{jn\alpha}$ ($n = 0, 1, ..., N - 1$),

$$f(\chi) = \sum_{n=0}^{N-1} a_n e^{jn(\alpha + \beta d \cos \chi)}$$

or, defining $u \equiv \alpha + \beta d \cos \chi$,

$$f_1(u) = \sum_{n=0}^{N-1} a_n e^{jnu} \tag{7}$$

The overall pattern function will be a maximum when $|f_1(u)|$ is a maximum, which occurs for $u = 0$. If $\alpha = 0$ (the individual antennas are all in phase), then $u = 0$ implies $\chi = \pm 90°$; i.e., peak radiation occurs at right angles to the line of antennas. This is called a *broadside* array. On the other hand, if the phasing $\alpha = -\beta d$ is imposed, $u = 0$ implies $\chi = 0°$; this is an *endfire* array.

A *uniform* array has all antenna currents equal in magnitude. For $a_0 = a_1 = \cdots = a_{N-1} = 1$, (7) becomes

$$f_1(u) = \frac{\sin(Nu/2)}{\sin(u/2)} e^{j(N-1)u/2} \tag{8}$$

Thus, the main peak or *lobe* of the radiation pattern, centered on $u = 0$, has "height" $|f_1(0)| = N$. The two *first nulls* of the pattern [zeros of $|f_1(u)|$], occur at $u = \pm 2\pi/N$. The separation of the two first nulls can be used to define the beamwidth. Concentrating on the plane $\theta = 90°$, one finds

$$\textbf{Broadside uniform} \qquad \Delta\phi = 2\sin^{-1}\frac{2\pi}{\beta Nd} \approx \frac{2\lambda}{Nd}$$

$$\textbf{Endfire uniform} \qquad \Delta\phi = 4\sin^{-1}\sqrt{\frac{\pi}{\beta Nd}} \approx \sqrt{\frac{8\lambda}{Nd}}$$

where the approximations are for the case $Nd \gg \lambda$.

The sidelobes occur approximately midway between the nulls. The ratio of the main lobe to the first sidelobe is $N\sin(3\pi/2N)$, which approaches the value $3\pi/2$ for large N.

17.11 Reflectors

The gain of an antenna element can be enhanced by means of a reflector. Gains of from 6 to 12 dB can be obtained by using a half-wave dipole and a corner reflector such as that shown in Fig. 17-12(*a*). (A flat sheet reflector results when $\psi = 180°$.)

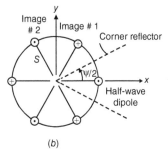

Fig. 17-12

The effect of a reflector with $\psi = 180°/N$ ($N = 1, 2, 3, \ldots$) can be calculated by the method of images. The actual reflector is replaced by $2N - 1$ image dipoles, which together with the actual driven dipole constitute an evenly spaced circular array, alternating in polarity [Fig. 17-12(*b*)]. Superposition of the far fields yields

$$\mathbf{E} = \frac{j\eta I_0 e^{-j\beta r}}{2\pi r} \frac{\cos\left(\dfrac{\pi}{2}\cos\theta\right)}{\sin\theta} \sum_{n=0}^{2N-1} (-1)^n e^{j\beta S \sin\theta \cos(n\psi - \phi)} \mathbf{a}_\theta \qquad (9)$$

For high-gain applications, the parabolic reflector driven by a source located at its focus, as shown in Fig. 17-13, is widely used. The directivity of the parabolic reflector is proportional to the aperture radius a and the aperture efficiency $\mathscr{E}$:

$$D_{\text{max}} = \left(\frac{2\pi a}{\lambda}\right)^2 \mathscr{E}$$

The aperture efficiency depends on a variety of design factors; a reasonable value is 55%. The half-power beamwidth can be estimated from the formula HPBW $\approx 117°(\lambda/2a)$.

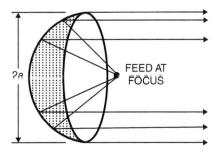

Fig. 17-13

SOLVED PROBLEMS

17.1. A center-fed dipole antenna with a z-directed current has electrical length $L/\lambda \ll \frac{1}{30}$. (*a*) Show that the current distribution may be assumed to be triangular in form. (*b*) Find the components of the vector magnetic potential **A**.

(*a*)   Since

$$\beta\left(\frac{L}{2}-|z|\right) < \beta\frac{L}{2} = \pi\frac{L}{\lambda} \ll \frac{1}{10}$$

we have

$$I(z') = I_m \sin\beta\left(\frac{L}{2}-|z'|\right)$$

$$\approx I_m\beta\left(\frac{L}{2}-|z'|\right) \approx \frac{2I_m'}{L}\left(\frac{L}{2}-|z'|\right) \text{ where } I_m' = I_m\frac{\beta L}{2}$$

(*b*) $$\mathbf{A} = \frac{\mu}{4\pi}\int_{-L/2}^{L/2} I(z')\mathbf{a}_z\left(\frac{e^{-j\beta r}}{r}\right)dz' = \frac{2\mu I_m' e^{-j\beta r}}{4\pi L r}\int_{-L/2}^{L/2}\left(\frac{L}{2}-|z'|\right)dz'\mathbf{a}_z = \frac{\mu I_m'}{4\pi r}\left(\frac{L}{2}\right)e^{-j\beta r}\mathbf{a}_z$$

from which

$$A_r = A_z\cos\theta = \frac{\mu I_m'}{4\pi r}\left(\frac{L}{2}\right)e^{-j\beta r}\cos\theta \qquad A_\theta = -A_z\sin\theta = -\frac{\mu I_m'}{4\pi r}\left(\frac{L}{2}\right)e^{-j\beta r}\sin\theta$$

and $A_\phi = 0$.

17.2. (*a*) Find the current required to radiate a power of 100 W at 100 MHz from a 0.01-m Hertzian dipole. (*b*) Find the magnitudes of **E** and **H** at (100 m, 90°, 0°).

(*a*) $$\lambda = \frac{3\times10^8}{10^8} = 3\text{m} \qquad R_{rad} = 790\left(\frac{d\ell}{\lambda}\right)^2 = 8.78\times10^{-3}\Omega$$

$$R_{rad} = \frac{2P_{rad}}{I^2} \qquad I = \sqrt{\frac{200}{8.78\times10^{-3}}} = 151\text{ A}$$

(This extremely high current illustrates that an antenna with a length much less than a wavelength is not an efficient radiator.)

(*b*) $$|\mathbf{E}| = \frac{\eta\beta I\,d\ell}{4\pi r}\sin90° = 0.95\text{ V/m} \qquad |\mathbf{H}| = 2.52\times10^{-3}\text{A/m}$$

17.3. Two z-directed Hertzian dipoles are in phase and a distance d apart, as shown in Fig. 17-14. Obtain the radiation intensity in the direction (θ, ϕ).

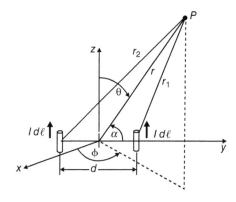

Fig. 17-14

Since $\cos\alpha = \sin\theta\sin\phi$,

$$r_1 \approx r - \frac{d}{2}\cos\alpha = r - \frac{d}{2}\sin\theta\sin\phi \quad \text{and} \quad r_2 = r + \frac{d}{2}\sin\theta\sin\phi$$

The far electric field is then $\mathbf{E} = E_\theta\mathbf{a}_\theta$, with

$$E_\theta = \frac{I\,d\ell}{4\pi r_2}e^{-j\beta r_2}(j\beta\eta\,\sin\theta) + \frac{I\,d\ell}{4\pi r_1}e^{-j\beta r_1}(j\beta\eta\,\sin\theta)$$

$$\approx \frac{j\beta\eta(I\,d\ell)}{4\pi r}e^{-j\beta r}\sin(e^{-j\beta(d/2)\sin\theta\sin\phi} + e^{j\beta(d/2)\sin\theta\sin\phi})$$

$$= \frac{j\beta\eta(I\,d\ell)}{2\pi r}e^{-j\beta r}\sin\theta\cos\left(\beta\frac{d}{2}\sin\theta\sin\phi\right)$$

Consequently,

$$U = r^2\left(\frac{E_\theta^2}{2\eta}\right) = \frac{\eta(\beta I\,d\ell)^2}{8\pi^2}\sin^2\theta\cos\left(\beta\frac{d}{2}\sin\theta\sin\phi\right)$$

For $d \ll \lambda$ the cosine term is nearly 1 and

$$U \approx \frac{\eta(\beta I\,d\ell)^2}{8\pi^2}\sin^2\theta$$

17.4. The far electric field of two Hertzian dipoles at right angles to each other (Fig. 17-15), fed by equal-amplitude currents with a 90° phase difference, is

$$\mathbf{E} = \frac{j\beta\eta(I\,d\ell)}{4\pi r}e^{-j\beta r}[(\sin\theta - j\cos\theta\cos\phi)\mathbf{a}_\theta + (j\sin\phi)\mathbf{a}_\phi]$$

Find the far-zone magnetic field, the radiation intensity, the power radiated, the directive gain, and the directivity.

$$H_\phi = \frac{E_\theta}{\eta} = \frac{j\beta(I\,d\ell)}{4\pi r}e^{-j\beta r}(\sin\theta - j\cos\theta\cos\phi)$$

$$H_\theta = -\frac{E_\phi}{\eta} = \frac{j\beta(I\,d\ell)}{4\pi r}e^{-j\beta r}\sin\phi$$

$$U = \frac{r^2\mathbf{E}\cdot\mathbf{E}^*}{2\eta} = \frac{\eta(\beta I\,d\ell)^2}{32\pi^2}(1 + \sin^2\phi\sin^2\theta)$$

$$P_{rad} = \int_0^{2\pi}\int_0^\pi U\sin\theta\,d\theta\,d\phi = \frac{\eta(\beta I d\ell)^2}{6\pi}$$

$$D(\theta,\phi) = \frac{4\pi U}{P_{rad}} = \frac{3}{4}(1 + \sin^2\phi\sin^2\theta)$$

$$D_{max} = D(90°,90°) = \frac{3}{2}$$

Fig. 17-15

17.5. A Hertzian dipole of length $L = 2$ m operates at 1 MHz. Find the radiation efficiency if the copper conductor has $\sigma_c = 57$ MS/m, $\mu_r = 1$, and radius $a = 1$ mm.

As defined in Section 17.4,

$$\epsilon_{rad} = \frac{P_{rad}}{P_{in}} = \frac{P_{rad}}{P_{rad} + P_{loss}} = \frac{R_{rad}}{R_{rad} + R_L}$$

where R_{rad} is the radiation resistance and R_L is the ohmic resistance. The radius a is much greater than the skin depth

$$\delta = \frac{1}{\sqrt{\pi f \mu \sigma_c}} \approx \frac{1}{15} \text{mm}$$

so that the current may be assumed to be confined to a cylindrical shell of thickness δ.

$$R_L = \frac{1}{\sigma_c} \frac{L}{(2\pi a)\delta} = 0.084 \text{ }\Omega$$

$$R_{rad} = (790 \text{ }\Omega)\left(\frac{L}{\lambda}\right)^2 = (790 \text{ }\Omega)\left(\frac{Lf}{u}\right)^2 = 0.035 \text{ }\Omega$$

$$\epsilon_{rad} = \frac{0.035}{0.119} = 29.4\%$$

17.6. Find the radiation efficiency of a circular-loop antenna, of radius $a = \pi^{-1}$ m, operating at 1 MHz. The loop is made of AWG 20 wire, with parameters $a_w = 0.406$ mm, $\sigma = 57$ MS/m, and $\mu_r = 1$.

At 1 MHz the skin depth is $\delta = 0.667$ μm. Assuming the current is in a surface layer of thickness δ, the ohmic resistance is

$$R_L = \frac{1}{\sigma}\left(\frac{2\pi a}{2\pi a_w \delta}\right) = 0.206 \text{ }\Omega$$

Taking the far-zone magnetic field from Section 17.5,

$$P_{rad} = \int_0^{2\pi} \int_0^{\pi} \frac{1}{2}\eta |H_\theta|^2 r^2 \sin\theta \, d\theta \, d\phi = \frac{\eta(\beta^2 \pi a^2)^2 I^2}{12\pi} = (10 \text{ }\Omega)(\beta^2 \pi a^2)^2 I^2$$

from which

$$R_{rad} = \frac{2P_{rad}}{I^2} = (20 \text{ }\Omega)(\beta^2 \pi a^2)^2 = 0.39 \text{ }\mu\Omega$$

and

$$\epsilon_{rad} = \frac{R_{rad}}{R_{rad} + R_L} = 1.89 \times 10^{-4}\%$$

17.7. Find the radiation resistance of dipole antennas of lengths (a) $L = \lambda/2$ and (b) $L = (2n-1)\frac{\lambda}{2}$, $n = 1, 2 \ldots$

(a) $$P_{rad} = \frac{1}{2}\int_0^{2\pi}\int_0^{\pi} \frac{|E_\theta|^2}{2\eta_0} r^2 \sin\theta \, d\theta \, d\phi = 30 I_m^2 \int_0^{\pi} \frac{\left\{\cos\left(\beta\frac{L}{2}\cos\theta\right) - \cos\left(\beta\frac{L}{2}\right)\right\}^2}{\sin\theta} d\theta$$

$$R_{rad} = \frac{2P_{rad}}{I_0^2} = \frac{60 I_m^2}{I_0^2}\int_0^{\pi} \frac{\left\{\cos\left(\beta\frac{L}{2}\cos\theta\right) - \cos\left(\frac{L}{2}\right)\right\}^2}{\sin\theta} d\theta$$

For the half-wavelength dipole $L = \lambda/2$ and $I_m = \dfrac{I_0}{\sin\left(\beta\dfrac{L}{2}\right)} = I_0$

$$R_{rad} = 60 \int_0^{\pi} \frac{\cos^2\left(\frac{\pi}{2}\cos\theta\right)}{\sin\theta} d\theta$$

Let $x = \cos\theta$

$$R_{rad} = 60 \int_{-1}^{1} \frac{\cos^2\left(\frac{\pi x}{2}\right)}{(1-x^2)}\, dx = \frac{30}{2} \int_{-1}^{1} \left\{ \frac{1+\cos\pi x}{1-x} + \frac{1+\cos\pi x}{1+x} \right\} dx$$

Since the integrals of the two terms within the brackets are equal

$$R_{rad} = 30 \int_{-1}^{1} \left(\frac{1+\cos\pi x}{1+x} \right) dx$$

letting $y = \pi(1+x)$

$$R_{rad} = 30 \int_{0}^{2\pi} \left(\frac{1-\cos y}{y} \right) dy = 30 \, \text{Cin}\,(2\pi)$$

$$R_{rad} = 30(2.48) = 73\ \Omega$$

(b) For $L = (2n-1)\frac{\lambda}{2}$, a similar approach yields

$$R_{rad} = 30 \, \text{Cin}\,[(4n-2)\pi]\ \Omega$$

17.8. Find the directivity D_{max} of a half-wave dipole.

From Section 17.6, for $\beta L/2 = \pi/2$,

$$|H_\phi| = \frac{I_0}{2\pi r} \left| \frac{\cos\left(\frac{\pi}{2}\cos\theta\right)}{\sin\theta} \right| \quad \text{whence} \quad |H_\phi|_{max} = \frac{I_0}{2\pi r}$$

the maximum being attained at $\theta = 90°$. It follows that

$$U_{max} = r^2 \frac{\eta}{2} |H_\phi|_{max}^2 = \frac{\eta I_0^2}{8\pi^2}$$

From Problem 17.7,

$$P_{rad} = \frac{\eta I_0^2}{8\pi} \, \text{Cin}\,(2\pi)$$

Thus,

$$D_{max} = \frac{4\pi U_{max}}{P_{rad}} = \frac{4}{\text{Cin}\,(2\pi)} = 1.64$$

17.9. A 1.5-λ dipole radiates a time-averaged power of 200 W in free space at a frequency of 500 MHz. Find the electric and magnetic field magnitudes at $r = 100$ m, $\theta = 90°$.

From Problem 17.7, $R_{rad} = (30\ \Omega)\,\text{Cin}\,(6\pi) = 105.3\ \Omega$, and so

$$I_0 = \sqrt{\frac{2P_{rad}}{R_{rad}}} = \sqrt{\frac{2(200)}{105.3}} = 1.95\ \text{A}$$

For a 1.5λ dipole, $|I_0| = |I_m|$.

From Section 17.6,

$$\left| H_\phi(100\,\text{m}, 90°) \right| = \frac{|I_m|}{2\pi r}\Big|_{r=100\,\text{m}} |F(90°)| = \frac{1.95}{2\pi(100)}(1) = 3.1\ \text{mA/m}$$

$$\left| E_\theta(100\,\text{m}, 90°) \right| = (120\pi)(3.1\times10^{-3}) = 1.17\ \text{V/m}$$

17.10. Obtain the image currents for a dipole above a perfectly conducting plane, for normal and parallel orientations.

The basic principle of imaging in a perfect conductor is that a positive charge is mirrored by a negative charge, and vice versa. By convention, electric currents are attributed to the motion of *positive* charges. Hence, for the two orientations, the image dipoles are constructed as in Fig. 17-16.

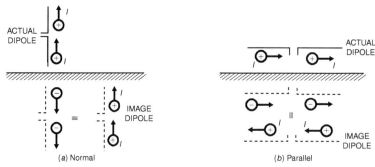

(a) Normal   (b) Parallel

Fig. 17-16

17.11. Calculate the input impedances for two side-by-side, half-wave dipoles with a separation $d = \lambda/2$. Assume equal-magnitude, opposite-phase feed-point currents.

The two feed-point voltages are given by

$$V_1 = I_1 Z_{11} + I_2 Z_{12} \qquad V_2 = I_1 Z_{21} + I_2 Z_{22}$$

where $Z_{12} = Z_{21}$; consequently,

$$Z_1 \equiv \frac{V_1}{I_1} = Z_{11} + \left(\frac{I_2}{I_1}\right) Z_{12}$$

$$Z_2 \equiv \frac{V_2}{I_2} = Z_{22} + \left(\frac{I_1}{I_2}\right) Z_{12}$$

For half-wave dipoles Fig. 17-8 gives $Z_{11} = Z_{22} = 73 + j42.5\ \Omega$ and Fig. 17-9 gives $Z_{12} = -12.5 - j28\ \Omega$. Then, with $I_1 = -I_2$,

$$Z_1 = Z_2 = 73 + j42.5 - (-12.5 - j28) = 85.5 + j70.5\ \Omega$$

17.12. Three identical dipole antennas with their axes perpendicular to the horizontal plane, spaced $\lambda/4$ apart, form a linear array. The feed currents are each 5 A in magnitude with a phase lag of $\pi/2$ radians between adjacent elements. Given $Z_{11} = 70\ \Omega$, $Z_{12} = -(10 + j20)\ \Omega$, and $Z_{13} = (5 + j10)\ \Omega$, calculate the power radiated by each antenna and the total radiated power.

From $V_1 = I_1 Z_{11} + I_2 Z_{12} + I_3 Z_{13}$,

$$Z_1 = \frac{V_1}{I_1} = Z_{11} + \left(\frac{I_2}{I_1}\right) Z_{12} + \left(\frac{I_3}{I_1}\right) Z_{13} = 70 + e^{-j\pi/2}(-10 - j20) + e^{-j\pi}(5 + j10) = 45\ \Omega$$

Similarly, $Z_2 = 70\ \Omega$ and $Z_3 = (85 - j20)\ \Omega$. It follows that

$$P_{\text{rad1}} = \frac{1}{2}|I_1|^2 \operatorname{Re}(Z_1) = \frac{1}{2}(25)(45) = 562.5\ \text{W} \qquad P_{\text{rad2}} = 875\ \text{W} \qquad P_{\text{rad3}} = 1065.2\ \text{W}$$

for a total of 2500 W.

17.13. Two half-wave dipoles are arranged as shown in Fig. 17-17, with #1 transmitting 300 W at 300 MHz. Find the open-circuit voltage induced at the terminals of the receiving #2 antenna and its effective area.

Fig. 17-17

For a half-wave dipole ($I_0 = I_{\max}$), Section 17.6 gives

$$h_e(\theta) = \frac{2}{\beta} \frac{\cos\left(\dfrac{\pi}{2}\cos\theta\right)}{\sin\theta}$$

and, at 300 MHz, $\beta = 2\pi$. For #1,

$$I_{01} = \sqrt{\frac{2P_{\text{rad1}}}{R_{\text{rad1}}}} = \sqrt{\frac{2(300)}{73}} = 2.87 \text{ A}$$

and the far field at angle θ_1 is of magnitude

$$|\mathbf{E}(\theta_1)| = \frac{\eta\beta I_{01}}{4\pi r} h_e(\theta_1) = \frac{\eta I_{01}}{2\pi r} \frac{\cos\left(\dfrac{\pi}{2}\cos\theta_1\right)}{\sin\theta_1}$$

Consequently,

$$|V_{OC2}| = h_e(\theta_2)|\mathbf{E}(\theta_1)| = \frac{\eta I_{01}}{\beta\pi r} \frac{\cos\left(\dfrac{\pi}{2}\cos\theta_1\right)\cos\left(\dfrac{\pi}{2}\cos\theta_2\right)}{\sin\theta_1 \sin\theta_2}$$

Substituting the numerical values gives $|V_{OC2}| = 0.449$ V.

The effective area of antenna #2 $A_e(90°) = \dfrac{u}{4R_{\text{rad}}}|h_e(90°)|^2 = 0.131$ m^2

17.14. For the antenna arrangement of Problem 17.13 find the available power at antenna #2.

From Section 17.9,

$$P_a = \frac{h_e(\theta_2)^2|\mathbf{E}(\theta_1)|^2}{8R_{\text{rad}}} = \frac{|V_{OC2}|^2}{8R_{\text{rad}}} = \frac{(0.449)^2}{8(73)} = 344 \ \mu\text{W}$$

17.15. Derive the array factor for the linear array of Fig. 17-11 (redrawn as Fig. 17-18).

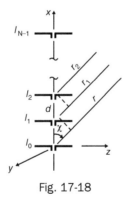

Fig. 17-18

The far electric field of the nth dipole ($n = 0, 1, \ldots, N - 1$) is, by Section 17.6,

$$\mathbf{E}_n = \frac{j\eta I_n e^{-j\beta r_n}}{2\pi r_n} F(\theta)\mathbf{a}_\theta \approx \frac{j\eta I_n e^{-j\beta(r - nd\cos\chi)}}{2\pi(r - nd\cos\chi)} F(\theta)\mathbf{a}_\theta$$

$$\approx \left[\frac{j\eta e^{-j\beta r}}{2\pi r} F(\theta)\mathbf{a}_\theta\right] I_n e^{j\beta nd\cos\chi}$$

By superposition, the field at P is

$$\mathbf{E}(P) = \sum_{n=0}^{N-1} \mathbf{E}_n = \frac{j\eta e^{-j\beta r}}{2\pi r}[F(\theta)f(\chi)]\mathbf{a}_\theta$$

where the array factor

$$f(\chi) = \sum_{n=0}^{N-1} I_n e^{j\beta nd \cos \chi}$$

acts as the modulation envelope of the individual pattern functions $F(\theta)$.

17.16. Suppose that Fig. 17-11 depicts a uniform array of $N = 10$ half-wave dipoles with $d = \lambda/2$ and $\alpha = -\pi/4$. In the xy plane let ϕ_1 be the angle measured from the x axis to the primary maximum of the pattern and ϕ_2 the angle to the first secondary maximum. Find $\phi_1 - \phi_2$.

For $\theta = \pi/2$, $\chi = \phi$ and the condition $u = 0$ for the primary maximum yields

$$0 = -\frac{\pi}{4} + \pi \cos \phi_1 \qquad \text{or} \qquad \phi_1 = 75.52°$$

The first two nulls occur at $u = 2\pi/N$ and $u = 4\pi/N$. The first secondary maximum is approximately midway between, at $u = 3\pi/N$; hence,

$$\frac{3\pi}{10} = -\frac{\pi}{4} + \pi \cos \phi_2 \qquad \text{or} \qquad \phi_2 = 56.63°$$

Then $\phi_1 - \phi_2 = 18.89°$.

17.17. A z-directed half-wave dipole with feed-point current I_0 is placed at a distance s from a perfectly conducting yz plane, as shown in Fig. 17-19. Obtain the far-zone electric field for points in the xy plane.

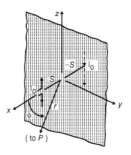

Fig. 17-19

The effect of the reflector can be simulated by an image dipole with feed-point current $-I_0$. We then have a linear array of $N = 2$ dipoles, to which Problem 17.15 applies. Making the substitutions

$$N \rightarrow 2 \qquad\qquad d \rightarrow 2s$$
$$\chi \rightarrow \phi \qquad\qquad I_0 \rightarrow -I_0$$
$$r \rightarrow r + s \cos \phi \qquad\qquad I_1 \rightarrow I_0$$

we obtain (to the same order of approximation)

$$\mathbf{E}(P) = \mathbf{a}_\theta \underbrace{\frac{j\eta e^{-j\beta(r + s \cos \phi)}}{2\pi r}}_{F(90°)} \cdot |\cdot \underbrace{2jI_0 e^{j\beta s \cos \phi} \sin(\beta s \cos \phi)}_{f(\chi)}$$

$$= -\frac{\eta I_0 e^{-j\beta r}}{\pi r} \sin (\beta s \cos \phi) \mathbf{a}_\theta$$

17.18. For the antenna and reflector of Problem 17.17, the radiated power is 1 W and $s = 0.1\lambda$. (*a*) Neglecting ohmic losses, compare the feed-point currents with and without the reflector. (*b*) Compare the electric field strengths in the direction ($\theta = 90°$, $\phi = 0°$) with and without the reflector.

(*a*) With the reflector in place, the input impedance at the feed point is

$$Z_1 = Z_{11} - Z_{12} = (73 + j42.5) - Z_{12}$$

But Fig. 17-9 gives, for $d = 2s = 0.2\lambda$, $Z_{12} = (51 - j21)$ Ω. Thus, $Z_1 = (22 + j63.5)$ Ω and so

$$I_{0\text{with}} = \sqrt{\frac{2P_{\text{rad}}}{R_{\text{rad}}}} = \sqrt{\frac{2(1)}{22}} = 0.302 \text{ A}$$

With the reflector removed, $Z_1 = (73 + j42.5)$ Ω and

$$I_{0\text{without}} = \sqrt{\frac{2(1)}{73}} = 0.166 \text{ A}$$

(b) At $P(r, 90°, 0°)$, one has, from Problem 17.17,

$$|\mathbf{E}_{\text{with}}| = \frac{\eta I_{0\text{with}}}{\pi r} \sin\frac{\pi}{5}$$

and, from Section 17.6,

$$|\mathbf{E}_{\text{without}}| = \frac{\eta I_{0\text{without}}}{2\pi r}$$

Hence, $|\mathbf{E}_{\text{with}}|/|\mathbf{E}_{\text{without}}| = 2(0.302/0.166) \sin 36° = 2.14$.

17.19. A half-wave dipole is placed at a distance $S = \lambda/2$ from the apex of a 90° corner reflector. Find the radiation intensity in the direction $(\theta = 90°, \phi = 0°)$, given a feed-point current of 1.0 A.

For $\psi = 90°$ and $\beta S = \pi$, (9) of Section 17.11 yields

$$E_\theta(90°, 0°) = \frac{j\eta I_0 e^{-j\beta r}}{2\pi r}(1)[-1 - 1 + (-1) - 1] = \frac{-j2\eta(1.0)e^{-j\beta r}}{\pi t} \quad (\text{V/m})$$

Then

$$U(90°, 0°) = \frac{r^2|E_\theta(90°, 0)|^2}{2\eta} = \frac{2\eta}{\pi^2} = 76.4 \text{ W/sr}$$

17.20. A parabolic reflector antenna is designed to have a directivity of 30 dB at 300 MHz. (a) Assuming an aperture efficiency of 55%, find the diameter and estimate the half-power beamwidth. (b) Find the directivity and HPBW if the reflector is used at 150 MHz.

(a) A directivity of 30 dB corresponds to $D_{\text{max}} = 1000$, and $\lambda = 1$ m at 300 MHz.

$$D_{\text{max}} = \left(\frac{2\pi a}{\lambda}\right)^2 \mathscr{E} \quad \text{or} \quad 2a = \frac{\lambda}{\pi}\sqrt{\frac{D_{\text{max}}}{\mathscr{E}}} = 13.58 \text{ m}$$

and HPBW $\approx (117°)(\lambda/2a) = 8.62°$.

(b) Halving the frequency doubles the wavelength; hence, from (a),

$$D_{\text{max}} = \frac{1000}{4} = 250 \approx 24 \text{ dB} \quad \text{and} \quad \text{HPBW} \approx 2(8.62°) = 17.24°$$

SUPPLEMENTARY PROBLEMS

17.21. The vector magnetic potential $\mathbf{A}(\mathbf{r}, t)$ due to an arbitrary time-varying current density distribution $\mathbf{J}(\mathbf{r}', t)$ throughout a volume V' may be written as

$$\mathbf{A}(\mathbf{r}, t) = \frac{\mu}{4\pi} \int\!\!\int\!\!\int_{V'} \frac{\mathbf{J}(\mathbf{r}', t - |\mathbf{r} - \mathbf{r}'|/u)}{|\mathbf{r} - \mathbf{r}'|} dv'$$

where $u = 3 \times 10^8$ m/s. Obtain $\mathbf{A}(\mathbf{r}, t)$ for a Hertzian dipole at the origin carrying current $\mathbf{I}(t) = I_0 e^{-t/\tau}\mathbf{a}_z$ ($\tau > 0$).

17.22. For the Hertzian dipole of Problem 17.21, determine $\mathbf{H}(r, \theta, \psi)$ under the assumption $|\mathbf{r}| \gg u\bar{t}$.

17.23. Consider a Hertzian dipole at the origin with angular frequency ω. Find the phases of E_r and E_θ relative to the phase of H_ϕ at points corresponding to (a) $\beta r = 1$, (b) $\beta r = 10$. Assume $0 < \theta < 90°$.

17.24. A z-directed Hertzian dipole $I_z\, d\ell$ and a second that is x-directed have the same angular frequency ω. If I_z leads I_x by 90°, show that on the y axis in the far zone the field is right-hand, circularly polarized.

17.25. Find the radiated power of the two Hertzian dipoles of Problem 17.3, if $d \ll \lambda$.

17.26. A short dipole antenna of length 10 cm and radius 400 μm operates at 30 MHz. Assume a uniform current distribution. Find (*a*) the radiation efficiency, using $\sigma = 57$ MS/m and $\mu = 4\pi \times 10^{-7}$ H/m; (*b*) the maximum power gain; (*c*) the angle θ at which the directive gain is 1.0.

17.27. Consider the combination of a *z*-directed Hertzian dipole of length $\Delta\ell$ and a circular loop in the *xy* plane of radius *a*, shown in Fig. 17-20. (*a*) If I_z and I_ϕ are in phase, obtain a relationship among I_z, I_ϕ, and *a* such that the polarization is circular in all directions. (*b*) Is linear polarization possible? If so, what is the phase relationship?

Fig. 17-20

17.28. A 1-cm-radius circular-loop antenna has *N* turns and operates at 100 MHz. Find *N* for a radiation resistance of 10.0 Ω.

17.29. A half-wave dipole operates at 200 MHz. The copper conductor is 406 μm in radius. Find the radiation efficiency and maximum power gain, if $\sigma = 57$ MS/m and $\mu = 4\pi \times 10^{-7}$ H/m.

17.30. Obtain the ratio of the maximum current to the feed-point current for dipoles of length (*a*) $3\lambda/4$, (*b*) $3\lambda/2$.

17.31. A short monopole antenna of length 10 cm and conductor radius 400 μm is placed above a perfectly conducting plane and operates at 30 MHz. Assuming a uniform current distribution, find the radiation efficiency. Use $\sigma = 57$ MS/m and $\mu = 4\pi \times 10^{-7}$ H/m.

17.32. Two half-wave dipoles are placed side-by-side with separation 0.4λ. If $I_1 = 2I_2$ and #1 is connected to a 75-Ω transmission line, find the standing-wave ratio on the line. [Recall that the reflection coefficient Γ is $(Z_1 - Z_0)/(Z_1 + Z_0)$ and the standing-wave ratio is $(1 + |\Gamma|)/(1 - |\Gamma|)$.]

17.33. A driven dipole antenna has two identical dipoles as parasitic elements; both spacings are 0.15λ. Given that $Z_{12} = (64 + j0)$ Ω and $Z_{13} = (33 - j33)$ Ω, find the driving-point impedance at the active dipole.

17.34. In Fig. 17-21(*a*) a half-wave dipole operates as a receiving antenna and the incoming field is $\mathbf{E} = 4.0e^{+j2\pi x}\mathbf{a}_y$ (mV/m). Let the available power be P_{a1}. In Fig. 17-21(*b*) a $3\lambda/2$ dipole lies in the *xy* plane at an angle of 45° with the *y* axis. The same incoming field is assumed, and the available power is P_{a2}. Find the ratio P_{a1}/P_{a2}.

(*a*)   (*b*)

Fig. 17-21

17.35. Find the effective area and the directive gain of a $3\lambda/2$ dipole that is used to receive an incoming wave of 300 MHZ arriving at an angle of 45° with respect to the antenna axis.

17.36. Consider a uniform array of 10 *z*-directed half-wave dipoles with spacing $d = \lambda/2$ and with $\alpha = 0°$. With the array axis along *x*, find the ratio of the magnitudes of the **E** fields at $P_1(100$ m, 90°, 0°) and $P_2(100$ m, 90°, 30°).

17.37. Eleven *z*-directed half-wave dipoles lie along the *x* axis, at $x = 0, \pm\lambda/2, \pm\lambda, \pm3\lambda/2, \pm2\lambda, \pm5\lambda/2$. Let the feed-point current of the *n*th element be $I_n = I_0e^{jn\alpha}$. A half-wave dipole receiving antenna is placed with its center at $(100$ m, 90°, 30°). (*a*) Determine α and the orientation of the receiving dipole such that the received signal is a maximum. (*b*) Find the open-circuit voltage at the terminals of the receiving antenna when $I_0 = 1.0$ A.

17.38. A half-wave dipole is placed at a distance $S = \lambda/2$ from the apex of a 60° corner reflector; the feed current is 1.0 A. Find the radiation intensity in the direction ($\theta = 90°$, $\phi = 0°$).

17.39. Two parabolic reflector antennas, operating at 100 MHz and 200 MHz, have the same directivity, 30 dB. Assuming that the aperture efficiency is 55% for both reflectors, find the ratios of the diameters and the half-power beamwidths.

ANSWERS TO SUPPLEMENTARY PROBLEMS

17.21. $\dfrac{\mu(I_0\, d\ell)}{4\pi|\mathbf{r}|} e^{-(t-|\mathbf{r}|/u)/\tau}\mathbf{a}_z$

17.22. $-\dfrac{\mu(I_0\, d\ell)}{4\pi u\tau|\mathbf{r}|}\sin\theta\, e^{-(t-|\mathbf{r}|/u)/\tau}\mathbf{a}_\phi$

17.23. (a) E_r lags H_ϕ by 90°, E_θ lags H_ϕ by 45°; (b) E_r lags H_ϕ by 90°, E_θ and H_ϕ are almost in phase.

17.24. By (3) the resulting electric field components have the same magnitude and 90 degrees phase shift. From Sections 1-12 and 1-13 one deduces the field is right-hand circularly polarized.

17.25. $\dfrac{4\pi\eta}{3}\left(\dfrac{I\, d\ell}{\lambda}\right)^2$

17.26. (a) 42%; (b) 0.63; (c) 54.71°

17.27. (a) $\dfrac{I_\phi}{I_z} = \dfrac{\lambda\Delta\ell}{2\pi a^2}$

(b) Yes. The currents must be out of phase by 90°.

17.28. 515

17.29. 99.26%, 1.63

17.30. (a) 1.414; (b) −1

17.31. 73.36%

17.32. 1.63

17.33. $(29.36 + j65.93)\ \Omega$

17.34. 0.748

17.35. 0.173 m², 2.18

17.36. 11.36

17.37. (a) $\alpha = -0.866\pi$; (b) 2.1 V

17.38. 76.4 W/sr

17.39. 1.414, 0.707

CHAPTER 18

Propagation of Electromagnetic Waves in the Atmosphere

18.1 Introduction and Summary

Transmission of signals by radio waves in the atmosphere is affected by air, ground, and sky, all of which influence the mechanisms of propagation. Their effects vary with weather conditions, spatial and temporal conditions of transmission, and frequency bands employed. The aim of this chapter is to present the basic features of propagation of radio waves in the atmosphere. The chapter does not discuss design aspects of transmission systems. For that purpose, and for further insight into atmospheric propagation, the reader may refer to the references listed at the end of the chapter.

Radio propagation in the atmosphere serves to transmit information and provide communication between points on the ground, in the air, or in outer space. The signals travel in the troposphere and ionosphere, and undergo attenuation, refraction, and scattering. They also are reflected or diffracted by the ground, sea, and ionosphere, and may travel through them. The chapter begins with a summary of wave equations, the parameters involved, and propagation mechanisms. It then briefly presents the tropospheric and ionospheric effects on propagation. Classes of waves such as ground and sky waves are presented. Finally, the ionospheric and tropospheric delays in satellite microwave ranging, and correction methods are briefly discussed.

18.2 Plane Waves in Homogeneous Media

Field Intensity. The electric field intensity of a plane wave having an x-component only and propagating in the z-direction at a sinusoidal angular frequency ω through a medium with zero net-charge ($\rho = 0$) is

time domain
$$E(z,t) = E_0 e^{-\alpha z} \cos(\omega t - \beta z + \phi)\mathbf{a}_x = \mathcal{RE}\{\hat{E}e^{-\gamma z}e^{j\omega t}\}\mathbf{a}_x \tag{1}$$

phasor domain
$$\mathbf{E}(z,t) = \hat{E}e^{-\gamma z}e^{j\omega t}\mathbf{a}_x \quad \text{and} \quad \mathbf{H}(z,t) = \sqrt{\frac{\sigma + j\omega\epsilon}{j\omega\mu}}\hat{E}e^{-\gamma z}e^{j\omega t}\mathbf{a}_y \tag{2}$$

propagation constant $\gamma = \alpha + j\beta$, $\gamma^2 = j\omega\mu(\sigma + j\omega\epsilon)$ (See Section 14.2, and Problems 18.1 and 18.2.) (3)

The phasor $\hat{E} = E_0 e^{j\phi}$ represents the magnitude and initial phase of the electric field. For simplicity, and without loss of generality, we assume $\phi = 0$. The attenuation coefficient, α, represents the loss in the medium. It is zero for a perfect dielectric. Its unit is Nepers per meter (Np/m). For $\alpha = 1$, the field amplitude is reduced by $e^{-1} = 0.368$ when it travels a distance of 1 m. β is the spatial phase coefficient so that for a distance of one wavelength, $z = \lambda$, the phase changes by the amount $\beta\lambda = 2\pi$. α and β are real numbers. In general, they depend on the medium properties (ϵ, μ, σ) and the frequency ω.

Converting attenuation coefficient from Np/m to dB/km. Reduction of the amplitude of a uniform plane wave traveling along a path is given by the attenuation coefficient α in Np/m. After traveling 1 km, the wave's amplitude is reduced by the factor $e^{-1000\alpha}$. The attenuation is also expressed in dB/km found from $-20\log[e^{-1000\alpha}] = 20\times1000\alpha\times\log[e] = 8686\alpha$ (dB/km).

354

EXAMPLE 1. The attenuation coefficient of a wave propagating in the z-direction is $\alpha = 0.01$ Np/m. Expressed in dB the attenuation is $8686\alpha \mid_{\alpha=0.01} \approx 87$ dB/km.

Phase velocity and travel time. The electric field may also be expressed as

$$E(z,t) = E_0 e^{-\alpha z} \cos[\omega(t - z/u) + \phi]\mathbf{a}_x$$

where $u = \omega/\beta$ is called the phase velocity. u is a measure of the degree to which a medium changes the phase of a sinusoidal field. It is not necessarily the same as group velocity; i.e., the speed at which an electromagnetic signal wave travels. Only when the phase velocity is independent of frequency, does it become equal to group velocity or the propagation speed of the electromagnetic signal.

EXAMPLE 2. Find travel time τ of a radio signal between two earth stations 1000 km apart and linked by a satellite orbiting at 36,000 km over the earth. The earth stations and the satellite form an equilateral triangle.

Solution. Assuming the speed of transmission to be 300,000 km/s and ignoring system delays, $\tau \approx 2 \times 36,000\,(\text{km})/300,000\,(\text{km/s}) = 0.240\text{s} = 240$ msec.

EXAMPLE 3. A transmitter sends a 1-MHz sinusoidal signal toward a passive reflector at distance d and receives its echo. The phase difference between the transmitted and received signals is $180°$. Assuming the speed of transmission to be 300,000 km/s, find the minimum value of d.

Solution. The electric field may be expressed by $E(z,t) = E_0 e^{-\alpha z} \cos\omega(t - z/c) = E_0 e^{-\alpha z} \cos(\omega t - \theta)$, where $\theta = \omega z/c$. For $z = 2d$ and ignoring system delays, we have $\theta = 2\omega d/c = \pi$. Therefore,

$$d = \frac{c}{\omega}\frac{\theta}{2} = \frac{3\times10^8}{2\pi\times10^6}\frac{\pi}{2} = 25 \text{ m}$$

Energy and Power. The density of stored energy in the electric and magnetic fields is $\frac{1}{2}\{\epsilon E_x^2 + \mu H_y^2\}$. The magnitude and direction of the instantaneous rate of energy flow per unit area is given by the Poynting vector

$$\mathcal{P} = \mathbf{E} \times \mathbf{H}^* \tag{4}$$

This represents the power per unit area that is carried by the wave. The time average of the magnitude of the Poynting vector gives the average power density.

$$P_{\text{avg}} = \frac{1}{2}\mathcal{RE}\{\mathbf{E} \times \mathbf{H}^*\} \quad (\text{W/m}^2) \tag{5}$$

In summary, a plane wave traveling a distance r in a homogeneous medium experiences a delay of r/u seconds. It is also attenuated by a factor $e^{-\alpha r}$ due to medium conductivity and losses. In a lossless medium (such as free space), the plane wave is not attenuated and field intensities remain the same from one location in the wave front to another. The Poynting vector and energy density do not diminish as the wave progresses in space.

18.3 Propagation Parameters

The propagation parameters of a plane wave with zero initial phase at a sinusoidal angular frequency ω in a medium with zero net-charge are summarized in Table 18-1.

High-Conductivity Media. In the case of $\dfrac{\sigma}{\omega\epsilon} \gg 1$, the attenuation and phase coefficients are approximated by $\alpha = \beta = \sqrt{\pi f \mu \sigma}$. See Problem 18-3.

TABLE 18-1 Propagation Parameters for Media with Zero Net-Charge

i)	electric field	$\mathbf{E}(z,t) = E_0 e^{-\gamma z} e^{j\omega t}\mathbf{a}_x$
ii)	propagation constant	$\gamma^2 = j\omega\mu(\sigma + j\omega\epsilon),\ \gamma = \alpha + j\beta$
iii)	attenuation coefficient	$\alpha = \omega\sqrt{\dfrac{\mu\epsilon}{2}\left(\sqrt{1+\left(\dfrac{\sigma}{\omega\epsilon}\right)^2}-1\right)}$
iv)	phase coefficient	$\beta = \omega\sqrt{\dfrac{\mu\epsilon}{2}\left(\sqrt{1+\left(\dfrac{\sigma}{\omega\epsilon}\right)^2}+1\right)}$
v)	wave length	$\lambda = \dfrac{2\pi}{\beta}$
vi)	phase velocity	$u = \dfrac{\omega}{\beta}$
vii)	refraction index	$n \equiv \dfrac{c}{u},\ c = 3\times 10^8$ m/s
viii)	intrinsic impedance	$\eta \equiv \dfrac{E}{H} = \sqrt{\dfrac{j\omega\mu}{\sigma + j\omega\epsilon}} = \lvert\eta\rvert\angle\theta,\ \tan(2\theta)=\dfrac{\sigma}{\omega\epsilon},\ 0° < \theta < 45°$

EXAMPLE 4. A 1-kHz uniform plane wave travels in the x-direction in sea water with $\sigma \approx 5, \mu_r = 1, \epsilon_r = 70$. At $x = 0$ the amplitude of the electric field is 100 V/m. Find the field intensity at i) $x = 10$ m, ii) $x = 20$ m, and iii) $x = 50$ m.

Solution. $\dfrac{\sigma}{\omega\epsilon} = \dfrac{5\times 10^9\times 36\pi}{2000\pi\times 70} = 12857 \gg 1$

$\alpha = \sqrt{\pi f\mu\sigma} = \sqrt{1000\pi\times 4\pi\times 10^{-7}\times 5} = 0.1405, E(x) = 100e^{-0.1405x}$

$E(10) = 100e^{-1.405} = 24.54$ mV/m

$E(20) = 100e^{-2.81} = 6.02$ mV/m

$E(50) = 100e^{-7.025} = 89\ \mu$V/m

Low-Conductivity Media.   In the case of $\frac{\sigma}{\omega\epsilon} \ll 1$, the attenuation and phase coefficients are approximated by $\alpha \approx \frac{\sigma}{2}\sqrt{\frac{\mu}{\epsilon}}$ and $\beta \approx \omega\sqrt{\mu\epsilon}$. See Problem 18-4.

EXAMPLE 5. A 1-MHz uniform plane wave propagates in an ionospheric layer. The conductivity and permittivity of the ionosphere at that height are $\sigma = 1\ \mu$S/m and $\epsilon_r = 0.9$. Find the attenuation of the intensity of wave after it travels a distance of 1 km in that layer.

Solution. $\dfrac{\sigma}{\omega\epsilon} = \dfrac{10^{-6}\times 10^9\times 36\pi}{2\pi\times 10^6\times 0.9} = 0.02 \ll 1$

$\alpha = \dfrac{\sigma}{2}\sqrt{\dfrac{\mu}{\epsilon}} = \dfrac{10^{-6}}{2}\sqrt{\dfrac{4\pi\times 10^{-7}\times 36\pi\times 10^9}{0.9}} = 0.19868\times 10^{-3}$ Np/m

$E(1000) = E_0 e^{-1000\alpha} = 0.8198E_0$

Attenuation $= -20\log[0.8198] = 1.72$ dB/km

Dielectric media and free space with zero charge. The propagation parameters in a media with $\sigma = 0$ and zero charge are summarized in Table 18-2.

TABLE 18-2 **Propagation Parameters for Dielectric Media and Free Space**

i)	field intensities	$\mathbf{E}(z, t) = E_0 e^{j\omega(t-z/u)}\mathbf{a}_x$	$\mathbf{H}(z, t) = \sqrt{\frac{\epsilon}{\mu}}E_0 e^{j\omega(t-z/u)}\mathbf{a}_y$
ii)	propagation constant	$\alpha = 0, \ \beta = \omega\sqrt{\mu\epsilon}$	free space $\epsilon_0 = \frac{10^{-9}}{36\pi}$ F/m, $\mu_0 = 4\pi \times 10^{-7}$ H/m
iii)	wave length	$\lambda = \frac{2\pi}{\omega\sqrt{\mu\epsilon}}$	free space $\lambda = \frac{2\pi c}{\omega} = \frac{c}{f}$
iv)	phase velocity	$u = \frac{1}{\sqrt{\mu\epsilon}}$	free space $u = \frac{1}{\sqrt{\mu_0\epsilon_0}} = 3\times10^8$ m/s $= c$
v)	refraction index	$n = c\sqrt{\mu\epsilon}$	free space $n = 1$
vi)	intrinsic impedance	$\eta \equiv \frac{E}{H} = \sqrt{\frac{\mu}{\epsilon}}$	free space $\eta_0 = 120\pi = 377\ \Omega$
vii)	average power density	$\frac{E^2}{2\eta}$	free space $\frac{E^2}{240\pi}$

18.4 Complex Dielectric Constant

Maxwell's equation (1) in Chapter 14 relates the curl of **H** to **E**:

$$\nabla \times \mathbf{H} = (\sigma + j\omega\epsilon)\mathbf{E} = j\omega\left(\epsilon - j\frac{\sigma}{\omega}\right)\mathbf{E} \equiv j\omega\epsilon_c\mathbf{E}$$

where $\epsilon_c \equiv \epsilon - j\frac{\sigma}{\omega}$ is the complex permittivity,

$\epsilon^* \equiv \frac{\epsilon_c}{\epsilon_0} = \epsilon_r - j\frac{\sigma}{\omega\epsilon_0}$ is the complex dielectric constant, and

$\epsilon_0 = 8.854 \times 10^{-12} = \frac{10^{-9}}{36\pi}$ (F/m) is the permittivity of free space.

The complex dielectric constant combines the permittivity of a partially conducting medium with its conductivity. It helps produce a unified form for the propagation equations and their parameters that simplifies calculations. We already have seen how Ampère's law may be written in terms of ϵ_c. Similarly, the propagation constant for a partially conducting medium may be written in the same form as a perfect dielectric, with ϵ replaced with $\epsilon_0\epsilon^*$, that is:

$$\gamma = j\omega\sqrt{\mu\epsilon_0\epsilon^*}$$

Also, ϵ^* may be incorporated into the reflection coefficients at the boundary between two conductive media. In this case however, the calculations become laborious and a computer may be employed.

In addition to the above features, the complex dielectric constant provides an indication of the degree to which the material behaves as a dielectric, a poor conductor, or a good conductor. The real part of the complex dielectric constant is the relative permittivity ϵ_r of the material. Its imaginary part is $\sigma/(\omega\epsilon_0)$. Their relative values determine whether the medium is more like a dielectric or a conductor:

If $f \gg \frac{\sigma}{2\pi\epsilon}$, or equivalently $\epsilon_r \gg \frac{\sigma}{\omega\epsilon_0}$, then the material behaves almost as a dielectric.

If $f \ll \frac{\sigma}{2\pi\epsilon}$, or equivalently $\epsilon_r \ll \frac{\sigma}{\omega\epsilon_0}$, then the material behaves as a good conductor.

The frequency $f_c = \sigma/(2\pi\epsilon)$ is called the cross-over frequency. The real and imaginary parts of ϵ^* are equal-valued at f_c.

EXAMPLE 6.   Find the complex dielectric constant and cross-over frequency for i) sea water ($\sigma = 4$ S/m and $\epsilon_r = 80$), ii) moist land ($\sigma = 5$ mS/m and $\epsilon_r = 15$), iii) dry land ($\sigma = 1$ mS/m and $\epsilon_r = 4$).

Solution.

TABLE 18-3 **Complex Dielectric Constant** $\epsilon^* = \epsilon_r - j\dfrac{\sigma}{\omega\epsilon_0} = \epsilon_r - j18 \times 10^9\dfrac{\sigma}{f}$

Cross-Over Frequency $f_c = \dfrac{\sigma}{2\pi\epsilon} = 18 \times 10^9\dfrac{\sigma}{\epsilon_r}$

GROUND	σ (mS/m)	ϵ_r	(200 kHz)	ϵ^* (1 MHz)	(10 MHz)	f_c
sea water	4000	80	80-j360,000	80-j72,000	80-j7,200	900 MHz
moist land	5	15	15-j450	15-j90	15-j9	6 MHz
dry land	1	4	4-j90	4-j18	4-j1.8	4.5 MHz

18.5   Power Equation

Plane wave formulation is merely a model for a small section of the wave-front at a distance from the radiating antenna. In practical communications, in addition to possible media loss, the electric field and power density are also reduced due to the expansion of the wave-front with distance. On the other hand, with the transmitter and receiver antennas being directed toward each other, the radiated power is more concentrated toward the receiver making more power available to it.

Design of a communication system begins with a power budget that takes into account all of the above factors. We start the analysis with radiation from a hypothetical isotropic point source in free space. A point source that radiates electromagnetic waves equally in all directions is called isotropic and the electric field strength E_r at a distance r from such a source is

$$P_r = \frac{P_t}{4\pi r^2} \tag{6}$$

where P_t is the power radiated by the source.

EXAMPLE 7.   Find electric field strength E at a distance $r = 10$ km from an isotropic source that radiates $P_t = 100$ watts in free space, if i) P_t is the instantaneous power, or ii) if it is the average power.

Solution.

$$P_r = \frac{P_t}{4\pi r^2} = \begin{cases} \dfrac{E^2}{120\pi},\ E = \dfrac{\sqrt{30P_t}}{r} = \dfrac{\sqrt{3000}}{10,000} = 0.00548\ \text{V/m} = 5.48\ \text{mV/m}, & \text{if } P_t \text{ is instantaneous.} \\[3ex] \dfrac{E^2}{240\pi},\ E = \dfrac{\sqrt{60P_t}}{r} = \dfrac{\sqrt{6000}}{10,000} = 0.00775\ \text{V/m} = 7.75\ \text{mV/m}, & \text{if } P_t \text{ is average power.} \end{cases}$$

In practice, the transmitting and receiving antennas have preferred directions with gains G_t and G_r, respectively. The effective area of an isotropic receiving antenna is $\frac{\lambda^2}{4\pi}$ and the receiving antenna power is

$$P_r = (P_tG_t)\left(\frac{\lambda^2}{4\pi}G_r\right)\frac{1}{4\pi r^2} = (P_tG_t)G_r\left(\frac{\lambda}{4\pi r}\right)^2 \tag{7}$$

The term (P_tG_t) incorporates the transmitter antenna gain and power and is called the effective isotropic radiated power (EIRP). In the SI system, the unit of powers is the watt and the unit of distances is the meter.

Antenna gains are with respect to an isotropic antenna. The factor $(\frac{\lambda}{4\pi r})^2$ shows the effect of distance. Its inverse, called the basic loss and designated by L_b, may be described as basic spatial attenuation, or loss, in free space. The above power equation is also expressed in the logarithmic scale (dB units) and called a power budget:

$$P_r = P_t + G_t + G_r - L_b \ (\text{dB}) \tag{8}$$

$$L_b = 20\log\frac{4\pi r}{\lambda} = 20\log f + 20\log r - 147.55 \ (\text{dB}) \tag{9}$$

If frequency is expressed in MHz and distance in km the basic loss in dB units will be

$$L_b = 20\log f + 20\log r + 32.45 \ (\text{dB}) \tag{10}$$

In addition to L_b, the power equation may contain dissipative attenuation due to media conductivity or absorption, given by a_d. It is expressed in dB/m and related to the attenuation coefficient of the medium α by $a_d = 8.68\alpha$, where α is in Np/m. The dissipative attenuation for a path of length r is, therefore, $L_d = a_d r$. In addition to the above, the power budget may need to include other losses that depend on the frequency of transmission and mode of propagation. These will be addressed in the remainder of this chapter as they arise.

Converting W to dBW. The power of a transmitter W is also expressed in the logarithmic scale (dB units) and is called dBW.

$$P\,(\text{W}) \Rightarrow 10\log P\,(\text{dBW})$$

The reference level is 1 W corresponding to 0 dBW.

EXAMPLE 8. The power of a transmitter is 7 W. How much is it in dBW? Answer: $10\log(7) = 8.451\,\text{dBW}$.

EXAMPLE 9. The power of a transmitter is 45 dB below 1 W. How much is it in μW? Answer: $10\log(P) = -45\,\text{dBW}$, $P = 31.6\times10^{-6}\ \text{W} = 31.6\ \mu\text{W}$.

EXAMPLE 10. A 50-km link at 5-GHz is established between a 2-W transmitter and a receiver in free space. The antenna gains are 40 dB each. Construct the power budget to include i) transmitted power P_t in dBW, ii) basic spatial loss L_b in dB, and iii) received power P_r in dBW and μW.

Solution. $\quad P_r = (P_t G_t) G_r \left(\dfrac{\lambda}{4\pi r}\right)^2$

$P_t = 10\log 2 = 3.01\,\text{dBW}$

$L_b = 20\log f + 20\log r + 32.45 \ (\text{dB}) = 20\log 5000 + 20\log 50 + 32.45 = 140.41\,\text{dB}$

$P_r = P_t + G_t + G_r - L_b = 3.01 + 40 + 40 - 140.41 = -57.4\,\text{dBW} = 1.82\ \mu\text{W}$

18.6 Refraction

Refraction index n of a medium is defined as

$$n = \frac{c}{u} \tag{11}$$

where u is the phase velocity of wave propagation in that medium and c is the speed of light in vacuum. For a perfect dielectric we have $u = 1/\sqrt{\mu\epsilon}$. For a nonmagnetic material, $\mu = \mu_0$ and the refraction index of the dielectric becomes $n = \sqrt{\epsilon_r}$, where $\epsilon_r = \epsilon/\epsilon_0$ is the relative permittivity (also called the dielectric constant) of the medium. The index of refraction manifests itself in two ways: i) A wave traveling in a medium with an index of refraction greater than unity experiences greater delay than in free space. ii) A wave incident on a planar interface between two nonmagnetic media with refraction index changing from n_1 to n_2 will bend according to *Snell's law of refraction:*

$$\frac{\sin\theta_t}{\sin\theta_i} = \frac{n_1}{n_2} \tag{12}$$

where θ_i and θ_t are the incidence and transmission angles, respectively, with respect to the normal to the plane. The transmitted wave will refract away from the normal if $n_2 < n_1$, and toward it if $n_2 > n_1$.

EXAMPLE 11.   A layer of dielectric with refraction index $n_2 = 1.005$ is sandwiched between two dielectric media with refraction indexes $n_1 = 1.05$ and $n_3 = 1$. See Fig. 18-1. Given the incidence angle $\theta_1 = 30°$, find θ_2 and θ_3. Summarize your conclusions.

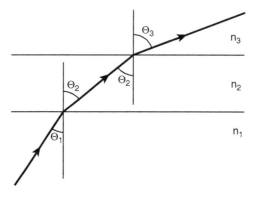

Fig. 18-1

Solution. $\sin\theta_2 = \sin\theta_1 \dfrac{n_1}{n_2} = 0.5\dfrac{1.05}{1.005} = 0.522388, \theta_2 = 31.5°$

$\sin\theta_3 = \sin\theta_2 \dfrac{n_2}{n_3} = 0.522388\dfrac{1.005}{1} = 0.525, \theta_3 = 31.66°$

The wave bends as it goes from a high-n region to low-n region.

For $n_2 < n_1$ and the critical angle of incidence $\theta_c = \sin^{-1}(\frac{n_2}{n_1})$ the transmission angle becomes $90°$ and the wave does not penetrate the second medium but propagates along the interface plane. Such a phenomenon may occur within both the troposphere and ionosphere.

EXAMPLE 12.   Given $\epsilon_{r2} = 1$, find θ_c for i) $\epsilon_{r1} = 1.05$, and ii) $\epsilon_{r1} = 1.005$.

Solution.   i) $\theta_c = \sin^{-1}\left(\dfrac{n_2}{n_1}\right) = \sin^{-1}\left(\dfrac{1}{\sqrt{1.05}}\right) = 77.4°$, ii) $\theta_c = \sin^{-1}\left(\dfrac{1}{\sqrt{1.005}}\right) = 86°$

18.7   Reflection, Diffraction, and Scattering

Reflection.   In passing from one medium to another, a radio wave may also reflect back from the plane of incidence as in Fig.18-2. Snell's law of reflection states that the angle of reflection is equal to that of incidence. The relationship between the intensities of incident and reflected waves are derived from Maxwell's equations with the following boundary constraints: i) The tangential components of E and H fields are continuous across the interface, and ii) The normal components of the D and B fields are also continuous across the surface. Reflection of electromagnetic waves is discussed in Sections 14-8 through 14-11 of this book. Radio waves reflect from the ground, sea, and ionosphere. The incident and reflected waves have the same frequency but different amplitudes and phases. (See Problems 18-27 and 18-51.) The received wave is a coherent wave made of their combination.

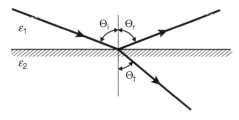

Fig. 18-2

Diffraction. Radio waves may be obstructed by objects casting a shadow but the shadow is not sharp. As an example, consider an absorbing object such as a wall located on the propagation path. Behind the object and near its edges the field intensity is not cut sharply from light to dark, but is reduced gradually. Moreover, the waves that pass over the wall are also affected by its edges. Radiation power develops noticeable ripples, as much as 1 dB, in the vicinity past the edges of the object. This phenomenon is called diffraction. The field is impacted by the geometry of the medium and its boundary. Diffraction by buildings, ground geometry, hills and mountains, and the earth's curvature contributes to the propagation of radio waves in the atmosphere.

Scattering. Scattering is produced by the ensemble of reflections from a large number of objects with different phases and amplitudes. Rough surfaces scatter radio waves. Local inhomogeneities in the troposphere may also produce variations in refraction indexes and reflected waves that have different phases and amplitudes but the same frequency. The result is tropospheric scattering. Scattering by the troposphere can create a mechanism for radio links between points beyond the horizon and at great distances. This, however, entails large attenuation. The mechanism requires a large transmitted power, powerful and efficient reception facilities, and an appropriate choice of frequencies (between 400 MHz and 7 GHz).

18.8 The Atmosphere

The earth's atmosphere extends to 10,000 km above the earth's surface and has a homogeneous composition up to about the 90-km mark. It contains, by volume, about 78% nitrogen, 21% oxygen, and 1% other gases. It contains a total of about 10^{44} molecules, 90% of which are in the 20-km thick shell surrounding the earth. The atmosphere is divided into five layers, reflecting the pattern of its temperature profile (see Fig.18-3). The lowest layer is called the troposphere. It extends from the ground to a height of 9 to 17 km, depending on weather conditions and location (the thickness of the layer being lower at the poles and higher at the equator). It contains 80% of the atmospheric air mass and almost all of its water vapor, clouds, fog, rain, and storms. Tropospheric pressure reduces with height. Its temperature also reduces with height at a rate of 6.5° C/km. The troposphere attenuates, refracts, and scatters radio waves, all of which are influenced by pressure, temperature, and humidity.

Above the troposphere and in ascending order lie the stratosphere (from 12 to 50 km), mesosphere (50 to 80 km), thermosphere (80 to 700 km), and exosphere (700 to 10,000 km; not shown in Fig. 18-3). Gas densities of the atmosphere decrease monotonously by height. Atmospheric pressure decreases exponentially with a height constant of about 8 km (also called scale height, i.e., the pressure at 8-km above the sea level is reduced by a factor $e^{-1} = 0.368$). The height profile of atmospheric temperature is not monotonous. It decreases throughout the troposphere at a rate of about 1° C per 100 m in dry air, increasing in the stratosphere, decreasing again in the tropopause and finally increasing in the thermosphere. See Fig.18-3.

Another important element of the atmosphere is the ionosphere created by ultraviolet and x-ray ionization of air molecules. Ionization produces concentration of electrons in several layers that span from 60 to 1000 km above the earth. Electron density in the ionosphere varies with height, day or night time, and latitude, among other factors. A typical example is sketched in Fig. 18-4. The electron density in the ionosphere makes it a low conductivity medium. It reflects radio waves or transmits them, depending on the frequency of the wave. In either case it becomes an important factor in both terrestrial and space communications.

EXAMPLE 13. The total air mass may be estimated from $ma = \frac{4\pi R^2 p_s}{g}$, where $R = 6400$ km is the radius of the earth, $p_s = 984$ mbar is the global mean pressure at the surface of the earth, and $g = 9.81$ m/s^2 is acceleration due to gravity. Using SI units we set $R = 6.4 \times 10^6$, $p_s = 984 \times 10^2$ pascal, $g = 9.81$ m/s^2 and obtain

$$ma = \frac{4\pi (6.4^2 \times 10^{12})(984 \times 10^2)}{9.81} = 5.16 \times 10^{18} \text{ kg}$$

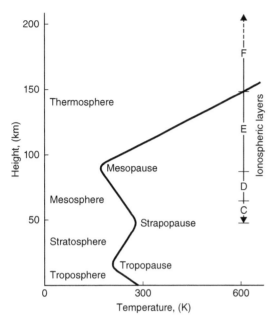

Fig. 18-3 Sketch of height profile of atmospheric temperature.

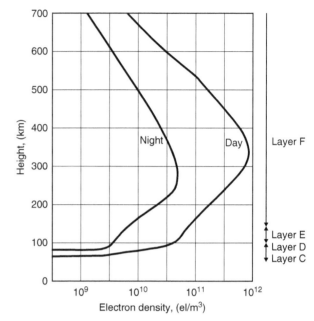

Fig. 18-4 Sketch of a typical height profile of electron density in the atmosphere.

18.9   Atmospheric Effects on Propagation of Radio Waves

The atmospheric influence on propagation of radio waves includes, but is not limited to, the following:

a)   The atmosphere attenuates radio waves by absorbing some of the radiated energy or scattering it. We will consider two causes for this phenomenon: i) gases and water vapor and ii) hydrometeors (rain, fog, and clouds).

b)   Atmospheric refraction changes the propagation path of radio waves and slows them down.

c)   The ionosphere reflects some radio waves. It also attenuates the waves that pass through it.

The above effects will be discussed in the remaining part of this chapter. Other atmospheric effects such as phase change and dispersion of radio signals will not be discussed.

18.10   Attenuation by Gaseous Absorption

Atmospheric gases absorb energy from the radio waves passing through them, thus causing some attenuation. The attenuation depends on the frequency of the radio wave. It is more pronounced at the resonance frequencies of gas molecules. The two components of specific attenuation, γ_o (for oxygen, also called the dry air component) and γ_w (for water vapor, also called the wet component), are shown in Fig.18-5 in dB per km, as functions of frequency. The total atmospheric loss due to gaseous absorption along a path is then

$$L_g = \int_{\text{path}} (\gamma_o + \gamma_w)\, dr$$

This requires a knowledge of the profile of specific attenuation, or its estimation. Assuming a constant specific attenuation along the path, for a distance r km the atmospheric loss is $(\gamma_o + \gamma_w)r$ dB. In both cases attenuation is small at frequencies below about 10 GHz and may be considered negligible compared to other terms in the power budget. For example, the total gaseous attenuation between ground and space stations is in general below 1 dB. Above 10 GHz, however, the total gaseous attenuation needs to be taken into account as a noticeable propagation loss. At frequencies above 10 GHz, the frequency bands that include resonance frequencies are avoided. Examples are the oxygen band from 58 to 62 GHz that contains the resonance frequencies

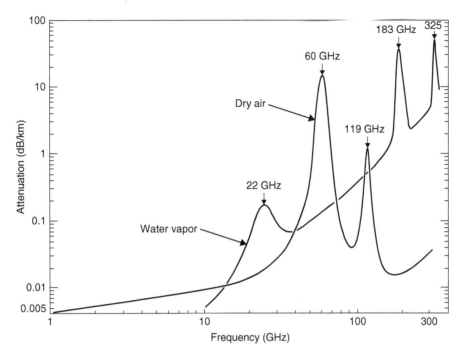

Fig. 18-5. Sketches of specific gaseous attenuation by oxygen and water vapor molecules in the air (in dB per km) as a function of frequency (pressure = 1013 mbar, temperature = 15° C, water vapor density = 7.5 g/m³).

of O_2 around 60 GHz, and also a second resonance band centered at 119 GHz. Similarly, water vapor spectral lines that cause high specific absorption are at 22, 183, and 325 GHz. Above 300 GHz there are many peaks with high absorption coefficients. In that frequency range transmission windows are chosen selectively to avoid high absorption.

EXAMPLE 14. A 10-GHz line-of-sight radio transmission link is established between two points that are 40 km apart. a) Calculate the free-space basic transmission loss. b) Determine the gaseous absorption loss assuming default values for pressure, temperature, and water vapor density along the path. Assume $\gamma_o = 0.008$ and $\gamma_w = 0.006$ dB/km at 10-GHz.

Solution.

a) From equation (10) $L_b = 20\log f + 20\log r + 32.45 = 20\log 10^4 + 20\log 40 + 32.45 = 145$ dB

b) From Fig. 18-5 at 10 GHz, $L_g = (\gamma_o + \gamma_w)r = (0.008 + 0.006) \times 40 = 0.56$ dB

18.11   Attenuation by Hydrometeors

In addition to water vapor, the atmosphere may also contain water particles of various sizes and shapes in the form of rain, snow, hail, cloud, and fog, collectively referred to as hydrometeors. A plane wave that travels through the atmosphere containing hydrometeors is both reflected from water particles and transmitted through them. Collectively, the water particles scatter the wave and, due to their conductivity, absorb energy from it as well. Both of these phenomena cause attenuation in the radio wave. Predictions of attenuation due to hydrometeors are based on models that take into account the size of the water particles, their shapes, their densities, and the precipitation rate. The models are calibrated and curve-fitted experimentally. Here are some examples.

Clouds and Fog. Within clouds and fog that consist of small water droplets (diameter of generally less than 100 microns), the specific attenuation for frequencies below 200 GHz is found from

$$\gamma_c = K_c \times M$$

where,

γ_c is the specific attenuation (dB/km),

K_c is the specific attenuation coefficient (dB/km)/(gr/m³), and

M is liquid water density in the cloud or fog (g/m³).

Typical liquid water density in fog ranges from 0.05 g/m³ (for medium fog with a visibility of about 300 m) to 0.5 g/m³ (for thick fog with a visibility of about 50 m). Specific attenuation coefficient K_c depends on temperature and permittivity and conductivity of water, and increases with frequency. It may be estimated from theoretical models and is also available in graphical or tabular forms. Sample values are given in Table 18-4.

TABLE 18-4 Sample Values of Specific Attenuation Coefficient K_c (dB/km)/(gr/m³) due to Clouds and Fog

FREQUENCY (GHz)	5	10	50	100	200
Specific Attenuation Coefficient K_c in (dB/km)/(gr/m³) at 0°C	0.025	0.1	2	5.5	10

EXAMPLE 15. Find the attenuation in dB for a 1-km path in medium fog at 0°C having liquid water density $M = 0.05$ g/m³ at a) 10 GHz, and b) 50 GHz.

Solution.

$$f = 10\,\text{GHz} \quad L_c = \gamma_c \times 1\,\text{km} = 0.1\,(\text{dB/km})/(\text{gr/m}^3) \times 0.05\,\text{g/m}^3 \times 1\,\text{km} = 0.005\,\text{dB}$$

$$f = 50\,\text{GHz} \quad L_c = \gamma_c \times 1\,\text{km} = 2\,(\text{dB/km})/(\text{gr/m}^3) \times 0.05\,\text{g/m}^3 \times 1\,\text{km} = 0.1\,\text{dB}$$

Rain. Rain scatters and absorbs radio waves. The effects depend on the size and geometry of the rain drops as well as rain rate, and conductivity. Rain models take into account the probability distribution of rain drops and their geometry, and estimate attenuation as a function of frequency. The results are plotted, tabulated, or curve-fitted for use. One model estimates the specific attenuation due to rain as a power-law function of the rain rate R in (mm/h)

$$\gamma_r = K_r R^\alpha\,(\text{dB/km}), \text{ where } R \text{ is in mm/h}$$

Coefficients K_r and α depend on frequency and wave polarization. They are obtained from calculations of scattering, given a size distribution for rain drops, and then curve-fitting the results. At lower frequencies of less than 20 GHz the specific attenuation grows with f. At higher frequencies of more than 100 GHz, it flattens, with some decrease with increasing f. In all cases, as expected, it increases with rain rate.

EXAMPLE 16. At around 10 GHz the attenuation coefficient due to rain is $\gamma_r \approx 0.02R^{1.25}$, where R is the rain rate in mm/h. Near 20 GHz it grows to $\gamma_r \approx 0.1R$. For a rain rate of $R = 10$ mm/h the attenuation coefficients become $\gamma_r = 0.35$ and 1 dB/km, at 10 GHz and 20 GHz, respectively.

18.12 Ground and Sky Waves

The space between the ground and the ionosphere constitutes the main corridor for the terrestrial transmission of waves. Transmission is between points on the ground, in the vicinity of the ground, or in the air. Propagation mechanisms are affected by attenuation, refraction, reflection, and scattering of the waves, all of which depend on the waveband, the ground and ionospheric conditions, and the location of transmitters and receivers. A simple classification of propagated waves is the following.

Ground waves. Consider a transmitter and a receiver above the ground at points A and B, respectively. See Fig. 18-6. The electromagnetic field at point B consists of three classes of waves (collectively called ground waves) arriving through i) the direct path AB, ii) the ground-reflected path AGB, and iii) the surface of the ground between A and B. The first two classes are called space waves. The effect of ground reflection and tropospheric influence on space waves can be understood and interpreted more simply. The third component is called a surface wave. It plays an important practical role in the HF band and lower frequencies. If the transmitter and receiver are close to the ground, the direct and reflected waves cancel each other and the surface wave is the one that dominates at point B. Its propagation mode, however, is more complex. Its propagation is shaped by the current in the surface of the conducting ground that tilts the wave-front toward the ground while it is attenuating the wave. Ground waves serve as the mechanism for radio propagation in the VLF, LF, and MF bands (3 kHz to 3 MHz), and some applications in the HF band. Ground waves reach beyond the horizon by diffraction around the curvature of the earth. They propagate best at long distances over seas with high conductivities. As frequency increases, attenuation reduces the propagation range of ground waves.

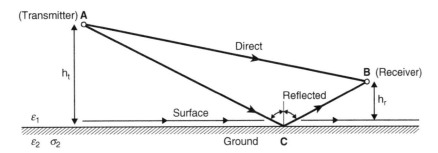

Fig. 18-6. Ground waves.

Sky waves. Ultraviolet and x-rays from the sun ionize air molecules. In the upper atmosphere where the air becomes thinner and mean free paths become longer, the ionization rate exceeds the recombination rate and this creates layers that contain free electrons. These layers constitute the ionosphere. The ionospheric layers start at heights of around 60 km and extend to 1000 km or more. The ionization depends on the time of day or night, season, and the sun's cycle. The ionosphere is a dielectric medium with poor conductivity. It may reflect the radio waves arriving from below it or transmit them on to space. By the refraction mechanism the ionosphere may also bend the incident waves back to earth. The returning waves, called sky waves, can be reflected back and forth several times between the earth and the ionosphere and propagate for long distances. The ionosphere is, therefore, the essence of the sky wave mode of propagation. The refraction index of the ionized region is modeled by

$$n = \sqrt{1 - 81\frac{N}{f^2}}$$

where N is the number of electrons per m^3 and f is the frequency of the incident wave. The refraction index is zero at $f = 9\sqrt{N}$. The maximum of that frequency is $f_c = 9\sqrt{N_{max}}$. This is called the *plasma frequency* or *critical frequency*. It is the highest frequency at which a normal incident wave is reflected from the ionosphere. Frequencies below f_c are reflected by the ionosphere regardless of their incident angles (i.e., the angle between the electromagnetic ray and the normal to the ionosphere layer). An HF oblique wave with $f > f_c$ may still be reflected if it reaches the ionosphere at an incident angle greater than a certain critical angle ϕ_c. For an oblique wave to pass through the ionosphere it is required that $f > f_c / \sin\phi_c$. For each frequency f there is a critical angle ϕ_c. Also, for each incidence angle there is a frequency called the *maximum usable frequency, MUF*, above which reflection does not occur. f_c, ϕ_c, and *MUF* depend on variations of the ionospheric electron contents (affected by diurnal, seasonal, geographical, and solar activity). Note that the above notations are defined in relation to the sky wave mode of HF propagation by ionosphere.

EXAMPLE 17. The following statements apply to the ionospheric reflection or transmission of radio waves.

i) Only frequencies greater than f_c can penetrate the ionosphere and pass through it.

ii) It is possible that a wave with $f > f_c$ is reflected from the ionosphere.

iii) Frequencies below f_c are reflected by the ionosphere.

iv) For each frequency $f > f_c$ there is a critical angle ϕ_c that the incident wave should not exceed in order for it to be reflected from the ionosphere.

v) For an oblique wave to pass through the ionosphere it is required that $f > f_c / \sin\phi_c$.

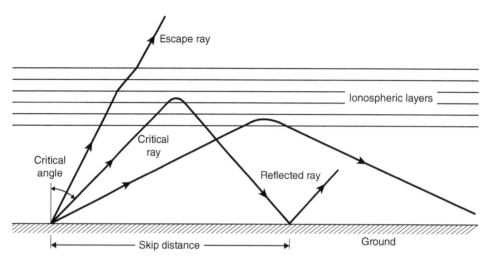

Fig. 18-7. Sky waves. Some radio waves escape through the ionosphere. Sky waves are reflected from it.

18.13   Models of the Troposphere

The troposphere may be considered to be a dielectric with a frequency-dependent attenuation coefficient and a refraction index slightly more than unity. Radio propagation in the troposphere undergoes attenuation, refraction, reflection, and scattering. Refraction causes bending and excess delay. Absorption and radiation by tropospheric particles cause scattering and attenuation. To account for these effects we need information about height profiles. In general, and except in special cases when inversion occurs, tropospheric pressure, temperature, humidity, and refraction index decrease with height. They vary with factors such as diurnal, seasonal, and weather conditions. Tropospheric profiles of pressure, temperature, and humidity are measured directly by radiosonde balloons or other similar methods at a number of weather stations worldwide once or more a day.

In system design and power budget planning one needs tropospheric models to calculate things such as path loss, delay, etc. In the absence of direct data, profiles are modeled by piece-wise linear and exponential functions. A hypothetical model called the *standard troposphere* is defined internationally and has the following specifications:

i)   Air pressure at sea level is 1013 mbar and decreases with height at the rate of 120 mbar/km.

ii)   Temperature at sea level is 290°K and decreases with height at the rate of 5.5°K/km.

iii)   A constant relative humidity of 60%.

Another hypothetical model with linear profiles for the first 1–2 km is characterized by the following:

$T(h) = 289 - 6.5h$ (°K) with h in km

$p(h) = 950 - 117h$ (mbar)

$e(h) = 8 - 3h$ (partial pressure of water vapor in mbar)

18.14   Tropospheric Refractivity

Relative permittivity and the refraction index at a location in troposphere at frequencies below 30 GHz are given by

$$\epsilon_r = 1 + 155.1 \times 10^{-6} \frac{p}{T} + 0.746 \frac{e}{T^2}$$

$$n = \sqrt{\epsilon_r} \approx 1 + \left(77.6 \frac{p}{T} + 3.73 \times 10^5 \frac{e}{T^2}\right) \times 10^{-6}, \quad \text{(approximation by binomial expansion)}$$

where

p is total pressure in mbar

e is partial pressure of water vapor in mbar

T is absolute temperature in °K

Because n is very close to unity a new index called *refractivity* is defined by

$$N = (n-1) \times 10^6 = 77.6 \frac{p}{T} + 3.73 \times 10^5 \frac{e}{T^2}$$

EXAMPLE 18. For $p = 1013$ mbar, $e = 20$ mbar, $T = 290$ °K we find

$$N = 77.6 \frac{1013}{290} + 3.73 \times 10^5 \frac{20}{290^2} = 271.065 + 88.704 = 359.77 \approx 360$$

Simple mathematical models for the height profile of refractivity are exponential or linear in nature. They use surface value N_0 and another parameter such as a scale factor or gradient of change. Some examples are the following:

i) A *general exponential model* which is expressed by $N = N_0 e^{qh}$, where h is in km and $-0.21 < q < 0.12$ with $dN/dh = -39$ at ground level. Another version of the above is $N = N_0 e^{-h/H}$, where h is height in km, H is a scale factor, and both are obtained from average data. An example is $N(h) = 315 e^{-0.136h}$ which gives a mean vertical gradient of -40 N/km.
ii) A *general linear model* which is expressed by $N = N_0 - bh$. The factor b is the height gradient. An example would be *standard linear model* $N = 324 - 40h$ that is used for heights less than 7 km. Another example uses the *standard linear atmosphere*, $N = 289 - 39h$, and is used for heights of less than 2 km.

For better accuracy more complex models such as the bi-exponential are used.

18.15 Tropospheric Excess Delay

The troposphere slows down propagation of radio waves. Excess travel time for a signal along a path ℓ, and the range error associated with the excess delay, are, respectively,

$$\Delta T = \frac{10^{-6}}{c} \int_\ell N d\ell, \text{ and } \Delta R = 10^{-6} \int_\ell N d\ell$$

EXAMPLE 19. Find the range error due to tropospheric excess delay for a zenith path between a satellite and an earth station at sea level with $N_0 = 360$. Assume an exponential height profile model of refractivity.

Solution. $$\Delta R = 10^{-6} \int_0^\infty N_0 e^{qh} dh = -10^{-6} \frac{N_0}{q}$$

$$\frac{dN}{dh}\Big|_{h=0} = qN_0 = -39, q = -\frac{39}{N_0}$$

$$\Delta R = 10^{-6} \frac{N_0^2}{39} = 3.32 \times 10^{-3} \text{ km} = 3.32 \text{ m}$$

Note: The exponential model uses only surface refractivity to provide a rough estimate of the range error. In many practical applications and for better accuracies, separate models are developed for the dry and wet components of the range error, as briefly described in Sections 18.19 and 18.20.

In addition to producing excess delay, tropospheric refractivity causes the path to bend, making it longer. The increase in path length, however, can be neglected except in special cases such as ground to space communication paths at low elevation angles.

18.16   Bending Effect of Tropospheric Refraction

The troposphere is stratified into horizontal layers and so is its refractivity. Therefore, a radio ray traveling through it bends. The curvature is defined as $C = 1/R$, where R is the radius of the circle modeling the curve. It may be shown that the curvature produced by bending the ray due to an incremental change in the refraction index with height is given by

$$C = -\frac{dn}{dh}\frac{\cos\theta}{n} \approx -\frac{dn}{dh}\cos\theta$$

where θ is the elevation angle of the incident wave. With $n \approx 1$ and the transmitter antenna beaming at a low elevation angle $\cos\theta \approx 1$, the path curvature is approximated by $C = -dn/dh$.

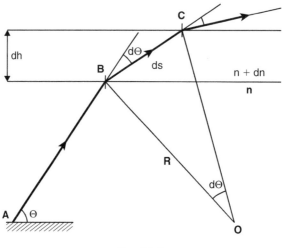

Fig. 18-8

Proof. From Fig. 18-8 and by Snell's law,

$$n\cos\theta = (n+dn)\cos(\theta - d\theta) = (n+dn)(\cos\theta + \sin\theta d\theta)$$

(where dn and $d\theta$ are incremental changes in n and θ, respectively)

from which $n\sin\theta d\theta + \cos\theta dn = 0$.

But, $\sin\theta = \dfrac{dh}{ds}$ and so

$$n\frac{dh}{dn} + \frac{ds}{d\theta}\cos\theta = 0.$$

Now $ds = Rd\theta$, where R is the radius of the path's curvature.

Therefore, $C \equiv \dfrac{1}{R} = -\dfrac{dn}{dh}\dfrac{\cos\theta}{n}$.

With $n \approx 1$ and $\cos\theta \approx 1$, $C = -dn/dh$.

4/3-Effective-Earth.   In the case of a standard linear troposphere with $dn/dh = -39 \times 10^{-6}$ per km, the path bends toward the ground with a curvature of $C = 39 \times 10^{-6}$ km^{-1}. The radius of the earth is 6378 km and its curvatures $1/6378 = 157 \times 10^{-6}$ km^{-1}. The curvature of the earth relative to the propagation path is $(157 - 39) \times 10^{-6} = 118 \times 10^{-6}$ km^{-1}. Effectively this corresponds to an earth with a radius of $1/(118 \times 10^{-6}) = 8{,}474$ km or 4/3 times the actual radius of the earth, and called 4/3-effective-earth. A ray propagating over the earth and bending due to tropospheric refraction is equivalent to one propagating on a straight line over the 4/3-effective-earth.

EXAMPLE 20. Find the distance to radio horizon d as a function of transmitter height h. See Fig. 18-9.

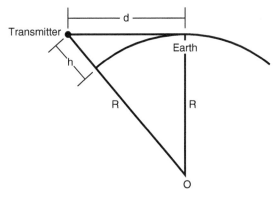

Fig. 18-9

Solution.

$R^2 + d^2 = (R+h)^2$. With $R \gg h$ we get $d = \sqrt{2R}\sqrt{h}$, where R is the 4/3-effective-earth radius = 8,474 km

$d = 4.12\sqrt{h}$, where h is in meters and d is in km.

18.17 Conductivity, Permittivity, and Refraction Index of the Ionosphere

Ionosphere is a partially conductive medium. The conductivity is due to the existence of free electrons that even at a comparatively low density (such as in the D layer where for every free electron there remain 10^{11} gas molecules) produce a conduction current. The three primary propagation parameters of the ionosphere (conductivity, relative permittivity, and the refraction index) may be obtained from the equation of motion of electrons and application of Ampère's law. Subjected to an electric field E an electron in the ionosphere experiences a force Ee. The electron moves at a velocity v, while colliding with other particles. The equation of motion of the electron is

$$Ee = m\frac{dv}{dt} + mvv$$

where e and m are the electron charge and mass, respectively, and v is the frequency of collision. In the above formulation, mvv is the frictional force due to electron collision with other particles. It acts against the motion. With $Ee^{j\omega t}$, the equation of motion in the phasor domain is

$$Ee = V(mv + jm\omega), \quad V = \frac{Ee}{m(v + j\omega)}$$

Motion of the electrons produces a conduction current density $J_c = Nev$, where N is the electron density.

The total current density is $\mathbf{J} = \mathbf{J}_c + \mathbf{J}_d = NeV + j\omega\epsilon_0 E$

Substituting for V: $\mathbf{J} = \left[\dfrac{Ne^2}{m(v + j\omega)} + j\omega\epsilon_0\right]E = \dfrac{Ne^2vE}{m(v^2 + \omega^2)} + j\omega\epsilon_0\left[1 - \dfrac{Ne^2}{\epsilon_0 m(v^2 + \omega^2)}\right]E$

From Ampère's law, $\mathbf{J} = \sigma E + j\omega\epsilon_0\epsilon_r E$

Therefore, $\sigma = \dfrac{Ne^2v}{m(v^2 + \omega^2)}$

and $\epsilon_r = 1 - \dfrac{Ne^2}{\epsilon_0 m(v^2 + \omega^2)} = 1 - \dfrac{\omega_c^2}{v^2 + \omega^2}$, where $\omega_c^2 = \dfrac{Ne^2}{\epsilon_0 m}$

If v^2 is much smaller than ω^2, it may be ignored and

$$\sigma = \frac{Ne^2 v}{m\omega^2} = \epsilon_0 v \frac{81N}{f^2}$$

$$\epsilon_r = 1 - \left(\frac{\omega_c}{\omega}\right)^2 = 1 - \frac{81N}{f^2}$$

$$n = \left\{1 - \frac{81N}{f^2}\right\}^{\frac{1}{2}}$$

where we have used the approximation $\frac{e^2}{4\pi^2\epsilon_0 m} = 80.5 \, \mathrm{m^3 s^{-2}} \approx 81$. The refraction index is zero at $f = 9\sqrt{N}$. At that frequency a normal incident wave gets reflected from the ionosphere. The maximum of that frequency is called the *critical frequency* $f_c = 9\sqrt{N_{max}}$, in which case

$$n = \left\{1 - \left(\frac{f_c}{f}\right)^2\right\}^{\frac{1}{2}}$$

Typically, higher values of N are at 10^{12} electrons per $\mathrm{m^3}$. They occur during the day time in the vicinity of the 300 km height of the ionospheric F layer. The corresponding critical frequency for such a density is 9 MHz. Under the worst case scenario, $f_c < 20$ MHz. For frequencies greater than 100 MHz, the refraction index given by the above expression may then be approximated by the first two terms of its Taylor series expansion:

$$n_p \approx 1 - \frac{1}{2}\left(\frac{f_c}{f}\right)^2 = 1 - 40.3\frac{N}{f^2}$$

Note: With $f > f_c$, we have $n < 1$ and a phase velocity $u > c$. This creates no contradiction with the laws of physics. The refraction index of a medium was defined based on the phase velocity (Table 18-1(vii)). The phase velocity is greater than c if the medium advances the phase of a simple sinusoidal input. The phase velocity does not reflect a signal's amplitude change, which carries information or energy. For that purpose we need to examine the group velocity u_g with which the frequency-components of the signal travel as a group ensemble.[1] The group refractive index is then defined as $n_g = c/u_g$. In the present case,

$$n_g = \frac{1}{n_p} \approx 1 + \frac{1}{2}\left(\frac{f_c}{f}\right)^2 = 1 + 40.3\frac{N}{f^2}$$

18.18   Satellite Microwave Ranging

The atmosphere reduces the speed of electromagnetic propagation to c/n. In addition, refraction can cause path bending, making it longer than the slant range. In some applications (such as broadcasting) the excess delay (and, in fact, the delay itself) can be neglected. In other applications (such as geodetic studies, remote sensing, and precise range measurements) the excess delay may not be ignored. It needs to be modeled, measured, and corrected for. The excess delay between an object in space and a ground location is

$$\Delta T = \frac{1}{c}\left[\int_\ell n \, d\ell - R_0\right]$$

where n is the refraction index along the path and R_0 is the true slant range. The contribution by path bending to excess delay may be ignored and so

$$\Delta T = \frac{1}{c}\int_\ell (n-1) \, d\ell$$

The following three components contribute to the (excess) delay: i) ionospheric and trans-ionospheric excess delay due to electrons, ii) tropospheric excess delay due to gas contents of the atmosphere (dry component),

---

[1]For a discussion of group and phase delays see Mahmood Nahvi, *Signals and Systems*, McGraw-Hill, 2014, pp. 560–564.

and iii) tropospheric excess delay due to water vapor (wet component). Each one of the above excess delays causes its own range error (ionospheric, dry, and wet range errors). These errors are corrected either by direct measurement or by modeling. In addition to the above, the uncertainty in satellite orbits and instruments also contribute to total range error. In precise-ranging systems it is desired that the total measurement uncertainty be of the order of 10 to 20 cm for a single pass.

18.19   Ionospheric Range Error

For frequencies above 100 MHz, the ionospheric refraction index may be given by a series. The first two terms of the series provide an approximation:

$$n \approx 1 - \frac{1}{2}\left(\frac{f_c}{f}\right)^2 = 1 - 40.3\frac{N}{f^2}$$

where N is the electron density. The term $\frac{1}{2}\left(\frac{f_c}{f}\right)^2$ results in 98% of the excess delay. The resulting range error is called a first order error:

$$\Delta R_1 \text{ (m)} = c\Delta T = \frac{40.3}{f^2}\int Nd\ell = \frac{40.3}{f^2}\times \text{TEC}$$

where TEC is the total electron content of a columnar path with a 1 m^2 cross section. TEC depends on the traversed path, time of the day, season, location, and sunspot cycle. A zenith column of TEC may vary from 10^{16} el/m^2 to 2×10^{18} el/m^2. Ionospheric range error corresponding to the above TECs for four frequencies are given in Table 18-5.

TABLE 18-5 First-Order Ionospheric Range Error ΔR_1 (in m) for Two TEC Limits at Four Frequencies

FREQUENCY	TEC = 10^{16} ℓ/m^2	TEC = 2×10^{18} ℓ/m^2
100 MHz	40	8000
400 MHz	2.5	500
2 GHz	0.1	20
10 GHz	0.004	0.8

The first-order range error is corrected by obtaining the TEC along the propagation path. This is done either by models or direct measurement. In the two-frequency measurement method, two signals of different carrier frequencies are transmitted to a target and the difference in their arrival times δT is measured.

$$\delta T = T_2 - T_1 = 40.3\frac{\text{TEC}}{c}\left(\frac{1}{f_2^2} - \frac{1}{f_1^2}\right),\ f_1 > f_2$$

$$\text{TEC} = \frac{c\delta T}{40.3}\times\frac{f_1^2\times f_2^2}{f_1^2 - f_2^2}$$

$$T_1 = \frac{f_2^2}{f_1^2 - f_2^2}\delta T$$

All high precision range and range rate measurements use the two-frequency method. Two examples are given in Table 18-6.

TABLE 18-6 Two-Frequency Systems for Ionospheric Correction

SYSTEM	f_1	f_2	T_1
Navstar GPS	1.57 GHz	1.23 GHz	$1.6\,\delta T$
Topex/Poseidon	13.6 GHz	5.3 GHz	$0.16\,\delta T$

Correction for ΔR_1 removes 98% of the error. The remaining part, called the Residual Range Error (RRE) which includes the contribution from the magnetic term, is estimated and corrected by more detailed methods. Beside these corrections, the change in ionospheric delay can also be measured using a single-frequency carrier modulated by a Pseudo Random Noise (PRN) signal. These methods will not be discussed here.

18.20 Tropospheric Range Error

For frequencies below 30 GHz, the refractivity $N = 10^6(n-1)$ of a non-ionized atmosphere was given in Section 18-13 to be

refractivity
$$N = N_d + N_w = 77.6\frac{p}{T} + 3.73 \times 10^5 \frac{e}{T^2}$$

dry range error
$$\Delta R_d = 10^{-6} \int N_d \, d\ell = 10^{-6} \int 77.6 \frac{p}{T} \, d\ell$$

wet range error
$$\Delta R_w = 10^{-6} \int N_w \, d\ell = 10^{-6} \int 3.73 \times 10^5 \frac{e}{T^2} \, d\ell$$

The dry gas composition of the atmosphere is more predictable in terms of latitude, time of the year, and height. On the other hand, water vapor is mostly within the first 1–2 km of the height of the troposphere, less mixed, and shows more variability. For the purpose of modeling and estimation, ΔR_d and ΔR_w are, therefore, treated separately.

Dry range error.   The zenith dry range error is

$$\Delta R_d = 77.6 \times 10^{-6} \int \frac{p}{T} \, dh$$

Assuming that the dry air obeys the perfect gas law $pv = RT$,

$$\int \frac{p}{T} \, dh = R \int \rho \, dh = \frac{R}{g} \int dp = \frac{R}{g} P_0$$

$$\Delta R_d(\text{m}) = 2.2757 \times 10^{-3} P_0 \, (\text{mbar})$$

In the above equation, ρ is the density of dry air at height h, P_0 is the surface pressure in mbar, and ΔR_d is the dry range error in m. Accordingly, the zenith dry range error is potentially predictable from the surface pressure. For example, the zenith dry range error at a location having surface pressure $P_0 = 1013$ mbar is estimated to be 2.3 m. For elevation angle $\theta > 15°$, ΔR_d may be estimated from

$$\Delta R_d(\text{m}) = \frac{2.2757 \times 10^{-3} P_0}{\sin \theta}$$

Note: The refraction index decreases with height and the refraction angle varies. The effect is a bending of the path, making it longer, which adds to the error. The path bending effect needs to be taken into account for low-elevation angles. In such cases the estimation of ΔR_d is done by more detailed modeling techniques.

Wet range error.   The zenith wet range error is obtained from

$$\Delta R_w = 0.373 \int \frac{e}{T^2} \, dh$$

By using the ideal gas law ($e = \rho_w R_w T$, $R = 461$ J kg^{-1} K^{-1}) the integral may be expressed in terms of water vapor density:

$$\Delta R_w = 1.72 \times 10^{-3} \int \frac{\rho_w}{T} \, dh$$

where ρ_w is the density of water vapor in gr/m^3 and T is the temperature along the path. ΔR_w depends on the height profiles of water vapor density (ρ_w) and temperature (T). An exponential decrease of a surface value $N_w = 48.5$ with a scale height of 2 km produces a typical value of $\Delta R_w = 10$ cm. The observed high value of $\rho_w = 37.6$ gr/m^3 over the Persian Gulf produces $\Delta R_w = 45$ cm. The magnitude of the wet range error is small compared to the other components of range error. However, because of its variability and unpredictability, its estimation by models is much harder and its effect on the total range error stronger. The typical range of the wet error is 3–30 cm. In precise ranging systems, ΔR_w is predicted with an uncertainty of less than 2 cm. Models based on surface data are used to estimate ΔR_w. The latter is also obtained by measuring sky brightness temperature.

SOLVED PROBLEMS

18.1. Given $\gamma^2 = j\omega\mu(\sigma + j\omega\epsilon)$, find $\gamma = \alpha + j\beta$.

$$j\omega\mu(\sigma + j\omega\epsilon) = (\alpha + j\beta)^2$$

$$j\omega\mu\sigma - \omega^2\mu\epsilon = (\alpha^2 - \beta^2) + j2\alpha\beta$$

From which:
$$\begin{cases} \alpha^2 - \beta^2 = -\omega^2\mu\epsilon \\ 2\alpha\beta = \omega\mu\sigma \end{cases}$$

Solve for α and β to obtain the expressions given in Table 18-1.

18.2. For a plane wave we have $\mathbf{E} = E_0 e^{-\gamma z}\mathbf{a}_x$, $\mathbf{H} = H_0 e^{-\gamma z}\mathbf{a}_y$, and $\gamma^2 = j\omega\mu(\sigma + j\omega\epsilon)$. Show that

$$H_0 = E_0\sqrt{\frac{\sigma + j\omega\epsilon}{j\omega\mu}}.$$

Start with $\qquad\qquad\qquad\qquad\qquad \mathbf{E} = E_0 e^{-\gamma z}\mathbf{a}_x$

Take the curl $\qquad\qquad\qquad\qquad\quad \nabla \times \mathbf{E} = \dfrac{\partial}{\partial z}\{E_0 e^{-\gamma z}\}\mathbf{a}_y = -E_0\gamma e^{-\gamma z}\mathbf{a}_y$

Use Faraday's law (equation (2) in Section 14.2) $\quad \nabla \times \mathbf{E} = -j\omega\mu\mathbf{H}$

Substitute for the curl $\qquad\qquad\qquad\quad E_0\gamma = j\omega\mu H_0$

Substitute for γ $\qquad\qquad\qquad\qquad\quad E_0\sqrt{j\omega\mu(\sigma + j\omega\epsilon)} = j\omega\mu H_0$

Simplify and get $\qquad\qquad\qquad\qquad H_0 = E_0\sqrt{\dfrac{\sigma + j\omega\epsilon}{j\omega\mu}}.$

18.3. High-conductivity media. Approximate the propagation constant γ and the intrinsic impedance η for media in which $\dfrac{\sigma}{\omega\epsilon} \gg 1$. Such media are classified as having high conductivity.

high conductivity $\qquad\qquad \dfrac{\sigma}{\omega\epsilon} \gg 1 \Rightarrow \sqrt{1 + \left(\dfrac{\sigma}{\omega\epsilon}\right)^2} - 1 \approx \dfrac{\sigma}{\omega\epsilon}$

propagation constant $\qquad\qquad \gamma = \alpha + j\beta$

attenuation coefficient $\qquad \alpha = \omega\sqrt{\dfrac{\mu\epsilon}{2}\left(\sqrt{1 + \left(\dfrac{\sigma}{\omega\epsilon}\right)^2} - 1\right)} \approx \omega\sqrt{\dfrac{\mu\epsilon}{2}\dfrac{\sigma}{\omega\epsilon}} = \sqrt{\dfrac{\omega\mu\sigma}{2}} = \sqrt{\pi f\mu\sigma}$

phase coefficient $\qquad\quad \beta = \omega\sqrt{\dfrac{\mu\epsilon}{2}\left(\sqrt{1 + \left(\dfrac{\sigma}{\omega\epsilon}\right)^2} + 1\right)} \approx \omega\sqrt{\dfrac{\mu\epsilon}{2}\dfrac{\sigma}{\omega\epsilon}} = \sqrt{\dfrac{\omega\mu\sigma}{2}} = \sqrt{\pi f\mu\sigma}$

propagation constant $\qquad \gamma = \alpha + j\beta = \sqrt{\dfrac{\omega\mu\sigma}{2}}(1 + j) = \sqrt{\omega\mu\sigma}\angle 45°$

intrinsic impedance $\qquad \eta = \dfrac{E}{H} = \sqrt{\dfrac{j\omega\mu}{\sigma + j\omega\epsilon}} \approx \sqrt{\dfrac{j\omega\mu}{\sigma}} = \sqrt{\dfrac{\omega\mu}{\sigma}}\angle 45°$

18.4. **Low-conductivity media.** Approximate the propagation constant γ, intrinsic impedance η, and average power density for media in which $\frac{\sigma}{\omega\epsilon} \ll 1$. Such media are classified as having low conductivity.

low conductivity
$$\frac{\sigma}{\omega\epsilon} \ll 1 \Rightarrow \sqrt{1+\left(\frac{\sigma}{\omega\epsilon}\right)^2} \approx 1+\frac{1}{2}\left(\frac{\sigma}{\omega\epsilon}\right)^2$$

propagation constant
$$\gamma = \alpha + j\beta$$

attenuation coefficient
$$\alpha = \omega\sqrt{\frac{\mu\epsilon}{2}\left(\sqrt{1+\left(\frac{\sigma}{\omega\epsilon}\right)^2}-1\right)} \approx \frac{\sigma}{2}\sqrt{\frac{\mu}{\epsilon}}$$

phase coefficient
$$\beta = \omega\sqrt{\frac{\mu\epsilon}{2}\left(\sqrt{1+\left(\frac{\sigma}{\omega\epsilon}\right)^2}+1\right)} \approx \omega\sqrt{\mu\epsilon}$$

intrinsic impedance
$$\eta = \frac{E}{H} = \sqrt{\frac{j\omega\mu}{\sigma+j\omega\epsilon}} \approx \sqrt{\frac{\mu}{\epsilon}}\angle\theta, \theta \approx \frac{\sigma}{2\omega\epsilon} \text{ (rad) (almost as a dielectric)}$$

average power density
$$\frac{E^2}{2|\eta|}\cos\theta$$

18.5. The amplitude of the electric field of a 1-MHz uniform plane wave at $z = 0$ is 100 V/m. Express the field in the time domain and obtain its average power density at $z = 0$ if the propagation medium is a) free space, and b) fresh water with $\sigma \approx 0, \mu_r = 1$, and $\epsilon_r = 80$.

Let the electric field be in the x-direction and propagation in the z-direction.

a) Free space: $\omega = 2\times10^6\pi, \alpha = 0, \beta = \omega\sqrt{\epsilon_0\mu_0} = \frac{\omega}{c} = 0.021, \eta_0 \equiv \frac{E}{H} = \sqrt{\frac{\mu_0}{\epsilon_0}} = 120\pi = 377\,\Omega$

$$E(z,t) = 100\cos(\omega t - \beta z)\,\mathbf{a}_x = 100\cos\omega(t - z/c)\,\mathbf{a}_x$$

$$H(z,t) = \frac{100}{\eta_0}\cos(\omega t - \beta z)\,\mathbf{a}_y = 0.2653\cos\omega(t - z/c)\,\mathbf{a}_y$$

$$P_{avg} = \frac{1}{2}\mathcal{RE}\{\mathbf{E}\times\mathbf{H}^*\} = \frac{E^2}{2\eta_0} = \frac{10^4}{2\times377} = 13.26\ \text{W/m}^2$$

Alternative calculation: $P_{avg} = \frac{100\times0.2653}{2} = 13.26\ \text{W/m}^2$

b) Fresh water: $\alpha = 0, \beta = \omega\sqrt{\epsilon\mu} = \omega\frac{\sqrt{80}}{c} = 0.187, \eta = \sqrt{\frac{\mu}{\epsilon}} = \frac{\eta_0}{\sqrt{80}} = 42.15\,\Omega$

$$E(z,t) = 100\cos\omega\left(t - \sqrt{80}z/c\right)\mathbf{a}_x,\ H(z,t) = 2.3725\cos\omega\left(t - \sqrt{80}z/c\right)\mathbf{a}_y$$

$$P_{avg} = \frac{E^2}{2\eta} = \frac{10^4}{2\times42.15} = 118.63\ \text{W/m}^2$$

18.6. Repeat Problem 18.5 for the case of fresh water at 2.5 GHz. At that frequency the constants of fresh water are $\sigma = 1\ \text{S/m}, \mu_r = 1$, and $\epsilon_r = 80$.

$\alpha = 21\ \text{Np/m}, \beta = 468.8, \eta = 42.06\angle2.57°\ \Omega$

$$E(z,t) = 100e^{-21z}\cos(5\times10^9\pi t - 468.8z)\,\mathbf{a}_x$$

$$H(z,t) = 2.3773e^{-21z}\cos(5\times10^9\pi t - 468.8z - 2.57°)\,\mathbf{a}_y$$

$$P_{avg} = \frac{E^2\cos(2.57°)}{2|\eta|} = 118.75\ \text{W/m}^2$$

18.7. Repeat Problem 18.5 for the case of sea water at 1 MHz. At that frequency the constants of sea water are $\sigma = 4$ S/m, $\mu_r = 1$, and $\epsilon_r = 80$.

$\alpha = 3.9716$ Np/m, $\beta = 3.9760$, $\eta = 1.405\angle 44.97°\ \Omega$

$E(z,t) = 100e^{-3.9716z}\cos(2\times10^6\pi t - 3.976z)\,\mathbf{a}_x$

$H(z,t) = 71.1763e^{-3.9716z}\cos(2\times10^6\pi t - 3.976z - 44.97°)\,\mathbf{a}_y$

$P_{avg} = \dfrac{E^2\cos(44.97°)}{2|\eta|} = 2517.9$ W/m^2

18.8. **Converting Np/m to dB/km.** A wave propagating in the z-direction is expressed in the time domain by $E(z,t) = E_0 e^{-z}\cos(\omega t - \beta z)$. Find the attenuation in dB/km.

After traveling 1 km, the wave's amplitude is reduced by the factor e^{-1000}. The attenuation is $-20\log[e^{-1000}] = 20\times1000\times\log[e] = 8686$ in dB/km.

18.9. The attenuation coefficient of low-conductivity media was found to be $\alpha = \dfrac{\sigma}{2}\sqrt{\dfrac{\mu}{\epsilon}}$. Find the attenuation in dB/km as a function of σ and ϵ_r. Assume $\mu = \mu_0$.

Attenuation in Np/m is: $\alpha = \dfrac{\sigma}{2}\sqrt{\dfrac{\mu}{\epsilon}} = 60\pi\sigma\epsilon_r^{-1/2}$

Attenuation in dB/km is: $-20\log[e^{-1000\alpha}] = 20\times60\pi\times\sigma\epsilon_r^{-1/2}\times10^3\log[e] = 1.6373\times10^6\sigma\epsilon_r^{-1/2}$

18.10. The electrical constants of a given fresh water is $\sigma = 5$ mS/m and $\epsilon_r = 70$. Find its attenuation coefficient α in Np/m and dB/km at i) $f = 100$ kHz and ii) $f = 100$ MHz.

i) $f = 100$ kHz, $\dfrac{\sigma}{\omega\epsilon} = 12.86 \gg 1$, (high-conductivity) $\alpha = \sqrt{\pi f\mu\sigma} = 0.0427$ Np/m $\Rightarrow 3721.2$ dB/km

ii) $f = 100$ MHz, $\dfrac{\sigma}{\omega\epsilon} = 0.013 \ll 1$, (low-conductivity) $\alpha = \dfrac{\sigma}{2}\sqrt{\dfrac{\mu}{\epsilon}} = 0.1126$ Np/m $\Rightarrow 978.4$ dB/km

18.11. At a) $f = 200$ kHz, b) $f = 1$ MHz, and c) $f = 10$ MHz, find the complex dielectric constant and crossover frequency for each of the following media: i) sea water ($\sigma = 5$ S/m and $\epsilon_r = 70$), ii) fresh water ($\sigma = 5$ mS/m and $\epsilon_r = 80$), iii) rocky land 1 ($\sigma = 5$ mS/m and $\epsilon_r = 7$), iv) rocky land 2 ($\sigma = 1$ mS/m and $\epsilon_r = 7$).

TABLE 18-7 Complex Dielectric Constant $\epsilon^* = \epsilon_r - j\dfrac{\sigma}{\omega\epsilon_0} = \epsilon_r - j18\times10^9\dfrac{\sigma}{f}$

Cross-Over Frequency $f_c = \dfrac{\sigma}{2\pi\epsilon} = 18\times10^9\dfrac{\sigma}{\epsilon_r}$

GROUND	σ(mS/m)	ϵ_r	(200 kHz)	ϵ^* (1 MHz)	(10 MHz)	f_c
sea water	5000	70	70-j450,000	70-j90,000	70-j9,000	1285.7 MHz
fresh water	5	80	80-j450	80-j90	80-j9	1.1 MHz
rocky land 1	5	7	7-j450	7-j90	7-j9	12.9 MHz
rocky land 2	1	7	7-j90	7-j18	7-j1.8	2.6 MHz

18.12. Express the complex dielectric constant of an imperfect dielectric in terms of its relative permittivity ϵ_r, conductivity σ, and wave length λ.

$\epsilon^* = \epsilon_r - j\dfrac{\sigma}{\omega\epsilon_0}$

$\dfrac{1}{\omega\epsilon_0} = \dfrac{1}{2\pi f\epsilon_0} = \dfrac{\lambda}{2\pi\epsilon_0 c}$

But $\epsilon_0 = \dfrac{10^{-9}}{36\pi}$ and $c = 3\times10^8$. Therefore, $\dfrac{1}{\omega\epsilon_0} = \dfrac{\lambda\times36\pi}{6\pi10^{-1}} = 60\lambda$

$\epsilon^* = \epsilon_r - j60\sigma\lambda$

18.13. The intrinsic impedance of a medium is defined by

$$\eta \equiv \frac{E}{H} = \sqrt{\frac{j\omega\mu}{\sigma + j\omega\epsilon}} = |\eta| \angle\theta, \ \tan(2\theta) = \frac{\sigma}{\omega\epsilon}, \ 0° < \theta < 45°$$

Given $\mu = \mu_o, \sigma = 5$ mS/m, and $\epsilon_r = 15$ for moist land, find the exact values of η at the following frequencies: a) 200 kHz, b) 1 MHz, c) 10 MHz, and d) 100 MHz. Compare these exact values with the results obtained from the approximation for a medium with low conductivity:

$$\eta \approx \sqrt{\frac{\mu}{\epsilon}} \angle\theta, \theta \approx \frac{\sigma}{2\omega\epsilon} \text{ (rad)}$$

TABLE 18-8 Exact and Approximation Values of Intrinsic Impedance η for a Low-Conductivity Medium ($\sigma = 5$ mS/m, $\epsilon_r = 15$)

INTRINSIC IMPEDANCE		200 kHz	1 MHz	10 MHz	100 MHz
exact value	η_a	12.77w +j12.35	30.11 +j25.51	86.86 +j24.06	97.20 + j2.91
approximation	η_b	−73.94 +j63.29	−96.36 +j13.73	92.99 +j28.76	97.29 + j2.91
difference	$\eta_b - \eta_a$	− 86.72 + j50.95	−126.48 − j11.77	6.13 +j4.71	0.09 + j 0.01

The approximation is acceptable at $f = 100$ MHz. At other frequencies the error is more than 10%.

18.14. Find the intrinsic impedance of a partially conductive medium in terms of its complex dielectric constant ϵ^*.

i) Direct approach $H = \sqrt{\frac{\sigma + j\omega\epsilon}{j\mu_0\omega}} E$

$$\eta = \frac{E}{H} = \sqrt{\frac{j\mu_0\omega}{\sigma + j\omega\epsilon}} = \sqrt{\frac{j\mu_0\omega}{j\omega\epsilon_0\left(\epsilon_r - j\frac{\sigma}{\omega\epsilon_0}\right)}} = \sqrt{\frac{\mu_0}{\epsilon_0}}\frac{1}{\sqrt{\epsilon^*}} = \frac{120\pi}{\sqrt{\epsilon^*}}$$

ii) By substitution $H = \sqrt{\frac{\epsilon_c}{\mu}} E = \sqrt{\frac{\epsilon^*\epsilon_0}{\mu}} E$

$$\eta = \frac{E}{H} = \sqrt{\frac{\mu}{\epsilon_0\epsilon^*}} = \frac{120\pi}{\sqrt{\epsilon^*}}$$

18.15. The power of a transmitter is 100 W. How much is it in dBW?

$$P_{dBW} = 10\log P_W = 10\log(100) = 20 \text{ dBW}$$

18.16. The power of a transmitter is 15 dBW. How many watts is it?

$$P_W = 10^{\frac{P_{dBW}}{10}} = 10^{1.5} = 31.6 \text{ W}$$

18.17. A radio transmitter radiates 50 W through an antenna with a 20-dB gain. Find $P_t G_t$ the effective isotropic radiated power (EIRP), in dBW and W.

$P_t = 50$ W $\Rightarrow$ $10\log 50 = 16.9897 \approx 17$ dBW
$EIRP = 17 + 20 = 37$ dBW $\Rightarrow$ $10^{3.7} = 5012$ W (The exact value is 5000 W.)

18.18. An isotropic source radiates 100 W in free space. Find electric field intensity E at a distance of 1 km from the source.

$$P_r = \frac{P_t}{4\pi r^2} = \frac{E^2}{240\pi}, \ E = \frac{\sqrt{60P_t}}{r} = \frac{\sqrt{6000}}{1000} = 77.5 \text{ mV/m}$$

18.19. A radio transmitter radiates 100 W in the atmosphere with a 40-dB antenna gain. Find i) the power density in dBW at a distance of 80 km in the direction of the antenna, and ii) electric field strength E. Ignore losses due to atmospheric absorption.

$$P_r = \frac{P_t G_t}{4\pi r^2}$$

$$P_r(\text{dBW}) = 10\log 100 + 40 - 10\log(4\pi \times 64 \times 10^8) = 60 - 109.0539 = -49.0539 \text{ dBW}$$

$$10\log P_r \approx -49.05, \ \log P_r = -4.905 \ P_r = 10^{-4.905} = 12.434 \ \mu W$$

$$P_r = E^2/(2\times 377), \ E^2 = 12.434 \times 2 \times 377 \times 10^{-6}, E = 96.8 \text{ mV/m}$$

18.20. A 50-km radio link operating at 5-GHz is established between a 2-W transmitter and a receiver in free space. The antenna gains are 40 dB each. Construct the power budget to include i) transmitted power P_t in dBW, ii) basic spatial loss L_b in dB, and iii) received power P_r in dBW and μW.

$$P_r = (P_t G_t) G_r \left(\frac{\lambda}{4\pi r}\right)^2$$

$$P_t = 10\log 2 = 3.01 \text{ dBW}$$

$$L_b = 20\log f + 20\log r + 32.45 \ (\text{dB}) = 20\log 5000 + 20\log 50 + 32.45 = 140.41 \text{ dB}$$

$$P_r = P_t + G_t + G_r - L_b = 3.01 + 40 + 40 - 140.41 = -57.4 \text{ dBW} = 1.82 \ \mu W$$

18.21. Repeat Problem 18.20, but with a 20-W transmitter.

$$P_t = 10\log 20 = 13.01 \text{ dBW}, 10\text{dB more than in Problem 18.20}$$

$$L_b = 20\log 5000 + 20\log 50 + 32.45 = 140.41 \ (\text{dB})$$

$$P_r = P_t + G_t + G_r - L_b = 13.01 + 40 + 40 - 140.41 = -47.4 \text{ dBW} = 18.2 \ \mu W$$

18.22. A 1-GHz microwave link is 40 km long. Transmitter power is 1 W and antenna gains are 20 dB each. Find the voltage at the terminal of a matched 50 Ω receiver.

$$P_t \ (\text{dBW}) = 10\log 1 = 0 \text{ dBW}$$

$$L_b = 20\log f + 20\log r + 32.45 \ (\text{dB}) = 20\log 1000 + 20\log 40 + 32.45 = 124.49$$

$$P_r = P_t + G_t + G_r - L_b = 0 + 20 + 20 - 124.49 = -84.49 \text{ dBW} = 3.55 \times 10^{-9} \text{ W}$$

$$P_r = \frac{V^2}{R} \Rightarrow V = \sqrt{P_r \times R} = \sqrt{3.55 \times 10^{-9} \times 50} = 421 \ \mu V$$

18.23. Calculate the scale height H for the exponential model of atmospheric pressure $p = p_0 e^{h/H}$, where

$p_0 = 1013$ mbar is sea level standard atmospheric pressure,

$H = \dfrac{R_0 \times T_0}{M \times g}$ is scale height,

$T_0 = 15°C$ is surface temperature,

$g = 9.81 \text{ m/s}^2$ is acceleration due to gravity,

$R_0 = 8.31447 \text{ J} \times \text{mol}^{-1} \times \text{K}^{-1}$ is the universal gas constant, and

$M = 0.0289644 \text{ kg} \times \text{mol}^{-1}$ is the molar mass of dry air.

Using SI units we set $p_s = 1013 \times 10^2$ pascal, $T_0 = 15 + 273 = 288$ K and obtain

$$H = \frac{[8.31447 \text{ J/(mol} \times \text{K)]} \times 288 \text{ K}}{[0.0289644 \text{ kg/mol}] \times 9.81 \text{ m/s}^2} = 8427 \text{ m} = 8.4 \text{ km}$$

18.24. a) Determine the gaseous absorption loss at 10 GHz from a ground station at sea level to a satellite at a height of 40,000 km. Assume default weather conditions at the ground. b) Repeat for 20 GHz.

$$L_g = \frac{1}{\sin\theta}\left(\int_{\text{path}} \gamma_o dh + \int_{\text{path}} \gamma_w dh\right) = \frac{\gamma_o h_o + \gamma_w h_w}{\sin\theta}$$

where h_o and h_w are the wet and dry "equivalent heights," respectively, in km. Their determination involves height profiles and is tedious. Therefore, they may be approximated. Here are some examples. (See references at the end of this chapter.)

TABLE 18-9 Sample Values of the Total Zenith Gaseous Attenuation at 10 and 20 GHz

		10 GHz	20 GHz
Dry	γ_o (dB/km)	0.008	0.012
	h_o (km)	5.2	5
	L_o (dB)	0.04	0.06
Wet	γ_w (dB/km)	0.006	0.1
	h_w (km)	1.7	2
	L_w (dB)	0.01	0.2
Total	$L_g = L_o + L_w$ (dB)	0.05	0.26

The total zenith gaseous attenuations at 10 and 20 GHz are 0.05 and 0.26 dB, respectively. These are small numbers compared to other path losses. However, at higher frequencies they become considerably larger.

18.25. Find the cloud attenuation of radio waves from a satellite to an earth station at a 30° elevation angle at 10 and 50 GHz. The cloud is 1 km thick with a density of 0.5 gr/m³ and is at 0 °C.

$$\gamma_c = K_c \times M \text{ (dB/km)}, \qquad L_c = \frac{\gamma_c \times 1}{\sin 30°} \text{ (dB)}$$

From Table 18-4 $f = 10$ GHz, $\gamma_c = 0.1 \times 0.5 = 0.05$, $L_c = 0.05 \times 2 = 0.1$ dB

$f = 50$ GHz, $\gamma_c = 2 \times 0.5 = 1$, $L_c = \gamma_c \times 2 = 2$ dB

18.26. Refractivity. Given $N_0 = 360$ at sea level, find N at i) $h = 1$ km and ii) $h = 2$ km.

Exponential model: $N = 360e^{qh}$, $\frac{dN}{dh}\big|_{h=0} = 360q = -39, q = \frac{-39}{360} = -0.108$, $\begin{cases} N(1) = 360e^{-0.108} = 323 \\ N(2) = 360e^{-0.108\times2} = 290 \end{cases}$

Linear model: $N = 360 - 39h$, $\begin{cases} N(1) = 360 - 39 = 321 \\ N(2) = 360 - 39 \times 2 = 281 \end{cases}$

18.27. Ground Reflection. A radio wave impinges on moist ground ($\sigma = 5$ mS/m, $\epsilon_r = 15$) at an incident angle of $\pi/6$ radians. Find the intensity ratios of reflected and transmitted electric fields to the incident field for a) $f = 200$ kHz, and b) $f = 100$ MHz.

Refer to Fig. 18-2 $n_1 = 1,\ n_2 = \sqrt{15} = 3.8730$ $\dfrac{\sin\theta_t}{\sin\theta_i} = \dfrac{n_1}{n_2}$

$\theta_i = \pi/6 = 0.5236$ $\theta_t = \sin^{-1}(n_1 \sin\theta_i /n2) = 0.1295$

Perpendicular polarization: $\dfrac{E_0^r}{E_0^i} = \dfrac{\eta_2 \cos\theta_i - \eta_1 \cos\theta_t}{\eta_2 \cos\theta_i + \eta_1 \cos\theta_t}$ $\dfrac{E_0^t}{E_0^i} = \dfrac{2\eta_2 \cos\theta_i}{\eta_2 \cos\theta_i + \eta_1 \cos\theta_t}$

Parallel polarization: $\dfrac{E_0^r}{E_0^i} = \dfrac{\eta_2 \cos\theta_t - \eta_1 \cos\theta_i}{\eta_2 \cos\theta_t + \eta_1 \cos\theta_i}$ $\dfrac{E_0^t}{E_0^i} = \dfrac{2\eta_2 \cos\theta_i}{\eta_2 \cos\theta_t + \eta_1 \cos\theta_i}$

TABLE 18-10 Intensity Ratios of Reflected and Transmitted Electric Fields to the Incident Field

f	η_1	η_2	PERPENDICULAR POLARIZATION $\dfrac{E_0^r}{E_0^i}$	$\dfrac{E_0^t}{E_0^i}$	PARALLEL POLARIZATION $\dfrac{E_0^r}{E_0^i}$	$\dfrac{E_0^t}{E_0^i}$
200 kHz	377	$12.77 + j12.35$	$-0.94 + j0.05$	$0.06 + j0.05$	$-0.92 + j0.07$	$0.07 + j0.06$
100 MHz	377	$97.21 + j2.91$	$-0.63 + j0.01$	$0.37 + j0.01$	$-0.54 + j0.01$	$0.39 + j0.01$

18.28. In an experiment the collision frequency v of electrons is plotted in logarithmic scale versus height in linear scale. The plot is a straight line from $v = 10^7\ \text{s}^{-1}$ at 60 km to $v = 10^3\ \text{s}^{-1}$ at 140 km, as shown in Fig. 18-10. Construct an exponential model $v(h) = v_0 e^{-h/h_0}$ for the above height profile by determining its constants.

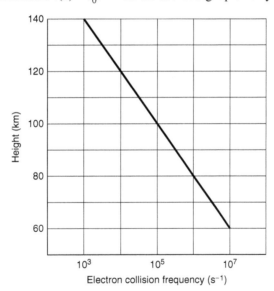

Fig. 18-10

From Fig. 18-10, $\dfrac{\log v - 7}{h - 60} = \dfrac{3 - 7}{140 - 60} = -\dfrac{1}{20},\ \log v = -\dfrac{h}{20} + 10$

$v = 10^{\left\{-\frac{h}{20}+10\right\}} = 10^{10} \times 10^{-\frac{h}{20}} = 10^{10} \times e^{-\frac{h}{H}}$, where $H = \dfrac{20}{Ln(10)} = 8.7$ km

Answer: $v(h) = 10^{10} e^{-\frac{h}{8.7}}$

Verification: $v(60) = 10^{10} e^{-\frac{60}{8.7}} = 1.011 \times 10^7$

$v(140) = 10^{10} e^{-\frac{140}{8.7}} = 1.026 \times 10^3$

The above model is to be considered only for the range $60 < h < 140$ km.

18.29. **Propagation properties of the ionosphere.** Find conductivity σ, critical frequency f_c, relative permittivity ϵ_r, intrinsic impedance η, attenuation coefficient α (in Np/m and dB/km), refraction index n, and group and phase velocities at 1 MHz in the D layer of the ionosphere, given an electron density $N = 10^{10}$ el/m^3 and collision frequency of $v = 10^6$ s^{-1}. (This is a maximum for the product Nv and may occur during daytime at a height of about 70 km.)

conductivity

$$\sigma = \frac{Ne^2 v}{m(v^2 + \omega^2)} = 6.95 \ \mu\text{S/m}$$

critical frequency

$$\omega_c^2 = \frac{Ne^2}{\epsilon_0 m} = 3.1781 \times 10^{13}, \quad f_c = 897.24 \text{ kHz}$$

relative permittivity

$$\epsilon_r = 1 - \frac{Ne^2}{\epsilon_0 m(v^2 + \omega^2)} = 1 - \frac{\omega_c^2}{v^2 + \omega^2} = 0.2149$$

intrinsic impedance

$$\eta = \sqrt{\frac{j\mu_0 \omega}{\sigma + j\omega\epsilon}} = 730.1 + j196.9 = 756.2\angle 15.1° \ \Omega$$

attenuation coefficient

$$\alpha = \frac{\sigma}{2}\sqrt{\frac{\mu_0}{\epsilon}} = 0.0028 \text{ Np/m}, \Rightarrow 24.52 \text{ dB/km}$$

refraction index

$$n = \sqrt{\epsilon_r} = 0.4635$$

phase velocity

$$u_p = \frac{\omega}{\beta} = \frac{c}{n} = 6.4722 \times 10^8 \text{ m/s}$$

group velocity

$$u_g = \frac{c^2}{u_p} = 1.3906 \times 10^8 \text{ m/s}$$

SUPPLEMENTARY PROBLEMS

Note: In the following problems *power* and *power density* refer to average values, unless specified to be instantaneous values.

18.30. A 1-MHz plane wave is propagating in the z-direction in a dielectric medium with $\epsilon_r = 1.2$. The amplitude of the electric field is 100 V with zero initial phase. Give expressions for $E(t, z)$ and $H(t, z)$.

18.31. Find the phase velocity and wavelength of the wave described in Problem 18.30.

18.32. Find the power density of the wave described in Problem 18.30.

18.33. A 1-MHz plane wave is propagating in the z-direction in a dielectric medium with $\epsilon_r = 15$. The amplitude of the electric field is 100 (V). Find i) the phase velocity, ii) wavelength, iii) amplitude of the H field, and iv) the average power density.

18.34. Repeat Problem 18.33 for the case of a 10-MHz plane wave.

18.35. A 1-MHz plane wave is propagating in the z-direction in a partially conductive ionized medium with $\epsilon_r = 1.2$ and $\sigma = 50 \ \mu$ S/m. The amplitude of the electric field is 100 (V) with zero initial phase. Give expressions for $E(t, z)$ and $H(t, z)$.

18.36. Repeat Problem 18.35 for a 10-MHz plane wave.

18.37. Find the amplitude attenuation, in dB/km, for the wave in i) Problem 18.35 and ii) Problem 18.36.

18.38. The attenuation coefficient α of electromagnetic waves in a medium is specified in Np/m. Find the attenuation in dB/km, given i) $\alpha = 0.001$ and ii) $\alpha = 0.005$.

18.39. The magnitude of the electric field of an electromagnetic wave at a location in free space at an instance is 2 V/m. Find its instantaneous power density in dBW at that location.

18.40. The power density of an electromagnetic wave in free space is 5 W/m². Find the electric field intensity E_0 for this wave.

18.41. An isotropic source radiates 100 W in free space. Find the electric field intensity E_0 at a distance of 5 km from the source.

18.42. A source radiates 200 W in the atmosphere with a 20-dB antenna gain. Find i) the power density in dBW at a distance of 50 km in the direction of the antenna, and ii) the electric field strength E. Ignore atmospheric losses.

18.43. A 5-W transmitter sends radio waves at a frequency of 2.5-GHz to a receiver located 40 km away in free space. The antenna gains are 20 dB each. Construct the power budget to include i) transmitted power P_t in dBW, ii) basic spatial loss L_b in dB, iii) received power P_r in dBW, and iv) received power in nW.

18.44. Repeat Problem 18.43, for a 50-W transmitter.

18.45. A ground type 1 is characterized by $\sigma = 20$ mS/m and $\epsilon_r = 30$. Find its complex dielectric constant ϵ^* at i) $f = 200$ kHz, ii) $f = 1$ MHz, iii) $f = 10$ MHz, and iv) its cross-over frequency f_c.

18.46. Repeat Problem 18.45 for a ground type 2 characterized by $\sigma = 20$ mS/m and $\epsilon_r = 15$.

18.47. Repeat Problem 18.45 for a ground type 3 characterized by $\sigma = 5$ mS/m and $\epsilon_r = 30$.

18.48. Repeat Problem 18.45 for a ground type 4 characterized by $\sigma = 10$ mS/m and $\epsilon_r = 4$.

18.49. The intrinsic impedance of a medium is defined by

$$\eta \equiv \frac{E}{H} = \sqrt{\frac{j\mu_0\omega}{\sigma + j\omega\epsilon}}$$

Find the intrinsic impedance of land ($\sigma = 5$ mS/m, $\epsilon_r = 15$) at i) $f = 200$ kHz, ii) $f = 1$ MHz, iii) $f = 10$ MHz, and iv) $f = 100$ MHz.

18.50. In Problem 18.14 it was shown that $\eta = 120\pi/\sqrt{\epsilon^*}$, where ϵ^* is the complex dielectric constant of the medium. Find ϵ^* and then η for a land characterized by $\sigma = 5$ mS/m and $\epsilon_r = 15$, at i) $f = 200$ kHz, ii) $f = 1$ MHz, iii) $f = 10$ MHz, and iv) $f = 100$ MHz. Compare with the results obtained in Problem 18.49.

18.51. A radio wave is incident on land ($\sigma = 5$ mS/m, $\epsilon_r = 15$) at an angle of $\pi/3$ radians. Find the intensity ratios of reflected and transmitted electric fields to the incident field for i) $f = 200$ kHz and ii) $f = 100$ MHz.

18.52. A radio wave is incident on a sea ($\sigma = 5$ S/m, $\epsilon_r = 70$) at an angle of $\pi/3$ radians. Find the intensity ratios of reflected and transmitted electric fields to the incident field for i) $f = 200$ kHz, and ii) $f = 100$ MHz. Compare with the results obtained in Problem 18.51.

ANSWERS TO SUPPLEMENTARY PROBLEMS

18.30. $E(t,z) = 100\cos(2\pi10^6 t - 0.0229z)\mathbf{a}_x$ and $H(t,z) = 0.29\cos(2\pi10^6 t - 0.0229z)\mathbf{a}_y$

18.31. $u = 2.7386 \times 10^8$ m/s and $\lambda = 273.86$ m

18.32. $P_{avg} = 14.53$ W

18.33. i) 7.746×10^7 m/s, ii) 77.46 m, iii) 1.03 A/m, iv) 51.37 W/m^2

18.34. i) 7.746×10^7 m/s, ii) 7.746 m, iii) 1.03 A/m, iv) 51.37 W

18.35. $E(t,z) = 100e^{-0.0081z} \cos(2\pi 10^6 t - 0.0243z)\mathbf{a}_x$
$H(t,z) = 0.3249e^{-0.0081z} \cos(2\pi 10^6 t - 0.243z - 18.43°)\mathbf{a}_y$

18.36. $E(t,z) = 100e^{-0.0086z} \cos(2\pi 10^7 t - 0.2296z)\mathbf{a}_x$
$H(t,z) = 0.2910e^{-0.0086z} \cos(2\pi 10^7 t - 0.2296z - 2.15°)\mathbf{a}_y$

18.37. i) 70.45, ii) 74.68, both in dB/km

18.38. i) −8.68, ii) −43.43

18.39. −19.74 dBW

18.40. 61.4 V/m

18.41. 15.5 mV/m

18.42. i) −61.96 dBW, ii) 21.9 mV/m

18.43. i) 6.99, ii) 132.45, iii) −85.46, iv) 2.84

18.44. i) 16.99, ii) 132.45, iii) −75.46, iv) 28.4

18.45. i) 30-j1800, ii) 30-j360, iii) 30-j36, iv) 12 MHz

18.46. i) 15-j1800, ii) 15-j360, iii) 15-j36, iv) 24 MHz

18.47. i) 30-j450, ii) 30-j90, iii) 30-j9, iv) 3 MHz

18.48. i) 4-j900, ii) 4-j180, iii) 4-j18, iv) 45 MHz

18.49. i) 12.77 + j12.35, ii) 30.11 + j25.51, iii) 86.87 + j24.06, iv) 97.21 + j2.91

18.50. ϵ^*: i) 15-j450, ii) 15-j90, iii) 15- j9, iv) 15-j0.9
η: Same values as in Problem 18.49.

18.51. **TABLE 18-11**

	PERPENDICULAR POLARIZATION		PARALLEL POLARIZATION	
	REFLECTION	TRANSMISSION	REFLECTION	TRANSMISSION
f	$\dfrac{E_0^r}{E_0^i}$	$\dfrac{E_0^t}{E_0^i}$	$\dfrac{E_0^r}{E_0^i}$	$\dfrac{E_0^t}{E_0^i}$
200 kHz	−0.965 + j0.032	0.035 + j0.032	−0.869 + j0.112	0.067 + j0.057
100 MHz	−0.766 + j0.006	0.234 + j0.006	−0.331 + j0.013	0.343 + j0.007

18.52. TABLE 18-12

f	PERPENDICULAR POLARIZATION		PARALLEL POLARIZATION	
	REFLECTION $\dfrac{E_0^r}{E_0^i}$	TRANSMISSION $\dfrac{E_0^t}{E_0^i}$	REFLECTION $\dfrac{E_0^r}{E_0^i}$	TRANSMISSION $\dfrac{E_0^t}{E_0^i}$
200 kHz	$-0.999 + j0.001$	$0.001 + j0.001$	$-0.996 + j0.004$	$0.002 + j0.002$
100 MHz	$-0.975 + j0.023$	$0.025 + j0.023$	$-0.906 + j0.080$	$0.048 + j0.041$

As expected, reflection ratio is stronger and transmission ratio is weaker compared to the values obtained in Problem 18.51.

Selected References for Further Reading

Kerr, Donald E., *Propagation of Short Radio Waves*, First Edition, McGraw-Hill Book Company, New York, 1951.

Griffiths, John, *Radio Wave Propagation and Antennas*, Prentice-Hall International, 1987.

Boithias, Lucien, *Radio Wave Propagation*, North Oxford Academic, 1987.

Davies, Kenneth, *Ionospheric Radio*, IEE Electromagnetic Wave Series 31, Peter Peregrinus Ltd., London, 1990.

Hall, M.P.M., ed., *Propagation of Radio Waves*, The Institution of Electrical Engineers, London, 1996.

International Telecommunication Union, *ITU Regulations, Recommendations, and other publications.*

APPENDIX

SI Unit Prefixes

FACTOR	PREFIX	SYMBOL	FACTOR	PREFIX	SYMBOL
10^{18}	exa	E	10^{-1}	deci	d
10^{15}	peta	P	10^{-2}	centi	c
10^{12}	tera	T	10^{-3}	milli	m
10^{9}	giga	G	10^{-6}	micro	μ
10^{6}	mega	M	10^{-9}	nano	n
10^{3}	kilo	k	10^{-12}	pico	p
10^{2}	hecto	h	10^{-15}	femto	f
10	deka	da	10^{-18}	atto	a

Divergence, Curl, Gradient, and Laplacian

Cartesian Coordinates

$$\nabla \cdot \mathbf{A} = \frac{\partial A_x}{\partial x} + \frac{\partial A_y}{\partial y} + \frac{\partial A_z}{\partial z}$$

$$\nabla \times \mathbf{A} = \left(\frac{\partial A_z}{\partial y} - \frac{\partial A_y}{\partial z}\right)\mathbf{a}_x + \left(\frac{\partial A_x}{\partial z} - \frac{\partial A_z}{\partial x}\right)\mathbf{a}_y + \left(\frac{\partial A_y}{\partial x} - \frac{\partial A_x}{\partial y}\right)\mathbf{a}_z$$

$$\nabla V = \frac{\partial V}{\partial x}\mathbf{a}_x + \frac{\partial V}{\partial y}\mathbf{a}_y + \frac{\partial V}{\partial z}\mathbf{a}_z$$

$$\nabla^2 V = \frac{\partial^2 V}{\partial x^2} + \frac{\partial^2 V}{\partial y^2} + \frac{\partial^2 V}{\partial z^2}$$

Cylindrical Coordinates

$$\nabla \cdot \mathbf{A} = \frac{1}{r}\frac{\partial}{\partial r}(rA_r) + \frac{1}{r}\frac{\partial A_\phi}{\partial \phi} + \frac{\partial A_z}{\partial z}$$

$$\nabla \times \mathbf{A} = \left(\frac{1}{r}\frac{\partial A_z}{\partial \phi} - \frac{\partial A_\phi}{\partial z}\right)\mathbf{a}_r + \left(\frac{\partial A_r}{\partial z} - \frac{\partial A_z}{\partial r}\right)\mathbf{a}_\phi + \frac{1}{r}\left[\frac{\partial}{\partial r}(rA_\phi) - \frac{\partial A_r}{\partial \phi}\right]\mathbf{a}_z$$

$$\nabla V = \frac{\partial V}{\partial r}\mathbf{a}_r + \frac{1}{r}\frac{\partial V}{\partial \phi}\mathbf{a}_\phi + \frac{\partial V}{\partial z}\mathbf{a}_z$$

$$\nabla^2 V = \frac{1}{r}\frac{\partial}{\partial r}\left(r\frac{\partial V}{\partial r}\right) + \frac{1}{r^2}\frac{\partial^2 V}{\partial \phi^2} + \frac{\partial^2 V}{\partial z^2}$$

Spherical Coordinates

$$\nabla \cdot \mathbf{A} = \frac{1}{r^2}\frac{\partial}{\partial r}(r^2 A_r) + \frac{1}{r\sin\theta}\frac{\partial}{\partial \theta}(A_\theta \sin\theta) + \frac{1}{r\sin\theta}\frac{\partial A_\phi}{\partial \phi}$$

$$\nabla \times \mathbf{A} = \frac{1}{r\sin\theta}\left[\frac{\partial}{\partial \theta}(A_\phi \sin\theta) - \frac{\partial A_\theta}{\partial \phi}\right]\mathbf{a}_r + \frac{1}{r}\left[\frac{1}{\sin\theta}\frac{\partial A_r}{\partial \phi} - \frac{\partial}{\partial r}(r A_\phi)\right]\mathbf{a}_\theta + \frac{1}{r}\left[\frac{\partial}{\partial r}(rA_\theta) - \frac{\partial A_r}{\partial \theta}\right]\mathbf{a}_\phi$$

$$\nabla V = \frac{\partial V}{\partial r}\mathbf{a}_r + \frac{1}{r}\frac{\partial V}{\partial \theta}\mathbf{a}_\theta + \frac{1}{r\sin\theta}\frac{\partial V}{\partial \phi}\mathbf{a}_\phi$$

$$\nabla^2 V = \frac{1}{r^2}\frac{\partial}{\partial r}\left(r^2\frac{\partial V}{\partial r}\right) + \frac{1}{r^2\sin\theta}\frac{\partial}{\partial \theta}\left(\sin\theta\frac{\partial V}{\partial \theta}\right) + \frac{1}{r^2\sin^2\theta}\frac{\partial^2 V}{\partial \phi^2}$$

INDEX

AC resistance, of transmission lines, 273
Air-gap line, negative, 224, 225
Air gaps, cores with, 217
Ampere (unit), 113, 216
Ampere turns (unit), 216
Ampere's law, 174
  for magnetic circuits, 216–217
Antenna parameters, 336–338
Antennas, 335–353
  available power of, 341
  directivity of, 337–338
  effective area for, 341
  effective length of, 339
  electric dipole, 335–336
  linear arrays of, 342–343
  monopole, 339–340
  ohmic loss of, 338
  power gain of, 338
  radiation efficiency of, 338
  receiving, 341–342
  self-impedance of, 340–341
  small circular-loop, 338
Array factor, 342
Arrays:
  endfire, 342
  linear, of antennas, 342–343
  uniform, 343
Associative law, 32
Atmosphere, 361–362
  attenuation by gaseous absorption, 362–363
  attenuation by hydrometeors, 363–364
  effects on radio waves propagation, 362
  layers of, 361
Attenuation of electromagnetic waves, 254, 255, 275, 323, 354,
    358–359, 362–364, 373–374
  atmospheric, 362–364
  coefficient of, 255, 265, 354–356
  gaseous absorption, by 362–363
  homogeneous media, in, 354
  hydrometeors, by 363–364
  good conductors, in, 255, 373
  partially conducting media, in, 254, 374
  plane waves, 354
  power equation, 358–359
  transmission lines, in, 275
  wave guides, 323
Attenuation, per-meter, 291
Attenuation factor, 322–323
  total, 323
Available power of antennas, 341
Avogadro's number, 122
Axial components, transverse components from,
  317–318
Axial fields, 316–318
  determination of, 318–319

B (see Magnetic flux density)
B-H curve, 215–216
Back-voltage in inductor, 212
Beam width, half-power, 337

Biot-Savart law, 172–174
Boundary, current sheet at, 177–178
Boundary conditions:
  across interface of two dielectrics, summary, 178
  at interface of two dielectrics, 136–137
  conductor-dielectric, 120–121
Boundary reflection coefficient, 277
Boundary relations, for magnetic fields, 176–177

Capacitance, 131–149
  definition of, 132–133
  equivalent, 133–134
  of transmission lines, 273
Capacitors:
  energy stored in, 134
  multiple-dielectric, 133–134
  parallel-plate, fringing of, 74–75
Cartesian coordinate system, 34–35
  curl in, 85
  del operator in, 79–80
  differential displacement vector in, 97
  divergence, curl, gradient, and Laplacian in, 354
  divergence in, 81
  electric flux density in, 70
  field vector in, 317
  gradient in, 78–79
  Laplace's equation in, 152
    in one variable, 153–154
    product solution of, 154–155
  Laplacian of vector in, 251
  Maxwell's equations in, solutions for, 252–253
  position vectors in, 36–37
Characteristic impedance, 276
Charge density, 46–47
  volume, 46
  surface, 47
  line, 47
Complex dielectric constant, 357
Conduction current, 114
Conduction current density, 114
Conductor:
  current-carrying, 194
  cylindrical, inductance of, 211
  good, Maxwell's equations solutions for,
    255–256
  in motion:
    through time-dependent fields, 235–236
    through time-independent fields, 234–235
  parallel, inductance of, 211
  perfect, imaging in, 347–348
Conservative fields, 98
Conservative property of electrostatic field, 98
Constant currents, 113
Continuity of current, 119–120
  equation of, 119
Contour, closed, 98
Convection current, 114
Convection current density (J), 114
Coordinate system, divergence, curl, gradient, and
  Laplacian in, 354

Coordinate systems, 34–35, (*see also* Cartesian coordinate
    system; Cylindrical coordinate system; Spherical
    coordinate system)
Coordinates, 34
Core lengths, 214
Cores, with air gaps, 217
Coulomb (unit), 2
Coulomb forces, 44–62
Coulomb's law:
    Scalar form of, 4, 138
    Vector form of, 44, 45
Critical wave number, 318
Cross product of two vectors, 4, 33
Curl, 80
    in coordinate systems, 354
    divergence of, as zero scalar, 85
    of gradient as zero vector, 85
    of vector field, 84–85
Current(s) (I), 116–117
    constant, 113
    continuity of (*see* Continuity of current)
    displacement (*see* Displacement current)
    time-variable, 113
Current density, 113
    conduction, 114–115
    convection, 114
    displacement, 11, 236–238
    magnetic field strength and, 174–175
    total, 238
Current elements, magnetic force on, 195
Current filament, vector magnetic potential for, 179
Current law, Kirchhoff's, 119
Current sheet, 118
    at boundary, 177–178
Current sheet density, 118–119
Current source, phasor fields outside, 335
Cutoff frequency, 319–320
Cutoff wavelength, 329
Cylindrical conductors, inductance of, 211
Cylindrical coordinate system, 34–35
    curl in, 85
    del operator and, 80
    differential displacement vector in, 97
    divergence, curl, gradient, and Laplacian in, 354
    divergence in, 81
    electric flux density in, 71
    field vector in, 312
    gradient in, 79
    Laplace's equation in, 152
        product solution of, 155–156
Cylindrical guides, 311, 321–324

D (*see* Electric flux density)
D'Arsonval meter movement, 200
DC resistance, of transmission lines, 273
Decibel (unit), 264
Del operator, 10, 79–80
Delay time, 288
Density:
    charge (*see* Charge density)
    current (*see* Current density)
    energy, 107–108
    flux (*see* Flux density)
Depth of penetration, 256
Determinants, 33
Dielectric-conductor boundary conditions, 120–121
Dielectric constant, 4
    complex, 365
Dielectric free-space interface, 139
Dielectric losses, 322–323
Dielectrics:
    boundary conditions across interface of two, 178
    boundary conditions at interface of two 136–137
    perfect, Maxwell's equation solutions for, 255

Dielectrics (*Cont.*):
    polarization of (*see* Polarization of dielectric materials)
    two, in multiple-dielectric capacitors, 133–134
Differential line element, 36
Differential surface element, 36
Differential volume, 35
Diffraction, 360–361
Diffusion, 315
Dipole:
    finite-length, 338–339
    magnetic, 338
Dipole antennas, electric, 335–336
Dipole moment, electric, 131
Directivity, of antennas, 337–338
Dispersive medium, 255
Displacement current, 11
    definition of, 236–238
Displacement current density, 237
Displacement flux, 63
Displacement vectors, 44
Distributive law, 32
Divergence, 10, 80–82
    in Cartesian coordinates, 81
    in coordinate systems, 385
    of curl as zero scalar, 85
    definition of, 80
    of electric flux density, 83
    of gradient of potential function, 151–152
    negative, 80
    of zero, 88–89
Divergence theorem, 83–84
Dominant mode of waveguides, 315–316
Dot product of two vectors, 32–33
Double-stub matching, 285–286
Drift velocity, 113

E (*see* Electric field intensity)
Effective area for antennas, 341
Effective earth, 368
Effective length of antennas, 339
Electric component of force, 194
Electric current (*see* Current *entries*)
Electric dipole antennas, 335–336
Electric dipole moment, 131
Electric field intensity (E), 5, 44–62, 151
    definition of, 5, 45–46
    due to point charges, 51–52
    fixed-charge, 135–136
    fixed-voltage, 135
    flux density and, 65–66
    motional, 234
    potential function and, 100–101
    tangential component of, 136
    units of, 5, 46
Electric fields:
    magnetic fields combined with, 194–195
    point charges causing, 51–52
    static, energy in, 101–102
    work done against, 97
    work done by, 97
Electric flux, 63–77
    definition of, 63–64
Electric flux density (D), 64–65
    antisymmetrical, 164–165
    divergence of, 83
    electric field intensity and, 65–66
    fixed-charge, 135–136
    fixed-voltage, 135
    normal component of, 136
Electric potential:
    of charge distributions, 99–100
    definition of, 99
    of point charges, 99
    between two points, 99

Electric susceptibility, 132
Electromagnetic waves, 251–261
    propagation of, 354–372
    spectrum of, 16
    propagation constant of, 252–253, 277, 354–357
Electromotive force, 212
Electron-gas theory, 113
Electron-hole pairs, 115
Electron mobility, 122
Electrostatic field, 97–112
    conservative property of, 98
Endfire arrays, 337
Energy:
    instantaneous rate of, leaving volume, 261
    in static electric fields, 101–102
    stored in capacitors, 134
Energy density, 107–108
Energy differences, 109
Equation of continuity for current, 119
Equipotential surfaces, 79
Equivalent capacitance, 133–134
Excess delay, 370

Farad (unit), 132
Faraday homopolar generator, 244
Faraday's law, 212
    integral form of, 233
    two-term form of, 235
    Ferromagnetic materials, 214
Field lines, 330–321
Field vector, 317
Fields:
    axial (*see* Axial fields)
    conservative, 98
    electric (*see* Electric fields)
    electrostatic, 97–112
    magnetic (*see* Magnetic fields)
    radial, 184
    time-dependent, conductors in motion through, 235–236
    time-independent, conductors in motion through, 234–235
    transverse, 317–318
    vector (*see* Vector fields)
Finite length dipole, 338–339
First nulls, 342
Fixed-charge electric field intensity and electric flux density, 135–136
Fixed-voltage electric field intensity and electric flux density, 135
Flux:
    displacement, 63
    electric (*see* Electric flux)
    magnetic, 175
Flux density:
    electric (*see* Electric flux density)
    magnetic (*see* Magnetic flux density)
Flux lines, 64
Flux linkage, 209
Forces:
    Coulomb, 4–5, 44–45
    electromotive, 212
    in magnetic fields, 193–208
    magnetomotive, 216
    moment of, 196–197
Fourier sine series, 166–167
Free charge, 120
Free space, Maxwell's equation solutions in, 255
Free-space interface, dielectric, 139
Free-space permeability, 175
Frequency of harmonic wave, 252
Fringing of parallel-plate capacitors, 74–75
Friss transmission formula, 342

Gauss' divergence theorem, 83
Gauss' law, 65

Gaussian surfaces, special, 66–67
Generator, Faraday homopolar, 244
Geometrical factor, 273
Gradient, 78–79
    in coordinate systems, 354
    curl of, as zero vector, 85
    divergence of, of potential function, 151–152
Ground waves, 364–365
Guide wavelength, 320

H (*see* Magnetic field strength)
Half-power beam width, 337
Half-power points, 337
Helical motion, 194–195
Henry (unit), 209
Hertzian dipole antennas, 335–336
High-frequency lines, 287
Homopolar generator, Faraday, 244

I (*see* Current)
Imaging in perfect conductor, 347–348
Impedance:
    characteristic, 276
    intrinsic, 218, 254, 257
    mutual, of antennas, 340–341
    self-impedance, of antennas, 340–341
    wave, 313
Impedance matching, 283–284
Impendance measurement, transmission line, 287
Incidence:
    angle of, 258
    normal, interface conditions at, 256–257
    oblique, 258
    plane of, 258
Induced voltage, 212
Inductance, 209–232
    definition of, 209–211
    internal, 212–213
    mutual, 213–214
    self-inductance, 212
    of transmission lines, 273–274
Inductor, back-voltage in, 212
Infinite line charge, 48
Infinite plane charge, 49
Infinity, zero reference at, 100
Instantaneous power, 266–267
Interface conditions at normal incidence, 256–257
Internal inductance, 212–213
Intrinsic concentration, 123
Intrinsic impedance, 254, 257
Intrinsic semiconductors, 115
Inverse-square law of point charge, 48
Ionosphere, 361–362
    conductivity of, 369–370
    height profile of, 362
    maximum usable frequency in, 365
    permittivity of, 369–370
    range error in, 371
    refraction index of, 365–366, 369–370
    two-frequency correction method for, 371
Iron-core magnetics, 214
Isotropic radiator, 332

J (*see* Conduction current density; Convection current density)

Kirchhoff's law, 119, 216

Laplace's equation, 151–171
    in Cartesian coordinate system (*see* Cartesian coordinate system, Laplace's equation in)
    definition of, 151
    explicit forms of, 151–152

Laplacian, in coordinate systems, 351
Legendre polynomial:
    higher-order, 167
    of order n, 156
Lenz's law, 233–234
Lever arm, 196
Line charge, 47
    infinite, 48
Line charge density, 47
Line element, differential, 36
Linear arrays of antennas, 342–343
Lorentz force, 194
Lossless lines, 278
    transients in, 288–289
Lossless waveguide, power transmitted in, 322
Lossy waveguide, power dissipation in, 322–333

Magnetic circuits, 214
    Ampere's law for, 214, 216–217
    parallel, 218
Magnetic component of force, 194
Magnetic dipole, 338
Magnetic field strength (H), 172, 177
    current density and, 174
    tangential component of, 177
Magnetic fields:
    boundary relations for, 176–177
    electric fields combined with, 194–195
    forces and torques in, 193–208
    static, 172
    time-variable, 236
Magnetic flux, 175
Magnetic flux density (B), 175–176
    normal component of, 177
Magnetic force:
    on current elements, 195
    on particles, 193–194
Magnetic moment:
    of planar coil, 197–198
    of planar current loop, 197
Magnetic potential, vector, 178–179
Magnetization curves, 215
Magnetomotive force, 216
Mass-action law, 123
Matching:
    double-stub, 285–286
    impedance, 283–284
    single-stub, 284–285
Maximum usable frequency, 365
Maximum value theorem, 153
Maxwell's equations, 10–11, 233, 238–239
    free-space set, 239
    general set, 239
    interface conditions at normal incidence, 256–257
    solutions for good conductors, 255–256
    solutions for partially conducting media, 254–255
    solutions for perfect dielectrics, 255
    solutions in free space, 255
Mean value theorem, 153
    in special case, 157–158
Method of images, 146–147
Microwave ranging, 370
Mho (unit), 117
Mil, circular, 124
Mobility, 113
    electron, 122
Mode cutoff frequencies, 319–320
Moment:
    electric dipole, 131
    of force, 196–197
    magnetic (see Magnetic moment)
Monopole, quarter-wave, 340

Monopole antennas, 339–340
Motion:
    charges in, 113–114
    conductors in (see Conductors in motion)
    helical, 194–195
Motional electric field intensity, 234
Multiple coils, 217–218
Multiple-dielectric capacitors, 133–134
Mutual impedance, of antennas, 340–341
Mutual inductance, 213–214

n-type semiconductor materials, 115
Negative air-gap line, 224
Neper (unit), 224
Neper to dB conversion, 264, 354
Net charge, 119
    in region, 63
Net charge density, 119–120
Newton (unit), 4
NI rise and NI drop, 216
Nulls first, 342

Oblique incidence, 258
Ohmic loss of antennas, 338
Ohm's law, 113
    point form of, 114
Operating wave length, 315
Operators, mathematical, 10, 78–96
    curl, 9–10, 84–85
    divergence 10, 13, 80–84
    gradient, 78–80
    Laplacian, 86
Orthogonal surfaces, 34–35

p-type semiconductor materials, 115
Parallel conductors, inductance of, 211
Parallel magnetic circuits, 218
Parallel-plate capacitors, fringing of, 74–75
Parallel plate geometrical factors, 274
Parallel polarization, 259–260
Parallel wire geometrical factors, 274
Particles, magnetic force on, 193–194
Pattern function, 332
Penetration, depth of, 256
Per-meter attenuation, 291
Period of harmonic wave, 252
Permeability, 175
    free-space, 175
    relative, 175
Permittivity, 4
    relative, 4, 132
Perpendicular polarization, 259
Phasor fields, 335
Phasors, 276
Planar coil, magnetic moment of, 197–198
Plane, of incidence, 258
Plane charge, infinite, 258
Plane waves, 12–14, 253, 354–357
    homogeneous media, in, 354–355
    polarization of, 15–16
    power flow and poynting vector, 14, 261, 322–323, 355
    propagation parameters of, 355–357
Point charges:
    causing electric fields, 51–52
    electric field intensity due to, 51–52
    electric potential of, 99
    inverse-square law of, 98
    in spherical coordinate system, 69
    work done in moving, 98
Point form of Ohm's law, 114
Points, 34
    electric potential between two, 99

Poisson's equation, 151, 164–165
Polar form, 276
Polarity, 233–234
Polarization of dielectric materials, 131–132
    parallel, 259–260
    perpendicular, 259
Position vectors, 36
Potential:
    electric (*see* Electric potential)
    vector magnetic, 178–179
Potential difference, 99
Potential function (V):
    divergence of gradient of, 151–152
    electric field intensity and, 100–101
Power:
    available, of antennas, 341
    complex, 261
    dissipated in lossy waveguide, 322–323
    instantaneous, 266–267
    Poynting vector and, 261
    transmitted in lossless waveguide, 322
    work and, 195–196
Power equation in atmospheric propagation, 358
Power gain of antennas, 338
Poynting vector, 261
    power and, 261
Propagation constant, 252
Propagation parameters, 355

Quarter-wave monopole, 340
Quarter-wave transformer, 296–297

R (*see* Resistance)
Radial fields, 184
Radiation efficiency of antennas, 338
Radiation intensity, 337
Radiation resistance, 336
Radiator, isotropic, 337
Range error, 370–373
Receiving antennas, 341–342
Rectangular-guide formulas, 326
Reflection:
    angle of, 258
    coefficient of, in transmission lines, 18, 275–277
    ionospheric, 365
    radio waves, 369
    Snell's law of, 258
Reflectors, 343
Refraction, 359–360
    index of 356–357
    ionospheric, 369–370
    tropospheric, 366, 368
    Snell's law of, 258
Relative permeability, 175
Relative permittivity, 4, 132
Relaxation time, 120
Reluctance, 216
Resistance (R), 117–118
    radiation, 336
    surface, 323
Resistivity, 113
    conductivity as reciprocal of, 124
Right-hand rule, 173

Satellite microwave ranging, 370
Scalar function, gradient of, 78–79
Scalar triple product, 38
Scalars, 31
    zero, divergence of curl as, 85
Scattering, 360–361
Self-impedance, of antennas, 340–341
Self-inductance, 212

Semiconductors, 115–116
Sheet charge, 47
Sheet current, vector magnetic potential for, 179
SI unit prefixes, 354
SI units, rationalized, 4
Sidelobes, 343
Siemens (unit), 114, 117
Smith Chart, 279–281
Single-stub matching, 284–285
Sinks, 80
Sinusoidal steady-state transmission-line excitation, 227–277
Skin depth, 256
Skin effect, 212–213
Sky waves, 364–365
Slotted lines, 287
Small circular-loop antennas, 338
Smith Chart, 279–281
Snell's law:
    of reflection, 258
    of refraction, 258
Solenoids, inductance of, 211
Sources, 80
Space, free (*see* Free space)
Spherical coordinate system, 34–35
    curl in, 85
    differential displacement vector in, 97
    divergence, curl, gradient, and Laplacian in, 354
    divergence in, 81
    gradient in, 79
    Laplace's equation in, 152
    product solution of, 156
    point charge in, 69
    potential in, 101
Spherical shells, concentric, 104
Standing-wave ratio, voltage, 276, 278
Standing waves, 260
Static electric fields, energy in, 101–102
Static magnetic field, 172
Stokes' theorem, 179–180
Surface charge density, 47
Surface element, differential, 36
Surface resistance, 323
Surfaces:
    equipotential, 79
    orthogonal, 34–35
Susceptibility, electric, 132

TE (transverse electric) waves, 318
Time constant, 120
Time-dependent fields, conductors in motion through, 235–236
Time-distance plots, 288–289
Time-independent fields, conductors in motion through, 234–235
Time-variable currents, 113
Time-variable magnetic field, 236
TM (transverse magnetic) waves, 318
Toroids, inductance of, 211
Torque:
    definition of, 196–197
    in magnetic fields, 193–208
Transformer, quarter-wave, 282–283, 300
Transients in lossless lines, 288–289
Transmission, angle of, 258
Transmission formula, Friss, 342
Transmission lines, 273–313
    distributed parameters, 273–274
    double-stub matching, 285–286
    impedance matching, 283–284
    impedance measurement, 287
    incremental model, 274–275
    per-meter attenuation, 295

Transmission lines (*Cont.*):
  single-stub matching, 284–285
  sinusoidal steady-state excitation, 276–278
  slotted, 287, 306
  uniform, 273
Transverse components from axial components,
    312–313
Transverse electric (TE) waves, 318
Transverse fields, 316–318
Transverse length, unit, charge transport per, 118
Transverse magnetic (TM) waves, 318
Traveling waves, 262
Triple product:
  scalar, 38
  vector, 38
Troposphere, 361–362
  bending effect of, 368
  excess delay due to, 367
  models of, 366
  range error due to, 372
  refractivity of, 366
Tuner circle, 285, 304

Uniform arrays, 337
Uniform transmission lines, 273
Uniqueness theorem, 152–153
Unit vectors, 4, 31, 35

V (*see* Potential function)
Vector(s), 4, 31
  absolute value of, 4, 31
  component form of, 4, 31
  cross product of two, 4, 33
  displacement, 44
  dot product of two, 4, 33
  position, 36
  Poynting (*see* Poynting vector)
  projection of one, on second, 37–38
  unit, 4, 31, 35
  zero, curl of gradient as, 85
Vector algebra, 14, 32–33
Vector analysis, 4, 31–43
Vector fields, 4, 78–80
  curl of, 84–85
Vector integral, 45, 46
Vector magnetic potential, 178–179
Vector notation, 4, 31
Vector sum, 45

Vector triple product, 38
Vector wave equations, 251
Velocity, drift, 113
Voltage:
  around closed contour, 212
  induced, 212
  of self-inductance, 212
Voltage drop, 117
Voltage standing-wave ratio, 277
Volume:
  differential, 35
  instantaneous rate of energy leaving, 261
Volume charge, 46
Volume current, vector magnetic potential for, 179

Wall losses, 317–318
Wave equations, 251–252
Wave impedance, 318
Wave number, 317
  critical, 318, 324
  of radiation, 335
Waveguides, 316–334
  dominant mode of, 320–321
  lossless, power transmitted in, 322
  lossy, power dissipation in, 322–323
Wavelength:
  cutoff, 329
  guide, 320
  of harmonic wave, 252
  operating, 320
Waves:
  electromagnetic (*see* Electromagnetic waves)
  plane, 12–14, 253, 354
  polarization of, 15–16
  standing, 260
  traveling, 262
Weber (unit), 175
Work:
  definition of, 97
  done against electric field, 97
  done by electric field, 97
  done in moving point charges, 98
  power and, 195–196

Zero, divergence of, 88–89
Zero reference at infinity, 100
Zero scalar, divergence of curl as, 85
Zero vector, curl of gradient as, 85

Book • Online • Mobile

SCHAUM'S®
outlines

To Access Your Online and/or Mobile Prep Course:

1. Go to www.schaums.com.

2. Click on the banner to launch the mobile web app.

3. Find your desired discipline and click through to your title.

4. Once you have opened your title, the videos or audio content will open on the main Dashboard page.

YOU ARE ALL SET!

ON YOUR DESKTOP/LAPTOP

- Type in Schaums.com, click through to your desired title, and start studying!

ON YOUR SMARTPHONE

- Just go to the app store, search for "Schaums," download the app, and start studying!

STEPS TO ACCESS EASY OUTLINE DIAGNOSTIC TEST:

1. Go to Schaums.com

2. Search for your book's title and then click on your book's cover.

3. Scroll down and click on the "Downloads & Resources" tab.

4. Click on the bullet labeled "Online Diagnostic Test".

Printed in the USA
CPSIA information can be obtained
at www.ICGtesting.com
LVHW082113210124
769418LV00010B/448